Food for the Journey

365-DAY DEVOTIONAL

Edited by Elizabeth McQuoid

INTER-VARSITY PRESS
36 Causton Street, London SW1P 4ST, England
Email: ivp@ivpbooks.com
Website: www.ivpbooks.com

First published as single volumes under name of theme 2020, 2021, 2022

First published as Omnibus edition, combining all twelve volumes, 2024

British Library Cataloguing-in-Publication Data
A catalogue record for this book is available from the British Library.

ISBN: 9781789744965
eBook ISBN: 9781789744972

Set in Avenir 11/15pt
Typeset in Great Britain by Westchester
Printed in Great Britain by TJ Books

Produced on paper from sustainable forests

Contents

Application and commentary for each day by Elizabeth McQuoid

Preface

You'll remember what happened. People of all kinds had been flocking from Jerusalem and all over Judaea into the desert to hear an electrifying preacher with a strange diet of locusts and wild honey. Not only did John preach, warning of judgement to come, he also baptised those who confessed their sins in the river Jordan. And he pointed to another who would come after him whose sandals he was not worthy to carry, who would baptise with the Holy Spirit and with fire.

One of those baptised was now a young adult from Nazareth, by the name of Jesus. But his baptism was like no other. For one thing, John tried to hinder him, saying it was the wrong way round. For another, as Jesus emerged from the water, the heavens opened and the Spirit of God descended on him like a dove. A voice from heaven declared, 'This is my Son, whom I love; with him I am well pleased.'

These events could hardly be more dramatic. The sense of expectation could hardly be greater. But no sooner had the Spirit come on Jesus at his baptism than that same Spirit led Jesus into the wilderness to be tempted by the devil. Not the kind of Spirit's leading we might have expected.

Alone, hungry, thirsty, confronted with choices, tempting choices. The ministry that would change the face of the world had not even started. Would Jesus, the Son of God, fail like Adam had failed in the garden, like Israel had failed in the wilderness?

We know what happened. At the moment of temptation, Jesus drew on the Scriptures he had grown up with, had learned, had meditated upon. And he resisted. Faced with gnawing hunger and the temptation to turn stones into bread, he recalled and declared 'man shall not live on bread alone, but on every word that comes from the mouth of God.'

Jesus' victory over diabolical temptation was vital for God's plan of redemption. That's the central message of the temptation narratives. But Jesus also provides for us an inspiration and example for our own discipleship. Being soaked in the Word of God and drawing on it is vital for our discipleship.

This *Food for the Journey* compilation helps you soak yourself in God's Word, so you are shaped by it and so you are ready to draw on it in hard days.

It is made up of 12 different 30-day devotionals, each of which focuses on a topic vital for discipleship. Nine have been published as individual devotionals, but three are only to be found here.

Each of these devotionals contains 30 carefully selected excerpts of messages from Keswick Convention speakers, past and present, on that topic. The choice of passages is wide, but of course not exhaustive! At the end of each daily excerpt, there is a fresh section by Elizabeth McQuoid that helps you apply God's Word to your own life and situation.

The topics are grouped into threes, with an introductory day at the start. The devotional starts looking at the **Cross** of Jesus Christ, the sole ground for our confidence, before turning to the **Holy Spirit**, the incomparably great power for us who believe, and then to **Faithful**, which paints a picture of the faithful God and the call for us, in turn, to be faithful.

The next group of three begins with **Suffering**, the experience of every believer in Jesus Christ as well as of every human being in a world awaiting God's renewal. It then focuses on **Grace**, the generous self-giving of God himself in Christ, and **Joy**, rooted not in the whim of personal circumstances but in the reality of God and his re-creating work.

The third cluster starts with **Pray**, in the Spirit, through the Son, to the Father. It moves then to **Persevere**, the call to every believer to keep going to the end, a call rooted in God's preserving of those who are his own. The final one in this group is **Holiness**, which opens our eyes afresh to God's holiness and to the lifelong pursuit of holiness he calls us to.

The final set of topics opens with **Confident**, renewing our confidence in the good news of the gospel, the unshakeable truths of

God's Word and the unchanging nature of his character. The second is **Love,** an invitation to bask in God's love, its depth and richness, allowing it to warm your heart and in turn empower your love of others and your service. The final topic is, fittingly, **Hope**, which will whet your appetite for what God has planned and instil a sense of hope that inspires you to keep serving as you pray, 'Your kingdom come on earth as in heaven.'

You'll notice, as you look through this book, that the devotions are not dated. Although there are 365 readings, you do not need to follow a particular order through, though you'll probably find it helpful to stick with a particular topic. Each topic is standalone. And because each topic includes passages from different Bible books, there is a brief introduction to that Bible book at the back of this volume to give you some context.

If you've found helpful either a particular devotion or these devotions in general, you can easily access, for free, on the Keswick Ministries' website under Resources, many of the talks that found their way into this book.

As you meet with the Lord day by day through his Word, it is our prayer that your own love for the Lord, for his people and for a broken and needy world will grow, that you will be renewed, reshaped and recalibrated, so you will be inspired and encouraged to love Christ and live for him in his world.

James Robson
Ministry Director, Keswick Ministries (2017–2023)

Food for the Journey

Day 1

Read: John 6:25–40
Key verses: John 6:35, 38–40

∙∙∙

> *Then Jesus declared, "I am the bread of life. Whoever comes to me will never go hungry, and whoever believes in me will never be thirsty . . . ³⁸ For I have come down from heaven not to do my will but to do the will of him who sent me. ³⁹ And this is the will of him who sent me, that I shall lose none of all those he has given me, but raise them up at the last day. ⁴⁰ For my Father's will is that everyone who looks to the Son and believes in him shall have eternal life, and I will raise them up at the last day."*

What do you really need? At the start of this new devotional perhaps it is worth asking that question.

The crowd had seen Jesus feed the five thousand and were enticed by the offer of free food and a military Messiah who would overthrow the Romans. They wanted Jesus to authenticate his claims by giving them a sign even greater than producing manna in the desert.

But Jesus challenged their short-sighted assessment of their needs. In the first of John's 'I AM' sayings, he explained that God was still sending down bread from heaven and he was that bread – a life-giving bread that would satisfy them longer than daily manna and more deeply than any regime change. He still offers all who believe in him lasting satisfaction for their greatest need – a restored relationship with God and eternal life.

Throughout this year you will have many needs and various options as to how to meet them. Jesus' declaration, 'I am the bread of life' invites us to come to him, not for sporadic gorging feasts, but to spend time with him in his Word daily, receiving nourishment, finding that he alone satisfies.

This Bible passage is also a helpful introduction to our first three devotional themes – *Faithful, The Cross* and the *Holy Spirit.* Jesus is *Faithful* to God's will, dying for our sins and raising us up on the last day. He is also promises faithfully to keep each one of us on our journey of discipleship until the end (verse 37). The 'work' God requires of us (verse 29) is to 'look to the Son' as he hangs on *The Cross* and 'believe' (verse 40). To experience the bread of life which Jesus offers, we must put our faith and trust in his person, Word, and work on the cross. Each one who believes receives the free gift of eternal life, which starts now by the power of the *Holy Spirit.*

A restful holiday, bigger income, better job, and good times with friends all fill up our hearts, but only temporarily. We soon find ourselves longing for more because we were designed to be fully satisfied only by Christ. As you make your way through this devotional, 'Do not work for food that spoils, but for food that endures to eternal life, which the Son of Man will give you' (verse 27). Receive 'the bread of life' and keep coming to Christ, finding in him endless nourishment for your longing soul.

The Cross

Contributors

Day 2

Read: Isaiah 53:1–12
Key verses: Isaiah 53:4, 10

....

> Surely he took up our pain
>   and bore our suffering,
> yet we considered him punished by God,
>   stricken by him, and afflicted.
> ¹⁰ Yet it was the LORD's will to crush him and cause him to suffer,
>   And though the LORD makes his life an offering for sin,
> he will see his offspring and prolong his days,
>   and the will of the LORD will prosper in his hand.

For whom did Jesus die?

You might answer, 'Jesus died for the world,' or 'Jesus died for sinners,' or you may personalize it and say, 'Jesus died for me.' All those statements contain truth, because we are the beneficiaries of his death, but we are not the primary reason why Jesus died and why the cross was necessary. In the first instance, Jesus died for his Father. Verses 4 and 10 indicate it was God who required the cross.

We would prefer a simpler remedy for sin. We would rather just say 'sorry' for our sin, and have God forgive us. But that is not enough, because the problem with sin is not just that it messes with our lives, but that it violates God's righteousness and provokes his wrath. It is that which is to be addressed. What lies behind the cross is not in the first instance the love of God, although love is his very nature, but his wrath. The brutality of the cross is an expression of God's anger at sin.

God put Jesus Christ forward to address and satisfy his wrath. A good word to describe this is 'propitiation', which means to turn away wrath by satisfying its demands and requirements. Romans 3:24–25 explains that we are 'justified by his grace as a gift, through the redemption that is in Christ Jesus, whom God put forward as a propitiation by his blood, to be received by faith' (ESV), and 1 John 2:2 says, 'He is the propitiation for our sins, and not for ours only but also for the sins of the whole world' (ESV).

We don't like the idea that God's anger needs to be addressed. But the Bible teaches that Jesus was not just stricken by evil men, but stricken by God (verse 4). Verses 6 and 10 say, 'The LORD has laid on him the iniquity of us all . . . Yet it was the LORD's will to crush him . . . the LORD makes his life an offering for sin.' The wrath of God was poured out on Christ as our substitute, standing in our place that we might be forgiven.

> I believe a word that forcefully captures the essence of Jesus' work of propitiation is the word exhausted. Jesus exhausted the wrath of God. It was not merely deflected and prevented from reaching us; it was exhausted. Jesus bore the full, unmitigated brunt of it. God's wrath against sin was unleashed in all its fury on His beloved Son. He held nothing back.
> (Jerry Bridges, *The Gospel for Real Life*, NavPress, 2002, p. 56)

Heavenly Father, thank you that you held nothing back. You poured out all of your wrath at my sin on your Son so that I would never experience it. Lord Jesus, thank you that you stood in my place willingly. Help me grow to hate sin as much as you do. Give me strength to tackle sins which have become habitual, and avoid temptations. May my obedience bring you pleasure today. Amen.

Day 3

Read: Isaiah 53:1–12
Key verse: Isaiah 53:11

. . . .

After he has suffered,
he will see the light of life and be satisfied;
by his knowledge my righteous servant will justify many,
and he will bear their iniquities.

What did Jesus accomplish on the cross? Scripture says he 'justified' us. What does that mean? It is more than saying we are forgiven.

Justified is a legal term meaning that justice has been served and satisfied. When Britain had capital punishment, in Scotland if a man was hanged, a notice was posted outside the prison announcing the hanging. It had certain required legal language and would say, 'On such-and-such a date, at Market Cross, so-and-so [naming the prisoner] was justified.' What did it mean? Did it mean the prisoner had been forgiven? No, it meant justice had been satisfied, the case had been closed and could never be resurrected in a court of law again.

Justification is much deeper than forgiveness. It means the case against us is over, it has been legally satisfied. It is finished.

Of course it is true that the mercy and love of God lie behind the cross, but if God were to forgive us on the basis of mercy alone, we might be forgiven, but we would not be justified. We are justified on the basis that Jesus satisfied the justice of God. We may wonder as we confess the same sin that we have confessed so many times before if we've come to the point of exhausting God's mercy. But we appeal not to his mercy, but to his justice! When we appeal to his justice, God is legally and morally obligated to forgive. 'He is faithful and *just* to forgive us our sins and to cleanse us from all unrighteousness' (1 John 1:9, ESV, emphasis added).

When we come in repentance and say, 'I have failed again. Father, would you forgive me?', he looks at the cross, and our sin is paid for. Don't let past sins condemn you any more. Because Christ has absorbed the justice of God, the case against you is over.

> As we come to Christ . . . empty-handed, claiming no merit of our own, but clinging by faith to His blood and righteousness, we are justified. We pass immediately from a state of condemnation and spiritual death to a state of pardon, acceptance, and the sure hope of eternal life. Our sins are blotted out, and we are 'clothed' with the righteousness of Jesus Christ. In our standing before God, we will never be more righteous, even in heaven, than we were the day we trusted Christ, or we are now.
> (Jerry Bridges, *The Gospel for Real Life,* NavPress, 2002, p. 107)

We are justified. The penalty for our sin has been paid, and the case against us is closed. Of course, in our daily lives we still sin and fall short of the perfect righteousness God requires. But don't give up. Keep on coming to God for forgiveness. The Puritans called this 'renewing our repentance' – asking God to take the forgiveness he has already granted through Christ's death and apply it to our sins today. And keep on pursuing holiness, asking for Holy Spirit power to become what we are – righteous in God's sight.

Day 4

Read: Isaiah 53:1–12

Key verse: Isaiah 53:9

....

He was assigned a grave with the wicked,
    and with the rich in his death,
though he had done no violence,
    nor was any deceit in his mouth.

Are you plagued with guilt for past sin?

We need to know that not only have we been justified, but our sin has been buried. At Calvary Jesus bore our sin, he satisfied the wrath of God, and he legally removed our guilt so that we are justified. And having died, he was buried. Because of our union with Christ, not only have we died with him; we – including our sin – are buried with him too (Romans 6:4).

Historically, Jesus should not have been buried, because in Jerusalem the bodies of criminals were thrown into a deep narrow gorge on the south side of the city, which is known as the Valley of Gehenna. In Jesus' day it was known as the rubbish dump of Jerusalem, where a fire burned continually. But Jesus was not placed there, because Joseph of Arimathea, a member of the Sanhedrin, approached Pilate to ask for the body of Jesus (John 19:38). With Pilate's permission, Joseph took Jesus' body away, buried him in his own tomb, and this remarkable prophecy in Isaiah 53:9 was fulfilled.

There is a finality to burial. The time between death and burial is usually a difficult period for loved ones. But once burial has taken place, it is final. In being 'buried with Christ', we don't need to feel guilt over our confessed sins because they have been fully and finally buried with Christ. 'Therefore, there is now no condemnation for those who are in Christ Jesus' (Romans 8:1).

So whenever we feel condemned, we can be sure it is not God speaking to us. The devil is the one who accuses us before God day and night (Revelation 12:10). There are two who speak to us about our sins: the devil and the Holy Spirit. The devil condemns but the Holy Spirit convicts. Here is the difference: condemnation is like a wet blanket that sits on us and we can't get out from under it; conviction makes us aware of our sin, but at the same time the Holy Spirit points us to the cross and offers cleansing and forgiveness.

Whose voice are you listening to?

When the devil whispers to us about our sin, he breathes hopelessness and despair. 'Your friends would be horrified if they knew what you had done.' 'With your track record, you can't possibly serve God.' 'You'll never escape this cycle of sin.' Don't listen to the devil's condemnation, but remind him your sin has been buried.

In contrast, when the Holy Spirit speaks, we are cut to the heart, realizing how much our sin grieves God and how much it cost the Lord Jesus. But this conviction comes with the offer of forgiveness, hope and renewal. It comes with the comfort that there is 'no condemnation for those who are in Christ'. Today listen for the Spirit's voice, repent when he highlights your sin, and rely on his strength to live out your new life 'in Christ'.

Day 5

Read: Isaiah 53:1–12
Key verse: Isaiah 53:12

....

Therefore I will give him a portion among the great,
    and he will divide the spoils with the strong,
because he poured out his life unto death,
    and was numbered with the transgressors.
For he bore the sin of many,
    and made intercession for the transgressors.

What is a transgressor? It is a law-breaker, and everyone has broken God's law (1 John 3:4; Romans 3:23).

At the cross Jesus was 'numbered among the transgressors'. He was identified as one of us. He became a sinner in his standing before the Father. He who knew no sin was made to be sin for us (2 Corinthians 5:21). He did this so that he might intercede for transgressors, speak to God on our behalf. So he says to the Father, 'Charles Price has sinned again. He has confessed. I'm on his side, I am his defender and advocate. On the grounds of my own death, he is forgiven; he is justified.'

This is the language of substitution. Christ was made sin and stood in my place, I am made righteous and stand in his place. His sin was not about him, but it was about me; and my righteousness is not about me, but it's about him. He received our infirmities, our sorrows, our transgressions, iniquities and punishment. And we received his peace, healing and righteousness (verses 4–5).

It is important to grasp this teaching on substitution.

First, it reminds us that our godliness has nothing to do with how well we perform, but everything to do with the sufficiency of what Jesus did on the cross. Second, it challenges us about doubting our forgiveness. It is not being humble to doubt your forgiveness, because you are actually doubting Jesus. Of course we don't deserve forgiveness, but when we doubt that we are clean before God, we doubt the effectiveness of the cross. It says in 1 John 4:17, 'This is how love is made complete among us so that we will have confidence on the day of judgement.'

On that final day we are going to stand before God with confidence – not self-confidence, pride or arrogance, but in utter humility, confident that Jesus Christ is enough.

Are you doubting whether God can really forgive your sins? Are you measuring yourself by your own goodness? Will you trust that Jesus' death in your place is sufficient – sufficient to make you clean before God now, sufficient one day to stand before him, blameless and approved, sufficient for him to be as delighted with you as he is with Christ?

> In Christianity, the moment we believe, God imputes Christ's perfect performance to us as if it were our own, and adopts us into His family. In other words, God can say to us just as He once said to Christ, 'You are My Son, whom I love; with you I am well pleased.' (Tim Keller, *The Freedom of Self-Forgetfulness*, 10 Publishing, 2017, p. 40)

Day 6

Read: Matthew 27:11–31
Key verses: Matthew 27:27–31

....

Then the governor's soldiers took Jesus into the Praetorium . . .
28 They stripped him and put a scarlet robe on him, 29 and then
twisted together a crown of thorns and set it on his head. They
put a staff in his right hand. Then they knelt in front of him and
mocked him. "Hail, king of the Jews!" they said. 30 They spat on
him, and took the staff and struck him on the head again and
again. 31 After they had mocked him . . . Then they led him away
to crucify him.

'Hail, king of the Jews!' the governor's soldiers jeered.

What takes place in verses 27–31 is not standard protocol, but barrack-room humour. The soldiers put a scarlet robe on Jesus, as if he were an emperor or some great leader. They set a crown of thorns on his head, pretending he's a king. Then they put a stick in his hand, pretending it's a sceptre, and kneel in front of him saying, 'Hail, your majesty!' Laughing, they bash the stick against his head again and again.

When they say, 'Hail, King of the Jews!', what they really mean is, 'You're a counterfeit. You're not really the King of the Jews at all!' Pilate makes sure this is the charge written against Jesus because this makes him out to be treasonous against Caesar (verse 37). Their message was: he's a scoundrel and this is what happens to scoundrels. They mean the charge to be deeply ironic. But God knows, Matthew knows and the readers know that Jesus really is the King of the Jews. The soldiers have got it right, and they don't even know it.

The idea of Jesus' kingship has been building from about 1000 BC, when 2 Samuel 7 records the founding of the Davidic dynasty. Over the years there is more revelation about this king. Isaiah 9:6–7 records, 'To us a child is born, to us a son is given . . . he will reign on David's throne.' He is described in spectacular ways: 'Wonderful Counsellor, Mighty God, Everlasting Father, Prince of Peace'.

So there arose a greater and greater expectation of the coming of a messianic figure – an anointed king in David's line who would one day rule. Significantly, the New Testament begins with the origins of Jesus Christ, the son of Abraham, the son of David. Matthew's Gospel starts with a genealogy, broken up, somewhat artificially, into three series of fourteens, and it is significant that the central fourteen names cover the years of the Old Testament Davidic dynasty. Jesus himself preaches about the 'kingdom of God', and in his parables, like the parable of the sheep and the goats (Matthew 25:31–46), he frequently mentions a king. When you read those narratives carefully, you see that the king cannot be anyone other than Jesus.

A king without soldiers, arms or a geographical domain; headed for death. Jesus is a King with a shatteringly different kingdom: 'The Son of Man did not come to be served, but to serve and to give his life as a ransom for many' (Matthew 20:28). Today Jesus calls his followers to live out the values of his kingdom. One thing this means is that we dare not stand pompously on the authority of our office or focus on ourselves, but rather, passionately seek the good of those in our care.

Day 7

Read: Matthew 27:32–44

Key verse: Matthew 27:32

• •

As they were going out, they met a man from Cyrene, named Simon, and they forced him to carry the cross.

'We all have our crosses to bear!' we say, referring to an ingrown toenail or an obstreperous mother-in-law. But in the first century, crucifixion was not a joking matter.

Usually the upright of the cross was left in the ground, and the condemned criminal carried the crossbar on his shoulder, out to the place of crucifixion. There you were stripped naked and tied or nailed down to the crossbar. The crossbar was hung up on the upright; your feet were fastened, and thus you were crucified. But Jesus is already so weak, he has been battered so badly he can't even carry the wood on his shoulder, so they have to conscript Simon of Cyrene. It's a picture of his utter weakness, his powerlessness.

The soldiers divide up his clothes and keep watch over him. At an earlier period of the empire they would sometimes just have left people hanging, without guarding them. Once or twice friends had come along and taken the victim down, who would then survive. So now it was imperial policy to leave a quaternion of soldiers (four soldiers) on duty until the crucified person had actually died. Carrying a cross signalled there was no hope at all any more. You were going to die the most excruciating death.

Jesus used this crucifixion image earlier in Matthew's Gospel: 'Whoever wants to be my disciple must deny themselves and take up their cross and follow me. For whoever wants to save their life will lose it, but whoever loses their life for me will find it' (Matthew 16:24–25). For the condemned individual, all that is left is ignominy, pain, shame and death. Jesus says, 'If you want to be my disciple, you have to be similarly crucified every day.'

Of course, for the overwhelming majority of Christians worldwide, Jesus' words have to be taken metaphorically; most of us don't die that way. Jesus speaks so starkly because he understands that what must happen for us to be disciples is, in a sense, equally deeply cutting: we die to ourselves. Jesus himself in the garden cries, 'Not what I will, but what you will!' Genuine disciples of Jesus learn to pray the same thing. We take up our cross. We die willingly, daily, to rise in newness of life, to serve the Lord Christ, who died – literally – on our behalf, emptying himself, burying our guilt so that we might live again.

> What are our crosses? They are not simply trials and hardships . . . A cross results from specifically walking in Christ's steps, embracing His life. It comes from bearing disdain because we follow the narrow way of Jesus Christ . . . It comes from living out the business and sexual ethics of Christ in the market place, the community, the family, the world. It comes from standing true in difficult circum-stances for the sake of the gospel. Our crosses come from and are proportionate to our dedication to Christ. Difficulties do not indicate cross-bearing, though difficulties for Christ's sake do. Do we have any difficulties because we are closely following Christ?
> (Kent Hughes, *Luke*, Crossway Books, 2015, p. 349)

Day 8

Read: Matthew 27:32–44
Key verses: Matthew 27:39–40

....

Those who passed by hurled insults at him, shaking their heads ⁴⁰*and saying, "You who are going to destroy the temple and build it in three days, save yourself! Come down from the cross, if you are the Son of God!"*

Did Jesus actually say that he would destroy the temple?

It was a dangerous charge, because destroying a temple, even just desecrating one, was a capital offence in the Roman Empire. There were so many religions in the empire that this was one of the ways that the Romans imposed peace. False witnesses reported that Jesus had said this (Matthew 26:61), but the charges didn't stick. In the end, as far as the Roman courts were concerned, the charge was that in claiming to be a king, he was a threat to Caesar.

So, what *had* Jesus said? This is one instance where you get a fuller picture if you read the Gospels together. At the beginning of his ministry John records Jesus as saying, 'Destroy this temple, and I will raise it again in three days' (John 2:19). Neither his opponents nor his disciples understood what he meant. Perhaps their confusion was understandable. Temple-building was a slow process. In Jerusalem you weren't allowed to use a hammer and chisel anywhere within hearing of the temple, which meant that everything had to be cut, measured and brought in without hydraulics – and then put in place. Construction took a long time.

But after Jesus had died and risen again, the disciples remembered his words and believed the Scriptures (John 2:22). They understood he was talking about his own body. The temple was the place where human beings were reconciled to God by the sacrifices that God himself had ordained, such as the sacrifice of Passover, the morning and evening sacrifice, the sacrifice of the Day of Atonement. Jesus now becomes the temple because he becomes the great meeting-place between a holy God and sinful people.

The people think they're being ironic, 'Oh, you're the great temple destroyer and temple builder!' By which they mean, of course, exactly the opposite. 'You are going to destroy the temple and build it in three days? Look at you! You can't do anything!' Their mockery is thick. But there's a deeper irony because God knows, Matthew knows and the reader knows that it's by staying on the cross that Jesus builds the new temple by which sinners like you and me are reconciled to God. The one who is powerless is in fact powerful, and he becomes the great temple that brings sinners and God together precisely by emptying himself and becoming a wretch on a cross.

> Christ was all anguish that I may be joy,
> cast off that I might be brought in,
> trodden down as an enemy
> that I might be welcomed as a friend,
> surrendered to hell's worst
> that I might attain heaven's best,
> stripped that I might be clothed,
> wounded that I might be healed,
> athirst that I might drink,
> tormented that I might be comforted,
> made a shame that I might inherit glory,
> entered darkness that I might have eternal light.
> (ed. Arthur Bennett, *Valley of Vision*, Banner of Truth Trust, 2016, p. 76)

Day 9

Read: Matthew 27:32–44
Key verses: Matthew 27:41–42

....

In the same way the chief priests, the teachers of the law and the elders mocked him. [42] *"He saved others," they said, "but he can't save himself! He's the king of Israel! Let him come down now from the cross, and we will believe in him."*

What does the verb 'to save' mean?

If you're a sports fan, it's what you're supposed to do to stop the ball dribbling into the net in a World Cup game. If you're a computer geek, it's what you had better do unless you want to lose an awful lot of data. But what does 'to save' mean in the New Testament? In Matthew 1:21 Joseph is told, 'You are to give him the name Jesus, because he will save his people from their sins.'

This announcement provides a grid for how we are supposed to read Matthew's Gospel. So when Jesus teaches in the Sermon on the Mount, he is presenting what the consummated kingdom will be like when he has saved his people from their sins. There will actually be perfection: 'Be perfect as your heavenly Father is perfect.'

In chapter 10 when Jesus sends out his disciples, and in chapter 28 when he issues the Great Commission, we learn how Jesus will save his people from their sins through the proclamation of the gospel. This message 'Jesus saves' is in every chapter of the Gospel and ties the entire book together.

Of course, when the chief priests jeered, 'He saved others, but he can't save himself!' they meant to be ironic. 'He can't be much of a saviour to be hanging on the cross, damned by God and human beings both!' But God knows, Matthew knows and the reader knows that there's a deeper irony. It is precisely by not saving himself that he saves others.

If he had stepped down from the cross, the chief priests would have had to backtrack. In one sense, they would have believed. But they wouldn't have been believing in the Son of God who offers his life as a sacrifice, because he wouldn't be offering his life as a sacrifice. It is precisely by staying there that he saves others. When the mockers say, 'He saved others, but he cannot save himself,' they think the 'cannot' is bound up with the nails. But Jesus has already declared in the previous hours: 'Do you think I cannot call on . . . twelve legions of angels?' (Matthew 26:53). A few rusty nails aren't going to mean all that much to twelve legions of angels. No, the 'cannot' is not physical, it's moral.

Jesus is constrained not by might, nails or loss of blood. He is constrained by his passionate commitment to do his Father's will. In that sense, he cannot save himself, and that is how he saves others.

Heavenly Father, thank you that the Lord Jesus stayed on the cross to save me; not held there by nails but his obedience to you. He suffered the soldiers' beatings, endured the religious leaders' mockery, wore the crown of thorns, and let sinful men crucify him because of his passionate commitment to his Father's will and his enduring love for us – 'Hallelujah, what a Saviour!' (Philip P. Bliss, 1875)

Day 10

Read: Matthew 27:38–54
Key verse: Matthew 27:46

....

About three in the afternoon Jesus cried out in a loud voice, "Eli, Eli, lema sabachthani?" (which means "My God, my God, why have you forsaken me?").

'He trusts in God. Let God rescue him now,' the religious leaders jeer (verse 43). Full of irony, what they really mean is, 'He can't really trust in God. If he did, God wouldn't have let him go to the cross!' Jesus' anguished cry, 'My God, my God, why have you forsaken me?' almost seems to justify their charges.

But the opposite is true. Jesus is quoting a psalm of David. Throughout Psalm 22 David simultaneously cries to God in the most abject despair, while demonstrating his trust in God. It's not that the despair means that David is not trusting in God. It's precisely in his despair that he trusts God all the more! Jesus understands the meaning of the text, and as David's royal heir, he now uses the same words. He is the Davidic King who is trusting in his heavenly Father as he cries out in a despair even greater than David's.

While he cries out, the heavens become dark, a way of symbolizing that the wrath of God is upon Christ as he goes to the cross. We remember Matthew's words laced throughout his Gospel that have anticipated this event. He speaks of Jesus as the One who will take away our sins, and who came not to be served but to serve and to give his life as a ransom for many (Matthew 1:21; 20:28). Just a few hours earlier on the night that he was betrayed, Jesus himself says that his blood 'is the blood of the new covenant, which is shed for many for the remission of sins' (Matthew 26:28, NKJV).

Jesus knew what he was doing when he went to the cross. He wasn't taken by surprise. But in the bleakness of the hour, as all our sin is upon him, and he feels utterly abandoned and alone, the person of the Godhead who bears our guilt cries out in the most amazingly bleak despair – while simultaneously trusting in God. God knows, Matthew knows and the readers know that it was that trust in God that prompted Jesus to say in the garden, 'Not my will, but yours be done.' Jesus' trust in God took him to this very place.

Jesus cried, 'My God, my God, why have you forsaken me?' so that for all eternity, you wouldn't have to. As the poet Elizabeth Barrett Browning wrote so eloquently,

> Yea, once, Immanuel's orphaned cry his universe
> hath shaken –
> It went single, echoless, 'My God, I am forsaken!'
> It went up from the Holy lips
> Amid His lost creation,
> That of the lost no son should use
> Those words of desolation.
> (Elizabeth Barrett Browning, 'Cowper's Grave', in *The Complete Poetical Works of Elizabeth Barrett Browning*, BiblioBazaar, 2009, p. 59)

Today, know that in your deepest moments of despair, ill health and grief, God will never forsake you. You can trust him in the darkness, you can cling to him in obedience, because just as at Calvary, he is working his purpose out and he is in control.

Day 11

Read: John 19:17–27
Key verses: John 19:17–18

. . . .

Carrying his own cross, he went out to the place of the Skull (which in Aramaic is called Golgotha). ¹⁸There they crucified him, and with him two others – one on each side and Jesus in the middle.

Imagine the scene:

Jesus carries his own cross, almost certainly only the cross-piece. Normally the upright was already in place in cities within the empire; crucifixions were depressingly commonplace. He staggers along the road, with help from Simon of Cyrene (Mark 15:21). No doubt overwhelmed with loss of blood from his scourging and beating, he collapses beneath the load.

They come to a small hill called Golgotha. There the soldiers crucify him, which means they would have laid Jesus on that cross-piece, driven a nail through each wrist, right through the central nerve as it runs down the arm. The pain would be unspeakable. Then, with some pulley arrangement, they would attach the cross-piece to the upright, fix it in place, and then the two feet, one on top of the other, would be nailed to the wood.

Hanging there in that position meant the chest cavity was hugely constricted, and so to open it to get breath, you had to pull and push, and the pain would sear through the body. A gasp of breath and then you sink down again, and then another and another. This strange and terrible dance of death went on until the victim, unable any longer to make the effort to breathe, would be mercifully delivered by asphyxiation. People hung on crosses sometimes for days. The Roman writer Cicero described it as 'a most cruel and disgusting punishment' (Michael Licona, *The Resurrection of Jesus: A New Historiographical Approach*, IVP, 2010, p. 304).

The Gospel writers do not dwell unduly on the physical agony of the crucifixion, and neither should we. However, it is worth pausing to reflect on the extent of Christ's suffering and what he endured to save us. Because Christ suffered, we can be sure he understands our suffering and stands with us in it.

> In the real world of pain, how could one worship a God who was immune to it? I have entered many Buddhist temples in different Asian countries and stood respectfully before the statue of the Buddha, his legs crossed, arms folded, eyes closed, the ghost of a smile playing round his mouth, a remote look on his face, detached from the agonies of the world. But each time after a while I have had to turn away. And in imagination I have turned instead to that lonely, twisted, tortured figure on the cross, nails through hands and feet, back lacerated, limbs wrenched, brow bleeding from thorn-pricks, mouth dry and intolerably thirsty, plunged in Godforsaken darkness. That is the God for me! He laid aside his immunity to pain. He entered our world of flesh and blood, tears and death. He suffered for us. Our sufferings become more manageable in the light of his. There is still a question mark against human suffering, but over it we boldly stamp another mark, the cross that symbolizes divine suffering.
> (John Stott, *The Cross of Christ*, IVP, 1986, p. 387)

Day 12

Read: John 19:17–27
Key verses: John 19:19–22

....

> *Pilate had a notice prepared and fastened to the cross. It read:*
> JESUS OF NAZARETH, THE KING OF THE JEWS. [20] *Many of the Jews read*
> *this sign, for the place where Jesus was crucified was near*
> *the city, and the sign was written in Aramaic, Latin and Greek.*
> [21] *The chief priests of the Jews protested to Pilate, 'Do not write,*
> *"The King of the Jews", but that this man claimed to be king*
> *of the Jews.'*
> [22] *Pilate answered, "What I have written, I have written."*

At that moment Jesus looked like a strange king.

Writhing in the darkness – because darkness had fallen upon the whole land – terrible minute upon terrible minute, hour after hour. He was the antithesis of dominion in every sense. But, despite appearances, Jesus is the greatest King. Pilate's sign, 'Here is the King', was written in three languages. Unintentionally appropriate, because Jesus claims the world!

The sign was written in Greek, the language historically associated with the realm of culture. The church at times has turned a jaundiced eye upon all things artistic and creative, but Christ claims the world of culture no less than any other. Human creativity surely is a gift from him who made all things, and these gifts, brought to his feet, can be made a vehicle of praise to him.

'Here is the King' was written in Latin, the language of government, law and institutions. Too often the church has been unwilling to get involved in the messy, sometimes evil world of business, politics and power, but Christ claims this world as his own too. He is able, through lives surrendered to his lordship, to bring the salt and light of his kingdom to the arenas of public life.

The final inscription was written in Aramaic, and Christ claims the world of religion, which that language represents, as his own. He alone is the way to God; he calls us to acknowledge him, and in his name to call the lost millions who follow the empty gods of other religions, to bow before this King, exalted on a cross. Jesus himself promised, 'And I, when I am lifted up from the earth, will draw all people to myself' (John 12:32).

One of the great limitations that have beset human saviours, who over the centuries have dreamed dreams and flung their empires around the world, is that too often they lose sight of the individual. Our little personal universe of hope, pain, struggle and achievement is irrelevant to the great plan. The individual becomes expendable. Not to this King. Jesus rules in all the world, and yet he also comes to us in our personal world; our King is the King of the world.

Jesus was never more kingly than when he was dying to save us. One day his kingship over every sphere of life will be recognized – everyone will bow before him and confess he is Lord (Philippians 2:10–11). Until then we worship him and submit to his rule, praying that others would acknowledge his kingship willingly, while there is still time.

Day 13

Read: John 19:17–27
Key verses: John 19:23–27

••

When the soldiers crucified Jesus, they took his clothes, dividing them into four shares, one for each of them, with the undergarment remaining. This garment was seamless, woven in one piece from top to bottom.

24 "Let's not tear it," they said to one another. "Let's decide by lot who will get it."
This happened that the scripture might be fulfilled that said,
*   "They divided my clothes among them*
*   and cast lots for my garment."*
So this is what the soldiers did.

25 Near the cross of Jesus stood his mother, his mother's sister, Mary the wife of Clopas, and Mary Magdalene. 26 When Jesus saw his mother there, and the disciple whom he loved standing nearby, he said to her, "Woman, here is your son," 27 and to the disciple, "Here is your mother." From that time on, this disciple took her into his home.

If this was a scene from a film, the spotlight would be intently focused on Jesus. However, around the cross, some others played minor roles, which John captured in intricate detail. He presents us with four cameos which add to our understanding of what went on that first Good Friday.

Cameo one. Other criminals on each side, Jesus in the middle (verse 18). It is appropriate that, to the very last, Jesus is among sinners.

Cameo two. The Jewish high priests urged Pilate, the Roman governor, to change the sign he had prepared and fastened to the cross: 'Jesus of Nazareth, the King of the Jews' (verse 21). But Pilate would not be pushed any more. (To learn about Pilate's role in Jesus' crucifixion, read John 18:28–19:16.) He would not change the truth into a lie.

Cameo three. The soldiers distributed Jesus' belt, sandals, head turban and outer garment among themselves. But his undergarment was rather special; it was seamless, woven in one piece from top to bottom, and so they gambled for it. Psalm 22, written a thousand years before, is fulfilled astonishingly to the very letter: 'They divided my clothes among them and cast lots for my garment.' Such fulfilment of Scripture is an indication of God's presence and sovereignty, even in the midst of all this darkness.

Cameo four. We see the women who cared for Jesus standing near the cross. 'A sword will pierce your soul,' the old man Simeon had said to Mary when she and Joseph took Jesus to the temple for the first time (Luke 2:35). Now that sword was turning. What pain for Mary, for any mother, to be there, and yet, where else would she be? She's there for him. And, in his last moments of life, Jesus ministers to his mother in infinite love, commissioning John to look after her: 'Here is your son; here is your mother.'

If you had been at Calvary that first Good Friday, how would you have responded? What part do you think you would have played? I hope I would have been like that other soldier in Mark 15:39: 'When the centurion, who stood there in front of Jesus, saw how he died, he said, "Surely this man was the Son of God!"'

Day 14

Read: John 19:28–37
Key verses: John 19:28–30

. . . .

Later, knowing that everything had now been finished, and so that Scripture would be fulfilled, Jesus said, "I am thirsty." ²⁹ *A jar of wine vinegar was there, so they soaked a sponge in it, put the sponge on a stalk of the hyssop plant, and lifted it to Jesus' lips.* ³⁰ *When he had received the drink, Jesus said, "It is finished." With that, he bowed his head and gave up his spirit.*

What does Jesus mean when he cries out, 'It is finished'?

- *His obedience to his Father's will is finished.* Jesus said, 'My food . . . is to do the will of him who sent me and to finish his work' (John 4:34).

- *His defeat of his Father's enemy is finished.* Jesus triumphed over Satan once and for all. 'Having disarmed the powers and authorities, he made a public spectacle of them, triumphing over them by the cross' (Colossians 2:15).

- *The revealing of his Father's heart is finished.* There is no God behind the back of Jesus, but Jesus reveals all that God is to us. Jesus had said, 'Anyone who has seen me has seen the Father' (John 14:9). He prayed to his Father, 'I have revealed you to those whom you gave me out of the world' (John 17:6). At the cross we see the climax of that revelation. We see how holy God is because he cannot overlook, forget or ignore sin. We also see God's infinite and everlasting love thundering from Calvary across the generations. Look at the cross and tell yourself: this is not just what God thought about me two thousand years ago, but this is exactly what God thinks and feels about me now.

- *The redeeming of the Father's world is finished.* Jesus died in Jerusalem at Passover, a feast commemorating that moment in Egypt when for the liberation of the Israelites a spotless lamb was slain. Now all these centuries later the perfect Lamb of God is slain on the cross and his blood is shed so that we might be free. It is appropriate that this scene ends with Jesus taking a drink and then saying, 'It is finished.' In his death he is taking another cup from the hand of his Father, a cup of wrath and judgement (Isaiah 51:17). He drinks that cup until not a drop is left, and then cries out, 'It is finished.' On the cross Jesus' finished work achieved salvation, full and free, for all his people for ever more.

> The Lord Jesus could die on the cross a thousand times, yet no salvation would be accomplished until God in heaven was satisfied . . . If the work of Christ is to be finished, it is essential that it be finished in the estimation of God.
>
> 'Is it truly finished?' the Father might be pictured asking himself. 'Did he do all that I sent him to do? Was he perfect in his character and life . . . and – above all – did he really save the sinners I sent him to save?' And on the third day the Father raised him from the dead, so that we might know the estimate he placed on his Son.
> (Alec Motyer, *Lord Is King: Keswick 1979*, STL, 1979, pp. 131–132)

Day 15

Read: John 19:28–37
Key verses: John 19:33–37

....

But when they came to Jesus and found that he was already dead, they did not break his legs. ³⁴ Instead, one of the soldiers pierced Jesus' side with a spear, bringing a sudden flow of blood and water. ³⁵ The man who saw it has given testimony, and his testimony is true. He knows that he tells the truth, and he testifies so that you also may believe. ³⁶ These things happened so that the scripture would be fulfilled: "Not one of his bones will be broken," ³⁷ and, as another scripture says, "They will look on the one they have pierced."

Could Jesus simply have been unconscious on the cross?

Many Muslims and others still believe the 'swoon theory', that Jesus did not die on the cross – he simply fainted, or swooned, and was presumed dead. But this is absolute nonsense.

Let's look at the facts.

The Jews were anxious to clear the crosses for Passover, so the soldiers were given permission to break the legs of the crucified. When individuals could no longer push up on the cross and breathe, they expired quickly. By the time the soldiers came to Jesus, they realized he was already dead. To make absolutely sure, they pierced him with a spear. The Roman soldiers knew a dead body when they saw one. That same spear had probably been thrust through dozens before Jesus. Besides which, how could Jesus, having barely escaped death, a few days later have filled the disciples with a radiant conviction that he'd not only come back, but he'd conquered death (see John 20–21)? It's impossible. Jesus was dead.

The blood pours from Jesus' side. But there's something else – water. Because Jesus probably died of cardiac arrest, as the final act of taking the world's sin upon him, there is a gathering of fluid around the lungs, and so water flows out. John sees it and knows it is water, the great symbol of the Spirit, the water of life. Jesus talked to Nicodemus about it. He talked to the woman of Samaria about it. He spoke of the Spirit they would receive and, wonderfully, even as Jesus dies, the Spirit is stirring.

These marvellous prophecies from Zechariah 12:10, Psalm 34:20 and Exodus 12, given five hundred, a thousand and thirteen hundred years earlier, are fulfilled to the letter. God is in control; the Spirit is moving.

Jesus truly died, and evil appeared to have triumphed. But, in reality, God's sovereignty was undiminished, and his Spirit was at work. The cross testifies to the unshakeable truth that God is not only in control of dire circumstances, but can use them to further his eternal purposes. Praise God that in our darkest times, in our deepest suffering, he is in control and at work.

> The sovereignty of God is the one impregnable rock to which the suffering human heart must cling. The circumstances surrounding our lives are no accident; they may be the work of evil, but that evil is held firmly within the mighty hand of our sovereign God . . . All evil is subject to Him, and evil cannot touch His children unless He permits it.
> (Margaret Clarkson, *Grace Grows Best in Winter*, Eerdmans, 1984, pp. 40–41)

Day 16

Read: Romans 8:28–39
Key verse: Romans 8:30

....

And those he predestined, he also called; those he called, he also justified; those he justified, he also glorified.

Imagine a wedding.

The man says 'I do' and the woman says 'I do', and then the minister pronounces them 'husband and wife'. It's an objective declaration. It is this kind of objective declaration that Paul is talking about when he says in verse 30 that we are 'justified'. As Jesus bore our sins on the cross, God looked at his death and said, 'There is a legal payment for sin, and I am satisfied.' When you believed in Jesus, God saw a legal transaction take place: all Christ's righteousness was credited to you. This doesn't mean that when you put your faith in Jesus, you are perfect in character. It means that you are suddenly perfect in status. Like a marriage, it is a declaration, not a transformation.

The technical term for attributing righteousness is 'impute'. The Bible says that if I have called on the Lord, put my faith in him, God has credited to me, imputed to me, not only forgiveness, but righteousness.

So, being justified means:

• *You can be sure of your salvation.* Your salvation is not dependent on how you feel or perform. God's declaration is based on the death of Jesus.

• *You can be sure you are accepted by God.* Acceptance in society is based on how you look and succeed. The hunger to be accepted is never satisfied because you can never sustain the position of beauty and success – it is a momentary thing. In contrast, God's acceptance of the believer is fixed, secure, profound and for ever.

- *You can be sure of the final verdict.* Christianity is very simple. You say 'no' to Christ, and one day he will say 'no' to you. You say 'yes' to Christ, and one day he will say 'yes' to you. It is not pride to say, 'I am going to heaven'; it is pride to doubt God's verdict on your life when Christ has died and God has spoken.

- *You can be sure God is for you.* Isaiah 30:18 says, 'Yet the LORD longs to be gracious to you; therefore he will rise up to show you compassion. For the LORD is a God of justice. Blessed are all who wait for him!' Suffering does not have an attack built into it. God may use suffering to shape and transform, but it is wielded by God who works for your good and loves you through to the end.

If you are dealing with doubts and difficulties, remind yourself of the truth of the gospel. Meditate on the certainties of what God's declaration of being 'justified' means for your life. Cling to the truth that your salvation is sure, you are accepted by God, the final verdict is not in doubt, and God is for you.

Day 17

Read: 1 Corinthians 1:17—2:5
Key verses: 1 Corinthians 1:17–18

....

For Christ did not send me to baptise, but to preach the gospel –
not with wisdom and eloquence, lest the cross of Christ be
*emptied of its power. *[18]*For the message of the cross is foolish-*
ness to those who are perishing, but to us who are being saved
it is the power of God.

How can we get right with God?

Other religions say, 'Here is what you must *do*. Go to the temple,
church or mosque. Perform religious duties. Give money away. Be
nice to those who are in trouble.' But the Christian message says,
'No. You will never be able to *do* enough.' There's a massive barrier
of sin that cuts off sinful people from the holy God. We will never be
able to *do* enough to get over that barrier. Yet wonderfully, uniquely,
it has all been done for us. Christ himself, through his death on the
cross, has blazed a trail through that great barrier of sin, and he's
taken upon himself all the things that we've done wrong, as well as
the judgement of his Father, so that we might be forgiven.

This message of the cross is rejected by most. In terms of human
wisdom, it is foolishness (1:18). But the weakness of the message of
the cross has divine mighty power (verse 17). One day we will look
around God's throne and see millions from every tribe, race and
nation, there because of the message of the cross. In the meantime,
how are we going to reach our friends, neighbours and those around
the world with the good news of Christ? Are we going to rely on
church planting, new buildings, seeker courses or brilliant speakers?
Those things might help, but they're just a means to the end. We
need to rely on the message of the cross. That is, the power of God.

Of course, this is not the message people are asking for. Just as the Jews demand miraculous signs (verse 22), there are still those who say, 'Go on, prove God. Unless you prove him to me, I won't believe in him.' The Greeks looked for wisdom, and there are millions today who say, 'Just impress me with something that makes sense and fits with the mindset of the world.' It is tempting to present a message that is soft on sin, judgement and the uniqueness of Christ, but strong on affirmation: 'You're wonderful; God loves you just as you are!' That message might be popular, but it's not powerful. Loads of people might come and hear it, but it saves none. We need to follow the example of the apostle Paul: 'We preach Christ crucified: a stumbling block to Jews and foolishness to Gentiles, but to those whom God has called, both Jews and Greeks, Christ the power of God and the wisdom of God' (verses 23–24).

Could it be that our evangelism is powerless because we have compromised the message? Pray for gospel conversations that you will have this week with family and friends, at church on Sunday, in the gym or at the school gate. Ask God to be at work as, in his strength, you present the message of 'Christ crucified'.

Day 18

Read: 1 Corinthians 1:17—2:5
Key verses: 1 Corinthians 2:2–5

....

For I resolved to know nothing while I was with you except Jesus Christ and him crucified. ³I came to you in weakness with great fear and trembling. ⁴My message and my preaching were not with wise and persuasive words, but with a demonstration of the Spirit's power, ⁵so that your faith might not rest on human wisdom, but on God's power.

'All God's giants have been weak people' (Vaughan Roberts, *True Spirituality*, IVP, 2011).

Those were the words of Hudson Taylor, the great nineteenth-century missionary to China. And he was right. Paul explains in 1 Corinthians 1:27, 'God chose the foolish things of the world to shame the wise; God chose the weak things of the world to shame the strong.' Choosing weak people is God's deliberate strategy. Why? 'So that no one may boast before him' (verse 29). It's quite clear that the power of God, bringing people to conversion, has worked through weak people. No one will exalt those weak people and say, 'Aren't you marvellous!' But they will glory in God, so that no one may boast before him.

When Paul first visited Corinth, he knew that he'd be much more acceptable if he gave them what they wanted: human wisdom. But quite deliberately, having thought it through, he resisted that temptation: 'When I came to you, I did not come with elegance or [superior] wisdom as I proclaimed to you the testimony about God. For I resolved to know nothing while I was with you except Jesus Christ and him crucified' (2:1–2). Paul was fearful speaking to the Corinthians because he knew that the world mocks and hates the message of the cross (verse 3). And yet a church was founded there by a weak man proclaiming a weak message in the power of the Spirit of God.

The devil tells us that if we want to see people becoming Christians, we need to pay attention to human personalities, techniques and oratory. His message is seductive: 'You want to reach the world, don't you? You want to see people saved! They're really not going to listen to you.' Paul's testimony is that God's power is seen in our weakness. Spiritual power is unleashed when weak men and women speak out the message of Christ and his cross.

If we are not fit to hold such a glorious treasure as the gospel, then why in the world would God entrust it to us?! 'To show that the surpassing power belongs to God and not to us.' We are unfit, breakable, disposable vessels, and God has decided to use our weakness to display his power and love. A jar of clay may be cracked in a few places, making it unusable in the world's eyes, but God sees these deficiencies as a means to pour out and reveal more of himself.

The pastor and author Mark Dever hits the nail on the head when he says,

When we rely on God, and God shows himself to be faithful, he gets the glory. This is what he has always intended. He does not intend us to be strong, self-reliant and without need of turning to him . . . He intends for us to be weak and oppressed, and then to turn and rely on him, because then he can provide what we need and thereby be glorified.
(Mark Dever, *The Message of the New Testament*, p. 203; quoted in Kirsten Wetherell and Sarah Walton, *Hope When it Hurts*, The Good Book Company, 2017, pp. 26–27)

Day 19

Read: Philippians 2:1–18

Key verses: Philippians 2:5–8

· ·

In your relationships with one another, have the same mindset
as Christ Jesus:
⁶who, being in very nature God,
   did not consider equality with God something to be used to
      his own advantage;
⁷rather, he made himself nothing
   by taking the very nature of a servant,
   being made in human likeness.
⁸And being found in appearance as a man,
   he humbled himself
   by becoming obedient to death –
   even death on a cross!

Is disunity and rivalry in a church and grumbling among Christians really that serious? Surely it isn't as serious as doctrinal heresy.

Paul's emphatic answer is: 'Yes, it is!' It is so serious that he urges the believers in Philippi to tackle their infighting and dissent (Philippians 1:15, 17; 2:14; 4:2) by adopting the same 'mindset as Christ'. Jesus plunged downwards from the heights of the Godhead. He was in very nature God, but made himself nothing, humbling himself to become a man, and more than that, to be a suffering servant who died on a cross.

Sharing the mindset of Christ means we too must travel the way of the cross. We don't move on from the message of the cross as soon as we become Christians, but rather, it must shape our lives more and more. That's why Paul retold the gospel to these Philippian believers. He did the same thing when he wrote to Titus to remind the converts in Crete to show humility to all. The believers were behaving as if they were superior to the non-Christians around them. To help them see they were no better than the non-Christians, but were simply forgiven, Paul goes back to the cross to teach them how to live. He explains, 'At one time we too were foolish, disobedient, deceived and enslaved by all kinds of passions and pleasures . . . But when the kindness and love of God our Saviour appeared, he saved us' (Titus 3:3–5). In Titus 3:4–7 Paul reminds them of the gospel and what the cross has achieved.

The apostle Peter also preaches to believers about the cross. In 1 Peter 2:24 he states, '"He himself bore our sins" in his body on the cross, so that we might die to sins and live for righteousness.' Why is Peter reminding Christians that they are saved through the cross of Christ? Because he is struggling with the issue: 'How can I get people who are employed to serve faithfully in the workplace?' Throughout the letters of the New Testament we find issues of Christian conduct resolved by returning to the message of the cross.

Gossip, family feuds, complaints about leaders, rotas, sermons . . . all are accepted, even expected, in our churches. But it shouldn't be this way. Jesus died to reconcile us to God and to each other. The cross makes reconciliation possible and shows us how it is achieved. As you serve alongside other believers, meet as a home group or talk with a Christian friend over coffee, what does it look like for the cross to shape your interactions and for you to share the mindset of Christ?

Day 20

Read: Philippians 2:1–30
Key verse: Philippians 2:12

....

Therefore, my dear friends, as you have always obeyed – not only in my presence, but now much more in my absence – continue to work out your salvation with fear and trembling . . .

What does Paul mean, 'continue to work out your salvation'?

He is not saying you have to save yourself. The cross saves us. But he is saying that we need to work out what it means to adopt a cross-shaped life. In verses 12–30 he gives us three examples of lives shaped by the cross:

• *Himself.* Paul says, 'Even if I am being poured out like a drink offering on the sacrifice and service coming from your faith, I am glad and rejoice with all of you' (verse 17). When the contents of a bottle are poured out, it empties itself and eventually there is nothing left. Paul is pouring out his life in service to God and others, reminding us of Jesus who 'made himself nothing' (verse 7).

• *Timothy.* Paul remarks, 'I have no one else like him [Timothy], who will show genuine concern for your welfare. For everyone looks out for their own interests, not those of Jesus Christ' (verses 20–21). Timothy was sharing the mindset of Christ as he overlooked his own interests for the sake of others (verses 4–5).

• *Epaphroditus.* Paul urges the Philippians to welcome and honour Epaphroditus because 'he almost died for the work of Christ' (verse 30). He was being shaped by the cross to the extent that he was prepared to risk his life in the service of others. Epaphroditus reminds us of Christ, who humbled himself, going all the way to the cross to give up his life for us.

The apostle does not see the rivalries and dissensions in church life and just cry, 'Work it out!' He portrays the cross of Christ and says, 'This is the way.' He gives us examples of humility, service, suffering and sacrifice, lives shaped by the cross of the Lord Jesus Christ. But more than that, he reminds us that though we stumble and fail, God is at work in us to will and to act according to his good purpose (verse 13). By the power of the Holy Spirit, God will help us make the cross-shaped life more and more of a reality.

Take to heart God's promise that as you live this cross-shaped life, you will shine like a star in the night sky (verses 15–16) – your life authenticating the gospel message to unbelievers; your transformation proving the gospel is true and God is at work.

Use the ACTS acronym to guide your prayers:

- *Adoration*. Worship Christ for his humility, coming to earth to die on a cross for our sake.
- *Confession*. Confess the particular ways you have failed to live a cross-shaped life this week.
- *Thanksgiving*. Thank God for Paul, Timothy, Epaphroditus and the men and women he has put into your life who are godly examples of cross-shaped living.
- *Supplication*. Ask for Holy Spirit power to live the way of the cross in all your dealings today.

Day 21

Read: Colossians 1:15–20
Key verses: Colossians 1:19–20

....

For God was pleased to have all his fullness dwell in him, [20] *and through him to reconcile to himself all things, whether things on earth or things in heaven, by making peace through his blood, shed on the cross.*

We do not need to be convinced that there is something fundamentally wrong with our world and with ourselves. The natural world is in disarray. Human society is marked by discord and disorder. Physical decline pursues us even from youth, and death comes to too many, too soon. The Bible says the reason for this is that ever since the first humans rebelled against God, our relationship with him has been severed.

We ourselves have been under God's judgement, but the implications are even wider than that. Human beings were given a stewardship over the world, but when we turned away from the Lord, the whole world over which we had responsibility came under judgement too. Thankfully God's redemption plan did not simply extend to plucking individual human souls out of this world and then placing them in heaven. It was not like the rushed airlifts in the final days of the Western withdrawal from Afghanistan when a few souls were rescued from the airport in Kabul while the city descended into chaos and destruction. No, God's plan was much grander and more comprehensive than that.

The first human beings, Adam and Eve, led the way in establishing a situation of enmity with God, disrupting the created order, and making the mess in which we find ourselves today. By contrast, the first born of the new creation, the Lord Jesus Christ, died on the cross to make peace with God and rose from the grave to open the door to new life. In doing so he led the way in reconciling us to God and establishing a new order where creation and people would be at peace with him.

This new creation begins with the resurrection of Jesus Christ. It comes to us as we receive forgiveness and new life in him, and it will come to fruition when Jesus brings us to a new heavens and a new earth – a place where all things are as God intended them to be, where there is no sin, suffering, death or disorder. The promises of God all point to this. But the key to it and the basis upon which it is all possible, is the work of Jesus at the cross of Calvary. Through Jesus, God the Father was reconciling the world to himself.

Step back and take in the panoramic view. Not only does Jesus' death reconcile to God all who believe, but there is nothing in the universe outside the range of God's reconciling work in Christ accomplished on the cross. Christ, the fullness of God, who was there in the beginning, who created and sustains all things, will, through his death on the cross, usher in the new creation. Praise God today for the power of the cross and the glorious message of the gospel.

Day 22

Read: Colossians 1:15–23
Key verses: Colossians 1:21–22

• •

Once you were alienated from God and were enemies in your minds because of your evil behaviour. [22] *But now he has reconciled you by Christ's physical body through death to present you holy in his sight, without blemish and free from accusation.*

Don't you love hearing testimonies or stories of how people came to put their trust in Christ?

In these verses Paul is giving the Colossians' testimony for them. He describes what they were like before they came to Christ (verse 21). 'Alienated from God' means separated and distanced from him. 'Enemies in your minds' is having a mindset of hostility to God. 'Evil behaviour' indicates living lives which were rebellious to him. Paul's strong language makes us wonder if there was something particularly bad about these Colossians. But there's no evidence in the letter that the Colossians were worse than anybody else. These are just the terms the apostle Paul uses to speak about people before they come to faith: 'All of us also lived among them at one time, gratifying the cravings of our flesh and following its desires and thoughts. Like the rest, we were by nature deserving of wrath' (Ephesians 2:3; see also Romans 8:7).

According to the Bible, we don't just need a bit of moral improvement, we have a sinful mindset and are hostile to God, and that's why we desperately need a Saviour. In his autobiography, *Surprised by Joy*, C. S. Lewis described the first time he looked into his own heart:

For the first time I examined myself with a seriously practical purpose. And there I found what appalled me: a zoo of lusts, a bedlam of ambitions, a nursery of fears, a harem of fondled hatreds. My name was Legion.
(Collins, 2016, p. 263)

Even if we can't think of a time when we weren't a Christian, the Bible says we still have a 'sinful nature' (Romans 7:25). Imagine what we would be like if it weren't for the work of the Spirit of God within us. We'd be alienated from God. That doesn't just mean us keeping God out of the picture, but God, in response to our hostility to him, separating himself from us.

However, Paul says, God has 'reconciled' us (Colossians 1:22). God took the initiative to deal with the consequences of our sin, and turned his face back towards us as Jesus died on the cross and bore the penalty for our sins. Then he sent his Holy Spirit to turn us round so we were in a situation of reconciliation with him. Paul takes us to the cross. He's not talking about a concept; he's talking about a real historical event. Salvation is not us turning over a new leaf. It's Jesus dying, bearing our sins, that we might be forgiven and reconciled to God.

Our reconciliation to God is permanent and eternal. Because Christ accomplished it for us, there is no possibility it can ever be undone. Though we continue, even as believers, to do those things that in themselves deserve God's displeasure, we can never revert to a state of divine alienation. For the sake of Christ, God will always accept us. And even when God deems it necessary to discipline us for persistent disobedience, He always does so out of love to restore us to the way of obedience (see Hebrews 12:4–11).
(Jerry Bridges, *The Gospel for Real Life*, NavPress, 2002, p. 96)

Day 23

Read: Colossians 1:15–23
Key verses: Colossians 1:21–22

••

Once you were alienated from God and were enemies in your minds because of your evil behaviour. ²²*But now he has reconciled you by Christ's physical body through death to present you holy in his sight, without blemish and free from accusation.*

Are you reticent about sharing the story of how you came to faith?

Some of us shy away from telling our testimony because it seems too uninteresting or mundane. You may have been saved as a child, and perhaps you don't have a dramatic conversion story. But every Christian's testimony is powerful. We were once alienated from God, but when we put our trust in Christ, our sins were forgiven, fully and freely.

At the cross God 'has reconciled you by Christ's physical body through death to present you *holy in his sight*'. Paul could have finished there, couldn't he? Present you holy in his sight, just as if you'd never sinned – but he goes on: 'without blemish'. The idea is of something completely unstained, no sign of a mark at all. Perfect. Imagine a car when you pick it up from the showroom; there are no scratches on the bodywork at all. Gradually, over the years, the blemishes pile up. In God's sight we are absolutely without blemish *and* free from accusation. There's no possibility that we could be held to account for our sins before the holy God, because he has dealt with them entirely. The devil, who loves to accuse us of our sins, has no ground to stand on because our sins have been wiped away by Christ's sacrifice. All our sin – past, present and future – has been dealt with at Calvary. Every skeleton in the cupboard that you worry about has been forgiven.

In these verses Paul is retelling the Colossians' story.

He describes what they were before they came to Christ, and what they are now because of Jesus' work on the cross. These believers have been saved from alienation from God into this marvellous reconciled relationship, from which no one can separate them. In verses 13–14 Paul tells their testimony in another way: 'For he has rescued us from the dominion of darkness and brought us into the kingdom of the Son he loves, in whom we have redemption, the forgiveness of sins.'

Because of what Jesus did on the cross this can be our story too, if we trust in him.

Your testimony may not seem very glamorous or exciting. You may not even remember the exact moment when you trusted in Christ. But don't let that stop you telling other people about what God has done for you. He has brought you from death to life, from alienation to reconciliation, from sinner to saved. Many other religions and life philosophies can change your life for the better, but only the gospel can reconcile you to God and 'present you holy in his sight . . . free from accusation' (verse 22). Don't reduce your testimony to how God has made you more fulfilled and given you a purpose. Put the focus on the Lord Jesus, his cross and the message of the gospel, and your testimony will never seem mundane again.

Day 24

Read: Colossians 1:15–23
Key verses: Colossians 1:22–23

....

But now he has reconciled you by Christ's physical body through death to present you holy in his sight, without blemish and free from accusation – 23 if you continue in your faith, established and firm, and do not move from the hope held out in the gospel. This is the gospel that you heard and that has been proclaimed to every creature under heaven, and of which I, Paul, have become a servant.

Do you realize just how good the good news is?

The Colossians were being bombarded by some unhelpful teaching, so Paul wrote to urge them not to move, not to be dissuaded, from the gospel (verse 23). We have to read through the letter to try and work out what's going on (2:2, 8), but it seems this teaching can best be summarized under the heading of 'gospel plus' (2:16). These were not woolly liberals, but zealous people saying, 'Yes, what you've heard is all very good, but you need this extra thing in order to lead a godly life.'

Paul responds by saying that, in Christ, you have everything you need. Jesus' absolute sufficiency is the powerful message throughout the letter (see 1:15–18). If I add to the gospel, I'm really taking away from it because I'm saying that who Jesus is, and what he's done, are not sufficient for me to live a godly life.

Of course, there's always room for growth in the Christian life. It is a tremendous battle to grow to be more like Christ, but it's a great mistake to think that we need something more than Christ to be saved or to be sanctified. Christian history is littered with people who have made these kinds of suggestions. Some argue for special religious rituals. Others promote asceticism, or harsh treatment of the body (2:23). Yet others promote a kind of elitism: 'You've got to join *our* church or *our* group. We're the only ones who've really got it.'

It's very damaging when this kind of 'gospel plus' practice goes on in churches, because when we speak to non-Christians about Christ, they automatically think we are wanting to make them religious rather than give them good news. But Paul has much better news: Jesus has done everything necessary to put us right with the Father. There is no other gospel – Jesus' saving blood is the only place of atonement for our sins, and our only ground for hope before a holy God.

Are you personally persuaded by the absolute sufficiency of Jesus' death on the cross? Get this matter settled in your heart, because it is like a mainspring in a clock – it drives and motivates our Christian gratitude and obedience. It also helps us not to be nibbled away at by the devil. When he reminds us of our sins, we can look to that empty cross and remember the Saviour who has paid the price in full.

What an unspeakable gift we have been given through the perfect sacrifice of God's own Son, Jesus Christ. Hence, every single Christian should be filled with gratitude. No matter what our age, race, culture, language, social status, or life circumstances, all Christians should be known as characteristically grateful people. We, above all [other] humans, have overwhelming cause to be thankful.

(Mary Mohler, *Growing in Gratitude*, The Good Book Company, 2018, p. 15)

Day 25

Read: Titus 2:11–14
Key verses: Titus 2:13–14

· ·

We wait for the blessed hope – the appearing of the glory of our great God and Saviour, Jesus Christ, ¹⁴who gave himself for us to redeem us from all wickedness and to purify for himself a people that are his very own, eager to do what is good.

Why did Jesus have to die?

Paul says Jesus 'gave himself for us'. In Galatians 2:20 he makes it even more personal: the Lord Jesus 'loved *me* and gave himself for *me*'. Why?

Christ 'gave himself to redeem us'. The word 'redemption' comes from the marketplace, where slaves were purchased for a price. Jesus paid the price for our sins, purchased our salvation, through his death on the cross. This theme runs throughout all Paul's writing. Galatians 1:4 reminds us, 'He gave himself for our sins', as does Ephesians 5:2: 'He gave himself up for us.' Peter says that we were once enslaved, committed to an empty way of life, and then at just the right moment – as Paul says in Romans 5:6 – God sent Christ to be our Saviour: 'For you know that it was not with perishable things such as silver or gold that you were redeemed from the empty way of life handed down to you from your ancestors, but with the precious blood of Christ' (1 Peter 1:18–19).

Jesus' death purchased our redemption. His death was voluntary – he was not coerced by his Father; it was substitutionary – he took my place; and it was propitiatory – it satisfied God's wrath.

From all eternity God planned to purchase your redemption. But we have not been purchased to sit on a shelf and be dusted. We are now 'in Christ', and we are to be pure: 'For the grace of God has appeared that offers salvation to all people. It teaches us to say "No" to ungodliness and worldly passions, and to live self-controlled, upright and godly lives' (Titus 2:11–12). Our redemption is the foundational truth that motivates this practical holiness: 'You are not your own; you were bought at a price. Therefore honour God with your bodies' (1 Corinthians 6:19–20).

> Jesus is our kinsman-redeemer with the right to redeem us – made like us in every way, yet without sin (see Hebrews 4:15). He has the resources to redeem us – possessing all authority over nature and nations, disease and demons, sin and Satan, suffering and death. Finally, He has the resolve to redeem us. His resolve drove Him to take responsibility for our sin, enduring the wrath of God that we deserve, so that through faith in Him, we might no longer be outcasts separated from God, but instead we might be called sons and daughters of God.
> (David Platt, *Counter Culture*, Tyndale House, 2015, p. 104)

Thank God for such a costly redemption, and today respond by living in grateful obedience:

May these words of my mouth and this meditation of my heart
 be pleasing in your sight,
 LORD, my Rock and my Redeemer.
(Psalm 19:14)

Day 26

Read: Titus 2:11–14
Key verses: Titus 2:13–14

. . . .

We wait for the blessed hope – the appearing of the glory of our great God and Saviour, Jesus Christ, ¹⁴who gave himself for us to redeem us from all wickedness and to purify for himself a people that are his very own, eager to do what is good.

Jesus died to make you his. He didn't just die to 'redeem us *from* all wickedness', he died to 'purify *for* himself a people'.

From eternity God's purpose was to have a people of his own, and repentant sinners are privileged to be part of that people. We only need to listen to Jesus' preaching to learn about God's plan. For example, in John 6, Jesus says, 'All those the Father gives me will come to me, and whoever comes to me I will never drive away . . . And this is the will of him who sent me, that I shall lose none of all those he has given me, but raise them up at the last day' (John 6:37, 39). Jesus' prayers also reveal God's plan: 'Father, I want those you have given me to be with me where I am, and to see my glory' (John 17:24).

There was no one more surprised at Saul's conversion than Saul of Tarsus himself. But God was not surprised.

He said to Ananias: 'This man is my chosen instrument to proclaim my name to the Gentiles and their kings and to the people of Israel' (Acts 9:15). In the same way, you have not been purchased indiscriminately. God's purpose for your life is constrained and kept safe by God's eternal will.

If we are Jesus' 'very own' people, that means we don't belong to anyone else. Our hearts, minds, desires, motives are to be set apart for him, and this has consequences in our work places, homes and schools. Our salvation is meant to make a difference: 'At one time we too were foolish, disobedient, deceived and enslaved by all kinds of passions and pleasures. We lived in malice and envy, being hated and hating one another. But when the kindness and love of God our Saviour appeared, he saved us . . . ' (Titus 3:3–4).

The problem is that today the church is at pains to tell the world that we're no different from it. We are like the world in its need, but we're not to be like the world in its sin. The danger is that we become like it in its sin, and so we have nothing to say to its needs.

'They will be my people and I will be their God' is the refrain which began in the Old Testament (see Exodus 6:7; Ezekiel 36:26–28; 37:27; Jeremiah 32:38), and will reach a crescendo in the new heavens and new earth:

> Look! God's dwelling place is now among the people, and he will
> dwell with them. They will be his people, and God himself will be
> with them and be their God.
> (Revelation 21:3)

Jesus died to make us his 'very own people', and we are now caught up in God's glorious purpose. As you go about your day, remember – you belong to God. Let that truth sink deep into your heart. Pray also that your church family would grasp this truth, and together you would strive to be people of integrity, authenticity and purity, living unashamedly in obedience to God's Word.

Day 27

Read: Titus 2:11–14
Key verses: Titus 2:13–14

• •

We wait for the blessed hope – the appearing of the glory of our great God and Saviour, Jesus Christ, ¹⁴who gave himself for us to redeem us from all wickedness and to purify for himself a people that are his very own, eager to do what is good.

Has Jesus' death on the cross so gripped you that you are passionate about living a God-honouring, self-giving life? Has it profoundly shaped your values and priorities?

We have been redeemed to be God's own people and to do 'good'. Doing what is 'good' (verse 14) has been Paul's message throughout this letter. The older women are to 'teach what is good' (2:3). 'Similarly, encourage the young men to be self-controlled. In everything set them an example by doing what is good' (2:6–7). In 3:1 Paul urges these believers to be 'ready to do whatever is good'. In 3:8 he says, 'I want you to stress these things, so that those who have trusted in God may be careful to devote themselves to doing what is good', because that is how these individuals will be distinguished from those who 'claim to know God, but by their actions they deny him. They are detestable, disobedient and unfit for doing anything good' (1:16). What a disaster! To claim to know God and yet to be useless for him.

But Paul's emphasis here is not only on doing good, but on being *'eager* to do what is good'. The word here is translated 'zealous, devoted'. We are to say 'no' to worldly passions, but we're not to be passionless. What a tragedy a passionless church is – insipid and bland – when Jesus said we are to be involved and bold.

Are you useful to God? Do your actions affirm that you know God? Do they point believers and unbelievers to Jesus?

When our efforts go unnoticed or unrewarded, when there is no obvious fruit for our labours, we can easily become disillusioned and weary of doing good. If your zeal is fading, go back to Calvary, spend time at the cross. Jesus' death is the grounds for our devotion; he is our motivation. Serve others, be devoted to them, seek out opportunities, and be willing to sacrifice to bring good to others – but do it all with your eyes firmly fixed on Christ. We do good 'to' others, but we don't ultimately do it 'for' them – it is Christ we are serving. Let's learn to say with Paul, 'We make it our goal to please him' (2 Corinthians 5:9).

Today press on, eager to do good: 'Always give yourselves fully to the work of the Lord, because you know that your labour in the Lord is not in vain' (1 Corinthians 15:58).

Day 28

Read: Hebrews 10:8–18

Key verses: Hebrews 10:8–10

. . . .

First he said, "Sacrifices and offerings, burnt offerings and sin offerings you did not desire, nor were you pleased with them" – though they were offered in accordance with the law. ⁹Then he said, "Here I am, I have come to do your will." He sets aside the first to establish the second. ¹⁰And by that will, we have been made holy through the sacrifice of the body of Jesus Christ once for all.

We realize that Jesus could have died a thousand times and promised a thousand pardons and still not accomplished our salvation. Because, if God's wrath was not satisfied, then Jesus' death on the cross was pointless.

But the writer to the Hebrews assures us that Calvary does indeed satisfy God because it was his idea. Verse 10 explains that the salvation of sinners arises out of the will of God. In his first sermon Peter says that the crucifixion took place by God's 'deliberate plan and foreknowledge' (Acts 2:23). Wicked men crucified Jesus, and nothing will ever absolve them of the responsibility of doing that, but Jesus went to the cross because of the deliberate plan and foreknowledge of God. Our salvation is rooted in his will. As Isaiah prophesied, on the cross the sins of the world – past, present and future – are gathered up by the Father and laid upon his Son: 'The LORD has laid on him the iniquity of us all' (Isaiah 53:6; see Day 2).

We also know that Jesus' death satisfies God because of the welcome he gave to Jesus. Would God have welcomed Jesus to sit at his right hand, that place of exaltation (verse 12), if he had failed to accomplish his Father's purpose? The Holy Spirit also testifies that God is satisfied (verse 15). No member of the Trinity can keep silent on this theme!

The substance of God's testimony is: 'Their sins and lawless acts I will remember no more' (verse 17).

Yes, God's wrath is wholly satisfied. And to demonstrate this, on Good Friday he tore apart the veil of the temple (Matthew 27:51). The separation between God and man was now over, and God was inviting sinners into his presence through the precious blood shed on Calvary. Today we can come boldly into God's presence in the full assurance of faith, because of the Christ of Calvary.

Heavenly Father, thank you that today I can come into your presence because my sin has been paid for and your wrath has been satisfied. Lord Jesus, thank you for obeying your Father's will, dying in my place, taking the punishment I deserved. May I be forever grateful for this amazing 'grace in which we now stand' (Romans 5:1–2).

In his death on the cross, Christ becomes the place of refuge, the place in the world where the full wrath of God has already been spent. Therefore, to stand in Christ is to stand in a place where the wrath of God will never be felt, because it has already been there. (Rory Shiner, *One Forever*, Matthias Media, 2013)

Day 29

Read: Hebrews 10:11–18
Key verses: Hebrews 10:11–12

· ·

Day after day every priest stands and performs his religious duties; again and again he offers the same sacrifices, which can never take away sins. ¹²But when this priest had offered for all time one sacrifice for sins, he sat down at the right hand of God.

'I haven't sat down all day!'

When we hear someone say this, we get the message that they have been busy. Sometimes you can be busy while sitting down, but generally speaking, if you're standing, you're busy, and sitting down is a signal that you have finished for the day. The writer to the Hebrews depicts the Lord Jesus as sitting down for that very reason – he has finished his work.

He will never again stretch out his hands to be nailed to a cross. He doesn't need to make another sacrifice because this one was effective for sins – *plural* – the sum total of the sins of all the sinners whom he came to save. The Bible gives three categories of sin: outward acts of wrong-doing, rebellion against God, and the inner state of our fallen nature – and Jesus died once for all those sins. If the world should last a thousand more years, or a thousand times a thousand, there will still only be one sacrifice for sin for ever. Eternity itself will require no more than the Son of God accomplished in his work on Calvary. He deserves to sit down!

In contrast, the Old Testament priests never sat down. They had to deal with a never-ending stream of sinners, sacrifices and blood, because the animal sacrifices couldn't take away sin (Hebrews 10:4). We could well ask why God ordained such ineffectual sacrifices. What was he trying to teach through this useless repetition? God wanted to make sure that we understand three things:

- *The helplessness of the sinner.* Doing good works can never deliver us from sin. We can't deal with the offences of the past by the good deeds of the future. Doing our best is not an option. We can't even achieve our best, let alone achieve anything adequate in God's sight. Sin can only be dealt with if God deals with it himself.

- *The seriousness of sin.* The animal sacrifices show that sin and death are inseparable. The lamb was killed, its life terminated, because of the filthiness of sin. It was the blood of the sacrifice that paid the penalty for sin. As Paul said, 'The wages of sin is death' (Romans 6:23).

- *The need for substitution.* The sinner brings the sacrifice, an animal without spot or blemish, to the altar. The beast is innocent, but by laying his hands on it, the individual transfers his sin, guilt and rebelliousness on to the animal, which then dies in his place. Jesus stands as the perfect substitute, and does what an animal never could: he dies for us willingly, consenting to be identified with sinners, and with understanding, freely undertaking to bear our sin.

Today give thanks that Christ is 'seated at the right hand of God' (Colossians 3:1). Sin has been dealt with, and his work is finished.

Day 30

Read: Hebrews 10:11–18
Key verses: Hebrews 10:12–13

••

But when this priest had offered for all time one sacrifice for sins, he sat down at the right hand of God, ¹³ and since that time he waits for his enemies to be made his footstool.

The Lord Jesus is not only sitting (see Day 29), but also waiting – for his enemies to cave in, to surrender to his rule. Only one who has already achieved victory waits for the enemy to submit. It is folly to wait for submission if the battle has not yet been won. But Jesus has no more fighting to do. He is perfectly at rest at the right hand of God, simply waiting for the submission of his defeated foes.

Calvary was where Satan was defeated. On the cross the Lord was locked in single combat with the prince of this world. His disciples had abandoned him, and his Father turned his back on him, because he could not look on sin. As darkness descended, and Jesus breathed his last, it looked as if hope had died. The disciples took his body down from the cross and buried it, until, on the third day, he rose throbbing with the life of God, radiant, glorious, from the tomb.

Satan's apparent victory was short-lived. The victory lay eternally with the Son of God because the Father heard his cry on the cross, 'It is finished!' We can imagine the Father's response – 'Is it? Is Satan really dealt with?' From Good Friday and all through the quietness and solemnity of the Saturday the Father was calculating, estimating whether our sin had truly been paid for. And on the third day, with the cry 'It is finished!' still ringing in his ears, the Father cried, 'Amen!', and raised his Son from the dead, evidence that the victory lies with the Christ of Calvary.

Do you know this victorious Lord Jesus in your life? Whatever temptations and trials Satan confronts you with, look upwards at

Jesus on the throne and remember that no temptation can defeat him, and no trial unseat him.

Satan still prowls around like a roaring lion seeking to devour us (1 Peter 5:8). But don't lose heart. The Lord Jesus' decisive victory over Satan on the cross means that we can resist his attacks. The same power that raised Jesus from the dead is available to you. Today pray that you would treat Satan like the defeated enemy he is – don't give him room in your life, don't listen to his lies, don't give in to the temptations he puts before you, don't believe the doubt and despair he sows in your heart. Instead, pray for resurrection power to live the holy life Christ died to give you (Hebrews 10:14).

> I pray that the eyes of your heart may be enlightened in order that you may know . . . his incomparably great power for us who believe. That power is the same as the mighty strength he exerted when he raised Christ from the dead and seated him at his right hand in the heavenly realms.
> (Ephesians 1:18–20)

Day 31

Read: 1 John 3:1–10
Key verses: 1 John 3:5–6

•••

But you know that he appeared so that he might take away our sins. And in him is no sin. ⁶No one who lives in him keeps on sinning. No one who continues to sin has either seen him or known him.

What is the bull's-eye of the gospel?

Jesus died to 'take away our sins' (verse 5). The cross of Christ is a picture of the horror of my sin and the length that a holy God had to go to to deal with it. He died to take the punishment we deserve for our rebellion against a holy God. He absorbed the righteous wrath of God against human sin.

John is telling us this not just so we get our theology about the cross right, but so that we will learn to hate sin in our own lives. He is unsettled by how easily Christians learn to live with the sin that nailed the Saviour to the cross. It is a complete contradiction, in John's mind, to call yourself a child of God, yet have a lax view of sin (verses 4–6). He says that when we sin, we actually live like children of the devil (verses 7–10).

John is not claiming, in verse 6, that we can be sinless in this life (1 John 1:8–10). He is saying that as Christians mature, they will – must – become more and more intolerant of sin in their lives. 'The reason the Son of God appeared was to destroy the devil's work' (verse 8), so how can we play with, tolerate, the very thing that Christ despises? The mark of the children of God is that they hate sin because they have fallen in love with Jesus.

Today come to the cross for the forgiveness and grace Christ offers. 'If anybody does sin, we have an advocate with the Father – Jesus

Christ, the Righteous One. He is the atoning sacrifice for our sins, and not only for ours but also for the sins of the whole world' (1 John 2:1–2).

With God's strength, deal ruthlessly with the greed, lust, pride – whatever sin you have been complacent about – and strive for holiness. One day soon your transformation will be complete: 'When Christ appears, we shall be like him, for we shall see him as he is. All who have this hope in him purify themselves, just as he is pure' (1 John 3:2–3).

How do you fight the pleasure of sin? I'll tell you: with another pleasure. Holiness is not attained, at least not in any lasting, life-changing way, merely through prohibitions, threats, fear, or shame-based appeals. Holiness is attained by believing in, trusting, banking on, resting in, savouring, and cherishing God's promise of a superior happiness that comes only by falling in love with Jesus. The power that the pleasures of sin exert on the human soul will ultimately be overcome only by the superior power of the pleasures of knowing and being known, loving and being loved by God in Christ.

(Sam Storms, *Pleasures Evermore*, NavPress, 2000, p. 20)

For further study

If you would like to read more about the cross, you might find the following selection of books helpful:

- Don Carson, *Scandalous* (IVP, 2010)

- Tim Chester, *The Ordinary Hero* (IVP, 2009)

- Kevin DeYoung, Richard Coekin, Yannick Christos-Wahab, *The Cross in Four Words* (The Good Book Company, 2020)

- Tim Keller, *King's Cross* (Hodder and Stoughton, 2014)

- Mike McKinley, *Passion* (The Good Book Company, 2012)

- Jeremy and Elizabeth McQuoid, *The Amazing Cross* (IVP, 2012)

- Mark Meynell, *Cross-Examined* (IVP, 2021)

- Marcus Nodder, *Why Did Jesus Have to Die?* (The Good Book Company, 2014)

- John Stott, *The Cross of Christ* (IVP, 2006)

- Rankin Wilbourne and Brian Gregor, *The Cross Before Me: Reimagining the way of the good life* (David C. Cook Publishing, 2019)

The Holy Spirit

Contributors

Day 32

Read: John 7:37–44
Key verses: John 7:37–39

· ·

> *37 On the last and greatest day of the festival, Jesus stood and said in a loud voice, "Let anyone who is thirsty come to me and drink. 38 Whoever believes in me, as Scripture has said, rivers of living water will flow from within them." 39 By this he meant the Spirit.*

We can't see the Holy Spirit; he is invisible. So Jesus paints a picture of the Spirit as 'rivers of living water' to help us understand what he is like.

This image features through the whole of Scripture. From Eden it flows through the history of God's people as he brings them across the River Jordan into the Promised Land. The river flows on into the book of Psalms. It is a 'river whose streams make glad the city of God, the holy place where the Most High dwells' (Psalm 46:4) and beside which the man or woman of God flourishes (Psalm 1).

The river flows on in Ezekiel's magnificent vision: 'Where the river flows everything will live . . . Fruit trees of all kinds will grow on both banks of the river . . . Every month they will bear fruit, because the water from the sanctuary flows to them. Their fruit will serve for food and their leaves for healing' (Ezekiel 47:9, 11–12).

This vision is what John, at the very end of the Bible, sees again. The angel showed him, 'the river of the water of life, as clear as crystal, flowing from the throne of God and of the Lamb down the middle of the great street of the city. On each side of the river stood the tree of life, bearing twelve crops of fruit, yielding its fruit every month. And the leaves of the tree are for the healing of the nations' (Revelation 22:1–2).

What does this picture of a watered garden, with land which is fresh and green, mean? It is certainly a picture of what humanity wants. By the river our needs are met, our emptiness filled, and our thirst quenched. But this river also supplies what God wants for us. The people of God in the Promised Land, and believers down through ages, only enjoy the benefits and blessings of the river when they are obeying God and living on his terms. Then we discover that what God wants for us is even better than what we want for ourselves. It is in and by that river that we find all possible refreshment, the quenching of every thirst and fruitfulness in the service of the Lord Jesus.

We are thirsty for many things – love, joy, peace, significance – and the world offers to quench our thirst through family, friends, holidays, sex, jobs, and money. But even the good things we enjoy leave us longing for more. Jesus is the ultimate thirst-quencher and he invites us to come – and keep coming – to him, to live life on his terms and experience lasting satisfaction. Come and drink deeply of Christ today: 'I am the Alpha and the Omega, the Beginning and the End. To the thirsty I will give water without cost from the spring of the water of life' (Revelation 21:6).

Day 33

Read: John 7:37–44
Key verses: John 7:37–39

....

37 On the last and greatest day of the festival, Jesus stood and said in a loud voice, "Let anyone who is thirsty come to me and drink. 38 Whoever believes in me, as Scripture has said, rivers of living water will flow from within them." 39 By this he meant the Spirit.

What does Jesus promise about the Holy Spirit?

He promises that 'rivers of living water will flow from within [us]'. This means the power of the Spirit of God will flow out of us and produce –

• The fruit of the Spirit
   The Spirit flows from you to other Christians. Other people will be affected if you are producing the fruit of the Spirit; if there is love, joy, peace, long-suffering, kindness, goodness, faithfulness, gentleness and self-control in your life. All these flow out from you to others and they will be blessed as God's Holy Spirit blesses you.

• The fellowship of the Spirit
   As the Spirit flows out from you to other believers, and from them back to you, you will find that you are bound together in the kind of fellowship that overcomes all sorts of natural barriers, and brings together people who normally wouldn't mix.

• The unity of the Spirit
   As the Spirit produces fruit and creates fellowship, he creates unity. We belong to a community of Christian people.

But Jesus also promises that the rivers of living water will flow out from beyond the confines of the church, out into the unbelieving world. The river will convict the world of sin, righteousness and judgement (John 16:8). How will it do that? Jesus told his disciples, '"As the Father has sent me, I am sending you." And with that he breathed on them and said, "Receive the Holy Spirit"' (John 20:21–22). Jesus promised that as we go out in the power of the Holy Spirit from the church into our communities, the Spirit will flow out, like a river of living water into the unbelieving world.

This pattern is replicated as we pass from the Gospels into the book of Acts. Jesus promises that his people will first be baptised in the Holy Spirit, and then they will go out and witness in the power of the Spirit. When the church prays, the Holy Spirit says, 'Set apart for me Barnabas and Saul for the work to which I have called them' (Acts 13:2). And so, all down through history, the Spirit directs, because the Spirit is flowing through his people, into the world that needs his message.

Praise God for the Holy Spirit's fruit, fellowship and unity in your church. Think of the encouragements and practical help you have received from church members as well as the ministry and faith you share. Pray that more and more the Holy Spirit would flow out of us and impact those in our communities as we live out God's values and share the good news in word and deed.

Day 34

Read: John 16:1–15
Key verses: John 16:5–7

....

> Now I am going to him who sent me. None of you asks me,
> "Where are you going?" ⁶ Rather, you are filled with grief because
> I have said these things. ⁷ But very truly I tell you, it is for your
> good that I am going away. Unless I go away, the Advocate will
> not come to you; but if I go, I will send him to you.

'It's a good thing Jesus is not here', seems almost a scandalous claim.

The disciples certainly struggled to believe it. Within the hour, Jesus
would be betrayed. Within twenty-four hours he would be crucified.
In the upper room, on the threshold of these events, the disciples
are 'filled with grief' because they love Jesus. Since chapter 13 Jesus
has been seeking to prepare the disciples for the tragedy that will
engulf them. He's predicted that he will be betrayed by Judas,
denied by Peter and they will run away when he faces his arrest and
trial. Even though they are going to desert him he comforts them
with the promise of another comforter, the same as him, who will
help and strengthen them. He says:

> I will ask the Father, and he will give you another advocate to help you
> and be with you forever – the Spirit of truth. The world cannot accept
> him, because it neither sees him nor knows him. But you know him, for
> he lives with you and will be in you.
> (John 14:16–17)

Jesus teaches his disciples that though they will not see him any
more in his earthly body, their connection with him will be as real as
the connection of the branches to a vine. They are not alone, the
presence of the Holy Spirit will dwell within them.

This is especially important because the world is going to hate them. The world hates Jesus' unique claims, his high and holy standards, and his free offer of salvation. It hates Christ, his purity and wants to earn salvation on merit. In such a world, the disciples not only need to keep going but they must testify to Christ (John 15:27) and the personal cost will be high (John 16:2).

It is the requirement of the church in every generation to testify to the Lord Jesus, whatever the cost. The Holy Spirit is the linchpin in our efforts to witness about Christ in a hostile world. Jesus doesn't just leave us with techniques but with a person who is far more powerful than any situation we may find ourselves in.

Jesus going away hasn't left us alone. We now have the personal indwelling presence of the Holy Spirit. God is with us, in us – he sustains us in trying times, draws close in our grief, helps us testify about the gospel, and keeps our eyes fixed on Christ when the cost of following him seems overwhelming. Thank God for sending his Spirit so that we would truly know 'Immanuel' – God with us.

Day 35

Read: John 16:1–15
Key verses: John 16:8–11

....

When he [the Holy Spirit] comes, he will prove the world to be in the wrong about sin and righteousness and judgement: ⁹about sin, because people do not believe in me; ¹⁰about righteousness, because I am going to the Father, where you can see me no longer; ¹¹and about judgement, because the prince of this world now stands condemned.

How does the Holy Spirit work in the hearts of unbelievers?

The word 'prove' or 'convict' (ESV) comes from the law courts. It is the word used in the Greek-speaking world for cross-examination in the dock. The Holy Spirit comes to cross-examine people. He is the Spirit of truth (verse 13) and he presses home to people the truth about their lives. He shows them what they are really like. He's not after a 'guilty' verdict, that is already there – rather he is concerned that they see their desperate state before God and their need of mercy.

The Spirit convicts people that sin is deeper than they ever thought. People who once saw sin as someone else's problem, as naughty but nice, as just a religious word about lust and laziness, suddenly see it is far more penetrating than that. They stop saying, 'If you knew my circumstances you'd understand why I have to do this.' Most strikingly of all, they begin to see that the essence of sin is a declaration of independence against God. Sin is saying with Adam and Eve in the garden, 'It may be your world, God, but I will run my life my way.'

As the Holy Spirit opens people's eyes they begin to see they have treated Jesus with utter contempt. They have ignored him. Jesus said, 'people do not believe in me' (verse 9) – this is the ultimate yardstick of sin. They reject Christ as God, and therefore Lord of their lives. They also refuse to believe in Jesus' rescue. He died that people might have eternal life and so to reject Jesus is not an intellectual exercise, it is sin. When the Holy Spirit begins to work in a person's life, he shows them that they have been wrong about Jesus and that their unbelief is going to be their undoing.

If we really cared about loving Jesus, as the Spirit does, if we really were on the Spirit's wavelength, then we would be horrified that people refuse to believe in Jesus, that they suppress the truth by their wickedness (Romans 1:18). In Romans 9 Paul even wept because his people refused to believe in Jesus.

Many of us weep because close family members are not believers. But sometimes it is hard to keep on praying for them – their eyes seem so blind, their hearts closed to the truth and it is painful to consider their future without Christ. Ask God for strength to persevere in prayer for these loved ones. Pray for the convicting work of the Holy Spirit in their lives. Don't give up hope – if the Holy Spirit did the miracle of saving you, he can definitely save your non-Christian family and friends.

Day 36

Read: John 16:1–15
Key verses: John 16:8–11

....

When he comes, he will prove the world to be in the wrong about sin and righteousness and judgement: ⁹ about sin, because people do not believe in me; ¹⁰ about righteousness, because I am going to the Father, where you can see me no longer; ¹¹ and about judgement, because the prince of this world now stands condemned.

No one can bluff it with Jesus.

Jesus knew how many husbands the Samaritan woman had and that the man she was living with was not her husband (John 4:17). He told the religious hypocrites who were about to stone a woman caught in adultery to survey their own consciences: 'Let any one of you who is without sin be the first to throw a stone at her' (John 8:7). When Jesus was around, there was no problem persuading people that God's righteousness was higher than they could ever reach. People who met Jesus had the same response as the apostle Peter who shouted, 'Go away from me Lord; I am a sinful man!' (Luke 5:8).

So how do you convince people of the absolute and inescapable moral claim of God when Jesus has gone to the Father? How do you persuade people that righteousness is beyond them then? The Holy Spirit. He comes to press home to people the righteousness of God (verse 10). He causes the unbeliever to see that Jesus is the only way by which sinners like us can ever be made right with a holy God.

People go through life thinking that they are good enough and they can get right with God on their own. They cite moral reasons – 'I give to charity', 'I don't steal.' Sometimes they give religious reasons, 'I've been baptised', 'I go to communion', 'I read the Bible . . . for all these reasons I'm good enough.' But when the Spirit of Jesus does his work and teaches us about righteousness, people say, 'None of this will do me any good. I cannot be right before God because I'm moral or religious. The Holy Spirit reveals to me that my sin is so great that all I can do is trust in what the Lord Jesus has done and receive his gift of salvation.'

The Holy Spirit persuades unbelievers that they are not good people going to heaven but sinners going to hell. They flee to the cross as the Spirit causes them to see that Christ's righteousness alone is what they must depend on. The mark of the Christian therefore is constant awareness of sin and gratitude for the righteousness of Christ that has been won for us on the cross.

Thank God that he doesn't leave us thinking, 'I'm good enough.' He sent the Holy Spirit to convict us of our sin, show us the futility of our moral and religious excuses, and open our eyes to see that Christ alone makes us right with God. Praise God for sending his convicting Spirit and a righteous Saviour.

Day 37

Read: John 16:1–15
Key verses: John 16:8–11

....

When he comes, he will prove the world to be in the wrong about sin and righteousness and judgement: ⁹about sin, because people do not believe in me; ¹⁰about righteousness, because I am going to the Father, where you can see me no longer; ¹¹and about judgement, because the prince of this world now stands condemned.

Do you think about the future?

Many unbelievers are not interested in talking about the future until the Holy Spirit does his convicting work and then their eyes are opened. Christ's Holy Spirit is able to convince non-Christians that judgement is closer than they ever imagined (verse 11). Satan is called the 'prince of this world' because the world largely follows his delusions by rejecting Christ. He and the world which follow him face judgement. The person who is under the conviction of the Spirit will realize that judgement is not something like cancer, which may happen, and if it does, I'll face it then. The person under conviction realizes the wrath of God – his settled, controlled, personal hostility to all that is wicked and sinful – is hanging over them.

The Holy Spirit injects an imperative call for decision into our consciences. We see that in the Bible God's judgement is not set against his goodness. It is proof of his goodness. He will not co-exist with evil. The Spirit persuades unbelievers that one day they will stand before a righteous God (Hebrew 4:13) so they need to get right with him.

Amid all this miraculous work of conviction and conversion by the Spirit, what is my job? 'You must also testify' (John 15:27). We need to speak to people about sin and judgement and its seriousness. As we do so we know we have an ally in their hearts, the Holy Spirit of God doing battle with their conscience, convicting them that the message is true.

The terrible tragedy is that we've stopped believing the Holy Spirit can do this convicting work. We aren't telling people with tears and love that the gospel is about being saved from hell through the cross. We are not telling people that Christ saves us from the wrath to come. We change the gospel because we're embarrassed by it. In doing so we demonstrate that we don't believe the Holy Spirit can do his work, which is terrible blasphemy, and we show people we don't love them enough to tell them the truth.

Ask yourself:

- Do I believe the Holy Spirit can do his convicting work among the people I rub shoulders with?
- When I share the gospel, do I change the message in any way?
- Do I love people enough to tell them the truth?

Today, ask the Holy Spirit to do his work, lead you to those whose hearts he has prepared and give you strength and wisdom as you testify to the good news of the gospel.

Day 38

Read: Acts 1:1–8
Key verses: Acts 1:1–2

••

In my former book, Theophilus, I wrote about all that Jesus began to do and to teach ²until the day he was taken up to heaven, after giving instructions through the Holy Spirit to the apostles he had chosen.

Did Jesus need the Holy Spirit?

In the opening verses of Acts, Luke talks about Jesus 'giving instructions through the Holy Spirit to the apostles' (verse 2). Does that mean that Jesus, the Son of God, the risen Lord, needed the Holy Spirit to do his ministry? Yes! Jesus conducted his mission from beginning to end in the power of the Spirit. In fact, if you read through Luke's gospel – Acts is the second half of the story that Luke began in his gospel – he talks about the Holy Spirit coming on Jesus at his baptism (Luke 3:22), Jesus being led by the Spirit into the desert (Luke 4:1) and then going into Galilee to begin his ministry of preaching in the power of the Holy Spirit (Luke 4:14).

Jesus does his ministry in the power of the Holy Spirit and now he gives that Spirit to us. We do the ministry Jesus gives us with the same power he did. Jesus said: 'You will receive power when the Holy Spirit comes on you; and you will be my witnesses in Jerusalem, and in all Judea and Samaria, and to the ends of the earth' (verse 8).

Perhaps the best indicator of whether we are doing ministry in the power of the Spirit is our prayer life. Have you ever begun praying only to be distracted by your 'to-do' list? With your head full of the day's tasks, you stop praying and start answering your emails and getting on with work. It is not a conscious thought but when that happens we are really saying that our work is more important than God's work, that it is in our resources that the task of ministry will be done. When I don't give time to prayer, I'm saying either I don't want intimacy with the Father or I don't think I need his help. How wrong could we be! If Jesus needed to rely on the Holy Spirit to do his work, how much more do we?

Today, *especially* if your 'to-do' list is long, pray for the people you'll meet, decisions you'll make, meetings you will be part of – all the opportunities to serve God's mission – and ask for the Holy Spirit's wisdom and power to live faithfully, witness boldly and bring God glory.

Oh, without prayer what are the church's agencies, but the stretching out of a dead man's arm, or the lifting up of the lid of a blind man's eye? Only when the Holy Spirit comes is there any life and force and power.

(C. H. Spurgeon, *The Metropolitan Tabernacle Pulpit Vol. III*, Passmore and Alabaster, 1863, p465)

Day 39

Read: Acts 2:1–41
Key verses: Acts 2:16–18

....

This is what was spoken by the prophet Joel:
17 "In the last days, God says,
  I will pour out my Spirit on all people.
Your sons and daughters will prophesy,
  your young men will see visions,
  your old men will dream dreams.
18 Even on my servants, both men and women,
  I will pour out my Spirit in those days,
  and they will prophesy."

Are they drunk?

That's what some people wondered as they surveyed the scene on the first day of Pentecost. The Holy Spirit has been poured out and fifteen different language groups hear the apostles, 'declaring the wonders of God in our own tongues' (verse 11).

In the first apostolic sermon, Peter explains that what is happening is actually the fulfilment of God's purpose outlined in the Old Testament. The prophet Joel had predicted that the day would come when God would pour out his Spirit without distinction on men and women, young and old, regardless of social standing (verse 17–21). It would be a day of access and opportunity, everybody who hears and calls on the Lord will be saved.

Peter now focuses on how God accredited Jesus (verse 22) and raised him from the dead (verse 24). Death is the wage of sin but because of Jesus' sinless life, death had no wage to pay and couldn't keep him down. Being a Jewish audience, Peter quotes to them their psalms. He recites David's Psalm 16: 'You will not abandon me to the realm of the dead, you will not let your Holy One see decay' (verse 27). King David is buried in Jerusalem, but he was speaking prophetically about Jesus' resurrection (verse 31). Peter also quotes Psalm 110: 'Sit at my right hand.' David wrote that but he didn't sit at God's right hand! Peter's point is clear: 'God has made this Jesus, whom you crucified, both Lord and Messiah' (verse 36).

Here is a Pentecostal sermon which is all about Jesus. You think a Pentecostal sermon has got to be about the Holy Spirit. No, the Pentecostal sermon is all about Jesus because the Holy Spirit always points away from himself to the Lord Jesus. When Paul finds the disciples of John the Baptist who had never heard of the Holy Spirit, what does he do? He teaches them about Jesus because when they trust in Jesus, they'll receive the Holy Spirit. The great preacher Spurgeon explained it like this: 'I look to the dove [the symbol of the Spirit] and the dove flew away. But I look to the cross and the dove flew into my heart.'

The coming of the Holy Spirit at Pentecost means the fulfilment of the Scriptures – Joel and the Psalms – and that Jesus is Lord: 'Exalted to the right hand of God, [Jesus] has received from the Father the promised Holy Spirit and has poured out what you now see and hear' (verse 33).

Praise God that we are still in the day of opportunity when the long-awaited Holy Spirit is poured out unstintingly on all who repent and believe that Jesus is Lord: 'The promise is for you and your children and for all who are far off – for all whom the Lord our God will call' (verse 39).

Day 40

Read: Acts 4:1–31

Key verses: Acts 4:8–10

....

Peter, filled with the Holy Spirit, said to them: "Rulers and elders of the people! ⁹*If we are being called to account today for an act of kindness shown to a man who was lame and are being asked how he was healed,* ¹⁰*then know this, you and all the people of Israel: It is by the name of Jesus Christ of Nazareth, whom you crucified but whom God raised from the dead, that this man stands before you healed."*

Can you imagine the scene?

Peter and John had healed a lame man in the temple and he was walking and leaping around. A crowd gathers and as Peter is preaching the temple guard arrest them. The next day Peter and John are brought before the religious leaders and Peter, 'filled with the Holy Spirit' explained the gospel to them (verse 8). 'When [the religious leaders] saw the courage of Peter and John and realized that they were unschooled, ordinary men, they were astonished and they took note that these men had been with Jesus' (verse 13). This is what the Holy Spirit does – he takes ordinary people, with no education and empowers them to speak God's Word with courage.

The religious leaders release Peter and John, threatening them not to speak in the name of Jesus. The two go back to the disciples and pray together (Acts 4:23–31). This is the first time that the church has been threatened. But the believers don't pray for an end to persecution, they pray for boldness and miracles: 'Now, Lord, consider their threats and enable your servants to speak your word with great boldness. Stretch out your hand to heal and perform signs and wonders through the name of your holy servant Jesus' (verses 29–30). It is as if they are saying, 'Lord if you are going to perform miracles and heal people then you had better give us boldness because we are going to get into trouble!' And what happens? 'After they prayed, the place where they were meeting was shaken. And they were all filled with the Holy Spirit and spoke the word of God boldly' (verse 31). When you pray for boldness, God fills you with his Spirit. And when God fills you with his Spirit you proclaim the Word of God with boldness.

But that is not the end of the process. The Spirit also gives faith when people hear God's Word. Remember Peter who went to Cornelius' house and preached the gospel to all the family and friends gathered. Luke records, 'While Peter was still speaking . . . the Holy Spirit came on all who heard the message' (Acts 10:44). The Holy Spirit came upon Cornelius' family and gave them faith in the Lord Jesus.

We are often reticent to explain the gospel to people because, like the early disciples, we face hostility and rejection. But God is still at work, the Holy Spirit still answers prayers. So rather than shrink back, let's pray for boldness and miracles – boldness to share the gospel and the miracle of saving faith.

Day 41

Read: Acts 7:51–60
Key verses: Acts 7:54–56

....

When the members of the Sanhedrin heard [Stephen's sermon], they were furious and gnashed their teeth at him. ⁵⁵ But Stephen, full of the Holy Spirit, looked up to heaven and saw the glory of God, and Jesus standing at the right hand of God. ⁵⁶ "Look," he said, "I see heaven open and the Son of Man standing at the right hand of God."

Where do you go to find comfort and joy in hard times?

Many of us turn to family and friends, familiar places and favourite hobbies. But throughout the book of Acts Luke is keen to remind us that the Holy Spirit is the one who brings true and lasting comfort and joy to God's people.

Stephen, as he is speaking, is brought before the religious council. He bravely proclaims the gospel and the members of the Sanhedrin respond with fury. They gnash their teeth (verse 54). 'But Stephen, full of the Holy Spirit, looked up to heaven and saw the glory of God, and Jesus standing at the right hand of God' (verse 55). Stephen dies as the first martyr. Why does God not rescue him? I think because God gets so much glory from the faithful suffering of his people. But in God's kindness, the Holy Spirit gives Stephen a vision of the glory that is waiting him. In the depths of his suffering the Spirit gives Stephen out-of-this-world comfort and joy.

Soon after this, Luke reports that, 'the church throughout Judea, Galilee and Samaria enjoyed a time of peace and was strengthened. Living in the fear of the Lord and encouraged by the Holy Spirit, it increased in numbers' (Acts 9:31). A similar scenario is described in Pisidian Antioch. Paul and Barnabas preached the gospel and then had to flee to Iconium to avoid persecution. The believers who remained would undoubtedly face opposition but Luke records these new Christians were: 'filled with joy and with the Holy Spirit' (Acts 13:52). When the Spirit comes he gives comfort and joy to God's people.

When the Holy Spirit comes into our lives he brings joy. But so often that joy is stifled by hardship, busyness, or bitterness. We take our eyes off Jesus and try to live in our own strength. Today, focus on your spiritual blessings and eternal realities and ask God to restore the joy of your salvation. Then, like Stephen and those early Christians, experience the encouragement of the Holy Spirit as you depend on him.

And assuredly, if our faith shall be well grounded in God, and shall be thoroughly rooted in his word; and, finally, if it shall be well fortified with the aid of the Spirit as it, ought; it shall nourish peace and joy spiritual in our minds, though all the world be in an uproar. (John Calvin and Henry Beveridge, *John Calvin's Bible Commentaries On The Acts of the Apostles 1–13*, Jazzybee Verlag, 2017, p. 358)

Day 42

Read: Acts 8:26–40
Key verses: Acts 8:26–29

....

*Now an angel of the Lord said to Philip, "Go south to the road –
the desert road – that goes down from Jerusalem to Gaza."
²⁷ So he started out, and on his way he met an Ethiopian eunuch,
an important official in charge of all the treasury of the Kandake
(which means "queen of the Ethiopians"). This man had gone
to Jerusalem to worship, ²⁸ and on his way home was sitting in
his chariot reading the Book of Isaiah the prophet. ²⁹ The Spirit
told Philip, "Go to that chariot and stay near it."*

What exactly is the Holy Spirit's role in evangelism?

Luke records simply that an angel tells Philip to go to the Gaza road.
An Ethiopian official comes along and the Spirit tells Philip to go and
stand by the chariot. Philip sees that the Ethiopian is reading from
the Scriptures and he asks, 'Do you understand what you are
reading?' The official replies, 'How can I unless someone explains it
to me?' So Philip gets into the chariot and explains the message of
Jesus from the Old Testament. The Ethiopian is baptised and takes
the gospel message back to his country.

A little while later a man called Cornelius, who longs to know God,
has a vision and is told to send people to Simon Peter, one of the
apostles. Meanwhile Peter also has a vision: 'While Peter was still
thinking about the vision, the Spirit said to him, "Simon, three men
are looking for you. So get up and go downstairs. Do not hesitate to
go with them, for I have sent them"' (Acts 10:19–20).

The Spirit tells Peter to go to these men just like he told Philip to go
to the Ethiopian. What is striking is that not only does the Spirit
bring Christians to unbelievers, he brings unbelievers to Christians.
The Spirit says to Peter, 'Do not hesitate to go with them, for I – the

Holy Spirit – have sent them.' The Spirit is working in the lives of unbelievers, preparing them to hear the gospel and bringing them into contact with those who can tell them the gospel.

There is tremendous confidence and freedom in knowing that the Holy Spirit is the great mission strategist; he directs the mission of God's people. If you offer yourself, if you are open to the leading of God's Spirit, if you are faithful in what is before you, then the Spirit will use that as part of the big picture he oversees.

What a relief! It is not up to us to artificially engineer evangelistic conversations. The Holy Spirit is the mission strategist, directing the mission of God's people.

Today, pray that the Holy Spirit would be working in the lives of unbelievers in your sphere of influence, bringing across your path the ones who are ready to hear about the good news of Jesus Christ. Pray too that you would be ready to seize the gospel opportunities the Spirit gives and leave the results up to him.

Day 43

Read: Acts 13:4–12
Key verses: Acts 13:8–11

. . . .

But Elymas the sorcerer (for that is what his name means) opposed them [Paul and Barnabas] and tried to turn the proconsul from the faith. ⁹Then Saul, who was also called Paul, filled with the Holy Spirit, looked straight at Elymas and said, ¹⁰"You are a child of the devil and an enemy of everything that is right! You are full of all kinds of deceit and trickery. Will you never stop perverting the right ways of the Lord? ¹¹Now the hand of the Lord is against you. You are going to be blind for a time, not even able to see the light of the sun."

What happens when we face opposition?

When Paul and Barnabas went to Paphos, they had the opportunity to preach to the governor but a sorcerer called Elymas opposed them and tried to turn the proconsul away from the faith. Paul, filled with the Holy Spirit, looked straight at Elymas and called him a 'child of the devil and an enemy of everything that is right' (verse 10). Paul accused him of perverting the ways of the Lord and declared that because the Lord's hand was against him he'd be blind for a period of time. 'Immediately mist and darkness' came over Elymas and he had to be lead away (verse 11). The gospel is being preached, the sorcerer is trying to disrupt what is happening, Paul is filled with the Spirit and the opposition is confounded.

The same thing happened in Acts 6. Stephen performed miraculous signs, and the members of the synagogue opposed him. They tried to argue with him, 'But they could not stand up against the wisdom the Spirit gave him as he spoke' (Acts 6:10). It's a very striking phrase. When people belittle your faith, or when they pick holes in what you say, imagine the Spirit speaking through you in a way that no one can refute. Imagine people saying they could not stand against your wisdom or the power by which you spoke.

Why are we unable to confound those who reject God's Word? Why do we so rarely share Paul and Stephen's experience and speak with irrefutable wisdom from the Holy Spirit? Back in Acts 4, Peter and John spoke to the crowd with such boldness and clarity and the religious leaders noted, 'these men had been with Jesus' (Acts 4:13). The key to bold speech – whether confronting false teaching or sharing the gospel – is spending time with Jesus. When we learn from his Word, share more of his purpose and listen more to his Spirit, we are bound to speak more boldly. Today, if you face opposition for being a Christian – passed over for promotion at work, marginalized at school or university, the target of hurtful comments from family – spend time with Jesus. Enjoy his presence, ask for his Spirit of wisdom and the power to confound the opposition.

Day 44

Read: Romans 8:1–17
Key verses: Romans 8:13–16

....

For if you live according to the flesh, you will die; but if by the Spirit you put to death the misdeeds of the body, you will live. ¹⁴ For those who are led by the Spirit of God are the children of God. ¹⁵ The Spirit you received does not make you slaves, so that you live in fear again; rather, the Spirit you received brought about your adoption to sonship. And by him we cry, "Abba, Father." ¹⁶ The Spirit himself testifies with our spirit that we are God's children.

What are you allowing in your life that keeps you from personal reality with God?

Don't be afraid to return to him. He won't turn you away. Indeed, he promises to lead you forward into more of his love. To be 'led by the Spirit' (verse 14) is not guidance in decision-making. Paul is talking about our hearts being freed more and more from the anxiety of the flesh, so that we walk according to the Spirit and put to death our sinful impulses and *live*. The Spirit leads us back to our Father, where we start to feel like children again. We feel loved again. He makes the truths in our heads into the experience of our hearts.

This is how it happens. Verse 13 says, 'If by the Spirit you put to death the misdeeds of the body, you will live'. Verse 14 is talking about the same thing, but now in terms of what God does. Both verses are about us growing in freedom from the past and becoming more settled in the love of God. Verse 13 tells us our part. Verse 14 tells us God's part.

The gospel is not that we are forgiven slaves but that we are beloved children. The Holy Spirit helps us see and feel the difference. God adopted us. He sent his Spirit into our hearts to give us a new sense of family identity and belonging. Our hearts crying 'Abba! Father!' – that is what justification *feels* like.

We need that inner assurance, don't we? Knowing the personal love of God with grace-guaranteed, non-delusional certainty helps us not to panic when we suffer. With the felt love of God in our hearts, we don't fear commitment, need escapism, or run from life, because we know where this journey is headed. Our pathway to future glory in Christ looks like ordinary, vulnerable, unimpressive, sometimes boring everyday life – changing nappies, waiting in traffic, paying bills. On the outside, Christianity brings no advantages. But deep within, God gives us *himself* (verse 16). The Spirit himself enters our awareness to assure us that our heavenly Father is committed to us with all his mighty heart.

Sometimes the awareness of sin leaves us cowering before God like a slave dreading an angry master. There is still a lot inside us that needs to die. But the Spirit has come bringing new life and he witnesses to our hearts that we are loved and that we belong to God. Thank God that the Spirit of adoption brings a new awareness of who God is, so that even in our sorrows, our hearts cry, 'Abba! Father!'

Day 45

Read: 1 Corinthians 2:6–16
Key verses: 1 Corinthians 2:10–11

. . . .

The Spirit searches all things, even the deep things of God.
11 For who knows a person's thoughts except their own spirit
within them? In the same way no one knows the thoughts of
God except the Spirit of God.

Should we refer to the Holy Spirit as 'it' or 'he'?

The verb 'searches' shows clearly that the Holy Spirit is personal. You can't search unless you have got a mind, and if you've got a mind, you must be a person. Because the Holy Spirit is a person, we must never refer to him as 'it'. He is a 'he', as Jesus made clear in his own teaching.

This person of the Holy Spirit has unique understanding of God because he is God. Paul explains that the Holy Spirit searches the depths of God and knows the thoughts of God.

• He searches the depths of God (verse 10).
  The verb 'searches' is the very same word Jesus used about the Jews who study the Scriptures diligently (John 5:39). It refers to thorough investigation. In a third-century AD papyrus the 'searchers', using the same word, are custom officials who rummage about in our baggage. Also, the Greek word for 'deep things' became a favourite term used by the Gnostic heretics, who claimed to have been initiated into the deep things of God. It is just possible that Paul deliberately borrowed from the Gnostic vocabulary, which had by now become more widely accepted, insisting here that the deep things of God were known and investigated by the Holy Spirit alone. The Holy Spirit is depicted as a restlessly inquisitive research worker, even a deep-sea diver who is seeking to fathom

the deepest depths of the infinite being of God. The Holy Spirit is God exploring the infinity of God.

- He knows the thoughts of God (verse 11).
  The 'thoughts' are literally the 'things' of man or the 'things' of God. The 'things of man' are what we would call humanness. Nobody understands humanness except human beings. Teenagers may complain, 'No one understands me!' It's true nobody understands us fully, we don't even fully understand ourselves. Yet to some degree human beings are self-conscious and self-aware and have some understanding of what humanness means. This is the concept of self-awareness and self-consciousness that applies to the Holy Spirit. The Holy Spirit is like the divine self-consciousness or the divine self-understanding. Just as no one can understand a human being, except that human being himself, so nobody can understand God, except God himself. Only God knows God.

> The bottom line is this: the Holy Spirit can't be pumped and scooped. He can't be slung around, gathered up, or dispensed. He's not pixie dust. There's no such thing as the Holy Spirit, because the Holy Spirit is not a thing at all, but the very presence of the personal God himself – with us, in us, and around us.
> (Jared Wilson, *Supernatural Power for Everyday People*, Nelson, 2018, p. 29)

Day 46

Read: 1 Corinthians 2:6–16
Key verses: 1 Corinthians 2:12–13

....

What we have received is not the spirit of the world, but the Spirit who is from God, so that we may understand what God has freely given us. [13] *This is what we speak, not in words taught us by human wisdom but in words taught by the Spirit, explaining spiritual realities with Spirit-taught words.*

In what way was the Holy Spirit involved in the writing of Scripture?

Paul claims the Holy Spirit gave the apostles the very words to use in their communication with others (verse 13). We call this, 'verbal inspiration'. This doctrine is often misunderstood.

- Verbal inspiration does not mean every word of the Bible is *literally* true. The Bible contains poetry and apocalyptic literature and each has to be interpreted according to its own literary style. Jesus himself was an opponent of biblical literalism when he was speaking symbolically. For example, when he told Nicodemus he needed to be 'born again' he explained he wasn't talking about a second physical birth (John 3).

- Verbal inspiration does not mean verbal dictation. Muslims believe that Allah, through the angel Gabriel, dictated the Koran to Mohammed. All he had to do was take down the dictation. In contrast, Christians believe the biblical authors were in full possession of their human faculties. Every biblical author has his own literary style and theological emphasis, and these were not ironed out by the process of inspiration. Many authors were historians. This history was not supernaturally revealed; they did their own research (Luke 1:1–4).

- Verbal inspiration does not mean that every text of Scripture is true even in isolation from its context. The Bible is without error in all that affirms, but not everything in Scripture is affirmed by Scripture. For example God says Job's friends did not speak the truth about him (Job 42:7). Their words are included to be repudiated, not endorsed. The book of Job is the infallible Word of God if you take it as a whole, if you allow it to interpret itself, but each text is not the Word of God apart from its context.

- Verbal inspiration means that what the Holy Spirit spoke through the biblical authors – understood according to its literary genre, understood according to the plain, natural meaning of the words used, understood according to its context and the intention of its authors – is true and without error.

The Holy Spirit spoke his Word through the apostles' words in such a way that their words were simultaneously his words. This is the double authority of Scripture: God spoke, as the author, through human authors; his words were their words at the same time.

Are you wrestling with doubts? Does your faith feel fragile? Don't leave your Bible sitting on the shelf. The Holy Spirit's words are trustworthy and true; they are the bedrock of our faith and our daily nourishment. Read, believe, and apply these words of life and hope and watch the Holy Spirit transform you from the inside out.

Day 47

Read: 1 Corinthians 2:6–16

Key verses: 1 Corinthians 2:13–16

....

This is what we speak, not in words taught us by human wisdom but in words taught by the Spirit, explaining spiritual realities with Spirit-taught words. ¹⁴ *The person without the Spirit does not accept the things that come from the Spirit of God but considers them foolishness, and cannot understand them because they are discerned only through the Spirit.* ¹⁵ *The person with the Spirit makes judgements about all things, but such a person is not subject to merely human judgements,* ¹⁶ *for,*
"Who has known the mind of the Lord so as to instruct him?"
But we have the mind of Christ.

How is the Holy Spirit at work when we read the Bible?

We are not inspired, as the prophets and apostles were, when we preach and teach but the Holy Spirit illuminates our minds to understand the inspired Word of God. This is implied at the end of verse 13, which the NIV translates, 'explaining spiritual realities with Spirit-taught words.' Different English versions explain this complicated phrase in different ways but I think the best translation is, 'interpreting spiritual truths to those who possess the Spirit' (RSV). In other words, the possession of the Holy Spirit is not limited to the biblical authors. The Holy Spirit's work of inspiration was unique to the prophets and apostles but his work of illumination is shared by Bible readers.

Illumination is the subjective process by which the Holy Spirit enlightens our minds to understand the revelation that he has given in Christ and in Scripture. The person with the Spirit has not become omniscient or infallible; it's not that everything in the Bible is clear, but whereas he was spiritually blind (verse 14), now God's Word makes sense in a way that it had not done before (verse 15).

Charles Simeon, the vicar of Holy Trinity in Cambridge for 54 years, used the illustration of a sundial. He explained that if you go out into the garden on a cloudy day when the sun is not shining, and you look at the sundial, all you see is figures but no message. But if the sun breaks through the clouds and shines on the sundial, immediately the finger points. If I come to Scripture on a cloudy day, with sin between me and God, I will not receive any message from the Word of God; it is just ink and paper. But if the sunlight of the Holy Spirit breaks through on the printed page of my darkened mind and God says, 'Let there be light,' then the finger points and I receive a message that I would never have otherwise received.

Can you remember seeing a new Christian's joy as God's Word came alive for the first time and they read the Bible with fresh eyes? This is the illumination that only the Holy Spirit can bring. Today, pray for more 'sundial moments' – that the Holy Spirit would open the eyes of our non-Christian friends and family; those on the fringes of our church or attending evangelistic courses.

Day 48

Read: 1 Corinthians 12:1–11

Key verses: 1 Corinthians 12:1–3

. . . .

Now about the gifts of the Spirit, brothers and sisters, I do not want you to be uninformed. *²You know that when you were pagans, somehow or other you were influenced and led astray to mute idols.* *³Therefore I want you to know that no one who is speaking by the Spirit of God says, "Jesus be cursed," and no one can say, "Jesus is Lord," except by the Holy Spirit.*

What makes a Christian truly 'spiritual'? Being in church leadership, exercising a particular spiritual gift, being a proficient prayer . . . ?

Paul's letter answers this question that the Corinthians must have asked about. When Paul talks about the 'gifts of the Spirit' in verse 1 he's really speaking in a general way about Christian spirituality and what it means to be a spiritual person.

He says, 'No one can say "Jesus is Lord" except by the Holy Spirit.' Clearly it is possible for any sort of person to say the three words 'Jesus is Lord'. But Paul's point is that the Holy Spirit never does Jesus down. He will exalt Jesus. So, the truly spiritual person is anyone who makes the basic Christian assumption that Jesus is Lord. To be spiritual is to exalt Jesus. How do we exalt Jesus? We acknowledge him as Lord, King, Ruler, the one and only God. The truly spiritual are not – as the Corinthians thoughts – people who speak in tongues or exercise some other special spiritual gift. All Christians are truly spiritual because all make the basic affirmation 'Jesus is Lord' by the one Spirit.

The greatest miracle God's Spirit works on earth is conversion. If you are converted, then God's Spirit worked the greatest miracle inside you when he brought you to realize that Jesus is Lord. If you are not a believer, then pray for that miracle. Ask God's Spirit to open your eyes and lead you to make the affirmation: 'Jesus is Lord'. It is the Spirit who converts, he leads us to Christ. It isn't the other way around. The terminus is Jesus, and the Spirit always points to him. He has a burning desire to glorify the Lord Jesus. And so, we have a sure test for true Christian spirituality: does it exalt Jesus?

> Exulting in Christ is evidence of the Spirit's work! The focus of the church is not on the dove but on the cross, and that's the way the Spirit would have it. As J.I. Packer puts it, "The Spirit's message to us is never, 'Look at Me; listen to Me; come to Me; get to know Me,' but always, 'Look at Him, and see His glory; listen to Him, and hear His word; go to Him, and have life; get to know Him, and taste His gift of joy and peace.'"
> (Kevin DeYoung, *The Holy Spirit*, Crossway, 2011, p. 17)

Day 49

Read: 1 Corinthians 12:1–11
Key verses: 1 Corinthians 12:4–7

• •

There are different kinds of gifts, but the same Spirit distributes them. ⁵There are different kinds of service, but the same Lord. ⁶There are different kinds of working, but in all of them and in everyone it is the same God at work.
⁷Now to each one the manifestation of the Spirit is given for the common good.

What does God do when he freezes water? He makes snowflakes, every single one of them different. What do humans do when we freeze water? We make ice cubes, every one the same. God makes every one of us quite different in our mothers' wombs, and having made us he breaks the mould, saying: 'I'm not going to make that one again, I'm going to make a different one next time.'

We start as different people by nature, and then the Spirit of God makes us even more different as Christians. The Corinthians wanted everyone to speak in tongues, to the exclusion of the other gifts but it's not the Spirit's work to clone us. He delights in variety, but also in teaching us to get on with each other. When people of different temperaments, education, colour, gender, and social background get together, it is the Spirit of the living God who has brought them together. When you and I have nothing in common except Jesus Christ, then our fellowship begins to become really deep. Diversity, not uniformity, is essential for a healthy church because the church must be like God, and diversity has its roots in God himself.

How does God's Spirit make us more diverse than we already are? By giving each Christian a gift for the benefit of others (verse 7). Paul lists some gifts in verses 8–11. There are six other lists of gifts in chapters 12–14 and none of them match. A comparison with other

New Testament lists of spiritual gifts (Romans 12, Ephesians 4, 1 Peter 4) makes it clear that none of these lists is exhaustive, that there is no great significance in the order and that there is no clear distinction between what we might call natural and supernatural gifts.

Paul refuses to define spiritual gifts narrowly. If we try to make him do so, we miss the point – when we Christians meet together, the Holy Spirit goes to work among us to meet our many needs in a huge variety of ways. It is all at the initiative and under the sovereignty of God (verse 11), and each one of us has a part to play.

If Paul is right, that God has placed us in our local churches to minister to others, most of us need to change our mind set. Rather than wondering, 'What do I get out of church?' we need to be asking, 'What do I bring?' God has uniquely gifted you – it may be teaching children, welcoming a stranger, counting the collection or encouraging another believer – if you don't use your gift, the church misses out. This Sunday, will you go to church looking for ways to bless and serve?

Day 50

Read: 1 Corinthians 12:12–31
Key verses: 1 Corinthians 12:12–13

....

Just as a body, though one, has many parts, but all its many parts form one body, so it is with Christ. ¹³*For we were all baptized by one Spirit so as to form one body – whether Jews or Gentiles, slave or free – and we were all given the one Spirit to drink.*

Would you describe yourself as competitive?

In so many different subtle ways, we gently vie with one another. We compete through our careers, children, looks, intellect, achieve-ments, and possessions. There is a deep human need to feel just a little superior. And so, we take God-given diversity, essential to the body of Christ, and twist it by creating spiritual hierarchy and pecking orders within the church. Paul recognized this pervasive human tendency to one-upmanship in the Corinthians, so he wrote to them with this teaching about the body (verse 12).

Do you remember when Paul first encountered Jesus Christ? As he hurried to Damascus to imprison Christians, a light shone, he fell to the ground and a voice spoke.

'Saul, Saul, why do you persecute me?'
'Who are you, Lord?' Saul asked.
'I am Jesus, whom you are persecuting.'
(Acts 9:4–5)

Jesus identified himself with his followers on earth. So, Paul is not just saying that the church operates like a body; he is saying it is a body. It is Jesus's body on earth now.

It is the Spirit who makes the body one (verse 13). There is only one way into the body of Christ, and that is by being baptised by the

Spirit and by being given the one Spirit to drink. We only get converted one way, when the Spirit causes us to realize and declare that Jesus is Lord (verse 3). And because there is only one way into the Christian life, we all belong together from that moment on. The church cannot exist without the Spirit. A hundred religious people knit together by good administration do not make a church any more than eleven dead men in a coffin make a football team. It is the Spirit of Christ who converts us and brings us to new life. He brings us into the body and gives it life.

Being the body of Christ means:

• We don't give in to either self-pity because our gifting seems inferior or resentment because someone else's gift appears superior (verses 14–16).

• We trust that God has specifically arranged the parts of the body: 'every one of them, just as he wanted them to be' (verse 18) to fulfil his purposes.

• We realize that our differences make us indispensable to each other and we are all of equal value to God (verses 21–26).

Father, forgive me for the times prideful gossip has been disguised as passing on a prayer request, when family rivalry has prevailed, when I've acted as if my gift was superior, when I've wallowed in self-pity because my gift was not publicly appreciated, and when I've not valued believers like you do. Holy Spirit, extinguish competition from my church. Help us to live like the body you created us to be, bringing glory to Christ and showing the world what belonging to him looks like. Amen.

Day 51

Read: 1 Corinthians 12:12–31
Key verses: 1 Corinthians 12:27–30

....

Now you are the body of Christ, and each one of you is a part of it. [28] *And God has placed in the church first of all apostles, second prophets, third teachers, then miracles, then gifts of healing, of helping, of guidance, and of different kinds of tongues.* [29] *Are all apostles? Are all prophets? Are all teachers? Do all work miracles?* [30] *Do all have gifts of healing? Do all speak in tongues? Do all interpret?*

'No!' Is the answer to Paul's questions in verses 29–30. Clearly, we don't all exercise these gifts. Paul wants the Corinthians to stop expecting everyone to speak in tongues, making one gift a measure of spirituality for everyone, and start exercising a much wider diversity of gifts. In this chapter he is at pains to stress there is no inferiority or superiority in the body of Christ.

He determinedly ducks the question we want to ask: 'What's my spiritual gift?' It seems a reasonable question but Paul is not interested in answering it. Perhaps because my desire to know about my gifts may conceal a desire to know my status and where I come in the pecking order at church. Once I know my gifts I am likely to put myself above some people and below others. We tend to use our spiritual gift to gauge, 'How important am I in the church?' But that is an illegitimate question. I am infinitely important because Christ died for me. God does not arrange people in ranks in the church. He brought me into his church through his Spirit.

You may be wondering, 'How can I possibly exercise my gift in the church if I don't know what it is?' I think you can because this passage is teaching us to adopt the attitude, 'If I serve other people, God will equip me for service.' He will gift me for it, but the gift is his. In one sense it never becomes mine, I don't own it. The gifting is God's business and he never gets it wrong (see verses 11, 18, 24).

So our challenge from this chapter is not to discover what our spiritual gifts are but to lay down our lives for one another. We say to ourselves, 'If only I knew my gifts, I'd love to serve other people.' But Paul turns this thinking on its head and invites us to start loving, serving and building up the body of Christ with whatever gifts and resources we've been given.

'What is my spiritual gift?' is a question God rarely answers in a vacuum or through a personality and skills analysis test. Rather, it is in the context of serving in the church that we discover, use and hone our gifts. The type of gift matters little, only that we are using it to love others. The real question God wants us to ask today is, 'How can I grow in love for and service to the body of Christ?'

Day 52

Read: Galatians 5:13–26
Key verses: Galatians 5:16–18

. . . .

16 So I say, walk by the Spirit, and you will not gratify the desires of the flesh. 17 For the flesh desires what is contrary to the Spirit, and the Spirit what is contrary to the flesh. 18 But if you are led by the Spirit, you are not under the law.

How can I be a fruitful Christian?

Paul says: 'walk by the Spirit' (verse 16); be 'led by the Spirit' (verse 18); 'keep in step with the Spirit' (verse 25). All these expressions refer to the continuous outworking of what the Holy Spirit is doing within the believer. The initiative is all his. He provides the resources, and we are to walk or live relying on those resources by the power of the Spirit. He sets the direction, and we are to be led by the Spirit. He controls the pace, and we are to keep in step with the Spirit. The verbs of Galatians 5 indicate progress, development and growth.

God designed the world that all life will bear fruit after its kind. So, in a very real sense, it is the most natural thing in the world that all Christians who are filled with the Spirit should be fruitful – not just a few special Christians. But the process happens gradually. It isn't just a matter of sudden crisis experiences. Like the apples on a tree our growth in Christlikeness develops and comes to maturity slowly.

Of course, the amount of fruit produced depends on the health of the tree, the conditions of the soil and the climate. And it is because Paul is so concerned about Christians living in a hostile environment that he says, 'Walk by the Spirit and you will not gratify the desires of the flesh. For the flesh desires what is contrary to the Spirit, and the Spirit what is contrary to the flesh' (verse 16–17). Someone who lives like this is not hard to recognize. If you are responding to the life of

God within you, you will demonstrate the character of the Lord Jesus and produce spiritual fruit.

As you seek to be a fruitful Christian in a hostile environment, walk by the Spirit and grasp God's promise today.

> The Spirit has landed to do battle with the flesh. So take heart if your soul feels like a battlefield at times. The sign of whether you are indwelt by the Spirit is not that you have no bad desires, but that you are at war with them! . . . When you walk by the Spirit, you will not let those bad desires come to maturity. When you walk by the Spirit, you nip the desires of the flesh in the bud. New God-centred desires crowd out old man-centred desires. Verse 16 promises victory over the desires of the flesh – not that there won't be a war, but that the winner of that war will be the Spirit.
> (John Piper – https://www.desiringgod.org/messages/the-war -within-flesh-versus-spirit accessed 31/5/22)

Day 53

Read: Galatians 5:13–26
Key verses: Galatians 5:22–23

••

> ²² *But the fruit of the Spirit is love, joy, peace, forbearance, kindness, goodness, faithfulness,* ²³ *gentleness and self-control. Against such things there is no law.*

Can you remember going into the exam room and finding the optimistic exhortation at the top of the exam paper: 'Attempt any four questions'?

God is not saying choose three or four of these characteristics and work on them. The word for 'fruit' is singular. This is what holiness, being like Jesus, looks like and there are nine expressions of it. You don't add these qualities one by one. They are all to be growing in our lives.

Love, joy and peace are the initial demonstration of the Holy Spirit in a new Christian's life. But we never grow out of them. Rather, we grow more and more into them. They are not abstract virtues but evidence of Christ living out his life, by his Spirit, in us. Jesus speaks of 'my love' (John 15:9), 'my joy' (John 15:11) and 'my peace' (John 14:27) because he alone imparts these virtues to his people by his Spirit.

The fullness of the Spirit means that each of these characteristics of the Lord Jesus is to be experienced to an increasing degree. So, Paul prays that we may know this love of Christ which surpasses knowledge that we might be filled with all the fullness of God (Ephesians 3:19). Peter writes, 'you love [Jesus]; and even though you do not see him now, you believe in him and are filled with an inexpressible and glorious joy (1 Peter 1:8). Paul also talks about 'the peace of God, which transcends all understanding, will guard your hearts and your minds in Christ Jesus' (Philippians 4:7). The purpose of the fullness of the Spirit is that we may know the love that passes knowledge, the joy that passes description, and the peace that passes understanding. Every new Christian knows something of this, but the believer who is being filled with the Spirit is increasing in each of these areas.

How can we be sure Christ's love is in us? How can we be joyful through life's trials? Jesus' answer is, 'keep my commands' (John 15:10). How can we know the peace of God in the midst of turmoil? 'Anyone who loves me will obey my teaching. My Father will love them, and we will come to them and make our home with them' (John 14:23). Do you see how it works? As we obey the Scriptures we are responding to the Holy Spirit who uses the Word of God to produce fruit in the children of God. And as we open our lives fully to Christ, he will produce in us his characteristics of love, joy and peace.

Our fruitfulness is directly dependent on our obedience. So, we need to examine ourselves and ask: Am I indulging in a relationship God would not approve of? Do my attitudes and thoughts honour God? Are there failures of integrity at home, work or at church? Ask for God's help to root out sin and obey him today.

Day 54

Read: Galatians 5:13–26
Key verses: Galatians 5:22–25

∙∙

But the fruit of the Spirit is love, joy, peace, forbearance, kindness, goodness, faithfulness, ²³gentleness and self-control. Against such things there is no law. ²⁴Those who belong to Christ Jesus have crucified the flesh with its passions and desires.²⁵Since we live by the Spirit, let us keep in step with the Spirit.

How are you doing at producing spiritual fruit? Are you patient (forbearing), kind and good?

Jesus went about doing good (Acts 10:38). In a sense he couldn't help it; it was his nature. That's what is so attractive about the work of the Spirit. He doesn't produce a busy do-gooder that everyone resents but the overflowing life of Christ that doesn't miss the opportunity to help, encourage, bear a burden or give. We can't do this in ourselves. It is only as the Spirit fills us that he makes us more like Christ. And people will notice.

What about faithfulness, gentleness and self-control? Notice that the Holy Spirit changes us from the inside out. He did that with the disciples. They weren't faithful. They ran away in the Garden of Geth-semane. They weren't gentle; in the Gospels they were always arguing about status, power and who was the greatest. And they certainly weren't characterized by self-control. Think about the sons of thunder and Peter's impetuosity. What changed them? They received the Holy Spirit. In the book of Acts we find the disciples faithfully preaching God's Word. There is no longer any room for pride. They are meek and lowly in heart, following a servant Lord. When the Holy Spirit came into their lives, every area came under his control. The horrifying list of sins in verses 19–21 is full of the failure of self-control. But the Christian is controlled by the Holy Spirit.

'Those who belong to Christ Jesus have crucified the flesh with its passions and desires. Since we live by the Spirit, let us keep in step with the Spirit' (verse 24–25). All the resources are available. The question is, 'Do you really want to be like Jesus?'

We live by the Spirit but for the fruit of the Spirit to grow in us, for us to become more like Jesus, we must 'keep in step with the Spirit'. This is not a sea change – we became Christians by trusting in Christ and his Word and this never stops. 'Keeping in step with the Spirit' means believing and obeying the Word which the Spirit inspired; setting our minds and hearts on what he desires; surrendering to his prompts; and being part of a church community where he dwells. Imagine being in a three-legged race, running perfectly in tandem with your partner (for some of us, this is a stretch!). The Holy Spirit is like that partner, his arm around our shoulder, joined with us for the whole of life's journey. He sets the pace and as we learn to lean on him and follow his lead we experience his strength and enabling.

Day 55

Read: Ephesians 1:1–13
Key verses: Ephesians 1:3, 13–14

. . . .

Praise be to the God and Father of our Lord Jesus Christ, who has blessed us in the heavenly realms with every spiritual blessing in Christ... When you believed, you were marked in him with a seal, the promised Holy Spirit, [14]*who is a deposit guaranteeing our inheritance until the redemption of those who are God's possession – to the praise of his glory.*

Did you know that the Holy Spirit is mentioned in each of the six chapters of Ephesians?

Paul begins his letter by declaring that every blessing of the Holy Spirit is ours if we are Christ's. These blessings are ours already; given by God when he joined us to Jesus. I would sum it up in these words: if we are in Christ, we have everything, because everything we need is in Christ.

The rest of the letter to the Ephesians recounts every spiritual blessing we have received and the implications for our lives. The first blessing is the seal of the Spirit. All who have heard the gospel and believed in Jesus have been sealed with the promised Spirit of God (verses 13–14). The same verb 'sealed' is used when Paul exhorts us, 'Do not grieve the Holy Spirit of God, with whom you were *sealed* for the day of redemption' (Ephesians 4:30). Clearly, this sealing happened in the past, when we first believed.

A seal is a mark of ownership: whether it be affixing some personal seal to a legal document, stamping your name upon some tool, or branding of sheep or cattle with a hot iron, the purpose of sealing is to mark something as belonging to us. And God's seal, by which he brands us as belonging for ever to him, is the Holy Spirit himself. The Holy Spirit is the identity tag of the Christian. If the Holy Spirit dwells within you, you are a Christian. If the Holy Spirit does not, you are not a Christian.

The seal is indelible: it cannot and will not be erased. We have been 'sealed for the day of redemption' (4:30), that is until the final day, when our bodies will be redeemed. God has branded us with his seal, the Holy Spirit, and he will never take him from us. This divine seal is God's guarantee that we will receive our inheritance one day.

There is so much uncertainty and insecurity in our world. If we look solely at the news and social media, we are paralysed with fear. But when we focus on 'the heavenly realms', the unseen world of spiritual reality, and the blessings we have because we belong to Christ, we find security and hope. Every evidence of the Holy Spirit in our lives is a sign we have been 'sealed for the day of redemption'; proof that we belong to God and our eternal future is guaranteed. Today, praise God for the confidence and peace his seal gives.

Day 56

Read: Ephesians 1:16–23
Key verses: Ephesians 1:17–19

···

I keep asking that the God of our Lord Jesus Christ, the glorious Father, may give you the Spirit of wisdom and revelation, so that you may know him better. [18] *I pray that the eyes of your heart may be enlightened in order that you may know the hope to which he has called you, the riches of his glorious inheritance in his holy people,* [19] *and his incomparably great power for us who believe.*

Did you know that each person of the Trinity – Father, Son and Holy Spirit – is invested in your discipleship?

In Paul's opening prayer in Ephesians 1 he asks God the Father to give us the Holy Spirit of wisdom and revelation so that we can know Christ better (verse 17). The Holy Spirit is pleased to do this because, above all else, he delights to bear witness to Jesus. He is the author of Scripture and the whole Bible is testimony to Jesus. Through the prophets of the Old Testament and the apostles of the New Testament, the Holy Spirit has bequeathed to the church his unique and definitive witness to Christ. But that doesn't mean that the Holy Spirit's work was finished when the Canon of Scripture was completed, only that his work has changed. Now his work is more illumination than revelation. His role is to illumine our minds and the eyes of our hearts to understand what he has revealed in Christ and in Scripture. And, in particular, he longs to open our eyes to the hope to which God has called us, the riches of his glorious inheritance, and the immeasurable greatness of his power that he gives to those who believe (verse 18–19).

Like the seal of the Spirit this spiritual blessing has been ours from the day we first trusted Christ. God has blessed us with the illumination of the Spirit and, throughout our Christian life, he will go on opening our eyes wider and wider to see and understand his Word.

> 'There must be Spirit in me as there is Spirit in the Scriptures, before I can see anything,' remarked the sixteenth-century Puritan Richard Sibbes
> (Derek Prime and Alistair Begg, *On Being a Pastor*, Moody Press, 2004, p. 121).

Thank God that the Holy Spirit literally 'turns the light on', illuminating the Bible for us, helping us understand and apply its truths. 'Open my eyes that I may see wonderful things in your law' (Psalm 119:18) should be our plea every time we sit down to study the Bible.

Today makes Paul's prayer in Ephesians 1:17–19 your own.

Heavenly Father please give me the Holy Spirit's wisdom and revelation so that I might know and obey Christ better. May the Holy Spirit fill my heart with the hope of my future inheritance and may this eternal reality increasingly shape my values and priorities. I pray that also I would experience more and more of the Holy Spirit's power enabling me, throughout this day, to say 'no' to sin and 'yes' to righteousness. For your glory, amen.

Day 57

Read: Ephesians 3:14–21
Key verses: Ephesians 3:16–19

....

I pray that out of his glorious riches he may strengthen you with power through his Spirit in your inner being, ¹⁷ so that Christ may dwell in your hearts through faith. And I pray that you, being rooted and established in love, ¹⁸ may have power, together with all the Lord's holy people, to grasp how wide and long and high and deep is the love of Christ, ¹⁹ and to know this love that surpasses knowledge – that you may be filled to the measure of all the fullness of God.

What are you praying for? What are you praying for yourself and for other Christians?

Paul begins his letter by praying for the believers:

'I pray that the eyes of your heart may be enlightened in order that you may *know* . . . his incomparably great power for us who believe. That power is the same as the mighty strength he exerted when he raised Christ from the dead and seated him at his right hand in the heavenly realms' (Ephesians 1:18–20).

In this first prayer Paul is asking the Holy Spirit to enlighten us so that we may *know* God's 'strength', 'might', and 'power'. In his second prayer in chapter 3:14–19 he uses the same words but this time he prays that the Holy Spirit would help us *experience* them.

The strength of the Holy Spirit is not a shallow thing; it is not a superficial work. He is able to penetrate into the innermost recesses of our personality, right into our inner being. You are able to be strengthened in your innermost being by the Holy Spirit, so that Christ may reside and reign in your heart by faith. He is able to deepen your love for righteousness, to strengthen your resolve, and fortify your will.

This strength of the Holy Spirit is another one of the spiritual blessings we received when we first trusted Christ. It is already ours because the Spirit dwells in our hearts. Pray that we would experience this strength in our inner beings more and more.

In Ephesians 3 one of the things Paul prays for is that the Holy Spirit would give us power to grasp 'the love of Christ' (verse 18). We acknowledge Christ demonstrated his love for us on the cross but often the feeling of being loved by God is fleeting. It is only the strength of the Holy Spirit at work in our hearts that can assure us that the love which took Christ to the cross is the love with which he loves us still.

> The Spirit's role . . . is to turn our postcard apprehensions of Christ's great heart of longing affection for us into an experience of sitting on the beach, in a lawn chair, drink in hand, enjoying the actual experience. The Spirit does this decisively, once and for all, at re-generation. But he does it ten thousand times thereafter, as we continue through sin, folly and boredom to drift from the felt experience of his heart.
> (Dane Ortlund, *Gentle and Lowly*, Crossway, 2020, (p. 126)

Day 58

Read: Ephesians 4:1–16
Key verses: Ephesians 4:3–6

....

Make every effort to keep the unity of the Spirit through the bond of peace. ⁴There is one body and one Spirit, just as you were called to one hope when you were called; ⁵one Lord, one faith, one baptism; ⁶one God and Father of all, who is over all and through all and in all.

We tend to think of our relationship with God exclusively in individualistic terms, but the Holy Spirit is also at work in the church.

In chapter 4 Paul draws our attention to the Trinity. There is only one God and Father of us all (verse 6); one Lord (verse 5), and one Spirit (verse 4). This unity of the Godhead is reflected in the unity of the church. There is only one Christian family because there is only one heavenly Father. There is only one Christian faith, hope and baptism, because there is only one Lord Jesus, in whom we have believed, into whom we have been baptised, and for whose coming we are waiting. And there is only one Christian body because there is only one Holy Spirit animating the body. The fundamental spiritual unity of the church is as indestructible as the fundamental unity of the Godhead. We may try to break it up in our different denominations but you can no more divide the unity of the church than you can divide the unity of the Godhead. The one Father creates the one family; the one Lord Jesus creates the one faith, hope and baptism; and the one Holy Spirit creates the one body.

Paul goes further and urges us to maintain the unity of the Spirit (verse 3). If there is only one body and one Spirit, how can we be exhorted to maintain that which can never be destroyed? I think the answer is, we are to maintain it *visibly*. We are to seek to exhibit visible unity that is indestructible because there is only one Father, one Lord Jesus, and one Holy Spirit. The unity of the Spirit is a spiritual blessing we have received from God. Our charge is to maintain this unity and enjoy this blessing more and more.

> Is the unity of the Spirit visible in your church or is your fellowship characterized by bickering, factions and jealousies? What can you do to promote and protect unity? Remember, the unity you are aiming for is not superficial, based on shared backgrounds and preferences, but on an unshakeable commitment to core Bible truths – that there is only one body, one Spirit, one hope, one Lord, one faith, one baptism, one God and Father of all. Strive to hold fast to these truths, 'until we all reach unity in the faith and in the knowledge of the Son of God and become mature, attaining to the whole measure of the fullness of Christ' (Ephesians 4:13).

Day 59

Read: Ephesians 6:10–20
Key verses: Ephesians 6:11, 16–17

....

Put on the full armour of God, so that you can take your stand against the devil's schemes... ¹⁶*take up the shield of faith, with which you can extinguish all the flaming arrows of the evil one.* ¹⁷ *Take the helmet of salvation and the sword of the Spirit, which is the word of God.*

Is your faith under fire? Some days we are acutely aware of the sustained attacks of the devil. As we wrestle with discouragement, opposition, temptation or anxiety, Paul reminds us of the antidote.

This last chapter of Ephesians describes vividly our warfare with the devil, principalities and powers. Paul's goal is for us to recognize the indispensable necessity of clothing ourselves from head to foot in the armour of God. Six pieces of armour are mentioned. There are the shoes and belt which are part of every soldier's equipment. There are the breastplate, the shield and helmet, which are essentially worn for protection. Only the sword of the Spirit could be called an offensive weapon, used in attack as well as defence. The sword of the Spirit is the Word of God – the Word that God has spoken, not only in the living Word, Jesus Christ, but in the words of Scripture that have been preserved for our learning. The Word of God is living, active and powerful. It pierces our mind and conscience. It exposes our motives. It divides soul from spirit, revealing the difference between what is natural and what is spiritual, and shows whether we are born again or not.

Are you exercising the sword of the Spirit? Are you using God's Word in combat with the devil? When tempted, do you use words of Scripture to frustrate the plans of the devil, just as Jesus did? Are you wielding the sword of the Spirit with skill in your witnessing? If you are a minister or someone who teaches the Bible, are you conscientious in speaking biblically, wielding the sword of the Spirit which is sharp and penetrates the conscience?

> We have one offensive weapon: the sword of the Spirit, the Word of God (Eph. 6:17). But what many Christians fail to realize is that we can't draw the sword from someone else's scabbard. If we don't wear it, we can't wield it. If the Word of God does not abide in us (Jn. 15:7), we will reach for it in vain when the enemy strikes. But if we do wear it, if it lives within us, what mighty warriors we can be! (John Piper, *Desiring God*, Multnomah, 2011, p. 151)

Today, in the heat of the battle, draw strength from God's Word:

> You will find it unfailing in all periods of your life, in all circumstances, in all companies, in all trials, and under all difficulties. Were it fallible, it would be useless in emergencies, but its unerring truth renders it precious beyond all price to the soldiers of the cross. (C. H. Spurgeon and Robert Hall, *Spiritual Warfare in a Believer's Life*, Emerald Books, 1993, p. 76)

Day 60

Read: Ephesians 4:17–32
Key verses: Ephesians 4:30–32

• •

Do not grieve the Holy Spirit of God, with whom you were sealed for the day of redemption. ³¹*Get rid of all bitterness, rage and anger, brawling and slander, along with every form of malice.* ³²*Be kind and compassionate to one another, forgiving each other, just as in Christ God forgave you.*

If God has given me every spiritual blessing (Ephesians 1:3), why does my Christian life frequently fall so far short of what it ought to be? The answer is quite simple. The problem is not that we have been denied any blessing but that we have not exploited the blessings we have already received.

You may know the story of the Native American who died of starvation. When he died they found round his neck a little bag containing an old yellow parchment. He had kept it as a kind of charm. He had no idea that it meant anything. But it turned out to be a document granting a pension to the man's grandfather for his bravery in the American War of Independence. The terms of the deed made a pension available to the first recipient, his son and grandson – the man who had died of starvation. The document had been signed by George Washington himself. The man had been blessed, but he had never exploited his blessing.

That is the case for many Christians, indeed all of us to a certain extent. To help us understand how we can enjoy the spiritual blessings we have already received, Paul gives two commands in this letter to the Ephesians. The first is 'Don't grieve the Holy Spirit' (4:30).

Don't sadden the Holy Spirit. Don't cause his grief or sorrow. The Holy Spirit is a sensitive Spirit. We cannot even begin to understand his sensitivity. He cannot bear contamination with any evil – lying, anger, bitterness, slander, malice, immorality – all the things mentioned in this chapter. Any unholiness makes the Holy Spirit withdraw, not from us, but within us; not out of the front door but into the attic or cellar.

If we have grieved the Holy Spirit, we need to repent, confess what we have done and turn from it; because when the Holy Spirit is grieved, he is not able to help us experience the spiritual blessings which are already ours in potential.

Heavenly Father, I confess I have become hardened to my own sin, immune to the grief I cause the Holy Spirit when I gossip, harbour bitterness, lose my temper, lie to avoid awkward conversations and flirt with immorality. Teach me to see my sin as the Holy Spirit does, sharing his revulsion at the things that offend you. Please forgive me, restore to me the joy of my salvation, deepen my relationship with you and help me to experience, in increasing measure, all the spiritual blessings that you have blessed me with. Amen.

Day 61

Read: Ephesians 5:1–20
Key verses: Ephesians 5:18–20

. . . .

Do not get drunk on wine, which leads to debauchery. Instead, be filled with the Spirit, [19] speaking to one another with psalms, hymns, and songs from the Spirit. Sing and make music from your heart to the Lord, [20] always giving thanks to God the Father for everything, in the name of our Lord Jesus Christ.

Why is my Christian life not all it should be? Why am I not experiencing all the spiritual blessings God has given me?

First, we must make sure we haven't grieved the Holy Spirit (Day 60). Second, we must be 'filled with the Spirit' (5:18). Paul contrasts drunkenness and being filled with the Spirit. Drunkenness is due to a lack of self-control and leads to a further loss of self-control. The fullness of the Holy Spirit leads to the exact opposite; self-control is actually the ninth fruit of the Holy Spirit in Galatians 5. Whereas excessive alcohol robs us of our humanity and makes us behave like animals, the Holy Spirit is the only person who can lead you into a fully human existence and make you the man or woman God wants you to be.

So, it's a great mistake to suppose that the fullness of the Holy Spirit is a kind of spiritual intoxication. The only reason why, on the day of Pentecost, Christians were thought to be drunk was not because they had lost their self-control, but because they were speaking in foreign languages that people couldn't understand. Drunkenness is lack of self-control and excess but being filled with the Holy Spirit leads to love, joy, peace, patience, kindness, goodness, faithfulness, gentleness and self-control.

The only similarity between drunkenness and being filled with the Holy Spirit is the way in which both states are reached. People get drunk by going on drinking. People are filled by the Spirit by going on drinking! Jesus said, '"Let anyone who is thirsty come to me and drink. Whoever believes in me, as Scripture has said, rivers of living water will flow from within them." By this he meant the Spirit' (John 7:37–39). John is saying that somebody filled with the Spirit is so full that the blessing overflows into the lives of others. How does that happen? You have to come to Christ, and keep coming to Christ – the verb is in the present tense – and keep drinking from him, asking him to fill you with the Holy Spirit.

Are you disappointed with the state of your Christian life? The remedy is repentance and faith. If you've grieved the Holy Spirit, repent and turn from your sin. Keep repenting every day, the moment you are conscious of grieving and hurting the Spirit. If you know you are not filled with the Spirit because you are thirsty, come to Jesus in faith, in simple trust, and drink. Whenever you are conscious of being thirsty, come to Jesus, asking him to fill you with his Spirit. Keep repenting; keep coming to Jesus so that you can keep enjoying all the spiritual blessings you have been blessed with.

For further study

If you would like to read more about the Holy Spirit, you might find this selection of books helpful.

- Christopher Ash, *Hearing the Spirit* (Christian Focus, 2012)

- Tim Chester and Christopher de la Hoyde, *Who on Earth Is the Holy Spirit? (And Other Questions about Who He Is and What He Does)* (The Good Book Company, 2005)

- David Jackman, *Spirit of Truth: Unlocking the Bible's teaching on the Holy Spirit* (2007, Christian Focus)

- J. I. Packer, *Keep in Step with the Spirit* (IVP, 2006)

- John Stott, *Baptism and Fullness: The work of the Holy Spirit today* (IVP, 2021)

- Jared Wilson, *Supernatural Power for Everyday People* (Thomas Nelson, 2018)

Faithful

Contributors

Day 62

Read: Genesis 15:1–21
Key verses: Genesis 15:5–7

....

> [5] He [God] took him outside and said, "Look up at the sky and count the stars – if indeed you can count them." Then he said to him, "So shall your offspring be."
> [6] Abram believed the Lord, and he credited it to him as righteousness.
> [7] He also said to him, "I am the Lᴏʀᴅ, who brought you out of Ur of the Chaldeans to give you this land to take possession of it."

Are you good at keeping promises?

God has been keeping – and is still keeping – the promise that he made more than four thousand years ago.

God had commanded Abraham to leave his home (Genesis 12), and now promises him a people and a land (Genesis 15:5 and 7). This promise is not just to Abraham but to his people, to us. In Galatians 3:8, Paul says that, through this promise made to Abraham, God 'announced the gospel in advance'. This promise comes to us in the Lord Jesus Christ. As Paul says, 'If you belong to Christ, then you are Abraham's seed, and heirs according to the promise' (Galatians 3:29). And so, in Christ, we receive the promise of a people and a land, except that by the time we reach Christ, the promise has grown even bigger. Paul says that Abraham received the promise that he would be heir of the world (Romans 4:13)! In Christ, we too are promised a home in the new creation.

Abraham wonders how this is all going to happen, as he is childless (Genesis 15:2). Instead of explaining or giving him a timetable, God says, 'Look up . . . count the stars – if indeed you can count them . . . So shall your offspring be' (verse 5). Now, in one sense, this is simply a reiteration of the promise. There's no new information there. But it's more than that, for God is saying, 'Don't just look at the problem. Don't just view things from your perspective. See the bigger picture! See my power spread across the skies! I have created a million, million burning suns, and I can create a million, million children to be my people.' And that's enough for Abraham. Abraham believed the promise because he trusted the promise-maker (verse 6).

Now God makes that promise to you. If you put your faith in Christ, then you can be part of God's new people, living in God's new world, a child of God and an heir of the world. Don't just look at your guilt and your shame. Don't just look at your fears and your doubts. Look up! Look up and see the power of God spread across the skies. See the million, million burning suns that God has made as a sign to us of his power to remake your life.

Look up! Look at the skies, the starry host. Look all around you at the evidence of God's faithfulness. Look back at how God kept his promise to Abraham by giving him a son, and the Israelites the Promised Land. Look at your own life and all that God has done – forgiving your sins and making you his child. Praise God; he is relentlessly faithful. Whatever fears, doubts or guilt threaten to overwhelm you, you can trust him for all that lies ahead today and for eternity.

Day 63

Read: Genesis 15:1–21
Key verses: Genesis 15:8–10

. . . .

> [8]*But Abram said, "Sovereign LORD, how can I know that I shall gain possession of it?"*
>
> [9]*So the LORD said to him, "Bring me a heifer, a goat and a ram, each three years old, along with a dove and a young pigeon."*
>
> [10]*Abram brought all these to him, cut them in two and arranged the halves opposite each other; the birds, however, he did not cut in half.*

A bride walks down the aisle to her groom. They've said their vows, exchanged rings and signed the register. The couple not only make promises to each other, but they also enter into a legally binding 'till-death-do-us-part' contract.

Today, we make a contract by writing some commitments on a piece of paper and signing at the bottom.

In Abraham's day, you sliced up an animal and walked between the pieces. In effect, you were saying, 'If I break this covenant, may the fate of these animals be my fate!' So here, God is not only making a promise but also binding himself to that promise. Why? So that we can be doubly confident. A divine promise ought to be enough, because God never lies. There's a lovely little phrase in Isaiah 25:1 that literally says God is 'faithfully faithful'. We have a faithfully faithful God. But we get the bonus of having his promises signed and sealed in a covenant! 'How can I know?' asks Abraham in Genesis 15:8, and God's answer to that question is to call for the animals and to make a contract. This is how you can be sure, because it is signed and sealed in blood.

On the night before Jesus died, that contract was remade and reaffirmed. Here's Matthew's account of the Last Supper:

Then [Jesus] took a cup, and when he had given thanks, he gave it to them, saying, 'Drink from it, all of you. This is my blood of the covenant, which is poured out for many for the forgiveness of sins.'
(Matthew 26:27–28)

What did Jesus promise? He promised to forgive our sin. Whatever guilt you're carrying or whatever shame stains your soul, Christ promised to forgive you and, indeed, all who come to him. But he didn't just make a promise. He made a covenant – he bound himself to his promise.

He signed and sealed it through bread and wine, and the following day, as he died on the cross, he delivered on that promise. He died in our place, that our sin might be forgiven. He shed his blood for us, and he remains true to that covenant to this day.

God is 'faithfully faithful' (see Isaiah 25:1). Meditate on this glorious truth. At the cross, we see God's covenant love and faithfulness in action. Jesus' broken body and shed blood are our guarantee that, no matter how heinous our sin or how frequently we have offended God, he will forgive us when we come to him. He knows how frail we are, how battered by sin. Today, accept God's invitation to bring your weary, burdened soul to him and receive afresh his promise of forgiveness.

Day 64

Read: Genesis 15:1–21
Key verse: Genesis 15:1

. . . .

> After this, the word of the LORD came to Abram in a vision:
> "Do not be afraid, Abram.
>   I am your shield,
>   your very great reward."

It's not easy being a Christian. In fact, it can be really difficult. So is it really worth it?

What does Abraham get from this new covenant? First of all, he gains a son, Isaac. He also gets the people and the land that God had promised. But he receives much, much more. In chapter 14, Abraham has just restored to the king of Sodom what had been lost in battle. The king then tries to reward Abraham. It's really an invitation to come under his lordship. But Abraham refuses, saying to the king, 'You will never be able to say, "I made Abram rich"' (Genesis 14:23). Then chapter 15 begins: 'After this, the word of the LORD came to Abram in a vision . . . "I am your shield and your very great reward."' In other words, it's not the king of Sodom who will be Abraham's protector and benefactor; it is God himself. What is it that Abraham receives? Abraham gets God! His reward is God himself.

Abraham's response of faith is then credited to him as 'righteousness'. This means being right with God, being in a relationship with him as we were meant to be and made to be. It means that Abraham can come into God's presence, enjoy a relationship with God, enjoy God's love!

What did I get on my wedding day? I got about £100, a few dresses and some Jane Austen novels. When my wife said, 'All I have I thee endow', that's what was on offer. But I didn't marry her to get my hands on some books and dresses. What I got from our marriage covenant was my favourite person in the world. Think about these words from Martin Luther, the great Reformer:

> Faith unites us with Christ in the same way that a bride is united with her husband. Our sins, death and damnation, now belong to Christ, while his grace, life and salvation are now ours. For if Christ is a husband, he must take on himself those things which belonged to his bride, and he must give to her, those things that are his. Not only that, he also gives us himself.
>
> (Martin Luther, 'The Freedom of a Christian, 1520', *The Roots of Reform*, The Annotated Luther, Fortress Press, 2015, pp. 499–500)

I love that last line; it's beautiful. Luther lists some of the benefits that come to us in the Lord Jesus Christ. But best of all, we get Christ himself.

As the true God who always tells the truth, God cannot help but be faithful to his character, promises, purposes and glory. This faithfulness graciously and gloriously extends to us. In the midst of our suffering and struggles, God gives the very best he could give us; he gives us himself: 'I am your shield and very great reward.' He will never leave or betray you. He will love you for ever. You will always be welcome in his presence. You are his. Today, take joy in this incomparable treasure that is unreservedly yours.

Day 65

Read: Genesis 15:1–21
Key verses: Genesis 15:17–18

....

> [17]When the sun had set and darkness had fallen, a smoking brazier with a blazing torch appeared and passed between the pieces. [18]On that day the LORD made a covenant with Abram and said, "To your descendants I give this land."

Can you picture the scene?

Laid out, on the ground, were the animals God had asked for. On one side: half a cow, half a goat and half a sheep, and a dove. There was no point cutting a dove in two, so it just goes off on one side. On the other side: the other half of the cow, the goat and the sheep, and a pigeon. The sun has set, darkness has fallen, then a 'smoking brazier' and a 'blazing torch' appear. They represent God. In fact, you might want to think of them almost as a kind of mini version of when God came down at Mount Sinai. So, God appears and passes through the animals, and it's in that key moment that the covenant is made (verse 17).

But what's missing from the picture? Abraham. He's not playing any part in the action. What is his role as this covenant is made? Absolutely none! 'As the sun was setting, Abram fell into a deep sleep, and a thick and dreadful darkness came over him' (verse 12). Abraham is asleep! He's out for the count. This is one of the key moments in the whole Bible story, in the whole of human history, and Abraham sleeps through it all.

To be fair to him, I don't think it was a normal sleep. It seems that it was a supernaturally induced sleep. The point is this: it's a one-way agreement. All the commitments are made by God. All the action is done by him. All Abraham does is receive: 'Abram believed the LORD, and he credited it to him as righteousness' (verse 6). His role is simply to receive the promises by faith. And when it comes to receiving Christ and his promises, here's what you have to do to be worthy – nothing. Absolutely nothing. There is nothing you need to do. No level of morality that you have to attain, no feat that you have to accomplish. No religious duty to perform, no kind of intellectual level of understanding that you have to attain – all you must do, and all you can do, is receive the promises by faith. This is what my sinful, doubting, fearful heart needs more than anything else: for God to reaffirm his covenant promises to me. We come because God promises to forgive, because God covenants to forgive.

Come to the cross. See God's love and faithfulness on display, his personal and passionate commitment to you. Just as he walked among the carcasses to pledge his faithfulness to Abraham, he went to the cross to bring you salvation. He did all that needed to be done – the penalty for sin has been done away with: 'It is finished' (John 19:30). Today, receive afresh this promise of forgiveness from a forever faithful God.

Nothing in my hand I bring,
Simply to Thy cross I cling;
Naked, come to Thee for dress,
Helpless, look to Thee for grace:
Foul, I to the fountain fly,
Wash me, Saviour, or I die.
(Augustus Toplady, 'Rock of Ages', 1763)

Day 66

Read: 1 Samuel 13:5–14
Key verses: 1 Samuel 13:11–12

....

[11]*"What have you done?" asked Samuel.*

Saul replied, 'When I saw that the men were scattering, and that you did not come at the set time, and that the Philistines were assembling at Michmash, [12]I thought, "Now the Philistines will come down against me at Gilgal, and I have not sought the Lord*'s favour." So I felt compelled to offer the burnt offering.'*

What should we make of believers who start the Christian life with great promise but end in failure?

Saul had every reason to be a champion for God. He was born into privilege, had exceptional physical attributes and was God's anointed king. But this first moment of crisis in his leadership signalled the beginning of his decline. The Philistine army was arrayed against him. 'All the troops with him were quaking with fear. He waited for seven days, the time set by Samuel; but Samuel did not come to Gilgal, and Saul's men began to scatter' (verses 7–8).

Saul thought that he had to take action or the whole army would desert. So he sacrificed the burnt offerings himself (verse 9). Commentators struggle to define the actual sin of which Saul is guilty. But there is disobedience at the heart of it. '"You have done a foolish thing," Samuel said. "You have not kept the command the Lord your God gave you"' (verse 13). The consequences were severe – Saul's dynasty would end (verse 14) and his relationship with Samuel was irrevocably damaged (verse 15). What is happening here? By sacrificing, was Saul attempting to extend his powers to include a priestly role as well as a military one? Had he lost confidence in God? Was he failing to rely on God? We are given a clue when he says to Samuel, '"I haven't even asked for the Lord's help!" So I felt compelled to offer the burnt offering myself' (verse 12, NLT). Saul didn't make time to listen to God and had taken matters into his own hands.

We see a similar scenario in chapter 14. The Philistines were in disarray so Saul shouted to Ahijah, 'Bring the ephod here' (verse 18, NLT). The ephod (a garment worn by the high priest) was used to discern God's will, and Saul was expecting God to give him orders about how to handle this situation. But while he was talking to the priest, confusion among the Philistines increased and Saul said, 'Never mind; let's get going' (verse 19, NLT). Essentially, he was saying, 'We should be waiting for divine orders, but too much is happening. We haven't got time to wait for God.'

Saul's tragic failure begins as self-sufficiency grows in his heart. He has no time to wait for God, no time to listen.

Today, we come before almighty God – our all-knowing, ever-present, eternally powerful, sovereign God. With all the choices, responsibilities and conversations that lie ahead in our waking hours, we can't afford to say, 'Never mind; let's get going.' Make time to linger in God's presence, prayerfully admit your dependence on him and ask him to speak to you through his Word. Over the long haul, it is this daily decision, more than any other, that results in a life of faithfulness.

If we think we can do life on our own, we will not take prayer seriously.
(Paul E. Miller, *A Praying Life*, NavPress, 2009, p. 59)

Day 67

Read: 1 Samuel 13:5–14
Key verse: 1 Samuel 13:13

....

*"You have done a foolish thing," Samuel said. "You have not kept the command the L*ORD *your God gave you; if you had, he would have established your kingdom over Israel for all time."*

Why didn't Saul just obey God?

Because Saul wasn't listening to God (see Day 66), his relationship with him had become distant, and so the confidence to trust and obey gradually eroded.

We see this pattern throughout Saul's reign. In 1 Samuel 15:2, God tells him, 'I have decided to settle accounts with the nation of Amalek' (NLT). The Amalekites had tried to prevent Israel from reaching Sinai after they had crossed through the Red Sea (see Exodus 17:14), so God was giving Saul the responsibility of carrying out the divine sentence. This wasn't a war of aggression or self-defence, but a truly holy war.

God decreed that the whole nation must be destroyed. This may seem harsh to us but it would not have seemed strange to the Israelites. They were carrying out God's judgement, and he would have the victory over the Amalekites. Saul engages in a great slaughter, but it was not the total destruction that the Lord had demanded. He spared Agag, the Amalekite king, and kept the best of the sheep and cattle (1 Samuel 15:7–9). What held Saul back from total obedience? We can't be sure, but no doubt it was similar to the things that hold us back. Perhaps saving the best of the livestock made him something of a hero in front of his men? It must have been to their advantage. Perhaps he hoped to negotiate a huge ransom for the release of King Agag?

In our materialistic, consumer-driven age, there is relentless pressure to hold back the best in our commitment to God. So often we have to choose between acceptance by our friends or total obedience to God. We rationalize our choices: 'To maintain this lifestyle for my family, I must achieve a certain income, which means I must work certain hours. I don't have any free time or money to give to God.' Although most of us could live comfortably with a much lesser lifestyle, we are reluctant to consider such a choice. Like Saul, we give God our leftovers rather than our best.

God held nothing back in his commitment to us – he gave his one and only Son to save us, and the Holy Spirit to live within us. Why would we hold back the best in our commitment to him?

Giving our best is not proved by one-off grand displays of devotion but, rather, in continuing obedience in the mundane and unremarkable routine of life. Part of this is faithfulness in giving from our finances.

If you are truly submitted to the lordship of Christ, if you are willing to obey Him completely in every area of your life, your giving will reveal it. We will do many things before we will give someone else, even Christ, the rights over every dollar we have and ever will have. But if you have done that, it will be expressed in your giving. That's why it's said that your chequebook tells more about you than almost anything else.

(Donald S. Whitney, *Spiritual Disciplines for the Christian Life*, NavPress, 2014, p. 177)

Day 68

Read: 1 Samuel 13:5–14

Key verses: 1 Samuel 13:13–14

. . . .

¹³*"You have done a foolish thing," Samuel said. "You have not kept the command the* LORD *your God gave you; if you had, he would have established your kingdom over Israel for all time.* ¹⁴*But now your kingdom will not endure; the* LORD *has sought out a man after his own heart and appointed him ruler of his people, because you have not kept the Lord's command."*

Is there a way back to God after failure?

Yes. But only if we repent. Unfortunately, Saul never learned how to do this. Instead, he justified his disobedient actions. He excused burning the offerings because his men were scattering and Samuel had not arrived at the appointed time (verse 11). In 1 Samuel 15, when Saul finally admitted that he'd disobeyed the Lord's commands, he was quick to justify himself and explain the mitigating circumstances: 'I was afraid of the people and did what they demanded' (verse 24, NLT).

Compare Saul's repentance to King David's. The moment Nathan the prophet exposed David's sins of committing adultery with Bathsheba and murdering her husband Uriah, David repented without any attempt at self-justification (2 Samuel 12). In Psalm 51:3–4, he confesses to God:

For I know my transgressions,
    and my sin is always before me.
Against you, you only, have I sinned
    and done what is evil in your sight;
so you are right in your verdict
    and justified when you judge.

As well as attempting to justify himself, Saul also tries to spiritualize his failures. In 1 Samuel 15:15, he says the army spared the best of the cattle and sheep to sacrifice them to God, so that, ultimately, God's command of total destruction would be fulfilled. Samuel, in verse 22, replies:

> Does the LORD delight in burnt offerings and sacrifices
>> as much as in obeying the LORD?
> To obey is better than sacrifice,
>> and to heed is better than the fat of rams.

Like Saul, we may attend public worship but God wants our faithfulness to be more than skin-deep. He is longing for our wholehearted devotion. If you have not been obeying God, turn back in repentance today. None of us has to finish like Saul. The example of David assures us of that. He fell spectacularly and, in some ways, his fall was greater than Saul's. But his repentance and determination to live once again in faithful obedience to God were equally spectacular and truly moving.

God's faithfulness to us is expressed, in part, in his readiness to forgive: 'If we confess our sins, he is faithful and just and will forgive us our sins and purify us from all unrighteousness' (1 John 1:9).

If you want to get back on the road of faithful obedience, follow the instructions Jesus gave to the Ephesian church in Revelation 2:5:

- *'Consider how far you have fallen!'* Think back to the days when you loved Jesus more. Reflect how and why your relationship with Jesus has changed.
- *'Repent.'* Turn back to God in sorrow. Find joy in his mercy and willingness to help you renew your commitment to him.
- *'Do the things you did at first.'* When you were walking closer with God, no doubt you had a hunger for his Word, spent time in his presence, told others about him and loved being with your church family. Start doing these things again and begin to enjoy an intimate relationship with the Father who is waiting to restore you.

Day 69

Read: Psalm 119:97–104
Key verses: Psalm 119:101–102

....

> [101] *I have kept my feet from every evil path*
>   *so that I might obey your word.*
> [102] *I have not departed from your laws,*
>   *for you yourself have taught me.*

Imagine that you're on a plane and the pilot announces, 'Good morning, ladies and gentlemen. As you know, we are committed to your safety. I want you to know that I don't plan on crashing very much.' How about not crashing at all? The objective must be 'I don't plan on crashing at all!'

Are we as clear about our objectives when it comes to sinning? The psalmist is uncompromising. We are to keep our feet from '*every* evil path' so that we can obey God's Word.

This principle is not just a moralistic one. Rather, it is written in the same tone as Paul's words to the Colossians: 'Now, let's become what we are in Christ. You are united to Christ. Therefore, seek those things from above where Christ is seated. Your life is hidden with Christ in God. This is who you are, your identity, and God has given you his Word to help you to become who and what he has designed you to be' (a paraphrase of Colossians 3:1–10).

Psalm 119:102 reminds us that we will never stop sinning because someone else persuaded us to do so; it will take the Word of God, by the Spirit of God: 'You yourself have taught me.' But there is no contradiction between the declarations in verses 101 and 102. We are both, at the same time, entirely dependent on the work of the Holy Spirit and yet entirely responsible for keeping our feet from 'every evil path'.

God has never yet turned a television programme off for me! The Lord has never taken a book right out of my hands! But I have heard the Spirit of God say, 'I thought you were reading Psalm 119, where it says keep yourself from "every evil path". And have you read Philippians 4, where it says, "Whatever is pure, whatever is lovely, whatever is admirable, think about these things"?'

The reason why you and I have not deviated from our course and lost connection with the source of God's grace is not because of superior virtue or peculiar discernment. It is because we have not departed from God's laws, for he himself has taught us (Psalm 119:102). We have to make sure we are listening to, meditating on and applying God's Word to our lives because it is the source of wisdom and the means of faithfulness.

This theme is consistent throughout the Bible. John says, 'See that what you have heard from the beginning remains in you. If it does, you also will remain in the Son and in the Father' (1 John 2:24). Similarly, Paul says to Timothy, 'Continue in what you have learned and have become convinced of, because you know those from whom you learned it, and how from infancy you have known the Holy Scriptures, which are able to make you wise for salvation' (2 Timothy 3:14–15).

Meditate on Psalm 119:101–102.

Thank God for the ways in which he has kept you from evil, by teaching you through his Word and by the power of the Holy Spirit. Ask for God's help to be uncompromising as you tackle sin in your life. Pray that you would continue to obey God's Word, so that you remain faithful to him.

Day 70

Read: Acts 20:17–38
Key verses: Acts 20:17–19

....

> ¹⁷ *From Miletus, Paul sent to Ephesus for the elders of the church.*
> ¹⁸ *When they arrived, he said to them: "You know how I lived the whole time I was with you, from the first day I came into the province of Asia.*
> ¹⁹ *I served the Lord with great humility and with tears and in the midst of severe testing by the plots of my Jewish opponents."*

Does what you do match what you say? Does your walk match your talk?

For Paul, it certainly did (verses 18 and 33–35). He was able to appeal to the Ephesian elders as witnesses of the way in which his life matched his words. Such integrity was the essential ingredient for proclaiming a credible gospel message (verse 24) and also for making mature disciples.

This faithful conduct allowed Paul to remind the Thessalonians of how he and his fellow workers *lived*. The 'gospel came to you not simply with words but also with power, with the Holy Spirit and deep conviction. You know how we lived among you for your sake' (1 Thessalonians 1:5). The gospel that Paul was proclaiming was bearing fruit in his own life, and it was this combination of word and life that made his gospel communication so effective.

That is why he urges the Ephesian elders to 'keep watch over' themselves (Acts 20:28). He pleads with them to take their spiritual condition seriously. It is only when the leaders themselves remain faithful to God in their discipleship that they can expect others to be so too. It is only as they grow in grace and in the knowledge of the Lord Jesus, pressing on in the faith, that they can appeal to others to do so. Neglect in this area leaves us spiritually dry, often drifting morally, prone to mere professionalism, and passing on information without any real connection to our own spiritual life and maturity. Paul's words to Timothy should ring in our ears:

> Set an example for the believers in speech, in conduct, in love, in faith and in purity . . . Watch your life and doctrine closely. Persevere in them, because if you do, you will save both yourself and your hearers. (1 Timothy 4:12, 16)

There was nothing in Paul's life that could be used as an excuse by other people for not believing the gospel. His message was wedded to a godly life that made his ministry credible. In just the same way, our lives must embody the truth of the gospel. Faithful gospel proclamation and consistent living must go hand in hand in whatever area of mission or ministry God calls us to – the combination is vital.

Always living with integrity – so that what you say about the gospel truly resonates with how you live your life – is a huge responsibility. You can't do it on your own, but you don't need to. God, in his faithfulness, gives us his grace to live faithfully!

> Now this is our boast: our conscience testifies that we have conducted ourselves in the world, and especially in our relations with you, with integrity and godly sincerity. We have done so, relying not on worldly wisdom but on God's grace.
> (2 Corinthians 1:12)

Today, rely on God's grace to put his truth on display in your life faithfully.

Day 71

Read: Acts 20:17–38
Key verses: Acts 20:22–24

....

> [22] *"And now, compelled by the Spirit, I am going to Jerusalem, not knowing what will happen to me there.* [23]*I only know that in every city the Holy Spirit warns me that prison and hardships are facing me.* [24]*However, I consider my life worth nothing to me; my only aim is to finish the race and complete the task the Lord Jesus has given me – the task of testifying to the good news of God's grace."*

'I have fought the good fight, I have finished the race, I have kept the faith' (2 Timothy 4:7). Paul's words to Timothy sum up his faithfulness to God and to all that God had called him to do. But this faithfulness was costly.

In Acts 20:3, Luke refers to the plots of the Jews against Paul. In verse 19, Paul says, 'I served the Lord with great humility and with tears and in the midst of severe testing by the plots of my Jewish opponents.' Like the Lord Jesus who called him, if obedience required it, Paul was willing to suffer, which is the only way that you can make sense of the two apparently contradictory messages of the Spirit in verses 22 and 23. Verse 22 describes how the Spirit compels Paul to go to Jerusalem, yet in the very next verse the same Spirit warns Paul that he will suffer if he does go. How can such an apparent contradiction be reconciled? Only by Paul's statement of purpose in verse 24: 'However, I consider my life worth nothing to me; my only aim is to finish the race and complete the task the Lord Jesus has given me – the task of testifying to the good news of God's grace.' Paul was willing to suffer – to give everything he had – to make disciples, precisely because he knew that God had called him and given him an urgent task to fulfil.

Paul's motivation was absolutely clear. He knew the purpose of his life and calling, and he was willing to lay down his life if necessary. He wasn't after fame or money. His ambition was not to climb an ecclesiastical ladder but to finish the race, to complete the task of proclaiming the gospel and making disciples.

Similarly, our calling to serve God today, with its privilege of bringing the good news to others, should not be driven by self-fulfilment but by the calling of Jesus Christ himself. Acts 20 shows us that there are no false promises, no immediate rewards, save knowing that we serve Christ faithfully as we fulfil the task he has given us.

'Go and make disciples' (Matthew 28:19) was Jesus' charge to his disciples and, in turn, to the church. For pastors and ministry leaders, the mandate is clear (although the outworking may be more of a challenge!). But each of us, with our own unique set of circumstances and relationships, can be disciple-makers as we invest spiritually in children, grandchildren, those in our home groups or the young person interning in our church. Investing in others for the long haul is costly but part of our calling as disciples. Today, pray for God's help to be faithful in the task of pointing others to the Lord Jesus.

Day 72

Read: 1 Thessalonians 2:1–12
Key verses: 1 Thessalonians 2:1–2

....

¹You know, brothers and sisters, that our visit to you was not without results. ²We had previously suffered and been treated outrageously in Philippi, as you know, but with the help of our God we dared to tell you his gospel in the face of strong opposition.

How can we effectively engage with our culture while, at the same time, staying faithful to the gospel message?

Paul's secret was that while he contextualized the gospel, he never relativized it. To relativize the gospel is to wrap it up and put it in the culture. To contextualize the gospel is to understand it and make sure it connects with the culture without changing the message.

A great example of contextualization is Paul's engagement with those seeking the 'unknown god' at Mars Hill (Acts 17:16–34). He didn't start the conversation by telling the people of Athens all the ways in which they were wrong in their understanding. Instead, he said, 'I see you have an altar here; you are seeking the truth. Let me begin with where you are and take you on a journey, so that you can see the truth for what it really is.'

The fundamental challenge for us today is whether we believe the Scriptures speak the true Word of God and therefore have the power to transform culture. Alternatively, do we believe culture should transform our understanding of what the Bible teaches?

Our job is not to fit into the culture or change our core message to be popular. As Christians, we often think society should welcome and embrace us. Instead, the New Testament tells us that we will be challenged, mocked and persecuted (John 16:33). Paul says, 'With the help of our God we dared to tell you his gospel in the face of strong opposition' (1 Thessalonians 2:2). Acts 16 records Paul's being thrown into prison in Philippi because of his faithfulness to the gospel. Wherever he went, there was either a revival or a riot!

Will you dare to be faithful to God – at work, as a local church or in your family – in the face of strong opposition? Will you live out what you believe, not expecting the culture to embrace you but recognizing that it probably won't? We have a choice: we can be faithful to what God has called us to be and do, or we can be absorbed into our culture, quickly losing our effectiveness as the body of Christ and our witness in the world.

Heavenly Father, thank you that the Lord Jesus was faithful to you and to me – enduring the mocking, the betrayal, the nails and then dying in my place. He is not just an example to follow but is praying for me and is with me, by the power of the Holy Spirit, enabling me to be faithful.

Today, I pray for myself and my church community.

Help us to stay faithful to you in the face of opposition, whether we are being mocked for our faith by family members, challenged at work because of our beliefs or feeling the sting of increasing marginalization in society. Help us to stay faithful to the gospel, in the way we present it to others and the way in which we live our lives. May our conversations be marked with love, kindness and wisdom, so that the only offence is that of the cross. For Jesus' glory we pray. Amen.

Day 73

Read: 1 Thessalonians 2:1–12

Key verses: 1 Thessalonians 2:2 and 4

∙∙

> ²*With the help of our God we dared to tell you his gospel in the face of strong opposition . . .* ⁴*we speak as those approved by God to be entrusted with the gospel. We are not trying to please people but God, who tests our hearts.*

What is the gospel?

Paul says, 'With the help of our God we dared to tell you *his* gospel' (verse 2, emphasis added). You could translate it 'the gospel of God', which Paul does in verses 8 and 9. In verse 4, he talks about being entrusted with the gospel and, in verse 13, he speaks twice about the power of the Word of God. For the apostle, there is the conviction that the gospel cannot be changed; it is something he is entrusted with.

We think that the gospel is ours, in the sense that we own it, or we redefine it to make it sound as if God calls us just to be nice people – but that is not the gospel! We don't have to guess the gospel message or try to work it out. Paul tells us exactly what it is:

> For what I received I passed on to you as of first importance: that Christ died for our sins according to the Scriptures, that he was buried, that he was raised on the third day according to the Scriptures, and that he appeared to Cephas, and then to the Twelve.
> (1 Corinthians 15:3–5)

The good news of the gospel is that Christ died in our place, paying the penalty our sins deserved. All we must do – all we can do – to be reconciled to God is to repent of our sins and trust in Christ's work on the cross. He not only died for us; his resurrection is the guarantee that one day we too will rise to new life and spend eternity with God. No wonder Paul could say with confidence: 'I am not ashamed of the gospel, because it is the power of God that brings salvation to everyone who believes' (Romans 1:16). Paul's radical faithfulness was built on these truths and his conviction that the gospel worked.

Our faithfulness hinges on the same things. We are not free to change the gospel. It is a baton that has been handed to us, one that we must pass on to the generation that comes after us. We can't dilute it or turn it into something else because this is the only message that has the power to break the power of sin, transform lives and conquer death. We are not called to be nice people or just to make a difference. We are called to make disciples and point people to this glorious good news.

Have you ever found yourself wanting to soften the edges of the gospel when sharing it with someone? Have you wanted to lessen the demand for repentance, the brutality of the cross or the wrath of God? While we don't have to convey all the elements of the gospel in every conversation, we do need to make sure it is God's gospel we're sharing, otherwise we have nothing to offer people. And this message of good news is not just for unbelievers! Meditate on 1 Corinthians 15:3–5; speak it to your own soul and hold fast to this gospel, which proclaims freedom from sin and death, forgiveness and eternal security, and the power of God at work in you today.

Day 74

Read: 1 Thessalonians 2:1–12
Key verses: 1 Thessalonians 2:3–7

....

> ³For the appeal we make does not spring from error or impure motives, nor are we trying to trick you. ⁴On the contrary, we speak as those approved by God to be entrusted with the gospel. We are not trying to please people but God, who tests our hearts. ⁵You know we never used flattery, nor did we put on a mask to cover up greed – God is our witness. ⁶We were not looking for praise from people, not from you or anyone else, even though as apostles of Christ we could have asserted our authority. ⁷Instead, we were like young children among you.

What was at the heart of Paul's life that made him so faithful to God?

Essentially, Paul understood that God had commissioned him to proclaim the gospel message, and his life was now about pleasing him. So, Paul refused to dabble in error, or with impure motives or misunderstanding. He didn't want to make money; he wasn't interested in persuading people unfairly; he wasn't going to tell them a lie; and he wasn't going to water down the message. His actions weren't driven by the strength of his personality and he wasn't swayed by what people thought of him.

We may not share Paul's particular commission, but we are called by God to live for God alone. So, don't allow yourself to lower the standard of the gospel just to be popular. Don't turn the gospel into something you make money out of. Don't turn the church into a glorified social club. Instead, have confidence in the fact that when God calls, he equips and enables us to live for him.

Paul's confidence in God's calling meant that he acted with integrity and faithfulness, regardless of the circumstances or occasion. We have a glimpse of what this looked like in the 'holy' and 'blameless' (verse 10) way he lived among the Thessalonians – comforting, encouraging and urging them to continue in the faith. He explains that he didn't try to manipulate them: 'Instead, we were like young children among you' (verse 7). This is a picture of innocence and trust. Then he switches to three other pictures.

He says that he was like a nursing mother caring for them. His language is tender, gentle and kind. Next, he addresses them as brothers and sisters, bringing an equality into his relationship with them. He also uses the image of a father, as he challenges, guides and helps believers to understand how they are to live for God in the world in which they find themselves.

Your faithfulness matters! Your children, parents, spouse, friends and work colleagues are watching your life. They notice how you cope with suffering, how you treat others, your attitude to money, your integrity, your commitment to church and your passion for the gospel. Your example to others is never neutral – it is either positive or negative. If, like Paul, you live for an audience of One, you will spur others on in their faith. Put your name in the following verse and pray for God's help to live a life worth imitating.

Remember _____, who spoke the word of God to you. Consider the outcome of their way of life and imitate their faith. (Hebrews 13:7)

Day 75

Read: 1 Thessalonians 5:1–28
Key verses: 1 Thessalonians 5:6–8

••

> *6So then, let us not be like others, who are asleep, but let us be awake and sober. 7For those who sleep, sleep at night, and those who get drunk, get drunk at night. 8But since we belong to the day, let us be sober, putting on faith and love as a breastplate, and the hope of salvation as a helmet.*

Are you an early bird or a night owl?

In Paul's terms, believers are all daytime people. We are to be clear-headed and alert, not morally and spiritually asleep, so that we can live for the day when Jesus returns. The verb translated 'sleep' in these verses refers to moral laxity, not death (see Mark 13:36). We are no longer in spiritual darkness by circumstance or by nature (Colossians 1:13, 21–22). We have a new position, nature and loyalty (Galatians 2:20). Consequently, we have a responsibility to be morally alert and to have a distinctive way of life (Ephesians 5:8–15).

Paul likens our new lifestyle to warfare and urges us to 'Put on the full armour of God, so that you can take your stand against the devil's schemes' (Ephesians 6:11). We are to wear the armour that is our characteristic hallmark as believers – faith, hope and love.

This is the third time Paul has reminded the Thessalonian believers about this trio. In 1 Thessalonians 1:3, he looked back and acknowledged the genuineness of their salvation because he saw their faith, hope and love. In verses 6–10, Paul was delighted because the believers had resisted temptation. What was the victory? They were standing firm in the Lord. They were people of endurance, going on with the Christian basics of faith and love.

For us, the return of Christ requires nothing dramatic by way of preparation. We are just to go on – with faith, hope and love – trusting God, come what may, and living in the obedience of faith. We must go on loving our fellow believers and reaching out beyond them in love to the world. And we go on with endurance and hope, as we keep our eyes fixed on the Lord Jesus who is returning. That's our armour. We put on the breastplate of faith and love, and the hope of salvation as our helmet, so that we are protected, equipped and ready to live for the day of Christ's return.

God is 'abounding in love and faithfulness' (Exodus 34:6): he has redeemed us (Colossians 1:14) and reconciled us to himself (Colossians 1:22), and he will return (Acts 1:10–11; Revelation 22:20). He now 'lives' in us (Galatians 2:20) and gives us the resources to be faithful to him (2 Peter 1:3).

What does God want in return? Not an extravagant display of devotion – he has already provided that – but moment-by-moment faithfulness. This requires daily putting our armour on:

> God is strong, and he wants you strong. So take everything the Master has set out for you, well-made weapons of the best materials. And put them to use so you will be able to stand up to everything the Devil throws your way. This is no afternoon athletic contest that we'll walk away from and forget about in a couple of hours. This is for keeps, a life-or-death fight to the finish against the Devil and all his angels.
> (Ephesians 6:10–12, MSG)

Day 76

Read: 1 Thessalonians 5:1–28
Key verses: 1 Thessalonians 5:9–11

. . . .

⁹For God did not appoint us to suffer wrath but to receive salvation through our Lord Jesus Christ. ¹⁰He died for us so that, whether we are awake or asleep, we may live together with him. ¹¹Therefore encourage one another and build each other up, just as in fact you are doing.

Imagine if, on the day when Jesus chooses to return, we are having a spiritual 'day off', that we are not living for the Lord Jesus as we should be doing. We are dozing spiritually. And our lives are showing some evidence of moral and spiritual slackness. Imagine that the day before Jesus' return is a Sunday, when we are passionately 'on fire' for God. The next day, Monday, when he comes back, we are below par, spiritually speaking. What will happen to us when the Lord returns?

Paul deals with this very issue in verse 10. 'Asleep' is not the verb that means we are dead and living with Jesus; it indicates the possibility of moral and spiritual slackness. And 'awake' means what it has meant in previous verses: being alert for the coming Lord. The apostle offers us the most intense, remarkable and glorious comfort. He says our great confidence in relation to Christ's coming is not anything that we do or are, but what God in Christ has done for us. We have been appointed eternally for the personal and full possession of salvation, through our Lord Jesus Christ who 'died for us' (verse 10).

His death covers all our sins, including those sins of spiritual slackness. Of course, we are to spur one another on to live in faith, love and hope (see Day 75), and some of what that looks like is described in 1 Thessalonians 5:12–22. But we can look forward to the second coming of Christ with confidence because the One who returns is that perfect mediator who knows both God's requirements and our needs. By his knowledge, this 'righteous servant' has justified many (Isaiah 53:11). We stand before Christ, clothed in his righteousness alone.

Your eternal destiny is not dependent on whether you are having a good or a bad day, spiritually speaking, when Jesus returns. In fact, it is not dependent on what *you do* at all. It is solely dependent on what *Jesus has done* on the cross. His faithfulness guarantees the security of our salvation:

> He was pierced for our transgressions,
>   he was crushed for our iniquities;
> the punishment that brought us peace was on him,
>   and by his wounds we are healed.
> (Isaiah 53:5)

Let this truth amaze, humble and comfort you. And as you meet others today who are also conscious of their wandering hearts and disappointed by the coolness of their affection for Christ, let the reminder of Christ's faithfulness encourage you and build you up (verse 11). Allow it to spur you on in your devotion to him.

Day 77

Read: 1 Thessalonians 5:1–28
Key verses: 1 Thessalonians 5:23–24

....

> ²³ May God himself, the God of peace, sanctify you through and through. May your whole spirit, soul and body be kept blameless at the coming of our Lord Jesus Christ. ²⁴ The one who calls you is faithful, and he will do it.

'I'll never be ready for when Jesus comes!'

Paul issues a whole raft of different commands – some with expansions and additions (verses 15–22). There are commands about how we are to treat leaders, and others about our personal obligations. All of these are about how we are to live in readiness for Christ's return. They describe the lifestyle required of a church family, and believers are to behave this way to everybody, all the time. Some commands relate to our character – we are to be patient, non-retaliatory and good (verses 14–15); others relate to our spirituality and how to live before God – we ought to be rejoicing, praying and giving thanks (verses 16–18).

The bar is high. The range of commands seems overwhelming. How can we be faithful to all God's requirements and so be ready for Jesus' second coming?

Paul concludes his letter by reminding the Thessalonians, and us, of a vital truth: we have God himself on our side. Verse 23 means that the heavenly Father will see to it that no single blemish will spoil the day of his Son's return.

As Paul says in Philippians 1:6, 'He who began a good work in you will carry it on to completion until the day of Christ Jesus.' God will go on putting the finishing touches to the work he has begun in our lives and, when the day of Christ comes, everything will be ready for his return.

God himself promises that he will sanctify you. God will preserve you, in an all-embracing, completed holiness that touches every part of your being and covers all that you are. That's what the two words 'sanctify' and 'keep' mean in verse 23. He will preserve you in relation to himself (your 'spirit'); he will preserve you in relation to your personality (your 'soul'); and he will preserve you in holy living in your body. We can have every confidence in God's promise to do this because he is the faithful and sufficient God: 'The one who calls you is faithful, and he will do it' (verse 24). Praise God!

Is our faithfulness important if, ultimately, it all depends on God's faithfulness? Yes! How we live as Christians matters. The genuineness of our salvation is proved by a new desire to obey God. Our spiritual transformation to become more like Jesus testifies to God's power at work in us, changing our hearts, minds and wills. God grants us the privilege of being his 'fellow workers' (2 Corinthians 6:1).

But – thank God – at every point our fragile and often wavering faithfulness is enabled, undergirded and completed by the faithfulness of Christ. Today, meditate, rest and rejoice in the truth that 'The one who calls you is faithful, and he will do it' (verse 24).

Day 78

Read: 2 Timothy 4:1–22
Key verses: 2 Timothy 4:6–7

• •

*⁶For I am already being poured out like a drink offering, and the
time for my departure is near.
⁷I have fought the good fight, I have finished the race, I have
kept the faith.*

How do we make sure that we finish life well?

Paul is a great example for us. In this poignant farewell chapter, he
describes himself as a sacrifice, 'a drink offering' poured out before
his Lord (verse 6). He knows that he is about to die: 'The time of my
departure is near.' The Greek word for departure conveys the idea of
being set free. It is the word used when a boat leaves harbour. For
Paul, it is not a reluctant departure but a purposeful one. He is
packed, ready to go and looking forward to all that lies ahead.

He uses three pictures derived from 2 Timothy 2 to describe his
faithfulness: the retiring soldier – 'I have fought the good fight'; the
retiring athlete – 'I have finished the race'; the retiring farmer – 'I
have kept the faith', which means literally 'I have persevered', like a
farmer who has fulfilled his tasks. Jesus ran the race before him,
enduring the cross and despising the shame (Hebrews 12:2). Now
Paul is writing in chains but looking at the joy set before him, the
'Well done!' garland given to God's servant by the righteous judge.

Paul's example and his teaching encourage Timothy – and us – to run
the race in the same way. People will come and go. There will be
those, such as Demas, who love this present world (2 Timothy 4:10).
There will be people like faithful Luke, practical Mark and evil
Alexander (verses 11 and 14). There will be practical needs, such as
for clothing and books, and there will be periods of living simply and
tough times (verses 13 and 16–17). There will be love and

encouragement from various Christian families, and there will be those, such as Trophimus, who will fall ill and won't be healed (verses 19–20). In the midst of it all, we must commit ourselves to the Lord and keep the gospel central. As individuals, we must come to God for daily cleansing and equipping. As a body of believers, we must spur one another on and invest in training, so that each and every man and woman in the church, by God's grace and mercy, might be able to say at the end of their lives, 'I have fought the good fight, I have finished the race, I have kept the faith.'

Paul's final word to Timothy and to the church was: 'The Lord be with your spirit. Grace be with you all' (verse 22). In this race of life, we can press on and finish well, knowing that God is with us personally and his grace is with us all for ever.

The Greeks had a race in their Olympic games that was unique. The winner was not the runner who finished first. It was the runner who finished with his torch still lit. I want to run all the way with the flame of my torch still lit for Him.

(Joseph M. Stowell, *Fan the Flame*, Moody Press, 1986, p. 32)

Day 79

Read: 2 Timothy 4:1–22
Key verses: 2 Timothy 4:9–10

. . . .

⁹Do your best to come to me quickly, ¹⁰for Demas, because he loved this world, has deserted me and has gone to Thessalonica.

Last words are important.

These verses in 2 Timothy 4 are among the last known words of the apostle Paul. He is in prison in Rome, facing certain death. But as he writes his own epitaph – he has fought the fight, kept the faith, run the race and finished the course – he also pens one for another dear friend, Demas: 'Demas . . . has deserted me.'

Paul is not writing as a megalomaniac growing old in his loneliness but as the pastor of this man's soul. These two verses summarize nearly all that we know about Demas (he is mentioned in passing in Colossians 4:14 and Philemon 1:24 as a fellow worker with Luke and John Mark). He serves as a warning of the grave possibility of spiritual decline in professing servants of God.

Demas deserted his divine call. 'Demas has left me in the lurch' might serve as a translation of verse 10. Demas had abandoned Paul in his hour of greatest need. When Paul made his pleas before Caesar, no one stood with him. Unlike the other men Paul mentions in this chapter, Demas hadn't left him to take the gospel message elsewhere. Rather, he had deserted Christ's cause. Perhaps Thessalonica (where he had gone) was Demas' home town, the place where he was brought to Christ (Acts 17). In the mighty work of God there, perhaps Demas was one of those who had 'turned to God from idols to serve the living and true God' (1 Thessalonians 1:9). When he joined Paul, no doubt there were high hopes for him in Christian ministry. But this sense of destiny came to nothing because he deserted his divine calling.

Demas deserted the apostle Paul. Demas had been in a privileged position. He'd seen Paul's suffering and the Lord standing by him; he had heard Paul preaching and witnessed him applying God's Word; he had seen answers to prayer, the glory of God and the power of the Holy Spirit coming down on men and women. And he had been drawn into intimate companionship with this great servant of God. But still he had deserted him.

Demas deserted the place of sacrifice and suffering. He left Paul in Rome to face the judgement of Caesar. Demas would not face the tribulation, persecution and cost of following Christ. He was like the rocky soil in Jesus' parable of the sower (Matthew 13:1–23). There the Word of God is received with gladness but then, when the noon-day sun of trials and persecution begins to emerge, the Word fails to flourish in the life of the believer; it withers and fades and seems to die. We never find out whether Demas returned to Christ or had committed the final apostasy.

It is one thing to begin enthusiastically; it is another to continue.

> Be sure to fear the LORD and serve him faithfully with all your heart; consider what great things he has done for you.
> (1 Samuel 12:24)

Meditate on the 'great things [God] has done for you'.

Pray that God's faithfulness would spur you on to 'serve him faithfully'.

Pray for family members and friends who professed to be Christians but have wandered away from the faith. Ask God to bring these prodigals home.

Pray for your pastor, elders, small group leaders and young people involved in ministry to stay faithful to God, to finish the Christian race well.

Day 80

Read: 2 Timothy 4:1–22
Key verses: 2 Timothy 4:9–10

. . . .

⁹Do your best to come to me quickly, ¹⁰for Demas, because he loved this world, has deserted me and has gone to Thessalonica.

Have you ever noticed how quickly the opportunity to sin arises once you have decided to give in to temptation?

Demas fled to Thessalonica. Perhaps he was returning to his home town (see Day 79). It may have been that Thessalonica, rather than Rome, was the place God seemed to be blessing, and so was a much cosier place in which he could serve Christ. Yet it is striking that not only did Demas head to Thessalonica but also, in those difficult circumstances, that he was able to get there at all. How often, in the life of a professing child of God, the desire to flee the place of God's calling and appointment is almost invariably followed by the opportunity to do so. There is a catalogue of names in Scripture that bear witness to this undying tactic of Satan.

Remember David. It was the time when kings go to war. But he ignored his place of duty, at the head of the army (2 Samuel 11:1). Soon afterwards, he committed adultery with Bathsheba and had her husband Uriah murdered. It all started because he saw the woman from his rooftop when he should have been at war.

Think of Jonah. He was fleeing from the Word of God and looking for an opportunity to escape it. He went to the port of Joppa and found a ship bound for Tarshish (Jonah 1:1–3).

Simon Peter wanted to flee from the cost of serving Christ, and then a servant-girl asked him if he had been with Jesus (Matthew 26:31–35, 57–58, 69–75). Demas-like, out of his heart and mouth, came the denial of the Lord Jesus.

It is true, in a very profound sense, that in the spiritual life you get what you want. When the desire to sin – to flee from God, his Word and his will – arises, the opportunity to do so will soon follow. Paul's highlighting that Demas 'loved this world' may imply that he turned away entirely from following Jesus. If so, Demas illustrates to us that when someone desires to turn away, he or she has no security with which to strengthen the soul against the onslaught of the devil. The immediate consequence of this spiritual decline was the opportunity to flee from Christ.

What do you really want? In spiritual terms, what are you aiming for?

There is a Cherokee tale about a man teaching his grandson about the war that wages in our souls. He explained that there are two wolves battling inside each one of us. One is evil – he is anger, envy, greed and resentment. The other wolf is good – he is joy, peace, hope and love. The young boy thought for a moment and then asked, 'Which wolf wins?' The old man replied simply, 'The one you feed.'

If we want to be like Christ, instead of fleeing *from* God as soon as temptation strikes, we need to flee *to* him – feeding on his Word and finding nourishment for our souls in prayer, worship, fellowship and service. Today, sinful desires *will* wage war within you, but don't feed them. Rather, keep your goal of Christlikeness in mind as you flee to him, finding strength for your soul.

Day 81

Read: 2 Timothy 4:1–22
Key verses: 2 Timothy 4:9–10

. . . .

⁹Do your best to come to me quickly, ¹⁰for Demas, because he loved this world, has deserted me and has gone to Thessalonica.

What causes backsliding?

Paul's answer in this case is that 'Demas loved this world'. The apostle is not speaking of the world around us, the cosmos in all its beauty and glory. He is thinking of the age in which we live, which is given over to the powers of evil and darkness. In Galatians 1:4, Paul calls it 'the present evil age'. It may be better to translate verse 10 as 'Demas has forsaken me because he fell in love with this age'.

Like Paul, Demas had professed to look forward to the crown of righteousness that would never fade away. He had preached and proclaimed that he was longing for the age to come and the return of the Lord Jesus Christ (2 Timothy 4:8). But now he was turning his back on the crown of righteousness and, instead of loving Christ's appearing, he had fallen in love with this present age.

Perhaps the world had come to him in the guises most suited to the desires lying latent in his heart. He had begun to feel the strings of his heart being tugged towards the pleasures of this age. His grip on the age to come had been released, he had fallen back into the embraces of this age and he had gone to Thessalonica.

As a pastor, Paul's heart was broken because he didn't know whether Demas had just backslidden or whether he had committed the final apostasy. Even now, we don't know the end of Demas' story. However, there is still hope and encouragement in these verses. For Demas is not the only name mentioned here; in verse 11, John Mark is mentioned. We might call him the Demas of Paul's earlier life. He deserted Paul (we can only guess why) but he was restored.

Here then is the message: there is restoration and forgiveness for returning deserters. In Christ, there is a welcome for people like Demas, people like you and me, when we return to the Lord in repentance and faith.

Do you feel the strings of your heart being tugged by the pleasures of this age? Can you sense yourself losing focus on the crown of righteousness and the age to come? Today, turn back to God. The restoration offered to John Mark and Demas is still available. God is ready and waiting to welcome you.

There is hope for the backslider. God especially describes his grace to backsliders in Hosea 14. God is so amazing! Even though our backsliding insults him, dishonours him, grieves him, and pushes away his love, still he calls us to return to him. This requires repentance: coming to grips with the badness of our sins against God and turning away from them to the Lord, with a firm resolution to follow his commands. It requires turning from our reliance on ourselves (and other mere men) and renewing our trust in Christ alone. Such trust does not use Christ as a means to get something you want, but rests in Christ as what you want above all else.

(Joel Beeke, 'Getting Back into the Race', 8 November 2011, <www.thegospelcoalition.org/article/getting-back-into-the -race>, accessed 6 January 2021)

Day 82

Read: Hebrews 3:1–6
Key verses: Hebrews 3:5–6

••

[5]*"Moses was faithful as a servant in all God's house," bearing witness to what would be spoken by God in the future. [6]But Christ is faithful as the Son over God's house. And we are his house, if indeed we hold firmly to our confidence and the hope in which we glory.*

What attributes of God should Christians share?

'Faithful' is one of the Bible's great descriptions of God towards us, and also of all those who are in Christ.

Paul speaks in Ephesians 1:1 of those who are 'faithful in Christ Jesus'. In his parable of the talents, Jesus speaks of the faithful and wise servants. Hebrews 11 is a catalogue of those who lived by faith, who were faithful in all the different circumstances of life. And Revelation 2:10 challenges us to 'Be faithful, even to the point of death', so that we may receive life as our 'victor's crown'.

Jesus is our supreme pattern of faithfulness, and we are to 'fix' our 'thoughts on' him (Hebrews 3:1). But we are also to consider Moses as a pattern of faithfulness (verse 2), a faithful servant of God (verse 5). He faced Pharaoh, led the Israelites across the Red Sea and remonstrated with the people about the golden calf.

It is easy to look over the fence and say, 'If only I were so-and-so. If only this hadn't happened to me . . . ' But God has called you where you are, and it is there that he wants you to be faithful. Moses wouldn't have chosen the life of a leader of escapee slaves; he had been pretty comfortable in Egypt. But God called him to lead the Israelites, and he stands out through the whole Old Testament as the supreme example of faithfulness.

Christ was also a faithful servant to God (verse 2). But he was more than that. He was faithful as 'the Son over God's house' (verse 6). For the Jews who read this letter, there was no one who had ever walked closer to God than Moses. But the writer says, 'Yes, there is – Jesus!' Moses was part of the house, but Christ was the builder and therefore worthy of greater honour.

Like Christ, we are God's sons and daughters. We share the wonderful privilege of being members of the eternal family, as 'holy brothers and sisters, who share in the heavenly calling' (verse 1). And our faithfulness, our perseverance, is the evidence that we are children of God, part of God's household: 'We are his house, if indeed we hold firmly to our confidence and the hope in which we glory' (verse 6).

For the doubters, the drifters and the weary, the encouragement is to 'fix your thoughts on Jesus' (verse 1). Greater even than Moses, he is worthy of our trust and obedience. Through him, God built his household: a community of believers saved by faith in Christ's death on the cross. Jesus' faithfulness on the cross means that our salvation is secure – now and for eternity. Today, praise God for Jesus' faithfulness, which means that we can 'hold firmly to our confidence and the hope in which we glory'.

Day 83

Read: Hebrews 3:7—4:13
Key verse: Hebrews 4:1

....

Therefore, since the promise of entering his rest still stands, let us be careful that none of you be found to have fallen short of it.

Most of us need the carrot-and-stick approach: encouragement to remain faithful but also warnings against complacency.

Here we have a warning – three symptoms of falling away – so that we can recognize and prevent unfaithfulness.

A hardening heart. Hebrews 3:7–11 quotes Psalm 95, which refers to the Israelites' lack of faith after they had escaped from Egypt. Joshua and Caleb believed God's Word that Israel could enter the Promised Land, but the rest did not. This unbelief led to thirty-eight years of wandering in the desert because people hardened their hearts towards God's Word. How well do we listen to and obey God's Word?

A turning away. A consequence of hardening our hearts is that we turn away from the living God. We develop 'sinful, unbelieving' hearts (Hebrews 3:12). If we don't want to hear God, we soon don't want to have contact with him. We stop reading the Bible, attending our small groups and, perhaps, eventually don't go to church at all. Our turning away progresses because we do not want to be convicted by the Word. Therefore, we avoid it.

The Israelites quickly turned away from God while Moses was on the mountain receiving the Ten Commandments. In his absence, they fashioned a golden calf and had an orgy (3:16–18). Aaron's excuse was this: 'So I told them, "Whoever has any gold jewellery, take it off." Then they gave me the gold, and I threw it into the fire, and out came this calf!' (Exodus 32:24). Aaron and the Israelites were deceived by their sin. When we begin to turn away from God, we also deceive ourselves and shut our ears to the truth we know so well.

> *A falling away.* We believe that once we have turned to Christ, we have 'crossed over from death to life' (John 5:24) and that no one can snatch us from the Father's hand (John 10:28–29). We have eternal life, beginning now, and nothing can separate us from the love of God in Christ Jesus (Romans 8:38–39). But you can't negate the force of Hebrews 4:11: 'So let us do our best to enter that rest. But if we disobey God, as the people of Israel did, we will fall' (NLT). This message is written to Christians: beware, in case you fall away!

If you are so hardened that you feel you could never fall away, you are probably more likely to do so. But if you are humble before God as a sinner saved by grace, although still wrestling with the sinful nature within you, you will hold to the wonderful doctrine of the preservation of the saints. You'll never be complacent as you look at the sin that can easily deceive, even in a Christian.

Because God is faithful, the promise of entering into his eternal rest still stands. With such a glorious future ahead, don't give in to complacency. Rather, press on all the more in faithfulness. Keep your heart soft towards God: obey his Word, pray often, join with your church family for worship and service, and spur one another on.

> I have chosen the way of faithfulness;
>   I have set my heart on your laws.
> (Psalm 119:30)

Day 84

Read: Hebrews 3:7—4:13
Key verses: Hebrews 3:12–13

....

[12] See to it, brothers and sisters, that none of you has a sinful, unbelieving heart that turns away from the living God. [13] But encourage one another daily, as long as it is called "Today", so that none of you may be hardened by sin's deceitfulness.

How well does your church look after new Christians? What care and provision are in place? This stage after birth is most important. We must invest in new believers for weeks and months, as what God has begun in them grows and takes root.

The writer to the Hebrews gives us four vital measures to put in place for ourselves and in the lives of those starting out on their Christian journey. It is never too early to guard our wayward hearts. He explains that unfaithfulness is prevented by four things.

Examination (3:12). The New International Version of the Bible says, 'See to it'; the English Standard Version says, 'Take care'. Self-examination is required. Will you stop and review your life? Will you ask yourself straight questions about where you are before God? Give yourself a spiritual check-up and say to God, 'Have I slipped up? Have I gone forward? What do you want to say to me?'

Encouragement (3:13). Have you encouraged someone today with a comment, a note or a text? Each of us has a ministry of encouraging the good, true and positive things in other Christians. Sin deceives us and Satan is seeking to destroy us, but encouragement from another Christian can strengthen us against temptation. Each morning, ask God, 'Whom can I encourage today?'

Effort (4:11). The writer is talking about the effort of learning, thinking, training, developing and applying the faith, moving towards a greater maturity and usefulness for God. Never stop wanting to learn more about the Lord. We must keep making this God-blessed effort because we have to look to 'him to whom we must give account' (4:13).

Exposure (4:12–13). Scripture is described as a double-edged sword, a short dagger, like a surgeon's knife that gets into where the problem is. It is 'living and active'; it is made personally alive to us by the Holy Spirit's action. It 'penetrates' us, reaching the deep recesses of the heart, and our inmost thoughts, subconscious motives and hidden agendas. 'It judges the thoughts and attitudes of the heart.' The Greek word for 'judges' here is one used in wrestling. God's Word grabs you, overthrows you just like a wrestler. Will you spend time reading and studying God's Word, letting it do its work in your heart?

There is nothing mystical about faithfulness. It is not a fluke, but the result of grace-driven effort.

Apart from grace-driven effort, people do not gravitate toward godliness, prayer, obedience to Scripture, faith and delight in the Lord. We drift toward compromise and call it tolerance; we drift toward disobedience and call it freedom; we drift toward superstition and call it faith. We cherish the indiscipline of lost self-control and call it relaxation; we slouch toward prayerlessness and delude ourselves into thinking we have escaped legalism; we slide toward godlessness and convince ourselves we have been liberated.

(D. A. Carson, *For the Love of God*, vol. 2, IVP, 2011, 23 January)

Day 85

Read: Hebrews 4:14—5:6
Key verses: Hebrews 4:14–16

. . . .

> [14] *Therefore, since we have a great high priest who has ascended into heaven, Jesus the Son of God, let us hold firmly to the faith we profess.* [15] *For we do not have a high priest who is unable to feel sympathy for our weaknesses, but we have one who has been tempted in every way, just as we are – yet he did not sin.* [16] *Let us then approach God's throne of grace with confidence, so that we may receive mercy and find grace to help us in our time of need.*

Are you a confident person?

Whatever your personality, there are two things that the writer to the Hebrews urges us to do confidently that will build and establish our faithfulness: to hold firmly to the faith we profess and approach the throne of grace.

> **Let us hold firmly to the faith we profess.** Many people today are scathing of Christianity. We, however, can be confident because our faith rests not on human philosophy but in Christ, the Son of God. He is already triumphant in resurrection and ascension; he is the King of kings. What is more, this faith works. We can look around and see evidence of how the gospel message transforms lives.

> **Let us approach God's throne of grace.** Don't just stand there, saying, 'Isn't it marvellous?' Be confident about this privilege and use it. Before Jesus' death, the way to approach God was via the tabernacle, the temple and through a high priest. But the cross changed all that, and it was a game-changer for first-century Jews. A revolution had taken place: the temple curtain had been torn in two and the way into the holy of holies had been opened by the

blood of Jesus. We must use this privilege to approach God's throne of grace directly, so that we may receive mercy and also find grace in time of need.

And when you come to his throne, come honestly and openly, as you are. Nothing is hidden from God's sight, so don't hold anything back as if he can't see the recesses of your life. Come because Jesus shared in our humanity and has 'sympathy'. The Greek word used here is found only in the New Testament; it means to 'suffer with'. Jesus has understood our temptation; therefore we can come before God knowing that he understands.

We can hold on tightly to the faith and come into God's presence because of Jesus' faithfulness as God's Son and as our high priest. Living as a Christian is not a matter of crossing our fingers and hoping everything will work out in the end. Our faithfulness is not dependent on human wisdom, favourable circumstances or how confident we feel, but on the character and work of Jesus Christ.

Today, use the privilege Christ bought for you on the cross and approach God's throne with confidence. While conscious of his presence, meditate on Christ's character, tell yourself the gospel message, receive mercy and grace, and ask for help to press on and hold fast.

Day 86

Read: Hebrews 6:11–20
Key verses: Hebrews 6:17–18

....

> ¹⁷ *Because God wanted to make the unchanging nature of his purpose very clear to the heirs of what was promised, he confirmed it with an oath.* ¹⁸*God did this so that, by two unchangeable things in which it is impossible for God to lie, we who have fled to take hold of the hope set before us may be greatly encouraged.*

Who is the most faithful believer you know?

The writer of Hebrews presents Abraham as an example of one who had 'faith and patience' (Hebrews 6:12). He left his home believing God's promise that he would give him a new land, make him into a great nation and bless him (Genesis 12). Many years later, his wife gave birth to Isaac, whom, Abraham was told, was the heir of the promise. In Genesis 22:2, God says to Abraham, 'Take your son, your only son whom you love . . . Sacrifice him.' Abraham knows that it is through his son that the promise will come, but he obeys God, reasoning that God can bring Isaac back from the dead (Hebrews 11:19). And so, Abraham draws the knife, holds it high and is about to sacrifice his beloved son. Then a voice says:

> Do not lay a hand on the boy . . . because you have not withheld from me your son, your only son . . . I swear by myself, declares the LORD, that . . . I will surely bless you and make your descendants as numerous as the stars in the sky and as the sand on the seashore . . . through your offspring all nations on earth will be blessed, because you have obeyed me.
> (Genesis 22:12, 16–18)

God has already promised, but now he swears on oath that he will bless all nations through this son. In a court of law, you might say, 'I swear by almighty God that the evidence I shall give shall be the truth, the whole truth and nothing but the truth.' To swear an oath is to say that if I lie, God may deal with me ever so severely. But why does God swear? Is his promise not enough?

God's promise is certain; he does not lie. But here he makes his purpose to bless doubly clear. He didn't swear for Abraham's sake: Abraham already trusted the promise, and he had been willing to offer up his own son. But it's for us – the heirs of the promise – so that, by the promise and the oath, we have a double assurance: 'God did this so that we who have fled to take hold of the hope before us may be greatly encouraged' (Hebrews 6:18).

If you are feeling lazy and sluggish in your Christian life (verses 11–12), if you are tempted to let your relationship with Jesus slip, remember the promise and oath of God and be 'greatly encouraged'. He does not lie; he cannot break his oath; he cannot break his promise – he is completely trustworthy.

Jesus' death and resurrection are the proof that any promise God has ever made, he keeps (2 Corinthians 1:20). We can bank our eternity on the promises of God. Today, be 'greatly encouraged' by the faithfulness of God. Because he is faithful in his character, and therefore faithful to his promises and purposes, we can trust him completely – now and for eternity.

Day 87

Read: Hebrews 6:11–20
Key verses: Hebrews 6:19–20

. . . .

> ^{19}*We have this hope as an anchor for the soul, firm and secure. It enters the inner sanctuary behind the curtain, ^{20}where our forerunner, Jesus, has entered on our behalf. He has become a high priest for ever, in the order of Melchizedek.*

How do we make sure that we don't drift away from Christ?

We have seen from a variety of Bible passages that effort is required on our part. The writer to the Hebrews underlines this:

> We want each of you to show this same diligence to the very end, so that what you hope for may be fully realized. We do not want you to become lazy, but to imitate those who through faith and patience inherit what has been promised.
> (Hebrews 6:11–12)

However, the great encouragement in these verses is that we have an anchor that will hold us fast. We have 'an anchor for the soul' that is 'firm and secure' (verse 19). Anchors bury themselves in the bed of the sea to make sure that the ship doesn't move. But, in an unusual feat of geography and gravity, this 'anchor' goes up, rather than down. It's as if it's whirled above the head and launched into the heavens, into the sky, into the holy of holies, the throne room of God, the very place where God himself dwells.

The promise of God comes from heaven to Abraham. It is fulfilled in Jesus Christ, in his death and resurrection, and then he returns through the curtain, into the presence of God, where he goes before us. He is the forerunner, opening the way for us to follow. The Lord Jesus Christ is an anchor, the promise of our sure and certain hope of an eternal inheritance. This is God's unchangeable and unstoppable promise to bless his people, that we might be eternally secure.

Think of a ship in a storm, tossed and thrown about, drifting, in real danger of hitting the rocks. That is what life is like if we let go of the anchor, if we let go of Christ, if we let go of his promise. Now, imagine being in that storm as you drop anchor. It's still choppy; you still go up and down; the storm may still cause you to be seasick. But you are safe and secure. You will not hit the rocks as long as that anchor is secure.

Perhaps you find yourself under pressure from circumstances. It could be that you feel alone and fearful. You might find yourself saying, 'I'm not sure if I can keep going with Christ.' God's Word says, 'You have an anchor for your soul – Christ.' Cling to him – devote yourself to prayer, grow in your relationship with him through God's Word, obey him through the power of the Holy Spirit – and he will hold you fast.

Jesus' faithfulness is our anchor. Nothing, or no one else, can offer the security our souls crave. As our forerunner, Jesus blazed a trail for us into the presence of God; as our high priest, he offered the perfect sacrifice of himself at Calvary. Now he sits at the right hand of God praying for us (Romans 8:34). Whatever storms you face today, remember, you have an anchor that cannot fail – Christ himself.

Day 88

Read: Revelation 2:18–29
Key verses: Revelation 2:20

....

I have this against you: you tolerate that woman Jezebel, who calls herself a prophet. By her teaching she misleads my servants into sexual immorality and the eating of food sacrificed to idols.

Do your words and worship on Sunday match your behaviour and values on Monday?

Jesus saw the love, faith, service and perseverance of the church at Thyatira (Revelation 2:19), but he also called them out on their compromise.

The city's commerce was operated by trade guilds. If you wanted to progress, you had to network in these guilds. But their meetings involved offering food to idols and emperor worship. What should Christians do? It seems that a prophetess in the church was saying, 'It's not a big deal. On Sunday, pledge allegiance to Jesus as Lord. On Monday, say that Caesar is lord.'

But the risen Christ calls this compromise spiritual adultery.

'Immorality' (verse 20) may refer to immoral acts in pagan rituals but, usually, in the book of Revelation, it refers to spiritual adultery (see Revelation 17:1–2; 18:1–3; 19:1–2). That's why Jesus calls this prophetess Jezebel. Jezebel was the foreign-born queen who had married the Israelite king Ahab. She had introduced the worship of Baal alongside the worship of the Lord (see 1 and 2 Kings). The Israelites didn't abandon worshipping the Lord to worship Baal; instead, they bowed to the two side by side. In the same way, the Jezebel of Thyatira was not *outside* the church; she was *inside* the church, worshipping Jesus on Sunday but also, on Monday morning, worshipping other gods.

How about us? Do we have two sets of values? On Sunday, do we believe God's Word as it speaks of Jesus Christ and yet, on Monday, give credence to the adverts that say life, identity and fulfilment are found through what we can buy? On Sunday, do we trust our future to the sovereign Lord but, on Monday, trust our future to the bank?

We can sympathize with Jezebel. After all, how can we prosper in the workplace, how will we find a marriage partner, unless we are prepared to compromise a bit? But Jesus says that the prophetess 'misleads' her servants. The Greek word for 'misleads' is one that is used in Revelation only of Satan, his false prophet and Babylon the Prostitute (Revelation 12:9; 13:14; 18:23; 20:3, 8, 10). Ultimately, compromise led to judgement for Jezebel and her followers (Revelation 2:22–23).

Christ will not tolerate spiritual adultery. When addressing the church, he opens with 'These are the words of the Son of God' (verse 18). Caesar was called a son of god or a son of Zeus. The Son of God challenges these claims head on. There can be no accommodation between Christ and Caesar, between Christ and the world.

Today, the risen Christ, the Son of God, sets his eyes 'like blazing fire' (Revelation 2:18) on our lives. He sees our love, faith, service and perseverance. But, jealous for our wholehearted devotion, he also wants to expose any spiritual adultery. Do your conversations at home, your behaviour at work and your bank balance reflect your trust in God and in his Word or do they mirror the concerns and priorities of the world? Ask God to reveal your areas of compromise and give you strength to be as faithful to God's will as Jesus was.

Day 89

Read: Revelation 2:18–29
Key verse: Revelation 2:23

....

*Then all the churches will know that I am he who searches hearts
and minds, and I will repay each of you according to your deeds.*

Worldliness is whatever makes sin look normal and righteousness look
strange.
(Kevin DeYoung, *The Hole in Our Holiness*, Crossway, 2012, p. 37)

It would be very easy to define worldliness in terms of activities that
Christians shouldn't do and places that they shouldn't go. But the
risen Lord has eyes 'like blazing fire' (Revelation 2:18), and he is
looking at our hearts because that is where the true battle for faithful,
holy living takes place.

There are Christians leading respectable lives with exemplary
behaviour who are losing the battle for the heart. Their actions arise
from duty instead of grace, and they act out of self-righteousness
instead of glory for God. Verse 23 is a quote from Jeremiah 17:

The heart is deceitful above all things
    and beyond cure.
    Who can understand it?

And the answer comes:

'I the LORD search the heart
    and examine the mind,
to reward each person according to their conduct,
    according to what their deeds deserve.'
(Jeremiah 17:9–10)

In Jeremiah 17:5–8, the Lord explains why the heart is so important.
Adversity, trials, suffering and problems will come to us all. What

makes the difference is how our hearts respond. If our hearts turn away from the Lord when the heat comes, we will be like a bush in the desert (verse 6). But if we trust in the Lord, we will be like a tree planted by water (verse 8).

The key to holy living is not circumstances but a heart that trusts the Lord:

> Teach me your way, LORD,
>   that I may rely on your faithfulness;
> give me an undivided heart,
>   that I may fear your name.
> (Psalm 86:11)

Elsewhere, the psalmist speaks of a fixed heart and a heart that is steadfast. We live at a time when people change their sets of values in different contexts. The challenge for believers is to have hearts that are fixed on faithfully serving Jesus.

And we are in this together. Holiness is a community project. This is how the writer to the Hebrews puts it:

> See to it, brothers and sisters, that none of you has a sinful, unbelieving heart that turns away from the living God. But encourage one another daily, as long as it is called 'Today', so that none of you may be hardened by sin's deceitfulness.
> (Hebrews 3:12–13)

Outwardly, you may look holy – you go to church, help with Sunday school and serve on rotas. But true holiness is a matter of the heart – it is being faithful to God when no one is watching, faithful when your circumstances are difficult and faithfully obedient in the little things.

> Holiness is the sum of a million little things – the avoidance of little evils and little foibles, the setting aside of little bits of worldliness and little acts of compromise, the putting to death of little inconsistencies and little indiscretions, the attention to little duties and little dealings, the hard work of little self-denials and little self-restraints, the cultivation of little benevolences and little forbearances.
> (Kevin DeYoung, *The Hole in our Holiness*, Crossway, 2012, p. 145)

Day 90

Read: Revelation 2:18–29
Key verses: Revelation 2:24–25

....

> [24] Now I say to the rest of you in Thyatira, to you who do not hold to her teaching and have not learned Satan's so-called deep secrets, "I will not impose any other burden on you, [25] except to hold on to what you have until I come."

'Hold on!' That is Jesus' command.

The risen Christ commends the church at Thyatira for not following the 'deep secrets'. Verse 24 may be ironic; it may be that Jezebel talked about the deep secrets of God, and Christ says that they are really the deep secrets of Satan. Or it may be that Jezebel's followers claimed to follow the way of Satan so that they could take part in pagan rituals without being affected.

Either way, the point is that Jesus rejects so-called deep things. We already have the wisdom and power of God in the message of Christ crucified. There is no higher way, no special teaching, no advanced message. The secret of holiness is no secret at all; it is to hold on to the gospel, goodness, grace and sovereignty of God.

That doesn't mean it is easy; it's still a battle. Behind every sin is a lie, a false promise. The battle for holiness is a battle to believe the truth, the truth that only God can bring true joy and justify us through his grace. But don't think of this battle for holiness as some kind of dreary struggle in which you have to give up pleasure. It's not! It is a battle to delight in God. 'The fight of faith is the fight to keep your heart content in Christ, to really believe and keep on believing that he will meet every need and satisfy every longing' (John Piper, *Future Grace*, Multnomah Press, 2012, p. 222).

When we can't see God's hand or feel his love, and his return seems very far away, it is a struggle to hold on to gospel truths. In our battle-weary moments, the happiness that the world offers – money, sex and personal satisfaction – seems very tempting. But these are precisely the times not to lose our grip on the gospel but to hold on even tighter, to ask God to strengthen us to delight in his truth, so that we remain faithful till the end.

> We . . . thank God for you, brothers and sisters loved by the Lord, because God chose you as firstfruits to be saved through the sanctifying work of the Spirit and through belief in the truth. He called you to this through our gospel, that you might share in the glory of our Lord Jesus Christ.
>
> So then, brothers and sisters, stand firm and hold fast to the teachings we passed on to you, whether by word of mouth or by letter.
>
> May our Lord Jesus Christ himself and God our Father, who loved us and by his grace gave us eternal encouragement and good hope, encourage your hearts and strengthen you in every good deed and word.
> (2 Thessalonians 2:13–17)

Day 91

Read: Revelation 2:18–29
Key verses: Revelation 2:26–28

....

²⁶ To the one who is victorious and does my will to the end, I will give authority over the nations – ²⁷ that one "will rule them with an iron sceptre and will dash them to pieces like pottery" – just as I have received authority from my Father. ²⁸ I will also give that one the morning star.

What motivates you to remain faithful?

The promise of rewards can encourage us all. In these verses, John gives us a vision of the future in which Christians are victorious and have authority. The morning star is the planet Venus, a Roman symbol of victory. The generals erected temples to the goddess Venus and carried her symbols on their standards. But look closely, because the risen Christ turns our ideas of success and victory upside down. Verse 27 is a quote from Psalm 2 and, in that psalm, God gives his Son authority over the nations. Now Jesus says that he is giving that authority to his people. In the Great Commission, Jesus sends us, with his authority, to teach the nations to obey his commands (Matthew 28:18–20). We exercise authority over the nations through the Word of God.

The same words from Psalm 2 are quoted in Revelation 12:11, where we are told what it means to overcome:

They triumphed . . .
>   by the blood of the Lamb
>   and by the word of their testimony;
> they did not love their lives so much
>   as to shrink from death.

How do we overcome? How do we exercise authority? By the blood of the Lamb. God revolutionizes our criteria for success: we rule by serving; we conquer by loving; we overcome by suffering.

And our greatest reward, our ultimate success, will be to receive the morning star (verse 28). In Revelation 22:16, Jesus says that he is the 'Morning Star'. The star is seen in the sky just before dawn. Jesus tells us that he himself is the sign of a new day. He is assuring us that we will be part of God's new dawn, God's new age. We will see God's kingdom, share in his banquet and, on that day, we will see Jesus.

The Christians in Thyatira had to choose between success in life and remaining faithful to God. It's the decision that we all have to make between worldliness and holiness.

As we face that choice, Jesus is raising our sights. Faithfulness might mean suffering and hardship in this life, but beyond that is the dawn of a world made new, in which God dwells with his people.

One day soon, the morning star will appear. On that great day, all God's promises will be fully and finally realized, and we will receive the reward for our faithfulness – the Lord Jesus himself. As we wait for the return of Christ and his unveiling of the new heavens and new earth, persevere a little while longer. In the darkness before that glorious new dawn, keep choosing faithfulness to Christ over success in this life – whatever the cost – knowing that, very soon, we will be with Jesus, enjoying him for ever.

Further study

If you would like to read more on the theme of faithfulness, you might find this selection of books helpful.

Books on the theme of staying faithful to God for the long haul:

- Christopher Ash, *Zeal without Burnout: Seven keys to a lifelong ministry of sustainable sacrifice* (The Good Book Company, 2016)

- Paul Mallard, Staying Fresh: Serving with joy (IVP, 2015)

- Trillia J. Newbell, *Sacred Endurance: Finding grace and strength for a lasting faith* (IVP, 2019)

Biographies of faithful men and women to inspire and encourage your own spiritual journey:

- John Piper, *21 Servants of Sovereign Joy: Faithful, flawed, and fruitful* (Crossway, 2018)

- Noël Piper, *Faithful Women and Their Extraordinary God* (Crossway, 2005)

- Dr Helen Roseveare, *Living Faith: Willing to be stirred as a pot of paint* (Christian Focus, 2007)

Books on the theme of staying faithful to the gospel while engaging with culture:

- Timothy Keller and John Inazu, *Uncommon Ground: Living faithfully in a world of difference* (Thomas Nelson, 2020)

- Rebecca Manley Pippert, *Stay Salt: The world has changed – our message must not* (The Good Book Company, 2020)

Day 92

Read: Romans 5:1–11
Key verses: Romans 5:1–4

• •

Therefore, since we have been justified through faith, we have peace with God through our Lord Jesus Christ, [2] through whom we have gained access by faith into this grace in which we now stand. And we boast in the hope of the glory of God. [3] Not only so, but we also glory in our sufferings, because we know that suffering produces perseverance; [4] perseverance, character; and character, hope.

Can you remember when you became a Christian?

You might be a new Christian or decades along your discipleship journey. You might remember a specific date you trusted Christ or perhaps it was more of a gradual acceptance of gospel truths. For some it was a dramatic event but for many it was unremarkable.

However you became a Christian, even if you felt no different at all, nothing will ever be the same again. That declaration of 'not guilty' by God when you trusted in Christ's work on the cross to forgive your sins opened the door to a new life. We are now no longer enemies of God, our relationship with him is restored and we can come into his presence boldly as his dearly loved children. We are now forever 'standing' in God's grace, living in the sphere of his unrelenting favour. God never stops being gracious to us, even when we face suffering.

Every one of us will suffer, either because of our faith or because we live in a fallen world. This shouldn't cause us to doubt God's love, in fact even in suffering we can experience joy – not an inane triumphalism but a deep-seated happiness rooted in our new relationship with God and the future he has in store for us. As believers, we 'boast in the hope of the glory of God' – this means, 'we confidently and joyfully look forward to sharing in God's glory' (verse 2, NLT). On our darkest days we can be joyful because we know a glorious future awaits and that God is preparing us for it. Through suffering, God is at work in us, developing perseverance and shaping our character. Like a sculptor's chisel, God uses suffering to whittle away our sinfulness and shape us into the image of Christ.

This passage is replete with our next three devotional themes – *Grace, Joy* and *Suffering* and it reminds us that, even on days where our life appears no different from those around us – when we are facing hardship and juggling the mundane – we have a new life in Christ. One day our present hope will be rewarded, the goal of our salvation complete – we will be like the Lord and with him forever.

Joyful people are usually well-acquainted with suffering. In the depths they have met with God, proved his faithfulness, and experienced his loving care. Suffering has started to loosen the ties that bind them to this world and their eyes are more keenly focused on the world made new. Today, whatever your suffering, rejoice in these unchangeable truths – you are standing in God's grace and you have a glorious future that even now he is preparing you for.

Suffering

Contributors

Day 93

Read: Psalm 63
Key verse: Psalm 63:1

••

You, God, are my God,
earnestly I seek you;
I thirst for you,
my whole being longs for you,
in a dry and parched land
where there is no water.

Is your faith faltering under the weight of your suffering?

When bereavement, tragedy or some sort of testing hits, it often exposes the reality that although we've put our trust in Jesus as Saviour, we still tend to think of God like a genie in the lamp, there to do our will. When God doesn't change our situation, doubts and disappointment set in.

The writer of Psalm 63 is facing suffering. He speaks of the dry and parched land, the desert, and his desperate need both in body and soul. But, his faith is unshaken in adversity. Why? He believes in God – the true God, not one who simply does his bidding.

This kind of faith means: 'Though the earth gives way . . . and the mountains quake' – though the whole world seems to be in chaos around us, you can – 'Be still and know that I am God' (Psalm 46:1–2, 10). The earth still trembles, the mountains are still shaking – circumstances are not changing – but in the midst of it you can know that God is God.

Hebrews 11 is a wonderful chapter about faith. The writer recalls the faith that carried men like Noah, Abraham and Moses to go out into the unknown, pursue thrilling adventures and prove God faithful.

He remembers the faith of those who conquered kingdoms and shut the mouths of lions (11:33). But he also mentions those who:

> Faced jeers and flogging, and even chains and imprisonment. They were put to death by stoning; they were sawn in two; they were killed by the sword. They went about in sheepskins and goatskins, destitute, persecuted and ill-treated – the world was not worthy of them.
> (Hebrews 11:36–38)

These individuals had faith but there was no great deliverance, no great exploits; there was destitution, death and suffering. The greatest faith of all is that which lays hold of God when there is no break in the clouds. Isn't it true that some of the greatest Christians you have known are people who have gone through suffering and glorified God? This is the type of faith that the writer of Psalm 63 had. When he cries out 'You, God, are my God' he is clinging to God even in disaster. He is loving God and rejoicing in him even in the darkest circumstances.

Suffering tests our faith as it forces us to ask the question: 'Am I really trusting in God or do I simply want him to do my will?' Like the psalmist, put your faith in God – cling to him, trust his character, know his peace, seek him in his Word and in prayer. Even if your circumstances don't change, even if the worst should happen, you have everything you need: 'You, God, are my God.'

Day 94

Read: Psalm 63
Key verse: Psalm 63:2

....

I have seen you in the sanctuary
and beheld your power and your glory.

How can I persevere through suffering?

David was sustained because he grasped the power and the glory of God. The writer of Psalm 73 had a similar experience. The psalmist is angry that evil prospers and those who do good don't. It's only when he goes into the sanctuary and his perspective is reoriented that he acknowledges, 'Whom have I in heaven but you? And earth has nothing I desire besides you' (Psalm 73:25). The same happens here; in the sanctuary David beholds the power and glory of God.

You get into a terrible mess if you believe that with sufficient faith and prayer, every illness, trouble and problem can be put right. The New Testament does not say this. God can heal, he does cure, he does solve, he does prevent but he is also glorified as he comes alongside those not healed.

Paul is miraculously snatched away when a plot endangers his life; Stephen is stoned to death. Peter is delivered from prison; John the Baptist is beheaded. Jesus comes to his disciples in the storm on the lake and it is stopped; Paul is shipwrecked, though they are rescued. There are times when God miraculously delivers, and times when he doesn't. We don't fully understand but we know that if we throw ourselves more deeply on God's love and grace we will receive inward blessing and he will receive glory (Romans 5:3–5).

If we recognize this then we know he *can* heal, deliver and preserve us and so we pray for it. We don't give up praying for it, just as Paul prayed three times for his own deliverance (2 Corinthians 12:8). And yet we also submit to the power and glory of God. The answer for Paul was that he was going to keep the thorn in the flesh; then he began to glory in his infirmities, because that's the way the power of God was going to rest on him. His suffering was going to glorify God and that was Paul's overriding aim, not his deliverance from the thorn in the flesh.

Very often the things that God wants to do for us are subordinated to a bigger purpose. Zechariah and Elizabeth prayed for a child, but God delayed it until his moment in his purposes. Job had fixed ideas about sin and suffering; he argued with God. Suddenly God started questioning Job: 'Where were you when I laid the earth's foundations?' (Job 38:4). Then eventually Job answered, 'I know that you can do all things'; that's the *power* of God.'. . . and no purpose of yours can be thwarted'; that's the *glory* of God (Job 42:2). Job had to go through that experience until he could bow before the power and glory of God.

Suffering can make us inward looking and self-absorbed. Today, look up and look out. Behold God's power and glory – in the teaching, singing, and fellowship at church; in creation; in his Word; in Jesus; even in your own circumstances. Then, like Paul, make it your overriding ambition that your life displays, and points others to, the power and glory of God – through sickness and health, good times and bad.

Day 95

Read: Psalm 63
Key verse: Psalm 63:3

....

Because your love is better than life,
my lips will glorify you.

You are loved!

The psalmist delights in God's steadfast, covenant love. This love can be traced through the Old Testament. It's this love that the prophets got hold of again after the exile. All their hopes for the people of God seemed to be shattered, Jerusalem had fallen and the people had been taken away as prisoners in exile. How could God do this to his people? Although the prophets couldn't explain it, they clung to the truth of God's unchanging love.

You see this in the book of Lamentations. The devastation of Jerusalem and the horrors the people faced because of their rebellion against God are difficult to read, until you get to Lamentations 3:22–23. Like a rocket cascading into the darkness comes the tremendous statement, 'Because of the Lord's great love we are not consumed, for his compassions never fail. They are new every morning; great is your faithfulness.' The circumstances haven't altered. What's changed is that the author of Lamentations has grasped the steadfast love of God.

Romans 8 gives the same message to believers. Paul asks, 'Who shall separate us from the love of Christ?' (verse 35). The New Testament does not say: 'You are a Christian, therefore you will avoid these things.' You are going to share with the rest of the world suffering and distress. But none of them can separate you from the love of God.

In fact, there is nothing about your circumstances that can alter God's love for you at all. The Bible says you are anchored by Christ through his Spirit into the love of God for ever. That is steadfast love. This is the love that saved us; the love that brought Jesus Christ into the world to die on the cross for our sins. This is the love that hung on the cross at Calvary. This is the love that brought us into God's family as we repented, received forgiveness and believed.

David's response to this love is heartfelt praise (verse 3–5). He then meditates on God (verses 6–7) and acknowledges: 'I cling to you; your right hand upholds me' (verse 8). As we cling to God, he upholds us. This is the anchor for our soul, the foundation of our faith. What a promise!

Enjoying good circumstances doesn't mean God loves you more; suffering under difficult circumstances doesn't mean he loves you less. God's love for you is the same today as it was when Jesus died for you. Praise God for his unfailing love which is new every morning:

> Oh, you are not dealing with trifles when you are dealing with the love of God to you. It is not a spare corner of the heart of God that He gives to you . . . but the great, inconceivably vast heart of God belongs as much to every Christian as if there were not another being in the world for God to love! Even as Jehovah loves His Only-begotten, so does He love each one of His children.
> (C. H. Spurgeon, *The Treasury of the Old Testament*, III.568)

Day 96

Read: Isaiah 52:13—53:12
Key verses: Isaiah 53:5–7

....

> But he was pierced for our transgressions,
>   he was crushed for our iniquities;
> the punishment that brought us peace was on him,
>   and by his wounds we are healed.
> We all, like sheep, have gone astray,
>   each of us has turned to our own way;
> and the Lord has laid on him
>   the iniquity of us all.
> ⁷He was oppressed and afflicted,
>   yet he did not open his mouth;
> he was led like a lamb to the slaughter,
>   and as a sheep before its shearers is silent,
>   so he did not open his mouth.

Why did Jesus not object to his suffering?

Pontius Pilate was mystified by the same thing (Mark 15:4–5). He had Jesus in front of him on trial and asked, 'Why are you not going to offer a defence? Don't you have anything to say?'

Jesus suffered silently because he was doing it for you and me. Do you see the 'he' and 'us' language in verse 5? 'He was pierced for our transgressions' where we overstepped God's law; 'he was crushed for our iniquities', our whole sinful mindset; 'the punishment that brought us peace' – that is, forgiveness, peace with God – 'was on him, and by his wounds we are healed'.

I deserve the punishment from God for the way that I've lived, but Jesus wonderfully, lovingly, absorbs that punishment instead. And he offers no defence because he does it willingly. It is in the plan of God and Jesus knew this. Isaiah writes: 'The Lord has laid on him the iniquity of us all' (verse 6). The great reformer Martin Luther put it this way:

> Our merciful Father sent his only Son into the world and laid on him the sins of all men, saying, 'Be Peter, that denier; Paul, that persecutor, blasphemer and cruel oppressor; David, that adulterer; that sinner that ate the apple in Paradise; that thief who hanged on the cross; and briefly be the person who has committed the sins of all men. See, therefore, that you pay and satisfy for them.
> (Martin Luther, *A Commentary on St. Paul's Epistle to the Galatians*, Cambridge: Clarke, 1953, p. 272)

Right from early on in the Gospels, Jesus tells his disciples he must go to Jerusalem and die. I remember hearing a vicar say that Jesus had hoped to change the world but, when that didn't work out, he had to go for plan B, which was to go to the cross. But Isaiah, 700 years in advance, is telling us that this is God's plan A and the Lord Jesus knows this. Jesus' death on the cross was not cosmic child abuse as if God was doing something horrible to his Son against his will. The Lord Jesus suffered willingly and voluntarily for us. That's why he offered no defence.

The Lamb of God was led like a lamb to the slaughter for *us*. Pause, be still and thank him.

> When they hurled their insults at him, he did not retaliate; when he suffered, he made no threats. Instead, he entrusted himself to him who judges justly. 'He himself bore our sins' in his body on the cross, so that we might die to sins and live for righteousness; 'by his wounds you have been healed.' For 'you were like sheep going astray,' but now you have returned to the Shepherd and Overseer of your souls (1 Peter 2:23–25).

Day 97

Read: Isaiah 52:13—53:12
Key verses: Isaiah 53:8

••

By oppression and judgement he was taken away.
Yet who of his generation protested?
For he was cut off from the land of the living;
for the transgression of my people he was punished.

Does God understand our suffering?

Yes! Jesus experienced loneliness, opposition, heartache, abandon-
ment by friends, and a cruel death. He understands our sufferings,
but that is not the main point of the cross. If it had been, why not
have Jesus come and die in a famine, natural disaster or war? Instead,
he dies in a process of judicial execution to demonstrate that
something judicial is happening. Humanly speaking, his trial is a
travesty of justice (see verse 9). But at another and more glorious
level, God is working out his process to sentence human sin and
have the Lord Jesus executed as the sentence is passed.

In every way Jesus was perfectly qualified to stand in for you and me.
As a human being, he had no sin of his own to die for, so could die
in our place. As God he was the judge taking the penalty on himself
in an extraordinary way. Isaiah is very clear about the purpose of
Jesus death: 'It was the LORD's will to crush him and cause him to
suffer . . . The LORD makes his life an offering for sin' (verse 10). This
is the language of the guilt offerings in the book of Leviticus, and
Jesus is that offering.

The New Testament understands Jesus' death in the same way. Peter
writes, '"He himself bore our sins" in his body on the cross, so that
we might die to sins and live for righteousness; "by his wounds you
have been healed"' (1 Peter 2:24). Paul startlingly says, 'God made

him, who had no sin, to be sin for us so that in him we might become the righteousness of God' (2 Corinthians 5:21).

Why do you think the Gospel writers tell us about the criminal Barabbas? It seems like a slight distraction. Surely it is because when Barabbas saw Jesus on the cross he thought to himself, 'That could've been me! The crowd were allowed to have one person released. If they had released Jesus, it would be me on that cross. But because he's there, I'm free!' Around the cross the mockers jeered: 'He saved others but he can't save himself.' Of course he couldn't. He saved you and me; that's why he couldn't save himself.

John also calls Jesus 'The Lamb of God', stressing the connection with the Passover. That night the lamb died and its blood was daubed on the door so that God would pass over the house. The lamb dies so that the firstborn son does not need to die. Again and again the Gospel writers affirm Jesus died in our place as our substitute.

Some people find the idea of God punishing anybody unpalatable. Others find it incomprehensible or unnecessary that Jesus would die in their place. They would rather put themselves right with God.

But, if you've come in God's grace to understand that you are a sinner urgently in need of forgiveness, then it is the most wonderful news in the world.

Bearing shame and scoffing rude,
in my place condemned he stood,
sealed my pardon with his blood:
Hallelujah, what a Saviour!
(P. P. Bliss, Man of Sorrows, 1875)

Day 98

Read: Isaiah 52:13—53:12

Key verses: Isaiah 53:10–11

....

Yet it was the Lord's will to crush him and cause him to suffer,
and though the Lord make his life an offering for sin,
he will see his offspring and prolong his days,
and the will of the Lord will prosper in his hand.
[11]After he has suffered,
he will see the light of life and be satisfied
by his knowledge my righteous servant will justify many,
and he will bear their iniquities.

What did Christ's suffering achieve?

Isaiah says that God's Servant 'will see his offspring'. Jesus' saving death will lead to many people becoming offspring. As one commentator puts it: 'We strayed as sheep and we return as sons.' We have the privilege of belonging to this great worldwide family, which is Christ's achievement. Look around your church or small group and you see just a small outpost of the vast, multi-million-people family that this suffering servant has bought by hanging and dying on a cross.

What exactly did Jesus do for us? God says, 'My righteous servant will justify many'. 'Justify' means 'Just as if I'd never sinned' or, in fact, even better: 'Just as if I'd lived like the Lord Jesus himself.' Jesus' blood brought us full forgiveness. There is nothing for us to pay if we're in Christ. He has paid our debt of sin in full and all the benefits of the gospel flow from that: adoption as his children; glory in the future. Why? Because he bore our iniquities (verse 11). Isaiah is using the image of the scapegoat. In the days of the Old Testament a goat was sent out into the desert after the priest laid his hands on it and confessed the sins of the people. This scapegoat would go far away, out into the desert, and die as if to symbolize the sins of the people had gone far away.

Jesus' death means that we don't need to 'hope for the best' when it comes to our eternal future. The apostle John says, 'If we confess our sins, [God] is faithful and just to forgive us our sins and to cleanse us from all unrighteousness' (1 John 1:8–9, ESV). We might have expected John to write that God is 'faithful and merciful'. No, he 'is faithful and *just*' because the debt having been paid once by Jesus, on our account, God will not require it a second time. How marvellous! If, like me, you're a sinner, conscious of some of your sin (and your family might be conscious of even more of it!), how marvellous to know that the Lord Jesus has dealt with it.

Praise God for the assurance Christ's death brings – our sins are forgiven, we are justified before the Father, brought into God's family and our eternal future is guaranteed. Not only are we thrilled with all that Jesus accomplished on the cross, God is too. Amazingly, Jesus himself will look at us, the ones he died for, and he'll think all his suffering was worth it – 'He will be satisfied'.

Day 99

Read: Psalm 6:1–10
Key verses: Psalm 6:1–3

....

Lord, do not rebuke me in your anger
  or discipline me in your wrath.
²Have mercy on me, Lord, for I am faint;
  heal me, Lord, for my bones are in agony.
³My soul is in deep anguish.
  How long, Lord, how long?

What is causing you tears and heartache?

Sin brings deep sorrow into the world. You, or those whom you love, may be struggling with debilitating illness, the dull pain of a broken marriage, the tears of childlessness, the razor-sharp sword of a false accusation. All manner of things make us sad.

In this Psalm David is weeping: 'All night long I flood my bed with weeping and drench my couch with tears' (verse 6). We don't know exactly what was going on in his life, only that he feels himself under the anger of God (verse 1). These words, 'anger' and 'wrath' are used in Deuteronomy 29 about the destruction of Sodom and Gomorrah. David uses these strong words because he has seen the holy anger of God break out (2 Samuel 6) and knows to take it seriously.

How do you respond when something goes wrong? It might be trivial like a washing machine breaking down or something serious like bullying in the workplace or the onset of dementia. David understands that everything that goes wrong in the world happens because we are sinners in a world under God's righteous judgement and curse. The particular difficulties don't always come from particular sins, but that is the big picture. So David doesn't grumble, he doesn't try and be stoical or bottle it up; he takes it to the Lord.

There's nothing particular in this psalm that David confesses but he knows he is the king of a people under sin and that hurts; his soul is greatly troubled, his body is in pain and he cries, 'How long, Lord?' (verse 3). He knew that every death and disease is because of sin, often not individual sin, but still sin. Today's mishap, tomorrow's setback, yesterday's sadness – sin lies behind them all, and behind sin, the righteous anger of God.

Today ask God to soften your heart so that you grieve for sin like King David did. Feel the weight of God's wrath for your sin, the sin in the church, and the sin in our world. But also rejoice in the hope of the gospel. We no longer have to face the wrath of God because Jesus took our place. For the soft and tender heart of Jesus, who treasured the Father's love, the wrath of God was infinite agony. With no sin in his own flawless soul, he felt the full weight of the righteous anger of God. When he cried out, 'My soul . . . is greatly troubled', it was troubled for us. He felt the full weight of God's wrath so we would never have to!

Day 100

Read: Psalm 6:1–10
Key verses: Psalm 6:4–7

. . . .

Turn, Lord, and deliver me;
*   save me because of your unfailing love.*
⁵Among the dead no one proclaims your name.
*   Who praises you from the grave?*
⁶I am worn out from my groaning.
All night long I flood my bed with weeping
*   and drench my couch with tears.*
⁷My eyes grow weak with sorrow;
*   they fail because of all my foes.*

Have you ever tried to repent?

We say, 'I'm going to turn over a new leaf. I'm going to fight that sin – that grumbling, that bitterness, that lust' but it is hard. 'We find it a tough and uphill struggle to twist ourselves away from the gloom of earthbound desires' (Augustine). We need God to turn his face to us if we are ever to turn to him in faith. And so, David cries out, 'Turn, Lord, and deliver me'.

Although this is traditionally a penitential psalm, David makes no explicit confession of sin. The grief he feels is for a world under sin and he weeps. Verse six is literally something like, 'I caused my bed to swim around the room.' It's an extraordinary amount of weeping that causes a flood and dissolves his couch. Even his eyes waste away because of his grief. The eye in Bible imagery, as in our imagery, is an index of life. We talk about somebody having a twinkle in their eye. You may have seen the dull eyes of somebody who has been suffering for a while or the empty eyes of one who has died. David's grief for sins is mirrored in his eyes. Calvin wrote that it was as if

David 'sees hell open to receive him, and the mental distress which this produces exceeds all other sorrows.'

Jesus also wept for sins. Jesus, who lived to bear the shadow of death and then death itself for sinners, wept. He wept at the grave of Lazarus. He wept over Jerusalem. He was overwhelmed with sorrow in the garden of Gethsemane. He prayed, 'with loud cries and tears' (Hebrews 5:7). I don't think we even begin to know how much Jesus wept for sins.

Are you grieving over sin in your life? Are you weeping because of the wasted years before you came to Christ or some unfaithfulness, greed or deceit you deeply regret. It is good to weep for our sins and the sins of others. But remember, 'If you have felt anguish of spirit under a sense of deserved wrath, let it cease when you find the Man of Sorrows presenting all his anguish as the atonement for your soul' (Andrew Bonar, *Christ and His Church in the Book of Psalms*).

He took my sins and my sorrows,
and made them his very own.
He bore the burden to Calvary
and suffered and died alone.
(Charles Hutchinson Gabriel, 'I stand amazed in the presence', 1905)

Day 101

Read: Psalm 6:1–10
Key verses: Psalm 6:8–10

....

Away from me, all you who do evil,
*   for the Lord has heard my weeping.*
⁹The Lord has heard my cry for mercy;
*   the Lord accepts my prayer.*
¹⁰All my enemies will be overwhelmed with shame and anguish;
*   they will turn back and suddenly be put to shame.*

Are you fed up with suffering?

For those who share King David's sentiment: 'I am worn out from my groaning' (verse 6), the final verses of this psalm offer comfort and hope.

The King speaks, 'Away from me, all you who do evil.' Does that remind you of anything? 'On that day', says Jesus at the end of the Sermon on the Mount, the Son of Man will say to people who thought they were insiders, 'Away from me you evildoers' (Matthew 7:22–23). Again, in Luke 13:27, speaking to the same people, the Son of Man will say, 'Away from me, all you evildoers.' Jesus' words echo King David's.

It is a paradox that at the end of this psalm, Jesus, who felt the anger of God against sinners, now expresses that anger against impenitent sinners. In his human nature, he felt that wrath; in his divine nature, he now demonstrates it in final judgement.

Jesus knows God hears and answers his prayers (verse 8–9) so, at the end of time, he will speak these words of confident authority to all who will not turn from sin: 'Away from me.' Jesus can be sure that, 'All my enemies will be overwhelmed with shame and anguish' (verse 10). The choice is stark – you can either have an anguished soul for sins in this life (verse 3) or an anguished soul for all eternity.

Those of us who belong to the Lord Jesus ought to share this longing that evil will be a long way away from us. By God's grace we must not give up the battle against our own sin. While we grieve at the evil that's still in our hearts – and will be until the day of resurrection – and the sadness that sin brings into the world we can rejoice with great hope because one day the Lord Jesus will say, 'Away from me, all you who do evil'. At that point all causes of sin, and therefore all causes of suffering and tears, and therefore, everything that causes trouble and sadness in this life will be banished forever. Jesus will gather into his kingdom every man, woman, and child who's been grieved by sin, and in the new heavens and the new earth everything that causes tears, suffering, sadness, sickness and pain will be excluded for ever.

> We know, O Lord Jesus Christ, that while you were on earth, you did every night water your couch with tears for us: grant us so to repent for our iniquities, that we may hereafter attain to that place where all tears are wiped from all eyes. Amen.
>
> (J. M. Neale, *Rev. J. M Neale Collection*, Aeterna Press, 2016)

Day 102

Read: 2 Corinthians 1:1–11
Key verses: 2 Corinthians 1:1–3

....

*Paul, an apostle of Christ Jesus by the will of God, and Timothy
our brother,
To the church of God in Corinth, together with all his holy people
throughout Achaia:
²Grace and peace to you from God our Father and the Lord
Jesus Christ.
³Praise be to the God and Father of our Lord Jesus Christ, the
Father of compassion and the God of all comfort.*

How can we praise God when we are weighed down with suffering?

Paul has been pushed to the limits of his endurance in his Christian
service (see 2 Corinthians 11–12), and yet he starts his letter to the
Corinthians with thanksgiving. This is not the power of positive
thinking. Paul needed more than this. The ability to praise God when
under pressure can only come from an experience of God's
strengthening comfort. The word 'comfort' is found ten times in five
verses (verses 3–7). The same word describes the Holy Spirit's
ministry in John's Gospel. The Spirit's ministry is to draw alongside,
to strengthen us and equip us when we are tested. No matter what
pressure of affliction we might suffer as Christians, this is more than
matched by God's strengthening presence.

This happened time and again for Paul, and it is true for you and me.
However dark the night or ferocious the storm, God does not
abandon us. When Paul finally arrived in Rome, he was nearing the
end of his life, sitting in a Roman dungeon, cold, lonely, deserted
and close to martyrdom. Yet he wrote to Timothy: 'But the Lord
stood at my side and gave me strength' (2 Timothy 4:17).

We need this word of encouragement because many of us face demanding pressures and carry some heavy burdens. The costs of discipleship are very real, so we shouldn't miss the comforting certainty which runs right through the Bible: 'Even though I walk through the darkest valley, I will fear no evil, for you are with me' (Psalm 23:4).

Paul refers to the source of that comfort in three phrases in verses 2 and 3. Just as grace and peace come 'from God our Father and the Lord Jesus Christ', so our comfort comes from 'the Father of our Lord Jesus Christ, the Father of compassion and the God of all comfort'. They are great descriptions of the God who cares. They are not simply technical or religious phrases, but they describe a profound intimacy with God. It is true for all Christians: we often come to know our Father best through suffering.

However deep your suffering, however dark the valley, you can be certain of this – God has not abandoned you. Our loving Father is an endless source of compassion and comfort. When you're at the end of your own physical and emotional resources, when the way ahead seems too overwhelming, when you feel abandoned and alone, you can put your trust the promises of God: the Lord is standing at your side, giving you strength.

Day 103

Read: 2 Corinthians 1:1–11
Key verse: 2 Corinthians 1:5

....

For just as we share abundantly in the sufferings of Christ, so also our comfort abounds through Christ.

What does the gospel say about suffering?

The heart of the gospel message is that God is at work through the weakness of the crucified Jesus; God's power is displayed in the apparent foolishness of the cross. It should not be a surprise then that God chooses to reveal his power through the weakness of his followers (2 Corinthians 12:9).

We're often quick to minimize suffering, assuming that true faith should be able to overcome difficulties. In contrast, Paul came to understand that his suffering was a mark of true discipleship, the result of fellowship with Christ. He was under attack by some in Corinth who doubted he was a genuine apostle. His missionary work, with its consequent catalogue of sufferings listed in 2 Corinthians 11, was quite literally killing him, and he deliberately and graphically connects those sufferings with Christ: 'For just as we share abundantly in the sufferings of Christ, so also our comfort abounds through Christ' (verse 5).

Suffering is the inevitable result of being united to Christ. It is a natural and normal part of life for Christians. Paul develops the idea in chapter 4: 'We always carry around in our body the death of Jesus . . . we who are alive are always being given over to death for Jesus' sake' (verse 10–11). Paul is explaining that he is sharing his master's earthly experience. Four times in those two verses (4:10–11) he refers to 'Jesus' the man, emphasising his humanity. And the word he uses in verse 10 could be better translated 'we carry around in our body the *dying* of Jesus'. Given the extent of his suffering Paul probably did look like someone in the process of dying. If you are a Christian, united to Jesus Christ, there is no avoiding this identification with his suffering.

In chapter 1 Paul is making the point that far from being evidence of his lack of spirituality, or casting doubts on his leadership, suffering was a badge of his discipleship. It was a clear indication that he was fulfilling his God-given ministry in serving Christ. Sharing 'abundantly in the sufferings of Christ' (verse 5) does not imply that Christ's sufferings in securing our redemption need extending or completing through the experience of Christians. Christ's suffering was unique, complete and once and for all (Romans 5:17–19). No, Paul is describing the intimate relationship between Christ and those who bear his name. Our life is his life. It is no wonder that Paul 'boasted' about his weaknesses (2 Corinthians 12:9). The more he suffered, the more it was evidence of the privilege of being identified with Jesus Christ.

Wounds, particularly from other believers, cut deeply but they shouldn't surprise us. Being united with Christ means as we live for him we will share his suffering, but, praise God, it also means we share in his life. Even now, as you respond to suffering and hurt, God's grace is sustaining you and his power is being displayed in your weakness. Today, ask God for help to see your suffering as part of your service, part of the privilege of being identified with Christ.

Day 104

Read: 2 Corinthians 1:1–11
Key verses: 2 Corinthians 1:3–4, 6–7

....

Praise be to . . . the God of all comfort, ⁴who comforts us in all our troubles, so that we can comfort those in any trouble with the comfort we ourselves receive from God . . . ⁶If we are distressed, it is for your comfort and salvation; if we are comforted, it is for your comfort, which produces in you patient endurance of the same sufferings we suffer. ⁷And our hope for you is firm, because we know that just as you share in our sufferings, so also you share in our comfort.

You are not alone!

If we are united to Christ we are therefore united to one another. Christians are bound to Christ and bound to every believer. So there is a community dimension the Christian experience, including our experience of suffering and comfort.

As we experience the Lord standing alongside us in times of pressure, so we become qualified to bring encouragement and help to others (verse 4). We might not experience the same pressures and troubles as others, but that does not limit our ministry. The experience of comfort itself is the basis for helping others. We are able to help one another 'in any trouble' (verse 4).

In Paul's case it is more than encouragement. 'If we are distressed, it is for your comfort and *salvation*' (verse 6). He says the same in chapter 4: 'So then, death is at work in us, but life is at work in you' (4:12); 'All this is for your benefit' (4:15). His experience of dying actually serves to bring life and salvation to the Corinthians. They are beneficiaries of all that Paul went through. Similarly, our suffering and weakness can be for the eternal benefit of those whom we serve.

Paul knew personally the importance of Christian community. He acknowledged not just his dependence on God (verse 9) but his dependence on God's people: 'you helped us by your prayers' (verse 11). We can do many things to help each other practically but we shouldn't forget to pray. Our prayers for each other achieve something in God's hands.

When we are suffering it is never easy to have the presence of mind to assess objectively how God has helped us. But it is good to remember that, when the pressure is on, God can redeem those experiences and use them for his good purpose of strengthening others in the Christian family.

> When you've passed through your own fiery trials, and found God to be true to what he says, you have real help to offer. You have firsthand experience of both his sustaining grace and his purposeful design. He has kept you through pain; he has reshaped you more into his image... What you are experiencing from God, you can give away in increasing measure to others. You are learning both the tenderness and the clarity necessary to help sanctify another person's deepest distress.
> (ed JohnPiper and Justin Taylor, *Suffering and the Sovereignty of God*, Crossway, 2006, p166)

Day 105

Read: 2 Corinthians 1:1–11
Key verses: 2 Corinthians 1:8–9

．．

We do not want you to be uninformed, brothers and sisters, about the troubles we experienced in the province of Asia. We were under great pressure, far beyond our ability to endure, so that we despaired of life itself. ⁹ Indeed, we felt we had received the sentence of death. But this happened that we might not rely on ourselves but on God, who raises the dead.

Why does God let good people suffer?

Paul describes the hardships he had suffered in Asia, and although the detail of that suffering isn't clear, the severity is (verse 8). For two years he struggled to proclaim Christ in a context of active opposition from others, and the pressures were unbearable: 'We were completely overwhelmed, the burden was more than we could bear, in fact we told ourselves that this was the end' (J.B Phillips).

Why was God allowing Paul to go through such experiences of despair and deep depression? 'This happened that we might not rely on ourselves but on God, who raises the dead' (verse 9). That is God's purpose. Throughout Scripture we find that God takes us through afflictions in order to bring us to a recognition of our own helplessness, to bring our self-confidence to an end, and to teach us exclusive trust in God. In desperate times we learn to hold him fast. If we didn't face these challenges, we would so easily revert back to living independently of God.

Paul says God can be trusted as the one who 'raises the dead' (verse 9). He is not describing a future hope but a daily reality. We are united to Jesus in his death but also in his resurrection life: 'We who are alive are always being given over to death for Jesus' sake, so that his life may also be revealed in our mortal body' (2 Corinthians 4:11).

God can raise up Christians who, like Paul, are despairing of life. Because God had delivered him from 'such a deadly peril', Paul knew God could be trusted for further deliverance, now and in the future: 'On him we have set our hope that he will continue to deliver us' (verse 10).

Of course, it is only a partial deliverance. One day we will face death, though with the same hope of resurrection to which Paul refers. Meanwhile, in times of despair we can trust God's purpose. He is the God of compassion and resurrection. He will not let go of his hold on us. He will deliver us now, in the days ahead, and on the final day of resurrection.

Suffering smashes our illusions of strength and control. It offers a daily opportunity to rely more deeply on God's resurrection life to sustain and comfort us. Today, praise God for the ways he has delivered you and will keep on delivering you until your full and final resurrection. Pray Paul's prayer for yourself and those you know who are suffering:

> I pray that . . . you may know . . . his incomparably great power for us who believe. That power is the same as the mighty strength he exerted when he raised Christ from the dead and seated him at his right hand in the heavenly realms.
> (Ephesians 1:18–20)

Day 106

Read: 2 Corinthians 4:1–18
Key verses: 2 Corinthians 4:16–18

....

Therefore we do not lose heart. Though outwardly we are wasting away, yet inwardly we are being renewed day by day. ¹⁷*For our light and momentary troubles are achieving for us an eternal glory that far outweighs them all.* ¹⁸*So we fix our eyes not on what is seen, but on what is unseen, since what is seen is temporary, but what is unseen is eternal.*

Are you losing heart?

You may be facing unjust criticism; your actions might be being misunderstood and even misrepresented; you may be facing opposition in your family, workplace, or even in your local church.

Paul was dealing with a similar situation. The Corinthian believers are questioning his integrity, in particular his handling of money. They are even now wondering whether they can trust the gospel he has brought to them. Their criticisms are very personal and extremely vicious. Some people complained, 'His letters are weighty and forceful, but in person he is unimpressive and his speaking [or his preaching] amounts to nothing' (2 Corinthians 10:10).

How does Paul cope with being opposed by those he led to faith and having his actions constantly misinterpreted? He focuses on future hope. He writes about how his future hope of the new heavens and the new earth impacts the way he lives in the present. He understands that he can't always expect immediate consolation. He won't always be encouraged by his circumstances but he knows that nothing and no one can touch his certain future. This emphasis in the letter reaches its highest point in 2 Corinthians 4:14–16, some of the most magnificent verses in the whole of the Bible.

Paul urged suffering and stressed Christians to fix their eyes, not on the visible and temporary, but on the unseen and eternal. Is your attention focused on visible things? Or even on the criticisms and poor treatment you have received from those from whom you'd expected help and encouragement? Paul would say if your eyes are on those things, they're on the temporary. Some of these things may seem wonderful, others devastating, but the reality is they are all temporary. Change your focus. Fix your eyes on the eternal glory that awaits you.

> If we are devoid of a theology of suffering, we are in danger of marginalizing our expectations of heaven . . . If we conclude that we are now to experience total healing, unfettered joy, unparalleled success, and freedom from pain, then why be concerned about heaven? How did Paul handle his sufferings and encourage the church to face theirs? Not by trying to produce heaven on earth but by recognizing that for the Christian the best is yet to be. He took the moment and put it in the larger context of God's unfolding purpose, not only for time but also in eternity.
>
> (Alistair Begg, *Made For His Pleasure*, Moody Press, 1996, p. 116)

Day 107

Read: Hebrews 12:4–11
Key verses: Hebrews 12:4–6

. . . .

In your struggle against sin, you have not yet resisted to the point of shedding your blood. ⁵And have you completely forgotten this word of encouragement that addresses you as a father addresses his son? It says,
"My son, do not make light of the Lord's discipline,
and do not lose heart when he rebukes you,
⁶because the Lord disciplines the one he loves,
and he chastens everyone he accepts as his son."

Some of us were promised that becoming a Christian meant we'd be healthy and wealthy every day of our life. So, when life goes wrong, when there is illness, poverty or that blindsiding upset that comes out of the blue, knocking the wind out of our sails, we want to throw in the towel. In contrast, the writer to the Hebrews makes a profound but quite simple point: suffering and opposition are part of normal Christian life.

The key word in this passage is 'discipline'. God disciplines his children for the same reason a parent disciplines a child; it's corrective. The suffering mentioned here is not just persecution it's a struggle against sin. Following Christ involves suffering because it's costly to live life God's way. It may cost you a promotion or a friendship, it may impact your spending or your home life. But there is also a price to pay when we make the wrong choice. Sin charges you far more than you ever expected to pay in lost time, peace, joy and relationships.

We shouldn't make light of these struggles; neither should we be surprised. By taking us back to the ancient words of Proverbs in verses 5–6, the writer is reminding us that discipline has always been part of the ordinary life of following God, from the earliest days of the Old Testament.

Discipline is God – in a variety of ways – saying 'no' to us indulging our passions. We are rebuked (verse 5); we are chastened (verse 6); we pay a price. Perhaps we should avoid calling it a punishment, as Scripture teaches that our punishment has been borne by Christ on the cross. We know 'there is now no condemnation for those who are in Christ Jesus' (Romans 8:1). The punishment has been taken. This divine correction is God saying, 'I love you too much to let you get away with indulging your sinful nature.'

If life has obstacles that God is using to correct us, what should we do? The writer says, 'Do not lose heart' (verse 5). Don't lose heart – it's because he loves you that he rebukes. Don't lose heart – it's because you're a true son of God that he chastens you. Don't lose heart – God loves you too much to leave you as you are.

Are you facing God's discipline today? Don't be surprised, don't make light of it, and, most of all, don't lose heart. Be encouraged that this divine correction is a sign of your Father's relentless love for you and his desire to shape you into the image of Christ. Ask God what he wants you to learn in this season of suffering and be willing to respond in humility and obedience.

Day 108

Read: Hebrews 12:4–11
Key verses: Hebrews 12:7–9

. . . .

[7] Endure hardship as discipline; God is treating you as his children. For what children are not disciplined by their father? [8] If you are not disciplined – and everyone undergoes discipline – then you are not legitimate, not true sons and daughters at all. [9] Moreover, we have all had human fathers who disciplined us and we respected them for it. How much more should we submit to the Father of spirits and live!

I know how to keep my children happy. I know what sweets they like; we've got a TV; we've got computer games. And if I'm working from home and my wife's out, the temptation is to think, 'Anything for an easy life!'

But keeping our children happy is not our responsibility. A caring parent is more interested in their child's character than in their comfort alone. Developing honesty, thoughtfulness, courage and patience is not the same thing as keeping them comfortable. Those characteristics don't come naturally to a child. Sometimes discipline is needed to grow a child's character and prevent them from making wrong decisions.

In the same way, God is more concerned with our character than with our comfort. He disciplines us to make us more like Christ and protect us from harm. So the writer to the Hebrews encourages us to 'endure' discipline rather than trying to avoid it or find the soft option. An indifferent father wouldn't care, but God disciplines us because he loves us. He wants to guard us from dabbling in trouble. His discipline proves that we belong to him and remain in his protection.

Our tendency is to seek comfort, to opt for the easy life. When it comes to moral or ethical issues, we ask 'How far can I drift before I get into sin?' But the Bible's moral foundations are given to show us a vision of the holiness of God so that we say 'This is the one I want to honour with my sexuality, with my time, with my money, with my relationships.' God uses discipline to change our perspective from 'What can I get away with?' to 'How can I best honour God?'

Generally, often in retrospect, we respect the discipline our human fathers gave us (verse 9). The same is true for God's discipline. We accept it because, 'later on . . . it produces a harvest of righteousness and peace for those who have been trained by it' (verse 11). The discipline isn't pleasant but painful. However, the alternative is far worse. To be allowed to indulge our senses, emotions and passions leads to far worse pain in the long run. Those who fall away and those who drift into sin, don't come back with badges of honour to share in Christian fellowship. They come back with regret; they come back with wasted years.

We may never know all the ways God's discipline has kept us from sin and held us back from foolish decisions. Today, thank God for his protection over your life. Commit to 'enduring' rather than avoiding discipline, looking forward to the 'harvest of righteousness and peace' it will produce in your life. And, if you are living with the regret of wasted years, know that it is never too late for forgiveness and to ask, 'How best can I honour God?'

Day 109

Read: Hebrews 12:4–11
Key verses: Hebrews 12:9–10

....

Moreover, we have all had human fathers who disciplined us and we respected them for it. How much more should we submit to the Father of spirits and live! [10] *They disciplined us for a little while as they thought best; but God disciplines us for our good, in order that we may share in his holiness.*

Children have a remarkable sense of fairness. It's amazing how a six-year-old child suddenly becomes a brilliant mathematician when it comes to adding up how much money has been spent on their older sibling, whether it's Christmas presents or sweets.

Parents try their best to be fair (verse 10). But, inevitably, we get it wrong and are uneven in our parenting. But God is fair. It may not look fair in the way he disciplines us; we may feel like the second child, but he knows what he's doing. The unusual expression used to describe God – 'Father of spirits' (verse 9), provides a parallel with earthly fathers. Our heavenly Father, the Father of spirits, unlike us, knows exactly what he's doing. When earthly parents are fair, they command respect. How much more respect is due the Father of spirits, who is always fair?

The problem is that God's discipline can *seem* unfair. What you are going through is different from the person sitting next to you and you don't know why. We question, 'Why does God give *me* these obstacles? Why do *I* have these challenges?' The writer says, God disciples us 'for our good' (verse 10). We tend to go for the easiest route in life, the way a stream always follows the softest earth as it makes its way down the fells. But, the reality is that so much of character growth happens when the challenges are great and we grow to meet them.

Why is God using this discipline in our lives? Why does he allow us to face all these obstacles and trials? Because he wants to make something out of us that is far better than would have been possible in a life of comfort. God has far higher expectations of us than any earthly parent could ever have. Ultimately, it's in order to 'share in his holiness'. God's great intention, his workmanship in our lives, is to make us saints. It contributes to his glory that we partake of his holiness, that we become the people that God wants us to be.

God wants you to 'share in his holiness' – what an amazing thought! It is hard to grasp – but it's true – that as we become more like the Lord Jesus we contribute to God's glory. Yes, discipline is hard to bear; yes, what God allows us to suffer sometimes seems desperately unfair. But knowing God's ultimate goal is for our holiness changes our question from 'Why me?' to 'Who am I Lord, that you should be so concerned about me?' That God would love us so much and have such glorious plans for us surely is a cause for endless adoration.

Day 110

Read: James 1:1–12
Key verses: James 1:1–3

....

James, a servant of God and of the Lord Jesus Christ,
To the twelve tribes scattered among the nations:
Greetings.

²Consider it pure joy, my brothers and sisters, whenever you face trials of many kinds, ³because you know that the testing of your faith produces perseverance.

Is it really possible to, 'consider it pure joy, when you face trials'?

James, the brother of Jesus, the leader of the church in Jerusalem, was writing to Jewish Christian communities scattered across the Roman world. James had seen what Jesus had suffered and he knew the struggles these young believers were facing. Many were subsistence farmers who were being exploited. They faced persecution for their allegiance to Jesus and some were being carried off to court. They were poor and marginalized, described as, 'the brother in humble circumstances' (verse 9). These communities were facing hostile persecution and economic oppression.

Our situations will be very different. But where James has talked about 'trials of many kinds' (verse 2), we can be absolutely sure that he covers your situation and mine – whether that is the pressure of hostility in the workplace or in your family, the loss of somebody you love, the pain of a broken engagement, the disappointment of redundancies or the challenges of deteriorating health.

What do we make of James' charge that we respond with joyfulness? He is not advocating false comfort that denies the pain of the trial we are going through. It is not a celebration of the presence of evil. It is not a trivial remark to be used insensitively in pastoral contexts.

Rather, James is explaining that trials bring particular benefits to those who experience them. The testing of our faith is valuable because it produces perseverance (verse 3). By God's grace, it produces the strength to stand firm and not give up. It builds spiritual muscle. One commentator says the picture is of a person who successfully carries a heavy load for a long time. This is the perseverance that comes from caring for somebody for the long haul, or facing an ongoing battle with illness, or bearing the weight of long-term Christian ministry.

Jeremiah, the prophet, endured a great catalogue of difficulties for forty years, facing trials of all kinds. God promised him, 'Today I have made you a fortified city, an iron pillar and a bronze wall to stand against the whole land' (Jeremiah 1:18). God was inserting vertebrae into Jeremiah's elastic spine. He was strengthening him with this kind of tenacity. Of course we would rather run away from trials. But the wise way to confront a trial is to see that, however painful it is, it is productive because it produces perseverance.

God is not asking us to put a 'fake it till you make it' smile on our face. Our joyful response in the face of suffering is a considered one – it is something we have reflected on and evaluated. Today, take time to consider what God is seeking to achieve in you through your particular suffering. Rejoice that even now he is making 'you a fortified city, an iron pillar and a bronze wall' – a believer shot through with perseverance, faithful for the long haul.

Day 111

Read: James 1:1–12
Key verses: James 1:2–8

....

Consider it pure joy, my brothers and sisters whenever you face trials of many kinds, ³because you know that the testing of your faith produces perseverance. ⁴Let perseverance finish its work so that you may be mature and complete, not lacking anything. ⁵If any of you lacks wisdom, you should ask God, who gives generously to all without finding fault, and it will be given to you. ⁶But when you ask, you must believe and not doubt, because the one who doubts is like a wave of the sea, blown and tossed by the wind. ⁷That person should not expect to receive anything from the Lord. ⁸Such a person is double-minded and unstable in all they do.

What has suffering got to do with Christian maturity?

James' answer is that we persevere under trials 'so that [we] may be mature and complete, not lacking anything' (verse 4). He uses a cluster of words. Sometimes our Bibles may translate 'mature' 'perfect', but it doesn't mean sinless; it means fully complete. The idea of completeness, of integrity and of wholeness, is a central theme for James and runs right through the letter. James' big concern is for integrated Christian living such that the values we profess shape every area of our lives, both public and private. He wants every aspect of our Christian life and Christian community to demonstrate the reality of our faith. In other words, he doesn't want us to compromise with worldly values but to give ourselves wholeheartedly to the Lord. A Christian marked by such maturity and integrity is the opposite of the person he is going to describe in verses 6–8: the wavering, divided person.

The point James is making is that, when a crisis comes or when we are living under sustained trial, it can generate a staying power which in turn means we are on our way to Christian maturity, to the rounded character which God longs to produce. In this demanding process we are not alone: God is providing what we need. James says that we are lacking nothing as God works to make us what we should be.

When you meet believers who have endured trials, often over an extended period, you can spot this kind of Christian maturity. They aren't easily blown off course. They have been carrying a heavy load for many years. The clear result has been the development of their character and their experience of God's grace. They have grown to become more and more like Jesus.

> The way to stronger faith usually lies along the rough pathway of sorrow. Only as faith is contested will faith be confirmed . . . I'm afraid that all the grace I have gotten out of my comfortable and easy times and happy hours, almost lies on a penny. But the good that I have received from my sorrows and pains and griefs is all together incalculable. What do I not owe to the hammer and the anvil, the fire and the file? Affliction is the best bit of furniture in my house.
> (C. H. Spurgeon, *The Complete Works of C. H. Spurgeon Vol. 34*, Delmara Publications, 2015)

Day 112

Read: James 1:1–12
Key verses: James 1:5–8

∙∙

If any of you lacks wisdom, you should ask God, who gives generously to all without finding fault, and it will be given to you. 6But when you ask, you must believe and not doubt, because the one who doubts is like a wave of the sea, blown and tossed by the wind. 7That person should not expect to receive anything from the Lord. 8Such a person is double-minded and unstable in all they do.

The great Puritan writer, John Owen, stressed that what we need in times of trial is 'godly judgement'.

This is because when we are under trial we very easily lose our bearings. We can feel guilty and blame ourselves. We can feel depressed, hopeless and angry towards God and others. Trials can sometimes paralyse us. And, perhaps most common of all, it produces a kind of confusion; a disorientation when our world is shaken and our questions remain unanswered. Soon it all becomes debilitating, and so we need to see things from God's point of view. We need his wisdom.

Wisdom in the Bible is not head knowledge; it is the way of obedience, knowing how to live God's way in God's world (Proverbs 3:6). If we lack wisdom, if we don't know how to single-mindedly obey, James says, 'ask God, who gives generously to all' (verse 5). It's a wonderful promise. God gives generously, freely, as we ask for his grace and his help. Even if you're angry or confused about what's happening, he gives 'without finding fault'.

When James talks about prayer, as he does several times in this letter, he always introduces the conditions. In this case, we are not to come in two minds when we ask for wisdom. Don't be like the doubter, tossed about like the waves of the sea. 'Such a person is double-minded and unstable in all they do' (verse 8). They are suffering from a kind of distracted restlessness that prevents them from learning from the Lord. They try to rely on all kinds of other things, and what is the end result? 'That person should not expect to receive anything from the Lord' (verse 7).

However, James assures us that God's goodness and generosity can be relied upon. If you seek God's wisdom in the middle of this situation, he will be a generous giver. He won't find fault with your angry words or your questions. He won't stop you from beating him on the chest. He's big enough to take all of this. By his grace, he will give you what you need.

When life is going well we rely on our own wisdom, good health and finances, under the illusion that we are in control. Trials bring back into laser focus our need to depend on God and his wisdom. Don't waste this trial. Instead use it as an opportunity to pray, to seek God's face, to lean on him. Bring your questions and doubts with the full assurance that you will receive all the grace and help you need for this trial. Praise God he is so generous with his wisdom and gives 'without finding fault'.

Day 113

Read: James 1:1–12

Key verses: James 1:9–12

. . . .

Believers in humble circumstances ought to take pride in their high position. ¹⁰*But the rich should take pride in their humiliation – since they will pass away like a wild flower.* ¹¹*For the sun rises with scorching heat and withers the plant; its blossom falls and its beauty is destroyed. In the same way, the rich will fade away even while they go about their business.*
¹²*Blessed is the one who perseveres under trial because, having stood the test, that person will receive the crown of life that the Lord has promised to those who love him.*

Have you noticed how suffering changes your perspective?

James gives an example of the kind of change of perspective we need: 'Believers in humble circumstances ought to take pride in their high position' (verse 9). One of the main reasons for instability, for double-mindedness, is our attempt to serve God as well as money and worldly ambition, to live life on our terms, to live life with a secular perspective. Of course, there are dangers with both riches and poverty in this regard. The rich can become too independent of God. The poor can succumb to despair. So James urges the believer in humble circumstances to recognize their status as God's dearly loved child. Equally, he tells the rich that they should be grateful if God humbles them – if the tendency to depend on other things or the desire to accumulate more and more is stripped away and no longer dominates them.

James concludes this section: 'Blessed is the man who perseveres under trial, because when he has stood the test, he will receive the crown of life that God has promised to those who love him' (verse 12). Trials provoke a change in perspective because they help us realize what really matters. What is worth living for? What is worth dying for? James says the final outcome for the person who perseveres under trial – the final proof of the genuineness of their faith and, ultimately, their maturity – is the promised crown of life. James is urging us to take the long-run perspective. When you are facing difficulties, have in mind that final horizon, that crown of life. Keep your eyes on eternity.

Do you remember Job's profound declaration? After going through 'trials of all kinds' he declared what really mattered to him:

> I know that my Redeemer lives,
>   and that in the end he will stand upon the earth
> And after my skin has been destroyed,
>   yet in my flesh I will see God.
> (Job 19:25–26)

Job's new perspective gave him hope, a vital ingredient in walking wisely under trial. That's the sequence that Paul also explains in Romans 5. He asks, 'Why do we rejoice in sufferings?' Because, 'suffering produces perseverance; perseverance, character [maturity]; and character, hope' (Romans 5:3–4). James is saying exactly the same thing.

Trials may strip us of many things – health, loved ones, reputation, finances – but for those who love the Lord the outcome of faithful suffering is the crown of life, eternity with Christ. Today, let this eternal perspective renew your hope, galvanize your obedience and thrill your heart.

Day 114

Read: 1 Peter 1:1–12
Key verses: 1 Peter 1:1

. . . .

Peter, an apostle of Jesus Christ,
To God's elect, exiles, scattered throughout the provinces of
Pontus, Galatia, Cappadocia, Asia and Bithynia.

So much has changed. Once, Christianity was at the centre of our culture. The world felt like our home, like we belonged, but not anymore. Those days are gone, at least in Europe. The letter of 1 Peter was written to people like us: people who were living on the edge of their culture. Peter has a great image to capture this sense of dislocation, of disorientation. He calls his readers 'exiles'; later on, he describes them as 'foreigners and exiles' (1 Peter 2:11). Verse 1 is literally, 'exiles of the scattering or diaspora'. It's a technical term. Five or six hundred years before the Lord Jesus, King Nebuchadnezzar defeated Jerusalem and carried the Jewish people away into exile so that they were scattered among the nations. It's that word 'scattered' that Peter is using. We are the diaspora, the scattered people. Christians are like those exiles in Babylon – we are outsiders, we don't belong any more in our society.

At the end of the letter, Peter sends greetings from Babylon. He's probably making a cryptic allusion to Rome. His point is that this is a letter from exile to exile. Peter feels like he's in exile in Babylon and he's writing to readers who are exiles. It's not that Christians have moved from one country to another. We're exiles because our identity has so radically changed that we're no longer at home, even in the country of our birth.

Now, at this moment in history, it feels like the reason we no longer feel at home is because our culture has changed. But, really, we're the ones that have changed. Peter explains: 'Praise be to the God and Father of our Lord Jesus Christ! In his great mercy he has given us new birth into a living hope through the resurrection of Jesus Christ from the dead, and into an inheritance that can never perish, spoil or fade' (verse 3–4). If you're a Christian, you were reborn as a citizen of heaven. You have a new family, with a new homeland; an inheritance in heaven. We feel like exiles because the world as it is, is not our home. One day the meek will inherit the earth. One day heaven and earth will be renewed. But just not yet.

Living on the margins of society and culture is an uncomfortable place to be. The sense of dislocation and homesickness is a persistent reminder that we're exiles. But this is not news! Believers have always been exiles. We shouldn't be striving to recapture the imagined glory days of the past when we were more accepted by society nor should we be passive, withdrawing from culture altogether. We are exiles with a purpose, reaching out to others with the good news of the living hope found in the counter-cultural gospel of Christ.

Day 115

Read: 1 Peter 1:1–12
Key verses: 1 Peter 1:3–6

. . . .

Praise be to the God and Father of our Lord Jesus Christ! In his great mercy he has given us new birth into a living hope through the resurrection of Jesus Christ from the dead, ⁴and into an inheritance that can never perish, spoil or fade. This inheritance is kept in heaven for you, ⁵who through faith are shielded by God's power until the coming of the salvation that is ready to be revealed in the last time. ⁶In all this you greatly rejoice, though now for a little while you may have had to suffer grief in all kinds of trials.

How do people respond when they find out that you're a Christian?

Some will be kind and affirming, but often people don't like the new values, culture and priorities that come with our new identity.

The sufferings that Peter's readers were facing were not state-sponsored persecution. They were not being imprisoned or martyred. That would come. But they were facing the suspicion and abuse of their neighbours. Peter describes the hostility: 'they accuse you of doing wrong' (2:12); he talks about the 'ignorant talk of foolish men' (2:15) and 'those who speak maliciously against your good behaviour in Christ' (3:16). These Christians are being slandered, abused, marginalized and verbally attacked.

Our experience is very similar in the UK today. We're not persecuted by the state but, every day, we face slander and insult. Our convictions on sexuality, gender, the uniqueness of Christ, and the reality of judgement are viewed as immoral. They 'accuse us of doing wrong', as Peter puts it. But, this shouldn't surprise us. Peter wrote, 'Dear friends, do not be surprised at the fiery ordeal that has come upon you to test you, as though something strange were happening to you' (4:12).

The whole message of the Bible – spoken by the prophets through the Spirit, preached in the gospel, and marvelled on by angels – is this: 'the sufferings of the Messiah and the glories that would follow' (verse 10–12). In other words, according to the Old Testament, we should expect suffering. This pattern of suffering followed by glory is the pattern for God's king, and it's the pattern for those who would follow him. Jesus experienced the ultimate marginalization. We pushed him out of this world and on to the cross. Now we are called to take up our cross and follow him to the margins.

Initially, Peter had raged against the idea of a suffering Messiah being part of God's plan. When Jesus first told the disciples that he was going to suffer and die, Peter said, 'Never Lord! This shall never happen to you!' (Matthew 16:22). But Peter had seen the Messiah die and he was experiencing suffering in his own life. Now, more than ever, he was convinced that suffering 'grief in all kinds of trials' should not come as a surprise to us.

Don't be surprised when you are mocked or marginalized! Suffering for being a Christian isn't the exception to the rule; it *is* the rule. Today, hold fast to God's values and priorities, knowing that you are identifying yourself with Christ; you are carrying your cross and following his pattern of suffering then glory. Your present suffering is the prelude to the eternal inheritance God is keeping for you. Take heart and rejoice – your 'grief in all kinds of trials' is only for a 'little while'; glory is just around the corner!

Day 116

Read: 1 Peter 1:1–12
Key verses: 1 Peter 1:3–6

· ·

Praise be to the God and Father of our Lord Jesus Christ! In his great mercy he has given us new birth into a living hope through the resurrection of Jesus Christ from the dead, ⁴and into an inheritance that can never perish, spoil or fade. This inheritance is kept in heaven for you, ⁵who through faith are shielded by God's power until the coming of the salvation that is ready to be revealed in the last time. ⁶In all this you greatly rejoice, though now for a little while you may have had to suffer grief in all kinds of trials.

Are you rejoicing today?

'In all this' – that is, in this new inheritance, this new homeland into which we've been born; all that Peter has said in verses 3 to 5 – 'you greatly rejoice' (verse 6). We may have to suffer but we have great joy. We may not be at home in the culture any more but we have a new home kept in heaven for us. We may be strangers here on earth, but we're not strangers in heaven. We belong where it matters most – in God's kingdom. We can be joyful because our inheritance is kept for us in the safest of all places; it's in heaven (verse 4). And we are kept safe for our inheritance. We 'are shielded by God's power until the coming of the salvation that is ready to be revealed in the last [day]' (verse 5). Despite all the hostility we might face, God's power sustains us and will bring us home.

How can we be so certain of all of this? Because of Jesus' resurrection: 'He has given us new birth into a living hope through the resurrection of Jesus Christ from the dead' (verse 3). Jesus has gone ahead of us and opened up the way. In fact, he *is* the way. He has defeated sin and one day he will return to take us home.

Peter recognizes that we've staked a lot on someone whom we have never seen. But, he says, a day is coming when Jesus Christ will be revealed. On that day, we will receive the salvation of our souls (verse 9) and our faith in the face of suffering will bring praise; it's praiseworthy. We will be vindicated but, more importantly, Jesus will be vindicated. He will receive praise and glory and honour (verse 7).

When you accept hostility because you're a Christian, you're saying to Jesus, 'I count it an honour to suffer disgrace for your name.' When you accept the sufferings of this life without bitterness, you're saying that Jesus is worth it. At the moment, you may be the only person that sees this. But when Jesus Christ is revealed, your suffering will result in praise, glory and honour and it will be worth it.

Even in the depths of suffering we have cause for great joy – our new home is being kept in heaven for us, we belong to God's kingdom and are being shielded by his power until Christ returns. But our 'inexpressible and glorious joy' now is miniscule compared to the joy we will experience when Jesus returns. Finally the value of our suffering will be seen and we will be caught up in the endless praise of Christ. What a wonderful day!

Day 117

Read: 1 Peter 1:1–12
Key verses: 1 Peter 1:1–2

....

Peter, an apostle of Jesus Christ,
To God's elect, exiles, scattered throughout the provinces of
Pontus, Galatia, Cappadocia, Asia and Bithynia, ²who have
been chosen according to the foreknowledge of God the
Father, through the sanctifying work of the Spirit, to be
obedient to Jesus Christ and sprinkled with his blood:
Grace and peace be yours in abundance.

How can we serve God in the midst of suffering?

In the introduction to his letter, instead of the usual reference to Father, Son, Spirit, Peter deliberately changes the order to Father, Spirit, Son (verse 2). Why? Peter was retelling the exodus story to these suffering believers. It was during the exodus that God's people were first called his 'son', his children. Israel was led out of Egypt to Mount Sinai by the pillars of cloud and fire which represent a picture of the Holy Spirit. There God calls them a holy nation and they are led by the Spirit to be sanctified as God's people; displaying his character to the wider world. Later on in Exodus, a covenant is made when the people are sprinkled with blood to confirm this new identity.

The Israelites are set apart from all the other nations to live under God's reign in such a way as to make him known and display his character to the world around them. God sanctifies them so that there will be one place on earth where people can see the goodness of God's reign. Peter recalls this in verse 2 because he's saying that this story is replayed in the formation of every local church. We are God's people, chosen by the Father, sanctified by the Spirit, sprinkled by blood for obedience to our King, the Lord Jesus, so that we might display the goodness of God's reign to the world around us.

The people around us think that God is a tyrant and that they would be better off without him. Our job is to obey Christ so that people see that life under God's rule is the good life because God is the good Father. All of which means that we are not just exiles; we are also ambassadors. An ambassador is a foreigner by definition. They're sent to a foreign country to represent their homeland; to represent their king. Their job is to live and speak in such a way that people think well of their king. And that's our job – to live and speak in such a way that people think well of our King, the Lord Jesus Christ.

Suffering often means our plans are shelved, our spiritual gifts are not used and our capacity is limited. How can we possibly serve God? It is in our suffering – not just our happy days – that God calls us to be obedient, to live a holy life, to display his goodness. Your love for the Lord, joy in your faith, lack of bitterness and complaining is a testimony to the power of the gospel. Just think of the impact your godly suffering could make on a young person in your church, a colleague at work, or your own children. Today, pray for God's help to live and speak in such a way that people think well of your King.

Day 118

Read: Revelation 2:8–11
Key verse: Revelation 2:8

....

To the angel of the church in Smyrna write:
These are the words of him who is the First and the Last, who
died and came to life again.

One in eight Christians – 340 million Christians – face high levels of persecution and discrimination for their faith. A global pandemic has made the situation worse. Violence has increased, and food supplies in some parts of the world simply don't get to you if you are a Christian.

The Christians in Smyrna knew all about persecution. The city [now called Izmir and the third largest city in Turkey] was known, not only for its impressive architecture, but also for its idol worship. In 26 AD, Smyrna beat ten other cities for the honour of building a temple to the emperor Tiberius. Worship of Roman royalty was strong and, because this state religion was tied up with trade, those who resisted had difficulty making a living and often found themselves destitute.

What made it worse was that this persecution came from within the Jewish community. Jesus says, 'I know about the slander of those who say they are Jews and are not, but are a synagogue of Satan' (verse 9). Christ is not questioning the ethnicity of these Jews but their spirituality. They claim to be the people of God but their behaviour seems more in line with the devil, 'the accuser' (Revelation 12:10). They are accusing Christians, Jews who believe in Jesus, before the Roman authorities. Consequently believers who refused to worship idols were put in prison and many were killed.

What does Jesus say to those who are facing persecution?

To this small church in Smyrna, Jesus says: 'These are the words of him who is the First and the Last' (verse 8). In other words: 'I am the forever God. I am eternal. I was there before the first bacteria came into existence and, while dinosaurs and dodos have become extinct, I remain for ever. I took on a human body; I grew up in it; I ate in it; I worked in it; I was put to death in it. But, I "died and came to life again" – that body now lives for ever by the power of an indestructible life. Suffering Christians, remember that your faith is grounded on my indestructible life. I came back to life so that all who trust in me can live for ever.'

What a hope to have when things seem hopeless!

Today pray for Christians around the world who are being persecuted (for more information go to www.opendoorsuk.org). Pray that they, like us, would draw comfort and strength from knowing that their faith is rooted in the indestructible life of the risen Christ. Pray that our brothers and sisters would have assurance that God knows and cares about every detail of their struggle (verse 9) and is, even now, present with his church (verse 1). Pray that they would persevere and hold fast to the gospel, certain that even in suffering: 'The eternal God is [our] refuge, and underneath are the everlasting arms' (Deuteronomy 33:27).

Day 119

Read: Revelation 2:8–11
Key verse: Revelation 2:9

....

I know your afflictions and your poverty – yet you are rich! I know about the slander of those who say they are Jews and are not, but are a synagogue of Satan.

Imagine a church with no weaknesses at all.

When Jesus speaks to the churches in Revelation 2–3 there is a pattern – a commendation, something the church is doing well; a correction, something they need to repent of; and a motivation, a pointer to eternal life to keep them trusting. But, for Smyrna, the pattern changes. There is no correction. Philadelphia is the only other church without a correction. It's telling that these two churches were the least significant in terms of numbers and influence, signalling that it is more important to be faithful than to be powerful.

To this faithful, suffering community, Jesus says, 'I know your afflictions and your poverty – yet you are rich! I know about the slander of those who say they are Jews and are not' (verse 9). That word 'afflictions' means extreme afflictions; that word for 'poverty' means destitute. Isn't it striking that what Jesus commends as strengths – afflictions, poverty and slander – are the very things we think of as problems. But Jesus says, 'I see. I know. Well done.'

Instead of correction Jesus offers these believers comfort by reminding them that they are rich. He's saying, 'In spite of the affliction that you're going through, God has given you a spiritual treasure chest: spiritual riches that are beyond your wildest dreams!' In a similar way, the apostle Paul describes going through his own struggles as: 'having nothing, and yet possessing everything' (2 Corinthians 6:10).

In 160 AD, years after John wrote this letter, Polycarp, the Bishop of Smyrna, was martyred for not burning incense to the imperial gods. He was offered freedom in exchange for renouncing his faith but he was said to have replied, 'Eighty-six years I have served him [Jesus] and he has done me no wrong. How can I blaspheme my King and my Saviour?' These spiritual riches were so deeply felt in his soul that all he could see was blessing. More than that, troubles actually increase our riches. Paul explained, 'Our light and momentary troubles are achieving for us an eternal glory that far outweighs them all' (2 Corinthians 4:17). Suffering is making our experience of the new creation even better than it would have otherwise been. On that final day we won't begrudge someone who has been steamrollered for their faith being closer to Jesus than we are; or someone who's spent years in prison for their faith being in charge of more heavenly cities than we are.

If you are counting the cost of upholding God's values in your workplace or among friends you may not feel rich. But you are! Not only do you have 'an inheritance that can never perish, spoil or fade' (1 Peter 1:4); you have life with Christ now – sins forgiven, righteousness applied, daily grace. You know the peace and presence of Christ; you have hope and a purpose. Suffering cannot erode this; it only makes eternal glory even sweeter. Praise God for the 'boundless riches of Christ' that are yours, now and for ever (Ephesians 3:8).

Day 120

Read: Revelation 2:8–11
Key verse: Revelation 2:10–11

. . . .

> *Do not be afraid of what you are about to suffer. I tell you, the devil will put some of you in prison to test you, and you will suffer persecution for ten days. Be faithful, even to the point of death, and I will give you life as your victor's crown.*
> ¹¹*Whoever has ears, let them hear what the Spirit says to the churches. The one who is victorious will not be hurt at all by the second death.*

God never promised life would be easy.

For believers in Smyrna the suffering is going to get worse. The Romans are going to put them in prison, they are going to be persecuted and some will even die. Things are not going to get better in the short term. But, the persecution is limited. Jesus says that they will suffer for 'ten days' (verse 10). Ten days was the standard time that people were put in prison before they were sent into the arena as a gladiator to fight to their death. But, more likely, the figure is symbolic for the fullness of the suffering that they would experience and also a reminder that it was limited; that Jesus is in control.

If trouble is going to come to you today, it is going to have to come through Jesus Christ. When it's over, if we stay faithful, there is eternal life to come. Jesus will give you, 'life as your victor's crown' (verse 10). In Smyrna the famous Street of Gold curved around the top of the mountain that went up 500 feet from the harbour. It was said to look like a necklace on a statue of a goddess but, more commonly, it was known as the 'Crown'. Jesus' point is that the real crown is not achievement in this life but the permanent life given to faithful Christians: tears wiped away; bodies made new; crowns on our heads; seeing the brilliance of the face of Jesus for ever.

For believers, eternal life means the second death – the day of judgement before God – is nothing to fear (see Revelation 20:14 – 15). Our existence will not end in suffering and death, although it will be part of our story this side of glory. We don't know the hardships that God will call us to walk through. But we can persevere in suffering, knowing that it's worth it because it is the gateway to eternal life and to unending joy.

It's tempting to avoid suffering at all costs – choosing tolerance over truth, keeping silent when we should speak out for Christ, living such indistinct lives that our worldliness contradicts any claims we make about his uniqueness. Ask God to reveal how you might be compromising in order to avoid persecution at work or in your community. Trust God that any trouble you face because of your allegiance to him will be filtered through his hands. Pray for help to persevere today as you look forward to receiving 'life as your victor's crown'.

Day 121

Read: Revelation 21:1–27
Key verses: Revelation 21:1–5

....

Then I saw "a new heaven and a new earth," for the first heaven and the first earth had passed away, and there was no longer any sea. ²I saw the Holy City, the new Jerusalem, coming down out of heaven from God . . . ³And I heard a loud voice from the throne saying, 'Look! God's dwelling-place is now among the people, and he will dwell with them . . . ⁴"He will wipe every tear from their eyes. There will be no more death" or mourning or crying or pain, for the old order of things has passed away.' ⁵He who was seated on the throne said, "I am making everything new!"

What does God promise suffering Christians?

John, himself exiled on the island of Patmos, is writing to persecuted believers. Imagine standing alongside John while God draws the curtains back to reveal a brief glimpse into heaven. What does John see? That evil will not triumph, the Lamb is on his throne, and Jesus and his people are and will be victorious. Alongside this, God gives the most glorious promise: 'I am making everything new!' (verse 5).

There is going to be a 'new heaven', a 'new earth', and a 'new Jerusalem'. The word translated 'new' means 'new in kind'; not a new edition of the same thing. We're looking ahead to complete transformation. Part of this transformation will be the removal of seven evils. The first is very interesting: 'there was no longer any sea' (verse 1). Of course, this is picture language and the sea is a picture of restlessness. In the book of Revelation, the Beast comes up out of the sea. Isaiah says, 'The wicked are like the tossing sea, which cannot rest' (Isaiah 57:20). So there is going to be rest in the new heaven, but not the rest of idleness. It will actually be rest from restlessness. Our deepest spiritual needs will be finally satisfied: 'To the thirsty I will give water without cost from the spring of the water of life' (verse 6).

There's also going to be rest from evildoers, the cowardly, and the unbelieving (verse 8). The holy city is described as having 'a great, high wall with twelve gates . . . twelve angels at the gates' (verse 12). Clearly, these angels are controlling who goes in and who goes out, guaranteeing 'nothing impure will ever enter in' (verse 27). There will be rest from evil and evildoers in the total security of the heavenly city.

When God makes everything new the other six evils will also be vanquished. There will be no mourning, weeping, death, or pain (verse 4). There will be an end to the curse (verse 27, see also Revelation 22:3). There will be no night and no more of the fears and doubts associated with the night (verse 25). For those who are suffering, this is the precious promise we cling to: 'I am making everything new.'

> The hope of Scripture acknowledges our loss and . . . offers this heart-expanding response: As dark as life is, the light will be greater still. Scripture does not minimize the sorrow; it maximizes the promise. God's victory and the world's renewal will be so perfect and eternal that it will be worth it in the end.
> (Eric Tonjes, *Either Way, We'll Be All Right*, NavPress, 2021, p. 159)

Day 122

Read: Revelation 21:1–27
Key verses: Revelation 21:1–4

....

Then I saw "a new heaven and a new earth," for the first heaven and the first earth had passed away, and there was no longer any sea. ²I saw the Holy City, the new Jerusalem, coming down out of heaven from God, prepared as a bride beautifully dressed for her husband. ³And I heard a loud voice from the throne saying, 'Look! God's dwelling-place is now among the people, and he will dwell with them. They will be his people, and God himself will be with them and be their God. ⁴"He will wipe every tear from their eyes. There will be no more death" or mourning or crying or pain, for the old order of things has passed away.'

What will the best thing about the new heaven and new earth be?

God holds back the curtain and allows the apostle John, and us, a glimpse into eternity future, and we see God himself is with his people (verse 3). This is the end of a very long journey. The God who came to his people in the tabernacle and the temple; who became flesh and lived among us; who then, through the presence of the Holy Spirit, made our bodies his temple; is finally with us, among his people. God is where he has always wanted to be. Our sins and our wanderings away from him cannot hinder him from drawing close.

And when God is among us one of the things he will do is wipe every tear from our eyes (verse 4). You can't live this life without the experience of loss and pain, in fact it increases as you grow older. You may be facing the loss of someone you love; the pain of illness; the shame of failure in your life; the sheer difficulty of standing for Christ in your situation; the trials of Christian ministry. In the darkness of such moments, a brilliant light blazes. It's the light of our certain future; the reward for the faithful. It's the security of God's presence and his personal consolation as he – not an angel – wipes away every tear from our eyes. Chrysostom, an early church Father, summed it up well, 'If one man (Christian) should suffer all the sorrows of all the saints in the world, yet they are not worth one hour's glory in heaven.' (Martin Manser, *The Westminster Collection of Christian Quotations*, John Know Press, 2001, p. 330)

The God who wept at Lazarus' tomb, who is with us in our broken-ness, comforting us in our grief, will, one day, once-and-for-all, wipe away our tears. Today we can look forward with joy to that future day when at last God will be with us, redeeming our suffering.

Christ and His cross are not separable in this life; howbeit Christ and His cross part at heaven's door, for there is no house-room for crosses in heaven. One tear, one sigh, one sad heart, one fear, one loss, one thought of trouble cannot find lodging there.
(Samuel Rutherford and Andrew Bonar, *Letters of Samuel Rutherford*, Robert Carter and Bros, 1863, p. 384)

Further Study

If you would like to read more on the theme of suffering, you might find this selection of books helpful.

- Catherine Campbell, *Broken Works Best* (10Publishing, 2018)

- Timothy Keller, *Walking with God through Pain and Suffering* (Hodder and Stoughton, 2015)

- Paul Mallard, *Invest Your Suffering* (IVP, 2014)

- Amy Orr-Ewing, *Where Is God in all the Suffering?* (The Good Book Company, 2020)

- Matt Searles, *Tumbling Sky* (10 Publishing, 2017)

- Eric Tonjes, *Either Way, We'll Be All Right* (NavPress, 2021)

- Paul David Tripp, *Suffering: Gospel hope when life doesn't make sense* (Crossway, 2018)

- Kristen Wetherell and Sarah Walton, *Hope When It Hurts* (The Good Book Company, 2017)

Grace

Contributors

Day 123

Read: Titus 2:11–14
Key verses: Titus 2:11, 14

....

11 For the grace of God has appeared that offers salvation to all people . . . 14 [Jesus Christ] gave himself for us to redeem us from all wickedness and to purify for himself a people that are his very own, eager to do what is good.

Whom does grace save?

All kinds of people, without distinction, are saved by grace (verse 11). There is no other way to be saved. But you need to realize you need saving. The Bible tells us that we all need rescued from the tidal wave of God's wrath against our wickedness (verse 14). God's wrath is his settled, just, controlled, personal hostility to all that is wicked in the world, including us. One day God is going to bring justice to bear in a way that is completely comprehensive and, when we look at our lives, we know we have much to fear. Those who were saved in Crete saw Titus' assessment of themselves and agreed: 'At one time we too were foolish, disobedient, deceived and enslaved by all kinds of passions and pleasures. We lived in malice and envy, being hated and hating one another' (Titus 3:3).

How does grace save?

The word 'redeem' (verse 14) comes from the slave market. Imagine I get into terrible debt. My wife, myself and my children are sold into slavery because we can't pay the debts. But I have a brother who loves me very much and he works night and day, year after year, to pay off my debts. One day he redeems me, he buys me back. It's nothing that I've done; all I've done is build up debt. But my brother has paid my debt.

That is what Jesus Christ has done. He has paid off our debt. He has redeemed us by dying on the cross. All God's righteous anger and his punishment for the sins of the world – the selfishness, hatred, envy, greed and arrogance, dishonesty, the lies in your heart and mine – hit one man, at one moment in history, with such terrible force that he cried out, 'My God, my God why have you forsaken me?' Jesus redeems us by saving us from God's anger through the cross so I don't have to perish and pay for my sins in hell.

How does God feel about us today? He is delighted with us. Why? Because he's delighted with Jesus and now we relate to God through Christ's performance, not our own, we're given Christ's righteousness. When God sees me, he sees Christ. That's the wonder of the gospel, the wonder of grace.

> In the New Testament, grace means God's love in action toward people who merited the opposite of love. Grace means God moving heaven and earth to save sinners who could not lift a finger to save themselves. Grace means God sending his only Son to the cross to descend into hell so that we guilty ones might be reconciled to God and received into heaven.
> (J. I. Packer, *Knowing God*, Hodder & Stoughton, 1975, p. 280)

Today, thank God for his redeeming grace.

Day 124

Read: Titus 2:11–14
Key verses: Titus 2:11–12

....

[11] For the grace of God has appeared that offers salvation to all people. [12] It teaches us to say "No" to ungodliness and worldly passions, and to live self-controlled, upright and godly lives in this present age

What happens after we are saved?

Titus faced a mountainous job in Crete. He had to plant churches, select the leadership and set standards for Christian integrity in a city where one of their own prophets said, 'Cretans are always liars, evil brutes, lazy gluttons' (Titus 1:12).

Again and again Titus appealed for a lifestyle that adorns the message of Christ. 'Urge the younger women . . . to be pure, to be busy at home, to be kind, and to be subject their husbands' Why? 'So that no one will malign the word of God' (verse 5). 'Encourage the younger men to be self-controlled' (verse 6). Why? 'So that those who oppose you may be ashamed because they have nothing bad to say about us' (verse 8). Even slaves must not 'steal . . . but . . . show they can be trusted' Why? 'So that in every way they will make the teaching about God our Saviour attractive' (verse 10).

If this message of Christ actually transforms people's lives, consistently and repeatedly, if the Cretans of chapter 1:12 become self-controlled, upright and godly (2:12), then people will stop and take note. But where is the power to go from Titus 1:12 to Titus 2:12? How can we live out the Christian message so there is no credibility gap between what we believe and how we behave? The power is in understanding verses 11–14. The key word is grace: 'for the grace of God that brings salvation has appeared to all men.'

Grace is generosity, unmerited favour, being given freely something that I don't deserve. Understanding God's grace to us in Christ motivates a change of behaviour. Grace also empowers our transformation and good deeds. John Stott often said, 'Grace is love that cares, and stoops and rescues.' This doesn't stop at salvation. We will still fail God but he goes on caring, stooping and rescuing. God knows all that I've done and he loves me anyway – that's the wonder of grace.

> If other people knew you like God knows you, all your faults, all your vain thoughts, all your sins, all the wrong things in your heart, all the wrong thoughts you ever had, would they trust you with the kind of work God trusts you with? Here is the supreme confidence that God has in his own grace, that he takes the likes of you and me and gives us the privilege of being his saints.
> (Australian Bishop Alf Stanway to men entering the ministry in Pittsburgh in the 1950s).

Every time you tell the truth, offer forgiveness, don't give in to temptation, avoid gossip – and a host of other things – you are leaning on God's grace and modelling gospel transformation. Your life is adorning the gospel; you are closing the credibility gap.

Today, thank God for his unstoppable grace toward you displayed in his 'love that cares, and stoops and rescues'.

Day 125

Read: Titus 2:11–14
Key verses: Titus 2:11–14

....

> [11] *For the grace of God has appeared that offers salvation to all people.* [12] *It teaches us to say "No" to ungodliness and worldly passions, and to live self-controlled, upright and godly lives in this present age,* [13] *while we wait for the blessed hope – the appearing of the glory of our great God and Saviour, Jesus Christ,* [14] *who gave himself for us to redeem us from all wickedness and to purify for himself a people that are his very own, eager to do what is good.*

Why does grace save?

So that Christ might have a new people that are not caught up in wickedness but are now living righteous transformed lives. Jesus redeemed us in order 'to purify for himself a people that are his very own, eager to do what is good' (verse 14).

Our lives here are to be lived between two events: the cross where we are redeemed, where we're forgiven because Christ has paid for our sin, and the new creation. We wait, and either we will die and be woken by Jesus, or he will return to rule. When Christ died he redeemed me, he saved me from the penalty of sin and I'm now waiting to be rescued from the presence of sin.

It's as though I'm drowning, and the lifeguard plucks me out of the sea and puts me on the life raft. He says to me, 'Hang on, I'll be back soon to haul you into land.' I've been saved. I'm no longer in danger, but I am now sitting on the life raft in the sea. And that's true of us. We're safe because of the cross, but now we are waiting and as we wait on the life raft what do we do? The one thing we should not do is plunge back into the wickedness. I say to other people that I can see drowning, 'Come to the raft' and they look up and they see how we're living and they say, 'That's where the truth is. I must swim to the raft.'

Grace 'teaches us to say "No" to ungodliness and worldly passions, and to live self-controlled, upright and godly lives in this present age' (verse 12). Don't leap back into ungodliness. Ask mature brothers and sisters in Christ to help you say 'No' to sin. And resolve, in God's strength, to be eager to do good deeds and to present grace to a dying world.

Imagine yourself on the life raft. You're relieved to be saved but anxious for those still drowning. Whose faces do you see in the water – family members, friends, work colleagues?

Today, pray that you'd have the opportunity to share the gospel with these loved ones and encourage them to, 'Come to the raft'. Pray that the purity of your life and your good deeds would make God's grace attractive to them.

Day 126

Read: Ephesians 2:1–10
Key verse: Ephesians 2:4–5

....

But because of his great love for us, God, who is rich in mercy,
⁵made us alive with Christ even when we were dead in
transgressions – it is by grace you have been saved.

What does it mean to be 'saved by grace'?

We were living a life of sin, not necessarily an openly scandalous one; it might have been a very respectable, useful, even an admired life. But it was profoundly sinful because God was not at the centre; self was enthroned. Paul explains, we were 'dead in our sins' (verse 1) meaning dead toward God, separated from him and without the eternal life he gives. It means guilty and condemned, with a guilt that cannot be denied and a condemnation that cannot be removed by any human means: not by tears, good works, religious practices, therapy or mysticism. We were utterly helpless to save ourselves.

But God sent Jesus to die in our place and 'in him we have redemption, the forgiveness of sins' (Ephesians 1:7). At every point where we failed, Jesus succeeded. He lived the sinless life we could not live and he died the atoning death we could not die. God raised him from the dead on that first Easter Sunday morning. Now we who were far off have been brought near by the blood of Christ. We who were dead are made alive to God, his sons and daughters by the adoption of grace. At the moment of our conversion the Spirit of God comes into our hearts and unites us with the living Christ; the sinner on earth united with the Saviour in heaven. The Holy Spirit himself is the link: permanent, unbreakable, and utterly adequate.

In that act of union we are no longer chained to a great defeat (either Adam's or our own), no longer trapped in a doomed world or bound to a great condemnation. Instead, we share Christ's past: his perfect obedience and his once-and-for-all atonement for sin, his resurrection and his heavenly life and glory with the Father. We also have a new future – a new life, a new Lord and a new allegiance and it is all because of grace (verse 5, 8–9). Grace is mentioned over one hundred times in the writings of Paul. It is at the very heart of the gospel. Grace is the unmerited favour of God, his undeserved help, his free gift of salvation. The stress is always on the freeness of what is given. Grace speaks of God's initiative, patience and love for the unworthy. Grace doesn't leave you desperately trying to earn the love of God, unsure and exhausted. Rather it puts wings on your feet and a song in your heart knowing that nothing in life or death can separate you from this divine commitment.

It is the most counterintuitive aspect of Christianity, that we are declared right with God not once we begin to get our act together but once we collapse into honest acknowledgment that we never will. (Dane C. Ortlund, *Gentle and Lowly: The heart of Christ for sinners and sufferers*, Crossway, 2020, p. 78)

Thank God that our salvation and God's eternal commitment to us is not based on anything we have done – or not done – but wholly achieved and guaranteed by God's amazing grace.

Day 127

Read: Ephesians 2:1–10
Key verse: Ephesians 2:8–10

....

> [8] *For it is by grace you have been saved, through faith – and this is not from yourselves, it is the gift of God –* [9] *not by works, so that no one can boast.* [10] *For we are God's handiwork, created in Christ Jesus to do good works, which God prepared in advance for us to do.*

Grace is not merely an attitude in God, it is an action by God. It is not only his activity at the start of our Christian lives lifting us out of condemnation, it is his ongoing activity in our lives: in our days and nights, in our advances and set-backs, in our victories and defeats, in our youth and old age.

And as such it means God isn't finished with us yet. Grace is God, who began a good work in us, continuing it all the way to completion (Philippians 1:6). Grace is God at work persistently in our lives, enabling, empowering and encouraging us. Paul calls us, 'God's work of art' (verse 10 Jerusalem Bible). We are a work in progress certainly, very unfinished and incomplete. But God himself is at work in us, conforming us more perfectly into the image of his Son. Developing that image, deepening it, growing, maturing and perfecting us. He is like a sculptor chiselling away, getting rid of the surplus and the useless.

At our conversion we are callow saints, full of inconsistencies and areas of real weakness. So God continues the work that he has begun. Sanctification is our growth in holiness, our resemblance to God, our family image. God, who sets us apart for himself at the start, claims more and more of our lives. Only when we are sanctified are we safe. Every unsanctified area is a danger area, a gap in our defences, a wound open to disease and ruin. It may be a relationship which is unwise or forbidden. It may be an element of our character or behaviour which is potentially harmful to our self or others. It may be a stage in our career, a talent or an opportunity. And God says, 'I want that area of your life.'

God is in the business of changing people. He's not a static observer, an invigilator in life's exam or a marker at the end. He's an active participator, saying, 'I myself will be with you. I myself will sanctify you through and through.' What a transition, what a change! From dead in trespasses and sins to alive in Christ; from following the course of this world to reigning with Christ in the heavenly realms; from an object of wrath to a dearly loved child; from a life lost, to a work of art developed and perfected through eternal ages. What grace!

You may be conscious of your sin and how imperfectly you bear God's image. But don't be discouraged, God has committed himself to your transformation. The same grace that saved you is today at work in you, changing you into Christ's likeness. Even now, you are his work of art! A 'display of his splendour' (Isaiah 61:3), showcasing the triumph of his grace to everyone who watches your life.

Day 128

Read: Romans 6:1–14
Key verses: Romans 6:1–2

. . . .

What shall we say, then? Shall we go on sinning so that grace may increase? ²By no means! We are those who have died to sin; how can we live in it any longer?

Does it matter if we keep on sinning?

Paul has just explained that our inability to keep the law means it can't save us. The law, although good, only points out how far we fall short of God's standards; the greater our distance from God's perfect standards, the greater God's grace is in saving us (Romans 5:20–21).

If increased sin means increased grace, should we just carry on sinning? Paul answers, 'By no means!' (verse 2). Salvation is not like a kidney donor card – only there to be used at your death, if necessary. It is not a certificate of justification that says, 'This person is right with God'. It is not a decision that makes no difference to life between the moment of your conversion and your glorification. That idea massively diminishes what salvation is all about. You've received not just a new status but a whole new life. You're a new person. You've experienced a death and a resurrection through union with Christ.

The New Testament's favourite way of describing the Christian is someone who is 'in Christ'; 164 times in Paul's letters, we find the expression: 'in Christ'. By faith we've been united to Christ by the Spirit as a tree has been united to its branches, as a limb is united to the body, as a husband is united to his wife, as the Father and the Son are united in the Trinity; these are all analogies that the Bible uses. We are in Christ, bound up with him.

So when Paul urges us, 'Count yourselves', understand yourselves, 'dead to sin but alive to God in Christ Jesus' (verse 11), he's not saying 'dead to sin' in the sense of being incapable of sinning (our experience tells us what nonsense that is) but, rather, 'dead to sin' in the sense of not being any longer under its tyranny because we've been united to Christ.

Paul is not saying that sin is impossible for the Christian but that it is completely inappropriate. It should be unthinkable for us. Don't you know who you are? You are no longer simply descended from Adam, you've been joined to Jesus Christ. You're a new person in him. You've died and risen with him. Now, as someone who no longer belongs to the old tyranny of sin, death and law but someone who's under the liberating reign of grace, live accordingly.

Today begin to grasp the magnitude of your salvation and:

Embrace the flooding liberations of the gospel all the way down – not the decaffeinated grace that pats us on the hand, ignores our deepest rebellions, and doesn't change us, but the high-octane grace that takes our conscience by the scruff of the neck and breathes new life into us with a pardon so scandalous that we cannot help but be changed.

(Dane Ortlund, *Surprised by Jesus,* Evangelical Press, 2021, p. 18)

Day 129

Read: 2 Corinthians 12:7–10
Key verse: 2 Corinthians 12:9

....

⁹But he [God] said to me, "My grace is sufficient for you, for my power is made perfect in weakness." Therefore I will boast all the more gladly about my weaknesses, so that Christ's power may rest on me.

What are you counting on?

Paul uses the perfect tense in Greek – '[God] *has said* to me, "My grace is sufficient for you."' In the past, God had spoken to Paul about the sufficiency of his grace so Paul knew this great truth before he went through the experience described in these verses.

Whatever suffering we pass through, whatever questions we have, there is one basic fixed point and that is God's grace towards us. Paul knew this. Everything which was good about him, he attributed not to himself but to the undeserved favour with which God looked at him.

He attributed his conversion not to a sudden change of heart or stroke of genius on his part but because God, in his sovereign grace, broke into his life and revealed Jesus not only *to* him but *in* him: 'When God, who set me apart from my mother's womb and called me by his grace, was pleased to reveal his Son in me' (Galatians 1:15–16).

He spoke in exactly the same way about his subsequent service. 'By the grace of God I am what I am' (1 Corinthians 15:10). Though he could rightly point out his hard work and effort it was with the rider, 'Yet not I, but the grace of God that was with me.' He owed every-thing to God's favour toward him.

When Paul was suffering, he prayed to God but he didn't get the answer he wanted. Instead God reminded him of what he had already said, 'My grace is sufficient for you.' There were many things Paul did not understand about his 'thorn in the flesh,' but what mattered more than anything else was that God didn't look upon him as he deserved but according to his grace. This applies to us too: what matters most is that God looks on us with grace and that really is sufficient for us. We can pray, 'Lord, even though I long to get the answer I want to my prayers, I realize that, though I don't deserve it and I have made mistakes, you still look on me with favour and I rejoice in that.'

The perfect tense of the Greek verb also indicates that it has present significance. What God has said in the past about his grace is still true now and it goes on being true; it will never not be sufficient. Our relationship with God is based on what is sometimes called, 'The covenant of God's grace'. It is a covenant (promise) that will never break, a grace that never fails. In our darkest days we might cry out like the psalmist, 'Has God forgotten to be gracious?' (Psalm 77:9 ESV). But Paul reminds us of the answer here. God would never forget to be gracious.

My name from the palms of His hands
Eternity will not erase;
Impressed on His heart, it remains
In marks of indelible grace.
('A Debtor to Mercy Alone', Augustus Toplady, 1740–1778)

Day 130

Read: 2 Corinthians 12:7–10
Key verse: 2 Corinthians 12:7–9

....

In order to keep me from becoming conceited, I was given a thorn in my flesh, a messenger of Satan, to torment me. [8] Three times I pleaded with the Lord to take it away from me. [9] But he said to me, "My grace is sufficient for you, for my power is made perfect in weakness." Therefore I will boast all the more gladly about my weaknesses, so that Christ's power may rest on me.

Do you ever think, 'If only this problem was taken away from me, I would be a much better Christian'?

Paul felt like this. We don't know whether his 'thorn in the flesh' was an illness, a difficult circumstance, a personal weakness, or something else, but it was something the devil could exploit to cause Paul to sin and he felt he'd be a much better Christian without it. Three times he asked God to remove it and the answer was, 'My grace is sufficient for you.' This is the way he would prove the sufficiency of God's grace.

God said to Paul, 'my power is made perfect in weakness.' 'Perfect' means, 'to achieve its purpose'. The way God's power achieves its purpose in us is so often through our weakness. That doesn't mean we are to make life deliberately difficult for ourselves to prove God's power. Paul says the thorn was 'given' to him. It was something that the devil did which God, in his overriding sovereignty, was able to repeatedly turn to his own good purpose. The purpose was, 'so that Christ's power may rest on me', literally 'pitch his tent upon me', just as God's glory dwelt in the Old Testament tabernacle. It seems: 'The greater the servant's weakness, the more conspicuous is the power of the Master's all sufficient grace' (Philip Hughes, *The Second Epistle to the Corinthians*, NICNT, Eerdmans, 1962, p. 451).

Paul explains that this thorn was given to him to prevent him becoming conceited after he'd had a great revelation from God (2 Corinthians 12:1–7). He had to learn not to boast in his spiritual experience which set him apart from other believers but in the weakness that proved God's power. Sometimes we can be in danger of developing a 'holier than thou' attitude, thinking we know it all and God has to deal with our spiritual pride by reminding us of our weakness.

No doubt Paul had very different ideas when he offered his prayer to God. But God said to him, 'My grace is sufficient for you, my power is made perfect in weakness.' So Paul responds to God's Word, 'I will boast all the more gladly about my weaknesses, so that Christ's power may rest on me.'

How do you respond when, despite your prayers, God doesn't take away your suffering or change your circumstances? Instead of getting stuck wishing things were different, will you accept your weaknesses as an opportunity to prove again and again the power of God and that God's favour towards you is what matters most of all?

Day 131

Read: 1 Peter 5:1–15
Key verses: 1 Peter 5:10–12

∙∙

¹⁰And the God of all grace, who called you to his eternal glory in Christ, after you have suffered a little while, will himself restore you and make you strong, firm and steadfast. ¹¹To him be the power for ever and ever. Amen.
¹²With the help of Silas, whom I regard as a faithful brother, I have written to you briefly, encouraging you and testifying that this is the true grace of God. Stand fast in it.

For years I was told that there must be something wrong with me because God would never allow my disability, if I had faith. But I find it hugely helpful that Peter is writing to a suffering church to tell them that suffering is normal for Christians. It is true that God heals, and I pray for healing every day, but the true grace of God that Peter has described throughout his epistle is like the J-Curve (Paul Miller, *J-Curve: Dying and Rising with Jesus in Everyday life*, Crossway, 2019).

The letter J goes down like Jesus going down into suffering, death and the grave and curves up as he's resurrected by the Spirit's power and ascends to glory. What we see in Jesus' life is suffering first, then glory, and that's the pattern we should expect too (verse 9). We follow Christ's example of going down into suffering, waiting for the Spirit's power to bring resurrection life into our life. We are not looking for glory right now, but we know there will be glory one day when Jesus returns. This is the true grace of God. We stand firm in this grace through, amongst other things, prayer, reading Scripture, meditating on it and applying its truth to our lives.

This suffering will only last a little while (verse 10). When life is hard and painful it may seem like God isn't working. But this is being at the bottom of the curve and it's actually the true grace of God. Wait there, knowing that Christ himself did the same thing. He went to the cross and down into the grave for you, so that this would not be the end of your story. So that the suffering you are going through now and eternal suffering in hell would not be the end; so that there would be a new chapter in your life, where you would live with Jesus in the new heavens and earth for all eternity. This is what Jesus has done for us so we can wait a little while at the bottom of the curve in hope, knowing that Jesus is with us and will bring resurrection life into our situations.

God's grace is not only evident in healing, answered prayers and happy times. Your suffering – now or in the future – is not a tragic mistake or a lapse in God's control, it is true grace. Today will you stand firm in the faith, full of hope, strong in God's strength and believing his promise: 'the God of all grace, who called you to his eternal glory in Christ, after you have suffered a little while, will himself restore you and make you strong, firm and steadfast.'

Day 132

Read: 2 Timothy 2:1–7
Key verse: 2 Timothy 2:1

....

You then, my son, be strong in the grace that is in Christ Jesus.

Paul was leaving Timothy in a very tough situation.

Paul is in prison, probably days away from death, and dealing with the massive disappointment of the defection of all the believers in Asia (1:15). Timothy is separated from his mentor and isolated in Ephesus because he remains faithful to God and to Paul. What last words does Paul say to Timothy to encourage him at such a difficult time?

Paul is not anticipating that Timothy would join the crowd of defectors. He says, 'You then, my son, be strong'. This can also be translated, 'But as for you' Paul expected Timothy to stand against the tide. How can he do this? Paul explains: 'Be strong in the grace that is in Christ Jesus'. He uses exactly the same word in Ephesians 6:10, 'Finally, be strong' – then he adds the words, 'in the Lord and in his mighty power.'

We know that the meaning of the word grace is unmerited favour. When we were utterly unable to help ourselves, sinners dead in our sins, cut off from God, we received his grace. That's why we are Christians, not because of our resolve or commitment, but because of his grace. That same grace, the unmerited help of Christ, is there to strengthen us for daily Christian living. John Stott says, 'It's not only for salvation that we are dependent on grace. We are dependent on grace for service as well' (John Stott, *The Message of 2 Timothy: Guard the Gospel*, Bible Speaks Today series, IVP, 2021).

Throughout the epistles, Paul seems to be encouraging Timothy to stand firm. In the context of using his spiritual gifts Paul tells him,

'For the Spirit God gave us does not make us timid, but gives us power, love and self-discipline' (1:7). In chapter 2 he urges, 'Join with me in suffering' (2:3). There are many other references which show Timothy is not naturally resilient. But still, in this incredibly difficult situation, Paul is confident that Timothy can stand strong because of the grace that is in Christ Jesus. The grace that is in Christ Jesus is available to all who are in Christ Jesus.

Thank God that in our darkest moments, when we feel weak and helpless, when we are tempted to give up or give in, we can lean upon God's grace. The same grace that saved us is available daily to strengthen us for service.

Before we can learn the sufficiency of God's grace, we must learn the insufficiency of ourselves. The more we see our sinfulness, the more we appreciate grace in its basic meaning of God's undeserved favour. In a similar manner, the more we see our frailty, weakness, and dependence, the more we appreciate God's grace in its dimension of His divine assistance. Just as grace shines more brilliantly against the dark background of our sin, so it also shines more brilliantly against the background of our human weakness. (Jerry Bridges, *Transforming Grace*, NavPress, 2017 p. 162)

Day 133

Read: 2 Timothy 2:1–26
Key verses: 2 Timothy 1:1

....

You then, my son, be strong in the grace that is in Christ Jesus.

How does grace make us strong?

In Ephesians 6:10, instead of saying 'Be strong in the grace that is in Christ Jesus', Paul says 'Be strong in the Lord and in his mighty power'. From time to time, when Jesus was on earth, that mighty power would break forth. As the detachment of soldiers come to arrest him, and make it clear who they are after, Jesus says: 'I am he' (John 18:5). Those words from the lips of Jesus were all it took for the soldiers to fall to the ground, helpless. Whatever situation, easy or difficult, we may be moving into, we have the grace, the mighty power that is in Christ. That is a challenge as well as an encourage-ment, because Paul expects Timothy to stand in that grace. We can be very quick to excuse ourselves as Christians. 'We're only human . . . These are tough times . . . my church isn't up to much.' But there is actually no excuse because the grace is in Christ. We are strengthened, enabled, through our relationship with Jesus. As Peter puts it, 'His divine power has given us everything we need for a godly life through our knowledge of him who called us by his own glory and goodness' (2 Peter 1:3).

Paul then gives Timothy six little pictures to help him realize what is needed if he is to stand firm. First there is the picture of the soldier calling us to wholehearted devotion (verse 4). Then the athlete reminding us of the discipline required to run the race to the end (verse 5). Verse 6 introduces us to the farmer and the sheer hard graft required in Christian living and service. We have the grace that is in Christ Jesus but that does not deliver us from the need to work hard at this business of Christian living. The picture of a diligent workman underlines this point (verse 14–19). The specific work in mind here is the work of the teacher, correctly handling the Word of truth. If preachers want mighty power in their preaching, they need to be diligent about their preparation.

Then there is the picture of the clean vessel; a reminder that all our work will be ruined unless the vessel, the worker, by the power of Christ, keeps his or her life pure and holy (verses 20–21). Finally the description of the Lord's bondservant; a challenging picture of the gentleness required in the Christian worker (verses 24–25). These six pictures build up a powerful image of what will be required of Timothy, if he is to remain faithful and fruitful, in the most trying of circumstances.

God's grace doesn't put an end to trying. We must open our Bibles, make time to pray, avoid the people, places or internet sites that tempt us to sin, make the effort to attend church, and – in a myriad of other ways – pursue godliness. But we do so knowing even our most feeble effort is undergirded and enabled by God's grace. This is for God's glory – that from beginning to end, our Christian life is dependent on his grace.

Day 134

Read: Hebrews 12:14–17
Key verses: Hebrews 12:15–16

••

15 See to it that no one falls short of the grace of God and that no bitter root grows up to cause trouble and defile many. 16 See that no one is sexually immoral, or is godless like Esau, who for a single meal sold his inheritance rights as the oldest son.

Are you falling short of the grace of God?

The grace of God leads his people on; it is sufficient for all that we need to live holy lives, and those who want to live that kind of life follow hard upon the leading of that grace. But some of us fall behind in this pursuit of grace (verse 15a). Once we were going strong but now we're lagging behind. It's as if your first attempts at shooting at the target, in those early days of being a Christian, scored bull's-eye after bull's-eye; but increasingly, as time has gone by, you don't hit the bull quite so often, you're falling short of the grace of God, you are not quite where you should be. And that quest for a holy life is not as realistic or as constant an experience as it once was.

The writer to the Hebrews urges us to avoid this great danger happening to ourselves or those near and dear to us. To help us understand, the writer phrases the warning another way, 'See to it that no bitter root grows up to cause trouble and defile many' (verse 15b). When you were newly converted, you were very alert to sin; quick to take it to the cross of Jesus to receive forgiveness and cleansing. You were on it like a terrier on a bone. But now that doesn't happen so much. Some little root has grown up in your heart. Perhaps you haven't noticed it or, if you have, you've ignored it and the root keeps growing.

'Let me put it another way,' says the writer to the Hebrews, 'See to it that no one is immoral or godless' (verse 16a). He's talking about the same thing; these are the two primary causes of falling away from grace and letting a bitter root bury deep down within us. Immorality is being careless about the kind of person that I am in myself, and godlessness is being careless about my attitude to God and his demands on me. If we give in to these two sins, bitterness will take root and we shall fall away from the grace of God.

Do you recognize these tell-tale traits of falling short of God's grace? You are not as passionate about being holy as you were when you first became a Christian; you're indulging in private sins; you're no longer quick to cut sin dead; you're half-hearted in the way you think and speak about God. Don't let the root of bitterness grow any more – repent and turn back to God. He is waiting with a fresh supply of grace to renew your heart and enable your obedience: 'Let us then approach God's throne of grace with confidence, so that we may receive mercy and find grace to help us in our time of need' (Hebrews 4:16).

Day 135

Read: Hebrews 12:14–17
Key verses: Hebrews 12:15–17

....

15 See to it that no one falls short of the grace of God and that no bitter root grows up to cause trouble and defile many. 16 See that no one is sexually immoral, or is godless like Esau, who for a single meal sold his inheritance rights as the oldest son. 17 Afterward, as you know, when he wanted to inherit this blessing, he was rejected. Even though he sought the blessing with tears, he could not change what he had done.

It would be great to be mentioned in the Bible, unless of course you are Esau. Esau is the outstanding Bible illustration of a man who is falling away from the grace of God.

His father was Isaac, his grandfather was Abraham; he was brought up in a godly home, with a godly heritage. He had immense privileges and was lined up to receive the birthright (inheritance rights of the firstborn) and the blessing from his father. All grace was his. But gradually those privileges turn sour and, by the end of the story, Esau has missed the mark, he's lagged behind, he's out of the race.

Back in his youthful days, Esau thought nothing of his birthright and he traded it for a bowl of his brother's soup (Genesis 25). Probably only Jacob knew about the incident but it was the beginning of a bitter root. The years went by and Esau never repented, he never pulled up the root. Then, when Isaac was near death and it was time for him to confer the blessing on his eldest son, Jacob pretended to be Esau and Isaac gave him the blessing. Nothing could be done, there was only one blessing and Esau had missed out (Genesis 27). He lost the blessing for the price of a single meal!

Esau illustrates what immorality or godlessness can do. To complain that Hebrews gets it wrong because we don't know that Esau was an immoral man misses the point. Hebrews is saying that either of these two areas is a danger area for this kind of carelessness. It just so happened that it was his relationship to God that was careless. It might just have well been his relationship to his own inner integrity, his inner purity.

We can see the Esau sequence in our own lives. If we're careless about our attitude to God and don't come to the cross daily to repent, the root of bitterness grows. If we're careless about our inner integrity and indulge in things which compromise that, there are consequences for ourselves and others. We think these things don't matter but they do and we lose the blessing.

Thank God for all the evidence of his grace in your life – your salvation, forgiveness, spiritual privileges and material provisions. Some of us have been blessed with godly parents; all of us have been blessed with a spiritual family. We've all been overloaded with grace. Take care not to squander this grace by careless living and lack of repentance. Today, crush the Esau sequence by acknowledging your complete dependence on God's grace not only for salvation but for daily obedience and holy living.

Day 136

Read: Hebrews 12:14–17
Key verses: Hebrews 12:14–16

....

> [14] *Make every effort to live in peace with everyone and to be holy; without holiness no one will see the Lord.* [15] *See to it that no one falls short of the grace of God and that no bitter root grows up to cause trouble and defile many.* [16] *See that no one is sexually immoral, or is godless like Esau.*

How do we know if we are taking God's grace for granted?

The test is whether we are pursuing holiness. The call to holiness is given in verse 14 and then the phrase 'see to it' lies behind both halves of verse 15 and the beginning of verse 16. It is as if the writer to the Hebrews is saying, 'Holiness – see to it!' In Greek the word used for 'see to it' is the same word from which our term 'bishop' comes. A bishop is one who is supposed to oversee the welfare of God's people. The writer to the Hebrews is saying that it is my responsibility to see to it that I am right with God and seeking the holy life he wants me to live, but also that my brothers and sisters seek holiness.

There has never been a time when the message 'holiness – see to it!' has not been applicable. There has never been a time without the danger of failing the grace of God; of letting a root of evil remain where it is and start to grow; of allowing ourselves just a little latitude in that realm of carelessness towards God or ourselves.

Whatever stage of the Christian life we are, we must see to holiness. If we treat sin lightly and put off dealing with it we are despising the cross of Christ. Neither is there any spiritual experience or gifting that moves us beyond the basics of holiness. We can never leave the cross behind. We come to the cross at the beginning of our Christian life, and the cross will pursue us until the end. Daily we have to turn to God and say, 'Lord, I've failed again. I've sinned again. How I praise you for the cross that cleanses me and the grace which forgives me again!'

God, in his grace, reminds us of our sinful hearts. He reminds us that the goal of holiness still lies ahead of us. Today we must see to that bitter root, be careful about those areas of immorality and godlessness and pursue holiness.

'You in your small corner and I in mine' is a line in an old children's chorus (Susan B. Warner, 'Jesus Bids Us Shine', 1864) but it is often how we think of holiness. Yes, we are responsible for our personal holiness but it is not an individual pursuit. Our love for God, commitment to his Word, eagerness to repent and avoid temptation – or not – impacts others. Our behaviour either spurs people towards holiness or puts them off. Today, pray and look for ways to encourage your children, a young person in the youth group, or a member of your small group to press on toward holiness, seeking God's transforming grace.

Day 137

Read: Psalm 119:9–16
Key verse: Psalm 119:9–11

....

> *How can a young person stay on the path of purity?*
>   *By living according to your word.*
> *¹⁰I seek you with all my heart;*
>   *do not let me stray from your commands.*
> *¹¹I have hidden your word in my heart*
>   *that I might not sin against you.*

How can we overcome sin?

The psalmist is not offering us a quick fix: 'Just read your Bible every day, make your mind up not to sin, and think positive.' He's not that naïve. The idea that rules or techniques alone can solve the problem of sin is in fact the essence of legalism. Psalm 119 and the Old Testament as a whole are often accused of legalism but that couldn't be further from the truth.

The psalmist does not say, 'I have memorised all the rules so that I won't break any of them.' He says, 'Lord, your word is in my heart and I don't want to sin against you.' This is relational language. The only answer to the problem of sin that the psalmist offers is God himself.

We might be tempted to say, 'Isn't the God of the Old Testament the God of wrath and judgement? Surely the psalmist is going to have to wait until the New Testament; he's not going to find any answer to his sin until he's able to read the gospel and hear the word of grace and salvation that will come through the cross of Calvary and the blood of Christ.' What a lie, what a travesty! It is a mistaken view of Scripture to assume that there's nothing but law and wrath in the Old Testament and you have to wait for grace until the New Testament.

Let the psalmist speak for himself. 'Keep me from deceitful ways; be gracious to me and teach me your law' (verse 29). 'May your unfailing love come to me, Lord, your salvation, according to your promise' (verse 41). 'Turn to me and have mercy on me, as you always do to those who love your name' (verse 132). 'Your compassion, Lord, is great; preserve my life according to your laws' (verse 156).

Did you hear those words? Grace, mercy, love, salvation, compassion – and this is the Old Testament! This is what made the psalmist come to life. He praises God for his law, but he says, 'Lord, I find in your Word that you are gracious, loving, compassionate and merciful; and that is the answer to my sin. I can do all that I can with my mind, heart, will and emotions, to keep myself from sin; but I know that in the end I have got to come back to you because you are the God of compassion, love, mercy and grace.'

Hide God's Word in your heart, meditate on it, seek to obey it. Make every effort to avoid sin. But when you fail – and you will – don't hesitate to come back to God in repentance. You will always be welcomed; you will always be showered with his bountiful love, grace, compassion and mercy. The well of God's forgiveness will never run dry because his character never changes.

Day 138

Read: Psalm 119:25–32
Key verse: Psalm 119:29

....

Keep me from deceitful ways;
be gracious to me and teach me your law.

How do we reconcile law and grace?

We write systematic theology books with all the law in one chapter and all the grace in another as if they were somehow totally different. Yet, here in the Old Testament, the psalmist is so filled with gratitude for what he finds in God's law that he says, 'Lord, I know you can be gracious to me because I've read it in your law.'

Where does the law mention the grace, love and mercy of God? We need to remember that when the Psalmist talks about 'the law' he's talking about the whole of the Torah – Genesis, Exodus, Leviticus, Numbers and Deuteronomy. It's there that we read about God's mercy when he saved Noah and his family from judgement it's there where we read the amazing story of the Exodus, that great act of grace, salvation and redemption.

In Exodus 34:6, God, speaking to Moses says, 'The Lord, the Lord, the compassionate and gracious God, slow to anger, abounding in love and faithfulness'. That verse echoes all the way through the Old Testament. You'll find it in the book of Numbers, the Psalms, Nehemiah, Daniel and in the prophets.

So, if you asked the psalmist, 'How do you know that God is gracious?' he would say, 'Let me take you to the law and tell you the stories about this God.' Of course, we know of the righteous mercy of God ultimately from the cross. But if the Old Testament believers had stood at the cross they would have said – and some of their successors did say – 'Yes, it's as we expected. That's our God: the God of love, patience, grace and mercy who we knew in our Scripture, in our history.'

They would also say to us, 'Look, it is we who gave you all the words you need to express this – words like grace, love, forgiveness and mercy, which flow through the Scriptures of the Old Testament and flood into the New.' You won't find any better way of expressing God's forgiveness of sin than Psalm 103:9: 'He will not always accuse, nor will he harbour his anger forever; he does not treat us as our sins deserve or repay us according to our iniquities.' Thank God for that. That's the gospel in the Psalms, the word of grace, the pure grace of the Lord himself.

Today, think about Old Testament stories and thank God for all the evidence that he is, 'The Lord, the Lord, the compassionate and gracious God, slow to anger, abounding in love and faithfulness.' The psalmist looked at God's law and knew he was the Saviour, healer and restorer of Israel. We too can look at God in the Old Testament and see that he alone has the words of eternal life, the words of grace that forgive, cleanse and heal.

Day 139

Read: Jonah 4:1–11
Key verses: Jonah 4:1–3

••

But to Jonah this seemed very wrong, and he became angry.
² He prayed to the Lord, "Isn't this what I said, Lord, when I was still at home? That is what I tried to forestall by fleeing to Tarshish. I knew that you are a gracious and compassionate God, slow to anger and abounding in love, a God who relents from sending calamity. ³ Now, Lord, take away my life, for it is better for me to die than to live."

Do you find it hard to relate to Jonah in chapter 4?

Jonah was a prophet, sent by God to Nineveh, a city in Assyria, the great enemy of Israel, to preach repentance. Not wanting to go, he got on board a ship going in the opposite direction. A storm arose. Jonah knew God had sent the storm because he was angry with him so he told the sailors to throw him overboard and they would be safe. God, in his mercy, sent a great fish to swallow Jonah up. After three days and nights inside the fish he was vomited on the shore and then went to Nineveh and proclaimed: 'Forty more days and Nineveh will be overturned.' The Ninevites repented and turned to God. In his grace God relented and the threatened destruction did not occur. Instead of being overjoyed, Jonah was very angry.

He had been forgiven for refusing God's commission to preach to Nineveh. He had been rescued by the fish and then delivered on the dry land just days before, yet here we find him justifying his sin. How could the chastened Jonah, praying a prayer of thanksgiving in the belly of the fish, humbled by the grace of God, full of gratitude to him, so quickly turn into this proud, bitter, self-obsessed man?

Before we condemn Jonah too quickly we need to face some uncomfortable facts. Like Jonah, those who trust in Christ have experienced an amazing rescue. We too were at the bottom of a deep pit, cut off from God, because of our sins. And yet, because of the death and resurrection of Christ, we have been raised from that pit (Jonah 2:6) and are enjoying new life with Christ, friendship with God. For a time, like Jonah in chapter 2, we are full of gratitude and sing, 'Amazing Grace, how sweet the sound that saved a wretch like me' (John Newton, 1779). But that experience of being rescued does not take away the sin in our hearts. It is possible to be on a spiritual high one day, praising God for rescuing us, and the next day fighting against that same God and resisting his will for our lives. We have received the Spirit of God but the sinful nature still remains and drags us down. There is a lot of Jonah in each of us.

We enjoy new life with Christ now but until we meet Jesus and become like him, our hearts often stray toward rebellion rather than obedience. Today, if you find yourself justifying sin and resisting God's will, remember how he rescued you and how much you have been forgiven, practice gratitude, let go of pride and allow yourself to be once again humbled by God's grace.

Day 140

Read: Jonah 4:1–11
Key verses: Jonah 4:1–3

....

But to Jonah this seemed very wrong, and he became angry.
²He prayed to the Lord, "Isn't this what I said, Lord, when I was
still at home? That is what I tried to forestall by fleeing to
Tarshish. I knew that you are a gracious and compassionate
God, slow to anger and abounding in love, a God who relents
from sending calamity. ³Now, Lord, take away my life, for it is
better for me to die than to live."

Do you have a problem with God's grace?

Jonah was battling against the great truth of this book: 'Salvation comes from the Lord' (Jonah 2:9). In his head he knew that God was sovereign and could do what he liked. He knew God's loving concern for himself and the people of Israel was all of grace. He knew that his rescue by the fish and then onto dry land was just as undeserved as the mercy God showed to the Ninevites. But, in his heart he still had God all boxed up. There were certain people who were outside the confines of God's grace – possibly all Gentiles, certainly those dreadful Ninevites who were known for their depravity and were great enemies of Israel. Very likely it wasn't just racism that motivated Jonah's anger, it was a warped sense of moral indignation. How could a holy God possibly forgive such wicked people? Surely justice demands that he punish them? What would people think of a God who let such evil people off scot-free?

Jonah's problem was with God's sovereign mercy – his grace. In chapter 2 he is full of praise inside the fish in response to the grace God showed him. However, in chapter 4 he is full of anger at the grace God showed to the Ninevites. He took God's grace to the Israelites for granted, but resented when it was shown to others.

He couldn't see that he and the people of Israel stood in the same place as those Ninevites, as sinners deserving nothing but God's destruction. He had no compassion on them, no desire that they should be saved.

Like Jonah, in our heads we believe all the right things. We know God is sovereign in his exercise of mercy. We know we deserve it no more than anyone else. But it is easy to take that mercy for granted and cease to identify with those outside it. We have little concern for those who don't belong to our group or type, those we find it hard to relate to – the critical boss or judgemental neighbour. We want God to exercise mercy on those we long to see saved, but others we consign quite happily to his hand of judgement. We're more like Jonah than we care to admit.

We stop having a problem with God showing grace to others when we realize how very much we need it ourselves. Today ask God to wipe away any sense of entitlement and show you afresh the offense of your sin, your need of redemption and the scandal of his grace. Knowing God has lavished his grace on you, joyfully extend it others. Grace is never diminished – only multiplied – when shared.

Day 141

Read: Jonah 4:1–11
Key verses: Jonah 4:10–11

....

*But the Lord said, "You have been concerned about this plant,
though you did not tend it or make it grow. It sprang up
overnight and died overnight. ¹¹And should I not have concern
for the great city of Nineveh, in which there are more than a
hundred and twenty thousand people who cannot tell their right
hand from their left – and also many animals?"*

Will God come to his senses and destroy Nineveh?

That was Jonah's hope as he angrily leaves the city, sets up camp
and waits to see what will happen. He had been unable to accept
God's exclusive right to have 'mercy on whom He will have mercy'
(Exodus 33:19) and so God provided a visual aid to illustrate his
sovereignty. God miraculously accelerated the growth of a vine
which provided extra shade in the hot climate. 'Jonah was very
happy about the plant' (verse 6). Possibly he saw it as divine
confirmation that God had come round to his way of thinking. If so,
his hopes were dashed when the next day God sent a worm to chew
the plant so that it withered. God also summoned a scorching wind
which, combined with the relentless blaze of the sun, made Jonah
feel terrible. Jonah is angry because he is convinced that he is right
about Nineveh and God is wrong; the city should be judged. And he
is equally convinced that God is wrong in the way he has treated him
by callously taking away that vine.

God points out how foolish and small-minded Jonah is being. He
draws a contrast between the plant and the people of Nineveh.
'Jonah you didn't make that vine or sustain it. You only knew it for
one day and yet you were very upset when it was destroyed. Can
you understand how I feel for the thousands of people of Nineveh

whom I created and have sustained for years?' And that is where the book ends.

We aren't told how Jonah responds. We are deliberately left feeling uncomfortable with that final question ringing in our ears, 'Should I not be concerned about that great city?' and with the implied question burning in our hearts – should we not be concerned as well? The book presents us with a God who is sovereign in mercy, who won't be boxed in, who refuses to show his grace only to those we regard as kosher, who 'rejoices over every sinner that repents' (Luke 15:7, 10).

How do we fare when we compare ourselves to God? Aren't we more like Jonah? We believe in evangelism in theory but when it comes to the crunch, we prefer church to be a cosy club for insiders; we don't want the trouble of trying to reach those outside.

Will you take God's grace to 'outsiders'? Will you strip away unhelpful church traditions, find relevant ways to introduce the gospel, offer practical support, pray fervently, give sacrificially, and go out of your comfort zones to reach people with the good news. Today, ask God to increase your compassion until you share his concern for the lost.

Day 142

Read: Matthew 18:1–6
Key verse: Matthew 18:1–3

....

At that time the disciples came to Jesus and asked, "Who, then, is the greatest in the kingdom of heaven?"
He called a little child to him, and placed the child among them. And he said, "Truly I tell you, unless you change and become like little children, you will never enter the kingdom of heaven."

'I want to be the greatest!'

We might not dare say it, but sometimes we think it. Jesus' answer is, if you want to be great in the kingdom of God you need to learn to be a nobody, like a slave (Matthew 20:26–28) or a child. The little children in this chapter represent the Christian believer. The point is not that the children are innocent; you don't have to be a parent long to work that out. It isn't even that children are naturally humble; most are remarkably self-centred. The point is that in the first century children were insignificant. They didn't count.

What do you do when you are face to face with a nobody? What would grace do? 'Welcome' says Jesus. 'Whoever welcomes one such child in my name welcomes me' (Matthew 18:5). Whose company are you willing to keep? This is a sure test of our self-importance. Will you welcome the one who is awkward or slow, the rebel or the one with a disability? Will you welcome those who don't count in the community? Do you speak to one of these people on the margins of the Christian community but all the time you are looking over their shoulder for the 'important person' in order to have a conversation that really matters? Or do you just avoid difficult people with whom you disagree? Their worldview is so profoundly different, the way they have dealt in business is damaging, or their sexual history is an anathema, so you just steer clear.

What would grace do? Welcome, not trip up. 'If anyone causes one of these little ones – those who believe in me – to stumble, it would be better for them to have a large millstone hung round their neck and to be drowned in the depths of the sea' (verse 6). I used to think that verse had to refer to some appalling abuse or led into gross immorality and it certainly includes that. But it must also include the cold-shouldering that will stop the little children from growing in Christ. Jesus' words remind us that showing the grace of welcome is part of kingdom life.

Who do you sit next to at church or talk to after the service? Grace extends that welcome beyond people who are just like us to those considered the last and the least. Grace supports and nurtures these little ones to grow as believers – not just to avoid God's punishment but because in doing so we are welcoming God himself. Don't let the converse be true – that we are so caught up in our own self-importance that we fail to welcome Christ, shunning him from our churches and homes.

Day 143

Read: Matthew 18:10–14
Key verse: Matthew 18:12

....

What do you think? If a man owns a hundred sheep, and one of them wanders away, will he not leave the ninety-nine on the hills and go to look for the one that wandered off?

How should the Christian community operate? What difference should grace make?

To teach us Jesus tells this famous story. He asks you to put yourself in the man's shoes. If you owned a hundred sheep and one of them wanders away, what would you do? Adopt the cost efficiency approach? 'It's a much better use of my time to carry on looking after ninety-nine sheep than go wandering after one . . .' Make the logical judgement? 'If he chooses to wander off, he must learn that there are consequences.' Or leave the door open a bit? 'If he comes back, we'll welcome him with open arms.'

Or put it another way, if one of your children went missing what would you do? You would search and search until you found them. The man in the story did that and when he found the lost sheep 'he is happier about that one sheep than about the ninety-nine that did not wander off' (verse 13).

'Well' says Jesus, 'it's like that with God. God is that kind of shepherd, he always has been (see Ezekiel 34).

The challenge of this parable is very clear. Do we reflect the heart of God? Do we show grace? Do we care for other believers in our church or do we despise those who are not like us? Those who are awkward, those with a past, those who are needy. If they don't turn up at church we breathe a sigh of relief but God breathes a sigh of concern. He says, 'These people are just my type. They couldn't matter more. Where is she? Where is he?' The challenge of caring in this chapter is matched with a warning, 'See that you do not despise one of these little ones. For I tell you that their angels in heaven always see the face of my Father in heaven' (verse 10).

Why does God count sheep? It is not because he's trying to get to sleep! It's because he has a heart for the stray; he doesn't want to lose any. And if you feel that you are on the edge of the Christian community, that you don't matter, listen and believe God's Word to you: 'In the same way your Father in heaven is not willing that any of these little ones should perish' (verse 14).

God has counted his sheep and will not let any one of us go. We are his treasured possession, held safe in his hands. As we interact with believers today let's take care not to look down on anyone but treat each other as who we truly are – trophies of God's grace, made in his image and bought by his blood.

Day 144

Read: Matthew 18:15–22
Key verses: Matthew 18:15–17

....

If your brother or sister sins go and point out their fault, just between the two of you. If they listen to you, you have won them over. ¹⁶ But if they will not listen, take one or two others along, so that "every matter may be established by the testimony of two or three witnesses." ¹⁷ If they still refuse to listen, tell it to the church; and if they refuse to listen even to the church, treat them as you would a pagan or a tax collector.

How do you show grace to another Christian who has sinned against you?

Do you avoid them for a bit and make sure no one else gets hurt by them? No. Grace means we 'go and point out their fault, just between the two of you. If they listen to you, you have won them over.' Grace will try and win over. The mark of the kingdom is not that we're all perfect, so we don't need to go on pretending we are to one another. It's actually how we handle the offence. Wrongs are faced, they are not ignored. The wronged person has a responsibility to take deliberate action; not to grumble to friends, not to put the other person down but to win over. If you do go to show someone their faults, remember why you are going; not to make all the points that have been brewing but to win them over. And if someone comes to explain how you have offended them, please listen sensitively. You may think you are very approachable, but it takes a huge effort to initiate this type of conversation. The words might come out wrong, the person may get tense and aggressive. I need to listen well and show grace to the one trying to win me over.

Unfortunately, reconciliation won't always happen. If the person you are trying to win over won't listen to you, take along one or two others as witnesses who can also help facilitate dialogue. 'If they still refuse to listen, tell it to the church; and if they refuse to listen even to the church, treat them as you would a pagan or a tax collector' (verse 17). There may need to be discipline. The behaviour here is unacceptable to kingdom community but the issue is less the original fault, nor the refusal to face it, but the refusal to engage with grace.

Despite being forgiven, in a church comprised of sinful, broken people we are bound to hurt each other. We can ignore the hurt, lash out in anger or extend grace and work towards restoring the relationship. The power of our witness doesn't depend on church members being perfect – or even pretending to be – but on us being transformed by the 'the gospel of God's grace' and extending it, again and again to each other. In a world where grace is lacking, you and I – the church – can be a beacon, drawing people to God and the wonder of his amazing grace.

Day 145

Read: Matthew 18:21–35
Key verses: Matthew 18:23–25

....

Therefore, the kingdom of heaven is like a king who wanted to settle accounts with his servants. ²⁴As he began the settlement, a man who owed him ten thousand bags of gold was brought to him. ²⁵Since he was not able to pay, the master ordered that he and his wife and his children and all that he had be sold to repay the debt.

10,000 bags of gold is an awful lot of debt. Each bag was worth a 'talent', equal to 20 years of a day labourer's wages. You have to work hard to run up this kind of debt.

Out of options and facing slavery, 'the servant fell on his knees before [his master]. "Be patient with me," he begged, "and I will pay back everything"' (verse 26).

I don't know how many weeks he'd have to win the National Lottery to pay off this debt but more than is ever going to happen. But the master, 'took pity on him, cancelled the debt and let him go' (verse 27). This wasn't financial restructuring; the debt was cancelled. Put yourself in the servant's shoes; face up to the reality of the ruin that lies ahead and then recapture the wonder of grace.

Imagine the relief and astonishment the servant experienced. And yet he went and found a fellow servant who owed him a hundred denarii – nothing – and demanded to be paid back. The man begged him, 'Be patient with me, and I will pay it back' (verse 29). These are the exact words the servant himself had used. You'd think it would bring back memories but it doesn't seem to. He had the man thrown into prison until he could pay the debt. We're shocked; so are the servants and their master.

'You wicked servant,' he said, 'I cancelled all that debt of yours because you begged me to. Shouldn't you have had mercy on your fellow servant just as I had on you?' In anger his master handed him over to the jailers to be tortured, until he should pay back all he owed (verse 32–34).

The power of the parable cuts deeply: 'This is how my heavenly Father will treat each of you unless you forgive your brother or sister from your heart' (verse 35). We can't be the kind of people who receive grace from God and then don't show it to others. Jesus told this parable because Peter had asked how many times we should forgive someone who repents. 'Up to seven times?' (Matthew 18:21) The moment you start counting you've missed the point! Grace forgives and forgives.

> How can we not forgive each other in light of all God has forgiven us? . . . I hear a loud whisper from the gospel that I did not get what I deserved. I deserved punishment and got forgiveness. I deserved wrath and got love. I deserved a debtor's prison and got instead a clean credit history. I deserved lectures and crawl-on-your-knees repentance; I got a banquet spread for me.
> (Philip Yancey, *What's So Amazing about Grace?* Zondervan, 1997, p. 64)

Day 146

Read: Luke 14:1–14
Key verses: Luke 14:12–14

¹²*Then Jesus said to his host, "When you give a luncheon or dinner, do not invite your friends, your brothers or sisters, your relatives, or your rich neighbours; if you do, they may invite you back and so you will be repaid.* ¹³*But when you give a banquet, invite the poor, the crippled, the lame, the blind,* ¹⁴*and you will be blessed. Although they cannot repay you, you will be repaid at the resurrection of the righteous."*

Who do you invite into your home for a meal?

Most people invite those who are naturally close to them, friends and relatives. But in Jewish society you also would invite rich neighbours – people who are significant and could invite you back. You would never invite people beneath your social standing, only those of equal standing or above, because they would give you prestige and further honour. Like many of the Jews of Jesus' day we tend to grade people according to their usefulness to us. But the kingdom of God is an upside-down kingdom. And instead of socially conventional behaviour, we ought to be people who engage in spiritually intentional behaviour, which is radically different.

The kingdom principle is to invite those who would never be able to invite us back. Luke lists them here: the poor, the crippled, the lame and the blind. The list is also found in Luke 4:16–30, echoing the Magnificat that Mary sang, recorded in Luke 1:46 onwards. The kingdom turning everything on its head is a recurring theme in Luke's gospel. The rich, powerful and well fed are dethroned from their positions, while those who are poor, hungry and of no social standing are lifted up.

Here is sheer grace in operation: giving without strings attached. This is not the ugly face of generosity that gives in order to control and exercise power over people. It is just free giving without any return expected. It is irrational according to any market economy and makes no sense in a capitalist economy. Giving for the sheer joy of giving leads to a state of blessedness, says Jesus. If you want to be blessed, then God will do it when you invite the poor, crippled, lame and blind. Kingdom disciples include these people, not by sending them a donation or supporting a charity that works with the poor but by inviting them in to have a meal and developing a relationship with them.

Maybe one of the reasons why there isn't blessing in many of our churches is not because we don't desire it or pray for it, but because we are just not putting into operation the plain, ordinary teaching of Jesus in an obedient fashion. If God's grace has flowed into our lives, it should turn us upside down and flow from us into the lives of others.

Who do you invite for Sunday lunch or to stay in your home – ex-offenders, ethnic minorities, alcoholics, those who are struggling to make it in life, those who could never return the invitation? Having received God's grace it must flow out from us to others. Grace operates like the best type of virtuous circle. It never runs out – as we offer grace to others, we receive even more from God as he delights to bless us.

Day 147

Read: Luke 14:15–24
Key verses: Luke 14:23–24

....

> [23] Then the master told his servant, "Go out to the roads and country lanes and compel them to come in, so that my house will be full. [24] I tell you, not one of those who were invited will get a taste of my banquet."

Who will be at the banquet at the end of time?

One of the guests is confident of a seat at the Messiah's banquet: the feast envisaged by Abraham and spoken of in Isaiah 25, when God reigns and everything in creation would be summed up. Jesus tells a story about a party to answer the problem of who will be there. This event was going to be the place to be seen, determining who was 'in' and who was 'out'. The host used the system of double invitation as Buckingham Palace does today. Potential guests were asked if they would accept an invitation if they were invited because no one, including the Queen, wishes to be turned down.

But, surprisingly, the guests who had already said, 'I'll be free on the night' reject the invitation with the strangest excuses (verses 18–20). In the first century no property or oxen would ever have been bought without being checked out first. No bride would have been allowed to stand in the way of an invitation like this. No wonder the host is angry. This is a deliberate slight which says that the host is of no value, he doesn't matter, he isn't where the action is.

The plot continues to unravel with the unexpected guests being invited and expected. Two categories of guest are now included: those who lived in the town and were unfit – the poor, crippled, blind and lame; and those who live outside the city and are homeless. 'Make them come in' says the host because he recognizes that such people would find it hard to believe that this invitation was genuine.

Jesus is saying, it's not the expected or the conventional people who will be found at the Messiah's banquet. This is a banquet of grace and love, which has been undeserved, but which has been fully accepted in faith by the undeserving. It is for the unworthy.

This is a terrifying word from Jesus. We might expect to be at the banquet but we need to make sure we don't reject his invitation. Not by saying, 'No,' but by disobeying him in the way in which we live.

There is still room at God's banquet of grace. It's for the unworthy; it's for you. What do you need to do to earn a seat at the table? Nothing! The invitation is based solely on the goodness of our heavenly Host. All we have to do is recognize our hunger, believe the invitation is true and accept it. Don't use possessions, experiences or even family as excuses to dismiss Jesus and his invitation. It's the invite of a lifetime; accept it while it's still on offer. And, as you wait for this great banquet, make sure you live in a way that honours your host.

Day 148

Read: Luke 15:1–2, 11–32
Key verses: Luke 15:1–2

••

Now the tax collectors and sinners were all gathering around to hear Jesus. But the Pharisees and the teachers of the law muttered, "This man welcomes sinners and eats with them."

Are there limits to God's grace?

It's the Sabbath and Jesus goes to eat in the house of a prominent Pharisee (Luke 14:1). Dr Luke tells us that Jesus is being carefully watched. The Pharisees are out to get him, they are watching his every move and listening to his every word. Jesus does nothing to allay the fears of these religious leaders or their desire to bring him down: he heals a man on the Sabbath (Luke 14:4), challenges the seating arrangements of the guests and calls them out for their lack of humility (Luke 4:7–12), tells a parable about a great banquet where God's grace extends to the outcast and undeserving (Luke 14:15–24) and teaches about the cost of being his disciple (Luke 14:25–35).

In chapter 15 we find Jesus surrounding himself by undesirables; tax collectors and sinners, and this confirms the Pharisees conviction that Jesus himself is an undesirable: 'This man welcome sinners and eats with them' (verse 2). The fact that Jesus ate with sinners would have upset the Pharisees. This implied much more than just associating with sinners: as he ate with them, he was welcoming them, he was saying, 'I am here for you'. Jesus was always clear about that: 'I came not to call the righteous but sinners to repentance . . . I came to seek and to save those who were lost' (Luke 5:32, 19:10). Never forget that Jesus remains, for all time, the sinner's friend. The author of Hebrews tells us, 'He always lives to intercede' for people like us (Hebrews 7:25).

The three parables in this chapter – the lost sheep, lost coin and the lost son – drive home this point. By welcoming sinners and eating with them Jesus is like a shepherd leaving his ninety-nine sheep and going out to find one lost sheep, like a woman searching diligently for that one coin that meant a day's wages to her, and like a father welcoming his lost son. Each of the parables ends with a party because God delights to welcome the worst of sinners and rejoices every single time one repents. Praise God because that includes me and you.

God's grace is not for those who think they have life sorted but for those who recognize they are lost and helpless. The grace-laden message of the gospel is that there is forgiveness for every sinner who repents. As you recognize your desperate need of God and come to him, Jesus welcomes you without reservation and rejoices over you. Today, Jesus says, 'I am here for you . . . here to forgive, here to draw alongside, here praying for you.'

Day 149

Read: Luke 15:11–32
Key verses: Luke 15:11–12

....

Jesus continued: 'There was a man who had two sons.
¹²The younger one said to his father, "Father, give me my share
of the estate." So he divided his property between them.'

We probably miss the magnitude of the son's request: 'Father, give me my share of the estate.' The custom was that the older son would receive two thirds of the estate and the younger one, one third. The Father would probably have had to sell off part of his land to meet the boy's request. As one commentator said, 'He was being asked to tear his life apart.' But more seriously than that, by asking for the inheritance while his father was still alive the son was essentially wishing his father dead. If any child ever made such a request, tradition dictated that the father should drive him from the home. So, Luke's observation, 'He divided his property between them' is remarkable.

Soon the hard-earned inheritance was blown completely. The young man 'squandered his wealth in wild living' (verse 13). Before he knows it, he is working the land again but this time, he has the lowest job, he's feeding pigs. He's no longer working as a son but as a hired hand. Perhaps it was shame or pride or fear of the reception he would receive that kept him away from home. But, at some point, he 'came to his senses' (verse 17) and decided to go back to his father.

He makes plans to return home and works on his speech: 'I will set out and go back to my father and say to him, "Father I have sinned against heaven and against you. I am no longer worthy to be called your son; make me like one of your hired servants"' (verse 18–19). You can sense his struggle: 'He's still my father. Nothing I've done can change that relationship, but I can't expect to be treated like a son, can I? Not after the disgrace I brought on my father, not after the way I've rejected his love and completely blown the inheritance he worked to provide for me. So, I'll ask him to make me one of his hired men. I'll work hard to earn his respect and maybe one day his love. I'll live the life of a servant right here in the home where I'm a son.' With his speech ready, he sets out for home, but nothing could have prepared him for what he would experience before the end of that journey.

If, for whatever reason, you are at a distance from God and you decide: 'I'm going to return to my Father, I'm going home because whatever I've done, however long I've been away, I'm still a daughter, I'm still a son' then you too will be utterly overwhelmed by what you experience before you get to the end of the journey. It will be amazing outrageous grace.

Day 150

Read: Luke 15:11–32
Key verses: Luke 15:20

· ·

But while he was still a long way off, his father saw him and was filled with compassion for him; he ran to his son, threw his arms around him and kissed him.

The first thing this prodigal son sees is his father running towards him. Middle Eastern men don't run but this man has been waiting for this moment from the minute his son left home. The father's acceptance of his son is immediate and total. Before he can get the first word of his speech on his lips, his father is all over him. The running father throws his arms around his son and kisses him, and that kiss of the father precedes the repentance of the son.

The young man begins to speak but he doesn't get very far before his father says to his servants, 'Quick! Bring the best robe put it on him. Put a ring on his finger and sandals on his feet' (verse 22). The robe and the ring were both signs of the position the son was being given in the home. To be barefoot would have been the sign of a slave. When the father said, 'Put sandals on his feet' the son knew how he was being received. There was no point in continuing his carefully prepared speech. Notice there is no mention of the young man's profligate lifestyle. His father does not wait for him to clean up his act before he receives him: 'Bring the best robe, that will clean him up.'

The Pharisees hadn't quite got it. They said of Jesus, 'This man welcomes sinners and eats with them.' But Jesus says, 'My father does much more than welcome sinners. He actively goes out searching for them.' In its day this would have been seen as revolutionary. The rabbis agreed that God would welcome the penitent sinner, but this was a wholly new idea that God would take the initiative. They didn't understand their own Scriptures which spoke of a seeking, searching shepherd: 'I myself will search my sheep and look after them . . . I will rescue them from all the places where they are scattered . . . I will search for the lost and bring back the strays' (Ezekiel 34:11, 12, 16).

God is the seeking, running God. We love him because he first loved us. We did not choose him, he chose us. Why does he run towards us? Why does he choose us? Because of his love and compassion for us and for his own pleasure and joy. All returning prodigals experience the same outrageous grace from an overjoyed heavenly Father.

Can you sense the compassion in God's heart, his delight in you, and his joy as he lavishes extravagant grace upon you? This grace is as revolutionary now as it was when Jesus first told the parable. We don't get what we deserve, we get the *opposite* of what we deserve. In Christ we receive forgiveness, an eternal welcome into God's embrace, and adoption into his family – 'grace upon grace' (John 1:16 ESV).

Day 151

Read: Luke 15:11–32
Key verses: Luke 15:28–30

....

> [28] *The older brother became angry and refused to go in. So his father went out and pleaded with him.* [29] *But he answered his father, "Look! All these years I've been slaving for you and never disobeyed your orders. Yet you never gave me even a young goat so I could celebrate with my friends.* [30] *But when this son of yours who has squandered your property with prostitutes comes home, you kill the fattened calf for him!"*

Which son was really the prodigal?

The parable paints a striking contrast between the two brothers. One is irresponsible, the other is hardworking. One wastes his life and comes home humbled, the other proudly refuses to celebrate his brother's homecoming. The story ends with one son in a joyful family celebration and his brother outside, bitter and unwilling to forgive.

Like the Pharisees, the older brother in the story could not begin to grasp grace. He says to his father, 'All these years I've been slaving for you and never disobeying your orders' (verse 29). His language is interesting. He's a son in the family but he's living as a slave. He's very proud of his obedience and goodness. He says, 'You never gave me even a young goat.' He was working, not because he loved his father, but so he would one day get something.

It's so easy to become like the older brother and assume God owes us. A number of years ago, my son Tim was very seriously ill and for a thirty-six-hour period we really didn't know if he was going to live or not. I lay on the bed with him and for those hours I slipped into entitlement thinking. 'You can't take my son, I'm your servant. I've made sacrifices for you. You owe me.' That's the attitude of the older brother, 'I'm not serving you because I love you. You owe me. I'm entitled to something.'

How does the father react? The father who had been out looking for the returning prodigal, goes out again for this self-righteous brother. As the young man sulks outside the party his father pleaded with him to come in (verse 28). He says to him, 'My son . . . everything I have is yours' (verse 31). At the start of the parable, the father divided his property between the boys. The inheritance was already his, but the elder brother continued to live as a slave.

Are you living like a slave or a son? Have you slipped into entitlement thinking, serving God out of duty and hoping to earn his favour? Some of us have lost sight of God's grace and are as lost at home as the other son was lost far away. Today, meditate on whose you are and what that means: in Christ God says to us, 'Everything I have is yours'. 'You are no longer a slave, but God's child; and since you are his child, God has made you also an heir' (Galatians 4:7).

Day 152

Read: John 2:1–12
Key verse: John 2:7–10

....

> [7] *Jesus said to the servants, "Fill the jars with water"; so they filled them to the brim.*
> [8] *Then he told them, "Now draw some out and take it to the master of the banquet."*
> *They did so,* [9] *and the master of the banquet tasted the water that had been turned into wine . . . Then [the master of the banquet] called the bridegroom aside* [10] *and said, "Everyone brings out the choice wine first and then the cheaper wine after the guests have had too much to drink; but you have saved the best till now."*

I love the fact that the very first story about Christ is that he goes to a party!

He had been invited to a wedding feast in Cana and finds out, from his mother, that they have run out of wine.

He could have walked away and said, 'It's none of my business. It is not my moment.' He could have said, 'Who planned this party? He'll never learn his lesson if we let him off the hook.' He might have thought, 'I've come to display God's grace on this planet and help in times of need. These people don't deserve it but I'll perform a miracle. Do a head count; we'll do one glass each because I've got three years ahead of me, I can't spend all of my grace at the first party I go to.' Do you know how much wine he provided? Three thousand, five hundred, six-ounce glasses of wine! Just to prove that grace is generous.

Whenever Jesus poured out his grace, it was lavish. F.B Meyer was spot on in his commentary on Psalm 23:5 and the phrase, 'my cup overflows': 'Whatever blessing is in our cup, it is sure to run over.

With [God] the calf is always the fatted calf; the robe is always the best robe . . . God's way is always characterised by multitudinous and overflowing bounty' (*The Shepherd Psalm*, Moody Press, 1976, p. 451–452).

The choicest wine sloshing over the brim of the ceremonial water jars points forward to a day the prophets' anticipated: 'new wine will drip from the mountains and flow from all the hills, and I will bring my people Israel back from exile' (Amos 9:13–14). It was a preview of the day God's grace reaches its climax when all of creation will be redeemed and God's saving mission complete.

But, it was also a taster of grace now.

> The old Jewish order of things, which was based on trying to observe the Law [was being replace with] the new Christian order of things which springs from the grace and truth brought into the world by Jesus the Messiah, and consists not in trying to be good but in rejoicing in the generosity of God
> (A. R. Vidler, *Windsor Sermons*, London, 1958, p. 68).

Thank God that he doesn't measure out his grace slowly and deliberately, drop by drop. His grace is – and always will be – bountiful. Like a powerful waterfall it is relentless, overwhelming, and utterly breath-taking.

For further study

If you would like to read more on the theme of grace, you might find this selection of books helpful.

- Jerry Bridges, *The Discipline of Grace: God's role and our role in the pursuit of holiness* (NavPress, 2007)

- Jerry Bridges, *Transforming Grace* (NavPress, 2017)

- Philip Ryken, *Grace Transforming* (IVP, 2012)

- John Piper, *Future Grace* (Multnomah, 2012)

- David Powlison, *God's Grace in Your Suffering* (Crossway, 2018)

- Philip Yancey, *What's So Amazing about Grace?* (Zondervan, 2002)

Joy

Day 153

Read: Nehemiah 8:1–18
Key verses: Nehemiah 8:10, 12

• •

Nehemiah said, "Go and enjoy choice food and sweet drinks, and send some to those who have nothing prepared. This day is holy to our LORD. Do not grieve, for the joy of the LORD is your strength . . . " 12 Then all the people went away to eat and drink, to send portions of food and to celebrate with great joy, because they now understood the words that had been made known to them.

How did you feel the last time you read your Bible? Comforted, challenged, joyful . . . ?

In Nehemiah 8, the Israelites had finished rebuilding the walls of Jerusalem and had gathered in the square before the Water Gate to listen to Ezra the scribe reading from the 'Book of the Law of Moses' (verse 1). The first reading of the Law provoked within them a sense of contrition as they realized that their lives had failed to match up to God's standards. But, intriguingly, Ezra and Nehemiah moved quickly to stop the people from mourning their failures (verses 9–10). Instead, they wanted the Israelites to see the bigger picture of God's purpose, accept joyfully all that God had done for them and recall his grace.

So the people went off to celebrate, to eat and drink 'with great joy' (verse 12). After standing listening to God's Word from 'daybreak till noon' (verse 3), they must have headed off to the party with added zest! They were back home in Jerusalem and had finally come to realize, from all that had been read, that God's desire was to bless them: 'They now understood the words that had been made known to them' (verse 12). It was for this reason that the 'joy of the LORD' was their strength – the word means their 'fortress', their 'stronghold'. It is the awareness that God has good purposes for us, that his Law is for our benefit, and that his actions of mercy and grace are for our well-being, our shalom.

Full appreciation of that cannot fail to generate a deep sense of joy and thanksgiving in our lives too.

Today, remember that God is *for* you. The eternal, sovereign God wants to bless you. Daily, he showers you with grace and mercy, and is acting in many, often unseen, ways on your behalf. His greatest blessing was sending Christ to die in your place, for your sins. Ultimately, God's good purpose is to make you like Christ, and even now he is working to conform you into the image of his Son.

> The LORD is my strength and my shield;
>   my heart trusts in him, and he helps me.
> My heart leaps for joy,
>   and with my song I praise him.
> The LORD is the strength of his people,
>   a fortress of salvation for his anointed one.
> Save your people and bless your inheritance;
>   be their shepherd and carry them for ever.
> (Psalm 28:7–9)

Day 154

Read: Nehemiah 8:1–18
Key verses: Nehemiah 8:17–18

••

The whole company that had returned from exile built temporary shelters and lived in them. From the days of Joshua son of Nun until that day, the Israelites had not celebrated it like this. And their joy was very great. ¹⁸Day after day, from the first day to the last, Ezra read from the Book of the Law of God. They celebrated the festival for seven days, and on the eighth day, in accordance with the regulation, there was an assembly.

Have you noticed how often the Bible talks about celebrating?

On the second day of their Bible study no less, the Israelites discovered the Feast of Booths, a harvest festival, when they specially remembered deliverance from Egypt and the long march to the Promised Land (verses 13–14). So, just as it was written in Leviticus 23, they went out and built their shanty huts. For seven days, they were not only celebrating the liberation of God's people from Egypt, but also their own return from exile (verse 17). Notice that their joy was inclusive: they cared for those without resources and showed compassion to those in need (verse 10).

Believe it or not, joy should be the hallmark of true Christian faith. Of course, how we express it is sometimes to do with our personalities and our culture, and God respects that. But what have we done to provoke so many people to imagine that the Christian faith is so joyless? Before his conversion, Ernest Gordon, the author of *Miracle on the River Kwai*, thought of Christians as people who had 'managed to extract the bubbles from the champagne of life'. He said he would prefer 'a robust hell to this grey, sunless abode of the faithful' (quoted in *To End All Wars*, Zondervan, 2001, p. 115). I know that when people describe the church as boring, it says as much about them as the church. But so often, there is the missing dimension of celebration. I like the remark of the German pastor and theologian, Helmut Thielicke: 'Should we not see that lines of laughter about the eyes are just as much marks of faith as are the lines of care and seriousness?' (quoted by R. Kent Hughes, *James*, Crossway, 2015, p. 115).

> God is particularly interested in our joy. He tells us, 'Be glad in the Lord, and rejoice, O righteous, and shout for joy, all you upright in heart!' (Psalm 32:11). When the church gathers, the sense of confident joy in God should be pronounced. When we fail to demonstrate delight and satisfaction in God, we're not only dishonoring God, we're disobeying Him. More than anyone else on earth, Christians have a reason to celebrate.
>
> (Bob Kauflin, *Worship Matters*, Crossway, 2008, p. 167)

Consider how you could incorporate more God-focused celebrations into your church and family life. Make time for joy! Celebrate well!

Day 155

Read: Psalm 1:1–6
Key verse: Psalm 1:1

....

Blessed is the one
   who does not walk in step with the wicked
or stand in the way that sinners take
   or sit in the company of mockers.

In every survey about what humans want out of life, you will find right at the very top of the list, or at least in the top five answers, that people of all ages will say, 'I would just like to be happy.' The pursuit of happiness and joy is relevant to every generation, and this psalm tells us how to find it.

'Blessed', or to put it another way, 'happy' or 'joyful', is the man or woman who 'does not walk in step with the wicked' (verse 1). Walking is a metaphor for lifestyle, and one that Paul frequently used: 'I urge you to walk in a manner worthy of the calling to which you have been called' (Ephesians 4:1, ESV). We need to read this psalm in the light of Paul's words. He is saying, 'You who are in Christ must no longer walk as the old man you were in Adam, because you are no longer the old man you once were.' And the practical expression of our new life in Christ will be displayed in the fact that we take our counsel, not from a world view that is alien to these things, but rather from the Word of God itself. We submit to the rule of the Lord Jesus and weed out everything that stands against his Word and his will.

The happy or joyful person does not 'stand in the way that sinners take'. That means we do not allow sinful thoughts or world views orientated without God to shape our thinking and way of life. Notice that the three negatives in verse 1 are not simply parallel statements, but progressive: there is a downward spiral of sin. The devil is deceitful, seducing us little by little, sowing seeds of doubt in our minds. He then tempts us to take a stand in matters contrary to God's Word so that it becomes customary to our way of life. And then, if possible, he urges us to take a seat, establishing ourselves there.

What is the secret to happiness? Blessing attends those who are not taking counsel from the wicked, are not parking their car in the car park of the sinner, and are certainly not sitting down to scoff at the things we know we ought to hold dear.

> The real secret of joy, the key to walking along the pathway of Psalm 1, is saying 'No' to what we should say no to, and saying 'Yes' to what we ought to say yes to. Pray for God's help and strength to do this today.
>
> For the grace of God has appeared that offers salvation to all people. It teaches us to say 'No' to ungodliness and worldly passions, and to live self-controlled, up-right and godly lives in this present age.
> (Titus 2:11–12)

Day 156

Read: Psalm 1:1–6
Key verses: Psalm 1:1–2

....

Blessed is the one
    who does not walk in step with the wicked
or stand in the way that sinners take
    or sit in the company of mockers,
²but whose delight is in the law of the LORD,
    and who meditates on his law day and night.

What is the secret to experiencing true joy?

Joy unfurls within us as we avoid sin (Day 155) and delight in God's Word. It is dependent on both these things. Verse 2: the individual's 'delight is in the law of the LORD'. The instructions of the law are a delight to this person. Delighting in the law of the Lord means that each part of my life is being brought into harmony with the Word and will of God. The people who are close to you will know that your life is increasingly being brought under the jurisdiction of Scripture, and delightfully so. And that delight leads to meditation 'on his law day and night'. This interest in God's Word is not just a passing fancy; it is not just a brief intrusion into the day or week. It is certainly not a twenty-minute talk once a week – it is far more significant than that.

Neither is the psalmist advocating Eastern meditative practices. Rather, he urges us to use our minds and bring our emotions once again into line with the truth of God's Word. The word 'meditate' is the same word translated 'plot' in Psalm 2. 'Why do the nations conspire and the peoples plot in vain?' (verse 1). In other words, why do they sit down and cogitate on what they could possibly do in order to undermine this king? You see, meditating is not something that causes us to sit quietly by ourselves, although there is great value in doing so. Rather, it is the thoughtful progression that leads to action. Think of Joshua, that man of action. You don't imagine him sitting around very much. What did God say to him? 'Keep this Book of the Law always on your lips; meditate on it day and night, so that you may be careful to do everything written in it' (Joshua 1:8).

Are you too busy for joy? With the relentless demands of our schedules and a never-ending 'to do' list, do we need to make a conscious decision to take time to 'delight' in God's Word? It is easy for our Bible reading to be like a fast-food snack rather than a gourmet meal. Try memorizing and meditating – chewing, cogitating on God's Word – so that your emotions are brought into line with God's truth and your behaviour reflects his will.

When the early believers converted to Christ, it never occurred to them to fit Him into the margins of their busy lives. They redefined themselves around a new, immovable centre. He was not an optional weekend activity, along with the kids' soccer practices. They put Him and His church and His cause first in their hearts, first in their schedules, first in their budgets, first in their reputations, first in their very lives. They devoted themselves (Acts 2:42).
(Ray Ortlund, blog post, 16 February 2010, www.thegospelcoalition .org/blogs/ray-ortlund/they-devoted-themselves/)

Day 157

Read: Psalm 1:1–6
Key verse: Psalm 1:3

••

That person is like a tree planted by streams of water,
*   which yields its fruit in season*
and whose leaf does not wither –
*   whatever they do prospers.*

If you had to paint a picture of what joy looks like, what would you paint?

The illustration in Psalm 1:3 comes pretty close with this image of the divine Gardener who plants and provides the irrigation essential for fruitfulness. The verse reminds us of Jesus' words: 'You did not choose me, but I chose you and appointed you so that you might go and bear fruit – fruit that will last' (John 15:16).

But there are seasons of fruitfulness. Our souls are not always in the full bloom of summer. Sometimes we look round and are envious at the prosperity of the wicked (Psalm 73:3). People who are not remotely interested in God, ignoring all the instructions in this psalm, seem to be prospering immensely. We, in turn, try our best to live under the rule of his law, joyfully obey his Word, and it certainly doesn't seem as if we are prospering. But from the perspective of eternity and viewed from the vantage point of the assembly of God, Psalm 73 explains what is really going on. Many things come into our lives that do not immediately fit with the notion of prospering, but the righteous will prosper, because the only prosperity that really matters is found on the pathway of God's appointing.

Ultimately, the wicked will perish. They will not be able to stand before the judging gaze of God. On that day, he will administer his fair and final judgement (Psalm 1:4–5). But for those who turn to the Lord now, there is mercy and salvation (Isaiah 55:6–7). There is also the promise: 'the Lᴏʀᴅ knows the way of the righteous' (Psalm 1:6 ᴇsᴠ). Psalm 139 explains that he knows when you sit down, when you stand up. He knows the words of your mouth before you even speak them. He has a whole universe to care for, and yet he knows you. Amazing!

Who can live Psalm 1 perfectly? Only Jesus. Who lives in perfect community with the Father? Only the Son. Who is it that delights in the Word of God and prospers? Jesus. In Christ, you may become a blessed, happy, joyful person, because he has fulfilled all the demands of the law, he has paid the penalty for all our sin, and he grants us his righteousness so that we, living in union with him, discover that our way is known to the Lord. Paul says, 'you are in Christ Jesus, who has become for us wisdom from God – that is, our righteousness, holiness and redemption. Therefore, as it is written: "Let the one who boasts boast in the Lord"' (1 Corinthians 1:30–31).

> If Christians do not rejoice, it is not because they are Christians, but because they are not Christian enough. Joy is the rational state of the Christian in view of his [or her] spiritual position in Christ.
> (Derek Prime and Alistair Begg, *On Being a Pastor*, Moody Press, 2013, p. 52)

Day 158

Read: Psalm 19:1–14
Key verses: Psalm 19:7–8

....

*The law of the L*ORD *is perfect,*
refreshing the soul.
*The statutes of the L*ORD *are trustworthy,*
making wise the simple.
[8] *The precepts of the L*ORD *are right,*
giving joy to the heart.
*The commands of the L*ORD *are radiant,*
giving light to the eyes.

In our culture of fake news, people find themselves asking, 'Can we trust anything we read?'

Here, the psalmist, David, says that you can trust the law of the Lord, because it is perfect, without flaw or error, and it is absolutely and directly suited to the needs of those who read it. The word for 'law' is a comprehensive term, essentially to do with everything God has revealed of himself. It involves not only the law itself, but also the prophets and the psalms. It wouldn't be wrong for us to read simply, 'The Word of the Lord is perfect.'

Scan your eyes down the words used to describe God's law in verses 7 and 8: perfect, trustworthy, right and radiant. These are synonyms. David is deliberately piling up these words that have the same meaning in order to drive home the value of the Scriptures and the need to obey them. Let's look at one phrase: 'The precepts of the LORD are right, giving joy to the heart.' Does reading the Bible fill you with joy?

People are searching for happiness and contentment in our world. The progress promised by the humanism of the past three centuries is now gravely threatened by an understanding of the human person that reduces our humanity to a cosmic chemical accident. If humanity has no intentional origin, if God didn't create us, then there is no ultimate destiny or way to make sense of life. Materialism – and all the other isms too – leave us high and dry. In contrast, the Bible, if you really understand its message, fills you with unspeakable joy.

David is saying, here is God's Word that has been given to you. It is perfect, it converts, revives and brings life. It is reliable testimony – you can base your life on it and it will make you wise. It is absolutely right. It brings joy to the heart and enlightens the eyes. In other words, the Bible shows us what we must believe. The precepts tell us what we need to do. The warnings tell us what we need to avoid. And the promises tell us what we are able to hope for and to trust.

Heavenly Father, help me learn to love your Word. In reading and studying it, revive, guide and keep me. Captivate my heart, mind and consciousness by its truth. In the pages of the written Word, reveal the Living Word, the Lord Jesus Christ. Help me to be able to say with the psalmist of your words:

They are more precious than gold,
    than much pure gold;
they are sweeter than honey,
    than honey from the honeycomb.
(Psalm 19:10)

Day 159

Read: Psalm 32:1–11
Key verses: Psalm 32:1–2

· ·

Blessed is the one
whose transgressions are forgiven,
whose sins are covered.
² Blessed is the one
whose sin the LORD does not count against them
and in whose spirit is no deceit.

What has a cover-up got to do with joy?

Psalm 32 is all about a cover-up. The context is most likely the time that King David seduced another man's wife while her husband was at war. Her name was Bathsheba, and David even went as far as arranging for her husband to be killed in battle so he could have her for himself (2 Samuel 11).

This massive cover-up of sin was destroying David. Psalm 32:3–4 describe him wasting away. His strength, joy, self-respect and energy were diminishing.

Relief only came when he confessed his sin and found that God was not harsh and vindictive, but full of grace and compassion (verse 5). It was the joy of knowing this forgiveness that led David to write this psalm. You could translate 'blessed' from verses 1 and 2 as 'happy'. He wanted others to know: 'What joy for those whose disobedience is forgiven' (verse 1, NLT). This joy is for all those 'in whose spirit is no deceit' (verse 2). David is not talking about perfect people, but about those who have confessed their sin to God and are no longer lying about it or covering it up.

When you confess your sins, you too find God's forgiveness is not conditional, lukewarm, distant, a concession somehow squeezed out of him reluctantly. It is total and unqualified. Because Jesus has dealt with your sins on the cross, they are not on your shoulders any more. He's covered over all their shame and paid the penalty for ever, so there is nothing left for you to pay. God has made you righteous in Christ. You are blessed, you're loved, you're family, you're free. That's the outrageous grace of God – no wonder we can be joyful.

The God whom David feared would expose and condemn him now surrounds him with songs of deliverance (verse 5). It may be that David is talking generally about God's protection, but the link with the previous verses is so strong that when we read about the rising flood waters, we should be recalling the great flood Noah experienced in Genesis 6. Those waters were an expression of God's judgement. Just as Noah, who trusted God, was protected from judgement through the Ark, lifted up above the flood water and saved, so we too are protected from the judgement of God as we ask for his forgiveness, open up the dark places of our lives to him, and trust ourselves to Christ for his mercy and protection.

David's urgent plea is for us to find the joy of forgiveness while there is still time: the opportunity won't last for ever.

Today, confess your sins to God, receive his gracious forgiveness, and know the joy of a renewed relationship with your heavenly Father.

> Repentance that renews precious fellowship with our incomparably wonderful God ultimately furthers our joy. Just as we cannot enter into true repentance without sorrow for our guilt, we cannot emerge from true repentance without joy for release from shame. (Bryan Chapell, *Holiness by Grace*, Crossway, 2011, p. 88)

Day 160

Read: Psalm 97:1–12
Key verses: Psalm 97:1–2

....

The Lord reigns, let the earth be glad;
   let the distant shores rejoice.
2 Clouds and thick darkness surround him;
   righteousness and justice are the foundation of his throne.

Is it possible to be truly joyful when our loved ones aren't Christians?

It is difficult to rejoice when we think of the judgement that is in store for them. Yet, strangely, in verses 1 and 2, we have joy co-existing with condemnation. In verse 1, the earth rejoices because God is King and, without any link, verse 2 gives us a picture of God's throne when he came to his people at Mount Sinai (Exodus 19). The darkness and smoke demonstrate his righteousness and justice, and portray the threatening, judgemental side of the holiness of God. Here is true joy existing alongside an earth that melts when the Lord appears.

Verses 3–5 speak of God's presence bringing destruction. 'Fire goes before him' – fire is the symbol of the holiness of God, and especially his antagonism to sin. Remember when Mount Sinai was surrounded by smoke because the Lord had descended on it in fire? The people were not allowed to approach because God had warned: 'Put limits around the mountain and set it apart as holy' (Exodus 19:23). In verse 5, the mountains melted like wax. Why? What did the Lord do? Well, he didn't do anything. He just came. The mere presence of God, and the whole physical fabric of the world begins to disintegrate.

One day, the preaching of the gospel will be finished. The sense of the Hebrew text in verses 6–7 is of a completed act: the Word has gone round the whole world. God speaks, in verse 7, of a universal opportunity that has been given, and a merited judgement. Everyone who has refused to give God their loyalty reaps the shame they deserved. The gods they have worshipped will also bow before God.

Zion now rejoices in judgement (verse 8). At the end of time, there will be those who fall under God's judgement. And yet, somehow, the joy of God's people will be undimmed. Verse 9 adds a word of explanation: 'For you, LORD, are the Most High over all the earth.' The people of God will be caught up in the vision of the glory of the supremacy of their God, who is most high over all the earth, and exalted far above all gods. This doesn't take away the mystery, but it goes far to explaining the joy.

You may wonder how you could possibly experience joy in eternity if your loved ones weren't with you. Today we weep, all the while praying that the Holy Spirit will open their eyes to the truth of the gospel and give us opportunities to witness and model Christ to them. But when God has completed his work, there will be no more tears, and our focus will be trained on him. We will be caught up in the vision of the glory of the supremacy of our God; rejoicing in his righteousness, justice and holiness. Praise the Lord!

Day 161

Read: Psalm 97:1–12
Key verses: Psalm 97:10–12

....

Let those who love the LORD hate evil,
  for he guards the lives of his faithful ones
  and delivers them from the hand of the wicked.
¹¹*Light shines on the righteous*
  and joy on the upright in heart.
¹²*Rejoice in the LORD, you who are righteous,*
  and praise his holy name.

Jesus is coming again. Those who 'love the LORD' have to get ready for this final day.

How should we prepare? The psalmist advises us to:

• Hate evil (verse 10).
  When Jesus returns and establishes the new heavens and the new earth, his abhorrence of sin will be unmistakable. Ephesians 5:5 makes it clear that evil will have no place in 'the kingdom of Christ and of God'. In the meantime, we must hate evil too. Our ethics, our moral principles, must derive their strength and conviction from what God will do on the last day. 2 Peter 3:11–12 makes the same point: 'Since everything will be destroyed in this way, what kind of people ought you to be? You ought to live holy and godly lives as you look forward to the day of God and speed its coming.' When we commit ourselves to God and his values, he in turn commits himself to us. His preserving grace guarantees our per-severance and rescues us from every enemy.

• Rejoice in the Lord (verse 12).
  Be joyful as you remember God's holiness. The psalmist urges us to remember the name of God and the meaning of that name, which indicates the kind of God he is (Exodus 3:15). In the realities

and difficulties of life, we are joyfully to remember that God is our deliverer and redeemer, and commit ourselves to him.

- Believe his faithful promises (verse 11).

The essence of verse 11 is: 'Light is sown for the righteous, and gladness for the upright in heart.' I think the translators took fright because they had never sown light in their gardens. But God is not afraid of mixing his metaphors! Sowing looks forward to the reaping of a crop. Light stands for all that is joyous, all that relieves, all that uplifts. God has *planted* it. And the day will come when God's righteous ones will reap the crop. In the meantime, as we wait for his coming, we rest on the promise that our joy is secure, and one day our salvation will be complete.

The events of the final day are as certain as if they had already happened. The joy we will experience in the new heavens and the new earth is a sure promise to cling to. In the meantime, as we live holy lives, we can find joy in God himself. Today, rejoice in God's great name and all that it signifies.

There exists a delight that is not given to the wicked, but to those honouring Thee, O God, without desiring recompense, the joy of whom Thou art Thyself! And this is a blessed life, to rejoice towards Thee, about thee, for Thy sake.
(Augustine, *Confessions* X, 32, quoted in John Piper, *When I Don't Desire God*, Crossway, 2018, p. 18)

Let all who take refuge in you be glad;
    let them ever sing for joy.
Spread your protection over them,
    that those who love your name may rejoice in you.
(Psalm 5:11)

Day 162

Read: Psalm 98:1–9
Key verse: Psalm 98:1

• •

Sing to the LORD a new song,
for he has done marvellous things;
his right hand and his holy arm
have worked salvation for him.

Psalm 98 is a call to joy. It rests on three exhortations. Verse 1: 'sing to the LORD a new song.' Verse 4: 'Shout for joy to the LORD, all the earth'. Verse 7: 'Let the sea resound.' Three great invitations to make an enormous noise!

The first exhortation is to be joyful because of our salvation. God has accomplished salvation (verse 1). It's a salvation that only he could have achieved: '*his* right hand and *his* holy arm have worked salvation for *him*'. Salvation begins in the mind of God: it is something he wants. It is done by his personal agency, 'his right hand', in keeping with his character. God doesn't wait for us to realize our need for salvation. He diagnoses the problem and provides the remedy. In verse 3, God has 'remembered' – salvation originates in God's unprovoked love, a love we could never have imagined or deserved. It has welled up in God's heart because he is like that. God's love was first for 'Israel', but its ultimate objective is the whole world: 'all the ends of the earth have seen the salvation of our God.' We can experience deep joy today when we trust in this divine, finished work of salvation.

The second exhortation invites us to 'Shout for joy to the King' (verses 4–6). The Lord's kingship is a source of joyful praise.

The third exhortation is: 'Let the sea resound'. Why? 'For he comes' (verse 9). Our joy will be completed by the coming of the Lord. At last, it's not just the sea and creation praising God, but a redeemed humanity using harps, voices, trumpets, horns – all means – to offer a great paean of praise. Today, the church – the fruit of the gospel – is full of people ready to roar out their appreciation 'before the Lord, the King'.

Whatever trials or difficulties you face, you can rejoice because of your salvation, because God is King, and because Jesus is returning. Today, turn up the volume on the worship songs and sing with heartfelt praise: 'Shout for joy before the Lord, the King . . . sing before the Lord, for he comes' (Psalm 98:6, 9).

I will sing the Lord's praise, for he has been good to me.
(Psalm 13:6)

I will sing of the Lord's great love for ever;
with my mouth I will make your faithfulness known
through all generations.
(Psalm 89:1)

Come, let us sing for joy to the Lord;
let us shout aloud to the Rock of our salvation.
Let us come before him with thanksgiving
and extol him with music and song.
(Psalm 95:1–2)

Day 163

Read: Psalm 100:1–5
Key verses: Psalm 100:1–2

....

Shout for joy to the LORD, all the earth.
2Worship the LORD with gladness;
come before him with joyful songs.

Have you ever wondered what songs Jesus would have sung?

No doubt Psalm 100 would have been a favourite. It invites all people on the earth to worship the Lord with gladness, because he is God and because he is good. The Israelites sang this psalm in the temple. Subsequently it was part and parcel of the worship within the synagogue services. And now, the choirmaster, as it were, invites us to add our voices to the crowd of singers.

Psalm 100 provides a climax to a series of psalms that extol God's kingship, and it is right that we should celebrate God's sovereignty with joyful praise. Amazingly, this King welcomes us into his presence. In verses 1–2, we have three commands or invitations, each indicating increasing access to God: 'Shout', 'Worship', 'Come before him'. We shout out from afar, we worship him, and then we come right to where he is. We come and stand before him. The people of God are welcomed into the presence of God.

And we come joyfully. Why? Because of what God has done for us. He has 'made us' (verse 3). This is a reference not to creation, but to redemption. We who were formerly sinners have now become the redeemed people of God. If that were not cause enough for rejoicing, God is our shepherd, we are his people, the sheep of his pasture. We look forward and see him as God; backwards and see the work of salvation he has accomplished; and around, to see his shepherding care. And we rejoice that we belong to him.

The second half of the psalm invites us to come nearer into the presence of God. 'Enter his gates . . . and his courts', and then 'give thanks' and 'praise his name'. We praise God for who he is. Verse 5 declares, 'The LORD is good and his love endures for ever; his faithfulness continues through all generations.' We look at him and see that he is essentially, wholly, completely, utterly good. We look at him in his unvarying attitude to us and learn that his steadfast love is everlasting. We look at our experience of life and find that God's faithfulness, his reliability, just goes on and on.

This psalm is completely God-centred and a reminder that joy isn't dependent on circumstances or feelings, but rather is rooted in God himself and all that he has done for us – past, present and future. Consequently, our joy is in proportion to our God-centredness:

> We minimize our joy when we neglect the daily worship of God in private. It is one of the great blessings of life that God does not limit our access to Him and enjoyment of His presence to only one day per week! Every day, the strength, guidance, encouragement, forgiveness, joy and all that God is, awaits us.
> (Donald Whitney, *Spiritual Disciplines for the Christian Life*, NavPress, 2014, p. 113)

Day 164

Read: Habakkuk 1:1–11; 3:16–19
Key verses: Habakkuk 3:17–18

....

Though the fig-tree does not bud
 and there are no grapes on the vines,
though the olive crop fails
 and the fields produce no food,
though there are no sheep in the sheepfold
 and no cattle in the stalls,
[18]*yet I will rejoice in the LORD,*
 I will be joyful in God my Saviour.

Everything has gone.

It is possible that Habakkuk is anticipating the ultimate Day of the Lord. But it is also highly likely that he is referring to the devastating impact of the predicted invasion of the Babylonians described in chapter 1. This was the judgement God had promised because his people refused to obey him. Verse 17 begins with the apparent luxuries of figs, grapes and olives, but moves very quickly to show that there is no food at all. Habakkuk is describing not simply a devastated economic and social infrastructure, but total destruction.

That's what makes this small word 'yet' all the more remarkable. Habakkuk is stripped of everything, but still this man of faith sings, 'Yet I will rejoice in the LORD' (verse 18). How can Habakkuk respond as he does? What was there left for him to rejoice in? It was not his possessions; it was certainly not his circumstances. Like Job, he was stripped of everything but God. And that is the key to his joy: it is finding that God the Creator, the Redeemer, the covenant-keeping God is enough.

When we become Christians, we are not protected from the hardships of the world. There is no guarantee that we will be immune from suffering or from God's discipline, from the oppression of enemies, or from the pains and dangers of living in this broken world. But we know that the Lord will not let go of his people, that he has not abandoned his world. He is still in control, and his purposes will be fulfilled. People of faith have discovered that Habakkuk's song rings true. When everything is taken away, we can still say, 'I will rejoice in God.'

It is relatively easy to be joyful when we are healthy, our careers are on track, we're enjoying our retirement, our children are happy, and our marriages are fulfilling. But when you face life's uncertainties and turbulence, will you respond like Habakkuk, '*Yet* I will rejoice in the LORD, I will be joyful in God my Saviour'? When everything you have come to rely on is stripped away, will you acknowledge that God is enough?

> Observe, it is our duty and privilege to rejoice in God, and to rejoice in Him always; at all times, in all conditions; even when we suffer for Him, or are afflicted by Him. We must not think the worse of Him or of His ways for the hardships we meet with in His service. There is enough in God to furnish us with matter of joy in the worst circumstance on earth . . . Joy in God is a duty of great consequence in the Christian life; and Christians need to be again and again called to it.
> (Matthew Henry, *Philippians*, CreateSpace Publishing, 2015, p. 60)

Day 165

Read: John 16:1–33
Key verse: John 16:7

....

But very truly I tell you, it is for your good that I am going away. Unless I go away, the Advocate will not come to you; but if I go, I will send him to you.

How can we experience the joy of Jesus when everything seems to be against us?

As we have discovered, in Scripture joy is much more than an emotion. It is a spiritual quality, grounded on God himself, and it comes from our relationship with him (Psalm 16:11; Philippians 4:4). Joy is also one of the fruits born in our lives, through the ministry of the Holy Spirit (Galatians 5:22–23). It is for me that deep underlying shalom peace; that deep sense of well-being; the assurance that a sovereign God has his hand upon my life, and that his Son has won eternal salvation for me; that I am 'in Christ', for ever united with him.

Jesus promised his disciples peace and joy (John 16:22, 33). This seemed an outrageous promise, given that he had just told them that greater persecution was on its way. They would be put out of the synagogue, ostracized from society and killed for their faith (verse 2). The disciples' fear and uncertainty is magnified when Jesus tells them he is leaving: 'It is for your good that I am going away' (verse 7).

You can imagine their confusion, even anger. 'You've just explained to us the struggles that we're about to face, and now you're walking out on us. How can that possibly be to our advantage?' Jesus replies, 'Unless I go away, the Advocate will not come to you; but if I go, I will send him to you.' Jesus must go away through death and resurrection to the glory of the Father's presence. Then he'll send the

Holy Spirit. In sending the Holy Spirit, he will usher in the powers of the promised kingdom of God in the world.

In his address on the day of Pentecost, Peter explained the coming of the Holy Spirit. Objecting to the suggestion that the disciples were drunk, he said: 'No, this is what was spoken by the prophet Joel: "In the last days, God says, I will pour out my Spirit on all people"' (Acts 2:16–17).

That's how my Saviour, my Friend, walks with me and you, through the dark times as well as the good. He does so in the person of the Holy Spirit. Despite the hardships and pressures they were experiencing, the Holy Spirit – the ever-present God – was a source of joy for the disciples, and he can be for us too.

The day we trusted in Christ, we received the Holy Spirit. He helps us live the Christian life, grow in Christ-likeness, and persevere through suffering. He is God's presence with us – a constant source of love, joy and peace.

Today, thank God for the gift of his Spirit. Pray that his presence may be increasingly evident in your life and that you may follow his leading (Galatians 5:22–25).

True joy comes only from God, and He shares this joy with those who walk in fellowship with Him.
(Jerry Bridges, *The Pursuit of Holiness*, NavPress, 2016, p. 124)

Day 166

Read: John 16:1–33
Key verses: John 16:16, 22

••

Jesus went on to say, "In a little while you will see me no more, and then after a little while you will see me. [22]*...now is your time of grief, but I will see you again and you will rejoice, and no one will take away your joy.*

'They worshiped together at the Temple each day, met in homes for the Lord's Supper, and shared their meals with great joy and generosity' (Acts 2:46, NLT). What changed the grief of John 16 to the joy of Acts 2?

In John 16, Jesus knew the disciples were suffering, but he was clear: 'You will see me no more, and then after a little while you will see me . . . and no one will take away your joy.' What does Jesus mean when he says, 'in a little while you will see me no more'? Interpreters are divided over whether 'the little while' refers to his second coming or to the resurrection. I lean to the view that he's referring to the resurrection, but both these statements are true. Verse 22 also seems to be referring to the resurrection.

What transformed the early Christians' grief into joy? How can we have such a joy that no power on earth can take it away? The answer is that Jesus is alive. Our joy is based on events that have happened in history, and that can never be reversed. Jesus has defeated death and sin, and his resurrection has set in motion a chain of events that no power on earth can stop. In 1 Corinthians 15, Paul explains that Christ's resurrection is only the beginning. He is 'the first fruits of those who have fallen asleep'. When he returns, those who belong to him will be made alive. Then, the next step in this inevitable process is that the end will come when he hands over the kingdom to God the Father, and God is 'all in all' (1 Corinthians 15:28). Paul says the resurrection of Christ has sealed this. There can be no turning back. A process has been set in motion which nothing and no one can thwart, and it ends in final, glorious and complete victory. The reality of the resurrection and the hope of final victory mean that, despite intense struggles, no one can take away our joy.

> I am the Living One; I was dead, and now look, I am alive for ever and ever! And I hold the keys of death and Hades.
> (Revelation 1:18)

> Jesus' resurrection defeated sin and death (1 Corinthians 15:54–57). He now lives in 'the power of an indestructible life' (Hebrews 7:16) and guarantees our eternal life (John 11:25–26). If he can never die and we can never die, then we will never be cut off from the source for our joy: Jesus.

> This huge, breathtaking promise of never-ending joy is the joy of being with Jesus. No hardships, no suffering, not even our physical death, can separate us from Christ, so our joy can never be taken away.

> Thanks be to God for his indescribable gift!
> (2 Corinthians 9:15)

Day 167

Read: John 16:1–33
Key verses: John 16:23–24, 26–27

....

In that day you will no longer ask me anything . . . my Father will give you whatever you ask in my name. ²⁴*Until now you have not asked for anything in my name. Ask and you will receive, and your joy will be complete . . .* ²⁶*In that day you will ask in my name. I am not saying that I will ask the Father on your behalf.* ²⁷*No, the Father himself loves you because you have loved me and have believed that I came from God.*

You weren't created for boredom or burnout or bondage to sexual lust or greed or ambition, but for the incomparable pleasure and matchless joy that knowing Jesus alone can bring. Only then, in Him, will you encounter the life-changing, thirst-quenching, soul-satisfying delight that God, for His glory, created you to experience.
(Sam Storms, *One Thing*, Christian Focus, 2010, p. 12)

Satan is a brilliant thief. He loves to rob us of the joy that Jesus died to purchase for us. He feeds us lies, and delights to distract us from the joy of a personal relationship with God the Father.

In verses 26–27, Jesus is talking about what this new, direct, intimate relationship with the Father looks like. In the name of Jesus, we can enter the presence of the One who loves us. Jesus encourages us to do this: 'Until now you have not asked for anything in my name. Ask and you will receive, and your joy will be complete.' Up until this point, the disciples had brought their requests directly to Jesus. But after his death and resurrection, he would remove the barrier of sin. From then on, with utter confidence, they could address the Father directly through Jesus, sure of the Father's love for them.

Not only can we speak directly to the Father, but he speaks to us. In verse 13, Jesus promises his disciples, 'When . . . the Spirit of truth comes, he will guide you into all the truth.' This was to be one of the special ministries of the Holy Spirit. It is a promise we must primarily apply to the apostles, and the books of the New Testament are the result of this promise. It's the promise of special, unique inspiration for the apostles to deliver the New Testament Scriptures to the people of God. Through all the ups and downs of life, as we move to the inevitable final victory of our Lord Jesus Christ, we have the wonderful companionship of the Holy Spirit, using Scripture to reveal more and more of the majesty of our God to us.

Don't let Satan rob you of the true joy that only comes from a relationship with God. Be intentional about cultivating this relationship, meeting God in his Word and through prayer.

> The preservation of our joy in God takes work. It is a fight. Our adversary the devil prowls around like a roaring lion, and he has an insatiable appetite to destroy one thing: the joy of faith. But the Holy Spirit has given us a sword called the Word of God for the defense of our joy. Or, to change the image, when Satan huffs and puffs and tries to blow out the flame of your joy, you have an endless supply of kindling in the Word of God.
> (John Piper, *Desiring God*, Multnomah Press, 2011, p. 144)

Day 168

Read: John 16:1–33
Key verse: John 16:28

....

I came from the Father and entered the world; now I am leaving the world and going back to the Father.

What is the core reason for our joy?

The answer is found in the simplicity of verse 28. It is almost a summary of Jesus' whole mission. 'I came from the Father' – his virgin birth, his incarnation. 'I entered the world' – his identification with us, his ministry among us. 'Now I am leaving the world and going back [by way of the cross] to the Father.' That phrase 'back to the Father' emphasizes the victory. His statement of what will happen, step by step, is further evidence of his absolute control of the situation. As Jesus said, when he spoke of dying and giving his life for us, 'No one takes it from me, but I lay it down of my own accord. I have authority to lay it down and authority to take it up again. This command I received from my Father' (John 10:18).

Our joy is that we know that everything Jesus came to do, he did perfectly and completely. On our good days, we can't add to our salvation; on our bad days, we can't subtract from it. Our salvation has been perfectly, completely secured by Christ's work on the cross. That's why Paul can write in Romans 8:1, 'There is now no condemnation for those who are in Christ Jesus.'

We are not appealing for mindless triumphalism. We need to be very real about our difficulties (as we've already seen). Living for Christ involves struggles. There are many things that happen to us, or to those whom we love, that we can't understand or explain. But the knowledge that Christ himself has secured our ultimate salvation is surely the key to our joy.

I delight greatly in the Lord;
   my soul rejoices in my God.
For he has clothed me with garments of salvation
   and arrayed me in a robe of his righteousness.
(Isaiah 61:10)

My Saviour wept that all tears might be wiped from my eyes, groaned that I might have endless song, endured all pain that I might have unfading health, bore a thorned crown that I might have a glory-diadem, bowed his head that I might uplift mine, experienced reproach that I might receive welcome, closed his eyes in death that I might gaze on unclouded brightness, expired that I might for ever live.
(Arthur Bennett, ed., *The Valley of Vision*, Banner of Truth, 1975, p. 42)

Day 169

Read: Romans 5:1–11
Key verses: Romans 5:1–4

....

> *Therefore, since we have been justified through faith, we have peace with God through our Lord Jesus Christ, ²through whom we have gained access by faith into this grace in which we now stand. And we boast in the hope of the glory of God. ³Not only so, but we also glory in our sufferings, because we know that suffering produces perseverance; ⁴perseverance, character; and character, hope.*

Pure joy? Really? You may think you have little to rejoice about, but Paul urges you to do the following:

* Rejoice in what God has done for you.
  You are justified. All the sin God held against you has been transferred to Jesus' account, and the sum total of the righteousness of the Lord Jesus has been transferred to your account. You have peace with God and are now standing in grace. God's unmerited favour is enveloping you, at any given moment, under any given set of circumstances.

* Rejoice in your future prospects.
  'We rejoice in hope of the glory of God' (verse 2, ESV). New Testament hope is overwhelming confidence. We can rejoice because we are totally confident that God will establish a new heaven and a new earth, and we will be with him for ever.

* Rejoice in your present problems.
  We are not to ignore difficulties, but 'rejoice' (ESV) in them because of what they do (verses 3–5). *Suffering produces perseverance.* It is one thing to trust in Christ when everything is going great. It is entirely different to trust him when things are difficult. *Perseverance produces character.* The word means the evidence of being approved or tested. As we trust in Christ under pressure, the stamp

of his approval appears in our lives. *Character produces hope* or confidence. You came through one testing time and found God faithful. There is evidence of his power at work in a new way in your life, so you go into the next testing with an entirely different mindset.

When you know all this, your attitude to pressure changes dramatically. You know what God is allowing and why he is doing it. And all the time, the Holy Spirit is pouring the love of God into your heart (verse 5). He is saying to you, 'I love you so much that I want you to have a little more pressure, so that I can drive you deeper into Christ, so that you can grow up and reflect his glory.' This is how Christians get round to saying, 'I accept it. I don't understand it. I don't appreciate it. But I will rejoice in you in it, because I trust in you and what you are going to accomplish through it.'

• Rejoice in God.
So often, we rejoice in God's blessings, but Paul urges us to rejoice in God himself (verse 11, ESV). He repeats this exhortation in Philippians 4:4: 'Rejoice in the Lord always. I will say it again: rejoice!'

Today, practise cultivating joy by rejoicing in one of these – what God has done for you, your future prospects, your present problems, God himself.

Bring joy to your servant, Lord, for I put my trust in you.
(Psalm 86:4)

Day 170

Read: Galatians 5:16–26
Key verses: Galatians 5:22–23

....

But the fruit of the Spirit is love, joy, peace, forbearance, kindness, goodness, faithfulness, [23]gentleness and self-control. Against such things there is no law.

Imagine bringing a newborn baby back from hospital. Her presence will soon affect your lifestyle and your home. You can no longer do as you choose. A nursery has to be decorated, and sleepless nights will be the norm. But you also witness the miracle, and know the joy of seeing a life develop.

In the same way, when the Holy Spirit resides within you, unless he is neglected or confined to a tiny part of your life, the signs of his presence will soon be evident. He will produce his fruit in your life. This fruit is not something we can manufacture, and it takes time to grow. Sometimes, it involves painful pruning. So don't be discouraged if you haven't produced that perfect supermarket-quality fruit in your life yet. Don't give up. Allow the master gardener, the master pruner, to do his work (John 15:1–17).

Joy is one of the fruits of the Spirit. And this is not enforced jollity or superficial cheerfulness that is liable to change with the weather, but that uncontrived expression of deep trust in God which gives rise to thankfulness and the delight that comes from knowing God is in charge and can be trusted.

It expresses itself in all sorts of ways. Some of us are more extrovert than others, so don't measure the genuineness of someone's joy by whether or not they dance, or swing from the chandeliers! Emotions are not always best judged by outward expression.

This remarkable basket of fruit is composed of nine different kinds, but they all belong together. The picture is rather like one of those blended fruit juice drinks where you can detect the peach, mango, apple and pear that go to make up one rich harmonious mixture. Except this is not extracted juice, but the real fruit. The image is of a fruit basket where all the fruit needs to be displayed. It's not a box of chocolates where you can select your favourite and leave the rest for others to eat. We cannot specialize in joy and so excuse our lack of patience. We may naturally tend towards some fruit rather than others, but we need to let the Spirit cultivate those areas where we are weakest.

What a wonderful picture of a Christlike character this gives!

Do you want to be more joyful, more patient, more self-controlled? These Christlike character qualities can't be manufactured, but a significant element of our present experience of the Spirit is dependent on the next verse in this passage: 'Those who belong to Christ Jesus have crucified the flesh with its passions and desires' (Galatians 5:24). When we became Christians, we were crucified with Christ – our old self (our pre-converted way of life) died, and Christ's death freed us from slavery to sin (Romans 6:6–7). That decisive act gives way to a lifelong process of dying daily, renewing our commitment to reject the impulse to live self-centred lives, and obey the Master Gardener.

Whoever wants to be my disciple must deny themselves and take up their cross daily and follow me.
(Luke 9:23)

Day 171

Read: Philippians 1:1–11
Key verses: Philippians 1:3–4

....

I thank my God every time I remember you. ⁴In all my prayers for all of you, I always pray with joy.

My kids used to groan when I asked them to write 'thank-you' letters at Christmas. Here Paul is writing a thank-you letter, but he's not groaning. Rather, he is full of joy. His joy is even more remarkable when you recall that he is actually in prison.

In Rome, he is chained to the prison guard and writing to the Philippian church. This church – of all the churches – had been most faithful and supportive of his ministry. When Paul responded to the call to go to Macedonia during his second missionary journey, he landed in Philippi.

Philippi was significant because it was the first city in Europe that Paul evangelized. His first convert was Lydia. Then he ran into trouble when he cast out an evil spirit from a slave girl. He was arrested, beaten and thrown into prison. He was singing praises at midnight when an earthquake shook the building and, in the aftermath, the jailer was amazingly converted (Acts 16:25–34).

In prison, Paul couldn't do anything for these new converts except pray. His prayer life is marked by thanksgiving and joy: 'I thank my God every time I remember you. In all my prayers for all of you, I always pray with joy.'

Like most people, I struggle with prayer. One of the things that I've discovered is that if I begin my prayers with rejoicing in the Lord, intercession then becomes easier. So begin your prayers with praise and thanksgiving, by reflecting on what God has done for you and rejoicing in his mercy.

The letter to the Philippians is all about joy. Sixteen times Paul mentions joy, and Philippians 1:4 is the first of those. Joy is to be an essential characteristic of the Christian's life. Paul writes in Galatians 5:22–23, 'The fruit of the Spirit is love, joy, peace, forbearance, kindness, good-ness, faithfulness, gentleness and self-control' (see Day 170). Paul is saying that that fruit characterizes every Christian. Joy is not a matter of temperament, circumstances or mood. Our joy is in the Lord; we rejoice in God's goodness. And so Paul is in prison, he's facing an uncertain future, but he is full of joy.

Today, start your prayers by rejoicing in God.

O blessed Jesus, Your love is wonderful! It is the admiration, joy and song of glorified saints . . . It was love which moved You to . . . become obedient unto death, even the death of the cross! . . . You sought and found me when I sought You not. You spoke peace to me in the day of my distress, when the clouds of guilt and darkness hung heavy on my soul . . . You have borne with all my weakness, corrected my mistakes, restored me from my wanderings, and healed my backslidings. May Your lovingkindness be ever before my eyes to induce me to walk in Your truth. May Your love be the daily theme of my meditations, and the constant joy of my heart! (John Fawcett, *Christ Precious to Those Who Believe*, Bottom of the Hill Publishing, 2013)

Day 172

Read: Philippians 1:1–11
Key verses: Philippians 1:4–6

....

In all my prayers for all of you, I always pray with joy ⁵*because of your partnership in the gospel from the first day until now,* ⁶*being confident of this, that he who began a good work in you will carry it on to completion until the day of Christ Jesus.*

What is Paul joyful about?

As he sits in his prison cell praying, he is praising God 'because of your partnership [your fellowship, Greek *koinonia*] in the gospel from the first day until now' (verse 5). Paul is thrilled as he reflects on his fellowship with the Philippians. From the very beginning, the moment that God began a work in Philippi, the believers began to care for him. The first convert was Lydia (see Day 171). The Lord opened her heart, and what did she do? She opened her home (Acts 16:13–15). The Lord opened the heart of the Philippian jailer, and what did do? He opened his home (Acts 16:34). Even after Paul left Philippi, this church continued to care for him. The Christians prayed for him and sent financial support. Indeed, part of the reason he writes this letter is to thank them for their generosity and faithfulness (Philippians 4:10–20). Paul even mentions the sacrifice of these believers when he's writing to the Corinthians:

> And now, brothers and sisters, we want you to know about the grace that God has given the Macedonian churches. In the midst of a very severe trial, their overflowing joy and their extreme poverty welled up in rich generosity. For I testify that they gave as much as they were able, and even beyond their ability.
> (2 Corinthians 8:1–3)

The Philippians gave in great joy, despite their poverty. They gave more than they could afford to give because they loved Paul so much. The believers stood shoulder to shoulder with Paul, and it brought him tremendous joy. It is still a blessing to the Lord's people and to the ministry of the Lord's people when we give.

We often wrestle with giving. We worry whether we will have enough money left over and whether our sacrifice is actually worth it. But financial giving is part of our discipleship, and our bank statements are a reflection of what is most precious to us. God himself is a lavish giver – he sent his beloved Son to die for us – and we mirror his character when we cheerfully give generously to his people.

Who is thanking God today for you and your partnership in the gospel? To whom are you bringing joy because of your prayers, love and financial support? Don't miss out on the joy – give yourself and your resources to God's people and his work.

I know, dear God, that you care nothing for the surface – you want *us*, our true selves – and so I have given from the heart, honestly and happily. And now see all these people doing the same, giving freely, willingly – what a joy! O GOD, God of our fathers Abraham, Isaac, and Israel, keep this generous spirit alive for ever in these people always, keep their hearts set firmly in you.
(1 Chronicles 29:14–19, MSG)

Day 173

Read: Philippians 1:1–11
Key verses: Philippians 1:4–6

••

In all my prayers for all of you, I always pray with joy ⁵*because of your partnership in the gospel from the first day until now,* ⁶*being confident of this, that he who began a good work in you will carry it on to completion until the day of Christ Jesus.*

There is something bigger, more profound, that causes Paul's joy.

Yes, he is delighted by the Philippians' financial support, but he is much more thrilled that they have been saved by God. Look at verse 6: who is the author of the work? It is God.

The underlying, constant theme of the Bible is that salvation is of the Lord. God is the one who planned, and who executes and applies salvation. When I was converted at the age of eleven, I thought that I had come to God; that's what it felt like. But as I look back and reflect, I know it was God who drew me to himself. The Bible sometimes speaks of salvation as a work of God *for* you (you are justified); it also speaks of a work of God *in* you (you are sanctified, transformed into the likeness of God).

The phrase 'work of God' is from the Greek word that can be used of creation. Just as God created the universe, God creates something in our lives. One of my friends put it like this: 'God created the universe by preaching a sermon.' It's true, isn't it? He spoke, and the words of God had such power that the universe came into existence. In the same way, God began to create a new work in your life by a sermon, by his Word and his Spirit together. This good work within us will be brought to completion on the day of Jesus Christ.

Philippians 3:20 describes the ultimate outcome of salvation: 'Our citizenship is in heaven. And we eagerly await a Saviour from there, the Lord Jesus Christ, who, by the power that enables him to bring everything under his control, will transform our lowly bodies so that they will be like his glorious body.' The completion of God's work will be a brand new, transformed, spiritual body like the body of Christ. It will not just be an immortal body, bereft of aches and pains, but it will be a perfect body, unable to sin. God will finish what he started; his work is from conversion to consummation.

So Paul, in his prison cell, is able to rejoice that he can leave these Philippian believers in the hands of God.

Today, praise God for evidence of his transforming power in the lives of those around you. Rejoice in his promise to complete the work in their lives and yours.

> If we are saved by grace alone, this salvation is a constant source of amazed delight. Nothing is mundane or matter-of-fact about our lives. It is a miracle we are Christians, and the gospel, which creates bold humility, should give us a far deeper sense of humour and joy. We don't take ourselves seriously, and we are full of hope for the world.
> (Tim Keller, *Loving the City: Doing Balanced, Gospel-Centered Ministry in Your City*, Zondervan, 2016, pp. 50–51)

Day 174

Read: James 1:1–8
Key verses: James 1:2–3

· ·

Consider it pure joy, my brothers and sisters, whenever you face trials of many kinds, ³because you know that the testing of your faith produces perseverance.

Pure joy? Really?

James is advocating something completely counter-intuitive. Nothing stuns the unbeliever more than seeing a Christian able to be joyful in the midst of suffering. It is not a matter of 'Hallelujah anyway', but it is a joy very deep within, present regardless of the circumstances.

There wasn't a lot of joy in the Jewish tradition. Elements came through in the Old Testament, like Habakkuk's declaration: 'Though the fig-tree does not bud . . . and the fields produce no food . . . yet I will rejoice in the LORD, I will be joyful in God my Saviour' (Habakkuk 3:17–18; see Day 164). And when we come to the New Testament, we find James challenging us in the same way as his brother, his Lord, did. In John 16:22, for example, when Jesus says, 'No one will take away your joy', the context is suffering. Jesus' point was that those who oppose you may hurt you, they may persecute you, they may kill you, but no one can take away your joy. And so, in the context of suffering, Jesus is able to promise, 'Ask . . . and your joy will be complete' (John 16:24; see Day 167).

This joy is an anchor for our soul. Remember Luke 10, where the seventy-two had been sent out on mission and came back over-whelmed with all that had happened: 'They . . . returned with joy and said, "Lord, even the demons submit to us in your name"' (verse 17). But Jesus' response is significant: 'Do not rejoice that the spirits submit to you, but rejoice that your names are written in heaven' (verse 20). If your success or failure is dependent on circumstances – how well your ministry is doing, how well your children are behaving, how robust your finances are – you are going to be on a rollercoaster, forever tossed about by your feelings. But if you are focused on the thing that can never change, your name being written in heaven, your joy will be full, all the time, even in the midst of suffering.

This joy also gives tremendous assurance. Jesus said, 'Blessed are you when people insult you, persecute you and falsely say all kinds of evil against you because of me. Rejoice and be glad, because great is your reward in heaven' (Matthew 5:11–12). Amid the harsh realities and overwhelming uncertainties of life, we can be joyful because the Lord knows what we are facing, cares about us and will reward our faithfulness.

> Joy in God in the midst of suffering makes the worth of God – the all-satisfying glory of God – shine more brightly than it would through our joy at any other time. Sunshine happiness signals the value of sunshine. But happiness in suffering signals the value of God. Suffering and hardship joyfully accepted in the path of obedience to Christ show the supremacy of Christ more than all our faithfulness in fair days.
> (John Piper, *Feed My Sheep*, Evangelical Press, 2009, p. 139)

Day 175

Read: James 1:1–8
Key verses: James 1:2–3

••

Consider it pure joy, my brothers and sisters, whenever you face trials of many kinds, ³because you know that the testing of your faith produces perseverance.

When tragedy strikes or when suffering comes, it is often difficult to summon up joy. That is why it is startling that James starts his letter with the words: 'Consider it pure joy . . . whenever you face trials.' The sentiment is, 'Consider it nothing but joy'. To 'consider' implies a settled conviction. In a sense, you need that conviction before the problems strike. It means you have thought about suffering, you have looked at what the Bible teaches, and you have decided that when difficulties arise, whatever life throws at you, you are going to trust the Lord.

In part, this conviction comes because 'you know' the value of these trials (verse 3). You are convinced they have a benefit. James says the trials you face – of various kinds – will result in perseverance. We can have deep-seated joy even in trials because we know that they are growing our Christian character. Peter has a similar message: 'In all this [i.e. the suffering] you greatly rejoice, though now for a little while you may have had to suffer grief in all kinds of trials.' Why? 'These have come so that the proven genuineness of your faith – of greater worth than gold, which perishes even though refined by fire – may result in praise, glory and honour when Jesus Christ is revealed' (1 Peter 1:6–7; see Days 176–178).

Do you have this settled conviction that James talks about? Are you ready to 'consider it pure joy' when trials come? Will you follow the example of the Apostle Paul: 'sorrowful, yet always rejoicing'

(2 Corinthians 6:10)? The writer to the Hebrews urges believers – then and now – to hold fast to this conviction:

> Remember those earlier days after you had received the light, when you endured in a great conflict full of suffering. Sometimes you were publicly exposed to insult and persecution; at other times you stood side by side with those who were so treated. You suffered along with those in prison and joyfully accepted the confiscation of your property, because you knew that you yourselves had better and lasting possessions. So do not throw away your confidence; it will be richly rewarded.
> (Hebrews 10:32–35)

We can be joyful, even in suffering, because we know God is working out his purposes in us; he is making us more like Jesus. And as we become more like the Christ and press on in obedience, there is even more joy!

> Jesus said, 'If you obey My commands, you will remain in My love, just as I have obeyed My Father's commands and remain in His love. I have told you this so that My joy may be in you and that your joy may be complete' (Jn. 15:10–11). In this statement, Jesus links obedience and joy in a cause and effect manner; that is, joy results from obedience. Only those who are obedient – who are pursuing holiness as a way of life – will know the joy that comes from God.
> (Jerry Bridges, *The Pursuit of Holiness*, NavPress, 2016, p. 123)

Day 176

Read: 1 Peter 1:1–12
Key verses: 1 Peter 1:3–6

· ·

Praise be to the God and Father of our Lord Jesus Christ! In his great mercy he has given us new birth into a living hope through the resurrection of Jesus Christ from the dead, ⁴and into an inheritance that can never perish, spoil or fade. This inheritance is kept in heaven for you, ⁵who through faith are shielded by God's power until the coming of the salvation that is ready to be revealed in the last time. ⁶In all this you greatly rejoice, though now for a little while you may have had to suffer grief in all kinds of trials.

We might like to imagine that the hopeful person is the optimist, who lives above the hassles of this world in the perennial pleasure of watching things get better. But in these verses, Peter places hope – our certain hope of Jesus' return, our resurrected bodies like his, our inheritance kept in heaven for us and us for it – in the context of suffering. He says we have only been introduced to hope; we are now receiving the goal of our faith, the salvation of our souls, yet we have not seen Jesus Christ and we still live with trials and opposition. In these verses, Peter provides several reasons why, while we may have to suffer, Christians actually rejoice in this hope.

The first reason is intrinsic. The suffering is temporary: it is transient. 'Though now for a little while you may have had to suffer grief in all kinds of trials', over against the fruitfulness and inheritance of an eternity with God. Small wonder then that, in 2 Corinthians 4, after many brutal experiences imposed both by the world and by churches that had gone astray, Paul can speak of his light and momentary afflictions, which cannot be compared with the eternal weight of glory:

Therefore we do not lose heart. Though outwardly we are wasting away, yet inwardly we are being renewed day by day. For our light and momentary troubles are achieving for us an eternal glory that far outweighs them all. So we fix our eyes not on what is seen, but on what is unseen, since what is seen is temporary, but what is unseen is eternal.
(2 Corinthians 4:16–18)

This is not how I'm inclined to see things when I am suffering. My entire horizon can be consumed by some small aggravation. Anyone who has ever served in church for any period of time knows full well that sooner or later you get kicked in the teeth, and then it is difficult to imagine any reward compensating for it. But that's not the way Peter saw it. No, the 'light and momentary troubles' Paul writes of, and this 'little while' Peter writes of, cannot be compared with the eternal weight of glory.

Don't let suffering extinguish your joy. Imagine your grief as simply a drop in the bucket compared to the ocean of eternal glory that is waiting for you. Today, determine to rejoice in the hope of your eternal inheritance.

May the God of hope fill you with all joy and peace in believing, so that by the power of the Holy Spirit, you may abound in hope.
(Romans 15:13, ESV)

Day 177

Read: 1 Peter 1:1–12
Key verses: 1 Peter 1:6–7

....

In all this you greatly rejoice, though now for a little while you may have had to suffer grief in all kinds of trials. ⁷ These have come so that the proven genuine-ness of your faith – of greater worth than gold, which perishes even though refined by fire – may result in praise, glory and honour when Jesus Christ is revealed.

Imagine if you had a really rough time before you became a Christian, but afterwards everything was smooth sailing. Would that increase your faith, in this broken, self-centred world? No, not at all! In these verses, Peter gives another reason why we can rejoice in trials. He explains that the tension between present pressures and the ultimate glory to come is precisely what strengthens our faith and produces endurance. It demonstrates that our faith is genuine, and it deepens that faith (verse 7).

This is a fairly common theme in New Testament writings. For example, 'Consider it pure joy, my brothers and sisters, whenever you face trials of many kinds' (James 1:2). That doesn't mean we are masochists. It tells us we should rejoice: 'because you know that the testing of your faith produces perseverance. Let perseverance finish its work so that you may be mature and complete, not lacking anything' (James 1:3–4; see Days 174 and 175). With God in charge, what this is really designed to do is to make us become enduring. Just as the endurance that an athlete pushes himself towards will produce endurance characteristic of his very being, so also with trials on the Christian way. And Christians prize endurance becoming part of our very being, just as an athlete does.

But it is not just strengthening in maturity and endurance in this life. There is something more: 'Blessed is the one who perseveres under trial because, having stood the test, that person will receive the crown of life that the Lord has promised to those who love him' (James 1:12). In other words, Christians do not have the same sort of values as the secular world that knows nothing of the rewards of heaven. We can look at trials in a different way, we can rejoice in them, precisely because we have this Christian hope.

> Paul and James both say that we should rejoice in our trials because of their beneficial results. It is not the adversity considered in itself that is to be the ground of our joy. Rather, it is the expectation of the results, the development of our character, that should cause us to rejoice in adversity. God does not ask us to rejoice because we have lost our job, or a loved one has been stricken with cancer, or a child has been born with an incurable birth defect. But He does tell us to rejoice because we believe He is in control of those circumstances and is at work through them for our ultimate good.
> (Jerry Bridges, *Trusting God*, NavPress, 2017, p. 175)

Day 178

Read: 1 Peter 1:1–12
Key verses: 1 Peter 1:7–9

....

These [trials] have come so that the proven genuine-ness of your faith – of greater worth than gold, which perishes even though refined by fire – may result in praise, glory and honour when Jesus Christ is revealed. 8Though you have not seen him, you love him; and even though you do not see him now, you believe in him and are filled with an inexpressible and glorious joy, 9for you are receiving the end result of your faith, the salvation of your souls.

Why rejoice in suffering? In this passage, Peter gives one further reason: the rewards are spectacular and actually begin now.

According to verse 7, our faith is proved genuine under trial and results in praise, glory and honour when Jesus Christ is revealed. Is this praise, glory and honour for us or for God? Commentators are divided over this, and you can make sense of the text either way. In his writings, Peter constantly says that the ultimate praise goes to God or Jesus (1 Peter 2:9; 4:11). Yet he also says we will receive a crown of glory at the end (1 Peter 5:4). Of course, our glory and Christ's glory are bound together. Any glory we ultimately receive is still a sharing of Christ's glory. So the thought of all praise being directed to God at the end is essential to this passage. And now, Christians already delight to see whatever praise and honour and glory come to God through Jesus Christ, even in our sufferings.

There will certainly be joy at Christ's second coming, but we can also rejoice now because the rewards start now. Christians are related to Jesus already, hence verses 8–9. Peter had seen Jesus, but he writes to people like us who have never seen him, yet who, by faith, love him. We are in a relationship with Jesus; we have been saved by him;

the new birth has been given to us; the Holy Spirit has come upon us because of all God's design work in sending Jesus to sprinkle his blood on us and clean us up. We do not see him now, but we believe in him, and we are filled with an inexpressible and glorious joy. Why? We are receiving the goal of our faith, the salvation of our souls.

When asked what the rewards for Christians were, the fourth-century church father Gregory of Nyssa (c.335–c.395) answered,

> It seems to me that for which we hope is nothing other than the Lord himself.
> For He himself is the judge of those who contend, and the crown for those who win.
> He is the one who distributes the inheritance, he himself is the good inheritance.
> He is the good portion and the giver of the portion; he is the one who makes riches and is himself the riches.
> He shows you the treasure, and is himself your treasure.
> (Gregory of Nyssa, *The Beatitudes*, Homily 8)

Day 179

Read: 1 Peter 4:12–19
Key verses: 1 Peter 4:12–13

. . . .

Dear friends, do not be surprised at the fiery ordeal that has come on you to test you, as though something strange were happening to you. ¹³But rejoice inasmuch as you participate in the sufferings of Christ, so that you may be overjoyed when his glory is revealed.

Imagine you did a small painting and suddenly, to your surprise, you found it on exhibition in London alongside great masters like Rembrandt and Van Gogh. You wouldn't say, 'Didn't I add to that occasion!' You would probably say, 'Why did they choose my work to put up there?' But you would certainly look at your painting in a different way from then on.

Similarly, we don't add anything to the sufferings of Christ, but when we suffer, we are privileged to have our suffering placed at the same level as his. Peter is saying, 'When you suffer, make no mistake; your suffering goes into the same hall of fame as the suffering of Jesus. So don't just put up with it – rejoice in it!' This is hard to do, but I have come to believe that it is possible to rejoice with tears in your eyes; when your heart is broken; when you actually feel so numb you wonder whether you will ever feel again – because you know that it is going to be all right, because, in God's hands, it *is* all right.

You can rejoice through the tears and pain, and that is precisely what Peter is commending here, 'so that you may be overjoyed when his glory is revealed'. You see, Christians are in effect putting all their eggs in one basket. They are saying, 'If the gospel message isn't true, I'm sunk.' But the other side of that is, when it is proved to be true, we'll be overjoyed.

Every bit of suffering is leading to the day when we'll join in the glad song of praise, to the glory of the Lord. We rejoice now, but on that great glory-day, when Jesus Christ is unveiled, we will be overjoyed. With this in mind, keep telling people the good news of the gospel so that they too can share in this joy.

Today, lift your eyes from your present troubles and focus on the future. Consider your suffering and gospel witness in the light of that great glory-day when you will be overjoyed in the presence of Christ.

If there lurks in most modern minds the notion that to desire our own good and earnestly hope for the enjoyment of it is a bad thing, I submit that this notion has crept in from Kant and the Stoics and is no part of the Christian faith. Indeed, if we consider the unblushing promises of reward and the staggering nature of the rewards promised in the Gospels, it would seem that Our Lord finds our desires not too strong, but too weak. We are half-hearted creatures, fooling around with drink and sex and ambition when infinite joy is offered us, like an ignorant child who wants to go on making mud pies in the slum because he cannot imagine what is meant by the offer of a holiday at the sea. We are far too easily pleased.

(C. S. Lewis, *The Weight of Glory*, William Collins, 2013, p. 26)

Day 180

Read: 1 John 1:1–10

Key verses: 1 John 1:1–2

• •

That which was from the beginning, which we have heard, which we have seen with our eyes, which we have looked at and our hands have touched – this we proclaim concerning the Word of life. *² The life appeared; we have seen it and testify to it, and we proclaim to you the eternal life, which was with the Father and has appeared to us.*

Is your joy complete?

John writes this letter 'to make our joy complete' (verse 4). He's not merely talking about fullness of joy here and now. He's looking forward to all that will be ours in the future too, since 'in your presence is fullness of joy; at your right hand are pleasures forevermore' (Psalm 16:11, NKJV). Such joy mirrors something at the very heart of deity, the mutual delight that the triune God has in himself. This 'joy of the Lord' in turn becomes 'our strength' (Nehemiah 8:10; see Day 153). While happiness depends on happenings, God's joy depends on Jesus!

There can be no real joy if what Christians believe is not true. John wants believers to know, beyond a shadow of a doubt, that they are loved by their Father, redeemed by his Son, indwelt by his Spirit, and headed for eternal life. So he carefully sets out how the gospel is based on apostolic, eyewitness testimony. He testifies that 'we have *heard* . . . we have *seen* with our eyes . . . we have *looked at*'. Then, amazingly, he adds, 'our *hands have touched*'. This echoes the scene in which the resurrected Christ appeared to the apostles and said, 'Touch me and see; a ghost does not have flesh and bones, as you see I have' (Luke 24:39). This apostle had taken a long, hard look at the risen Christ, and elsewhere affirmed: 'we *beheld* his glory' (John 1:14, KJV).

Notice the interplay in these verses between 'we' and 'you'. You and I are not eyewitnesses of the risen Christ. We were not there in the first century. But, thank God, we rely on the testimony of the men and women who were.

We do well to remember that the Christian faith's credibility has been contested from its earliest days. Today, we are Christians because 'we did not follow cleverly devised stories' (2 Peter 1:16). There are good, rock-solid, reasons why we have the writings that make up our New Testament. These documents have apostolic authority, as John, for example, reminds us here: 'The life appeared; we have seen it and testify to it, and we proclaim to you the eternal life' (1 John 1:2). Here is a first-century eye-witness testifying to who Jesus Christ is, and what he has done. We'll never have joy if we think the whole Christian story might just be a tissue of lies. Our joy is grounded in knowing that the gospel is true, resting as it does on apostolic authority.

Eternity has invaded time; the eternal has become one of us! This is a truth to rejoice in.

The happy life is joy based on truth. This is joy grounded in you, O God, who are the truth.
(Augustine, *The Confessions*, ed. Henry Chadwick, OUP, 2008, p. 199)

Day 181

Read: 1 John 1:5–10
Key verses: 1 John 1:5–6

• •

This is the message we have heard from him and declare to you: God is light; in him there is no darkness at all. ⁶If we claim to have fellowship with him and yet walk in the darkness, we lie and do not live out the truth.

Our joy can be extinguished when we are confronted with God's holiness and purity. How could we approach a God like this? How could we ever stand before One who is described as 'a consuming fire' (Hebrews 12:29)?

One option, found in these verses, is to deny the problem of human sinfulness. People don't like the word 'sin', or to admit their own sinfulness. Notice here three 'if we claim' statements (verses 6, 8 and 10). Verse 6 highlights how sin can lead us into self-deception: 'If we claim to have fellowship with him and yet walk in the darkness, we lie and do not live out the truth.' Verse 8 is a flat denial that sin exists in our nature: 'If we claim to be without sin, we deceive ourselves and the truth is not in us.' 'Sin' here is in its singular form, indicating that this is our human condition; we have sinful natures before we commit sins in particular. Finally, in verse 10, there is a denial of our sinful actions: 'If we claim we have not sinned, we make him out to be a liar and his Word is not in us.'

How do we make God a liar? Well, God's Word consistently affirms: 'There is no one who does not sin' (1 Kings 8:46); 'All have sinned and fall short of the glory of God' (Romans 3:23). We are all part of a broken, fallen, sinful race. We sin and we are sinned against. If we insist on our own righteousness and goodness, then we'll never need Jesus Christ who came to seek and to save that which was lost (Luke 19:10). But without Jesus, we'll never know the joy of eternity invading our hearts. In effect, we're saying: 'Maybe Jesus' death was for really bad people or folks who are a bit unhinged, but it isn't for nice, law-abiding people like me.' In doing so, we make God a liar, because he tells us we are all sinners in his holy sight. No one likes to be told they're in the wrong, but that's the truth about us all before a holy God. But when we own our sinfulness, trusting that Christ's death on the cross has paid the penalty for our sin, then we can come into God's presence with confidence, with joyful and thankful hearts.

Light and darkness cannot coexist. Today, ask God to shine his light on your life and expose sins that need his forgiveness – secret sins, unknown sins, habitual sins: 'Search me, God, and know my heart . . . See if there is any offensive way in me' (Psalm 139:23–24). Then, with joy and gratitude, live consciously in God's holy presence.

> Blessed are those who have learned to acclaim you,
>   who walk in the light of your presence, LORD.
> They rejoice in your name all day long;
>   they celebrate your righteousness.
> (Psalm 89:15–16)

Day 182

Read: 1 John 1:5—2:2
Key verses: 1 John 1:7, 9

. . . .

But if we walk in the light, as he is in the light, we have fellow-ship with one another, and the blood of Jesus, his Son, purifies us from all sin . . . ⁹If we confess our sins, he is faithful and just and will forgive us our sins and purify us from all unrighteousness.

Guilt is a major thief of joy. Many people are consumed by it for sins that may have haunted them for five, twenty-five, forty-five years, and even more. But the gospel tells us that in the violent, sacrificial, atoning death of Jesus – that's what 'blood' means in verse 7 – we can be cleansed from sin and guilt.

What a promise verse 9 contains: 'If we confess our sins, he is faithful and just and will forgive us our sins'.

The word translated 'confess' is literally to 'say the same', 'agree'. When we confess our sins, we're simply agreeing with God who knew all about our sins anyway! But our sins can only be covered if we will uncover them to God: 'Whoever conceals their sins does not prosper, but the one who confesses and renounces them finds mercy' (Proverbs 28:13). As we confess our sins, God is faithful to his promise to forgive. On what basis? All is based on the ultimate sacrifice, the death of Jesus Christ, his eternal Son, in our place, to bring a rebel people home to God for ever.

Christians are wise to remember three things about sin: don't 'expect', excuse or excite it. John, with a pastor's heart, reminds us, 'if anybody does sin, we have an advocate with the Father – Jesus Christ, the Righteous One' (1 John 2:1). The word 'advocate' is the same one used of the Holy Spirit's ministry (John 14:16). It conveys the idea of having someone alongside you, one who may speak and act in your defence. The astonishing message of the gospel is: we are guilty as charged. However, in heaven's court, our 'defence lawyer' speaks up for us, and he never loses a case.

Jesus is not only our advocate but 'the atoning sacrifice for our sins, and not only for ours but also for the sins of the whole world' (1 John 2:2). He has turned aside the wrath of God. Automatically and for everyone? Not quite! Rather, it is for all who confess their need, relying on the blood of Jesus as sufficient to cleanse from every sin.

Do we want 'our joy complete' (1 John 1:4)? Then accept his gift of forgiveness, relying alone on Christ. Then in his sight, we are clean and whole again. Hallelujah!

Jesus has died in our place, satisfied God's wrath, and is now interceding for us before his Father. We are forgiven, so let's not hold on to our guilt a moment longer. Take God at his word when he says he will 'cleanse us from all sin'. Pray with King David, 'Restore to me the joy of your salvation, and make me willing to obey you' (Psalm 51:12, NLT).

When Satan tempts me to despair
and tells me of the guilt within,
Upward I look and see him there,
who made an end of all my sin!
Because the sinless Saviour died,
my sinful soul is counted free
For God the just is satisfied
to look on him and pardon me.
(Charitie Lees Bancroft, 'Before the Throne of God Above', 1863)

For further study

If you would like to read more on the theme of joy, you might find the following selection of books helpful.

- Tim Chester, *Enjoying God* (Good Book Company, 2018)

- Tim Keller, *The Freedom of Self-Forgetfulness: The path to Christian joy* (10Publishing, 2012)

- Paul Mallard, *Staying Fresh: Serving with joy* (IVP, 2015)

- John Piper, *When I Don't Desire God: How to fight for joy* (Crossway, 2013)

- Mike Reeves, *The Good God: Enjoying Father, Son and Spirit* (Paternoster, 2013)

- Helen Roseveare, *Count It All Joy* (Christian Focus, 2017)

Day 183

Read: John 17:6–19
Key verses: John 17:15–17

··

My prayer is not that you take them out of the world but that you protect them from the evil one. 16 They are not of the world, even as I am not of it. 17 Sanctify them by the truth; your word is truth.

Who or what are you praying for?

The night before Jesus died he chose to pray for himself, his disciples and all subsequent believers. John allows us to listen in on Jesus' prayer and discover his heartfelt desires for his followers.

Strikingly Jesus doesn't pray that his disciples would be immediately transported to heaven to avoid suffering and hardship. Rather, he asks that they would be 'protected' on earth, in their everyday lives and situations. Jesus uses the word 'protect' or 'keep' three times. The disciples needed this divine protection and keeping so that they could persevere, keeping the faith whatever hurdles they would face. They were already hated for their allegiance to Jesus and all he stood for (verse 14) and they were being sent out into the unknown to share the gospel (verse 18).

When he was on earth Jesus protected his followers (verse 12), but now he prays that God would 'protect them from the evil one' (verse 15) 'by the power of his name' (verse 11). God's name represents his character, the entirety of his being. Jesus is asking that all of who God is protects the disciples from the devil's power. The devil's power is real, but it is limited and restrained and pales in comparison to the matchless protection of Almighty God.

Jesus also prays that God would 'sanctify' his followers. Jesus asks that God would make the disciples holy through his Word. Only God can make us holy but our role in sanctification is to read God's Word often, study it carefully, and meditate on it deeply; believing its truths, clinging to its promises, and obeying its challenges. We can only resist the devil, persevere, and grow in holiness as we hold fast to God's Word.

Jesus' prayer introduces us to our next set of three devotional themes – *Pray*, *Perseverance* and *Holiness*. This prayer in Gethsemane is echoed now in heaven (Hebrews 7:25): 'This prayer which he made on earth, is the copy and pattern of his prayer in heaven. What a comfort is this; when Satan is tempting, Christ is praying. This works for good' (Thomas Watson, *A Divine Cardinal*, Counted Faithful Publishers, 2018, p22). When you feel like giving up, when it seems like the devil is winning, when the hurdles you are facing look insurmountable, don't lose heart. Remember, Jesus is praying for you.

God answers every one of Jesus' prayers because he always prays in line with his Father's will. If Jesus is praying for us, we can be certain that we will persevere and grow in holiness until the final day. Then perseverance will be replaced by endless praise in the presence of God and our sanctification will be fully and finally complete. Thank you Jesus for praying for us on earth and in heaven!

Pray

Contributors

Nehemiah 1:1–11 and Habakkuk 1:1–17 and 3:1–19	Jonathan Lamb
Psalm 51:1–19	David Coffey
Daniel 6:1–28	Alistair Begg
Luke 22:7–23:49	Raymond Brown
John 17:1–26	Bruce Milne
Ephesians 1:1–23	Rico Tice
Ephesians 6:10–20	Calisto Odede
Philippians 1:1–11 and 1 Thessalonians 3:6–13	Paul Mallard
James 1:1–18 and 5:13–20	Michael Baughen

Day 184

Read: Nehemiah 1:1–11

Key verses: Nehemiah 1:4–6

....

> ⁴*For some days I mourned and fasted and prayed before the God of heaven.* ⁵*Then I said:*
> *"Lᴏʀᴅ, the God of heaven, the great and awesome God, who keeps his covenant of love with those who love him and keep his commandments,* ⁶*let your ear be attentive . . . to hear the prayer your servant is praying . . . for your servants, the people of Israel."*

'Why pray when you can worry?' seems to be the maxim of our day. In contrast, when he heard about the devastation in Jerusalem, Nehemiah committed himself to weeks of prayer. There was nothing else he could do – no-one but God could accomplish what needed to be done.

One great value in facing desperate situations is that we are forced to hold fast to God. 'I have been driven many times to my knees by the overwhelming conviction that I had nowhere else to go. My own wisdom and that of those about me seemed insufficient for the day' are words attributed to Abraham Lincoln. That is how Nehemiah felt, and that is the attitude we need to cultivate throughout the Christian life, especially in our praying.

Verse 5 introduces us to a model of how to pray in a desperate situation. 'Lord, the God of heaven' is always the right place to begin. Nehemiah cries out to the Lord, Yahweh, the personal God, the God of the exodus who had saved his people (verse 10) and defeated their enemies. He prays to the God of heaven, the Sovereign Lord who has universal supremacy, the transcendent Creator, the God above all others, who has the power to fulfil his purposes (see 2:4, 20; 4:14; 9:32).

For Nehemiah, this was neither theoretical nor formal. He refers to the great and awesome God as 'my God' – a phrase that appears ten times in his memoirs. In the building programme he was to lead, in the opposition he was to confront and in the reforms he was to introduce, he would depend on 'my God' at every turn. Like Moses, 'he persevered because he saw him who is invisible' (Hebrews 11:27).

Some of us serve God in places where the human and financial resources are minuscule, and where the temptation to give up is a daily one. In such circumstances, we need to be able to 'see' the Lord, Yahweh, the God of heaven. It certainly makes a difference to the way we pray if, first of all, we raise our eyes to 'the God of heaven, the great and awesome God'.

Fast-forward to the New Testament and a prison cell . . . Peter and John had just spent a night in jail, persecution was set to increase, and yet, when the believers prayed, their first words were: 'Sovereign Lord . . . you made the heaven and the earth and the sea, and everything in them' (Acts 4:24). Their focus, like Nehemiah's, was not on the magnitude of the task but on the magnitude of their God. Whatever you have to deal with today, will you begin your prayers by acknowledging the sovereignty of God and your dependence on the 'Lord, the God of heaven'?

Day 185

Read: Nehemiah 1:1–11

Key verses: Nehemiah 1:5–7

. . . .

⁵ *Then I said:*

> *'L*ORD*, the God of heaven, the great and awesome God, who keeps his covenant of love with those who love him and keep his commandments, ⁶let your ear be attentive and your eyes open to hear the prayer your servant is praying . . . I confess the sins we Israelites, including myself and my father's family, have committed against you. ⁷We have acted very wickedly towards you. We have not obeyed the commands, decrees and laws you gave your servant Moses.*

It is never easy to say sorry. But, as he entered God's presence, Nehemiah knew it was vital to repent before God.

The judgement of God, which had resulted in the destruction of Jerusalem, was a result of the Israelites' sin. So it followed that, if Nehemiah was about to appeal to God for the restoration of the city and its people, it would have to be done on the basis of confession of those very sins that had led to its destruction.

Nehemiah doesn't distance himself from the people, but identifies with them and acknowledges his own sinfulness before God. There is nothing self-righteous or superior about him. Similarly, on discovering the unfaithfulness of the people, Ezra had prayed, 'I am too ashamed and disgraced, my God, to lift up my face to you, because our sins are higher than our heads and our guilt has reached to the heavens' (Ezra 9:6). This kind of solidarity is important. It is all too easy to criticize the church or distance ourselves from its failings, but when the Holy Spirit is at work, he will show us that we too are guilty.

Mourning over the state of our church and our country is one of the lessons of this chapter; coming in confession to a holy God is an essential part of that process. Nehemiah would know God's blessing only as he and the people expressed genuine repentance for their unfaithfulness. One of the recurring features of revival – those significant times of spiritual renewal and awakening among God's people – is this awareness of the awfulness of sin and a willingness to confront it in prayerful repentance. As we confront the challenges of God's Word and allow the Holy Spirit to review our attitudes, our behaviour, our habits, our motivations and our priorities, we too will begin to see sin as God sees it and pray as Nehemiah did.

Today, repent before God for the sins of our nation, using some words from Daniel:

> Lord, the great and awesome God, who keeps his covenant of love with those who love him and keep his commandments, we have sinned and done wrong. We have been wicked and have rebelled; we have turned away from your commands and laws . . . Lord, you are righteous, but this day we are covered with shame . . . because we have sinned against you . . . Lord, in keeping with all your righteous acts, turn away your anger and your wrath . . . hear the prayers and petitions of your servant . . . We do not make requests of you because we are righteous, but because of your great mercy. Lord, listen! Lord, forgive! Lord, hear and act! For your sake, my God, do not delay.
> (Daniel 9:4, 8, 16, 17, 18–19)

Day 186

Read: Nehemiah 1:1–11
Key verses: Nehemiah 1:8–9

. . . .

> [8]Remember the instruction you gave your servant Moses, saying, "If you are unfaithful, I will scatter you among the nations, [9]but if you return to me and obey my commands, then even if your exiled people are at the farthest horizon, I will gather them from there and bring them to the place I have chosen as a dwelling for my Name."

Often, we feel unable to pray because we are paralysed by a sense of our failure. We can't imagine that God would listen to us, let alone accept us back. It is then we return to the truth that, however tenuous our hold of him might seem, God will never let us go: he 'keeps his covenant of love' (verse 5).

One of the most distinctive ideas in the Old Testament is God's steady persistence in loving his people despite their extraordinary waywardness. That's what he promised, and he will remain faithful to that promise. The Bible uses the word 'covenant' to describe that relationship, and Nehemiah's prayer is based on that foundation: God can be trusted. God's covenants in the Old Testament were founded on his sovereign grace. He had chosen the Jews, revealed himself to them and rescued them – so he would never give up on them. That's why Nehemiah prays, 'Remember.' It is a key word in the book of Nehemiah (4:14; 5:19; 6:14; 13:14, 22, 29, 31) and it represents a call for God to intervene. Nehemiah is saying, 'If you have been faithful to your promise in sending us into exile because of our sinfulness, now – as we obey you – fulfil your promise to bring us back and restore us.' The same theme comes through in the prayer of chapter 9, which is saturated with that kind of covenant language – *your* people, *our* God, *my* God. Nehemiah prays: we belong to you, so please be faithful in fulfilling your covenant promise.

Of course, the greatest covenant of all is found in Jesus Christ. By faith in him, we have been brought into a covenant relationship with the living God and with his global family, founded on God's grace. So, when we pray, however inadequately, it is on the basis of God's having chosen us, having welcomed us into his family and having saved us through Christ's work. Like Nehemiah, we can appeal to the Lord: 'We belong to you, please don't give up on us but be faithful in keeping your promises.' Whatever our emotional or spiritual state, we can come to God knowing that his grace never ends. He is the faithful God who keeps his promises.

Shortly before he was assassinated, the deputy governor of the Maze prison in Northern Ireland, William McConnell, said,

> I have committed my life, talents, work and action to Almighty God, in the sure and certain knowledge that, however slight my hold of him may have been, his promises are sure and his hold on me complete.
> (Jonathan Lamb, *From Why to Worship*, Authentic Media, 2007, p. 53)

Today, come to God in prayer, knowing that you belong to him and that, despite your faithlessness, he remains faithful and will always keep his promises.

Day 187

Read: Psalm 51:1–19
Key verses: Psalm 51:1–2

. . . .

> ¹*Have mercy on me, O God,*
> *according to your unfailing love;*
> *according to your great compassion*
> *blot out my transgressions.*
> ²*Wash away all my iniquity*
> *and cleanse me from my sin.*

Psalm 51 is a prayer of repentance, modelling the way back to God when we have sinned. David wrote this psalm at a tragic time in his life, after Nathan the prophet confronted him over his adultery with Bathsheba and his murder of her husband, Uriah (2 Samuel 11–12). But this psalm is not just for murderers and adulterers, although it is certainly for them; it is for all who seek to regain the peace and presence of God that they have lost through sinning. Thousands of sinners have found their way back to God, long after they had given up hope, through the words of this psalm.

Where does this journey start?

- By remembering you belong to God
  For all his wretchedness, David knows that he still belongs to God and therefore he appeals to God's unfailing love (verse 1). God has made a commitment between himself and his people; although David has broken his part of the agreement, he still appeals to the mercy, grace and compassion of his covenant-keeping God.

- By recognizing your sin for what it is
  David cries out to God to 'blot out my transgressions'. He knows he has a record that needs to be cleared. 'Transgressions' carries the idea of a revolt, of self-assertion. David is asking God to 'blot out' his rebellion. In verse 2, he says, 'Wash away all my iniquity.'

Iniquity implies waywardness, a deliberate choosing of the wrong path. David asks God to wash him – a gentle rinse will not do; he needs to be thoroughly scrubbed because this waywardness has gone so deep. He knows he needs to be cleansed from his sin – his own failures and faults for which he cannot blame anyone else.

David was constantly aware of his sin (verse 3). He realized it was primarily an offence against God (verse 4) and that it had pervaded his existence from the beginning (verse 5). He admits that he knew God's plan for righteous living but chose to go his own way instead.

When Nathan the prophet confronted David with his sin, he declared bluntly, 'You are the man!' (2 Samuel 12:7). Invite the Holy Spirit to search your heart and, when he confronts you with your sin, respond humbly like David and say to the Lord, 'You [are] justified in your words and blameless in your judgement (Psalm 51:4, ESV).

Begin the journey of repentance today by confessing your sins before God:

Heavenly Father, I'm sorry for _____. I know my sin is an offence to you because you are pure and holy. Please forgive me for turning away from you and your Word. Thank you that though I am faithless, you remain faithful to me and to all your promises. Thank you for your unfailing love and mercy and that I am yours – now and for evermore. Help me today to live as your child, for your pleasure and glory. Amen.

Day 188

Read: Psalm 51:1–19
Key verses: Psalm 51:7–9

. . . .

> [7]*Cleanse me with hyssop, and I shall be clean;*
>   *wash me, and I shall be whiter than snow.*
> [8]*Let me hear joy and gladness;*
>   *let the bones you have crushed rejoice.*
> [9]*Hide your face from my sins*
>   *and blot out all my iniquity.*

What's next? When we have agreed with God about the severity of our sin, what happens next in this journey towards repentance?

David asks God to apply his cure: 'Cleanse me, wash me, speak to me, hide your face from my sin and blot out my record.' The cure in David's day was a branch of hyssop dipped in sacrificial blood and applied to the person concerned – then came the pronouncement: 'You are clean' (see Leviticus 14:1–7; Hebrews 9:19–22). David didn't want to hear: 'You are the man!' Rather, he wanted to hear the words: 'You are clean.'

Jeremiah talks about people discovering that soap and detergent will not touch the stain that is in them (Jeremiah 2:22). But Jesus' death on the cross would provide that once-and-for-all blood sacrifice for sin. 'If we confess our sins, he is faithful and just and will forgive us our sins and purify us from all unrighteousness' (1 John 1:9). Jesus says the words we need to hear: 'You are clean.' 'As far as the east is from the west, so far has he removed our transgressions from us' (Psalm 103:12).

From verse 10 onwards, the prayer is no longer focused on dealing negatively with sin. David is asking God to perform his miracle: 'Create in me a pure heart.' The word 'create' is only ever used in connection with God's work. This is something that human beings can never do for themselves. Today, we can read verses 10–12 as New Testament Christians. Thank God that the work of creating a new heart in the believer has happened: 'If the Spirit of him who raised Jesus from the dead is living in you, he who raised Christ from the dead will also give life to your mortal bodies because of his Spirit who lives in you' (Romans 8:11). This work of the Holy Spirit, begun on earth, will be completed in the new creation when Christ returns as King.

What are the results of this kind of prayer? Our new hearts will be full of praise, thanksgiving (verses 14–15) and meaningful worship (verses 16–17). Personal repentance will lead to corporate blessings (verses 18–19). Just as sin can spoil a family, church and nation, repentance and forgiveness can bless a family, church and nation. And there is a restored ministry, a second chance for fruitful service (verse 13). Who else better to lead other sinners back to God than a repentant prodigal?

> There's a way back to God
> from the dark paths of sin;
> there's a door that is open
> and you may go in:
> at Calvary's cross
> is where you begin,
> when you come as a sinner to Jesus.
> (E. H. Swinstead, 1882–1950)

Today, come to the cross. Ask God for his cleansing and forgiveness. Invite the Holy Spirit to do his work in your heart – renewing your love for God, reviving your worship, restoring you to fruitful service and making you a blessing to others.

Day 189

Read: Daniel 6:1–28
Key verse: Daniel 6:10

. . . .

Now when Daniel learned that the decree had been published, he went home to his upstairs room where the windows opened towards Jerusalem. Three times a day he got down on his knees and prayed, giving thanks to his God, just as he had done before.

It was the perfect trap.

'All [have] agreed that the king should issue an edict and enforce the decree that anyone who prays to any god or human being during the next thirty days, except to you, Your Majesty, shall be thrown into the lions' den' (Daniel 6:7). The 120 satraps who ruled Babylon couldn't find anything with which to discredit Daniel before King Darius. The only way they could topple Daniel from power was to use his faith against him.

But, despite the king's edict, Daniel kept on praying as he had always done (verse 13). This wasn't an act of defiance but a display of discipline. It was this unswerving discipline that made it possible for his colleagues to catch him in the act. In his daily regime of prayer, with his face towards Jerusalem, Daniel displayed to all who knew him his belief that salvation was to be found only in the God of Israel. If his prayer had been a triviality to him and his colleagues, no-one would have cared about it. But his prayer was symbolic of the deep-rooted conviction of his life concerning God and his desire to serve him.

When crises hit our lives – the loss of a job, bereavement, a relationship falling apart – there is a sense in which they do something in us: they forge character for the future. But they reveal more than they create. The crisis of Darius' edict did not make Daniel a man of prayer: it revealed him to be a man of prayer.

Daniel had made the habit of prayer such an integral part of his life that the momentum sustained him. Some days, he might have been excited or inspired; other days, a little bored, but he always prayed. It was his custom. Daniel knew the race of life was not a sprint but a cross-country run, and his steady disciplined commitment highlights the priority of developing holy habits. In the New Testament, we read how Jesus went up to the synagogue on the Sabbath 'as was his custom' (Luke 4:16). Jesus himself established holy habits. Some object, saying, 'But that is just legalism.' How is it that when you are doing physical exercises, it's liberation, but when you are doing spiritual exercises, it's legalism?

Are you cultivating the holy habit of prayer?

We don't drift into spiritual life; we do not drift into disciplined prayer. We do not grow in prayer unless we plan to pray. That means we must set aside time to do nothing but pray. What we actually do reflects our highest priorities. That means that we can proclaim our commitment to prayer until the cows come home, but unless we actually pray, our actions disown our words.
(D. A. Carson, *A Call to Spiritual Reformation*, IVP, 2011, p. 19)

Day 190

Read: Habakkuk 1:1–4
Key verses: Habakkuk 1:2–3

....

> ²*How long, LORD, must I call for help,*
>   *but you do not listen?*
> *Or cry out to you, "Violence!"*
>   *but you do not save?*
> ³*Why do you make me look at injustice?*
>   *Why do you tolerate wrongdoing?*
> *Destruction and violence are before me;*
>   *there is strife, and conflict abounds.*

Why? How long?

Do your prayers start like this? The prophet Habakkuk was over-whelmed by these questions. He was living in Jerusalem during the reign of King Jehoiakim, who reversed all the good work which his father Josiah had achieved. During Jehoiakim's reign, the people ignored God's laws, so moral and terrible spiritual decline set in. The priests, politicians and civil servants took their cue from the king and they too became perpetrators of violence and injustice, adding to the moral confusion rather than resolving it. Habakkuk concluded, 'The wicked hem in the righteous' (verse 4). The few who did remain faithful to God were completely surrounded by ungodly behaviour that threatened to snuff out all signs of spiritual life.

Habakkuk not only wrestled with the situation, he wrestled with God. There is an intensity to verses 2–3. They imply that Habakkuk shouted, screamed, 'Help, Lord! Why are you allowing people to drift away? Why are you not intervening?' The real crisis for Habakkuk was not simply the appalling deterioration he witnessed among God's people. The crisis was compounded by the fact that he petitioned again and again, but it seemed that God was not listening. Habakkuk was bewildered and cried out to God in pain. As the novelist Peter de Vries puts it, the question mark is 'twisted like a fish hook in the human heart' (*The Blood of the Lamb*, University of Chicago Press, 2005, p. 243).

It is very important that we follow Habakkuk's example and admit our bewilderment at the perplexing questions and mysteries of life. We must pray honestly. 'We need not attempt to bottle it up, because God invites us to pour it out' (John Goldingay, *God's Prophet, God's Servant*, Paternoster Press, 1984, p. 29). It is false spirituality to imagine that we must not ask these questions. If we try to exhibit a brave and cheerful face before other Christians or even before God, when inwardly we feel torn apart, it is almost certain to accentuate our distress. It is a mark of mature spirituality to confess these things to God.

> Why, LORD, do you stand far off?
>   Why do you hide yourself in times of trouble?
> (Psalm 10:1)
>
> My soul is in deep anguish.
>   How long, LORD, how long?
> (Psalm 6:3)
>
> Join Habakkuk, the psalmist and believers down through the centuries as you bring your own situation before God and cry out 'Why?' and 'How long?' Admit your bewilderment and lay out your complaint honestly before him. Don't be tempted to believe Satan's lie that God's apparent silence means that he is neither interested nor working on your behalf. Ask God to help you trust his character, and learn to live with unanswered questions and mystery.

Day 191

Read: Habakkuk 1:5–11

Key verses: Habakkuk 1:5–6

. . . .

> ⁵*Look at the nations and watch –*
> *and be utterly amazed.*
> *For I am going to do something in your days*
> *that you would not believe,*
> *even if you were told.*
> ⁶*I am raising up the Babylonians,*
> *that ruthless and impetuous people,*
> *who sweep across the whole earth*
> *to seize dwellings not their own.*

When we pray, we usually have in mind exactly how we would like God to answer our prayer. Habakkuk certainly did. But God told him to 'look' (verse 5), which picks up Habakkuk's complaint in verse 3: 'Why do you make me look at injustice?' God encourages Habakkuk to take a wider look, to gain a divine perspective, and see that God is working in ways 'you would not believe, even if you were told'.

God's solution to the problem which so concerned Habakkuk was to send the Babylonians to bring devastation on the Israelites. The Babylonians were guilty of international terrorism, ethnic cleansing and the exercise of ruthless power. What was so troubling for Habakkuk was that, although the Babylonians were in the driving seat of this great war machine, God was the Commander. Why was God doing this? It was part of disciplining his people. They had ignored his justice, so Babylonian justice was what they would receive. If God's people were guilty of perpetrating violence and destruction, violence was what they would have.

The Babylonians were not just under God's sovereign authority, they were an instrument for God's purposes. This is because God is the

God of history, in control of the movements even of pagan nations. It might have seemed that it was the military prowess of the Babylonians that would eventually result in their success, but it was God who had raised them up to fulfil his purpose.

Exactly the same truth is found in the New Testament. The early Christians were bewildered at what had happened when Jesus was crucified. In their prayer meeting, they stated that Herod, Pontius Pilate, the Gentiles and the people of Israel had conspired against Jesus. But then they added, 'They did what your power and will decided beforehand should happen' (Acts 4:28). They realized that the apparently disastrous events in Jerusalem when Jesus was crucified were not completely out of control. There was another story. It was all to do with God's power, his will and his decision.

If God is not answering your prayers as you'd hoped, will you ask him to help you to look at your situation with fresh eyes? Pray that you will be able to see the ways in which he is working, acknowledge his control and trust his good purposes.

When we don't receive what we pray for or desire, it doesn't mean that God isn't acting on our behalf. Rather, he's weaving his story. Paul tells us to 'continue steadfastly in prayer, being watchful in it with thanksgiving' (Colossians 4:2). Thanksgiving helps us be grace-centred, seeing all of life as a gift. It looks at how God's past blessings impact our lives. Watchfulness alerts us to the unfolding drama in the present. It looks for God's present working as it unfolds into future grace.

(Paul E. Miller, *A Praying Life*, NavPress, 2009, p. 187)

Day 192

Read: Habakkuk 1:12–17
Key verses: Habakkuk 1:12–13

....

> [12]LORD, are you not from everlasting?
>   My God, my Holy One, you will never die.
> You, LORD, have appointed them to execute judgement;
>   you, my Rock, have ordained them to punish.
> [13]Your eyes are too pure to look on evil;
>   you cannot tolerate wrongdoing.
> Why then do you tolerate the treacherous?
>   Why are you silent while the wicked
>   swallow up those more righteous than themselves?

Habakkuk could hardly believe his ears. As a prophet, he knew that judgement on the Israelites was inevitable. But he couldn't understand how, if God was meant to be the God of awesome purity, he could allow the ruthless Babylonians to do their worst (verse 13). The suspicion was that 'if God uses them, he must be like them'. The imagery of verses 14–17 underlines the ruthless behaviour of the Babylonians. Like a fisherman with rod and net, they sat beside the stream that God had generously stocked with human fish: 'he gathers them up in his dragnet; and so he rejoices and is glad' (verse 15). Habakkuk was appalled by the brutality. He wondered how it could possibly fulfil God's purposes and how long it would last.

But like many of the psalmists and other prophets, Habakkuk set his questions in the context of his certainties. In the midst of his perplexity, he affirmed what he knew to be true about God's character and purpose (verse 12). He expressed confidence in three things: God's commitment, God's eternity and God's purpose.

- God's commitment
  He spoke to God in direct and personal terms: 'My God, my Holy One'. He was implying, 'You are the faithful, covenant-keeping God. I belong to you.' This is our confidence too. God will not let go of us. Whatever happens, we belong to him. This security is not dependent on the strength of our faith but on God's faithful commitment to us.

- God's eternity
  'LORD, are you not from everlasting?' God is not only engaged in history, but he is also above all its turbulent ebb and flow. Whatever our fears and uncertainties, God is eternal, the Rock, the one stable element in an uncertain world. If things are shaking in our lives or in our world, we must hold on to God's changelessness.

- God's purpose
  Habakkuk realized that the coming Babylonian invasion was something that God had ordained. Other prophets, such as Ezekiel, Jeremiah and Isaiah, also realized that international events are not random but are all part of God's sovereign purpose. 'You, LORD, have appointed them . . . ' (verse 12).

When we are in difficult situations, it is very easy for questions and doubts to overwhelm us. We need to remind ourselves of the certainties of God's Word and repeat to ourselves the confident realities expressed in these verses. If we respond in prayer as Habakkuk did – even in the blackest moments of our lives – we will discover that God is our refuge and strength.

> Never doubt in the dark what God has told you in the light.
> (Warren Wiersbe, *Be Comforted*, David C. Cook Publishing, 2009, p. 148)

When your heart is breaking with unanswered questions, rehearse the certainties of God's Word, the rock-solid truths of the Christian faith. Pray these truths of Scripture back to God, speak them to your own soul. Cling to God in dependence and trust. Acknowledge that, regardless of the circumstances, he is your Lord, your Holy One, your Rock (see Habakkuk 1:12).

Day 193

Read: Habakkuk 3:1–19
Key verse: Habakkuk 3:2

....

Lord, I have heard of your fame;
  I stand in awe of your deeds, Lord.
Repeat them in our day,
  in our time make them known;
  in wrath remember mercy.

Sometimes we struggle to know how to pray for our community and nation. The needs are overwhelming, as is the sinfulness all around us. Chapter 3 provides us with a model prayer. Notice three things about Habakkuk's appeal: conviction, a call for action and a cry for mercy.

• A conviction about God's work: 'I stand in awe of your deeds'
  Habakkuk's tone has changed from the anxious prayers and appeals of chapter 1. Now he prays with a sense of humble commitment. He is no longer arguing, for he recognizes that everything God has said and done is just. Habakkuk has heard God's Word – the report of God's work in the past as well as the prophecies of what is to come. He has recognized that God is in control and now he accepts God's just purposes. When he prays, 'Lord, I have heard of your fame; I stand in awe of your deeds, Lord', it is a kind of 'amen' to all that God has been saying to him.

• A call for God's action: 'Repeat them in our day'
  Habakkuk longs for God's powerful work in the past to be seen in his own day, so that people would know God is in charge of their lives and history. Chapter 3 has many references to the story of the exodus, celebrated frequently by the psalmists and the prophets as Israel's finest hour. And so Habakkuk appeals, 'Lord, repeat that kind of redemption now.' And he is clear about what matters:

renew *your* work. He wants God's purposes fulfilled; God's work established in his day. Essentially, Habakkuk is saying, 'Your kingdom come, your will be done.'

- A cry for God's mercy: 'in wrath remember mercy'
  Habakkuk had heard of God's judgement on his own people in Judah, the fearful reality of God's anger against sin. So he prays that, alongside this, God would remember mercy. Once again, this is a model for us. The essence of prayer is to plead God's character in God's presence (see Numbers 14:10–19). Habakkuk is crying out to God to be true to his character. Wrath and mercy are both essential character traits of God. For example, in Exodus 34:6–7, God is described as 'the compassionate and gracious God . . . Yet he does not leave the guilty unpunished' (see also Romans 11:22). Wrath and mercy are also found together at the heart of the Christian gospel. We know that our rebellion deserves God's anger, so we too cry out for God to be merciful on the grounds of Christ's work on the cross. Habakkuk certainly teaches us about the inevitability of God's wrath, but how wonderful it is that he also points us towards the Lord who shows mercy, the Lord who redeems his people.

Is this the kind of prayer you normally pray? Today, use Habakkuk's prayer as a model for your own.

Thank God that he is in control of our lives and world.
Plead with God to renew his church and fulfil his purposes in our generation: 'Your kingdom come; your will be done.'
Appeal to God: 'in wrath remember mercy'.

Day 194

Read: Luke 22:7–34
Key verses: Luke 22:31–32

....

> ³¹ *Simon, Simon, Satan has asked to sift all of you as wheat.* ³² *But I have prayed for you, Simon, that your faith may not fail. And when you have turned back, strengthen your brothers.*

Prayer is a key theme in Luke's Gospel. It is Luke who tells us that Jesus was praying when he was baptized and when he was transfigured. Chapter 11 provides teaching about prayer, and chapter 18 recalls parables about prayer, such as that of the persistent widow. The passion narrative in chapters 22–23 goes further. Jesus is saying, 'I'm not just teaching you about prayer. I'm doing it, for you.'

This story in verses 31–34 was not included in the Gospel account simply to tell the early church that, at a particular moment, Jesus prayed for Simon Peter. Luke's a theologian, so he knows the great truths that the apostle Paul and others communicated regarding the high priestly ministry of Jesus, including the one given in Hebrews 7:25 that Jesus lives for ever to intercede for us. Indeed, it is fascinating that the New Testament letters addressed to persecuted believers extol the high-priestly ministry of Jesus. We find this not only in the letter to the Hebrews, written to Christians in danger of giving up under pressure, but also in Romans 8:34. Similarly, the book of Revelation, written to the seven churches in the province of Asia facing marginalization, prison and even death for their faith, portrays Jesus as a priest. John's vision shows Jesus clothed with a robe reaching to his feet, which was how priests dressed (Revelation 1:13). Luke included this story in his Gospel to remind the early church *that Jesus was praying for them*. In dark times, be encouraged, Jesus is praying for you. Your name has been mentioned in heaven today!

Jesus knew the pressures Peter would go through, so he prayed that his faith would not fail. This prayer was answered. Peter's courage failed but not his faith, unlike Judas, who abandoned his trust in Jesus. Peter was brought to a place of penitence, forgiveness, renewed grace and mercy. As a result, he did 'strengthen his brothers' – many churches all over Asia Minor received, and were blessed by, Peter's first and second letters.

No doubt reflecting on his personal experience of failure and betraying Jesus caused Peter to write, 'Your enemy the devil prowls around like a roaring lion looking for someone to devour' (1 Peter 5:8). You may hear the lion roar as you battle with ill-health, family struggles, temptations, conflict in the church, or mocking at work or at home. But remember that Jesus is praying for you. He is your advocate and, on the basis of his own obedience and righteousness, he is interceding for you. Without the Lord's prayers, we would all end up like Judas – giving up on God and giving in to sin. Today, thank Jesus for his never-ending commitment to you and for his prayers that strengthen and sustain.

Day 195

Read: Luke 22:39—23:49
Key verses: Luke 22:42; 23:33–34, 46

....

> ^{22:42} *"Father, if you are willing, take this cup from me; yet not my will, but yours be done"* . . . ^{23:33} *When they came to the place called the Skull, they crucified him there, along with the criminals – one on his right, the other on his left. ³⁴ Jesus said, "Father, forgive them, for they do not know what they are doing"* . . . ⁴⁶ *Jesus called out with a loud voice, "Father, into your hands I commit my spirit." When he had said this, he breathed his last.*

In his last few hours of his life, Jesus cried out to his Father three times, revealing to us his priorities in prayer.

In the Garden of Gethsemane, full of anguish as he thought of bearing the world's sin in his own body, Jesus prayed, 'Father . . . not my will, but yours be done.' He didn't want to please himself; he wanted to please God. In the same way, what should matter most to us, what should galvanize our praying, is doing the will of God.

The second time Jesus cried out to his Father was in Luke 23:34. When the soldiers drove the nails into his hands, the first thing he said was, 'Father, forgive them, for they do not know what they are doing.' They didn't realize the horror of crucifying the Son of God, the Lord of Glory. Stephen, the first Christian martyr, followed in Jesus' footsteps. As members of the Sanhedrin hurled great stones and accused him of blasphemy, he knelt down and prayed, 'Lord, do not hold this sin against them' (Acts 7:60).

Are you willing to pardon others? To do so must be a priority because our prayers cannot find a hearing in the presence of a holy, loving and just God if we are harbouring bitterness (Matthew 6:15). If you pardon those who have been unkind to you, you will pray for them, which will transform your attitude. Sadly, we find broken relation-ships where Christians have not prayed for one another. If they had, the breakdown most likely would not have happened.

The third time Jesus prayed to his Father was in Luke 23:46. The curtain of the temple had been torn in two, and he cried, 'Father, into your hands I commit my spirit.' On the cross, Jesus was quoting Psalm 31:5, expressing his trust in God. In the most bewildering and painful experiences of life, we can say to God, 'Into your hands I commit my spirit.' Jesus was on the threshold of death, facing a journey we will all make unless the Saviour comes first and takes us in triumph to himself. When faced with that journey, we can come to our Father who loves us and we can rest safely in his arms.

Of course, God wants us to ask for things in prayer, but he also wants us to have the right priorities because, if we have the right priorities, we ask for the right things.

Today, as you come to your heavenly Father in prayer, express your
  desire to do his will;
  love for his people;
  trust in his sovereignty.

Day 196

Read: John 17:1–26

Key verses: John 17:1–4

. . . .

> [1]Father, the hour has come. Glorify your Son, that your Son may glorify you. [2]For you granted him authority over all people that he might give eternal life to all those you have given him. [3]Now this is eternal life: that they know you, the only true God, and Jesus Christ, whom you have sent. [4]I have brought you glory on earth by finishing the work you gave me to do.

We are standing on holy ground. We are reading the words said by one member of the Trinity to another – Jesus' praying to his Father. He knows that the 'hour' – the time for the cross – has come. Out of the depths of his sorrow Jesus expresses his ultimate longing for this act of self-sacrifice to glorify his Father (John 12:27–28).

How does Jesus glorify the Father?

- By the giving of eternal life (verses 2–3)
  Human responsibility to respond to the gospel message is not denied, but these verses portray salvation, from the perspective of the Father and the Son, as God's sovereign gift of grace to us. The substance of eternal life is knowing God; that's what the Christian life is all about and that brings glory to the Father.

  How can we glorify God? God is supremely glorified by the mission of his Son (sent into the world by the Father), which becomes the mission of the church (sent into the world by the Son). For the Lord's glory, for his honour, we are motivated to share the good news that people might enter into eternal life.

- By the completion of the work (verse 4)
  Individually, we are not called to win the world for Christ. The church is called to win the world for Christ. We are called to find

out, within that total purpose of God, what our roles are and to fulfil them with all our might – this glorifies God. Remember, Jesus too had limitations set on him during his life: he didn't ever leave the Holy Land; his teaching and healing didn't reach more than a few thousand at any one time; he didn't ever know the intimacies of marriage, the struggles of parenthood, the challenges of middle age or the limitations of ageing. Yet he brought glory to the Father because he did what he was called to do perfectly and completely, with single-minded dedication and, at the end, he could say, 'I have glorified your name.'

When we can begin to pray 'Father, glorify your name' meaningfully, making it a fundamental motivation of our lives, we are maturing as Christians and becoming more like the Lord Jesus.

Heavenly Father, help me to glorify your name by sharing the gospel and living it out where you have placed me. Help me to be obedient to you today when I'm at work, looking after family, relaxing with friends and serving in church. May I be single-minded in my dedication to you, like King David who 'served God's purpose in his own generation' (Acts 13:36).

Day 197

Read: John 17:1–26
Key verses: John 17:11, 14–15

. . . .

¹¹I will remain in the world no longer, but they are still in the world, and I am coming to you. Holy Father, protect them by the power of your name, the name you gave me, so that they may be one as we are one . . . ¹⁴I have given them your word and the world has hated them, for they are not of the world any more than I am of the world. ¹⁵My prayer is not that you take them out of the world but that you protect them from the evil one.

What does Jesus pray for his friends?

Jesus prayed for protection from the world which hated them (verse 14). He spelled this out in more detail earlier (15:18–25). It is not that we go out of our way to make the world hate us. On the contrary, we love the world, we get involved in the world, we care for people and we are as winsome as we possibly can be in our witness. We don't set out to be hated but, inevitably, we are; we follow a different leader and our value system is necessarily different because of our loyalty to Christ.

We also need protection from the evil one (verse 15); we need to be alert to the real opposition of the devil. Jesus prays that the power of the name of God would protect the disciples. The name of God is the revealed character of God; our protection comes from committing ourselves to him and reminding ourselves of who he is. 'The name of the LORD is a strong tower. The righteous run in to it and are safe' (Proverbs 18:10, NKJV). Protection is in the name of the Lord, in the character of God and in who God is. Throughout his ministry, Jesus revealed the Father and did so in this prayer, which teaches us about the Father's love, his ownership of his people and his sovereign purpose. It is in these things, as we lay hold of them and affirm them, that we find our protection.

Notice that this protection is corporate. Verse 11 continues, 'so that they may be one as we are one'. We often forget that all the basic New Testament teaching is given in letters to churches and is meant to be understood corporately. The Christian life is not envisaged in terms of individuals living in isolation, but in terms of commitment to a community in which each one is loved, prayed for, supported and encouraged. It is in community that we find strength and protection too.

Jesus is praying for your protection, which is found in God alone. Today, turn to your heavenly Father for refuge, security and strength.

> Whoever dwells in the shelter of the Most High
> will rest in the shadow of the Almighty.
> I will say of the Lord, 'He is my refuge and my fortress,
> my God, in whom I trust' . . .
> He will cover you with his feathers,
> and under his wings you will find refuge;
> his faithfulness will be your shield and rampart.
> (Psalm 91:1–2, 4)

Day 198

Read: John 17:1–26
Key verses: John 17:13, 17–19

• •

[13]I am coming to you now, but I say these things while I am still in the world, so that they may have the full measure of my joy within them . . . [17]Sanctify them by the truth; your word is truth. [18]As you sent me into the world, I have sent them into the world. [19]For them I sanctify myself, that they too may be truly sanctified.

Amid all the grim, costly conflict of the Christian disciple's life, Jesus makes an astounding prayer request: he prays that you'll be delighted (verse 13). Our Lord wants his disciples to have 'the full measure of my joy within them'. He wants us to have the joy of the kingdom, Christ and his resurrection; the joy of his presence, heaven and the victories of his grace; the joy that he had, in spite of his suffering, when he went to the cross.

Perhaps less surprising is his final prayer for his disciples. He prays that they may be dedicated to God's mission in the world. Being set apart for mission is enabled on two fronts: through the truth – by living in and under the truth of God, illumined by the Spirit of God (verse 17); and by Jesus, who lays himself on the altar: 'For them I sanctify myself' (verse 19). It's in his sanctification that we find the resources for our being set apart for the sake of the world. This is a very holy moment. Here is the Son, coming again to the Father, in self-giving. Although our Lord came out of eternity in the purpose of God to give himself (which he affirmed again and again through his mission), he arrived at the cross and, once again, there was a need for another moment of commitment. We sometimes talk about giving our lives to God, but we can't give our lives in one moment. All we can give is that moment. It takes a lifetime to give a lifetime to God.

Jesus prays for us to have joy in our discipleship. He's not praying for us to have a moment of elation or a 'glass half-full' attitude; he is praying for us to love and obey him, the source of true joy:

As the Father has loved me, so have I loved you. Now remain in my love. If you keep my commands, you will remain in my love, just as I have kept my Father's commands and remain in his love. I have told you this so that my joy may be in you and that your joy may be complete.
(John 15:9–11)

Such love and obedience inevitably lead to our fulfilling God's mission in the world as we live in and under the truth of Scripture and rely on Jesus' resources. Like Jesus, our lifetime of surrender to God is given moment by moment. Today, meditate on Jesus' prayer for you and give this moment to God.

Day 199

Read: John 17:1–26
Key verses: John 17:20–23

....

> ²⁰ *My prayer is not for them alone. I pray also for those who will believe in me through their message,* ²¹ *that all of them may be one, Father, just as you are in me and I am in you. May they also be in us so that the world may believe that you have sent me.* ²² *I have given them the glory that you gave me, that they may be one as we are one –* ²³ *I in them and you in me – so that they may be brought to complete unity. Then the world will know that you sent me and have loved them even as you have loved me.*

Jesus prayed for us! He didn't just pray for his disciples but for all those who would believe through their message. He prayed for us to be united. This unity is supernatural, tangible and evangelical.

• Supernatural
  It is given by the Spirit. We are born again and therefore share this common life of God.

• Tangible
  The world has to see it to believe it.

• Evangelical
  It is not simply a unity of love; it is unity predicated on adherence to the revelation of the Father through the Son. There are moments, despite our commitment to this unity, when we might have to say 'no' if we believe that the revelation of God through Jesus is in question.

In our local churches, when people come to an enquirers' course, they need to encounter a unity that reflects the reality of Christ and his love. With all the divisions in our culture, we have a marvellous evangelistic opportunity to embody the values of the kingdom in our communities. Jesus finishes by praying that his mission would be completed by our sharing and seeing his glory (verses 24–26).

Read through John 17:1–26 again. Why does the Holy Spirit give us this prayer at this point in the biblical record? Look back to John 16:23–24: 'Very truly I tell you, my Father will give you whatever you ask in my name . . . Ask and you will receive.' Jesus is saying that prayer in Jesus' name is guaranteed an answer. The answer might be 'no', but God will always answer prayer in Jesus' name. If he's committed to do that, how much more will God answer Jesus' prayer in Jesus' name? Jesus, on the brink of his self-sacrifice, is gathering up in his arms all the generations of the people of God, all our witness, mission, ministry, service and faith, and he presents them before the Father. God the Father says 'amen' to it; the prayer of Jesus is irresistible. Despite calamities, terror and martyrdom, we will be protected, united, delighted, dedicated, completed and glorified because Jesus prayed for us.

As you meditate on the scope of Jesus' prayer for you in John 17, make this prayer your own:

Lord Jesus, because you ever live to pray for us, may we ever more quickly abandon ourselves to you and your advocacy. Certainly, anything and everything you pray for will come to pass. Your advocacy is our assurance; your intercession is our liberation; your prayers are our peace. Thank you, and hallelujah!
(Scotty Smith, *Every Season Prayers*, Baker, 2016, p. 66)

Day 200

Read: Ephesians 1:1–23
Key verses: Ephesians 1:15–16

....

¹⁵For this reason, ever since I heard about your faith in the Lord Jesus and your love for all God's people, ¹⁶I have not stopped giving thanks for you, remembering you in my prayers.

I reckon I use about 3% of the capacity of my mobile phone. I'm only scratching the surface of everything it could do for me. The same seems to be true when it comes to our spiritual blessings – we don't fully grasp what we've been given and the difference it could make. Ephesians 1 tells me I'm chosen, God is sovereign, I'm adopted as a son, God has filled me with his Spirit and I have a tremendous future ahead. We're spiritual millionaires and yet we live like paupers, pathetically unaware of how rich we really are.

Paul is thrilled as he prays, remembering these spiritual blessings and all that God has been doing behind the scenes of history for the Ephesian congregation. The church exists because God has been at work 'before the creation of the world' (verse 4). In terms of putting together a body of believers, Isaiah says that God carved my name and those of my brothers and sisters in his hand before the beginning of time (Isaiah 49:16). Talk about the value that God places on us!

Jesus' death brings us 'redemption through his blood, the forgiveness of sins, in accordance with the riches of God's grace' (verse 7). This means that, amazingly, believers are a family, despite the immense barriers of race, class, culture, intellect and age. Paul goes on, 'And you also were included in Christ' and his Spirit made you a new creation, having believed, 'you were marked in him with a seal, the promised Holy Spirit' (verse 13). So God carved my name in his hand and he sent the Lord Jesus to die. Then he sent the Holy Spirit to turn my heart around when I was fully against him, which is no small thing. One day, I'll stand before God and he'll say, 'Rico, it's good to see you. You've been on my mind a very long time.'

If Paul came to your church on a Sunday morning, he'd grab your arm and he'd say, 'Look at these people. This is the evidence that God's mighty plan for the redemption of the world is working out, and you're part of it! It's amazing!'

This prompts me to ask, do you love and marvel at your local church?

How often do you pray for your church? You may occasionally pray for church ministries or leaders, but most of us don't often pray that we would grasp our spiritual blessings fully!

Today, take time to meditate on Ephesians 1:3–14 and thank God for your church and all the spiritual blessings you enjoy. Allow these truths to seep deeply into your soul and affect not only your prayer life but also your actions and attitudes.

Day 201

Read: Ephesians 1:1–23
Key verse: Ephesians 1:17

. . . .

I keep asking that the God of our Lord Jesus Christ, the glorious Father, may give you the Spirit of wisdom and revelation, so that you may know him better.

In the midst of suffering, struggles and the challenges of everyday life, what are you praying for? Paul prays for spiritual enlightenment. He prays for the Ephesians to know God better. The original words translated 'knowledge' in our Bibles can have a much richer range of use than our word 'knowledge'. The King James Version helps us see this in the Old Testament because it says, 'Adam knew Eve . . . and she conceived'; 'Cain knew his wife and she conceived' (Genesis 4:1, 17). The Bible uses this word *yada* ('know') for sex. The Greek word here, like that Hebrew word, often speaks not of information but of personal encounter. Paul prays here that you may *know* God in the depths, that you may personally, intimately encounter him. Isn't that staggering?

Doubtless, along with persecution, the Ephesians faced economic, social and relational problems, and yet Paul does not pray for easier circumstances – rest for the stressed, health for the sick, success for the struggling. He doesn't pray for their circumstances at all. If that were me, I'd pray, 'Give me rest, health and success, because I feel stressed, sick and struggling!' When we pray for ourselves and others, we need to be praying more like Paul, 'Lord, you know that John is really struggling with his illness. You know how worried I am about the pressures of Claire's new job, and how stressed Paul and Fiona are about selling their flat. But thank you that they are Christian believers and you've blessed them in Christ with every spiritual blessing. Please open their eyes to grasp what you've done for them and help them know you better.' It may seem tame to pray for the grasping of invisible truths and the changing of inward character – what about the illness, the stress and the sale of the flat? But Paul knows that if people know God, then whatever issues arise stay in perspective.

The point is not that we never pray about our jobs, house moves or family issues, but that through all the circumstances of our lives – good and bad – our priority, our prayer, is that we may know God better. As Paul said in Philippians 3:8–11:

> I consider everything a loss because of the surpassing worth of knowing Christ Jesus my Lord, for whose sake I have lost all things. I consider them garbage, that I may gain Christ and be found in him, not having a righteousness of my own that comes from the law, but that which is through faith in Christ – the righteousness that comes from God on the basis of faith. I want to know Christ – yes, to know the power of his resurrection and participation in his sufferings, becoming like him in his death, and so, somehow, attaining to the resurrection from the dead.

Day 202

Read: Ephesians 1:1–23
Key verse: Ephesians 1:18

....

I pray that the eyes of your heart may be enlightened in order that you may know the hope to which he has called you, the riches of his glorious inheritance in his holy people.

I always wanted more. I never had enough milk or money or socks or sex or holidays or first editions or solitude or gramophone records or free meals or real friends or guiltless pleasure or neckties or applause or unquestioning love. Of course, I've had more than my share of most of these commodities, but it always left me with a vague feeling of unfulfilment.

These are the opening words of the autobiography of Barry Humphries (Dame Edna Everage), entitled *More Please* (Penguin, 2016).

The human heart is always asking for 'more, please'. We have an insatiable desire for beauty, peace, rest, happiness and love. We seek to satisfy these desires within the parameters of this world, but whatever we do never quite measures up, never quite quenches our thirst. The problem is we are looking to the world to satisfy eternal desires. The Bible teaches us that God has set eternity in our hearts (Ecclesiastes 3:11), and that desire for eternity will only be satisfied with the treasures of eternity. So, God means for that desire for beauty, rest, peace, love and happiness to be satisfied not just in him here on earth but in the full knowledge of God in the world to come. And it will *not* be satisfied anywhere else.

Paul particularly prays 'that the eyes of your heart may be [opened to] the hope to which he has called you' because, if we don't grasp what a great eternity each of us has ahead of us, our temptation will always be to build heaven here. Ephesians 1 reminds us that we are going to inherit the earth and, in Christ, the future is ours, so we shouldn't try to build heaven now. Instead, it is best to invest our time and energy in God's purposes.

If my aim is to build heaven here, then it becomes hard to submit to Christ, love him and share him with others. I don't speak about Christ because I don't want to cause any upset; I don't want to be drawn into other people's problems; I want heaven here. Financial giving? I can't do that because I'm building heaven here. God's going to have to be happy with the small change. Regular prayer and personal Bible reading are going to be a struggle because I've got heaven here to worry about. Involvement with small groups and discipleship courses is not an option. I'm casual about church membership because my focus is building heaven here.

What are your treasures? Where are you building?

Are you trying to build heaven on earth? Examine your relationships, bank statement and diary to find out in whom and what you are investing your life. Today, pray that you will fully grasp the hope and inheritance you have, and that these eternal realities will shape your life now.

If you read history, you will find that the Christians who did most for the present world were just those who thought most of the next.
(C. S. Lewis, *Mere Christianity*, Collins, 2016, p. 132)

Day 203

Read: Ephesians 1:1–23
Key verses: Ephesians 1:18–20

··

18 I pray that the eyes of your heart may be enlightened in order that you may know . . . 19 his incomparably great power for us who believe. That power is the same as the mighty strength 20 he exerted when he raised Christ from the dead and seated him at his right hand in the heavenly realms.

Do you feel trapped in a cycle of sin, a pattern of behaviour you just can't seem to escape from? Is there a secret sin you have been indulging in? Have you grown accustomed to excusing the so-called 'respectable sins', such as gossip, worry, gluttony and lack of contentment? There is hope; you can change. Here, Paul prays that these Ephesian believers – and we – might know that we are possessed by God's power. Paul wants us to see that not only do we have a glorious inheritance, a wonderful future, but we also have God's power at work in us now.

You are sitting on a gold mine! The power that raised Christ, seated him at God's right hand and placed him above every power and authority we might tremble at is already at work in us. This means that we can pray, 'Lord, I'm angry at this person, but thank you that the power that raised Christ from the dead is at work in me. Please help me to calm down and be godly. Please, Lord, give me your Spirit and your strength to comfort and calm me.' Don't look inwards at yourself or sideways at one another; look to Christ and know that you are possessed by the same power.

When you are feeling weak, insecure and struggling with sin, ask him for strength to control your tongue, temper, lust, greed, malice and jealousy. If you look to Christ and fill your heart with him, you can battle against your sinful nature as you need to each day. Do you think it is beyond the power of God, who raised Christ from the dead, to help you? It is beyond our power, yes, but it is certainly not beyond God's power.

Today, as you wrestle with the temptation to sin, will you remember that the same power that raised Jesus from the dead is available to you? Pray for God's 'mighty strength' to help you 'to say "No" to ungodliness and worldly passions, and to live self-controlled, upright and godly lives in this present age' (Titus 2:12).

A cry for help from the heart of a childlike [believer] is sweet praise in the ears of God. Nothing exalts Him more than the collapse of self-reliance which issues in passionate prayer for help. 'Call upon me in the day of trouble; I will deliver you, and you shall glorify me' (Ps. 50:15). Prayer is the translation into a thousand different words of a single sentence: 'Apart from me [Christ], you can do nothing' (John 15:5).

(John Piper, *Brothers, We Are Not Professionals*, Broadman & Holman, 2013, p. 70)

Day 204

Read: Ephesians 6:10–20
Key verses: Ephesians 6:18–20

. . . .

[18] And pray in the Spirit on all occasions with all kinds of prayers and requests. With this in mind, be alert and always keep on praying for all the Lord's people. [19] Pray also for me, that whenever I speak, words may be given me so that I will fearlessly make known the mystery of the gospel, [20] for which I am an ambassador in chains. Pray that I may declare it fearlessly, as I should.

Just as the armour of God is not reserved for the spiritual elite, neither is praying. Prayer is indispensable if we are to stand strong and resolute in our faith (Ephesians 6:10, 11, 13, 14).

Paul urges us to 'pray in the Spirit', that is, to pray prayers which are energized by the Spirit of God. Pray with thanksgiving, petitions and intercessions; pray silently, vocally, individually and corporately; fast from food, hold all-night prayer vigils – all these are included when Paul says pray 'with all kinds of prayers and requests' (verse 18).

In verse 19, he adds, 'Pray also for me.' Although Paul had written almost half the New Testament and preached throughout the then-known world, he is asking for prayer. Although he has raised a man from the dead (Acts 20:10) and cast out demons (Acts 16:18), he is asking for prayer. Although he has gone up to the third heaven and heard things that human beings are not allowed to hear (2 Corinthians 12:2–4), he is asking for prayer. Paul recognized his need for prayer. He acknowledged his utter dependence on God's power and enabling for his life and ministry. In contrast, we often become too *self*-focused in our ministries. We try to deal with problems in our own strength, to the extent that we almost stigmatize praying. We behave as if we believe that to need prayer is to need a crutch.

What did Paul want the believers to pray for? First, for his preaching to be energized by God as God's Word was proclaimed. Second, for fearless proclamation, that he would not be shy as he shared the 'mystery of the gospel'. Third, that he would be an ambassador for Christ, even in his prison cell. We need to pray for the things that burn in God's heart – concern for those who have not heard the gospel, the preaching of the Word – to burn in our hearts too.

We may pray for our church leaders occasionally but often only in a general sense. Today, will you pray specifically for the person who is preparing to preach in your church this Sunday? Pray for the

- preaching to be energized by God;
- proclamation of the gospel to be fearless, regardless of potential opposition;
- life to authenticate the message.

Pray too for your church congregation who will listen to the message this Sunday. Pray for unbelievers to accept the gospel joyfully and for believers to respond in obedience. Don't forget to pray for yourself – for the things that burn in God's heart to burn ever more strongly and brightly in yours.

Day 205

Read: Philippians 1:1–11
Key verse: Philippians 1:9

· ·

And this is my prayer: that your love may abound more and more in knowledge and depth of insight.

What is the biggest problem in the church? People!

We struggle to get on with one another. Philippi was the definition of a loving church and yet, even here, there are problems. In chapter 2, Paul has to say to the believers, 'Look, you need to have the mind of Christ, who humbled himself so much and was obedient to death.' In Philippians 4:2, we are told that there are two women who can't agree. Consequently, Paul's main prayer for this church is love. He prays for an *abounding* love. Paul wants the believers to demonstrate a love for one another that is growing, increasing, bubbling up and overflowing.

My family and I used to live near Malvern and, as far as I am aware, the Malvern spring has never run dry. Even in the driest periods, the water continues to bubble up and flow out. That's the kind of love that Paul is talking about here. Are there people in your fellowship with whom you don't get on? Are there people you don't speak to or have a certain level of bitterness towards? Well, you need to pray for the Lord to give you the kind of love that bubbles up and flows out.

What about our lost world? On a hot day, I would love to be in Malvern, standing under the Malvern spring, its cold, refreshing water flowing over me. Wouldn't you? In this world, where there is so much pain and sorrow, the church is supposed to be a spring of overflowing love. Yes, we must preach the truth in Christ. Even so, what makes people sit up and take notice of Christianity is seeing Christians who love one another – that's where it starts. Sooner or later, they can hear the gospel, but the thing that will attract them first and foremost is the life-refreshing spring of love that flows up and flows out.

Notice here that Paul is not only praying for an abounding love but also an *intelligent* love. In verse 9, Paul prays for a love abounding 'in knowledge and depth of insight'. Christian love is not mere sentiment; it knows the truth, and is rooted in knowledge and understanding.

Do you dare pray for more love? More love will result in more prayer! Watch out for this delightful pattern emerging in your life.

Prayer is the product of [our] passion for people . . .

Unaffected fervency in prayer is not whipped-up emotionalism, but the overflow of [our] love for brothers and sisters in Christ Jesus. That means that if we are to improve our praying, we must strengthen our loving. As we grow in disciplined, self-sacrificing love, so we will grow in intercessory prayer. Superficially fervent prayers devoid of such love are finally phony, hollow, shallow.

(D. A. Carson, *A Call to Spiritual Reformation*, IVP, 2011, p. 85)

Day 206

Read: Philippians 1:1–11
Key verses: Philippians 1:9–11

....

⁹And this is my prayer: that your love may abound more and more in knowledge and depth of insight, ¹⁰so that you may be able to discern what is best and may be pure and blameless for the day of Christ, ¹¹filled with the fruit of righteousness that comes through Jesus Christ – to the glory and praise of God.

Why should we pray for love? Because, if we love one another with God's overflowing love, three things will follow: discernment, purity and the fruit of righteousness.

• Discernment
Verse 10 says, 'so that you may be able to discern what is *best*' (my emphasis). If you have love from God for one another, you will be able to make a judgement about what is important and what isn't, the things that really matter and the things that don't.

Some years ago, I was President of the Fellowship of Independent Evangelical Churches (FIEC). There are almost 600 churches in FIEC and I travelled all over the country helping those in trouble. I still visit churches and I have yet to find one in which the things that divide Christians are actually fundamental, biblical or theological principles. Almost always, the division is over secondary things, issues of culture or preference, such as sung worship.

What are the things that are troubling your church at the moment? Are they *really* theological things? The Bible says that love covers a multitude of sins, a multitude of differences, and that love will give you discernment.

- Purity
  Verse 10 also says, '[so that you] may be pure and blameless for the day of Christ'. The word 'pure' means 'chaste'; the word 'blameless' conveys the idea of not causing other people to stumble. Paul prays for these believers to be abounding in love, because if you love your brothers and sisters in the church, you will make sure you do nothing to cause them to stumble. Why? Because you know that you are going to heaven together. You know that you belong to one another. You know that Christ is coming and, when he does come, every sin will be revealed in the blaze of his glory!

- The fruit of righteousness
  Overflowing love leads to being 'filled with the fruit of righteousness' (verse 11). Essentially, 'the fruit of righteousness' means being filled with love, grace and mercy towards one another. It means being filled with the fruit of the Spirit. And, as Galatians 5 emphasizes, the fruit of the Spirit is displayed within the context of relationships.

God wants to enlarge our hearts and increase our capacity for loving him and others.

Father, please pour out the Spirit upon us in increased measure. Save us from paddling around in the shallows of limited vision and understanding, and please sweep us up in the ocean of your matchless love. Lord, forgive my small view of your vast generosity, and grant that every thought of your Fatherly care may cause my love for your Son Jesus to deepen and then overflow, so that others may be caught up in your embrace. For the sake of Jesus, in whose name I pray, Amen.

(Alistair Begg, *Pray Big*, Good Book Company, 2019, pp. 83–84)

Day 207

Read: Philippians 1:1–11
Key verses: Philippians 1:9–11

....

> [9] *And this is my prayer: that your love may abound more and more in knowledge and depth of insight,* [10] *so that you may be able to discern what is best and may be pure and blameless for the day of Christ,* [11] *filled with the fruit of righteousness that comes through Jesus Christ – to the glory and praise of God.*

Why should we pray this prayer of the Bible for ourselves and make it our own? So that we may be 'to the glory and praise of God'. God's great concern is for his glory. All of creation, every starry constellation, displays God's glory. The psalmist declared, 'The heavens declare the glory of God' (Psalm 19:1). Supremely, God's glory is seen in the face of his Son, Jesus Christ (2 Corinthians 4:6). But, amazingly, God's glory is also seen in his people, the church, as Ephesians 3:20–21 highlights:

> Now to him to is able to do immeasurably more than all we ask or imagine, according to his power that is at work within us, to him be glory in the church and in Christ Jesus throughout all generations, for ever and ever! Amen.

Can you believe it – 'glory in the church'? Glory in your church, with all its foibles, failings and imperfections. Paul thought of this church in Philippi that had stood by him through thick and thin, and he prayed for its people to love one another. As they loved one another as he loved them, as they loved him, as they moved in the love of God, he prayed for the world to see it and for God to be glorified. This is the work of the church – to show people the glory of God.

On the walls of the Faith Mission building in Edinburgh there's a quote from the US evangelist, D. L. Moody: 'Out of 100 men, one will read the Bible, the other 99 will read the Christian.' What will the world see? Where will they see the gospel? They'll see it in you. Our job as individuals in the church is to make Jesus Christ visible, intelligible and desirable. That is the essence of Paul's prayer.

> Praying over the Word . . . has the effect of shaping our minds and hearts, so that we desire what the Word encourages us to desire, and not just what we desire by nature. That is why the prayers of Bible-saturated people sound so differently. Most people, before their prayers are soaked in Scripture, simply bring their natural desires to God. In other words, they pray the way an unbeliever would pray who is convinced that God might give him what he wants: health, a better job, safe journeys, a prosperous portfolio, successful children, plenty of food, a happy marriage, a car that works, a comfortable retirement, etc. None of these is evil. They're just natural. You don't have to be born again to want any of these. Desiring them – even from God – is no evidence of saving faith. So if these are all you pray for, there is a deep problem. Your desires have not yet been changed to put the glory of Christ at the centre. (John Piper, *When I Don't Desire God*, Crossway, 2013, p. 165)

Day 208

Read: 1 Thessalonians 3:6–13
Key verse: 1 Thessalonians 3:10

....

Night and day we pray most earnestly that we may see you again and supply what is lacking in your faith.

Are you growing?

Paul tells these Thessalonian Christians that he's heard about their faith, love and hope (1 Thessalonians 1:3).

His prayer is that these wonderful virtues may keep on growing (1 Thessalonians 5:8). If you're not growing as a Christian, then there's something wrong. You don't stand still in the Christian life. You either go forwards or backwards, but you never, ever, stand still.

The first aspect of Paul's prayer is that the Thessalonians' faith may be strengthened (verse 10). Persecution had forced Paul to leave Thessalonica in a hurry, and he longs to see the believers again. He's been praying for them, he's written to them, he's sent Timothy to them, but he longs to see them. Why? He wants to strengthen their faith. Paul is not talking about the experience of faith, more about Christian truth. There's something lacking in their understanding of Christian truth that he wants to teach them. One clear gap in their theology was the issue of what happened to people who died before the Lord's return (1 Thessalonians 4:13–17).

Paul prays for the Thessalonians' faith and their grasp of truth to grow. He wants them to have a better understanding of God's Word so that they can increase their knowledge of the Lord Jesus. The Bible is about Jesus, from beginning to end. The more we know of Jesus, the deeper our love for him becomes and the stronger we are in our Christian lives. Doctrine, the truth of God's Word, is not just for the academics who go to Bible college; it is the warp and weft of our lives. Doctrine is the truth that keeps us going in difficult times. It strengthens us and is the rock-solid foundation of our lives. Paul prays for these Thessalonians because he wants to fill up those bits that are missing in their faith. He wants them to be firmly established so that they will stand strong when trials come (1 Thessalonians 1:6; 2:14–15; 3:2–3).

Is your faith growing? Is your understanding of the Bible growing?

We may pray for health, for God's strength to deal with the challenges of the day, but rarely do we pray to grow in our knowledge and understanding of Christian doctrine. Will you pray that prayer today? What practical measures can you put in place to be the answer to that prayer and grow in your understanding of the Bible? Think about how you listen to sermons, prepare for Bible studies and approach your devotional times with God. Also, reflect on the opportunities you have to teach doctrine – reading Bible stories to your children before bed, singing Christian songs with your grandchildren in the car, leading a Bible study, speaking words of encouragement to another believer. Pray for God to use these moments to increase the faith of others.

Day 209

Read: 1 Thessalonians 3:6–13
Key verse: 1 Thessalonians 3:12

....

May the Lord make your love increase and overflow for each other and for everyone else, just as ours does for you.

Timothy had reported to Paul that the church in Thessalonica was a loving one (1 Thessalonians 1:3). But Paul is not content with the status quo. He prays for the believers, asking for their love for one another to overflow and for their love to overflow to a lost world.

• Their love for one another to overflow
Paul prays for the believers' love for each other to grow, to become stronger and deeper. His great prayer in the New Testament is that the church may demonstrate love between Christians to a lost world (see Philippians 1:9–11, Days 204 and 205). There are twenty-one letters in the New Testament and every single one, at some point, talks about the problem of relationships between Christians. Why? Because loving one another is important, which, because we're all different, is difficult. Do you love one another enough? Of course, our love for one another depends on our love for Christ. We cannot serve the Lord, the Lord's people and a lost world unless our hearts are right in our relationship with Christ.

In Revelation 2:1–7, John writes to the church at Ephesus. It is a busy, doctrinally sound church that has persevered despite persecution. It seems to be a great church, until you read verse 4: 'Yet I hold this against you: you have forsaken the love you had at first.' Literally, the Ephesians have deserted their first love. It is the same word that is used of Peter when he denied the Lord three times. They have denied their first love. Do you love Jesus as much as you used to? If you don't, ask him to give you that love. Only then will you be able to love others.

- Their love to overflow to a lost world
Imagine a spring from which the water never runs dry and to which people flock to quench their thirst. The church is supposed to be like that spring, flowing out of the life of Christ, pointing people to Jesus. Jesus said, 'Whoever believes in me will never be thirsty' (John 6:35). In this world, we're surrounded by lost men and women who are desperate, who go down into the gutter to drink the water. We have the gospel of Jesus Christ; the most loving thing we can do is to tell them this good news and show them it in action. This should be the focus of our prayers and our energies.

> Are you willing to say to God that He can have whatever He wants? Do you believe that wholehearted commitment to Him is more important than any other thing or person in your life? Do you know that nothing you do in this life will ever matter, unless it is about loving God and loving the people He has made?
> (Francis Chan, *Crazy Love*, David C. Cook Publishing, 2013, p. 97)

Day 210

Read: 1 Thessalonians 3:6–13
Key verse: 1 Thessalonians 3:13

....

May he strengthen your hearts so that you will be blameless and holy in the presence of our God and Father when our Lord Jesus comes with all his holy ones.

The motivation behind Paul's prayer is for the Thessalonian believers to be established and to grow in purity and holiness, ready for Christ's return.

We don't often hear sermons about holiness, despite the Bible's teaching that the purpose of God in salvation is holiness. Before the foundation of the world, the Father chose us in Christ to be holy (Ephesians 1:4). The Son died on the cross, shedding his blood to bring into existence the holy people of God (Colossians 1:12–14; Hebrews 13:12). The Holy Spirit – the secret is in the name – had the agenda to transform us, to make us holy. But what is holiness? It is quite simply the beauty of Christ shining through us. Holiness is being like Jesus. It is a passion for God and his purity, and it is seen in the lives of those who follow Christ.

Paul prays for the Thessalonians to become more and more pure, holy and blameless, because Jesus is coming back. The return of Christ is the heartbeat of 1 Thessalonians. Every chapter in the book begins or ends with this doctrine. If we don't speak about holiness very much, we speak even less about the Lord's return. Perhaps we're a bit confused about the details, but there is one great truth to cling to: Jesus is coming back. As he went, so he will return and when he comes, it will be glorious. He'll bring the angels of heaven and his people with him. The dead in Christ will rise and we will see the Lord for ever.

It is this great and glorious hope that directs our prayers and drives the church on. If we are to be the kind of Christians God wants us to be, we must look forward to the second coming of Christ. We must be like those Thessalonians who 'turned to God from idols to serve the living and true God, and to wait for his Son from heaven . . . Jesus' (1 Thessalonians 1:9–10).

> You ought to live holy and godly lives as you look forward to the day of God and speed its coming.
> (2 Peter 3:11–12)
>
> For the grace of God has appeared that offers salvation to all people. It teaches us to say 'No' to ungodliness and worldly passions, and to live self-controlled, upright and godly lives in this present age, while we wait for the blessed hope – the appearing of the glory of our great God and Saviour, Jesus Christ.
> (Titus 2:11–13)
>
> Today, pray that you would grow in holiness, ready for Christ's return. Ask for God's help to root out sin and to display, in increasing measure, the fruit of the Holy Spirit.

Day 211

Read: James 1:1–18
Key verses: James 1:5–8

. . . .

> *⁵If any of you lacks wisdom, you should ask God, who gives generously to all without finding fault, and it will be given to you. ⁶But when you ask, you must believe and not doubt, because the one who doubts is like a wave of the sea, blown and tossed by the wind. ⁷That person should not expect to receive anything from the Lord. ⁸Such a person is double-minded and unstable in all they do.*

Have you prayed for wisdom lately? Wisdom is discerning the right thing to do; it is seeing as God intends you to see. It is a gift from God and, like Solomon, we have to ask for it (1 Kings 3:9; 4:29). In Ephesians 1 and Colossians 1, we are encouraged to pray for fellow Christians, for them to have wisdom. When we ask, God promises to be so generous in doling out this wisdom that we will be stunned. We will receive so much more than we could ever 'ask or imagine' (Ephesians 3:20).

The problem is, however, that many people pray for wisdom – and other things – while hedging their bets. They don't really believe God is going to answer, but they pray anyway. Prayer is a safety net in case their other options fail. Remember John Bunyan's character in *Pilgrim's Progress*, Mr Facing-Both-Ways? The message of the Sermon on the Mount presses the point home: 'You can't serve God and money . . . You can't store up treasure on heaven and on earth . . . You can't be double-minded.' James explains that if you are double-minded, you have no anchor for your soul. You are like a boat tossed about on a rough sea. The only other place this word is used is in Luke 8, of the storm on the Sea of Galilee. In the middle of that storm, Jesus said to the disciples, 'Where is your faith?'

As we go through storms and turbulent times, Jesus asks us the same question: 'Where is your faith?' You can't fool God. Either you mean what you pray or you don't. If you don't mean it, save your breath and don't pray. James' invitation is to single-minded devotion to God, praying to him for wisdom because we trust him. Let's pray to God in faith, trusting him, ready to be obedient to his will, not trying to bend him to ours.

Praying for wisdom will never be something we outgrow. We need wisdom more than ever to navigate our way through life in a way that pleases God. The Bible urges us to pursue wisdom relentlessly.

Do not forsake wisdom, and she will protect you;
 love her, and she will watch over you.
The beginning of wisdom is this: get wisdom.
 Though it cost all you have, get understanding.
(Proverbs 4:6–7)

Wisdom allows us to pursue what is good in life, not as judged by our standards, but as judged by the Creator. Wisdom allows us to see what is important to God, what values He gives us for our benefit, and it allows Him to teach us how we can pursue them. (Tim Challies, *The Discipline of Spiritual Discernment*, Crossway, 2008, p. 56)

Day 212

Read: James 5:13–20
Key verse: James 5:13

. . . .

Is anyone among you in trouble? Let them pray. Is anyone happy? Let them sing songs of praise.

When should we pray? James tells us to pray when we are 'in trouble' and when we are 'happy'.

First, pray when you are in trouble. The word for 'trouble' here conveys the idea of suffering evil. The same word is used in James 5:10 of the prophets who suffered persecution and in 2 Timothy 2:9 of suffering for the gospel, even to the point of being chained like a criminal. James' point is that when we endure hardship, we don't just sit with folded hands or engage in violent resistance; we pray. We pray for our enemies, our persecutors and for God's hand in the situation. We don't despair of the evil; we bring it to God. If your ministry or church is dealing with bitter opposition, then James urges you to start praying for those standing against you.

Second, we are to praise God when we are 'happy', although 'happy' is perhaps not the best translation. The original term really means 'in good heart': when Paul is shipwrecked in the middle of a raging storm, this is what he says (Acts 27:22, 25). He doesn't come up on deck to ask if people are happy. What he says is what James uses here: 'keep up your courage' or 'take heart' (ESV). Be of good heart, keep looking to God, although the storm rages round you, and sing praises. James is urging us to rejoice in God in all circumstances. We are not praising God *for* the evil. We are praising God because, in the worst evil, he is with us. Paul has the same message for us in 1 Thessalonians 5:16–18: 'Rejoice always, pray continually, give thanks in all circumstances; for this is God's will for you in Christ Jesus.'

Grant me more and more
    to prize the privilege of prayer,
    to come to thee as a sin-soiled sinner,
    to find pardon in thee,
    to converse with thee;
    to know thee in prayer as
        the path in which my feet tread,
        the latch upon the door of my lips,
        the light that shines through my eyes,
        the music of my ears,
        the marrow of my understanding,
        the strength of my will,
        the power of my affection,
        the sweetness of my memory.
May the matter of my prayer be always
        wise, humble, submissive,
        obedient, scriptural, Christ-like.
Give me unwavering faith
    that supplications are never in vain,
    that if I seem not to obtain my petitions,
        I shall have larger, richer answers,
        surpassing all that I ask or think.
Unsought, thou hast given me
    the greatest gift, the person of thy Son,
    and in him thou wilt give me all I need.
(Arthur Bennett, 'The Prayer of Love', in *The Valley of Vision*, Banner
of Truth Trust, 2002, pp. 270–271)

Day 213

Read: James 5:13–20
Key verse: James 5:14–16

....

14 Is anyone among you ill? Let them call the elders of the church to pray over them and anoint them with oil in the name of the Lord. 15 And the prayer offered in faith will make the sick person well; the Lord will raise them up. If they have sinned, they will be forgiven. 16 Therefore confess your sins to each other and pray for each other so that you may be healed. The prayer of a righteous person is powerful and effective.

Is James saying that every time we pray for a sick person, he or she will be healed? We know from experience that God doesn't always work this way. So what do these verses mean?

Notice that the context of the whole chapter is the Lord's second coming, the end of life and meeting the Lord. We are not talking about ringing the pastor to come over because you have a sore throat. The reason the elders need to come to the patient's bedside is because the individual is too ill to go to church, literally 'at death's door'.

James says, 'The prayer offered in faith will make the sick person well.' The Greek word is actually 'save'. God may heal a person by bringing him or her back to full physical life or by saving the individual from the jaws of death. But he may also save someone by taking that person to be with him. This verse can mean both. Likewise, 'the Lord will raise them up' – he will raise the person up if there is physical healing, but he will also raise him or her up in the glorious resurrection. The role of the elders is to discern what God's will is. Is this a time when God will physically heal in a dramatic way or is this a moment when we sit, pray and read the Scriptures to a believer getting ready to meet the Lord? There are times when we sense God will heal and so we pray with confident faith because God has already given us extraordinary assurance. At other times, we leave a hospital bed knowing that we are on holy ground because a brother or sister has just walked into the presence of God.

The business of confession comes next because, when a person is preparing to pass into the presence of Jesus, it is important to know the assurance of the Lord's forgiveness. The interesting thing here is that, in verse 16, James uses the word 'healing'. Such is James the preacher: he uses 'saving' regarding sickness and 'healing' regarding confession because the full healing of God concerns the whole being. Healing is never to stand in the way of the full saving grace of the Lord because this body is going to be thrown away. The real person is eternal and will be for ever with the Lord.

Praying for the sick in your church is not solely the role of the elders. Today, pray that, if it is God's will, those who are unwell will be restored to full health. More importantly, pray for their spiritual healing. Pray for them to know the joy of their sins forgiven and to walk closely with God even in suffering.

For further study

If you would like to read more about prayer, you might find the following selection of books helpful:

- Alistair Begg, *Pray Big: Learn to pray like an apostle* (Good Book Company, 2019)

- D. A. Carson, *A Call to Spiritual Reformation: Priorities from Paul and his prayers* (IVP, 2011)

- Tim Chester, *You Can Pray* (IVP, 2014)

- Julian Hardyman, *Fresh Pathways in Prayer* (10Publishing, 2019)

- Tim Keller, *Prayer: Experiencing awe and intimacy with God* (Hodder & Stoughton, 2016)

- Paul E. Miller, *A Praying Life: Connecting with God in a distracting world* (NavPress, 2017)

Persevere

Contributors

Day 214

Read: Psalm 130:1–8
Key verses: Psalm 130:1–2

....

> ¹*Out of the depths I cry to you, LORD;*
>   ²*Lord, hear my voice.*
> *Let your ears be attentive*
>   *to my cry for mercy.*

Are you in the 'depths', full of despair and facing discouragement?

The Bible is honest and acknowledges how we feel. Psalm 130 was written by a man on his way to join the national celebrations in the temple. It is one of a group of psalms from 120 to 134 known as the 'Songs of Ascent' – songs the Jews sang on their pilgrimage to Jerusalem to meet God three times a year. Instead of sharing the excitement of the crowd, this man is crying to God 'out of the depths'.

There could be many reasons for his despair, but here it seems to be a growing consciousness of sin. Every step and every day take him nearer to a God he doesn't really want to face. Maybe it is a sense of national sin, but I suspect that it is more his own guilty conscience about the way he himself has been living. He is coming to an occasion when people gather from all over the country, and he knows he is going to hear the Word of God read and he will have to sing the praises of God. And there are aspects of his own life – selfishness and disobedience – that need to be dealt with before he gets to the end of the journey.

This happens to us too. Sin stops us running, as the psalmist puts it, 'in the way of your commandments' (Psalm 119:32, ESV). It is a great thing to get up in the morning and say, 'I want to run, Lord, in the way of your commands.' But sin hinders and so easily entangles us (Hebrews 12:1). The Lord graciously brings us to these points in our lives where we must face reality and not be anaesthetized any longer to how we have offended and hurt him.

It does not matter what depths of circumstances or sin you are in – cry out to God. He will hear you.

If you are in the depths today because of sin, will you cry out to God for mercy? If you are in the depths today because of hardship or loss, do the single most important thing you can do: cry out to the God who hears.

It little matters where we are if we can pray; but prayer is never more real and acceptable than when it rises out of the worst places. Deep places beget deep devotion. Depths of earnestness are stirred by depths of tribulation. Diamonds sparkle most amid the darkness. He that prays in the depth will not sink out of his depth. (C. H. Spurgeon, *Psalms, Vol. 1*, Crossway Classic Commentary, Crossway, 1994, p. 281)

Day 215

Read: Psalm 130:1–8
Key verses: Psalm 130:3–4

....

³*If you, L*ORD*, kept a record of sins,*
Lord, who could stand?
⁴*But with you there is forgiveness,*
so that we can, with reverence, serve you.

Is your heart feeling cold towards God? Have you lost the joy of serving him?

According to Psalm 130:4, the remedy we need is personal forgiveness. There is no law, no set of rules, no guilt trip that could motivate us to keep on living to please God. The only thing that makes our hearts run after the Lord Jesus is receiving God's forgiveness and appreciating his sheer grace and mercy towards us.

No one in the history of the world has ever come to God in heartfelt repentance and not received forgiveness. That was what the Old Testament declared in Exodus 34:6–7: 'The LORD, the LORD, the compassionate and gracious God, slow to anger, abounding in love and faithfulness, maintaining love to thousands, and forgiving wickedness, rebellion and sin.'

With me, sin; with the Lord, forgiveness. You may have grasped this wonderful truth and lived in the light of it for years; it's the anchor of your life. Or you may be aware of the stain of sin in your heart and wonder how you can possibly keep calling yourself a Christian. Do you know that you could write down everything about yourself that is an offence to God, and your friends and even the angel Gabriel could add to the list, but Christ forgives all your sins and doesn't keep the record?

If he doesn't keep the record, what does he keep in heaven? He keeps his wounds: 'Rich wounds, yet visible above, in beauty glorified' (Matthew Bridges, 'Crown Him with Many Crowns', 1852). And Jesus knows why his wounds are there: they are there so that you and I can be there. In heaven, Jesus has not forgotten that you and I are sinners, but rather he chooses not to keep the record. He will not hold our sins against us. Instead, we experience the kindness of God demonstrated at Calvary. Such extravagant forgiveness, such grace, melts our indifference and compels us to love and serve God with grateful hearts.

Mediate on the full and final forgiveness for sin that Christ achieved on the cross.

> When you were dead in your sins and in the uncircumcision of your flesh, God made you alive with Christ. He forgave us all our sins, having cancelled the charge of our legal indebtedness, which stood against us and condemned us; he has taken it away, nailing it to the cross. And having disarmed the powers and authorities, he made a public spectacle of them, triumphing over them by the cross. (Colossians 2:13–15)

Today, in view of this forgiveness, press on in loving and serving God.

Day 216

Read: Psalm 130:1–8
Key verses: Psalm 130:5–8

. . . .

> ⁵I wait for the LORD, my whole being waits,
>   and in his word I put my hope.
> ⁶I wait for the Lord
>   more than watchmen wait for the morning,
>   more than watchmen wait for the morning.
>
> ⁷Israel, put your hope in the LORD,
>   for with the LORD is unfailing love
>   and with him is full redemption.
> ⁸He himself will redeem Israel
>   from all their sins.

In general, we don't like waiting. It seems a waste of time, as well as an acknowledgment that we are not in control. But the waiting of the psalmist in Psalm 130 is not like the anxious waiting for test results from the hospital or the futile waiting in a traffic jam. It is completely different. It is eager and active; the psalmist is preparing himself to meet God.

The psalmist has decided, 'Whatever my circumstances, whatever's happening, I will wait for the Lord.' Notice that it's personal. He's not waiting for correct doctrine or a good meeting; he's not even waiting for forgiveness; he is waiting for the Lord. His soul is engaged; the innermost core of his being is going to wait for his coming. He is waiting for God's ultimate coming when the heavens are going to be unzipped and the Lord will appear with the angels. But he is also waiting for those other occasions when we meet God, the kind the Lord talked about in John 14:21: 'Whoever has my commands and keeps them is the one who loves me. The one who loves me will be loved by my Father, and I too will love them and show myself to them.'

'I am going to wait,' says the psalmist, 'for those manifestations of the Lord to my own soul. I am going to wait more than watchmen wait for the morning.' The watchmen would stand on the ramparts waiting for morning light. They knew the sunrise would come, so they waited with hopeful, trusting, patient expectation. So it is with that kind of hope that the psalmist waits.

Can you see how the psalm develops? The psalmist started off in the depths and then he began to pray. He found relief in God's unconditional forgiveness, began to hope that the Lord would visit him, and then his hope grew to expectancy because of the Lord's character – his unfailing love and full redemption (verse 7).

Likewise, we can wait on God because we know his character. We know and have experienced his forgiveness and unfailing love. We can also trust in God's Word. We have seen him keep his promises, not least in the full redemption he offers us in the Lord Jesus.

Are you, like the psalmist, putting your hope in God's Word and his character? Isaiah 26:8 teaches us how to wait well:

> Yes, Lord, walking in the way of your laws,
>   we wait for you;
> your name and renown
>   are the desire of our hearts.

Day 217

Read: Ephesians 1:3–23
Key verses: Ephesians 1:15–16

• •

15 For this reason, ever since I heard about your faith in the Lord Jesus and your love for all God's people, 16 I have not stopped giving thanks for you, remembering you in my prayers.

When you consider your church, what thoughts spring to mind? In Ephesians 1, Paul is reflecting on a congregation. And his reflection excites and overwhelms him so much that he falls into both prayer and praise. Why? Because, in that congregation, he sees what God has done behind the scenes of history.

So think of your church. It is there you meet because God has been at work since the beginning of time. He chose you before the beginning of time (verse 4). He sent Jesus to die for you (verse 7). Despite the immense barriers of race, class, culture, intellect and age, amazingly he's made you into a family (verse 13). And the Spirit was given to turn our hearts around when we were fully against him, which is no small thing (verse 14).

Do you think about the members of your church like that? Do you appreciate the value God has placed on them? If we're not thinking this about our own churches, then the devil's got hold of our thinking and resentment can come flooding through. You may have been hurt by painful experiences that have happened at church. You may be scraping around for self-esteem because there have been lies told about you and some horrible things have happened. That's why people who are committed Christians, or so-called Christians, just walk away from church.

But in these verses, Paul tells us how we can stay and persevere through the hard times in church life. You take the horrible things that have been said and you apply Ephesians 1. When it comes to church, the great aim of the devil is to cause resentment to grow in your heart. If you're constantly looking for problems in church life, you'll find them, and you'll become bitter. Instead, meditate on Ephesians 1 and all that God has done in, for and through the church. Reflect on God's love for the church, and let that shape how you think, feel and act towards your brothers and sisters in Christ.

How did Paul keep on loving the church? The key is thankfulness. He reflected on all that God had done for these believers in Christ and the value God had placed on them, and he couldn't help being thankful (verse 16). Will you try being more thankful? Perhaps every morning and night, kneel and give thanks to God. Why don't you start by thanking God for your church family and what Christ did for them? Watch how this one spiritual habit transforms your feelings and causes you to make very different choices.

Day 218

Read: 1 Thessalonians 3:1–13
Key verses: 1 Thessalonians 3:2–5

....

²We sent Timothy . . . to strengthen and encourage you in your faith, ³so that no one would be unsettled by these trials. For you know quite well that we are destined for them. ⁴In fact, when we were with you, we kept telling you that we would be persecuted. And it turned out that way, as you well know. ⁵For this reason, when I could stand it no longer, I sent to find out about your faith. I was afraid that in some way the tempter had tempted you and that our labours might have been in vain.

How can we resist the temptations offered by our secular society? How can we keep living for Jesus in a pluralistic context where he is denied?

The church in Thessalonica was facing all kinds of pressures. Paul had only been there for three weeks. What chance would such a church have of being established, let alone maturing? But notice verse 8: 'For now we really live, since you are standing firm in the Lord.' These believers were rock solid! How? They were 'standing firm *in the Lord*'. They sustained their steadfast commitment by being in close union with the Lord. He was the rock on which they stood, the one who strengthened their resolve to live with faith and love.

Paul wanted these young believers, and us, to know that the trials that threaten to unsettle our faith (verse 3) and the temptations of Satan (verse 5) are inevitable. It is not just a matter of chance or blind fate: the emphasis of verse 3 is that this is something within God's purpose. You are destined or appointed for these trials. Mysterious as it might seem, God's hand is in such trials, and he will use them for his particular purposes.

Whatever the source of the hardships, we can hold on to the truth that we are never beyond God's sovereign care; the situation is never out of control. We can hold on to the rock-solid certainties of God's good purposes and fatherly care. Pressures are part of living out the Christian life, and, if we allow them to, can strengthen our commitment to stand firm in the Lord.

In the trials and hardships you face, will you 'stand firm', trusting that God is in control and working out his good purposes? Will you seek to let these circumstances refine your faith and mould you into the character of Christ?

John Bunyan, the author of *The Pilgrim's Progress*, wisely (and quaintly) explained the value of trying days in the following:

> We are apt to overshoot, in the days that are calm, and to think ourselves far higher, and more strong than we find we be when the trying day is upon us . . . We could not live without such turnings of the hand of God upon us. We should be overgrown with flesh, if we had not our seasonable winters.
> (John Bunyan, *Seasonable Counsel*, CreateSpace Independent Publishing, 2014, p. 4)

Day 219

Read: 1 Thessalonians 3:1–13
Key verse: 1 Thessalonians 3:2

....

²We sent Timothy, who is our brother and co-worker in God's service in spreading the gospel of Christ, to strengthen and encourage you in your faith.

What do you talk about when you get together with Christian friends? Sport, the weather, church politics? What about making it your aim to encourage one another to persevere in the faith?

That is why Paul sent Timothy to Thessalonica. Paul was in Athens, about to face the philosophers and idolaters and perhaps another hostile reaction. But he writes, 'When we could stand it no longer, we thought it best to be *left* by ourselves' (verse 1, emphasis added). The Greek word translated 'left' is a strong word which can be used of being abandoned or even for dying. Paul's concern for his friends was such that he would send one of his closest friends and fellow workers – the very person who could have supported him in a new and challenging mission. What mattered most was the well-being of the small church in Thessalonica.

Look how he describes Timothy's ministry in verse 2: 'We sent Timothy . . . to strengthen and encourage you in your faith.' 'Strengthen' is a word from the building trade; it means to 'buttress'. Timothy's job was to build them up. This strengthening and nurturing is needed both by young Christians who are facing many new challenges and by older Christians who are in danger of becoming spiritually stagnant. He was also to 'encourage', exhorting and urging them to hold on to the apostolic teaching.

More than that, we see in verse 10 that, although they were standing firm, growing in faith and love, there was more to be done. Paul wanted to get back to see them again 'and supply what is lacking in your faith'. Here Paul uses a word that is used of mending nets in Mark 1 and of equipping Christians for the work of ministry in Ephesians 4. He wanted to make good the deficiencies, to restore and equip them for full maturity.

Both Paul's generosity and Timothy's ministry are examples of how to care for those who are under pressure and encourage them to stand firm. In fact, in verse 8, when Paul heard how well the believers were doing, he said, 'Now we really live.' In other words, his life was completely bound up with theirs. That is what Christian fellowship is all about. I feel the pressures that others are facing. And, under pressure myself, I need the encouragement of others who will remind me of God's promises, provoke my faith in the Lord and stand alongside me in the trials.

Remember Barnabas? 'When he arrived [at Antioch] and saw what the grace of God had done, he was glad and encouraged them all to remain true to the Lord with all their hearts' (Acts 11:23). Will you be like Barnabas? One who strengthens and encourages your friends, who urges them to hold on to the truths of the gospel, who reminds them they are not beyond the Spirit's comforting presence or the Father's compassionate care?

Day 220

Read: 1 Thessalonians 3:1–13

Key verses: 1 Thessalonians 3:10–13

....

¹⁰*Night and day we pray most earnestly that we may see you again and supply what is lacking in your faith.*

¹¹*Now may our God and Father himself and our Lord Jesus clear the way for us to come to you.* ¹²*May the Lord make your love increase and overflow for each other and for everyone else, just as ours does for you.* ¹³*May he strengthen your hearts so that you will be blameless and holy in the presence of our God and Father when our Lord Jesus comes with all his holy ones.*

A close friend is having a serious operation, or your child is in the middle of an important exam, and you are waiting for news of how it has gone. Every few minutes, it surfaces in your mind again, and you pray. You are so concerned about his or her situation and welfare that it naturally springs to mind.

That's exactly how it should be as we pray for one another. Paul expresses his affectionate concern and remarkable solidarity with these believers in prayer (verse 10). Christians under pressure need us to bring their situations to God. Prayer is deflecting all of our situations God-wards. I like the illustration that the preacher and Bible scholar Alec Motyer used: Christians are like mirrors, angled so that whatever meets us on our journey, we immediately deflect it to God, sending it up to our heavenly Father. Such praying helps us see our problems in proper perspective.

And notice how God-centred Paul's prayer is. Verses 10–13 are full of God's work, heralding what he can do. Think about our prayer meetings. Many of the prayers are: 'O Lord, we ask for . . . ', but the great Bible prayers are different. They are not: 'O Lord, we . . . ' but 'O Lord, you . . . ' Do you remember the prayer of the early Christians in Acts 4, when the small church was under pressure? How did they pray? 'Sovereign Lord . . . you made the heavens and the earth and the sea, and everything in them' (Acts 4:24).

Do you sometimes feel overwhelmed trying to live the Christian life? Do you feel it's impossible to overcome the pull of sin, or to live with integrity in your home or workplace when everyone else has different priorities? Do the problems at church or in your relationships seem beyond your control? Pray for God's mighty power. In Ephesians 1:19–20, Paul describes God's power at work in Jesus' resurrection: 'That power is the same as the mighty strength he exerted when he raised Christ from the dead.' God's power which overcomes death, which elevated Jesus far above all rule and authority, is the same power which is at work in us. It is the resource we need and for which we must pray.

In Ephesians 6:10, Paul urges us: 'Be strong in the Lord and in his mighty power.' Perhaps it would be better to say not 'be strong' but 'be strengthened': receive God's strength, and then you will be strong. Today, pray for yourself and those you know who are struggling. Pray that you would trust in God; that in his strength, you would persevere and live for him.

Day 221

Read: 1 Thessalonians 3:1–13
Key verses: 1 Thessalonians 3:11–13

....

> ¹¹ *Now may our God and Father himself and our Lord Jesus clear the way for us to come to you.* ¹²*May the Lord make your love increase and overflow for each other and for everyone else, just as ours does for you.* ¹³*May he strengthen your hearts so that you will be blameless and holy in the presence of our God and Father when our Lord Jesus comes with all his holy ones.*

In many parts of the world, Christians are in the minority, sometimes living under oppressive governments. Even in our increasingly secular culture, it is easy for believers to feel vulnerable. To stand firm and stay strong, we need to recover our conviction that God is unstoppable, that he will complete the work which he began. Paul's prayer reminds us:

• God directs (verse 11).
  Paul prayed for God to make it possible for him to visit the Thessalonians, and God answered his prayers. Paul was able to visit them on his way back to Jerusalem. Satan might hinder, but ultimately God's purposes are unstoppable.

• God equips (verse 12).
  Our spiritual growth is in God's hands. But this is a partnership. So, on the one hand, Paul sees it as God's work: 'May the Lord make your love increase' (verse 12). But on the other hand, in the next chapter, he says, 'You do love all of God's family . . . we urge you . . . to do so more and more' (4:10). There is a God-centredness, but that stimulates, not lessens, our sense of responsibility. We cooperate with God to activate his purposes in our lives.

- God completes (verse 13).

  God will complete the work which he has begun in our lives. 'Blameless' implies unblameable. On that future day when Jesus returns, nothing will stand against us; Satan's accusations cannot harm us. Surely there's no greater encouragement to live the life of faith – to live in holiness, to stand firm – than the prospect of Christ's return. Fixing our eyes on Jesus, the coming King, sets all of our trials and satanic pressures in perspective.

God helps us stand firm and persevere. However, ultimately it is not our hold of God that matters, but his hold of us:

> The eternal God is your refuge,
>   and underneath are the everlasting arms.
> (Deuteronomy 33:27)

In John 10:27–29, Jesus promises,

> My sheep listen to my voice; I know them, and they follow me. I give them eternal life, and they shall never perish; no one will snatch them out of my hand. My Father, who has given them to me, is greater than all; no one can snatch them out of my Father's hand.

Today, rejoice that, despite your present struggles, your eternal salvation is secure. You are held in the grip of God the Father and God the Son. There is no safer place to be.

Day 222

Read: 2 Timothy 2:1–13
Key verses: 2 Timothy 2:8–10

....

> [8] *Remember Jesus Christ, raised from the dead, descended from David. This is my gospel,* [9] *for which I am suffering even to the point of being chained like a criminal. But God's word is not chained.* [10] *Therefore I endure everything for the sake of the elect, that they too may obtain the salvation that is in Christ Jesus, with eternal glory.*

How can we cope when we face crises in our personal lives?

The apostle Paul was dying, and young, diffident Timothy found himself having to step into his mentor's shoes. Paul's encouragement in this trying circumstance was: 'Be strong in the grace that is in Christ Jesus.' He urged Timothy to press on with the commitment of a soldier and the determination of an athlete, and to work hard like a farmer. In a word, he was to endure.

Paul knew all about endurance. He himself was suffering for the gospel, wearing chains like a criminal, yet enduring that suffering and despising the shame for the sake of Christ (verse 9). Indeed, he put endurance top of the list when he wrote that great catalogue of ways to serve the Lord in 2 Corinthians 6:4.

But endurance was not just Paul's idea; it is one of the key words in the New Testament. The apostles Peter, James and John knew it in the context of persecution (1 Peter 2:20; James 5:11). In fact, at the same time as this epistle was being written, John was calling for the endurance of the saints, 'those who keep God's commands and hold fast their testimony about Jesus' (Revelation 12:17). John knew how persecution sought out the Christians who were strong in Christ, and those who were not.

Why does Paul say, 'Remember Jesus Christ' (verse 8)? Because Jesus calls us to endure. Listen to his words in Matthew 10:22: 'You will be hated by everyone because of me, but the one who stands firm to the end will be saved.' We also remember Jesus because he is our example and inspiration:

> let us run with perseverance the race marked out for us, fixing our eyes on Jesus, the pioneer and perfecter of faith. For the joy that was set before him he endured the cross, scorning its shame, and sat down at the right hand of the throne of God.
> (Hebrews 12:1–2)

Paul would not have suffered if he had not believed that the gospel was supremely worth the cost. Endurance is one of the qualities God wants. He wants every Christian to draw on the grace of Christ, to be committed, determined, working hard and ready to endure anything for the sake of the gospel and the Word of God that can never be chained.

It is easy to feel overwhelmed when we focus on our troubles. Today, lift up your eyes and fix them on Jesus rather than on your circumstances. 'Remember Jesus Christ', your:

- Creator (John 1:3)
- Saviour (John 3:16–18)
- Intercessor (Romans 8:34)
- Rescuer (Colossians 1:13)
- Comfort (2 Corinthians 1:3–4)
- Strength (Psalm 28:7)
- Sustainer (Isaiah 46:4)
- Guide (Psalm 139:9–10)

Day 223

Read: Hebrews 4:14–16
Key verse: Hebrews 4:14

....

14 Therefore, since we have a great high priest who has ascended into heaven, Jesus the Son of God, let us hold firmly to the faith we profess.

Disobedience, unbelief and hard hearts characterized the Israelites who wandered in the wilderness. The writer to the Hebrews urges us to learn from their mistakes and press on in wholehearted faith.

Look at the bookends that stand on either side of this section of Hebrews 4:14–16. The first is verse 13: 'Nothing in all creation is hidden from God's sight. Everything is uncovered and laid bare before the eyes of him to whom we must give account.' It is a warning. All the verses preceding this are a warning to take God's Word seriously. Why? Because to be exposed to the Word of God is to be exposed to God himself. The language used is that of nakedness. Everything is laid bare. The other bookend is 4:16: 'Let us then approach God's throne of grace with confidence, so that' – having been exposed and found wretched by God's Word – 'we may receive mercy and find grace to help us in our time of need.'

In moments of wretchedness, when God's Word has exposed our sin and guilt, we need to remember verse 14: 'we have a great high priest'. The writer emphasizes this as a present reality, not wishful thinking. He is not hoping it might happen; he is talking about that conscious possession of believers. We possess Jesus! We have this 'great high priest . . . Jesus the Son of God'. Notice the power behind these twin titles: Christ as fully man and fully God, Christ in his humiliation and exaltation, Christ in his sympathy and in his power and glory.

In Hebrews 1:2–3, we learn more about him: he is God's Son, heir of all things, maker and sustainer of the universe, the radiance of God's glory, God himself and an authentic representation of God the Father, our redeemer who has completed the work of redemption and is now ruling with God. No wonder the writer is inspired and wanting to inspire our hearts about what we possess. We possess Jesus, this great high priest.

Thank God that we possess Jesus, this great high priest, now. This means that the sacrifice he made once and for all is effectual *now*; if you confess your sins, he forgives you *now*; he is interceding for you *now*; he makes the way to the Father open *now*. In the light of this, and in the power of the Holy Spirit, 'hold firmly to the faith [you] profess'. Don't let doubt, disbelief or guilt throw you off course.

No condemnation now I dread;
Jesus, and all in Him is mine!
Alive in Him, my living Head,
and clothed in righteousness divine,
bold I approach th'eternal throne,
and claim the crown, through Christ my own.
(Charles Wesley, 'And Can It Be', 1738)

Day 224

Read: Hebrews 4:14–16
Key verse: Hebrews 4:14

....

¹⁴ *Therefore, since we have a great high priest who has ascended into heaven, Jesus the Son of God, let us hold firmly to the faith we profess.*

Red tape, protocols, months of planning and vetting are required for anyone meeting the royal family today. By contrast, we have permanent access to the King of kings. This is an amazing privilege.

How is such access possible? Because Jesus, our great high priest, has 'ascended into heaven'. We need to turn to the Old Testament for some context. Once a year, the high priest was allowed to enter the holy of holies through the temple curtain, beyond the eyes of the people, to atone for the sins of the nation. And on the day that Jesus died that temple curtain was torn from top to bottom (Matthew 27:51). The way to God's presence is now permanently open. In Hebrews 9:24, the writer explains that Christ did not enter a man-made sanctuary like the priests who had gone before. He entered heaven itself, and now he appears on our behalf in God's presence. That's what makes him a great high priest.

And when he talks about ascending into heaven, he is not giving you a cosmic geography lesson. He doesn't even want you to ponder where heaven might be. What he is really saying is that the one who ascended is the one who transcended all limits of time and space, so that, in accordance with Scripture, he is made higher than the heavens. And he has ascended far above all the heavens so that he might fulfil all things in that place of rule and authority, where the fight is over, the battle won and the victory secure.

Our great high priest has secured for us permanent access to God the Father because he passed through the heavens as the transcended Lord. The same Jesus who was born at Bethlehem, walked in Palestine, died on Calvary, rose in Jerusalem, ascended from earth and is now crowned with glory and honour is the great high priest who now appears on our behalf in God's presence.

It doesn't matter whether it is day or night, whether you have been obedient or have fallen into sin again, whether you are joyful or weighed down with cares – you have access to God. By his blood shed on the cross and his mighty resurrection to glory, Jesus has for ever opened the way to the Father. God wants you to come into his presence. Being with him – reading and meditating on his Word and praying – is vital if we are to persevere in our faith journey. He invites you today to come to him for forgiveness, strengthening, refreshment and comfort. The way is open; it is up to you to take the next step (Revelation 3:20).

Come near to God and he will come near to you. Wash your hands, you sinners, and purify your hearts, you double-minded.
(James 4:8)

Day 225

Read: Hebrews 4:14–16
Key verse: Hebrews 4:15

....

> ¹⁵*For we do not have a high priest who is unable to feel sympathy for our weaknesses, but we have one who has been tempted in every way, just as we are – yet he did not sin.*

What is your greatest temptation? Where are you vulnerable? What are the weak spots the devil targets again and again?

We are probably more secretive about our temptations than about any other aspect of Christian living, but Jesus knows all about them.

Verse 15 may be misunderstood in two ways. First, the verse does not say Jesus encountered every conceivable temptation. For example, he could not have experienced the temptations of those over forty, a married couple or a single woman. Second, this verse does not concede that if Jesus could be tempted and yet was incapable of sinning, his temptation in the wilderness, and in other aspects of his ministry, was nothing more than a charade. That is a ploy of the enemy to destroy your confidence in your great high priest. It is unthinkable that Jesus should have succumbed to that temptation that leads to sin, but never, ever, minimize the reality of the confrontation between Jesus and the tempter.

God restrains the power of temptation in the believer's life so we are not tempted beyond what we can bear; there is a way out. The temptation we meet is filtered through God's protecting hand: that's the way out. In Jesus' case, the filter was removed. His temptations were real: the forty days of unbroken temptation in the wilderness, where Satan offered him alternative routes to the kingdom (Matthew 4); the moment Satan tempted him through Peter, who refused to believe Jesus had to go to Jerusalem to die (Matthew 16:21–23); when he was tempted in the garden of Gethsemane to avoid the suffering ahead (Matthew 26:39); and his last hours on the cross and the temptation implicit in the invitation: 'Come down from the cross, if you are the Son of God!' (Matthew 27:40).

Have you grasped what happened at Gethsemane?

Our Saviour was praying with 'loud cries and tears' (Hebrews 5:7, ESV). Never doubt his close identity with those who are being tempted. We give in before temptation is fully spent in our bodies. Only the one who doesn't yield knows its full extent. What a great high priest we possess!

Jesus knows what it means to be tempted, and yet he never gave in. His determination to obey his Father overwhelmed his desire to succumb to temptation. Today, draw on his example and strength. As you encounter opportunities to sin, to give up, to be mediocre rather than wholehearted in your obedience, use Jesus' words as your fresh commitment to God: 'Yet not as I will, but as you will' (Matthew 26:39).

Day 226

Read: Hebrews 4:14–16
Key verse: Hebrews 4:15

. . . .

[15]*For we do not have a high priest who is unable to feel sympathy for our weaknesses, but we have one who has been tempted in every way, just as we are – yet he did not sin.*

Can Jesus – seated at the right hand of God in heaven, reigning in power and authority – really be a friend of sinners (Hebrews 1:3; Matthew 11:19)?

For those who doubt, the writer to the Hebrews uses explicit language to affirm we have a high priest who has gentle sympathy with our weakness. In his description in Hebrews 5:2, the writer describes the human tradition in which this great priest stands: 'He is able to deal gently with ignorant and wayward people because he himself is subject to the same weaknesses' (NLT). If a human priest is able to deal gently with those who are ignorant and are going astray, how much more so this great high priest?

Jesus' sufferings on earth have produced such sympathy in him that he has never forgotten them: the friends who forsook him in his hour of need (Matthew 26:40); the family who thought he was mad (Mark 3:21); the followers who deserted him, saying, 'We can't cope with teaching like that' (see John 6:66).

Jesus has gentle sympathy with those who are ignorant of the way and those who are ignoring the way. My experience through the years suggests that more Christians are tempted to despair, and even quit, because of the disappointments of life. This can be greater than almost any other temptation that besets us. And disappointment with your circumstances, if not curbed and dealt with, often leads to disappointment in the Lord himself. Don't be alarmed or ashamed if that is how you feel. You are coming to a high priest who is gently sympathetic to all conditions.

Are you disappointed with how your life has turned out? Are you disappointed with God? Don't despair; don't deviate from God's way. Rather, 'hold firmly to the faith [you] profess' (Hebrews 4:14). Come to Jesus, the great high priest and friend of sinners. Speak honestly to him, receive his comfort, listen to his Word.

> What a friend we have in Jesus,
> all our sins and griefs to bear!
> What a privilege to carry
> everything to God in prayer!
> O what peace we often forfeit,
> O what needless pain we bear,
> all because we do not carry
> everything to God in prayer!
> Have we trials and temptations?
> Is there trouble anywhere?
> We should never be discouraged;
> take it to the Lord in prayer!
> Can we find a friend so faithful
> who will all our sorrows share?
> Jesus knows our every weakness;
> take it to the Lord in prayer!
>
> Are we weak and heavy laden,
> cumbered with a load of care?
> Precious Saviour, still our refuge –
> take it to the Lord in prayer!
> Do your friends despise, forsake you?
> Take it to the Lord in prayer!
> In his arms he'll take and shield you;
> you will find a solace there.
> (Joseph Medlicott Scriven, 'What a Friend We Have in Jesus', 1855)

Day 227

Read: Hebrews 4:14–16
Key verse: Hebrews 4:16

• •

16Let us then approach God's throne of grace with confidence, so that we may receive mercy and find grace to help us in our time of need.

You may say, 'Who can cope with my misery, failure and despair?' God responds by saying, 'Come to the throne of grace and pour out to me all your needs.'

The way to read verse 16 is: 'Let us keep on approaching, again and again.' And we can come to this throne with 'confidence'. This indicates bold frankness, and open free speech. When this word is used in the Bible, it means, 'Come to the throne of grace and speak about everything; be unembarrassed, unrestricted; pour out your heart.'

I love the way that whenever people heard that Jesus was in a house or street, they approached him boldly. Jairus implored Jesus to help him because his twelve-year-old daughter was dying (Mark 5:22–24). The woman pushed her way through the crowds because she was haemorrhaging and no doctor could help her (Luke 8:43–48). This is boldly approaching the place of grace.

The writer to the Hebrews urges us to 'approach God's throne' to 'receive mercy and find grace to help us in our time of need'. Mercy to cover the sins of yesterday and grace to meet the needs of today. Remember the prodigal son, clutching his spiritual rags around him in his wretchedness and need (Luke 15:11–32)? He was weak, friendless, far from home. All he could do was cast himself upon the father's mercy, and he received a welcoming embrace. But it went beyond that. Here it says that we *receive* mercy and – to our surprise – we *find* grace. Grace is the unexpected blessing. All the prodigal asked for was that he might be able to find mercy. 'What shall I say to my father? "I have sinned, I am no longer worthy to be called your son. I just want to be in the house, in the servants' quarters – just let me come home."' He received mercy, and he *found* grace in the ring, the robe, the shoes, the banquet and the blessing he never deserved and certainly never expected.

Are you in need? Why don't you come to the throne of grace?

Grace goes beyond mercy. Mercy gave the prodigal son a second chance. Grace threw him a party . . . Mercy forgave the thief on the cross. Grace escorted him into paradise. Mercy pardons us. Grace woos and weds us . . . Saving grace saves us from our sins. Sustaining grace . . . surprises us in the middle of our difficulties with ample resources of faith. [It] does not promise the absence of struggle but the presence of God. And according to Paul, God has sufficient sustaining grace to meet every single challenge of our lives . . . *Grace* is simply another word for his tumbling, rumbling reservoir of strength and protection. It comes at us not occasionally or miserly, but constantly and aggressively, wave upon wave.
(Max Lucado, 'Grace: More Than We Deserve, Greater Than We Imagine', *Christianity Today*, 7 May 2013,
<https://www.christianitytoday.com/biblestudies/articles
/spiritualformation/grace-more-than-we-deserve-greater-than-we
-imagine.html>)

Day 228

Read: Hebrews 6:1–20
Key verses: Hebrews 6:7–8

....

> [7] *Land that drinks in the rain often falling on it and that produces a crop useful to those for whom it is farmed receives the blessing of God.* [8] *But land that produces thorns and thistles is worthless and is in danger of being cursed. In the end it will be burned.*

What evidence is there that you are a Christian? Fruitfulness is part of the proof that you are anchored to Jesus and persevering in the faith.

In this chapter, there is no encouragement for those whose lack of fruit shows a lack of faith. They are 'worthless . . . in danger of being cursed' (verse 8). The impossibility of their salvation is the judgement of God on their rebellion. By profiling these people, the author of Hebrews is giving us an important lesson. Their lack of progress is meant to be the spur we need to progress. Their danger of being cursed is meant to be the impetus that keeps us walking on the path to blessing. Their worthless fruit is meant to push us on to useful fruit.

God knows we are complex. He knows that on the journey of the Christian life we don't just need hope; we need warning. We don't just need good examples to follow; we need bad mistakes to learn from. We don't just need encouragement; we need fear. We need a carrot and a stick.

The point of reading about these people is not to make you doubt your salvation, but to make you diligent in your salvation. Because, as a pastor, the writer is not doubting them (verse 9). He is convinced they are saved because of their fruit. He has seen their work for the gospel, their love for the God of the gospel and how they helped the people of the gospel. And not just in the past; look at verse 10: 'you . . . continue to help them'. Genuine Christianity is never simply past tense. It's always present tense, always faithful to Christ today, trusting in Christ today. And the writer urges them to do this diligently until 'the very end' (verse 11).

Unbelievers need to know that religious works do not bring about eternal life, but believers need to know that religious works are a sign we are alive. Your faith in the gospel will always result in gospel fruit, which is why it is one of the grounds of the assurance of faith.

Are you producing fruit (John 15:5)? What is the evidence of your love for Christ? One proof is your diligence as a believer. It is stunning that the pastor to the Hebrews talks about laziness (verses 11–12). This church is being battered by persecution, and yet he sees one of the greatest threats to their persevering in the Christian life not in someone putting a knife to their throats and telling them to renounce Christ, but in the inclination of their hearts towards laziness. Don't give in to laziness! Put your faith into action today.

Day 229

Read: Hebrews 6:1–20
Key verses: Hebrews 6:13, 17

• •

13 When God made his promise to Abraham, since there was no one greater for him to swear by, he swore by himself . . . 17 Because God wanted to make the unchanging nature of his purpose very clear to the heirs of what was promised, he confirmed it with an oath.

We are not always good at keeping our promises, but God is. In verse 13, God throws down a promise built upon an unchangeable purpose (verse 17), and on top of that he builds an oath on the impossibility of him telling a lie. So what you have in Hebrews 6 is an oath on top of promise. Unchangeable purpose on top of unchangeable promise. A word that cannot fail on top of a word that cannot lie. And all of that built upon the unchanging, eternal character of God. Which means what? It's a promise you can bank everything on!

It was a promise Abraham did bank everything on. God had promised Abraham numerous descendants who would all come through Isaac. But hot on the heels of that promise, God tells him to sacrifice Isaac. How could Abraham kill not only his only son, but also the son of the promise? But Abraham is so confident in the promise of God that he would kill the child, knowing for certain that God would raise the child to keep the promise.

Let's put that in New Testament language: Abraham believes in resurrection. He knows that even if he were to sacrifice his son, God would raise him up. Faith, for Abraham, is not spread betting, it's not eggs in different baskets, it's all in. He raises a knife to kill his son. Why? He reasons that God can cause a resurrection. Some would call it risky or irrational. God calls it faith. Faith is a trust, a belief, in the promise of God – even in the face of death, and even when the only way out is resurrection.

We too can have faith in God's promises. Our salvation is as safe as Isaac's was when he was bound on the altar; not even death could finish him. That doesn't rule out suffering, but it guarantees hope. It doesn't rule out waves, but it promises an anchor. It doesn't rule out death, but it promises resurrection. The cross and the resurrection of Jesus are the proof that any promise God has ever made he keeps. Not even death can unearth the anchor of Christian salvation.

We can persevere during the darkest days because:

'no matter how many promises God has made, they are "Yes" in Christ. And so through him the 'Amen' is spoken by us to the glory of God . . . God . . . makes both us and you stand firm in Christ. He anointed us, set his seal of ownership on us, and put his Spirit in our hearts as a deposit, guaranteeing what is to come.'
(2 Corinthians 1:20–22)

Day 230

Read: Hebrews 6:1–20
Key verses: Hebrews 6:18–20

. . . .

[18] God did this so that, by two unchangeable things in which it is impossible for God to lie, we who have fled to take hold of the hope set before us may be greatly encouraged. [19] We have this hope as an anchor for the soul, firm and secure. It enters the inner sanctuary behind the curtain, [20] where our forerunner, Jesus, has entered on our behalf. He has become a high priest for ever, in the order of Melchizedek.

What does it mean to be a Christian? Verse 18 gives us a fascinating definition: someone who has fled to hope. Do you remember what your life was like before you were a Christian? Hebrews 9:27 explains you were destined to die and after that face judgement. That was my destiny, my life: I was hopeless. And when God's Word opened my eyes to my destiny, what did I have to do? I fled to Christ. Becoming a Christian is not a lifestyle choice. It's a life-or-death choice. Fleeing to Jesus is not like travelling to a holiday destination; it's like a Syrian refugee fleeing a war zone, knowing the only alternative is death.

So you flee to Christ. Why? Because on the cross, he takes your destiny of death and judgement and he bears it as his own. You flee to the one who dies your death, who takes the judgement of God on your behalf. He tears the temple curtain in two to show that you are no longer barred from the presence of God, but instead welcomed in. The curtain is torn; the job is done – he has achieved your salvation (see Day 224). And he has not just achieved your salvation, he has also anchored it:

'We have this hope as an anchor for the soul, firm and secure. It enters the inner sanctuary behind the curtain, where our forerunner, Jesus, has entered on our behalf' (verses 19–20).

As quickly as a Christian flees from hopelessness to hope, Jesus runs from the cross to heaven to anchor that hope. Jesus not only achieves our salvation, but he also anchors it in the presence of God, and there he sits to pray you home. Your salvation is anchored in the eternal presence of God – the place where there are no storms, no shame, no suffering and no sin. It's safe and it's secure.

You may be acutely aware of the storms of suffering and the storms of your own sin. But while you are in the storm, you have not only a high priest who died on your behalf at Calvary, but one who is also interceding for you in heaven. Can the cross be undone? Can the curtain be stitched back together again? No. It's anchored in the continuing priestly work of Christ. That is an anchor firm and secure, hope for your soul.

We have an anchor that keeps the soul
steadfast and sure while the billows roll;
fastened to the Rock which cannot move,
grounded firm and deep in the Saviour's love!
(Priscilla J. Owens, 'We Have an Anchor That Keeps the Soul', 1882)

Day 231

Read: Hebrews 12:1–17
Key verse: Hebrews 12:1

．．

¹Therefore, since we are surrounded by such a great cloud of witnesses, let us throw off everything that hinders and the sin that so easily entangles. And let us run with perseverance the race marked out for us.

The Christian life is never described as a stroll in the park or a jog around the block. One metaphor used in the New Testament is that of a race. In 1 Corinthians 9:24–26, Paul says, 'Do you not know that in a race all the runners run, but only one gets the prize? . . . Therefore, I do not run like someone running aimlessly; I do not fight like a boxer beating the air.' He talks about running the race with great commitment, vision and a sense of focus. In 2 Timothy 2:5, Paul talks about the athlete who will win the prize only because he has run according to the rules. And at the end of his life, he says, 'I have fought the good fight, I have finished the race, I have kept the faith' (2 Timothy 4:7).

When Paul, and the writer to the Hebrews, used this metaphor of athletics, people knew what they were talking about. They were familiar with the famous Isthmian Games in Corinth and the Ancient Olympics begun seven hundred years before Christ. But what made the author of Hebrews pick on this athletic contest to explain ordinary Christianity? The New Testament writers somehow saw that there were important similarities, but also differences, between the Christian life and an athletic contest.

The similarity was that both the professional athlete and the professing Christian had to subject themselves to extreme physical, emotional and psychological demands. Both had stringent requirements and both had to make enormous sacrifices because of these demands. The difference between the athlete and the Christian was that the reward, honour and glory were more tangible and obvious for the athlete. At the end of the race, he would receive the winner's crown. But in the case of the Christian, the reward was not obvious or tangible. The recipients of this letter could not see their rewards. And so the author had to write to encourage them to keep in mind that there *is* a reward and that it *will* be given.

How are you doing in the race? The finishing line is in sight. One day you will receive your reward and know that your sacrifice was worth it. Will you press on so that you can say with Paul,

> "I have fought the good fight, I have finished the race, I have kept the faith. Now there is in store for me the crown of righteousness, which the Lord, the righteous Judge, will award to me on that day – and not only to me, but also to all who have longed for his appearing."
> (2 Timothy 4:7–8)

Day 232

Read: Hebrews 12:1–17

Key verse: Hebrews 12:1

....

> [1] *Therefore, since we are surrounded by such a great cloud of witnesses, let us throw off everything that hinders and the sin that so easily entangles. And let us run with perseverance the race marked out for us.*

Are you beginning to flag and lose courage in the Christian race? The writer to the Hebrews urges us, 'Therefore, since we are surrounded by such a great cloud of witnesses . . . let us run with perseverance.' The 'therefore' causes us to look back to chapter 11 where we find the 'hall of fame' of the biblical world. The writer provides this long list of heroes of faith to inspire our own faith and to bolster our perseverance.

Over thirty-eight verses, the author patiently and persistently reminds his readers of story after story from the Old Testament. In fact, he mentions seventeen heroes by name, from Abel all the way to David. In addition, he talks about a few whole generations. A total of eighteen times in the Greek text of this chapter we read that the Christian race is to be run 'by faith'. You do not see the reward; you will not hold on to it; you will not have it as a tangible reality right now, so you need to have the ability to go 'by faith'.

Why does the writer go through such a lengthy commentary? He takes us back to the first human family, beginning with Abel, to underline that from the beginning of the human race until now, all our transactions with God have depended on the currency of faith. Faith is not something that began with the nation of Israel. We also learn that faith is not the gross simplification of the 'name-it-and-claim-it' religion that sometimes passes for Christianity today. Some Old Testament believers received tangible rewards in their lifetimes;

others saw only the price of their faith as they experienced humiliation and even death (see Hebrews 11:32–40). But they were 'all
commended for their faith' (verse 39). And faith, says Hebrews 11:6,
is believing that God exists and that he's a rewarder of those who
earnestly seek him. That's what chapter 11 records that these heroes
of the faith did. What an inspiring example they set for us today!

Over the last two thousand years, our cloud of witnesses has
expanded. We now have millions in the stadium watching us run
the race. Imagine the ones who are personally cheering you on
and calling out your name. It could be your Sunday school teacher,
youth leader, parents or grandparents – those faithful Christians
who prayed for you, explained and modelled the gospel for you,
and have now taken their seats in the stadium to watch you run.
Thank God for this cloud of witnesses. Today, let their testimony
and encouragement inspire you to keep running your race with
courage and perseverance.

Day 233

Read: Hebrews 12:1–17
Key verse: Hebrews 12:1

....

> [1]*Therefore, since we are surrounded by such a great cloud of witnesses, let us throw off everything that hinders and the sin that so easily entangles. And let us run with perseverance the race marked out for us.*

What is holding you back from running the Christian race? The author says in verse 1, 'Let us throw off everything that hinders and the sin that so easily entangles.' He is thinking of certain factors that can impede our progress and compromise our good intentions. He distinguishes between weights and sins, and both need to be thrown off.

For too long, Christians have focused only on right and wrong. We say that as long as what I am doing is not wrong, it is OK for me. But God wants us to go beyond that legalistic mentality. The apostle Paul's argument was that if what I do is a stumbling block to my brother – even though I have no conscience problem with it because it is not in itself a sin – still I will not do it for the sake of my brother (1 Corinthians 8). I am not simply asking, 'Is this right or wrong?' I am asking, 'Is this good; is this the best thing I can do?' Paul's point is that while something is permissible, it may not be beneficial.

The professional swimmer understands it is permissible to have long hair, but most male swimmers prefer to shave all the hair off their bodies! They want to ensure there is not a single weight that will add unnecessarily to the burden of their race. Athletes wear light clothes and shoes because they want to throw off every weight to ensure they have the best chance at the race.

But we don't only throw off the weights; we also throw off the sins. The author talks about 'the sin which so easily ensnares us' (NKJV). We recognize that sin can become our great obsession if we give it room. So don't nurture it, don't caress it, don't hide it. Simply throw it off and get rid of it. Jesus said that if your hand causes you to sin, cut it off (Matthew 5:30)! He is using hyperbole, but he is making a very important point: if your hand, which is so important to you, causes you to sin, do without it. Take radical and extreme steps to throw off sin from your life.

Friendship with a gossip, watching pornography, pride in your career . . . what sin do you need to stop nurturing and to get rid of? What weights – which relationships, priorities or activities, permissible but not necessarily the best choice – do you need to throw off if you want to make progress as a Christian? Take action today so that you can keep running your race with perseverance.

Day 234

Read: Hebrews 12:1–17
Key verses: Hebrews 12:1–3

∙∙

¹Let us run with perseverance the race marked out for us, ²fixing our eyes on Jesus, the pioneer and perfecter of faith. For the joy that was set before him he endured the cross, scorning its shame, and sat down at the right hand of the throne of God. ³Consider him who endured such opposition from sinners, so that you will not grow weary and lose heart.

While the cloud of witnesses inspires us, our eyes are not fixed on them. We don't look at Abraham, Moses or David, great as they are. We don't look at Rachel, Rebekah, Ruth or Hannah, great as they are. We fix our eyes on Jesus, because *he* is our example. The example of Jesus instructs us. Built into the definition of Christian discipleship is the idea of imitating Jesus. In his first letter, John says, 'Whoever claims to live in him must live as Jesus did' (1 John 2:6). Our claim to be disciples of Jesus must be matched by lives that emulate him.

When Jesus called people to become his followers, he called them with these words: 'follow me'. It didn't simply mean 'physically come after me', but 'learn to pattern your life after what you see in me'. And so Paul would later write, 'Imitate me' – mimic me – 'just as I imitate Christ' (1 Corinthians 11:1, NLT). Because after Jesus had ascended into heaven, the only way the early church could know how Jesus had lived was to look at the apostles, pastors and leaders who were imitating Christ and through them understand how to follow Christ.

It is important to learn to pattern our lives after Jesus, but here the author specifically wants us to look carefully at the way Jesus ran his race. His race, of course, was unimaginably demanding because it involved a Roman crucifixion, which was the most cruel and painful form of execution that had been devised. It was the most shameful way to be executed, since the victim was crucified naked after suffering terrible tortures. How did Jesus bear such humiliation and degradation? How was he able to endure such agony and shame? The author says, 'For the joy that was set before him he endured the cross, scorning its shame' (verse 2).

Amy Carmichael, suffered much over the course of her fifty-five years in India, rescuing more than a thousand young girls from prostitution. During the last years of her life, she was an invalid, writing books and poems from her bed. She wrote 'No Scar?'

No wound? No scar?
Yet as the Master, shall his servant be,
and piercèd are the feet that follow me.
But thine are whole; can he have followed far
who hast no wound nor scar?
(Amy Carmichael, *Toward Jerusalem*, Triangle, 1987, p. 85)

Suffering for being a Christian is part of what it means to follow Jesus. But *how* are you suffering? Are you imitating his endurance and single-minded obedience to God's purpose? Is the joy of future glory spurring you on?

Day 235

Read: Hebrews 12:1–17

Key verse: Hebrews 12:7

....

7 Endure hardship as discipline; God is treating you as his children. For what children are not disciplined by their father?

'Everyone who wants to live a godly life in Christ Jesus *will* be persecuted,' writes the apostle Paul (2 Timothy 3:12, emphasis added). Not 'maybe' or 'probably', but everyone who wants to live a godly life in Christ Jesus 'will' be persecuted, which means you and me. You will suffer in some form or other, whether it's psychologically, mentally, emotionally or physically.

In this first-century church, there has not yet been a martyr (Hebrews 12:4), but still these believers are extremely discouraged. As they suffer for being Christians, the author will reinterpret their Christian experience of suffering. And the word he will use for that is 'discipline'. In the New Testament, the word for 'discipline' occurs twenty-one times, eight of them in this short passage. The writer talks about these disciplines that God has brought into our lives. In verses 5 and 6 he quotes Proverbs 3:11–12. He wants us to see our suffering for the sake of the gospel as God's discipline. Like a father disciplining his children, it is an experience intended for our benefit and not for our harm.

In our own situations, we need to learn to stand before God and say, 'God, I want to endure this hardship as discipline, as a training, as a means by which you are forming Christ more in me.' To this end, I have found the following poem – which spans the genders – a great encouragement. It is by an unknown writer.

When God wants to drill a man,
and thrill a man,
and skill a man,
when God wants to mould a man
to play the noblest part;
when he yearns with all his heart
to create so great and bold a man
that all the world shall be amazed,
watch his methods, watch his ways!
How he ruthlessly perfects
whom he royally elects!
How he hammers him and hurts him,
and with mighty blows converts him
into trial shapes of clay which
only God understands;
while his tortured heart is crying
and he lifts beseeching hands!
How he bends but never breaks
when his good he undertakes;
how he uses whom he chooses,
and with every purpose fuses him;
by every act induces him
to try his splendour out –
God knows what he's about.
(Author unknown; cited in J. Oswald Sanders, *Spiritual Leadership*,
Moody Press, 1994, p. 151)

The Lord says, 'Those whom I love I rebuke and discipline. So be earnest and repent' (Revelation 3:19). Consider the hardships you are dealing with. What is God trying to teach you? What changes of attitude and behaviour do you need to make to be responsive, rather than resistant, to his discipline?

Day 236

Read: Hebrews 12:1–17
Key verses: Hebrews 12:10–11

....

> [10]*God disciplines us for our good, in order that we may share in his holiness.* [11]*No discipline seems pleasant at the time, but painful. Later on, however, it produces a harvest of righteousness and peace for those who have been trained by it.*

What are you looking forward to in your Christian life? As we run this race, the writer explains, there are rewards which, even now, we can receive. He outlines these rewards in verses 10–11. First, we begin to live holy lives, and second, we are drawn to a place of peace and righteousness.

God is holy, and those who live in Christ must live as holy people. 'Be holy, because I am holy,' says the Lord (1 Peter 1:16). He wants us to grow in our holiness so we may develop our friendship with him. 'Peace' suggests our relationships in society and in the church, that goodwill which grows as we learn to relate to one another. The writer says that as you go through this hardship, discipline and training, on the one hand, you will find yourself becoming more and more holy and walking closer with God; and on the other hand, you will find that your influence in the world will expand. In your family, your credibility will rise as you live faithfully, and as your credibility grows, your peace will grow, because the community that God has placed you in will begin to trust you and look to you more. Such credibility, however, will only result if we are willing to persevere, even in the face of misunderstanding and persecution (12:1–3). Often the faithful witness of an individual Christian, or the local Christian community, yields its fruit of credibility and peace only for the generation that follows. This is what makes persevering faith so crucial.

Now, in verses 14 to 17, the author reminds us that the race is a team effort. Of course, each one of us must make a strong personal effort to run our best race (verse 14). But don't think only of your race; think of other believers too (verses 15–16). Make sure you're looking out for those who need accountability and help. See to it that no one falls short of the grace of God. Never give up, and together let us run with perseverance the race that is marked out for us.

> Be careful then, dear brothers and sisters. Make sure that your own hearts are not evil and unbelieving, turning you away from the living God. You must warn each other every day, while it is still 'today', so that none of you will be deceived by sin and hardened against God. For if we are faithful to the end, trusting God just as firmly as when we first believed, we will share in all that belongs to Christ.
>
> (Hebrews 3:12–14, NLT)

Thank God for the Christian friends he has given you. Ask for his help as you hold each other accountable for living out the gospel. Pray for wisdom as you encourage your friends in the faith, share their struggles and help them recognize sin's hardening power. Speak Bible truth to each other, and spur one another on to finish the race well.

Day 237

Read: James 1:1–8
Key verses: James 1:3–4

....

> [3] *You know that the testing of your faith produces perseverance.*
> [4] *Let perseverance finish its work so that you may be mature and complete, not lacking anything.*

Sometimes, remembering God has a purpose in allowing our trials helps us to endure them. In Romans 5:3–5, Paul teaches,

> We also glory in our sufferings, because we know that suffering produces perseverance; perseverance, character; and character, hope. And hope does not put us to shame, because God's love has been poured out into our hearts through the Holy Spirit, who has been given to us.

For both Paul and James, there is this great sense that perseverance is a productive area in which we grow, because trials test faith (verse 3).

We need to be prepared for trials. When difficulties arise, there is no point wondering, 'Why has this happened to me?' Just being a Christian does not mean you are never going to have any problems or illnesses. If so, becoming a Christian would save on health insurance! Living in our world means we will suffer – believers and unbelievers alike.

What matters is how we meet trials. We meet them 'God with us' – and also with the recognition that they test us not to break us, but to grow us and strengthen us. As Peter says,

> You may have had to suffer grief in all kinds of trials. These have come so that the proven genuineness of your faith – of greater worth than

gold, which perishes even though refined by fire – may result in praise, glory and honour when Jesus Christ is revealed.
(1 Peter 1:6–7)

Perseverance is not just putting up with these trials. It is an active, not a passive, word. It's courage and robustness. It's saying, 'All right – let's go for it!' This passage teaches that perseverance is us cooperating with God. James urges us, 'Let perseverance finish its work.' This means saying to God, 'Come on, Lord; I understand that this is a way in which you are moulding me to be more like Jesus. I want to cooperate with you. Please grow me through this experience so that I become mature and complete.'

How are you coping with your trials? You can kick against them and blame God or you can persevere, cooperating with God's work. Will you grasp this trial as an opportunity to grow more like Christ? Will you view it as a means to get to know God better, pray more deeply and become more obedient?

In Christ's light, suffering is a ministry, not a millstone. It is a gift, not a glitch in the plan.
(Kristen Wetherell and Sarah Walton, *Hope When It Hurts: Biblical reflections to help you grasp God's purpose in your suffering*, The Good Book Company, 2017, p. 88)

Day 238

Read: 1 Peter 4:12–17

Key verses: 1 Peter 4:12–13

••

> [12]*Dear friends, do not be surprised at the fiery ordeal that has come on you to test you, as though something strange were happening to you.* [13]*But rejoice inasmuch as you participate in the sufferings of Christ, so that you may be overjoyed when his glory is revealed.*

Often suffering comes upon me as a surprise. And, in my default view, like many of us, I imagine, I'm looking and praying to get back to 'normal' as soon as possible. But these verses provide a radically countercultural perspective and a challenge to that default mode.

Peter explains that these trials are coming to test you. Your faith is more precious than gold; and gold is tested. It goes through fire, and then its purity is measured (1 Peter 1:6–7). It's not that you are stalked by a peril that's 'out to get you', but rather what is coming is to test you, and it is within God's plan and purpose.

In the midst of these trials, Paul calls us to 'rejoice'. I think the underlying meaning is: 'But *continue to* rejoice.' For me, rejoicing is gathering all the good things and being joyful about them. However, verse 13 says, 'But rejoice inasmuch as you participate in the sufferings of Christ.' How do we do that? It's not that we ignore the reality of sufferings, but that somehow we super-rejoice in the light of the future revelation of Jesus' glory: 'Rejoice inasmuch as you participate in the sufferings of Christ, so that you may be overjoyed when his glory is revealed.' So practise joy now, because we will be overjoyed then.

What Peter's saying here, from his own personal experience, is that fixing our eyes on the future helps us to face the present. How do you do that? You look back to the real Jesus of Nazareth, who died on the cross according to the Scriptures, and you look forward to his triumphant return. It's having our eyes trained not so much on the hardness of our circumstances, but on the foundation of the promises in Christ and the glorious revelation that is to come. It is the reality of what Jesus will do that is meant to flow back into our present – it breaks into our lives now, not removing our suffering, but helping us to live within it.

What are you praying for? It is not wrong to ask God to remove your suffering. But don't stop there. Try praying a bigger prayer – that if God does not choose to change your circumstances, he would use them to refine and prove your faith. Take encouragement from 1 Peter 1:3–9 as you consider the purpose of your trials and the future God has planned for you. Let the joy of Christ's return and the culmination of your salvation seep into your soul and have an impact on how you respond to your circumstances today.

Day 239

Read: 1 Peter 5:1–11
Key verses: 1 Peter 5:8–9

∙∙

⁸Be alert and of sober mind. Your enemy the devil prowls around like a roaring lion looking for someone to devour. ⁹Resist him, standing firm in the faith, because you know that the family of believers throughout the world is undergoing the same kind of sufferings.

The devil is not a box jellyfish, a deadly creature that floats through the sea and will sting you without thinking about it; you just drift into it. Our enemy, the devil, is not a stinging nettle that accidentally hurts you but has nothing against you personally. No! Our enemy is a 'roaring lion', a real, opposing enemy.

We're told to 'resist him, standing firm in the faith' (verse 9). This is not a call to aggressive spiritual warfare. Rather, as in Ephesians 6 and elsewhere in the New Testament, it is simply the call to stand faithfully for Jesus as his people – and to do so realizing that other Christians are going through the same thing.

Why is it important to realize that other Christians around the world are also suffering? Three reasons. First of all, it stops me seeing myself as a miserable exception. 'Woe is me! It's just me. The Lord is blessing all these other Christians and I'm the lousy exception.' Number two, it stops me seeing myself as a comfortable exception. 'Phew! I'm glad I live here and not there; I wouldn't like to go through that. I'll pray for them, but I'm glad it's not me.' Third, positively, I'm drawn into seeing myself as part of a worldwide fellowship. As believers, we're bound together as a whole, not just as a believing community but also as a suffering community. Remember Acts 14:22,

the one bit of teaching for believers that's recorded in the book of Acts: 'We must go through many hardships to enter the kingdom of

God.' This fellowship of suffering is about being brought to completion. And that's what Peter's saying here in verse 9.

Your suffering is not just an awkward little sting that accidently happened to you; it's personal. Be on your guard because the devil is prowling around, looking for someone to devour. Know that the same kinds of sufferings are being experienced by our brothers and sisters throughout the world, and it is part of God's purpose.

> This is . . . a life-or-death fight to the finish against the Devil and all his angels. Be prepared. You're up against far more than you can handle on your own. Take all the help you can get, every weapon God has issued, so that when it's all over but the shouting you'll still be on your feet. Truth, righteousness, peace, faith, and salvation are more than words. Learn how to apply them. You'll need them throughout your life. God's Word is an *indispensable* weapon. In the same way, prayer is essential in this ongoing warfare. Pray hard and long. Pray for your brothers and sisters. Keep your eyes open. Keep each other's spirits up so that no one falls behind or drops out.
> (Ephesians 6:12–18, MSG)

Day 240

Read: 1 Peter 5:8–14
Key verse: 1 Peter 5:10

....

> ¹⁰*And the God of all grace, who called you to his eternal glory in Christ, after you have suffered a little while, will himself restore you and make you strong, firm and steadfast.*

God knows what he is doing.

If God gives us decades to come, then that 'little while' of suffering may feel like an awfully long time. But in the span of God's things, if he would give us the eyes of faith, we'd see it as only 'a little while'. And in that little while, 'the God of all grace' – I think it is better translated as 'the God who produces and brings forth all grace' – has 'called you to his eternal glory in Christ'. He will comprehensively change things after you have suffered for a little while.

We're following in the footsteps of Jesus. The prophets looked to the 'sufferings of the Messiah and the glories that would follow' (1 Peter 1:10–11). We do not have a gospel of glory without suffering; we need to hold them both together. And we need to hold them in order: suffering for a little while, then glory to come for eternity.

Then what will this God of all grace do? He 'will himself restore, confirm, strengthen, and establish you' (verse 10, ESV). And it is 'you' plural. The spiritual house that's being built in your church fellowship, of which you are a living stone as you continue coming to Christ the living stone, might look shaky, but God will restore, confirm, strengthen and establish you (1 Peter 2:4–10). You are secure in Christ and in the purposes of God.

Peter concludes, 'I have written briefly to you, exhorting and declaring that this is the true grace of God. Stand firm in it' (verse 12, ESV). What is 'this'? 'This' is the message, the ethic, the worldview, the way of life in this letter. 'This' is the 'varied grace' (1 Peter 4:10) from God (5:10) that comes to us through Jesus (4:11). It's true, dependable grace, however beleaguered your Christian life might be. And variable grace trumps variable trials (see 1:6 and 4:10). 'This' is how things really are. The suffering that you face now or in the future for the faith is legitimate grace from God, not an awful mistake, not a tragic cul-de-sac; suffering for a little while, leading to glories to come – both bound up in grace. So stand fast, knowing it's for a little while, knowing that it's real, knowing that God's grace is even more real.

When faced with suffering, will you say to yourself, 'This is the true grace of God. [I will] Stand firm in it'? God will enable you to stand; his limitless grace is sufficient to match your current trial. Will you persevere, relying on his strength and believing his promise: 'My grace is sufficient for you, for my power is made perfect in weakness' (2 Corinthians 12:9)?

Day 241

Read: Revelation 22:8–21
Key verses: Revelation 22:8–9

. . . .

> [8]*I, John, am the one who heard and saw these things. And when I had heard and seen them, I fell down to worship at the feet of the angel who had been showing them to me.* [9]*But he said to me, "Don't do that! I am a fellow servant with you and with your fellow prophets and with all who keep the words of this scroll. Worship God!"*

The book of Revelation gives us a glimpse into the climax of history, the coronation of our Lord Jesus Christ. In 22:16, John gets to the end of this great revelation and explains its purpose by quoting the words of Christ: 'I, Jesus, have sent my angel to give you this testimony for the churches.' John realized that this revelation was for the church in every age and generation, so that we might be encouraged and strengthened knowing that history is heading towards an end point.

You can sense the anticipation (verse 20): 'He who testifies to these things says, "Yes, I am coming soon." Amen. Come, Lord Jesus.' We echo this, but in the meantime, in difficult church situations, at work where you are the only believer, how do you persevere?

The Bible warns us to avoid distraction. Did you notice that in verses 8–9 John falls down to worship at the feet of the angel who'd shown him the vision? It was such an amazing experience and he was so full of wonder that he fell at the angel's feet in worship. And the angel says, 'Don't do that! . . . Worship God!' (verse 9). The angel didn't want to be the focus of worship or the cause of distraction. Instead, he directed John to worship 'the Alpha and the Omega, the First and the Last, the Beginning and the End' (22:13).

In the same way, we need to make sure our focus is not in any sense captivated or sidetracked by the wrong things. It is possible to become distracted, even by good and godly things. We can be distracted about translations of the Bible, methods of church government and modes of baptism. We can major on minors, make mountains out of molehills and become distracted by the very things that are meant to lead us to love Jesus more and serve him better.

Jesus knows our perseverance in the faith gets tested when we're distracted, even by good things like Christian service. When we take our focus off Jesus, we tend to get anxious and stressed, and start to believe that our progress in the Christian life is all down to us. Look out for these tell-tale signs and be honest with yourself about what is distracting you. Relegate that distraction to its proper place and renew your allegiance to Christ. Through repentance, prayer and time in the Scriptures, get your focus back on him (Luke 10:41–42)!

Day 242

Read: Revelation 22:8–21
Key verses: Revelation 22:14–15

....

> [14] *Blessed are those who wash their robes, that they may have the right to the tree of life and may go through the gates into the city.* [15] *Outside are the dogs, those who practise magic arts, the sexually immoral, the murderers, the idolaters and everyone who loves and practises falsehood.*

Jesus is coming back soon! So what are the things we should keep on doing, and what must we avoid? Jesus warns us in Revelation 22:14–15 to beware of dirt.

If we look back to Revelation 7:14, we read about those who have washed their robes and made them white in the blood of the Lamb. The tense in the Greek language denotes a once-and-for-all action. When you trust the Lord Jesus, your sins are forgiven; they are washed away by the blood of Jesus, shed on the cross; they are blotted out, and your name is entered into the Lamb's book of life. But here in Revelation 22:14, the word 'wash' is in the present tense: it is not to do with your salvation but that daily cleansing that you and I need. We need cleansing for that hasty word, for that unkind response and selfish attitude. This sense of the Lord Jesus' imminent return encourages us to keep short accounts with God and with one another.

Verse 15 provides a sharp contrast to the previous verse. In the Bible, the word 'dog' is a symbol of things that are impure and unclean. 'Outside' doesn't necessarily mean that sinners are sitting at the doors of the heavenly Jerusalem. Rather, the sense is that the un-righteous are not part of what goes on inside the heavenly city. The list of sinful practices is not exhaustive, but conveys the difference between righteous and unrighteous living. We are called to live clean in a dirty world.

We are not called to live self-righteously, with a holier-than-thou attitude, but to live righteously. To live as Jesus lived. He hung around drunkards, gluttons and the immoral, and they were attracted to him because he didn't write them off or look down on them. There was no element of self-righteousness that said, 'I am holy and you are inferior.' Rather, his righteousness was winsome and attractive. Jesus lived clean in a dirty world, and that is his call to each of us today.

Are you still coming to God for daily cleansing? Are you still passionate about dealing with the sin in your life? It is easy to become complacent and excuse sin. But Jesus' call is to press on, to persevere in the life-long pursuit of holiness (Romans 6:11–14; Colossians 3:1–10). Today, reflect on how much God hates sin. Ask him to stir your heart and renew your strength to say 'no' to sin and 'yes' to righteousness (Titus 2:12). Pray that your 'walk' would match your 'talk', and your life would attract people to Jesus and the gospel.

Day 243

Read: Revelation 22:8–21
Key verses: Revelation 22:18–19

....

> [18]I warn everyone who hears the words of the prophecy of this scroll: if anyone adds anything to them, God will add to that person the plagues described in this scroll. [19]And if anyone takes words away from this scroll of prophecy, God will take away from that person any share in the tree of life and in the Holy City, which are described in this scroll.

What are the final words God wants to leave ringing in our ears as we press on in this life of faith?

First, there is a warning to watch out for deception (verses 18–19). This is a similar warning to the one the apostle John gave in 1 John 4:1–3:

> Dear friends, do not believe every spirit, but test the spirits to see whether they are from God, because many false prophets have gone out into the world. This is how you can recognise the Spirit of God: every spirit that acknowledges that Jesus Christ has come in the flesh is from God, but every spirit that does not acknowledge Jesus is not from God. This is the spirit of the antichrist, which you have heard is coming and even now is already in the world.

John explains that many false prophets have gone out into the world, and in order to recognize, test and refute them, we have to know our Bible. We must have an intimate relationship with God – Father, Son and Spirit – through Scripture. We need to know our history and be familiar with the story of the church and what God has been doing in different generations and ages. We need to be people of maturity, like the men of Issachar who understood the times and knew what Israel should do (1 Chronicles 12:32).

But after the warning comes an encouragement. Look at the very last verse in the book of Revelation. Verse 21 is a wonderfully simple ending: 'The grace of the Lord Jesus be with God's people.' Today, whatever you face, God's grace is with you. God's grace is not something you have to stockpile at a Christian convention. Neither is it something you can leave behind at the end of an event. God's grace goes with you, and it is sufficient for everything that you face.

John Bunyan, author of *The Pilgrim's Progress*, taught,

> 'Grace can pardon our ungodliness and justify us with Christ's right-eousness; it can put the Spirit of Jesus Christ within us; it can help us when we are down; it can heal us when we are wounded; it can multiply pardons, as we through frailty multiply transgressions.'
> (John Bunyan, *The Riches of Bunyan: Selected from His Works*, ed. Taylor Anderson, CreateSpace Independent Publishing, 2017, p. 39)

Today, trust in God's grace to persevere, and live the life of faith well.

> May our Lord Jesus Christ himself and God our Father, who loved us and by his grace gave us eternal encouragement and good hope, encourage your hearts and strengthen you in every good deed and word.
> (2 Thessalonians 2:16–17)

For further study

If you would like to read more on the theme of perseverance you might find the following selection of books helpful:

- Christopher Ash, *Zeal without Burnout* (The Good Book Company, 2016)

- Dale Ralph Davis, *Slogging along on the Paths of Righteousness* (Christian Focus, 2016)

- Dale Ralph Davis, *The Way of the Righteous in the Muck of Life* (Christian Focus, 2016)

- Sharon James, *Ann Judson, A Missionary Life for Burma* (Evangelical Press, 2015)

- Paul Mallard, *Invest Your Disappointments* (IVP, 2018)

- Paul Mallard, *Staying Fresh* (IVP, 2015)

- John Piper, *The Roots of Endurance* (IVP, 2003)

- Helen Roseveare, *Digging Ditches* (Christian Focus, 2012)

Holiness

Contributors

Day 244

Read: Leviticus 11:1–47
Key verses: Leviticus 11:43–44

....

43Do not defile yourselves by any of these creatures. Do not make yourselves unclean by means of them or be made unclean by them. 44I am the LORD your God; consecrate yourselves and be holy, because I am holy.

Finding the first call in Scripture to 'be holy, because I am holy' at the end of a list of food regulations is like digging over a scrap heap and suddenly finding a diamond ring buried in the muck and the rubbish!

Why were these regulations given? Perhaps it was to do with hygiene or that the banned animals were used in cultic practices by the Canaanites. Recently, the most popular explanation has been that whenever there's a lack of wholeness or something doesn't measure up to the norm, then it's considered impure and you are to steer clear of it (see Day 245). But even this reasoning is secondary to the Bible's own explanation.

God's holiness is the primary reason he gives for these regulations (see verses 44–45). The human mind always likes to explore further, but it ought to be enough that God says to his people, 'Live like this.' God says this is what you can eat and this is what you should avoid and, because these regulations somehow connect to holiness, we should obey.

However, these are not the demands of an impersonal, sovereign lord of the universe who woke up one day and decided to make life awkward for his creatures. This is a reflection of the personal, saving relationship that God has with the children of Israel. He says, 'I am the LORD, *your* God! [Verse 44, emphasis added.] I am your redeemer. Your obedience isn't mere drudgery or duty. It rises out of gratitude and is an expression of the relationship you have with me.'

In essence, holiness is resembling God. 'Be holy,' says God, 'because I am holy.' This is a staggering command, not just for the children of Israel but for us as well, since it's repeated in the New Testament (see 1 Peter 1:16). God calls us to be holy so that we might, to some extent, reproduce him in the world. We can never be perfect reproductions. We are not life-giving creators as he is. We do not have his matchless perfection or his power. There are qualities that belong to God alone. But we are called to resemble God not by following food regulations but by demonstrating his grace, compassion, mercy, goodness and moral purity to the world.[1]

This command to imitate God and be holy is absolutely breath-taking! It may seem overwhelming but consider this:

> Imitating Christ is no burden for genuine disciples who act out only what, or rather who, is in them. The disciple's mandate is simply 'Become who you already are [in Christ]' . . . The real work of discipleship, growing into our parts as little Christs, remains, not as a condition but as a consequence of our salvation . . . If disciples are to become Christlike, they must do more than learn their lines; they must also develop their characters.
> (Kevin J. Vanhoozer, *Faith Speaking Understanding*, Westminster John Knox Press, 2014, p. 129)

---

1. For further study on Leviticus, see Derek Tidball's *The Message of Leviticus* in IVP's The Bible Speaks Today series (listed in the 'For further study' section).

Day 245

Read: Leviticus 11:1–47
Key verses: Leviticus 11:1–3

••

> ¹ *The* Lord *said to Moses and Aaron,* ² *'Say to the Israelites: "Of all the animals that live on land, these are the ones you may eat:* ³ *you may eat any animal that has a divided hoof and that chews the cud."'*

When you're listening to a piece of music, you don't analyse every individual note. It is only as you listen to the whole piece that the theme and beauty emerge. In the same way, when we stand back from the details of Leviticus 11, we see a common theme: each example of impurity is where something doesn't quite fit as it should and where wholeness is lacking.

You expect farm animals to chew the cud and have divided hooves. If they lack one of those things, they're dealt with as animals that don't quite match your expectation and reach the standard. On that basis, eating cattle and sheep is fine but eating camels and pigs is not (verses 4–8). We naturally think that fish have fins and scales, so we are happy to eat haddock or salmon, but we're not quite so sure about eels, which don't (verses 9–12).

What about birds? There seem to be no real criteria except that the impure birds are the ones that live off the blood of others (verses 13–19). The impure insects are the swarming ones that seem a little uncertain about whether they fly or walk and don't fit one category of movement or the other (verses 20–23).

The next chapters of Leviticus cover a range of other examples of impurity or lack of wholeness: when damp undermines the integrity of your house; when your garments have a hole or are stained; when you have a skin disease. Each of these, in different ways, threatens the integrity of the species or of the person, and, by contrast, God is teaching his people that holiness stands for wholeness, for completion and for integrity. And God reveals himself, as he did in Exodus 15:26, to be the God who heals people's diseases: 'I am the LORD, who heals you.'

Holiness, throughout life, is a journey towards wholeness. The healing of our deficiencies, our sicknesses, the things that make us vulnerable – not just physically but also personally, psychologically and certainly spiritually – as God calls us increasingly forwards until the 'the day of Christ' (Philippians 1:6). On that day, God, who began a good work in us, will bring it to completion. Until then we're on a journey of holiness.

In our search for wholeness, we may turn to many things – a marriage partner, family, money or a career. Ultimately, however, only Jesus can make us whole. One day, he will finish the job but, for now, we grow in holiness through the routines, suffering and joys of life. Each day is an opportunity to keep our hearts fixed on Jesus – surrendering to his will, trusting his purposes, renouncing our sin and learning to love him more.

Jesus! What a friend for sinners!
Jesus! Lover of my soul;
friends may fail me, foes assail me,
He, my Saviour, makes me whole.
(J. Wilbur Chapman, 'Our Great Saviour', 1910)

Day 246

Read: Leviticus 11:1–47
Key verses: Leviticus 11:33–34

....

> [33] *If one of them [a rat or gecko] falls into a clay pot, everything in it will be unclean, and you must break the pot.* [34] *Any food you are allowed to eat that has come into contact with water from any such pot is unclean, and any liquid that is drunk from such a pot is unclean.*

Holiness is not a Sunday morning add-on.

Leviticus 11:33–34 is a snapshot of the teaching found in Leviticus 11–15. These chapters powerfully demonstrate that the call to holiness is comprehensive, involving every aspect of our lives. Holiness is required in the kitchen in terms of what we eat. Holiness relates to the bedroom, in terms of our sexual relationships and faithfulness. Holiness is to be found in the maternity ward as a child is born. Holiness is found in the sick room. Holiness is required on the building site and in the clothing store. Elsewhere in Leviticus, references are made to the market-place and the law courts, so business and public life are included, too.

There is no sacred–secular divide in Scripture. Every day, as you stand at the kitchen sink, go to work, relate to your family members or visit somebody in hospital, you are reminded that God presides over every aspect of your life. You can't compartmentalize what God has brought together. These verses teach that holiness is to do with how you vote in an election, your attitude towards economic injustice, how you spend your leisure time, what hobbies you adopt and how you behave as a father, auntie or grandparent. It has as much to do with your attitude as an employee or employer as it does with singing songs and arguing doctrinal points in church.

As Chris Wright explains:

> Holiness is thus a very comprehensive concept indeed.
> It is really not so much a religious aspiration or even just a moral code.
> Holiness is rather a way of living with God, in a Covenant relationship.
> It's a way of being like God in clean and wholesome living. It's a way of being God's people in the midst of an unholy and unclean world.
> (Christopher J. H. Wright, *Old Testament Ethics for the People of God*, IVP, 2010, pp. 286–287)

These regulations are designed so that, at every point in your life, you are reminded of God's call to be holy. Every time you cook, give birth, fall sick or deal with DIY problems in your house, there is a tutorial going on about being a reflection of the God who calls you to be holy. Paul says exactly the same thing in the New Testament: 'Whatever you do, whether in word or deed, do it all in the name of the Lord Jesus, giving thanks to God the Father through him' (Colossians 3:17).

Do you have a sacred–secular divide in your life? Has God's call to holiness had an impact on your finances, free time, work, retirement, parenting or hospital visits (to name just a selection)? Pray through your day, asking for God's strength to 'do it all in the name of the Lord Jesus'.

Day 247

Read: Leviticus 11:1–47
Key verses: Leviticus 11:39–40

....

> ³⁹*If an animal that you are allowed to eat dies, anyone who touches its carcass will be unclean till evening.* ⁴⁰*Anyone who eats some of its carcass must wash their clothes, and they will be unclean till evening.*

Does your life look any different from the lives of non-Christian friends and colleagues?

These Old Testament laws teach us that holiness is a call to distinctiveness. For Israel, this was demonstrated in a call to ritual purity (chapters 11–15). The laws were the ways in which, ritually in life, they were reminded about the call to be holy, hence the teaching being done by this dramatic, symbolic action. If they didn't live up to the call – if they touched a dead carcass, if they ate an unclean animal, if there was some mould in their houses that they hadn't eradicated or if there were emissions from their bodies – then it had to be dealt with. It didn't mean that they were immoral, because these were ordinary functions of life. But it did mean that they were ritually impure and needed to be cleansed. This usually involved washing and a period of 'time out', often until the evening (11:24–25, 39–40). Through these ordinary activities, the point was clear – God has a claim on the whole of your life; he desires purity in all dimensions.

God was teaching people at every level, in every way and in every area of life about the need to reflect his holiness. And that's the same call for us today. We are no longer, as New Testament Christians, called to manifest our distinctiveness in the world through our diet or the various ritual rules and regulations of Leviticus 11–15. We know this because Jesus said in Mark 7:1–23 that what matters is what comes *out* of us, not what goes *into* us. Peter (Acts 10–11) and Paul

(Galatians and Romans) also spend time explaining that these rituals were actually signposts to a different way of life. Now our distinction is in the way we live, the love we show, the forgiveness we demonstrate, the honesty we practise, the grateful speech that comes out of our mouths, the sexual chastity and faithfulness within heterosexual marriage, and our humility rather than the self-assertion often found in our society.

These food laws might be outdated, but they are powerful reminders that holiness is down-to-earth, practicable, everyday living. It is not abstract or ethereal spirituality; it reaches every aspect of our lives and every part of the world in which we live.

> If Christians were as serious about moral distinctiveness as Israel was about ritual cleanness, then our salt and light might have a greater power and impact in the world than it often does.
> (Christopher J. H. Wright, *Old Testament Ethics for the People of God*, IVP, 2010, p. 299)

> Heavenly Father, save us from having such an anaemic faith that we blend in with our culture. May our love for you and the distinctiveness of our lives provoke gospel conversations, bringing others to know you. Help us to be salt and light in our homes, workplaces and communities, for Jesus' sake and his glory. Amen.

Day 248

Read: Leviticus 19:1–37
Key verses: Leviticus 19:1–2

....

> [1] *The* L*ORD* *said to Moses,* [2] *'Speak to the entire assembly of Israel and say to them: "Be holy because I, the* L*ORD* *your God, am holy."'*

Leviticus 19 is one of the greatest ethical charters in the world. It is a wonderfully liberating and person-centred approach to how to live. It calls us to reflect God's character and be holy in a wide variety of scenarios. We are to demonstrate a concern for the poor, truthfulness in all our relationships and a respect for the disabled.

A concern for the poor (verses 9–10). At harvest time, the Israelites were told not to pick up every last grain of corn or every single grape. These were to be left for the poor. We can't literally fulfil this command today. But it's a window on to God's compassion for the marginalized, often the immigrants and foreigners. It matters little that we know the latest worship songs if we do not have compassion for those who are on the margins of our society. Biblically speaking, a concern for the poor is high on God's agenda.

Truthfulness in all our relationships (verses 11–12). We are called to be truthful in our speech as we speak to one another and about one another to other people. This integrity isn't just an integrity of words but of action. We are given these directives: 'Do not steal' (verse 11) and 'Do not use dishonest standards when measuring length, weight or quantity. Use honest scales' (verses 35–36). We are to reject all exploitation. Verse 13 says, 'Do not hold back the wages of a hired worker overnight.' It is not the mechanism that is important, but the principle of not exploiting those we employ. Our calling is to be distinct; we are not to contribute to the corrupt system of our economy, which says that people can be used, abused and not receive their just payment.

Respect for the disabled (verse 14). 'Do not curse the deaf or put a stumbling block in front of the blind, but fear your God. I am the LORD' (verse 14). People argued, 'Well, the deaf are deaf, so I can say what I like about them! And the blind can't see the banana skins that I put in front of them, so let's have a laugh at their expense!' But disabled people are made in the image of God. Any physical disability from which they suffer is yet another example of the multiplicity of disabilities from which we all suffer. Some happen to be physical, others emotional or mental, and we're all caught in the spiritually disabled trap. We must treat every human being, whatever his or her disability, with respect and not take advantage of anyone.

'Holiness is the biblical 'shorthand' for the very essence of God. This is what makes the command of Leviticus 19:2 quite breathtaking. Your quality of life, it said to the people of God, must reflect the very heart of God's character.'
(Christopher J. H. Wright, *An Eye for an Eye*, IVP, 1983, p. 27)

Does your quality of life – in particular, your integrity, compassion for the poor and respect for the disabled – reflect the very heart of God's character? Come to the Lord in prayer, to repent and seek his transforming Holy Spirit.

Day 249

Read: Leviticus 19:1–37
Key verses: Leviticus 19:1–2, 37

••

> ¹ *The L*ORD *said to Moses,* ² *'Speak to the entire assembly of Israel and say to them: "Be holy because I, the L*ORD *your God, am holy . . .* ³⁷ *Keep all my decrees and all my laws and follow them. I am the L*ORD.*"'*

What motivates us to be holy? The biggest reason is that we're like God (verse 2), but Leviticus 19 gives us three others.

We fear God (verse 14). This is not a cringing dread but a healthy respect. Seven times in this chapter we read, 'I am the LORD your God'; eight times, God simply says, 'I am the LORD.' The point is that he is God and we are his subjects. He is Creator and we are his creatures. He is infinite and eternal, and we owe everything to him. So we have no right to make up the law ourselves or live as we desire. Remember how Peter and John, when told not to preach the gospel, challenged the Sanhedrin: 'Which is right in God's eyes: to listen to you, or to him?' (Acts 4:19). Our society is continually saying, 'You can't live like that!' Our calling as the people of God is to listen to and obey God because we fear him.

We love our neighbour (verse 18). God has made us for community, and so many of these regulations invite us to invest in what the sociologists call 'social capital' – things that make society function smoothly. If only we lived like this, our society would not be falling apart with rampant individualism. We're called to love our neighbours not just when they like us or when they're fellow church members with the same educational level, professional background and interests. We are called to love our neighbours as ourselves when they have a very different social background, language, skin colour and past (see Matthew 22:39).

We recall our past (verse 34). We live like this, in our treatment of foreigners for example, because we remember that we were slaves in Egypt. It was the mercy and grace of God that delivered us and gave us freedom. It had nothing to do with our own goodness, merits or worthiness. While we might never have been foreigners in Egypt, we do have a past story, which means that our salvation, our acceptance by God, our liberty in Christ, is purely by God's grace. Paul never forgot this. He reminded Timothy that 'the grace of our Lord was poured out on me abundantly, along with the faith and the love that are in Christ Jesus' (1 Timothy 1:14). On that road to Damascus, when Paul was called to be an apostle, it wasn't because he was a Pharisee, a Jew and a well-educated Roman citizen. All that mattered was the grace of God.

If your motivation for holiness is flagging, dwell on these key truths:

• The 'Lord your God' – to whom you owe everything – calls you to reverent obedience.
• You were made for community – to demonstrate practical holiness by loving others with God's love.
• God has poured out his grace on you abundantly.

Day 250

Read: Psalm 99:1–9
Key verses: Psalm 99:1–3

....

¹ *The LORD reigns,*
    let the nations tremble;
he sits enthroned between the cherubim,
    let the earth shake.
² *Great is the LORD in Zion;*
    he is exalted over all the nations.
³ *Let them praise your great and awesome name –*
    he is holy.

'God is holy.'

This is the refrain of Psalm 99 (see verses 3, 5 and 9). The spotlight is on how God's kingship reveals his holy nature.

The opening verses describe the greatness of the King (verses 1–3). He doesn't have to do anything to be great – he just is. The mere fact of his being King makes the whole earth shake. He is great and high; he is awesome. The psalmist recognizes that, in the presence of such greatness, people tremble. His name spells fear in the hearts of men and women.

Rahab, the Canaanite woman who helped the Israelites to capture the city of Jericho, expressed similar sentiments:

> I know that the LORD has given this land to you and that a great fear of you has fallen on us, so that all who live in this country are melting in fear because of you. We have heard how the LORD dried up the water of the Red Sea for you when you came out of Egypt . . . When we heard of it, our hearts sank . . . for the LORD your God is God in heaven above and on the earth below.
> (Joshua 2:9–11)

Amazingly, this great God is near; he comes down to live among his people in Zion (Psalm 99:2). This reminds me of Isaiah 6 (which we will focus on later). Isaiah had a vision of the King in his holiness and he felt the earth tremble. He experienced first-hand the awe-inspiring nearness of the holy God.

But do you see God's graciousness? Where does he set his throne when he comes down to dwell? 'Between the cherubim' (verse 1). This is not the enthronement that the prophet Ezekiel saw (Ezekiel 10:20). Neither is God enthroned above the cherubim of Genesis 3:24 that turned every way to guard the tree of Life. These are the cherubim *in Zion* mentioned in Exodus 25:18–20: 'And you shall make two cherubim of gold . . . their faces one to another; towards the mercy seat shall the faces of the cherubim be' (ESV). God reigns on his throne in the place of mercy. The grace of this great, awesome and near God is that, when he comes down in all his holiness to be among his people, he takes up his throne in the place where mercy triumphs over wrath.

Praise God's 'great and awesome name – he is holy' (Psalm 99:3). Today, recover the awe and wonder of coming into the presence of the holy God, whose greatness makes the earth shake. Marvel that our God is near and that he invites us into his holy presence, where his mercy triumphs over his wrath. Come joyfully; come reverently.

Day 251

Read: Psalm 99:1–9
Key verses: Psalm 99:4–5

....

> [4] *The King is mighty, he loves justice –*
>   *you have established equity;*
> *in Jacob you have done*
>   *what is just and right.*
> [5] *Exalt the LORD our God*
>   *and worship at his footstool;*
>   *he is holy.*

How does a holy king rule?

The literal translation of verse 4 is: 'The King's strength loves justice.' All the power of this great King is wrapped up in the love and exercise of justice, in doing what is right. This links up with the fact that, in the Old Testament, the law is a manifestation of the image of God. The Lord chose to be known among his people not by visible representation but by the law that he spoke to them (Deuteronomy 4:12). Think back to Leviticus 19, where that amazing collection of laws is shot through with the refrain: 'I am the LORD.' If the people had asked, 'Why should we keep these laws?', the answer would come back: 'Because the law represents among you what I am.' Therefore, Leviticus 19:2 says, 'Be holy because I, the LORD your God, am holy.' The law is the perpetual image of God, and if any one follows it, he will be like God.

God is passionately concerned about establishing righteousness, justice and equity among his people (Psalm 99:4). The implementing of these holy principles and practices is the outflow of divine holiness. So he doesn't accommodate his principles to the inadequacies of his people. Rather, he insists his people keep his law, despite our incapacity. Perhaps the name 'Jacob' is used here to underline the helplessness of the people of God in keeping the law. Remember, Jacob deceived his father Isaac and cheated his brother out of his birthright. Although he was given a new name (Israel) and nature, he so often lived the old Jacob-life.

Like Jacob, we continually fall woefully short of God's demands. But, thankfully, those who face the obligation of the divine law also live ever under grace. It is 'Jacob' who is invited not simply to praise but to worship at God's footstool (verse 5), the mercy seat. God deliberately places his feet on the mercy seat where blood is sprinkled. No sooner is the law declared than sacrifices are initiated to pay the price for all the ways we failed to keep it. These Old Testament sacrifices point us to Christ: 'If anybody does sin, we have an advocate with the Father – Jesus Christ, the Righteous One. He is the atoning sacrifice for our sins' (1 John 2:1–2).

God's holy character means he is always just and always merciful. In the face of sin, how can these two elements be reconciled? Only by God himself, in the person of Christ, taking the punishment for our sins. The cross was the most profound display of God's holiness – out of sheer mercy, God forgave our sins, but divine justice was still carried out because the entire penalty for sin was paid. Today, worship God for his flawless standard of justice and righteousness, which sets us apart from him, and also for his boundless grace and mercy, which draw us close.

Day 252

Read: Psalm 99:1–9
Key verses: Psalm 99:6–9

. . . .

> ⁶*Moses and Aaron were among his priests,*
> *Samuel was among those who called on his name;*
> *they called on the L*ORD
> *and he answered them.*
> ⁷*He spoke to them from the pillar of cloud;*
> *they kept his statutes and the decrees he gave them.*
>
> ⁸*L*ORD *our God,*
> *you answered them;*
> *you were to Israel a forgiving God,*
> *though you punished their misdeeds.*
> ⁹*Exalt the L*ORD *our God*
> *and worship at his holy mountain,*
> *for the L*ORD *our God is holy.*

What does a personal relationship with a holy God look like?

Moses, Aaron and Samuel are mentioned as representatives, typical of what it means to be part of the people of God. We, like them, are each called to a life of praying and receiving, hearing and obeying, and forgiveness and chastisement.

A life of praying and receiving. The psalmist mentions Moses and Aaron, both priests with the privilege of having access to God. 'Samuel was among those who called on his name' (verse 6). Again and again, the hallmark of the people of God is that they are a praying people (Psalm 65:2; 138:1–3). The verbs indicate that their unwavering attitude was one of calling on God, and he continually answered them.

A life of hearing and obeying. The Lord's people live by supernatural truth, the Word of God: 'They kept his statutes and the decrees he gave them' (99:7). God's Word was authenticated by himself and graven into the tablets of rock brought down from Mount Sinai by Moses. It became the permanent standard of the way the people of God were to think and act.

A life of forgiveness and chastisement. We have 'a forgiving God' (verse 8), literally a 'God of sin-bearing'. This idea takes us back to Leviticus 16:22, when, on the Day of Atonement, Aaron the priest sent the live goat – the sin-bearer – into the wilderness. We also look forward to Isaiah 53:12: 'He [Jesus] poured out his life unto death, and was numbered with the transgressors. For he *bore* the sin of many, and made intercession for the transgressors' (emphasis added). Fast forward to the New Testament and John's cry: 'Look, the Lamb of God, who takes away [bears away] the sin of the world!' (John 1:29). God is forgiving, but punishment for misdeeds is also mentioned here because forgiveness without chastening would make us complacent, and chastisement without forgiveness would crush us. While, together, they are the guarantee that we can trust we will be forgiven, we can never take sin lightly.

It is staggering that a holy God would want to know us personally. Yet he answers our prayers, gives us his Word so that we know how to live in relationship with him, and he forgives our sins. Today, don't be afraid to bring your prayers to him, don't be slow to obey his commands and don't shrink away from repentance. Most of all, 'exalt' him; 'worship' our holy God (Psalm 99:9). The 'LORD our God' invites you into the deepest relationship of your life, so don't hold back.

Day 253

Read: Isaiah 6:1–8
Key verses: Isaiah 6:1–3

....

> ¹*In the year that King Uzziah died, I saw the Lord, high and exalted, seated on a throne; and the train of his robe filled the temple.* ²*Above him were seraphim, each with six wings: with two wings they covered their faces, with two they covered their feet, and with two they were flying.* ³*And they were calling to one another:*
> *"Holy, holy, holy is the L*ORD *Almighty;*
> *the whole earth is full of his glory."*

In the year the great king Uzziah dies, Isaiah the prophet catches a glimpse of God.

The apostle John writes, 'No one has ever seen God' (John 1:18; see Exodus 33:20). But throughout the Old Testament, the invisible, immortal God occasionally clothed himself, as it were, physically appearing and revealing aspects of his being and nature. Of course, this was pointing forwards to the day when God would become flesh and dwell among us in the person of Jesus Christ.

Isaiah sees God sitting on the throne, ruling with sovereign authority:

> He does as he pleases
> with the powers of heaven
> and the peoples of the earth.
> No one can hold back his hand
> or say to him: 'What have you done?'
> (Daniel 4:35)

God is reigning; he is majestic; he cannot be contained; he is immense and glorious. Before him the seraphim, the burning ones, veil their faces and cry out to one another: 'Holy, holy, holy is the LORD Almighty' (Isaiah 6:3).

Why do they say this? This is a unique expression in the Old Testament. When you want to make something a superlative in Hebrew, you repeat it: the 'Song of Songs' is the best of songs; the 'gold of gold' is the best gold. But here we have not just the holy of holies; this is a superlative of a superlative – the holiest of the holiest. The word 'holy' carries the idea of purity, so even the bright, burning seraphim discreetly cover themselves. Isaiah is encountering the transcendence of God. The God before whom he stands is immeasurable and incomprehensible. He is eternally the great I AM, who was, and is, and is to come.

'When we say that God is holy, we do not simply mean that He does not sin. That is true, of course . . . God is undefiled in all His ways. He is the supreme, the superlative moral majesty in the universe. But God's holiness refers to more than His ethics. Holiness refers to everything that distinguishes the Creator from His creation. It is the infinite distance between His deity and our humanity. Holiness is the very 'Godness' of God, the sum total of all His glorious perfections.'
(Philip Graham Ryken, *When You Pray*, Crossway, 2000, p. 67)

Today, marvel at the 'otherness' of God. Our human minds cannot comprehend 'the sum total of his glorious perfections'. All we can do is bow in awe and wonder and worship our 'holy, holy, holy' God.

Day 254

Read: Isaiah 6:1–8
Key verses: Isaiah 6:5–7

....

⁵ *"Woe to me!" I cried. "I am ruined! For I am a man of unclean lips, and I live among a people of unclean lips, and my eyes have seen the King, the Lᴏʀᴅ Almighty."*
⁶ Then one of the seraphim flew to me with a live coal in his hand, which he had taken with tongs from the altar. ⁷ With it he touched my mouth and said, "See, this has touched your lips; your guilt is taken away and your sin atoned for."

What would you do if you glimpsed God? Ask him a question? Tell him about a problem you need resolving?

Most likely, we would respond like Isaiah: 'Woe to me . . . I am ruined!' (verse 5). In the face of God's holiness and purity, Isaiah is acutely aware of his sin. He is saying, 'I am torn apart as I stand before this holy God who knows everything I've ever thought, said and done. I stand in need of mercy.'

The prophet realizes his own sin and also the disgraceful state of the nation of Judah: 'I am a man of unclean lips and I live among a people of unclean lips' (verse 5). The early chapters of Isaiah, which describe the Israelites, make for uncomfortable reading:

They are full of superstitions from the East;
    they practise divination like the Philistines
    and embrace pagan customs.
(2:6)

    The women of Zion are haughty,
walking along with outstretched necks,
    flirting with their eyes,
strutting along with swaying hips,

with ornaments jingling on their ankles.
(3:16)

By the time we reach Isaiah 5:20, it becomes apparent that there was widespread moral chaos: 'Woe to those who call evil good and good evil.'

Isaiah uses the metaphor of physical disease to describe his nation's spiritual sickness:

Your whole head is injured,
    your whole heart afflicted.
From the sole of your foot to the top of your head
    there is no soundness –
only wounds and bruises
    and open sores.
(1:5–6)

Isaiah stands before a holy God, knowing that he is sinful and part of a sinful race. In response, the seraphs fly with a live coal from the altar. This was the altar where they offered blood sacrifices for sin. It was the place of atonement, where you found forgiveness. The seraph touched Isaiah's mouth with the coal and cried, 'See.' Older translations say, 'Behold.' In the New Testament, the same idea is conveyed when John the Baptist sees Jesus and says, 'Look/behold, the Lamb of God, who takes away the sin of the world!' (John 1:29). Isaiah anticipates the cross of Jesus, where his substitution enables sinners to stand before a holy God: forgiven, welcomed and blameless in his sight.

When confronted with our sin, each of us also cries, 'Woe is me!' But, praise God, that is not the end of the story. Just as the coal from the altar brought Isaiah atonement, so we find full atonement at the cross.

Once, it was God's holiness that separated us from God, the holiness of his being. Now it is God's holiness that brings us to God, the holiness of the perfect sacrifice Jesus offered for our sins on the cross. God displayed his holiness by making us holy through his holy Son.
(Philip Graham Ryken, *When You Pray*, Crossway, 2000, p. 72)

Day 255

Read: Romans 12:1–21
Key verses: Romans 12:1–2

....

> ¹*Therefore, I urge you, brothers and sisters, in view of God's mercy, to offer your bodies as a living sacrifice, holy and pleasing to God – this is your true and proper worship.* ²*Do not conform to the pattern of this world, but be transformed by the renewing of your mind. Then you will be able to test and approve what God's will is – his good, pleasing and perfect will.*

Imagine your personal holiness, not like a bunch of cut flowers but as a garden where flowers grow. The Christian life is a living, growing thing, and the soil needed for growth is an increasing knowledge and understanding of, and obedience to, biblical truth.

That's why Paul begins chapter 12 with the word 'therefore'. Practical Christian living has to be rooted in the theology set out in his previous chapters. Romans 1–11 is the sum of the whole of the Scriptures' teaching on the subject of who God is, what humanity is and the dealings of one with the other. This theology is the basis on which Paul urges us to practise holy living.

You could sum up all the teaching of chapters 1–11 in the phrase 'in view of God's mercy'. Romans 11 climaxes with this amazing doxology:

> Oh, the depth of the riches of the wisdom
> and knowledge of God!
> How unsearchable his judgements,
> and his paths beyond tracing out!
> (verse 33)

But what sparks off this great anthem of praise? Look at the preceding verses:

Just as you who were at one time disobedient to God have now
received mercy as a result of their disobedience, so they too have now
become disobedient in order that they too may now receive mercy as
a result of God's mercy to you. For God has bound everyone over to
disobedience so that he may have mercy on them all.
(verses 30–32)

At the heart of the gospel is God's mercy to the sinner. If we are to
grow in holiness, we must grow in our knowledge of God's Word,
putting down deep roots. Whatever else we learn, we must keep
coming back to this grand, central truth.

Glance at the rest of Romans 12 and notice all the gifts God has
given us (verses 6–8). See all the experiences and relationships that
we may encounter (verses 9–16). See all the problems that we may
face (verses 17–21). But Paul is saying, 'First go back to that basic
theology and see at its heart the mercy of God. As you confront each
of these new things, come as an undeserving but believing sinner,
putting your trust in Jesus.'

Holiness flourishes as we grasp, believe and live in the goodness
of Bible truths. It grows as we daily remember God's mercy.
Although we are great sinners, he is a great Saviour. Come again
to him for cleansing, thankful for all that he has done and continues
to do for you, trusting him for all that lies ahead today.

Day 256

Read: Romans 12:1–21
Key verses: Romans 12:1–2

....

> [1]Therefore, I urge you, brothers and sisters, in view of God's mercy, to offer your bodies as a living sacrifice, holy and pleasing to God – this is your true and proper worship. [2]Do not conform to the pattern of this world, but be transformed by the renewing of your mind. Then you will be able to test and approve what God's will is – his good, pleasing and perfect will.

What is worship?

It is more than the church service on Sunday or the songs that we sing. Paul tells us that worship is the offering of our bodies as a sacrifice to God, which is another way of saying 'practical, holy, Christian living'.

For Paul's readers, sacrifice was common. Everyone, including pagans, took it for granted that religion involved going to a temple or holy place and taking an offering for the priest to slaughter. Often it was a living creature, an animal or bird, which was duly killed. The arresting thing about Romans 12:1 is not that worship involves sacrifice but that the sacrifice is your body! This is one of the differences between Christianity and all other religions. Most religions offer sacrifices, but only the Christian faith holds that what you are to offer to God is your body. We are to offer these bodies, which confront a mountain of work in the course of the day and which walk down the street and chat to neighbours. These bodies of ours, with their minds and limbs, are what we are to offer as our sacrifice, together with the ordinary, everyday lives that we lead.

Some translations say that this is your 'spiritual', 'reasonable' or even 'logical' worship. But I prefer the term 'intelligent' worship because Paul is talking about the worship of people who know what they are doing and why. They know Christian worship is the definition of what practical, holy living is. Worship is not simply what you find in verses 6–7: 'If your gift is prophesying, then prophesy in accordance with your faith; if it is serving, then serve; if it is teaching, then teach.' Worship is also described in verse 8: 'If it is to encourage, then give encouragement; if it is giving, then give generously.' The whole of life is to be a process of intelligent worship.

Fill Thou my life, O Lord my God,
in every part with praise,
that my whole being may proclaim
Thy being and Thy ways.

Not for the lip of praise alone,
nor e'en the praising heart,
I ask, but for a life made up
of praise in every part:

Praise in the common things of life,
its goings out and in;
praise in each duty and each deed,
however small and mean.

Fill every part of me with praise;
let all my being speak
of Thee and of Thy love, O Lord,
poor though I be and weak.

So shall no part of day or night
from sacredness be free,
but all my life, in every step,
be fellowship with Thee.
(Horatius Bonar, 'Fill Thou My Life', 1866)

Day 257

Read: Romans 12:1–21
Key verses: Romans 12:1–2

....

> *¹Therefore, I urge you, brothers and sisters, in view of God's mercy, to offer your bodies as a living sacrifice, holy and pleasing to God – this is your true and proper worship. ²Do not conform to the pattern of this world, but be transformed by the renewing of your mind. Then you will be able to test and approve what God's will is – his good, pleasing and perfect will.*

How does holiness happen?

Paul explains that sanctification, the process by which holy living develops, happens as you no longer '*conform* to the pattern of this world [and are] *transformed* by the renewing of your mind' (verse 2, emphasis added). These two verbs are significant: both are in the passive voice; both are commands; and both are in the present tense.

Both are in the passive voice. According to the Greek text, you are not being active or doing anything; rather, you are being passive and something is being done to you – you are 'being conformed' and 'being transformed'. The world is aiming to conform you to itself, but all the new nature that God, by his Holy Spirit, has implanted in you is aiming to transform you. There is a power around you that will conform you to the prevailing culture, if you let it. But there is also a power inside you that will renew you, if you let it. As J. B. Phillips said in his translation, 'Don't let the world around you squeeze you into its own mould, but let God re-mould your minds from within' (verse 2).

Both are commands. There is a force outside you, or inside you, doing something to you. Yet paradoxically, at the same time, you are told to do something about it. You are commanded to stop letting one thing happen and to make sure another thing happens to you: 'Be transformed by the renewing of your mind.' This is the conscious thought that says:

> Today, I must deliberately size up every situation I find myself entering and assess it according to what God's Word says about it. I must say 'no' to everything that forces me into the world's shape and 'yes' to the power of the Spirit, who wants to make me more like Christ.

This is a command and, therefore, something you can do and must deliberately embrace every day. Gradually, in this process of sanctification, you will become shaped less like the world and more like Christ.

Both are in the present tense. These verbs are happening now and will go on happening. There may be times of spiritual crisis and significant points of growth in your Christian life but, nevertheless, sanctification is a life-long process. Whether you are a new Christian or a mature Christian, every day will bring a new opportunity to say 'no' to being conformed to the world and 'yes' to being transformed by the renewing power of the Holy Spirit in your mind.

How is the world trying to squeeze you into its mould? What would it look like to say 'yes' to the Holy Spirit's work in particular areas of your life? Today, ask for God's help to believe and to apply his Word to your specific concerns. Pray that your responses and desires would be less like the world's and more like Christ's.

Day 258

Read: 1 Corinthians 1:1–3
Key verses: 1 Corinthians 1:2–3

....

> ²To the church of God in Corinth, to those sanctified in Christ
> Jesus and called to be his holy people, together with all those
> everywhere who call on the name of our Lord Jesus Christ –
> their Lord and ours: ³Grace and peace to you from God our
> Father and the Lord Jesus Christ.

How do you usually begin a letter or email?

Paul opted for a striking introduction when he wrote, 'To those
sanctified in Jesus Christ and called to be . . . holy' (verse 2). It was a
bold way to start any letter, especially one to the church in Corinth.
This Roman colony was renowned for its wickedness. So much so
that the Greeks used the term 'to Corinthianize' to mean 'to lead a
promiscuous life'. And wickedness had permeated the church:
immorality (chapter 5), law cases between Christians (chapter 6),
carelessness about the consciences of others (chapter 8), idolatry
(chapter 10) and improper behaviour at communion meals
(chapter 11).

'Sanctified' conveys the idea of being set apart, and because the
church is set apart *for* some things, it has to be set apart *from* others.
In the Old Testament, there were separated days, separated places,
separated people – called holy days, holy places and holy people.
Paul says to the people at Corinth, 'You are set apart like that.' God
sees even these believers, with all their history of bad behaviour, as
sanctified (set apart) in Christ Jesus. Because their faith is in Christ,
God sees them in Christ: that's their status before him.

The word for 'holy' comes from the same root as the word for
'sanctified'. Paul is saying that the church is holy and is called to be
holy. The journey of the Christian life is the process whereby God

changes us into the holy people he chose us to be the moment we accepted Christ. We see this wonderfully spelled out in 2 Corinthians 3:18. Paul had the image of a mirror in his mind. When you look into a normal mirror, you see the image of your own face. But, Paul says, the more you look at the image of Christ, the more you grow to resemble him. That's the process of becoming sanctified.

This call to holiness is not reserved for a select few; it goes out to 'all who call on the name of Christ'. Whatever our differences of church practice and tradition, the pursuit of holiness unites us with other believers. It is a lifelong priority for us all.

Thank God that when we fail, we are not dismissed! Thank God that when the church isn't as it should be, God doesn't say, 'They're hopeless.' He says, 'I see them in Christ Jesus, sanctified, and I will help them to become what they are.' Thank God that holiness is not a solitary pursuit; rather, God provides people to join us on the journey and spur us on. Keep looking to Christ today.

Day 259

Read: Galatians 5:16–26
Key verses: Galatians 5:22–23

....

²²But the fruit of the Spirit is love, joy, peace, forbearance, kindness, goodness, faithfulness, ²³gentleness and self-control. Against such things there is no law.

What is holiness? Not doing certain things or not going to certain places? Gaining victory over particular sins? No! Holiness is actually the transformation of our whole Christian character; it is Christlikeness. Holiness is a rainbow of many colours and the whole spectrum is portrayed in Galatians 5:22–23.

Love is the first fruit of the Spirit; there is no holiness without it. The remaining eight graces on this list are all aspects of love. Put love through a prism and its light breaks into these beautiful colours. There is no joy or peace without love. Partly because joy and peace prosper in fellowship – they never prosper in isolation – and partly because love is self-giving. Jesus taught that you'll never find yourself, never be fully satisfied, and never have joy and peace until you give yourself in love (Matthew 10:39).

Forbearance, kindness and goodness are next on the list. We know that the first two are expressions of love because Paul says, 'Love is patient, love is kind' (1 Corinthians 13:4). It is no use claiming to love people unless we are patient with those who irritate us, unless our minds are full of goodwill and kindness, and unless we engage in concrete acts of goodness. Love without these things is not love.

Faithfulness is another characteristic of divine love. Many times, in the Old Testament, we read of the 'steadfast love' of God that endures for generations (see 2 Chronicles 7:3, ESV). Just as nothing can separate us from God's love, nothing should be able to separate others from ours. True love is faithful; it goes on loving even when it is unrequited or met with a rude rebuff.

Finally, gentleness and self-control: love is not an uncontrolled passion. Today, much of what is called 'love' is actually a contradiction of it. If you really love, your love will be marked not by self-gratification but by self-control.

In contrast to the 'acts of the flesh', which are plural (Galatians 5:19–21), these nine graces of Christian character together form the one, indivisible fruit of the Holy Spirit. He doesn't produce one or two of these graces without the others: he doesn't produce joy without peace or faithfulness without self-control. He produces them all – a whole, integrated character. The Holy Spirit does not produce lop-sided Christians; he makes Christlike Christians. And Jesus Christ is the most balanced and integrated person who has ever lived. The Holy Spirit makes Christians who are mature in their Christian character.[2]

Holiness is not a list of places to avoid or a tinkering around the edges of our character – it is to be like Christ. Today, meditate on the beauty of Christ's character and the examples of his love, joy, peace, forbear-ance, kindness, goodness, faithfulness, gentleness and self-control.

> In seeking after holiness we are not so much seeking after a thing as we are seeking a Person . . . We want the Holy One in whom we have been counted holy and are now being made holy. To run hard after holiness is another way of running hard after God.
> (Kevin DeYoung, *The Hole in Our Holiness*, Crossway, 2012, p. 123)

---

2. For further study on Galatians, see John Stott's *The Message of Galatians* in IVP's The Bible Speaks Today series (listed in the 'For further study' section).

Day 260

Read: Galatians 5:16–26
Key verses: Galatians 5:22–23

....

22 But the fruit of the Spirit is love, joy, peace, forbearance, kindness, goodness, faithfulness, 23 gentleness and self-control. Against such things there is no law.

How do we become holy?

Holiness is the fruit of the Spirit. It is the Holy Spirit alone who can produce this fruit. Sanctification, the process of growing in holiness, is just as much the work of God as justification (the declaration of our righteous standing before God), except that he justifies through his Son and sanctifies through his Spirit. Both are the work of God. Paul quite clearly attributes the existence of these graces, of this balanced Christian character of love, to the Holy Spirit.

Holiness is not something we can inherit; it is not a matter of temperament; it is not just that some are born that way. Our fallen human nature, with which we were born, cannot produce holiness. Paul explains: 'I know that good itself does not dwell in me, that is, in my sinful nature' (Romans 7:18). Neither is holiness the fruit of education or effort. Men or women cannot make themselves holy by trying hard. Holiness is supernatural in its origin; only the Holy Spirit can make us holy. He is the Spirit of holiness; he can touch the inner parts of our characters and do a deep and lasting work in our personalities. It is the Holy Spirit who regenerates us, implanting life and a new nature within us; it is he who sanctifies us, causing the new nature to grow and to bear fruit.

Holiness does require grace-fuelled effort (see Day 262) but, ultimately, it is a work within us that only God, by his Spirit, can do. The Holy Spirit exposes our sin and gives us strength to turn away from it; he illuminates Scripture so that we understand its meaning and can apply it to our lives; and, increasingly, he helps us to appreciate the glory of Christ.

Heavenly Father, thank you for the continual presence of your Holy Spirit, who comforts and strengthens us, testifies to the truth of your Word, and guarantees that one day you will finish your work in us. We look forward to the day when we will stand in your presence blameless. Until then, thank you for all you are doing in our lives to make us more like the Lord Jesus. Have your way in our hearts and lives, we pray. Amen.

Day 261

Read: Galatians 5:16–26
Key verses: Galatians 5:22–23

....

²²But the fruit of the Spirit is love, joy, peace, forbearance, kindness, goodness, faithfulness, ²³gentleness and self-control. Against such things there is no law.

Imagine a Christmas tree.

The sparkling fairy lights and the shiny baubles look beautiful, but they are all attached to the tree by string or wire. The decorations don't grow on the tree; they don't belong to the tree. Artificial holiness is like that. It is a way of life imposed on you or you impose it on yourself from outside. The expectations of the Christian community, our church membership, the fear of what people think or the fear of consequences, society's taboos – all these influence external conduct. By effort, a man or woman can control his or her temper and avoid lashing out in anger, and so appear to be holy – but it is an artificial holiness. It has been tied on from outside; it doesn't grow from within. It is a matter of outward convention, not inward character. It is superficial, leaving the heart untouched. It is the decorations on a Christmas tree, not the fruit of the Spirit.

True holiness is not the artificial adoption of a pattern of behaviour; it is the natural ripening of the new and divine nature that has been implanted within us. And this takes time. Holiness is gradual in its growth. Like all fruit, the fruit of the Spirit ripens slowly, bit by bit. You can't think of holiness as a mechanical process; it doesn't suddenly appear at the press of a button or the flick of a switch.

It is true that God implants life suddenly and we are regenerated in a moment, but the development of this new life from a tiny seed to a ripe fruit is an unhurried, continuous and sometimes lengthy process. When you become a Christian, you don't suddenly find yourself able to love God with all your heart, mind, soul and strength, and your neighbours and enemies as yourself. Regeneration gives the capacity to love, but the new nature comes to fruition in love only by the gracious, continual operation of the Spirit. That's why Paul writes to the Thessalonians of their need to love 'more and more' (1 Thessalonians 4:10).

It would be so much easier (and quicker) if holiness were achieved simply by reading a Christian book, attending the church prayer meeting or serving on a rota. We might do these things as a result of growing in holiness, but they themselves are not signs of holiness. Holiness can't be hurried by adopting outward conventions; it can't be measured in days or minutes. It is the pursuit of a lifetime. Until we meet Jesus, there will always be room for growth. Today, ask the Holy Spirit to help you to live out your new nature and truly to become more and more of what you are – 'holy in [God's] sight' (Colossians 1:22).

Day 262

Read: Galatians 5:16–26
Key verse: Galatians 5:24

....

²⁴ *Those who belong to Christ Jesus have crucified the flesh with its passions and desires.*

What role do we play in becoming holy?

If we want the fruit of the Spirit to grow in our lives, we need to 'crucify the flesh' (see verse 24). This idea is not the same as the one conveyed in Romans 6, in which the old man, the former self, is crucified with Christ. Here, we are told that if we are Christians, we have crucified the old nature, that is the flesh. We did this at our conversion, when we denied ourselves and, in the language of Jesus, took up our cross and followed him to crucifixion. We killed our old nature, as it were. Although we have crucified the flesh, the Greek verb indicates that it is an attitude to be maintained. In Christ, we died to sin once, but we must die to ourselves every day. Jesus said that we are to take up our cross daily and follow him. That is, we are to take our self – our selfish, fallen, human nature – and crucify it every day. This means daily repentance.

One of the main reasons for our continued unholiness is that we are so soft in dealing with ourselves. The Holy Spirit cannot bear his fruit in our character because we are still toying with the flesh. We allow certain sins, attitudes, habits, thoughts and relationships to flourish in our lives instead of crucifying them. We treat our flesh, our fallen nature and its deeds, as the Israelites treated the pagan tribes in Canaan. Instead of slaying them, we make a truce with them or even sign a peace treaty.

We have to learn to be more ruthless with what we know to be wrong. Remember Jesus' imagery about plucking out an eye or cutting off a hand if it causes us to sin (Mark 9:43–49)? If temptation comes through our eyes, we shouldn't look. If temptation comes through places we visit, we shouldn't go. The way to deal with the flesh, our fallen nature, is not with compromise or a policy of co-existence. It is to declare war on it and put it to death. We will never bear the fruit of the Spirit unless we crucify the flesh and keep doing so in daily repentance.

> The Bible is realistic about holiness. Don't think that all this glorious talk about dying to sin and living to God [Romans 6] means there is no struggle anymore . . . The Christian life still entails obedience. It still involves a fight. But it's a fight we will win. You have the Spirit of Christ in your corner, rubbing your shoulders, holding the bucket, putting his arm around you and saying before the next round with sin, 'You're going to knock him out, kid.' Sin may get in some good jabs . . . It may bring you to your knees. But if you are in Christ, it will never knock you out. You are no longer a slave, but free. Sin has no dominion over you. It can't. It won't.
>
> A new King sits on the throne. You serve a different Master. You salute a different Lord.
>
> (Kevin DeYoung, *The Hole in Our Holiness*, Crossway, 2012, p. 105)

Day 263

Read: Galatians 5:16–26
Key verse: Galatians 5:25

....

²⁵ *Since we live by the Spirit, let us keep in step with the Spirit.*

Have you grieved the Holy Spirit?

If we want the fruit of the Spirit to grow in our lives, we need to 'crucify the flesh' (see verse 24, yesterday), but we also need to 'keep in step with the Spirit' (verse 25). Paul has already said, 'Live by the Spirit, and you will not gratify the desires of the flesh' (verse 16). Now he says, 'Since we live by the Spirit . . . keep in step with the Spirit.' We are to follow his direction and yield to his control. Holiness is the fruit of the Spirit; he cannot produce it in the lives of those who will not let him. The Spirit already dwells in every believer and he is ceaselessly active to cause the fruit to grow.

Picture God as the divine gardener. Remember how lovingly God described Israel as his vineyard? 'I, the LORD, am its keeper; every moment I water it' (Isaiah 27:3, ESV). God also promised, 'I will be like the dew to Israel; he shall blossom like the lily; he shall take root like the trees of Lebanon' (Hosea 14:5, ESV). But this blossoming and ripening of fruit occur only if God is the dew and if he waters us. This is the continual work of the Holy Spirit in our character. If he is not doing his work and producing his fruit, it must be that we have grieved him.

Is there a sin you have not repented of or forsaken? No wonder the Holy Spirit is not producing his fruit. How can he if you have grieved him? Is there rebellion, stubbornness or a refusal to surrender your will to his call and his demands? If by sin and self-will the Holy Spirit is grieved, he is effectively prevented from causing the fruit to grow.

Today, put things right. Set the Holy Spirit free to produce his fruit. It is only as you keep in step with the Spirit – surrendering to his control, setting your mind on him, sharing the Lord's Supper, and spending time each day in repentance, prayer and Bible reading – that he can cause the fruit to ripen and grow.

Heavenly Father, convict me if I have grieved the Holy Spirit and help me to put things right. From this moment on, help me always to be eager to repent, feast on your Word and obey your will. Thank you that the power of sin is cancelled, that I belong to Christ and that I'm united to him. Help me each day to keep in step with his Spirit so that the beauty of Jesus' character would be more and more on display in my life. Please bring forth an abundance of fresh fruit in me so that my friends and family can taste the goodness of God and experience the power of the gospel. For your glory. Amen.

Day 264

Read: Ephesians 5:1–14
Key verses: Ephesians 5:1–2

••

¹Follow God's example, therefore, as dearly loved children ²and live a life of love, just as Christ loved us and gave himself up for us as a fragrant offering and sacrifice to God.

How do we stay holy in an unholy world?

Much like our own society, first-century Ephesus was awash with immorality. Paul was understandably concerned that Christian converts from a Gentile background could easily slip back into their old way of sin. It's the same for us – much like those early converts, the pressure to lower our standards and go with the flow of the culture is ever present. So how do we overcome the pull of sin and live holy lives?

Paul's answer is simple yet profound: 'Follow God's example, therefore, as dearly loved children' (verse 1). The previous chapter ends by urging us to forgive, just as Christ forgave us. That leads directly to the call to 'follow God's example' – to love as God has loved us. So a fundamental reason for refusing to live immorally is that I am now God's dearly loved child. I've been adopted into his family. His love has been poured into my heart by the Holy Spirit. So I should imitate my Father; I should reproduce the family likeness.

In verses 3–4, Paul describes behaviour that is completely alien to a Christian lifestyle. The dominant characteristic of first-century pagan religion and the twenty-first-century sex industry is self-gratification. Its definition of love is self-centred and its motivation is self-fulfilment, not self-sacrifice. But if we know God as Father, then we will want to walk in the way of his love. And because we share the Father's nature, we can exhibit the Father's character. That's our new identity. It's in our DNA.

Whenever I feel the pull of sin, I should say, 'I am loved by the Father.' If I'm tempted to look to sex or to greedy self-indulgence for satisfaction, I say, 'I am loved by the Father.' If I am hurt by someone and want to retaliate, I say, 'I am loved by the Father.' In essence, provided we focus on how we have been loved – eternally, irrevocably, freely – then we will have a growing desire to live for God. That's because love like this changes us. It draws us towards God, and it makes living for him something to which we are deeply committed.

A holy life cannot be sustained by guilt or trying harder. It springs from the knowledge that we are truly loved by God. Dwell on the immensity of this love today.

Oh, you are not dealing with trifles when you are dealing with the love of God to you. It is not a spare corner of the heart of God that He gives to you . . . but the great, inconceivably vast heart of God belongs as much to every Christian as if there were not another being in the world for God to love! Even as Jehovah loves His Only-begotten, so does He love each one of His children.
(C. H. Spurgeon, *Spurgeon's Sermons*, vol. 19, ed. Anthony Uyl (Devoted Publishing), p. 165)

Day 265

Read: Ephesians 5:1–14
Key verse: Ephesians 5:2

....

²Live a life of love, just as Christ loved us and gave himself up for us as a fragrant offering and sacrifice to God.

Do you ever feel that holiness is out of reach? That you've failed God too many times and wandered too far away from him?

Paul's answer is to remind us of what Christ has done for us. Using the language of sacrifice, Paul declares that Christ 'gave himself up for us' (verse 2). He willingly gave himself as an offering for sin. 'A fragrant offering' implies the acceptability of Christ's sacrifice. It is such good news! I have been rescued; I have been purchased by Jesus' blood. I am not my own, since I have been bought for a price. In our continuing struggle against sin, this is a wonderful incentive to pursue holiness.

What has Christ rescued us from? Verses 5–6 describe a deliberate and sustained choice to live in opposition to God. People who live this way, giving themselves over to immorality, impurity and greed, are idolaters because, in effect, they have chosen another god – a false god. As a consequence, they are excluded from eternal life and subject to God's wrath. But Christ gave himself to deliver us from God's judgement. We have a wonderful new future: an inheritance in God's kingdom. Of course, this assurance is no excuse for presumption, for we are still responsible to Jesus, our Saviour and Judge. But Paul's point is to underline that we have been rescued from this way of life.

In 1 Corinthians 6:9–11, Paul again asserts that wrongdoers will not inherit the kingdom of God. He lists the sexually immoral, adulterers, thieves, slanderers and more. But then notice what he writes: 'And that is what some of you were. But you were washed, you were sanctified, you were justified in the name of the Lord Jesus Christ and by the Spirit of our God' (verse 11).

While we still feel the pull of sin, Paul describes a lifestyle that is in the past: 'That is what some of you were.' We must remember that we have been rescued by God's Son, that Jesus' sacrifice has been accepted, that we have been set free. Having been profoundly converted, the former slave trader John Newton held firmly to this truth. To ensure he kept God's grace at the forefront of his mind, he had Deuteronomy 15:15 displayed on the wall of his study: 'Thou shalt remember that thou wast a bond-man [slave] in the land of Egypt, and the LORD thy God redeemed thee' (KJV).

Today, don't dwell on what you have done – your sin, doubt and despair – but dwell on what Christ has done for you.

Light began to break over me when I realized in the depth of my spirit that I was forgiven, cleansed, accepted, justified because of what Christ had done for me. I found I was set free, free to be holy. To my astonishment, I discovered that I wanted to live a holy life far more than I wanted to sin. Forgiveness freed me to do what I wanted most.
(John White, *The Fight*, IVP, 2008, p. 170)

Day 266

Read: Ephesians 5:1–14
Key verse: Ephesians 5:3

....

3But among you there must not be even a hint of sexual immorality, or of any kind of impurity, or of greed, because these are improper for God's holy people.

You are not alone!

The exhortation to avoid immorality and impurity is based on the fact that we belong to God's holy people. We have been chosen; we have been set apart. So the kind of behaviour described in verse 3 violates God's standards – it has no place in God's holy family.

If we are loved by the Father (see verse 1) and if we belong to his holy people (verse 3), then our identity and therefore our motivation have changed. We resist temptation because our sights are set not on the tawdry impurity of our world but on the joy of serving a new master: one who loves us as fully as we can be loved and who has set us apart to belong to him.

There is no question that we face a daily struggle with sin. We feel its pull all the time and frequently experience the heat of the spiritual battle. So it is profoundly reassuring to remember that we are not fighting this battle alone, but are part of God's family, supporting and encouraging one another. The fellowship of believers is one where, through prayer and support, we help one another to keep on track.

But more than that, we have the Holy Spirit's help. Verse 14 is possibly a quotation from a hymn that the early church used at Easter or at a baptismal service: 'Wake up, sleeper, rise from the dead, and Christ will shine on you.' Conversion is waking from sleep, rising from death and being brought out of darkness into light. And the light that shines on believers is the empowering presence of the Lord. By the power of his Spirit, he enables us to resist the pull of sin and live a life of holiness.

In the heat of the battle against sin, we must remember that we are not alone. We have the fellowship of believers and the empowering Spirit of Christ.

Pursuing holiness in our own strength is exhausting and ultimately fruitless. We need the Holy Spirit's help, and the support and encouragement of Christian friends. The extraordinary act of becoming holy is enabled by God using very ordinary means – as we pray with others, hear the Bible being taught, study Scripture in a group (and individually), serve together, carry one another's burdens, share Communion and receive rebukes. Today, thank God for the particular group of 'holy people' he has given you. Pray that you would be a blessing to one another and that, with the Holy Spirit's help, you would be iron sharpening iron (Proverbs 27:17).

Day 267

Read: Ephesians 5:1–14
Key verses: Ephesians 5:3–4

....

³*But among you there must not be even a hint of sexual immorality, or of any kind of impurity, or of greed, because these are improper for God's holy people.* ⁴*Nor should there be obscenity, foolish talk or coarse joking, which are out of place, but rather thanksgiving.*

Do you know the power of thankfulness?

Paul has been writing about sexual morality, urging that there must be no place in our conversation for vulgarity, obscenity or even innuendo. As we grow up into God's family likeness, our attitudes and our conversation change, underpinned by one thing – 'thanksgiving' (verse 4). Sexuality is a subject for thanksgiving, not for joking. We should celebrate God's good gifts with grateful hearts rather than degrade them with coarse joking.

In fact, this should be our attitude to the whole of life. Thanksgiving means turning our attention away from ourselves towards God, and away from selfish desires and towards his good purposes. Indeed, some suggest that thanksgiving is a synonym for the Christian life. It's a mark of the Spirit's work, as Paul says in verse 20: 'Always giving thanks to God the Father for everything.'

Thankfulness is the exact opposite of self-centredness. It is a recognition of God's generosity. It's a response of gratitude for God's saving work – I am thankful for God's gifts, thankful that I have been saved from God's wrath, thankful for his redeeming, transforming, empowering grace. Grace produces gratitude. The answer to the question 'How do I overcome the pull of sin?' lies here, too, because it is very difficult to give thanks and sin at the same time. Thanksgiving is the antidote to giving in to sin.

It is impossible to be selfish, bitter or proud while at the same time saying 'thank you'. Thanksgiving alters our whole posture and attitude towards God. It signals that we are humbling ourselves, depending on God's goodness and trusting in his sovereignty. We have so much to be grateful for but, in our 'entitled' culture, thanksgiving is something we need to be deliberate about. As we cultivate this habit of being thankful, we grow in holiness because gratitude produces in us a whole host of other Christlike qualities, such as love, joy, patience, kindness and gentleness. We have seen before that there is no quick fix to becoming holy, but thankfulness certainly accelerates the process!

Today, be intentional about giving thanks to God often. And be specific. As the old hymn says, 'Count your blessings, name them one by one.'

> Thanksgiving will draw our hearts out to God and keep us engaged with Him; it will take our attention from ourselves and give the Spirit room in our hearts.
>
> (Andrew Murray, *The Prayer Life*, Aneko Press, 2018, p. 50)

Day 268

Read: Ephesians 5:1–14
Key verses: Ephesians 5:8–11, 13

• •

[8]*For you were once darkness, but now you are light in the Lord. Live as children of light* [9]*(for the fruit of the light consists in all goodness, righteousness and truth)* [10]*and find out what pleases the Lord.* [11]*Have nothing to do with the fruitless deeds of darkness, but rather expose them . . .* [13]*everything exposed by the light becomes visible – and everything that is illuminated becomes a light.*

Your holiness matters.

In Ephesians, Paul continually makes dramatic contrasts to describe what has happened to us. We have been brought from death to life and from being far away to being brought near. Here, he says that we've been rescued from the dominion of darkness and now we 'are light in the Lord' (verse 8). It is a radical change of identity. We have been transferred from one kingdom to another and from darkness to light. This section might have been used at baptismal services; it reminds us that we have an entirely new nature. This new nature leads to a different way of life. We're taken out of darkness and brought into God's marvellous light. As children of the day, we must live like those who are truly at home in the daylight.

Because we have a new orientation, identity and nature, we are not to get involved in the evil conduct of immoral people. Again, Paul presents us with the stark contrast: 'Have nothing to do with the fruitless deeds of darkness' (verse 11); instead, 'the fruit of the light consists in all goodness, righteousness and truth' (verse 9). The summary is in verse 10: 'Find out what pleases the Lord.'

Christians who truly live a life that pleases God will inevitably show up the darkness. Our light not only reveals; it exposes and it penetrates darkness (verse 11). And perhaps verse 13 implies that light not only illuminates, but it can truly change people: 'Everything that is illuminated becomes a light.' We're not just mirrors; we are conduits of light – light that blesses, educates and restores. If we are 'light in the Lord', we become light-bearers in this dark world. So we should ask, 'To what extent do our lives, our families and our local churches truly shed the light of Christ in our world?'

Holiness is cultivated by the myriad private and personal decisions you make each day – how you spend your money, which books you read, which programmes you watch, the time you set aside to read the Bible and pray, your choice not to participate in gossip or give in to lust, your commitment to grow in patience and exercise forgiveness, your investment in your community and your integrity at work. But holiness never stays private – your character, your actions, inevitably have an impact on others. The brighter your holiness shines, the more it will shed Christ's light in the world. The light is not always welcomed, since darkness rarely likes to be exposed. But today, as you live to please God, sharing his love and goodness with family, friends and work colleagues, pray that they will be drawn to God's light within you and be captivated by his truth.

Day 269

Read: 1 Thessalonians 3:11–4:8
Key verses: 1 Thessalonians 4:1, 7

....

> [1]As for other matters, brothers and sisters, we instructed you
> how to live in order to please God, as in fact you are living. Now
> we ask you and urge you in the Lord Jesus to do this more and
> more . . . [7]For God did not call us to be impure, but to live a
> holy life.

Just do it!

Paul prays that God would perfect the Thessalonians in holiness. Certainly, on the day Jesus returns, we will praise God because the full measure of holiness we will enjoy is the work of his mercy and grace (3:13).

Yet, Paul 'urges' (4:1), exhorts, us to pursue practical and progressive holiness now. Being Christian is not a dressing gown-and-slippers exercise. God brings us to holiness as we commit to realizing his will, which means living lives that are obedient, informed, reverent, trusting and enabled.

An obedient life (4:1–3). Paul says, 'We instructed you how to live in order to please God.' These instructions came 'by the authority of the Lord Jesus'. The command to obey God brooks no argument because it is not simply what the apostle wants; it is what God demands.

An informed life (4:4–5). One of the ways we demonstrate our holiness – our distinctiveness from the world and our dedication to God – is to avoid sexual immorality. Paul's point is that were the Gentiles only to know God, they wouldn't behave immorally. Knowing God – learning about him through his Word and loving him deeply – is the key to avoiding sin.

A reverent life (4:6). The Lord will punish those who take advantage of a brother or sister in the area of sexual morality. God is the avenger. With this in mind, we need to recover our fear of the Lord.

A trusting life (4:7). God has called us to 'live a holy life'. Holiness is not an external objective but the reality, the context, into which God has called us and we have got to learn how to become what we are. We say to him, 'I'm desperately unholy in all my inclinations; I desperately want to be holy. I believe that you have given me all that I need to be, therefore it is worth struggling and striving.'

An enabled life (4:8). God wants us to be holy, so he has given us his Holy Spirit. The holy life means enjoying the inward residence of the holy God, respecting that holy One and drawing upon his Spirit within us. God keeps on giving us the Holy Spirit to administer holiness to us as we walk with him.

> Some Christians are stalled out in their sanctification for simple lack of effort. They need to know about the Spirit's power. They need to be rooted in gospel grace. They need to believe the promises of God. And they need to fight, strive and make every effort to work out all that God is working in them. Let us say with Paul, 'I worked harder than any of them, though it was not I, but the grace of God that is with me' (1 Corinthians 15:10) . . . God wants us to get up and get to work (Philippians 2:12–13). Because when it comes to growth in godliness, trusting does not put an end to trying.
> (Kevin DeYoung, *The Hole in Our Holiness*, Crossway, 2012, pp. 90–91)

Day 270

Read: 1 Peter 1:13–2:3
Key verses: 1 Peter 1:13–16

∙∙

> *¹³Therefore, with minds that are alert and fully sober, set your hope on the grace to be brought to you when Jesus Christ is revealed at his coming. ¹⁴As obedient children, do not conform to the evil desires you had when you lived in ignorance. ¹⁵But just as he who called you is holy, so be holy in all you do; ¹⁶for it is written: "Be holy, because I am holy."*

What are you hoping for?

Peter calls us to set our hope on the grace we will receive when Jesus returns. The 'therefore' in verse 13 takes us back to the preceding verses which describe the glorious salvation God has provided. When Jesus is revealed, we will receive resurrection bodies, we will be ushered into a new heaven and a new earth, and we will be transformed into the likeness of Jesus. Peter now urges us to set our hope fully on this grace – the grace of perfection in the new heaven and the new earth. This is not a matter of hoping harder but, rather, of thinking again and again about the object of our hope. Setting our hope fully on the grace to be revealed is little different from thoroughly and increasingly believing the gospel message, particularly the good news about the life to come. For Peter, this means a diligent obedience that pursues practical holiness.

We Christians are moving towards the holiness that will be ours in the new heaven and the new earth. To claim that we have had our sins forgiven and that we are pressing on towards this climactic hope when Jesus is revealed, and yet deep down to cherish sin, is so massively inconsistent, so grotesque, that it puts a question mark over all our assertions.

Hope – what we eagerly anticipate – and our behaviour are connected. If what you hope for is a really big house in the Cotswolds, and it dominates your thinking and your priorities, then other things will be trimmed off so that you can press on in that direction. If you tell everybody that's what you want but, meanwhile, you spend every free moment and every free pound trying to buy a little fishing shack somewhere off the coast of Scotland, people are going to say, 'How can you say this over here when you do that over there? It doesn't make sense.'

That's the connection between hope and holiness. We are called to be holy. Objectively, we are moving towards climactic holiness in the new heaven and new earth, so we need to align our conduct with this ultimate Christian hope and set our hope on the grace to be revealed when Jesus comes.

We say our hope is in Jesus but, often, our everyday choices reveal that we're actually putting our hope in finances, health and family. Today, fix your hope on future grace; root out sin, trimming away even the good things that prevent you from pursuing holiness.

Day 271

Read: 1 Peter 1:13–2:3
Key verse: 1 Peter 1:17

....

17 Since you call on a Father who judges each person's work impartially, live out your time as foreigners here in reverent fear.

It is hard for us to hear the power of this verse because, in our culture, all opinions are considered intrinsically worthy; youth is promoted and the father figure is trivialized.

But in the ancient Jewish world there was more respect for the opinion of the elderly and informed than of the young. Youth were to be disciplined and taught, and the father was to be revered, because not only was he the family's authority figure, he was also its arbiter and judge. Yet because he was father, he was also compassionate.

Most sons ended up doing what their fathers did. If your father was a farmer, you were likely to become a farmer. Thus, not only were fathers the ones who passed on certain traditions, they were also the ones who took the children out to the fields. Personally and in a hands-on way, they instructed the new generation. They disciplined, they instructed and they held to account. They were compassionate but they were to be revered and even feared.

Obviously, sin could distort this particular cultural structure; fathers could be abusive and perverse. But if we are to understand the cultural connections that are bound up with the figure of God as Father, we need to understand that, in the Bible, they emerge from the first century, not from the twenty-first.

With this background in mind, we read this verse with fresh insight. Because God is our Father, we're part of his family and our home is elsewhere – where he is. We are introduced to this idea of being foreigners and strangers in 1 Peter 1:1. We are waiting for the new heaven and new earth. We don't quite belong here. We belong to this Father who judges each one's work in this family impartially. He has no favourites. He is our Father on whom we call. Yet he is also the Father whom we are to treat with reverent fear.

No doubt, perfect love casts out fear. But in this sinful world, when we are never all that far away from shoving our fists in God's face and singing with Frank Sinatra 'I did it my way', it's a good thing to have a bit of fear. The word 'reverent' is an addition – the Greek text just says 'fear'. This is not a cringing fear; we are not crouching down, waiting for the next blow to fall. No, this is a compassionate Father on whom we call. But we do fear him, and that's a good thing.

What draws us towards holiness? The commanding, demanding judgement of the Father, which completely fills us with both anticipation and fear. God holds us to account but provides us with a name on which we can call: our Father. This Father does not drive us from him but towards him in obedience, for this Father really does know best.

> When I regarded God as a tyrant, I thought my sin a trifle, but when I knew Him to be my Father, then I mourned that I could ever have kicked against Him.
> (C. H. Spurgeon, quoted by Bryan Chapell, *Holiness by Grace*, Crossway, 2011, p. 108)

Day 272

Read: 1 Peter 1:13–2:3
Key verses: 1 Peter 1:18–20

∙∙

18For you know that it was not with perishable things such as silver or gold that you were redeemed from the empty way of life handed down to you from your ancestors, 19but with the precious blood of Christ, a lamb without blemish or defect. 20He was chosen before the creation of the world, but was revealed in these last times for your sake.

Are you spitting in the face of Christ?

The connection in these verses is clear – not to pursue holiness is to despise and insult the inestimable value of Christ's sacrifice on our behalf.

Peter says that Jesus' death redeemed us. Redemption is an alien concept in our culture but it was not to the first-century world. Someone could pay money to the slave-owner and redeem the slave, and thus free the individual from slavery. Jesus redeemed us from the meaninglessness of a pagan life – the sheer slavery of it (see verse 18). The idea is not that we are redeemed from the odd little sin that we may have committed, but that our whole outlook, the whole heritage, the whole anti-God stance that we have inherited is a form of bondage from which we have to be set free.

We aren't redeemed with money but with 'the precious blood of Christ, a lamb without blemish or defect' (verse 19), like the prescribed sacrificial lambs in the Old Testament system by which people were made holy. Jesus was the lamb slain before the foundation of the world (see verse 20). He gave up his life, according to the plan of God, the just for the unjust, to bring us to God.

When we take the elements in Communion, we remember Christ's broken body and his shed blood. 'Do this in remembrance of me,' Jesus said. Suppose we were to take those elements and say by our participation, 'I remember Christ's death on my behalf', and then go and swear at the kids, gossip about the minister, nurture a little bitterness and cheat on our income tax forms. The very act of publicly remembering would not only be a contradiction in terms but it would also be like spitting on Christ all over again.

One of the functions of the Lord's Supper is to serve as a public renewal of the covenant (see Luke 22:14–20) by which we remember that we are redeemed by Christ's death and we pursue holiness. As we grow in grace and in our estimation of the worth of Christ, we are increasingly broken by the horror of our sin. The shame and ugliness of it are so great that only Christ's death was sufficient to pay for it. Focusing on the death of Christ becomes, of itself, a God-given means to pursuing holiness.

Today, when you face the temptation to sin, fix your mind on Christ on the cross: his beaten back, the nails driven through his hands and feet, and a crown of thorns piercing his brow. This was the price of your sin and mine. Don't let your behaviour or thoughts mock Christ's sacrifice any longer, but, remembering the agony of Calvary, say 'no' to sin and 'yes' to righteousness (see Titus 2:11–14).

Day 273

Read: 1 Peter 1:13–2:3

Key verses: 1 Peter 1:22–23; 2:2

∙∙

1:22 Now that you have purified yourselves by obeying the truth so that you have sincere love for each other, love one another deeply, from the heart. 23 For you have been born again, not of perishable seed, but of imperishable, through the living and enduring word of God . . . 2:2 Like newborn babies, crave pure spiritual milk, so that by it you may grow up in your salvation.

What's next after becoming a Christian?

Peter says that after you've submitted to Christ's lordship and embraced the gospel, you are to 'love one another deeply'. In other words, holiness (being devoted to God) is demonstrated by love for fellow believers. You cannot have one without the other. You cannot pursue holiness and not love brothers and sisters in Christ. And you cannot grow in love for brothers and sisters in Christ without also pursuing holiness before God.

How do we love deeply from the heart? You can demonstrate it in lots of ways, but it cannot simply be taught because Christian love comes from a regenerated heart (see 1:23) and is bound up with the gospel, which is the 'living and enduring Word of God'. This life-giving Word of God is the seed of life, sown in us to generate love through its eternal, enduring power. Since this Word is changeless, powerful and effective, a seed that generates and regenerates and transforms from within, we should 'rid [ourselves] of all malice . . . deceit, hypocrisy, envy . . . [and] crave pure spiritual milk' (2:1–2).

This 'spiritual milk', the Word of God, is not an optional extra. Like milk for a baby, it's what keeps us alive; it feeds us and makes us grow. And it tastes good (see verse 3)! When we devote ourselves to reading and studying the Bible, in due course the delight is not in the rhetoric but in beginning to taste the Lord himself. He reveals himself through his Word. Peter's message is clear: now that we have become Christians, we have tasted and seen that the Lord is good, so let's have more goodness; let's enjoy him all the more and crave this spiritual food, 'so that by it [we] may grow up in [our] salvation' (verse 2).

God's means of grace to pursue holiness is his Word. Remember how, on the night Jesus was betrayed, only hours before his cruci-fixion, he prayed, 'Sanctify them by the truth; your word is truth' (John 17:17). Jesus was praying for God to make us holy through his Word.

Imagine being the answer to one of Jesus' prayers.

If we want to grow spiritually, we have to stop starving ourselves. We have to stop believing that snacking on Christian blog posts or inspirational comments on Facebook is enough to nourish us, or that the Sunday sermon banquet will sustain us through the week. In God's strength, cultivate the daily habit of studying his Word. You may miss some days, but don't be discouraged. Return to the Scriptures again and again. Ponder and apply God's truth, allow it to purify, challenge and change you. Let God reveal Christ to you so that you taste his goodness and enjoy him more and more.

For further study

If you would like to read more about holiness, you might find this selection of books helpful.

- Jerry Bridges, *The Pursuit of Holiness* (NavPress, 2016)

- Kevin DeYoung, *The Hole in Our Holiness: Filling the gap between gospel passion and the pursuit of godliness* (Crossway, 2012)

- Jackie Hill Perry, *Holier Than Thou: How God's holiness helps us trust him* (B&H Publishing, 2021)

- R. C. Sproul, *The Holiness of God* (Tyndale House, 2000)

- John Stott, *The Message of Galatians*, The Bible Speaks Today (IVP, 2020)

- Derek Tidball, *The Message of Holiness*, The Bible Speaks Today (IVP, 2010)

- Derek Tidball, *The Message of Leviticus*, The Bible Speaks Today (IVP, 2021)

- Derek Tidball, *Transformed: Becoming like God's son*, Keswick Study Guides (IVP, 2016)

Day 274

Read: 1 John 3:1–10
Ke verses: 1 John 3:1–3

....

See what great love the Father has lavished on us, that we should be called children of God! And that is what we are! The reason the world does not know us is that it did not know him. ²Dear friends, now we are children of God, and what we will be has not yet been made known. But we know that when Christ appears, we shall be like him, for we shall see him as he is. ³All who have this hope in him purify themselves, just as he is pure.

Are you a confident person?

Some people are naturally confident, while others are more apprehensive and shy. At times, the state of our world and worry about finances, jobs and family relationships leave even the most confident of us reeling.

But, regardless of our personality type or our current situation, Christians can have a confidence about whose they are and where they are headed. This is not an arrogant boastfulness but a deep-seated trust that helps us weather dark days and gives us peace when we are troubled.

Our confidence is rooted in God's love. John's letter reminds us that God's lavish love towards us gives us assurance that we belong to him, we are his 'children'. The world does not recognize our true status. How could it, when it didn't recognize who Jesus was? Many of his own people, the Jews, including the leaders who had been waiting for the Messiah, didn't acknowledge who Jesus was (John 1:10–11). Despite how the world perceives us, God's love towards us in Christ means we are his children, even now.

And because we are children of God it follows that we can be confident in our hope for the future. Our eternity is secure. When Christ appears to usher in the new heaven and the new earth we will 'all be changed' (1 Corinthians 15:51). We will instantly be transformed, our sanctification finally complete. We will be like Christ and with him for ever.

By reminding us of whose we are and where we are headed, this passage introduces us to our next three devotional themes – *Confident, Love, Hope*. But what difference does this *confidence* in God's *love* and *hope* for the future make now? John says, while we wait for Jesus' return, the sure sign that we belong to him is that we purify ourselves (verse 3) and love other believers (verse 10). Because we have this hope in Christ, our lives are changed, we 'cannot go on sinning' without thought of God and we seek to 'do what is right' (verses 9–10). We can't help being who we are. Although not always welcomed, as children of God we will shine like stars, illuminating the darkness all around us.

Today, will you purify yourself, cut out sin and clothe yourself in God's character, as you prepare for your final transformation. Being a bright light in a dark place will not always be comfortable. Our light shows how dark the darkness really is. But don't shrink back; shine out, confident in God's love, your status as his child and the future that he has planned for you.

Confident

Contributors

Psalm 23:1–6	Keith Weston
Psalms 93:1–5 and 94:1–23, Philippians 2:1–13, Colossians 2:20—3:17 and 1 Thessalonians 2:1–20	Alec Motyer
Psalm 121:1–8	Andrew Dow
Habakkuk 2:1–20 and Revelation 2:8–11 and 4:1–11	Jonathan Lamb
Romans 8:18–30	Vaughan Roberts
Romans 8:31–39	Alistair Begg
Colossians 1:1–14	Steve Brady
1 John 4:7–21	Hugh Palmer
Revelation 1:4–8	Raymond Brown

Day 275

Read: Psalm 23:1–6
Key verses: Psalm 23:1–3

••

¹The LORD is my shepherd, I lack nothing.
²He makes me lie down in green pastures,
he leads me beside quiet waters,
³he refreshes my soul.
He guides me along the right paths
for his name's sake.

Are you confident that you have everything you need?

Satan has an arsenal of weapons at his disposal. One of his most popular tactics is to peddle the lie that if we yield ourselves to Christ completely, we will suffer incalculable loss. But we will not! Far from wanting to strip us of everything worthwhile in this life, the Good Shepherd wants to clothe us in riches. Indeed, when Jesus is our Shepherd, when we surrender ourselves to his lordship, we can say for certain, 'I shall not want' (Psalm 23:1, ESV).

How is it that we will lack nothing? Because the Shepherd is lord of infinite grace. In Psalm 34:10, David says, 'Those who seek the LORD lack no good thing.' In Romans 8:32, the apostle Paul adds, 'He who did not spare his own Son, but gave him up for us all – how will he not also, along with him, graciously give us all things?' In the magnificent opening of the letter to the Ephesians, Paul presses home the point: 'Praise be to the God and Father of our Lord Jesus Christ, who has blessed us in the heavenly realms with every spiritual blessing in Christ' (Ephesians 1:3). What an astonishing statement. He *has* blessed us – already – with every spiritual blessing that he has to give us. When we become Christians, we are united to Christ and that union means we receive every spiritual blessing available in the heavenly realms.

Peter writes, 'His divine power has given us everything we need for a godly life through our knowledge of him who called us by his own glory and goodness' (2 Peter 1:3). He makes over his riches to me now – in my situation – by refreshing my soul, by leading me by quiet waters and along the right paths (Psalm 23:2–3). He does this day by day, for his own name's sake, which means for his own honour and glory. If the Lord is your Shepherd, he has blessed you with every blessing; he calls you to surrender yourself to him and to enter into the fullness of those blessings. We can go all through life, to the grave and into eternity, and we will never exhaust the riches that are ours in Christ.

You may think that you lack many things – a spouse, children, health, finances, qualifications, recognition . . . To be without these things may be a source of pain, sadness and stress. But the Chief Shepherd invites you to follow him and find in him all the sustenance you need. Whatever your circumstances, you are rich beyond compare because you have every spiritual blessing in Christ. Today, keep your eyes on your Shepherd and allow him to refresh your soul. Listen to his voice through his Word and receive his limitless grace.

Day 276

Read: Psalm 23:1–6
Key verse: Psalm 23:4

....

Even though I walk
  through the darkest valley,
I will fear no evil,
  for you are with me;
your rod and your staff,
  they comfort me.

Are you, or is someone you love, walking through the 'darkest valley'?

Instead of 'darkest valley', some translations say 'valley of the shadow of death'. There are many dark valleys but, certainly, the valley of the shadow of death is the one we will all face if the Lord does not come back before we cross it. But the psalmist knows, even in death, that there is no need to fear because God is with him. Notice the change in pronoun from 'he leads me . . . he refreshes . . . he guides me' to 'you are with me' when the valley is reached – the relationship is even closer.

There is a related passage in Psalm 84:5–7:

Blessed are those whose strength is in you,
  whose hearts are set on pilgrimage.
As they pass through the Valley of Baka,
  they make it a place of springs;
  the autumn rains also cover it with pools.
They go from strength to strength,
  till each appears before God in Zion.

On their pilgrimage to Jerusalem, the Israelites passed through the Valley of Baka, a very dry and arid place, a 'dark valley', as Psalm 23 would say. What did they do? Did they just mope away their days in Baka? Did they turn bitter against the Lord and say, 'Why did you bring us here?' No, they made it a place of springs. They didn't sit idly under suffering but, we might say, they got out their shovels, dug wells and they found the grace of God. They went 'from strength to strength', and if the Lord had not led them through this valley, they would not have had their faith strengthened.

The end of verse 7 of Psalm 84 is reassuring. When you are going through the dark valley, God does not let go of you. He is with you 'till each appears before God in Zion'. His rod and his staff are your comfort. He will be with you in the valley and see you through the other side, tried but purified. You do not need to worry because God knows the path you take, the God of all wisdom directs your life and he is with you.

'You are with me.' Let the implications of that phrase sink deep into your soul today. God is not with you as an observer. He is there to lead (Psalm 23:2), refresh (verse 3), guide (verse 3) and comfort you (verse 4). In the person of the Holy Spirit, the almighty God of the ages, your heavenly Father, is forever present with you.

You may be serving God in a difficult situation, laid low with depression or approaching that final valley of the shadow of death. Whatever your valley, do not fear; the Chief Shepherd is carrying you on his shoulders and he will not let you go (Luke 15:5).

Day 277

Read: Psalm 23:1–6
Key verses: Psalm 23:5–6

....

> [5]*You prepare a table before me*
>   *in the presence of my enemies.*
> *You anoint my head with oil;*
>   *my cup overflows.*
> [6]*Surely your goodness and love will follow me*
>   *all the days of my life,*
> *and I will dwell in the house of the* LORD
>   *for ever.*

Does your wandering heart sap your confidence in your salvation and your suitability for Christian service? How can you get back on track?

The key is the opening statement of Psalm 23: 'The LORD is my shepherd.' In Old Testament times, 'shepherd' was the word used for kings and leaders (see Ezekiel 34). So David, the writer of the psalm, is saying, 'The Lord is my king', and he is surrendering to the kingship – the rule, priorities and values – of the loving Shepherd. Those, like David, whose lives are shaped by the Shepherd acknowledge that God's goodness and mercy follow them all their days. The Hebrew verb for 'dwell' in verse 6 could be future as well as present tense. I imagine here a man or a woman who, all through the ups and downs of an earthly pilgrimage, dwells consciously in the presence of the Lord.

When I acknowledge that the Lord is my Shepherd, and that goodness and mercy are following me all the days of my life, it is more difficult to wander. I *want* to dwell in God's presence every day. I once was God's enemy but now he is the dearest friend that I have. The apostle Paul sums up our relationship with God in Romans

5:1–2: Jesus' death on the cross blots out past sin, and brings us peace and reconciliation with God. We have access to God's grace, which sustains in all the circumstances of life. And what's more, looking ahead to the future, I rejoice in my hope of sharing the glory of God, guaranteed for me by the Shepherd, whose goodness and mercy follow me all the days of my life until, at long last, I am home.

God knows that your heart wanders. But he welcomes you into his presence regardless. Today, reflect on all his goodness and mercy to you. Ask for renewed dedication to live under his lordship:

> O to grace how great a debtor
> Daily I'm constrained to be!
> Let Thy goodness, like a fetter,
> Bind my wandering heart to Thee.
> Prone to wander, Lord, I feel it,
> Prone to leave the God I love;
> Here's my heart, O take and seal it,
> Seal it for Thy courts above.
> (Robert Robinson, 'Come, Thou fount of every blessing', 1758)

Thank God that, although we fail, the Chief Shepherd remains utterly committed to us:

> My sheep listen to my voice; I know them, and they follow me. I give them eternal life, and they shall never perish; no one will snatch them out of my hand. My Father, who has given them to me, is greater than all; no one can snatch them out of my Father's hand. (John 10:27–29)

Day 278

Read: Psalm 93:1–5
Key verse: Psalm 93:1

....

The LORD reigns, he is robed in majesty;
    the LORD is robed in majesty and armed with strength;
    indeed, the world is established, firm and secure.

What picture do you have in mind when you imagine God?

Do you see a baby in a manger, a rugged Galilean or a bloody body on a cross? The psalmist wants us to visualize and remember that the Lord is King.

- *He is an eternal King.* Verses 1, 3 and 4 affirm the present reality of his kingship. In verse 2, we stand by the throne and realize that there has never been a time when the Lord wasn't King. And verse 5 points forward to the Lord being King for 'endless days'.

- *He is a reigning King.* In the opening verses of the psalm, we see the throne, and then we let our eyes drop beneath it to the world over which the King reigns. The clear implication is that the created order depends for its stability on the security and changelessness of a reigning King. Verse 3 depicts a turbulent world but, when we look beyond the reality of the pounding waves, we see what the Bible insists is equally a reality – a reigning God.

- *He is an active King.* The Lord's kingship is neither idle nor ornamental, but real and active. He is wearing the kingly robes of majesty (verse 1) to indicate his capacity and commitment to rule.

- *He is an absolute King.* The psalm doesn't mention where God reigns. He reigns over this world and holds it in his hand. Neither does the psalmist specify enemies. He portrays them with the single image of the turbulent sea. The message is that over all his enemies, regardless of who they are, the Lord on high is mighty.

In verses 2 and 5, the people acknowledge the Lord as their King. In response, in verse 5, they commit themselves to the truth and reliability of the word that God has spoken and which he has vouched for. They also commit themselves to the holiness that he requires. We can respond in the same way because we know that the Lord is King. This great truth is our shield and strength, the armour to face the daily challenges of life.

Are you caught up in those swirling waves of Psalm 93? Our struggles are real, but there is an unseen reality of which we can be sure: the Lord is King. Don't become discouraged. God knows what is going on in your life, he cares and he is in absolute control. Let this truth be your shield today.

> Blessed are you, Israel!
>   Who is like you,
>   a people saved by the LORD?
> He is your shield and helper
>   and your glorious sword.
> Your enemies will cower before you,
>   and you will tread on their heights.
> (Deuteronomy 33:29)
>
> We wait in hope for the LORD;
>   he is our help and our shield.
> (Psalm 33:20)
>
> You are my refuge and my shield;
>   I have put my hope in your word.
> (Psalm 119:114)

Day 279

Read: Psalm 94:1–23
Key verse: Psalm 94:22

....

*But the L*ORD *has become my fortress,*
  and my God the rock in whom I take refuge.

'Your God doesn't care about what is going on in the world.'

How do you feel when people lambast God like this? In Psalm 94, God's people are dealing with enemies who were not afraid to speak against them, act with violence and hatred towards the helpless, and deny God's love. When we face similar opposition, this psalm bolsters our confidence by reminding us who God is.

- *We have a God of redemption.* In verse 5, the psalmist calls the Israelites 'your people'. They became God's people at the exodus, when he brought them out of Egypt. This was their redemption, when they were rescued from slavery. We too are the redeemed. We have been brought out of slavery to sin by Christ's blood, which was shed on the cross. And God cannot forget those for whom his Son died. His love will never fail us.

- *We have a God of creation.* God made the ear and eye (verse 9). The Bible tells us that the Creator is involved in his creation: he began all things, maintains all things, governs all things and guides all things to their appointed destiny. Can this God be absent or uninvolved?

- *We have a God of providence.* Verses 12–15 remind us of God's involvement, direction and control, even in the smallest details of the experiences of his people. In the thick of this hostility, the psalmist says, 'Blessed is the one you discipline' (verse 12). He speaks of this experience as purposeful: it is the way to peace, the loving way that God brings his people home, and a pit is being dug for the wicked (verse 13). Verse 14 emphasizes that, even in our present difficulties, we have an underlying confidence – 'the Lord will not reject his people'.

- *We have a God of tender care.* The psalmist found himself lonely (verses 16–17), dealing with the precariousness of life (verse 18) and afflicted with distracting thoughts, not knowing what to believe (verse 19). In those times, he found the Lord to be his help, support and comfort (verses 17–19). The New King James Version of the Bible says, 'Your comforts delight my soul.' This speaks of the indescribable inner communications of God whereby he comforts us.

- *We have a God of security and triumph.* God triumphs over the ungodly; he cuts them off. But, for the believer, there is complete security (verse 22). God is 'my fortress'. The Lord lifts his child up into a fortress because it is high and inaccessible to the enemy. He is also 'my . . . refuge' – he is there, available for me to run to.

Meditate on the character of God in Psalm 94. Whether you are suffering for being a Christian or simply because we live in a fallen world, rest secure in God's unfailing love, care, commitment and protection. Run to him; he is your refuge. Let him lift you up; he is your fortress. Surely, we say with the psalmist:

Who is like you, LORD God Almighty?
You, LORD, are mighty, and your faithfulness surrounds you.
(Psalm 89:8)

Day 280

Read: Psalm 121:1–8
Key verses: Psalm 121:7–8

....

>⁷The LORD will keep you from all harm –
> he will watch over your life;
>⁸the LORD will watch over your coming
>   and going
> both now and for evermore.

Do you have confidence in God's promises?

Psalm 121 is full of big promises. In verses 3–6, we follow the pilgrims on their way to Jerusalem and in their nightly camping. When they are on the move, the psalmist affirms, '[God] will not let your foot slip', and when they are at rest, 'he who watches over you will not slumber'. In those days in Israel, you hired a keeper to watch over you while you slept. The trouble was that those hired keepers would sometimes fall asleep themselves. Not so the Lord! He is totally reliable.

God will protect us (verse 6). In Old Testament times, people believed that the moon shed malignant influences on unsuspecting sleepers. So, God promises protection from real perils, such as sunstroke, and imagined perils, such as those from the moon. He protects us from our fears, whether they are reasonable or groundless. God's cover is fully comprehensive.

Then the psalmist's enthusiasm seems to have run away with him: 'The LORD will keep you from all harm' (verse 7). But surely this promise doesn't hold true when we place it next to the realities of life? The Christian has no divine immunity from hurt or trouble. You've only got to read about the sufferings of the apostle Paul to understand that. So what does this promise mean? Paul's answer would be that the Christian can be sure that any so-called evil is good 'with a veil on'. That's his point in Romans 8:28: 'And we know that in all things God works for the good of those who love him, who have been called according to his purpose.' Even when the Christian cannot understand what God is doing, he or she knows that God's love is in, and behind, his work.

To paraphrase Psalm 121:7 slightly, 'The Lord will keep you from the ultimate corruption of evil', from the devil, if you like. Whatever is thrown at you, you will not sink without a trace because you are being kept by the Master Keeper. This interpretation is supported by the second half of verse 7: 'he will watch over your life' – your soul, the deepest part of you. Jesus himself said not to worry about those who have the power to destroy the body; rather, fear the soul-keeper (Matthew 10:28). If you belong to God, he will keep your soul safe in this life and the next. That's a great assurance.

Insert your name into Psalm 121 and meditate on God's precious promises. He is watching over you and protecting you in ways that you may never know. In the face of overwhelming circumstances, know for sure that the devil's reach is limited. Cling to the certain hope that your soul is being kept by the Master Keeper.

Day 281

Read: Habakkuk 2:1–20
Key verses: Habakkuk 2:14, 20

....

> ¹⁴*For the earth will be filled with the knowledge*
> *of the glory of the* LORD
> *as the waters cover the sea . . .*
> ²⁰*The* LORD *is in his holy temple;*
> *let all the earth be silent before him.*

When your world is rocked by grief and loss, in whom or what do you put your confidence?

The prophet Habakkuk famously declared, 'Though the fig-tree does not bud and there are no grapes on the vines . . . yet I will rejoice in the LORD, I will be joyful in God my Saviour' (3:17, 18). But this declaration wasn't easy triumphalism. Habakkuk had wrestled with God to get to this point.

The first two chapters of the book see the prophet distraught at the violence and injustice in Judah, and wondering why God does not intervene. When God says he will send the Babylonians to judge the Israelites, Habakkuk is even more perplexed. How could a holy God appoint such an evil nation to execute judgement? They were even less righteous than the Israelites! In the midst of his despair, there are two shafts of light for Habakkuk (and for us) to cling to:

- *A present reality: 'The Lord is in his holy temple' (verse 20).* The Babylonians may be arrogantly asserting their power, but the Lord of the universe is reigning in the place of ultimate authority, high above his creatures. The deities that the pagans turn to are useless (verse 19), but God is in control and can be relied upon.

- *A future certainty: 'the earth will be filled with the knowledge of the glory of the Lord' (verse 14).* In the context of the power of empires and the pretension of human rulers, the Lord speaks of the certainty of what will be left on that final day: the universal knowledge of God. There is a similar phrase in Isaiah 11:9, when the prophet looked at that great messianic era, which pointed to Jesus himself, the One who would ultimately bring the victory of God's purposes, the destruction of evil, the salvation of his people, and the establishment of a new heaven and a new earth. Habakkuk adds the word 'glory' to Isaiah's phrase, perhaps because it encompasses the greatest goal of all human history – the glory of God. One day, all other glories will fade in the light of this supreme glory: his royal majesty. We can look forward to the final triumph of God, when the world will be filled with his purposes, presence and glory.

In the midst of suffering and grief, when all other certainties have been swept away, you can be confident that God is in control now and will ultimately triumph. These twin truths are like stakes in the ground, anchors that hold us fast in turbulent times. The psalmist captures the same truths for us to meditate on:

'Be still, and know that I am God;
   I will be exalted among the nations,
   I will be exalted in the earth.'
The LORD Almighty is with us;
   the God of Jacob is our fortress.
(Psalm 46:10–11)

Day 282

Read: Romans 8:18–30
Key verse: Romans 8:28

· ·

And we know that in all things God works for the good of those who love him, who have been called according to his purpose.

Have you ever heard this verse quoted glibly?

You have just received news that you've got an incurable disease or someone you love has died: 'Oh, don't worry . . . ' and someone quotes verse 28. 'Praise the Lord, anyway.'

Taking this verse out of context makes light of very real suffering. Not all things are good for Christians, and some things we experience are very bad indeed: bereavement, sickness, the largely hidden pain of childlessness, unwanted singleness, a difficult marriage, the psychological scars of bullying, emotional or sexual abuse, the desperation of depression, or an estrangement from family or friends. It is not that all things are good but that, in all things, God works *for good*, fulfilling his purposes.

The big question is, of course, what is this good? Verse 27 says, 'The Spirit intercedes for God's people in accordance with the will of God.' The good is God's will, which is described in verses 29–30: 'For those God foreknew he also predestined to be conformed to the image of his Son' (verse 29). This is his will for our lives – that we might be like Jesus once again, perfectly conformed to his image, perfectly reflecting his glory. Verse 30 continues, 'Those he predestined, he also called; those he called, he also justified; those he justified, he also glorified.' These two verses span eternity. God has an eternal purpose for our lives and he will not let anything stop him fulfilling it. That doesn't remove the pain but it does give great perspective within it.

Terrible things may happen, but God is at work and forming us into the likeness of Jesus. Of course, there is mystery: 'Why did God allow that to happen to me?' Or sometimes, even harder to deal with, when it's someone we love very much: 'Why did God allow that to happen to him or her?' It doesn't make any sense, and sometimes we don't see any good come from it. But we can trust our Sovereign God, that in all things he is at work, conforming his people into the likeness of Christ.

You may be dealing with many things in your life that are not 'good'. Today, will you cling to the certainty that God is sovereign and working out his eternal purposes? Will you ask God to help you to accept your suffering as his instrument to make you more like Christ? More than that, with God's enabling, will you join him in his work and strive to grow in godliness, even in these dark days?

Now may the God of peace, who through the blood of the eternal covenant brought back from the dead our Lord Jesus, that great Shepherd of the sheep, equip you with everything good for doing his will, and may he work in us what is pleasing to him, through Jesus Christ, to whom be glory for ever and ever. Amen.
(Hebrews 13:20–21)

Day 283

Read: Romans 8:18–30
Key verses: Romans 8:29–30

....

> [29] For those God foreknew, he also predestined to be conformed to the image of his Son, that he might be the firstborn among many brothers and sisters. [30] And those he predestined, he also called; those he called, he also justified; those he justified, he also glorified.

Are you confident that you will persevere in the Christian faith? Confident that you will be with Christ when you die?

Paul helps to answer these questions in verses 29–30, verses sometimes described as 'the golden chain'. It begins 'those whom God foreknew'. Paul is not speaking about the fact that God can tell in advance which choices we might make. This phrase speaks about an intimate, personal knowledge. God set his love on a group before they ever loved him, before they were ever born. The golden chain is not fastened ultimately by anything I do – if it were, it would be bound to break. It is fastened on God's gracious commitment. Before I was even born, God foreknew, and those whom he 'foreknew, he also predestined'. Having set his love on a people, he decided on his plan for them, and determined to fulfil it, that they might be conformed to the likeness of Jesus. 'Those he predestined, he also called' is not simply talking about putting out an invitation and nervously looking to see if anyone might respond. It speaks of listening to his voice – with God calling his own. 'Those he called, he also justified' – that we might be absolutely in the right with God. 'Those he justified, he also glorified' – it is as good as done; it is absolutely certain. He will keep us *all* the way.

There is great mystery in God's sovereignty. But it does not deny human responsibility; we must repent and believe. Neither does it excuse human passivity. We can't say, 'Oh, God will bring his own in; I don't have to pray or share the gospel.' God uses the prayers and proclamation of his people, and faithful preaching.

But I can be sure that if I have truly put my trust in Christ, I have been born again. The Spirit of God is in me and has given me a new heart, a new desire to please him, even though I don't do this as I should. I have a new intimacy, a sense that I'm a child of God. I can be sure that I am justified and will be glorified. Whatever happens in my life, I can be sure that all things work for good because all things lead to glory.

> Everything in these verses – all of God's work, his choosing you, predestining you, calling you, justifying you, sanctifying you, bringing you to final glory – is designed by God not mainly to make much of us, but to free us and fit us to enjoy making much of Christ forever. So I plead with you, set your mind's attention and your heart's affection on the glory of Christ, so that you will be changed from glory to glory into his image, so that you might fully enjoy what you were made for – making much of Christ.
> (Extract from a sermon by John Piper, 'Glorification: Conformed to Christ for the supremacy of Christ', 11 August 2002, <www .desiringgod.org>, accessed 23 November 2020)

Day 284

Read: Romans 8:31–39
Key verses: Romans 8:31–32

. . . .

> [31] *What, then, shall we say in response to these things? If God is for us, who can be against us?* [32] *He who did not spare his own Son, but gave him up for us all – how will he not also, along with him, graciously give us all things?*

Are you confident that God is *for* you?

There is no uncertainty in this verse: the God who calls and justifies is on our side. Therefore, whatever opposition comes our way is ultimately of no account. Paul is not suggesting that the opposition does not exist. He does not ask the question 'Who can be against us?' because many people can be against us. The evil one is against us and our conscience often accuses us. Paul asks, '*If God is for us,* who can be against us?' (emphasis added). He is saying that if we take all that is against us and set it alongside the fact of God's abiding presence on our behalf, we gain a proper perspective.

This is a lesson that the armies of Israel needed to learn. It took David the shepherd boy to remind them that the giant Goliath was of no account. 'If God is for us, you are nothing, Goliath.' The cry of God's people all the way through the Old Testament was this: 'If the Lord had not been on our side, what would have happened to us?' (see Psalm 124:1–5).

Paul picks up that Old Testament principle and reality, and brings it home to the believers in his day. 'Let me prove that God is for you,' says Paul. Here is the evidence: 'He . . . did not spare his own Son' (Romans 8:32). When Jesus prayed in the Garden of Gethsemane, 'If you are willing, take this cup from me' (Luke 22:42), the Father did not remove the cup of bitterness from him, so that those who are in Jesus might be able to drink the cup of blessing. Isaiah 53 says it was the will of God to crush him. God did not spare him; instead, he gave him up for us as a substitute. But never think of Christ as an unwilling participant in the Father's plan.

> It is true that the Father gave the Son; it is equally true that the Son gave himself. We mustn't speak of God punishing Jesus, or of Jesus persuading God. We must never make Christ the object of God's punishment, or God the object of Christ's persuasion. For the Father and Son are subjects, not objects, taking the initiative to save sinners. (John Stott, *The Cross of Christ*, IVP, 2006)

If God be for us, then who *can* be against us?

When we face opposition for our faith, when our conscience accuses us, it is tempting to throw up our hands and wonder, 'Is God *really* for me?' The cross is God's definitive answer. Jesus' death, of course, was a once-in-a-lifetime event but God – Father, Son and Holy Spirit – is still 'for us', with the same degree of passion and commitment. So, fix your eyes on the cross – see there God's ultimate demonstration of what he thinks of you. Today, marvel with the psalmist: 'If the Lord had not been on our side, what would have happened to us?' (Psalm 124:1, adapted).

Day 285

Read: Romans 8:31–39
Key verse: Romans 8:32

. . . .

He who did not spare his own Son, but gave him up for us all –
how will he not also, along with him, graciously give us all
things?

Do you remember when you were desperately hoping for a toy at
Christmas and, as you removed the toy from the box, you saw the
label 'Batteries not included'?

Your heart sank; you had this wonderful gift but it couldn't work.
Without batteries, the gift was useless and you were left to your own
devices.

That is certainly not a picture of what God has done for us in Jesus.
Paul uses unassailable logic to make the point in verse 32 that if God
has given us the greatest and the best gift in Jesus, he will not
withhold all the gifts and blessings of grace that complete the work
that his goodness has begun. In Christ, all the blessings are ours,
and the story of our Christian experience includes all that accompanies
the wonder of our salvation in the Lord Jesus Christ. Again, Paul is
asking us to think – would God have given us his Son, sent him to the
cross for us, and then be unwilling to give us all the things that
accompany his purposes?

Incidentally, 'give us all things' (verse 32) is a dangerous phrase if it
is unearthed from the context. 'All things' does not mean that
because God gave us salvation in Christ, he will give us everything
we want or everything we ask for. No. Paul's argument is that God
will give us all the things that are necessary to accomplish his purpose
of making us like Christ. He will give us all we need 'to be conformed
to the image of his Son' (verse 29).

We, like those first-century believers, can be fully confident that God finishes what he starts: 'he who began a good work in you will carry it on to completion until the day of Christ Jesus' (Philippians 1:6).

We often abandon DIY or gardening projects halfway through. We get tired, overwhelmed or just plain bored. But God is not like us. Hebrews 12:2 calls him 'the pioneer and perfecter' (NIV) or 'the author and finisher' (NKJV) of our faith. He promises to finish the work he started in us. Reflect on all that God has done in your life so far – these are wonderful examples of God's faithfulness and guarantee that he will finish his work. He will never abandon you.

> He will keep you strong to the end so that you will be free from all blame on the day when our Lord Jesus Christ returns. God will do this, for he is faithful to do what he says, and he has invited you into partnership with his Son, Jesus Christ our Lord.
> (1 Corinthians 1:8–9, NLT)

> May God himself, the God of peace, sanctify you through and through. May your whole spirit, soul and body be kept blameless at the coming of our Lord Jesus Christ. The one who calls you is faithful, and he will do it.
> (1 Thessalonians 5:23–24)

Day 286

Read: Romans 8:31–39
Key verses: Romans 8:33–34

....

> ^{33}Who will bring any charge against those whom God has chosen? It is God who justifies. ^{34}Who then is the one who condemns? No one. Christ Jesus who died – more than that, who was raised to life – is at the right hand of God and is also interceding for us.

Are you riddled with guilt, doubting that God can forgive your sin?

Satan comes in our imaginations and says to the Father, 'Look at that sinner. How can you declare this person justified?'

'Well, yes,' says the Father, 'this person is a sinner. The charges that you bring are valid. But will you look at my Son's hands and feet? Will you look at the wounds in his side? Who are you to condemn? It is Christ who justifies.'

Paul is not suggesting that no charge may be brought against us (verse 33). What he is saying is that any charge that is brought cannot stand because the case is closed. The verdict has been rendered. Indeed, Romans 8 begins: 'Therefore, there is now no condemnation for those who are in Christ Jesus.' Why? Because, having been justified by faith, we have peace with God. Remember the great exchange – all our demerits to Christ's account and all Christ's righteousness to our account? The righteousness that God requires of us, if we are ever to stand before him, is the righteousness that God reveals in the work of the gospel, the righteousness that Christ has achieved on our behalf and the righteousness that God bestows upon all who believe.

'Christ Jesus who died – more than that, who was raised to life.' Verse 34 is simply stating the facts: we serve a risen Saviour. What possible good would a dead one be? It is as the risen Christ, the living Lord, that Christ ensures the security of all who are in him. It is as if Paul is saying in these verses, 'The reason why I am able to say these things (about no condemnation, the reality of justification and the irrelevance of someone who comes to accuse you) is because we are dealing with Christ Jesus who died an atoning death, who was raised to life and is seated at the right hand of God.' Jesus is in the place of dominion and authority. He is physically present in heaven, interceding for us. Not only does the Holy Spirit intercede concerning the groanings in our hearts but Jesus also intercedes on our behalf on the basis of his once-for-all work of atonement. He continues to secure all the benefits of his death for his people.

Are you hanging on to guilt, raking over failures and believing Satan's accusations? Why are you remembering sins that God has chosen to forget? Today, take God at his word. Jesus' death and resurrection have dealt with your sins – past, present and future – once and for all. Will you trust that Jesus' blood was sufficient to wipe away your sin? Consider the psalmist's words:

> He does not treat us as our sins deserve
>   or repay us according to our iniquities.
> For as high as the heavens are above the earth,
>   so great is his love for those who fear him;
> as far as the east is from the west,
>   so far has he removed our transgressions from us.
> (Psalm 103:10–12)

Day 287

Read: Romans 8:31–39
Key verse: Romans 8:35

....

Who shall separate us from the love of Christ? Shall trouble or hardship or persecution or famine or nakedness or danger or sword?

Do you truly believe that God loves you?

When difficulties or suffering come, we often think, 'If God really loved me, he wouldn't allow this to happen.' But Paul turns our argument on its head and asks in verse 35, 'Who shall separate us from the love of Christ?' or 'What shall separate us from the love of Christ?' Then he lists enemies of our happiness and potential security in Christ. Once again, he returns to the sufferings that he mentioned at the very beginning, the sufferings of this present time. Trouble, hardship, persecution, famine, nakedness, danger and sword – Paul lists them all.

In verse 36, he quotes Psalm 44:22, underlining the fact that suffering has always been part of the experience of God's people. Without a theology of suffering, we will fall prey to all kinds of temptation, and we will find it far more difficult to speak to sufferers who come to our churches.

Remember the prophet Jeremiah's words:

I have been deprived of peace;
    I have forgotten what prosperity is.
So I say, 'My splendour is gone
    and all that I had hoped from the LORD.'

I remember my affliction and my wandering,
    the bitterness and the gall.
I well remember them,

and my soul is downcast within me.
Yet this I call to mind
    and therefore I have hope:

Because of the LORD's great love we are not consumed,
    for his compassions never fail.
They are new every morning;
    great is your faithfulness.
I say to myself, 'The LORD is my portion;
    therefore I will wait for him.'
(Lamentations 3:17–24)

Paul reinforces Jeremiah's point: 'Life is hard but God is good.'

Suffering doesn't separate us from God's love; in a strange way, it is proof of it. God longs for us to be like Christ. Suffering, if we allow it, imprints the likeness of Christ on us more deeply, as it forces us to rest, hope and trust in God alone.

John Newton, the former slave trader and author of the hymn 'Amazing Grace', helps us to understand this:

> Assurance grows by repeated conflict, by our repeated experimental proof of the Lord's power and goodness to save; when we have been brought very low and helped, sorely wounded and healed, cast down and raised again, have given up all hope, and been suddenly snatched from danger, and placed in safety; and when these things have been repeated to us and in us a thousand times over, we begin to learn to trust simply to the word and power of God, beyond and against appearances: and this trust, when habitual and strong, bears the name of assurance; for even assurance has degrees.
>
> (Tony Reinke, *Newton on the Christian Life*, Crossway, 2015, p. 220)

Day 288

Read: Romans 8:31–39
Key verses: Romans 8:35–37

....

> [35] Who shall separate us from the love of Christ? Shall trouble or hardship or persecution or famine or nakedness or danger or sword? [36] As it is written:
> 'For your sake we face death all day long;
>   we are considered as sheep to be slaughtered.'
> [37] No, in all these things we are more than conquerors through him who loved us.

Do you feel like a conqueror? Always, sometimes, almost never? (Delete as appropriate.)

The apostle Paul was very familiar with suffering and, as he rehearses the catalogue of difficulties that Christian believers face, he makes this amazing declaration: 'We are more than conquerors' (verse 37). The Greek word is *hypernikomen*, which sounds like some sort of computer game. Paul loads this word up: 'We are not just conquerors; we are more than conquerors. We are hyper-conquerors!' Now the reason why he uses this word is that it is the only word which does justice to the victory that is ours in the face of overwhelming odds. I am a hyper-conqueror in all the suffering and hardships outlined in verse 35.

But how can I be a conqueror in them? *In* them, *through* him – prepositions are important. In all these things I am more than a conqueror *through* him; 'through him who loved us' – a love that has been demonstrated in the cross, a love that is sustaining and everlasting. It is not that he started to love us and then he stopped along the way or that his love is a diminishing love. His love knows no end. There is no possibility of his bailing out on us.

Therefore, even though all hell can be set loose against us – the accusations of conscience, the challenges of life, the immensity of the diminution of physical powers, the loss of personal relationships, the disintegration that comes by way of the ravages of sin – 'In all these things I am more than a conqueror through him who continues to love us.'

Troubles will come, but you can be confident of this: you can face illness, slurs on your reputation, grief – in fact, all things – not by gritting your teeth and willing yourself to press on, or by relying on a fantastic network of family and friends, but through Christ. Encouragement and the love of friends are valuable but, ultimately, the only way we can stand in the face of suffering is through Christ who continues to love us. Whatever happens to us, Jesus' life, death and resurrection guarantee his forever love for us.

Today, you will be a conqueror – not by gliding through your 'to do' list, avoiding problems or bypassing sorrow, but through Christ, secure in his love. With Paul, we can say:

> I have been crucified with Christ and I no longer live, but Christ lives in me. The life I now live in the body, I live by faith in the Son of God, who loved me and gave himself for me.
> (Galatians 2:20)

Day 289

Read: Romans 8:31–39
Key verses: Romans 8:38–39

....

> ^{38}*For I am convinced that neither death nor life, neither angels nor demons, neither the present nor the future, nor any powers, ^{39}neither height nor depth, nor anything else in all creation, will be able to separate us from the love of God that is in Christ Jesus our Lord.*

Imagine trying to fly a plane through turbulence only by looking out of the window. You would be terrified; you wouldn't even know whether or not you were flying upside down. It is vital that the pilot flies while looking at the instruments because they tell the truth. The same applies in life: we must live not according to our feelings but by what we know to be true.

In this great declaration, Paul speaks of what he knows:

'I am convinced'. In the King James Version of the Bible, it says, 'I am persuaded'; in the English Standard Version, it is 'I am sure'. And it is a great encouragement when those to whom we look feel very confident about things. The early believers in Rome, reading this letter, would have been encouraged because, for them, tribulation, peril, sword and famine were not issues that they read about in missionary biographies – they were present realities. It would have been a tremendous encouragement for them to say, 'The one who is writing this letter to us knows about suffering, and he is convinced by the facts. He is persuaded by the truthfulness of what he knows.'

Paul says, 'I am sure that nothing can, and nothing will, separate us from God's love.' Then he runs through a list of potential or actual adversaries. 'Death nor life' – life, with all its battles, potential triumphs or temptations, and death, like an ever-rolling stream. We are either dead or alive; there is no middle ground. But the good news is that neither death nor life is going to separate you from God's love. 'Angels nor demons' – through the cross, Jesus has disarmed the powers of the unseen heavenly realms, whether they are of spiritual benefit or spiritual wickedness. 'Neither the present nor the future' – in other words, time is not going to erode God's love. The issues of time and space will not be able to impinge upon this. No chance. God is sovereign over both. 'Nor any powers' – don't worry about the forces of the universe or anything else in all creation. Nothing can – nothing will – 'separate us from the love of God, which is in Christ Jesus our Lord' (verse 39).

Are you convinced of God's love for you? As Christians, we may verbally assent to this truth but we don't always live as if we believe it. Our choices, priorities and behaviour are easily swayed by our feelings, circumstances and the opinions of others. How different would your life look if it were based on the same certainty Paul's was? If you were convinced of God's love for you, in what ways would it have an impact on the following aspects of your life?

• How you feel about yourself, your suffering and your failures
• Your devotional life and prayers
• Your relationships with family, friends and non-Christians
• Your involvement at work and in church

Day 290

Read: Philippians 2:1–13
Key verses: Philippians 2:12–13

....

¹²*Therefore, my dear friends, as you have always obeyed – not only in my presence, but now much more in my absence – continue to work out your salvation with fear and trembling,* ¹³*for it is God who works in you to will and to act in order to fulfil his good purpose.*

If you are a child of God, God dwells in you.

'Christ in you, the hope of glory' is a present reality, not wishful thinking (Colossians 1:27). It is not a promise dependent on something else happening, not a challenge requiring you to do anything, but a fact to believe.

God is not in us like a guest or a lodger but as a worker. The verb 'works' in Philippians 2:13 conveys the sense that he works ceaselessly. At any moment of day or night, throughout all your life as a Christian, God is at work. Other Bible verses that mention God's indwelling presence urge us to respect and reverence his holiness, such as Ephesians 4:30: 'do not grieve the Holy Spirit'. Clearly, the Christian who persists in sin is countering the action of God. However, the point of Philippians 2:13 is that, although we sin, God will never give up on us. That does not excuse our sin; it means that he stays faithful.

God works 'to will and to act in order to fulfil his good purpose' (Philippians 2:13). There are two sides to every action. There is the decision and there is the bringing it to pass. There is the will and the action. We are often so weak that we cannot even choose what is right. Sometimes, we can choose what is right but we can't make it happen. But God does both. His work is effective. God will accomplish his purpose; his work will achieve what it was designed to do. Philippians 3:21 explains that God has 'power that enables him to bring everything under his control'. The God who is working in us is conforming all things to his will – and that includes you!

Are you worried that God has abandoned you, that your sin and failure have finally pushed him away? God has not given up on you. He has promised to keep working in you to make you increasingly like Jesus. The challenge is this: will you join him in his work?

God wants you to be holy. Through faith, He already counts you holy in Christ. Now He intends to make you holy with Christ. This is no optional plan . . . God saved you to sanctify you. God is in the beautification business, washing away spots and smoothing out wrinkles. He will have a blameless bride. He promised to work in you; He also calls you to work out. 'The beauty of holiness' is first of all the Lord's (Ps. 29:2, KJV). But by His grace it can also be yours. (Kevin DeYoung, *The Hole in Our Holiness*, Crossway, 2012, p. 146)

Day 291

Read: Philippians 2:1–13
Key verses: Philippians 2:12–13

....

¹²Therefore, my dear friends, as you have always obeyed – not only in my presence, but now much more in my absence – continue to work out your salvation with fear and trembling, ¹³for it is God who works in you to will and to act in order to fulfil his good purpose.

Are you confident by now that God is at work in you, and using all the circumstances of your life to make you more like Jesus?

Imagine if God waited for our permission before he acted. There might be a few days a month when we would be fired up for God to work, but the rest of the time we might not be so keen. Thankfully, God is not waiting for our assent. Paul makes it clear that God is working to 'fulfil his good purpose'. Another Bible version, the King James Version, says he is working for 'his good pleasure'. Our wonderful God didn't wait for our good pleasure when he saved us, and he is not waiting for our good pleasure to bring us into conformity with his perfect design for us.

He is working for *his* good pleasure. Behind this ceaseless, effectual and complete work of our indwelling God, there is all his eternal purpose to save us and have us for himself. He is working for reasons that make sense to him, for a purpose he has mapped out in his own mind.

Paul reminds us, in Philippians 1:6, 'that he who began a good work in you will carry it on to completion until the day of Christ Jesus'. God began the good work in us when he chose us in Christ before the foundation of the world (Ephesians 1:4). Our standing in Christ depends solely on his will. And he will keep working until he finishes the good work on 'the day of Christ'. This means that our complete and final perfection is as certain as God's pledge to his Son to give him the glory. God has said that there is a day coming when Jesus' triumph will be made public and every knee will bow and every tongue confess him as Lord (Philippians 2:10–11). Only the Father knows the timing of that day. But God has promised that, on the day of Christ, he will have us ready; there will be no unsanctified believer. Everything and everybody will be prepared for the glorious triumph that God is preparing for his Son. In the meantime, he will continue putting the finishing touches on his 'good work'.

Sometimes we are discouraged by our slow progress towards holiness. We are keenly aware of our sin and how far short we fall of God's perfect standard. But that's a good sign! The deeper our relationship with God, the more we appreciate his beauty and perfection, and the more sensitive we are to all that offends him. Keep resisting sin, keep striving for holiness. Take heart, God is working in you and will have you ready for the great day of Christ.

> And we all, who with unveiled faces contemplate the Lord's glory, are being transformed into his image with ever-increasing glory, which comes from the Lord, who is the Spirit.
> (2 Corinthians 3:18)

Day 292

Read: Philippians 2:1–13

Key verses: Philippians 2:12–13

....

> [12] *Therefore, my dear friends, as you have always obeyed – not only in my presence, but now much more in my absence – continue to work out your salvation with fear and trembling,* [13] *for it is God who works in you to will and to act in order to fulfil his good purpose.*

If there is a lift to get us to the top of the building, then we don't need to bother to take the stairs. In the same way, if God is working in us to make us perfect on the day of Christ, then surely we should give up the effort and leave it to him.

But Scripture does not say that God is doing it all, therefore we can relax. It says that God is working to this amazing extent in every believer, therefore 'work out your salvation with fear and trembling' – with fear and trembling because we owe a responsibility to the Father who loves us. This is not fear of judgement but fear of displeasing the One who loves us so much.

What does it mean to 'work out your salvation'? We already have full salvation. Christ has made us right with God and, at the cross, our sins were forgiven and we were sanctified. Paul talks about 'your salvation' because it is something we already possess. So, when he says 'work out your salvation', he means that we should appropriate it, to make sure we are growing in our experience of it.

The Old Testament provides a perfect illustration of this. Remember when the Israelites stood on the border of Canaan? This was the land that God had promised to their ancestors. It was already theirs, but now they were charged to 'go in to possess' (Joshua 1:11, KJV). Similarly, after Abraham had separated from Lot, God showed him all the land that he was giving to him and his descendants, and told him to walk the length and breadth of it (Genesis 13:14–17). Abraham was possessing his possession. So, we too have to appropriate, and make real in our personal experience, everything that was accomplished for us on Calvary.

How do we do this? By obedience (Philippians 2:12). We follow the example of Christ (2:6–8). Jesus was in full possession of the divine nature, the outworking of which was a life of self-denial and self-sacrifice. God now lives in us; we are partakers of the divine nature. And just as the possession of the divine nature led Jesus on a self-denying path of submissive obedience to the will of God, so 'as you have always obeyed', carry on the good work.

Obedience is the way we 'work out our salvation' and are confident that we're pleasing God. Don't give up on it or grow weary of it – God is in you, spurring you on to follow in the footsteps of Jesus. Today, with God's help, take the step of obedience that is in front of you – cleaning up your thought life, taking part in a church rota diligently, demonstrating God's love to your children, caring for that elderly relative with respect, and being 'salt and light' to non-Christian friends.

Day 293

Read: Colossians 1:1–14
Key verses: Colossians 1:1–2

....

> ¹ *Paul, an apostle of Christ Jesus by the will of God, and Timothy our brother,*
> ² *To God's holy people in Colossae, the faithful brothers and sisters in Christ:*
> *Grace and peace to you from God our Father.*

Did you know that if you are a believer, you are a saint?

Paul is writing to 'God's holy people [literally 'saints'] in Colossae'. This was a phrase used of the ancient people of God, the Jewish nation. And now, writing both to Jews and Gentiles, Paul says, 'You are saints. You are set apart for God. You belong to him.' You can't make yourself a saint but God can and does, for in the New Testament, it is a term applied to every Christian without exception. And, as saints, we have a dual address: 'To God's holy people *in Colossae*, the faithful brothers and sisters *in Christ*' (emphasis added). Do you see that double emphasis? Christians are people who live at two addresses: they live in Colossae and they live in Christ.

Colossae was in the Lycus Valley, in what is now modern Turkey. It had seen better days. It didn't have the reputation of neighbouring towns such as Hierapolis or Laodicea. It was a bit of a backwater. But God knew the circumstances of these believers in Colossae. I love the verse in Revelation 2:13, written to the Christians in Pergamum: 'I know where you live – where Satan has his throne.' God knows where you live. And where you live will have a certain impact on who you are. Your background, your family, will colour some of your experience of Christ. But here's the key – your background mustn't be the thing that defines you.

Paul says, 'You are the saints in Colossae . . . in Christ.' He uses this phrase 'in Christ' many times in his letters. Why? Because it is the marker for Christian identity. What defines me is not where I've come from but to whom I belong and, as a result, where I am going. My identity is determined not by my gender, sexual orientation, achievements, job or background, but by who I am in Christ. I belong to Jesus – that's my identity.

Being a saint does not, however, negate the struggles of life. That's why Paul says, 'Grace and peace to you from God our Father.' God gives us every grace we need, no matter what the trouble may be. And he provides peace – not merely the absence of war but shalom, God's wholeness and well-being in our hearts and for our lives.

Your 'Colossae', wherever you live, will no doubt have shaped you. But don't let it define you. Your identity is securely based on your union with Christ. You belong to him. As you go through your day, be mindful of who you are and to whom you belong. Receive the grace and peace God has for you today; rely on his resources to live the life God designed you for.

Day 294

Read: Colossians 2:20–3:17
Key verses: Colossians 3:1–4

· ·

> ¹Since, then, you have been raised with Christ, set your hearts on things above, where Christ is, seated at the right hand of God. ²Set your minds on things above, not on earthly things. ³For you died, and your life is now hidden with Christ in God. ⁴When Christ, who is your life, appears, then you also will appear with him in glory.

Imagine a doctor standing by your hospital bed, telling you, 'You're cured. There is no longer any trace of the disease.'

You might not feel cured. In fact, you know that if you got out of bed, you would collapse with weakness. Nevertheless, the reality is that you are cured. In a similar way, as we struggle with sin, we don't always think that we are living the new life of Christ. But the reality is that we are united with Christ, and his finished work on the cross has been accredited to us. We don't need to feel this truth but we do have to believe it.

This passage outlines what is true about every Christian: 'you died with Christ' (2:20); 'you have been raised with Christ' (3:1); 'your life is now hidden with Christ in God' (3:3); 'you also will appear with him in glory' (3:4). What does it mean that when Jesus died, we died? It means that the fully paid penalty for sin has been credited to our account. Jesus' resurrection means that when he rose, the full reality of a new life was credited to us. The Father has granted to us, here and now, the eternal security of a life already established in heaven. We will share the heavenly place; we'll serve him and see his face. But that will not add to our security for, at this present moment, as those who have been identified with Jesus, our lives are hidden with

Christ in God. The consummation of all of this will be when we appear with him in glory.

When the Lord appears at his second coming, believers will be shown in their true colours at his side. This is a sure hope. Jesus won't put on any new glory for the occasion. He will show then the glory he possesses *now*. Likewise, we will shine with the glory we have now, which was purchased on Calvary: the glory of the ascended life, the glory that is our true reality at this present moment.

In *Pilgrim's Progress*, John Bunyan describes a man who could look only down:

> One stood above the man's head holding a celestial crown and he offered him that crown for his muck rake; but the man never looked up . . . Instead, he only raked bits of straw, the small sticks, and dust from the floor.
>
> (John Bunyan, *Pilgrim's Progress*, Aneko Press, 2015, p. 217)

Stop digging around in the dirt! 'Set your hearts . . . set your minds on things above': you have died and been raised with Christ; your life is hidden with Christ in God, and you will appear with him in glory. A heavenly crown and glory are yours.

Reflect on these truths; be confident in them and live as if you believe them.

Day 295

Read: 1 Thessalonians 2:1–20
Key verse: 1 Thessalonians 2:18

....

We wanted to come to you – certainly I, Paul, did, again and again – but Satan blocked our way.

Are you confident of God's authority over Satan? Alternatively, do you look at your life and what is going on in the world and wonder if Satan is running amok?

Clearly, there is a supernatural power ranged against believers, but we need to have a sense of proportion. In Paul's letters, Satan is mentioned by name only nine times. Compare that with the hundreds of times that Paul refers to 'Jesus', 'the Lord Jesus' and 'Jesus Christ'. We also need to remember that Satan does not operate as a free agent, but only within the sovereign purposes of God. Even in Revelation 20, where Satan is let loose, it is only to do what God pre-determined he should do.

The opening chapters of Job explain this to us. It wasn't Satan who said, 'I'm going to have a go at your servant Job.' No, it was the Lord who said, 'Have you considered my servant Job?' (Job 1:8). And it was God who put the boundary markers in place. Satan could touch Job's children, home, goods and even his health, but not his life. Somehow, great eternal issues are at stake here. The point is that Satan could only operate within the permission, direction and limitation of God.

Here in 1 Thessalonians 2, Paul wanted to go back to see the believers, but he says that Satan put a roadblock in his way. God allowed Satan to prevent Paul's visit. We don't know how he did it. But wasn't it good that Paul could not return to Thessalonica? As a result, he learned first-hand that our spiritual welfare rests in the hands of God, who is looking after his church.

It is well to remember that Satan's power is not inherent, but permitted (Rom. 13:1). It is not unlimited, but controlled (Job 1:12; 2:6). It is not invincible, but broken (Luke 11:21–22). It is not assured of success, but is surely doomed (Rev. 20:2–3). Satan knows well that there is no ultimate victory for him. The pronounced sentence has only been postponed. But he works to hinder and postpone Christ's final triumph. We can rejoice in the certainty of John's assurance: 'Greater is he that is in you, than he that is in the world' (1 John 4:4).

(J. Oswald Sanders, *Cultivation of Christian Character*, Moody Press, 1965, p. 86)

Heavenly Father, when it seems as if Satan has the upper hand, help me to remember that you are on the throne and in control, and that he operates only within the boundaries you have permitted. When I can't see how you are working, or why you have allowed Satan to turn his attention on me, help me to trust you. And if there are lessons you want me to learn, help me to learn them well and not to miss the opportunity to sink deeper roots into Christ. Amen.

Day 296

Read: 1 John 4:7–21
Key verse: 1 John 4:17

....

This is how love is made complete among us so that we will have confidence on the day of judgement: in this world we are like Jesus.

Are you ever tongue-tied in certain stressful situations?

Maybe you just can't find the right words to say when a particular relative or work colleague comes into the room. If any situation is going to leave us tongue-tied and cause us to hang our heads in shame, surely it will be the day of judgement (Revelation 6:15–17). But John says that God's love is designed to give us confidence on that day.

God's love is 'made complete' – in other words, it has accomplished its goal, reached its target in us, when we have confidence to face the day of judgement. The word 'confidence' conveys the idea of outspokenness, of freedom of speech.

How can we have this type of confidence? Verse 17 of 1 John 4 says that 'in this world we are like Jesus'. John writes as if we are just like Jesus, as if our relationship with the Father is just like his. Jesus doesn't come cringing and fearful into his Father's presence, and neither should we: 1 John 3:1–2 reminds us that we are not just *called* 'children of God' but that we *are* 'children of God'. Similarly, Romans 8:16–17 tell us that we are children of God and so 'heirs of God and co-heirs with Christ'. What he inherits, so shall we inherit. Because we are God's children, we can stand in his presence on the last day.

Clearly, there are differences between us and Christ.

One of the tensions between John and his opponents concerned the sense in which we are like Jesus. The opponents wanted to view themselves as little Christs. But John emphasizes that, unlike Jesus, we are not in glory yet. Judgement day is not behind us but ahead of us. In this world, we are not beyond the reach of sin, but we are cleansed from all unrighteousness. This is where we stake our confidence for the day of judgement: 'If we confess our sins, he is faithful and just and will forgive us our sins and purify us from all unrighteousness' (1 John 1:9). Indeed, God's love has accomplished its goal in us when we are confident on the day of judgement because we know we're cleansed from all unrighteousness.

> Nobody can produce new evidence of your depravity that will make God change his mind. For God justified you with (so to speak) his eyes open. He knew the worst about you at the time when he accepted you for Jesus' sake; and the verdict which he passed then was, and is, final.
>
> (J. I. Packer, *Knowing God*, Hodder & Stoughton, 2005, p. 310)

> Are you worried about judgement day? There is no need to be. We can be confident, not because of our own goodness and achievements but because Christ's sacrifice declares us righteous (Romans 3:22–24). It also guarantees that God will give us the same welcome he gave Christ. And as we grow in love and become more like Jesus, this is further assurance that we're saved – yet more reason to be confident as we approach that final day.

> In the meantime, keep coming to God for forgiveness, press on in love and obedience, becoming what you are – righteous in his sight.

Day 297

Read: 1 John 4:7–21
Key verse: 1 John 4:18

∙∙∙

There is no fear in love. But perfect love drives out fear, because fear has to do with punishment. The one who fears is not made perfect in love.

What is your biggest fear?

There is a right fear of God that we all ought to have. That is, treating him as God, as maker and sustainer of all, our Saviour and Sovereign to whom every one of us needs to give an account. But the fear John mentions here is linked to terror and punishment; it is a fear of what God might do to us. This type of fear has no place in Christian life because God's love drives it away.

When John describes God's love in this chapter, it's always in terms of the cross. God's love is no romantic gesture: it is practical and purposeful. So, 1 John 4:9–10 says:

This is how God showed his love among us: he sent his one and only Son into the world that we might live through him. This is love: not that we loved God, but that he loved us and sent his Son as an atoning sacrifice for our sins.

God demonstrates his love by sending Jesus to die for my sin and giving me eternal life. And, if I have eternal life, I don't need to fear eternal death. If my sins have been atoned for, I don't need to be terrified, even of a holy God. If I'm saved, I needn't be frightened about the day of judgement.

John is not asking us to believe that we're lovely enough for God. He's not even telling us that, if we love God enough, we can have confidence on that day. When John speaks of love, he's not thinking of our feelings at all but pointing us back to the cross. And when we look at the cross, we have assurance of eternal life.

Some of us are so conscious of our sins and shame that we almost refuse to believe that this confidence can be ours. But don't be more concerned about your sin than you are about God's love. Jesus says, 'Remain in my love' (John 15:9). Believe it and apply it to your heart each day, because this love was designed to give you confidence on the day of judgement.

> For God so loved the world that he gave his one and only Son, that whoever believes in him shall not perish but have eternal life. (John 3:16)
>
> Unless we're very intentional about meditating on these truths [that show God's love], they slip from our thoughts like misty dreams that evaporate in the morning light. That's why Luther said we must 'take heed then, to embrace . . . the love and kindness of God . . . [and] daily exercise [our] faith therein'.
> (Elyse M. Fitzpatrick, *Because He Loves Me*, Crossway, 2010, p. 36)
>
> Today, look to the cross and revel in God's love for you. Believe it, and stake your past, present and future on it. Let it banish your fear.

Day 298

Read: Revelation 1:4–8
Key verses: Revelation 1:5–6

. . . .

> [5] *To him who loves us and has freed us from our sins by his blood,* [6] *and has made us to be a kingdom and priests to serve his God and Father – to him be glory and power for ever and ever! Amen.*

Jesus loves you! Have you got that message by now?

John writes, 'To him who loves us' What a message for these first-century believers. Many who received this letter were slaves; they had no assurance of love; they could not look back to parents or family who loved them. They were flawed; they encountered difficulties. You only need to read Revelation 2–3 to realize that these were not model believers. And yet, despite all that, they, like us, could be confident of Jesus' love in all its glorious dimensions.

- *It is a costly love.* There is sacrifice at the heart of this love. It is not the love of a teacher who has marvellous ideas, although Jesus is the most superb teacher the world has ever known. It is not the love of someone who displays a glorious, morally upright example, although Jesus certainly did that. It is the love of someone who paid the greatest price ever, who demonstrated his love by giving himself to die in our place. The cross of Christ shows us not only the depravity of people but also the dignity of humankind. We are made in the image of God and, in the heart and mind of God, we are worth saving.

- *It is an unrequited love.* 'You have persevered and have endured hardships for my name . . . Yet I hold this against you: you have forsaken the love you had at first' (Revelation 2:3–4). Believers in Ephesus, like many of us, had understood the costly love of Christ and yet abandoned it. For all their many gifts, talents and skills, they had lost the thing that matters most of all.

- *It is a corrective love.* 'Those whom I love I rebuke and discipline' (Revelation 3:19). Jesus loves us enough to rebuke and chastise us. When you fail him, he still loves you and goes on loving you. He doesn't love you for the love he gets back, but because he can't help loving you; it is in his nature to love you. And he loves you so much that he corrects you.

Notice this love is in the present tense. It is not that he loved us once, at the cross, and demonstrated it by the shedding of his blood. No, he loves us today with the same love that drove him to Calvary. Although our love falters, his remains the same.

You can be confident of this: Jesus loves you. Nothing – no circumstances, no sin – can separate you from his love (Romans 8:38).

The gospel is this: We are more sinful and flawed in ourselves than we ever dared believe, yet at the very same time we are more loved and accepted in Jesus Christ than we ever dared hope. (Timothy Keller with Kathy Keller, *The Meaning of Marriage*, Hodder & Stoughton, 2011, p. 48)

Day 299

Read: Revelation 1:4–8
Key verses: Revelation 1:5–6

· ·

> ⁵*To him who loves us and has freed us from our sins by his blood,* ⁶*and has made us to be a kingdom and priests to serve his God and Father – to him be glory and power for ever and ever! Amen.*

Freedom!

We all want it, but not many of us experience it. In the first century, a number of people were captive as slaves; others were bound by traditions. Today, people still need liberating from a host of different tyrannies. And Christ is the only liberator. Even as believers, we frequently have to be reminded of the freedom we have in Christ.

In these opening chapters of Revelation, we see that the freedom Christ brings has both a negative and a positive element. Here in Revelation 1:5, it is freedom *from* our sins. The positive element comes in verse 6, which explains what we have been freed *for*: '[Christ] has made us to be a kingdom and priests to serve his God and Father – to him be glory and power for ever and ever! Amen.'

Revelation 5:9–10 portrays a similar scene. In his vision, John sees the living creatures and elders singing a new song to Christ:

> You are worthy to take the scroll
>   and to open its seals,
> because you were slain,
>   and with your blood you purchased for God
>   persons from every tribe and language and
>   people and nation.
> You have made them to be a kingdom and priests

to serve our God,
and they will reign on the earth.

We can be confident that Christ's work on the cross and mighty resurrection free us from the bondage to sin and guilt, from the things that held us captive in the past, from the habitual sins we struggle with, and from the sins we have committed today and will do tomorrow (Ephesians 1:7). But we can also be confident that we are redeemed for a purpose – 'for God'. He has made us 'a kingdom and priests'. There is an echo here of Exodus 19:6, when God brought the Israelites out of slavery in Egypt: 'you will be for me a kingdom of priests and a holy nation'. We are now members of a privileged kingdom. Our response must be to acknowledge the King's rule over every part of our lives – work, home, church and leisure. It doesn't stop there, for God has also made us priests to worship and serve him for the rest of our days. This is true freedom.

Today, live confidently in the freedom Christ has won for you – no longer shackled by the guilt of past sin, but choosing to obey God at every opportunity you get.

Since we're free in the freedom of God, can we do anything that comes to mind? Hardly. You know well enough from your own experience that there are some acts of so-called freedom that destroy freedom. Offer yourselves to sin, for instance, and it's your last free act. But offer yourselves to the ways of God and the freedom never quits. All your lives you've let sin tell you what to do. But thank God you've started listening to a new master, one whose commands set you free to live openly in *his* freedom! (Romans 6:17–18, MSG)

Day 300

Read: Revelation 2:8–11
Key verse: Revelation 2:8

....

To the angel of the church in Smyrna write:
These are the words of him who is the First and the Last, who
died and came to life again.

Have you received a personal letter recently? A hand-written envelope with a postage stamp?

It is much more significant than a generic email, isn't it? Perhaps unsurprisingly, Jesus' letters to the seven churches in Revelation 2–3 are personalized. In each, the designation or reference given to Christ is specifically appropriate to the situation of that church. Many of the phrases introducing Christ are borrowed from the earlier vision in Revelation 1.

When writing to Smyrna, the designation is: 'These are the words of him who is the First and the Last, who died and came to life again.' The phrase 'the First and the Last' is used of God himself in Isaiah 44:6. John uses it in Revelation 1:17, and also at the end of the book. Jesus, God's Son, is at the beginning and at the end. He is the Lord of life. Here (in Revelation 2:8), the tense of the verb refers to the moment of resurrection: 'he became dead and lived again'. The Christians in Smyrna would have listened attentively. They were living in a city that had been destroyed and rebuilt, that had died and been resurrected. And now death hung over them. So, the words of the One who had defeated death represented another great assurance, another great certainty in their Christian discipleship.

Similarly, our hope for the future is based on an event that has already happened. Usually, our hopes are to do with something that has not yet occurred. We look at possibilities and say, 'I hope it will be sunny tomorrow.' But there are no guarantees. Christian hope is radically different. It *will* be realized. It is totally certain. Why? Because it is based on an event that has already happened. We have hope because of the resurrection of Jesus Christ from the dead (1 Peter 1:3). Jesus died and sprang to life again; he is the First and the Last; he is the Lord of life – so we can be confident of death's defeat and of our resurrection.

'Everything will be all right in the end. If it's not all right, it's not the end' (Sonny, in the film *The Best Exotic Marigold Hotel*). Things were not all right for those suffering believers in Smyrna. But they, like us, can look forward with certainty to a day when everything will be all right – more than all right, absolutely perfect! Remember, we can be confident of our glorious future because Jesus defeated death, and his resurrection blazed the trail for us.

I am the resurrection and the life. The one who believes in me will live, even though they die.
(John 11:25)

I am the Living One; I was dead, and now look, I am alive for ever and ever! And I hold the keys of death and Hades.
(Revelation 1:18)

Day 301

Read: Revelation 2:8–11
Key verse: Revelation 2:9

....

*I know your afflictions and your poverty – yet you are rich! I
know about the slander of those who say they are Jews and are
not, but are a synagogue of Satan.*

'I know . . . '

Jesus knew all about these believers. He knew that they were
destitute. He knew that they were being slandered by members of
the Jewish synagogue following their conversion. He knew the
persecution, imprisonment and even death that members of this
small Christian community would face.

How did Jesus know? In John's vision (Revelation 1), we are told that
Jesus walks among the lampstands – among the churches. He is with
his people.

Down through the ages, God's people have testified to this truth.
Paul, in a Roman dungeon, cold, lonely, deserted and close to
martyrdom, stated, 'The Lord stood by my side and gave me strength'
(2 Timothy 4:17). The Puritan Richard Baxter (1615–1691) wrote a
hymn ('Lord, it belongs not to my care') that contains the line 'Christ
leads me through no darker rooms than he went through before'.
Betsie ten Boom, incarcerated in Ravensbrück concentration camp,
said to her sister Corrie, 'We must tell people . . . that there is no pit
so deep that he is not deeper still' (Corrie ten Boom with John and
Elizabeth Sherill, *The Hiding Place*, Hodder & Stoughton, 2004,
p. 202).

Today, we face demanding pressures and carry debilitating burdens.
The costs of discipleship are very real. So please don't miss the
comforting certainty of Christ's presence. What gives such pressure

its meaning is our vital connection with Jesus. We suffer in solidarity with Jesus, who took our sufferings upon himself.

The late Helen Roseveare was a medical missionary in the Democratic Republic of Congo. During the uprisings of the 1960s, she endured beatings, torture and rape. She told of one occasion when, as she was close to being executed, the Holy Spirit reminded her of her calling:

> Twenty years ago, you asked me for the privilege of being identified with me. This is it. Don't you want it? This is what it means. These are not your sufferings. All I ask of you is the loan of your body.

She was spared execution and later wrote:

> He didn't stop the sufferings. He didn't stop the wickedness, the cruelties, the humiliation or anything. It was all there. The pain was just as bad. The fear was just as bad. But it was altogether different. It was in Jesus, for him, with him.
> (Quoted in Philip Ryken, *The Message of Salvation*, IVP, 2001, p. 257)

The great certainty for those Christians in Smyrna, and for us, is that no matter what happens, the suffering and risen Christ is with us.

You are not alone. Through every trial, doubt and discouragement, God is with you. There is no situation too awful, no doubt too shocking, no failure too final to separate you from God. Lean on the truth of God's word:

> The LORD himself goes before you and will be with you; he will never leave you nor forsake you. Do not be afraid; do not be discouraged.
> (Deuteronomy 31:8)

Day 302

Read: Revelation 2:8–11
Key verse: Revelation 2:10

· ·

Do not be afraid of what you are about to suffer. I tell you, the devil will put some of you in prison to test you, and you will suffer persecution for ten days. Be faithful, even to the point of death, and I will give you life as your victor's crown.

Do you ever wonder why God allows you to suffer? Why you seem to be under such sustained attack?

Some believers live as if they are in a *Star Wars* adventure. They assume that they are surrounded by equal and opposite forces of good and evil. Neither good nor evil is quite strong enough, so they assign this part of life, or this event, exclusively to God and another part to the devil. It is almost as if there were two worlds of good and evil, with their lives swinging between the two. Other Christians believe that God is good, and whenever something evil enters their lives, God must remove it in response to the prayer of faith. If the evil doesn't disappear, it is because their faith is weak. Neither of these is a biblical perspective but, surprisingly, each is a common feature of supposed Christian spirituality.

It is clear from the New Testament that Christians experience satanic resistance. Twice in this short letter to the church in Smyrna, the risen Christ refers to Satan's work. In verse 9, Satan has inspired the actions of some Jews and, in verse 10, it is he who will put some of the Christians in prison. In verse 10, he is referred to as 'the devil', which means the accuser or slanderer, the 'father of lies' (John 8:44).

We can easily forget that there is a devil actively working against us, and that Christian discipleship is lived out in the context of a spiritual battle. But these verses make clear that this evil is not out of control. Notice that only some of the believers were put in prison, and the persecution was for a defined period. There were limits imposed. As in the story of Job, the situation was still under the Lord's oversight and care. We can be confident that nothing lies outside the scope of God's sovereignty and control, not even Satan. He can act only within the parameters that God has set.

No trouble, no hardship and no suffering can touch you, unless God, in his infinite wisdom, has allowed it. Imagine God sifting troubles through his hand like grains of sand. Some troubles he will keep from you, others he will allow into your life, with the express purpose of moulding you into the image of his Son. Today, be confident in God's good purposes for you.

I make known the end from the beginning,
    from ancient times, what is still to come.
I say, 'My purpose will stand,
    and I will do all that I please.'
(Isaiah 46:10)

Who can speak and have it happen
    if the Lord has not decreed it?
Is it not from the mouth of the Most High
    that both calamities and good things come?
(Lamentations 3:37–38)

Day 303

Read: Revelation 2:8–11
Key verses: Revelation 2:10–11

．．

[10]Do not be afraid of what you are about to suffer. I tell you, the devil will put some of you in prison to test you, and you will suffer persecution for ten days. Be faithful, even to the point of death, and I will give you life as your victor's crown.
[11]Whoever has ears, let them hear what the Spirit says to the churches. The one who is victorious will not be hurt at all by the second death.

Eighty and six years have I served him and he has done me no wrong. How then can I blaspheme my king who saved me?
(*Polycarp's Letter to the Philippians and His Martyrdom*, CreateSpace, 2016, p. 19)

These were the words of Polycarp, the leader of the small church in Smyrna, when he was commanded to hail Caesar as lord. Many years after John's letter had arrived, Polycarp was martyred, as Jesus had predicted in verse 10. Like countless others, he forfeited his reward in this life because of his confidence in something far better.

For him and for us, the promised reward is a 'crown of life' (verse 10, ESV). This is possibly the image of the crown of victory in the games or a laurel crown as a reward for service in the city. But it probably refers to the royal crown, the reward to faithful disciples who will rule with Christ.

And not only that, verse 11 assures us that the faithful disciple 'will not be hurt at all by the second death'. This phrase is used by John later in Revelation, which helps us to understand its meaning: 'Then death and Hades were thrown into the lake of fire. The lake of fire is the second death' (Revelation 20:14). The second death is by eternal judgement. It is the death after death. We will all die once, but the second death is an eternity separated from God. And for Christ's followers, this death will not touch us. It is an emphatic double negative in verse 11. There is no way you will ultimately be harmed. You are absolutely secure.

It is costly to be a disciple of Christ. As Paul and Barnabas reminded new believers, 'We must go through many hardships to enter the kingdom of God' (Acts 14:22). But troubles are not a dead end; rather, they are the gateway to life in all its fullness. So, 'Do not be afraid . . . Be faithful' (Revelation 2:10) because 'if we endure, we will also reign with him' (2 Timothy 2:12).

God is not oblivious to what it is costing you to follow him. He sees all your sacrifices, the acts of obedience no one else sees. Today, have confidence in his promise: one day you will be rewarded for your deeds of faith. You will receive a crown of life to lay at the feet of your Saviour whom you have loved and served.

Blessed is the one who perseveres under trial because, having stood the test, that person will receive the crown of life that the Lord has promised to those who love him.
(James 1:12)

Day 304

Read: Revelation 4:1–11

Key verses: Revelation 4:1–2

••

> ¹*After this I looked, and there before me was a door standing open in heaven. And the voice I had first heard speaking to me like a trumpet said, "Come up here, and I will show you what must take place after this."* ²*At once I was in the Spirit, and there before me was a throne in heaven with someone sitting on it.*

We know we need a physical health check once in a while, but have you had a spiritual check-up lately?

In Revelation 2 and 3, the Lord has been giving the church a spiritual check-up. There are lots of wonderful things to commend, but there are also some serious problems and challenges to address. The church is under attack; virtually all the seven churches are facing persecution. They are being invaded by false teachers, people who bring what the writer calls the deep teaching of Satan (Revelation 2:24). The spiritual decline within the churches is almost bordering on apostasy.

To the church in Sardis, God says, 'You have such a fantastic reputation! Everyone's talking about how alive you are. But it is only a reputation. You're spiritually dead.' To the church in Laodicea, he says, 'You are so compromised, you make me sick.' You can imagine the apostle John looking at the state of the church, hearing this word from the Lord and wondering, 'Has the church got a future?' And it is after these things that God takes John to heaven and shows him the great and glorious vision recorded in chapter four.

What is the point of this vision? To remind us that when the church is feeble and the world seems to have turned its back on God completely, the ultimate place of authority in the universe is the throne of God. And it is occupied. It has never been unoccupied. The word 'throne' is one of the key words in Revelation. It is used about sixty times in the New Testament, forty-seven of them in the book of Revelation and fourteen times in this chapter. The theme of this chapter and, indeed, the whole Bible is the absolute authority of the throne of God. We can be confident of this: when the church is in a state and things are going badly, God is still on the throne.

Father, our lives are broken. We're serving in difficult situations, and sometimes it feels as if the world is spinning out of control. It is so easy to become anxious, despondent and filled with doubt. Thank you that things are not as they appear. You are on the throne, high and exalted. You love us and are in control. Today, grant us peace in knowing you reign, faith that keeps our hearts focused on Christ, and hope because one day your authority will be gloriously on display and everyone will bow before you. Until that day, may our words and actions testify to Christ's rule in our lives and point others to the gospel. Amen.

For further study

If you would like to read more on the theme of confidence in Christ, you might find this selection of books helpful.

On the theme of assurance of salvation and our eternal destiny:

- Joel R. Beeke, *Knowing and Growing in Assurance of Faith* (Christian Focus, 2017)
- Ray Galea, *From Here to Eternity: Assurance in the face of sin and suffering* (Matthias Media, 2017)
- Greg Gilbert, *Assured: Discover grace, let go of guilt, and rest in your salvation* (Baker, 2019)

On the theme of confidence in God's love despite our failures:

- Matt Fuller, *Perfect Sinners: See yourself as God sees you* (The Good Book Company, 2017)

On the theme of confidence in God's sovereignty:

- Christopher Ash, *Where Was God When That Happened? And other questions about God's goodness, power and the way he works in the world* (The Good Book Company, 2017)
- Orlando Saer, *Big God: How to approach suffering, spread the gospel, make decisions and pray in the light of a God who really is in the driving seat of the world* (Christian Focus, 2014)

On the theme of dealing with doubt:

- John Stevens, *How Can I Be Sure? And other questions about doubt, assurance and the Bible* (The Good Book Company, 2014)

On the theme of confidence in the Scriptures:

- Daniel Strange and Michael Ovey, *Confident: Why we can trust the Bible* (Christian Focus, 2015)
- Lee Strobel, *The Case for Christ: A journalist's personal investigation of the evidence for Jesus* (Zondervan, 2016)
- Peter J. Williams, *Can We Trust the Gospels?* (Crossway, 2018)

Love

Contributors

Day 305

Read: Ruth 1:1–22
Key verses: Ruth 1:16–17

••

> ¹⁶ But Ruth replied, "Don't urge me to leave you or to turn back from you. Where you go I will go, and where you stay I will stay. Your people will be my people and your God my God. ¹⁷ Where you die I will die, and there I will be buried. May the LORD deal with me, be it ever so severely, if even death separates you and me."

What torpedoes love in our culture?

Capitalism, by its endorsement of self-interest, and the media, with their preoccupation with erotic images, have played a part. But the real problem is that, for the past fifty years, we have redefined the meaning of love. It is no longer a sacrificial commitment to another person. Love is now considered to be an intensity of feeling within us. This understanding is what makes Ruth, and the book that bears her name, such a candle in the darkness.

The events took place when the judges ruled: 'In those days Israel had no king; everyone did as they saw fit' (Judges 21:25). Society was utterly individualistic and hedonistic – just as it is today. The book of Ruth, even when it was written, would have been seen as very old fashioned because its message is that love is a sacrificial commitment; a laying down of your life for others. The book is about loyalty, duty and the cost that comes from putting the needs of others before your own. It demonstrates how God achieves his purpose in history through insignificant people who trust him enough to take the risks that sacrificial covenant love demands.

The story begins when Naomi and her family leave Bethlehem during a famine and go to Moab as economic refugees. Both her sons marry Moabite women but, sadly, her husband and sons die within a short period of time. Utterly destitute, Naomi plans to return to Bethlehem. Contrary to all good sense and her own best interest, Ruth, her widowed daughter-in-law, commits herself in love to Naomi. Rather than leave this old woman bereft, Ruth abandons her own country of Moab and her religion, and accompanies Naomi to Judah, the southern Israelite kingdom. In her speech, Ruth deliberately echoes the covenant vow (binding promises) of God to Israel in her own covenant vow to Naomi (Ruth 1:16). She declares her forever, come-what-may commitment to Naomi. This covenant relationship is what real love is about!

If Ruth had been interested only in self-fulfilment, she would have abandoned Naomi and gone in search of a husband among her own people. But she is determined to put loyalty to Naomi and Naomi's God first, whatever the sacrifice. Strikingly, Orpah, Naomi's other daughter-in-law, can't face such a cost and she returns to Moab. So two destitute widows, one a Moabite (considered an enemy of Israel), are heading straight for Bethlehem.

Ruth's sacrificial love for Naomi is a pale reflection of God's love and faithfulness to you. God has declared his forever, come-what-may commitment at the cross. There is nothing you can do to make God love you any more and no sin you can commit that would make him love you any less. Jesus laid down his life to save you – that is how loved you are!

Day 306

Read: Ruth 3:1–18
Key verses: Ruth 3:8–9

....

> [8]*In the middle of the night something startled the man; he turned – and there was a woman lying at his feet!*
> [9]*"Who are you?" he asked.*
> *"I am your servant Ruth," she said. "Spread the corner of your garment over me, since you are a guardian-redeemer of our family."*

It wouldn't rank very highly as a conventional (or romantic) marriage proposal.

Ruth had arrived in Bethlehem during harvest time and started gleaning in the fields to support herself and Naomi, which is what the homeless and the beggars did. She just happens to go to a field belonging to Boaz (2:3), who just happens to be a member of Naomi's family (2:20).

In the middle of the night, when the party to celebrate the harvest is over, Boaz wakes from sleep on the threshing floor to discover Ruth lying at his feet (3:8). She says to him, 'Spread the corner of your garment over me' (3:9), which means in essence, 'Marry me!'

When Boaz first met Ruth, he was moved by her kindness to Naomi and prayed, 'May you be richly rewarded by the LORD, the God of Israel, under whose wings you have come to take refuge' (2:12). Ruth is now saying, 'Just as you prayed that for me, Boaz, let me come under the protection of God's wings by coming under the protection of your garment!' The word translated 'corner of your garment' is the same word for 'wing'. In Ezekiel, God's spreading of the corner of his garment (that is, 'wing') is used of God when he makes a covenant with his people. Ruth is asking Boaz to be the answer to his own prayers. She's saying, 'Boaz, marry me, and please take care of my mother-in-law. I will not break my covenant and vows of love to her.'

Ruth's covenantal love and kindness to Naomi has impressed Boaz (3:10) but, more importantly, it transforms Naomi. This woman of faith has been devastated by family bereavements. She articulates the honest complaint of many believers who find themselves the innocent victims of God's judgement in a fallen world: 'The Lord has afflicted me' (1:21). But Naomi discovers that her cynicism is misplaced and she ends this story with her grandson, Ruth and Boaz's son, in her arms (4:16). What a joy!

How was Naomi's faith restored? By personally experiencing the human love and sacrificial service of Ruth. Her faith in the covenant love of God was restored because another human being demonstrated such love to her.

The kindness of God was real to Naomi because of the kindness of Ruth.

Have you come under the Redeemer's wing? Are you sheltering under the corner of his garment? If so, you are absolutely secure in God's covenant love in Christ. Today, thank him for the love he has lavished on you and consider to whom you will show that same covenant love. God calls us to love others with the love he has shown us. So who is your Naomi? What task has God asked you to do that will require you to lay down your life for the sake of others?

Day 307

Read: Ruth 4:1–22
Key verses: Ruth 4:5–6

· ·

⁵ Then Boaz said, "On the day you buy the land from Naomi, you also acquire Ruth the Moabite, the dead man's widow, in order to maintain the name of the dead with his property."
⁶ At this, the guardian-redeemer said, "Then I cannot redeem it because I might endanger my own estate. You redeem it yourself. I cannot do it."

What would you do for love?

Boaz is depicted as a servant-hearted, godly, self-sacrificing believer. He bore Ruth no resentment when she gleaned in his fields (2:8); he told his men not to harm her (2:9); he acknowledged and encouraged her godliness (2:12); and he sent her home with food (2:17). Naomi actually tells us that Boaz is famed for his kindness (2:20).

And now, just as Ruth was contrasted with her sister-in-law in chapter 1, Boaz is contrasted with another relative. This unnamed man wants the land that Naomi's husband, Elimelech, left when he went to Moab. He has first refusal and says that he will buy it. He ultimately shies away from covenant love, however, when he realizes that he'll have to support Ruth and Naomi, as well as provide an heir for Elimelech's family.

His excuse: 'I might endanger my own estate!' Never mind his duty to God's law or his responsibility to care for Elimelech's family, this man wants the land but not the widows. The same reasoning stops us caring. We think, 'I can't risk this sort of sacrifice and self-giving. What about me, what about my resources and what about my own boundaries?' This man walks away from Naomi and, in doing so, walks away from his duty, his calling. But Boaz does the right thing. He buys the field and takes on the care of Ruth and Naomi, too.

The big picture is that covenant love is going to put Boaz and Ruth right into the middle of salvation history. Their child Obed was the grandfather of David, whose descendent was Christ (4:17)! But Boaz and Ruth couldn't see how God was sovereignly working his purposes out. All they could see was Naomi and the call to obedience and covenant love.

This story is designed to deprogramme us from our selfish, individualistic, therapeutic attitudes towards love, a love that is about an intensity of feeling, rather than a sacrificial commitment to another person. The message was needed in the time of the judges and it is needed today. It's a story that is meant to encourage us; if we really want to know what love means, in its fullest and richest form, then we must be willing for commitment and sacrifice as the price of love, for we live in the shadow of Calvary.

Many times each day we face a choice: to be like the unnamed relative and preserve our resources and boundaries or be like Boaz and love sacrificially. Such love is costly, especially when our circumstances are difficult and God's purposes are hidden. But we mustn't stop loving. We must keep on laying down our lives. Our obedience reflects God's love, delights his heart and is being used by him in ways we could never imagine to work out his sovereign plan.

Day 308

Read: Hosea 10:1–11:11

Key verses: Hosea 11:1–2

....

¹When Israel was a child, I loved him,
and out of Egypt I called my son.
²But the more they were called,
the more they went away from me.
They sacrificed to the Baals
and they burned incense to images.

Most parents capture those early memories of a baby's first steps or first spoonful of solid food. In Hosea 10–11, it's as if God were taking out his photo album and poignantly remembering how Israel used to be before its fall from grace. He gives three snapshots, each designed to remind Israel of the great start it had in life.

The fruitful vine (10:1–8). God has planted and taken great care of the vineyard and the vine is heavy with luscious, ripe grapes. But, perversely, instead of giving God glory for all the prosperity that he has showered upon them, the Israelites turn from him and worship other gods. In fact, the more God blesses them, the more they praise the Baals, the fertility gods of the Canaanites, as if the Baals had provided their prosperity.

A prize cow (10:9–15). This young cow is well-trained, in prime condition and already loves to thresh (verse 11). God, as it were, brings this cow home, places a yoke upon her neck and starts her ploughing. The picture speaks of the early promise of Israel, chosen by God to do his work (verse 12). But instead of being willing to be used in God's service, growing the crop of holiness, Israel plants wickedness and reaps evil (verse 13). Such promise ends in tragedy.

A beloved child (11:1–11). The images have steadily become more intimate. We've moved from horticulture to the farmyard, and now we're in the family. The child, Israel, is so precious in the sight of God. God redeemed Israel out of slavery in Egypt to be his son. However, the fatherhood of God is not presented here to comfort Israel but to confront her with the awfulness of her sin (verse 2).

To underline the full horror of what they're doing, God takes out of the album a photograph that every parent treasures: an infant taking his first steps (verse 3). The child falls and hurts his knee; Dad picks him up and kisses it better. God says, 'I did that for you. You don't realize it was I who healed you.' The final photograph is of the child in his high chair. Dad is leaning down, feeding him and beaming again with pride and devotion (verse 4). It's a picture of divine love. And yet it's a love that has been spurned. We tend to think of sin in impersonal terms – as breaking certain laws and standards – but God, through Hosea, reminds us that sin is intensely personal. When Christians sin, we are spurning our divine Father. Sin is serious. It matters.

Your sin is not just a harmless outburst of anger or bout of selfishness; it's not just a quick glance at a web page or idle gossip. It's a spurning of God's love. Today, in your fight to resist sin, meditate on the immense privileges that you have: God has blessed you abundantly, chosen you to serve him and adopted you into his family. You are able to call the living God 'my Father'. You are precious to him.

Day 309

Read: Hosea 10:1–11:11
Key verse: Hosea 11:8

••

> [8] *How can I give you up, Ephraim?*
>   *How can I hand you over, Israel?*
> *How can I treat you like Admah?*
>   *How can I make you like Zeboyim?*
> *My heart is changed within me;*
>   *all my compassion is aroused.*

Do you really believe that God loves you?

We know how wicked we've been and the judgement we deserve, so believing that God loves us is often a hard truth to accept.

The book of Hosea is dominated by the themes of sin and judgement, and that message is underlined by powerful pictures of God as husband and father. Just like Hosea, who takes Gomer back, despite all that she has done, God can't switch off his love for his bride or, to use the image of chapter 11, his love for his child.

God is all churned up inside. On the one hand, he must judge the people (10:2, 13; 11:5). He made it clear before they entered the land that if they disobeyed him, they would be evicted. But on the other hand, he can't abandon them. Before they entered the land, God had promised Abraham: 'I will make you into a great nation, and I will bless you . . . all peoples on earth will be blessed through you' (Genesis 12:2–3). This is the great tension throughout the Old Testament. How can God meet the demands of his justice and, at the same time, the demands of his love? How can God be faithful to his covenant promises of love and remain just at the same time?

That tension is finally resolved only in Christ. Judgement came in 722 BC, when the Assyrians destroyed the nation of Israel. But that was not the end. Seven hundred years later, a baby boy was born in Bethlehem and taken by his parents to Egypt to protect him from Herod. Then he returned; Matthew quotes Hosea 11:1, 'And so was fulfilled what the Lord had said through the prophet: "Out of Egypt I called my son"' (Matthew 2:15). You see, Israel had blown it. They'd disobeyed God. They had to face his judgement. But then came the Lord Jesus Christ.

He was the 'true vine' (John 15:1). He was Israel as Israel should have been, the perfect son of God who always lived in obedience to his Father. Therefore, he didn't deserve to face the judgement that came upon Old Testament Israel. Yet willingly, in his infinite mercy and grace, he took the judgement that God's people deserved so that all who trust in him can become like Israel: God's son; forgiven and blessed.

The lion is roaring lovingly (Hosea 11:10), calling us back from Egypt, Assyria and wherever the nation has been scattered. Christ is inviting all people, Jews and Gentiles, to join God's Israel, his holy people, that we might know God as our Father. The exile is over and he's calling us back home.

Today, praise God that, because Jesus was the perfect Son, we can know God as Father. His obedience on the cross means that God does not look on us in judgement and anger but says, 'I love you; I sent my Son to die for you. You can call me "Father". I forgive you; I accept you. Come home.'

Day 310

Read: Matthew 5:43–48
Key verses: Matthew 5:43–44

....

> [43]*You have heard that it was said, "Love your neighbour and hate your enemy." * [44]*But I tell you, love your enemies and pray for those who persecute you.*

'Love your enemies' is a phrase known by people who would never darken the door of a church. It is one of the most quoted sayings of the early church and at the very heart of the Sermon on the Mount. At the core of the Christian ethic, we are called to love people as God loves them, without discrimination.

This call to love enemies is difficult to hear. Around the world believers are tortured and even killed for their faith. Many Christians have been wounded by toxic church battles and have faced discrimination in the workplace, and some are experiencing domestic abuse[3]. Loving enemies was no easier for first-century believers who lived with the brutal reality of Roman occupation.

Jesus' words were in stark contrast to the 'love your neighbour and hate your enemy' maxim invented by religious leaders to ease the burden of the law. The legal retribution of 'an eye for an eye' was transformed by Jesus' new initiative: 'do not resist an evil person' (see Matthew 5:38–42). If you're taken to court unjustly by someone who wants to shame you and he takes your coat, give him your shirt as well. As you stand almost naked, you will not be the shamed one, that person will be. If you meet a Roman soldier, who by law, was allowed to make you carry his backpack for a mile, carry it a second

---

3. Please understand that you are not required to remain in a dangerous home environment. If reading these verses causes you distress or confusion, seek the support of a trusted group of Christian friends to help you to understand how these verses might relate to you personally.

mile. This will leave the Roman soldier, one of the hated enemies, totally amazed.

How can anyone obey this seemingly impossible command? When Jesus tells us to 'love' our enemies, he uses the word *agape*. There are other Greek words that imply there is something attractive or desirable in the object of love, but to have *agape* is to love without reason. It is the love that can be born only by the power of the Holy Spirit. C. S. Lewis says that we shouldn't spend time pondering whether we love an enemy, we should behave as if we do, so that we 'will presently come to love him' (*Mere Christianity*, Collins, 2012, p. 131). That's what Jesus is saying. He knew that love could begin only when we pray for an enemy. Prayer is the action that moves the will. Don't wait to feel love in your heart; pray for God's power to bless a persecutor and forgive an enemy.

> 'When [God] tells us to love our enemies he gives, along with the command, the love itself.'
> (Corrie ten Boom, a prisoner at Ravensbrück concentration camp, from *The Hiding Place*, Hodder & Stoughton, 2004, p. 221)

Day 311

Read: Matthew 5:43–48
Key verses: Matthew 5:44–47

. . . .

[44]But I tell you, love your enemies and pray for those who persecute you, [45]that you may be children of your Father in heaven. He causes his sun to rise on the evil and the good, and sends rain on the righteous and the unrighteous. [46]If you love those who love you, what reward will you get? Are not even the tax collectors doing that? [47]And if you greet only your own people, what are you doing more than others? Do not even pagans do that?

Why should we love our enemies? Because it's Godlike.

We prove that we're children of our heavenly Father by displaying the family likeness. God loves without discrimination, and when we love like this, we share his character. He sends rain on evil people and good people, on the righteous and unrighteous. God is generous even to the morally undeserving. His sun and rain are a sign of his common grace, and they are intended to draw people to his saving grace in Jesus Christ.

Your own story proves that God loves without discrimination. While you were God's enemy, he died for you. He cleansed you of your sins, adopted you into his family and commissioned you to be an ambassador of the good news. Each follower of Jesus, saved by grace, is a living testimony that an enemy can be transformed into a friend and become part of God's family.

But Jesus doesn't stop there. We are to love our enemies, not just because it's Godlike but also because we are called to a life of 'more than' (verse 47). Jesus asks, 'What are you doing *more than* tax collectors who love their friends?' His point is that even cheats and swindlers have friends. They enjoy loving relationships, good marriages and are generous with their money. Jesus is saying, 'I want "more than" in my disciples.' There is nothing exceptional about loving your own kind and greeting your own friends. What is exceptional is loving your enemy and praying for those who persecute you. The world is crying out for examples of that kind of discipleship.

Is the way you love demonstrably different from your non-Christian friends? Are you living a 'more than' kind of life? This may mean:

- forgiving a Christian who has hurt you;
- praying and doing good to family members or work colleagues who ridicule your faith;
- finding ways to serve and share the gospel with people in your city who have backgrounds different from yours;
- intentionally praying for political and social groups that have an anti-Christian agenda;
- showing hospitality in your home and befriending those in church who are not 'your own people';
- being kind and respectful on social media to those who disagree with you.

Pray for God's help to share his character and live a 'more than' kind of life that draws Christians and non-Christians to him.

Day 312

Read: Matthew 5:43–48
Key verses: Matthew 5:43–45, 48

● ●

> [43]*You have heard that it was said, "Love your neighbour and hate your enemy."* [44]*But I tell you, love your enemies and pray for those who persecute you,* [45]*that you may be children of your Father in heaven . . .* [48]*Be perfect, therefore, as your heavenly Father is perfect.*

When our feelings have been hurt, the urge to get even is powerful and, in the spirit of retaliation, almost anything is excused in our culture. But God calls us to live radically different lives.

We are to love our enemies because we are called to be perfect (see Day 311 for the other reasons Jesus gives for loving our enemies). Jesus doesn't mean perfect in the sense of sinless perfection. According to the Sermon on the Mount, we can't have perfect lives without sin on earth. How could we if Jesus taught us to pray in the Lord's Prayer 'forgive us our debts [sins]' (Matthew 6:12; see Luke 11:4)?

Perfection, total life with God, will be ours in the new heaven and the new earth. Meanwhile, the command to be perfect is a call to maturity, to completeness and to wholeness. It means a life entirely at one with the will of God – a longing to fulfil the family likeness and reflect it in our living; a desire to love without discrimination.

How can we be perfect like this? How can we love our enemies and pray for those who persecute us? We look to Jesus on the cross, who, when he was mocked by his enemies, didn't retaliate. When his enemies beat him, he took the pain. When his enemies nailed him to the cross, he prayed for them: 'Father, forgive them, for they do not know what they are doing' (Luke 23:34). After Jesus died, the people on Golgotha, who had come to witness the crucifixion, 'beat their breasts and went away' (Luke 23:48). Would they have done this if Jesus hadn't prayed for them? Was it not this prayer for the enemy that distressed them? He could have cursed them. He could have threatened them. He could have called down his judgement on them. But he prayed for his enemies.

What is God's will for my life? In Matthew 5, God makes his will clear and it is a comprehensive, for-all-time command. Like God, we are to be perfect, reflecting his likeness by loving our enemies and praying for those who persecute us. In the light of this, whom do you need to love and pray for today? Draw strength and encouragement from the example of Christ on the cross. 'In your relationships with one another, have the same mindset as Christ Jesus' (Philippians 2:5).

Day 313

Read: Mark 12:28–34
Key verse: Mark 12:28

....

> [28] *One of the teachers of the law came and heard them debating. Noticing that Jesus had given them a good answer, he asked him, "Of all the commandments, which is the most important?"*

You would be forgiven for thinking that this was a simple question.

In fact, it was a massive contemporary debate. The Jewish rabbis had identified 613 commands in the Torah, the first five books of the Old Testament. The Mishnah, the written collection of the Jewish oral tradition, says that charity and deeds of kindness outweigh all the other commandments. Midrash (Jewish commentary) on the book of Haggai concludes that purity and temple service – sacrifices, rituals and offerings – are what count as Torah.

What does Jesus reply? He cites the Shema (Deuteronomy 6:4–5). Every good Jew prayed the Shema every day, 'Love the LORD your God with all your heart and with all your soul and with all your strength,' but Jesus adds, 'Love your neighbour as yourself,' a statement from Leviticus 19:18 encapsulating a whole list of laws. Jesus' summary of the whole law is love God; love neighbour.

Moses received the Ten Commandments on two tablets. The first tablet was concerned with a right relationship with God – don't make idols, don't blaspheme, observe the Sabbath. Tablet two was about right treatment of your neighbour: not murdering, stealing, coveting, lying or committing adultery. In Mark 12, Jesus is saying, 'Here's a summary of the two tablets. Tablet one: love God; tablet two: love your neighbour. They are inextricably and intrinsically bound together.' If you love God but fail to care for your neighbour, you don't really love God at all. If you love your neighbour and do acts of philanthropy and kindness but don't have a relationship with God, you're not loving your neighbour properly either.

In his magnum opus, *The City of God*, Augustine, a fifth-century North African bishop, asked, 'Is it OK to love yourself? Is it Christian?' You can't help loving yourself because it is natural simply to seek your own highest well-being, goodness, joy, satisfaction and happiness. Augustine concluded it was a good thing but added that you find the greatest satisfaction and your highest well-being as a creature in relationship to your Creator. So to love your neighbour as yourself means to seek the same thing for him or her. Augustine argued that you can't separate these two commands. You can't be a pious individual who hates your neighbour because you're not really loving God. And you can't love your neighbour without helping that person to find reconciliation with his or her Maker. You don't really love your neighbour if you don't love God.

'Which is the most important commandment?' Jesus' answer is that it's love. Having love for God and love for your neighbour is the way you fulfil the law.

Does your behaviour reflect the fact that love is the most important commandment? We believe God and we serve him, but do we really love him? At work or at home, are we known for our love? Without love, we accomplish nothing (see 1 Corinthians 13:1–3). Today, take time to delight in God, valuing him above all else and, in your interactions with others, make love the priority.

Day 314

Read: Mark 12:28–34
Key verse: Mark 12:30

....

³⁰Love the Lord your God with all your heart and with all your soul and with all your mind and with all your strength.

Do you love God with all your heart and soul?

I suspect that our culture's understanding of the heart and the Bible's understanding are different things. When the Bible uses the word 'heart', it's not talking about our emotions, moods or the tingly feeling that occurs when boy meets girl. In the Bible, the heart is the seat of the will; it's the decision-making centre. It's not a *feeling* towards something or someone; it's a *decision* towards something or someone. It's an act of the will with regard to the other person.

This is significant because if love were just a feeling, it would come and go. Jesus is saying that to love the Lord with all your heart is a *decision*. That means you don't just go to church when you feel like going to church. You don't just keep up your personal devotions when you're in the mood and you feel close to God. No. You *decide* that you will love God through thick and thin, not just when it feels good. Our culture says feelings lead to actions and, in some cases, that's true. The Bible says it's the other way round – we have to decide to love God and then the feelings and the emotions follow.

The second thing Jesus says is that you must 'love the Lord your God with all your soul'. In the Hebrew of Deuteronomy 6, the word *nephesh*, translated 'soul', actually means 'life'; it doesn't mean 'soul' at all. 'Soul' is not a particularly helpful translation for Western twenty-first-century people because we think of something immaterial and ghostly. We have this strict division between body and soul. Hebrew thought doesn't have that, so when it says, 'Love your God with all your *nephesh*', it means love God with all your life, with every fibre of your being and existence, every moment of every day. Nothing is off-limits to God. There's no part of your life that you can rope off, put a 'no entry' sign over and say, 'God, I love you but you just can't come here. Don't challenge me on this. It's private property.' To love God with all your soul means with every part of you; every bit of your life and existence is God's property and is for his glory.

Is there a relationship, hobby or possession that you have made 'off-limits' to God? Heed the Spirit's call and, in his strength, surrender this area of your life to God. But don't stop there. Loving God with all your heart and soul is not about a spectacular, one-off display of obedience but daily surrender in the routine of life, over years and decades – it is a 'long obedience in the same direction' (see Eugene Peterson, *Long Obedience in the Same Direction*, IVP, 2021). Pray: 'God, I want nothing to be off-limits to you. Whatever comes across my path today, help me to love you with all that I am and with all that I have. For your glory. Amen.'

Day 315

Read: Mark 12:28–34
Key verse: Mark 12:30

....

> *³⁰Love the Lord your God with all your heart and with all your soul and with all your mind and with all your strength.*

Are you loving God with all your mind and strength?

Interestingly, 'mind' isn't mentioned in Deuteronomy 6:5. The Hebrew of Deuteronomy 6 calls us to love God with all our heart, soul and strength. In the Greek translations of the Hebrew, you get a couple of variations in the translation of the last word, 'strength': some say 'strength' and others, 'mind'. I think Jesus is saying that both these traditions capture something of the essence of Deuteronomy 6, which is why I presume he pulls them together and turns the command into a fourfold, instead of a three-fold, one.

Loving God with your mind isn't theological study for study's sake; it's about getting to know a person. You can't love someone you don't have a personal relationship with. In the Bible, knowledge is never an abstract, cognitive thing. The Hebrew verb for 'know' connotes the intimate personal knowledge between a man and a wife. If you want to love God, you have to grow in your knowledge of him, which means daily reading, studying and meditating on the Bible.

The final element of this fourfold command is 'love the Lord your God . . . with all your strength'. Love God with all your power and energy. Love is not a feeling; it's an action. It's a verb. The Targum is the Jewish translation of the Hebrew Scriptures into the lingua franca of the day, which was Aramaic. It's fascinating that the Targum translates the word 'strength' in Deuteronomy 6 into the Aramaic word *mamona*: mammon – money or possessions. Jewish scholars looked at this word 'strength' and understood it to mean not so much physical strength and energy as resources.

The command is to 'love the Lord your God with all your heart . . . with all your soul . . . with all your mind and with all your *stuff*': to love God not only with every fibre of your existence but also with everything he has given you. Everything we have is a gift from God to be richly enjoyed and that includes loving God with our *things* – our possessions, time, talents and treasures.

The way we study the Bible, open our homes, share our meals, spend our money and use our time reveal the depth of our love for God. Most of us need to release our grasp on what we have, remembering that it is God's 'stuff', not ours, as Randy Alcorn discovered:

> If God was the owner, I was the manager. I needed to adopt a steward's mentality toward the assets He had entrusted – not given – to me. A steward manages assets for the owner's benefit. The steward carries no sense of entitlement to the assets he manages. It's his job to find out what the owner wants done with his assets, then carry out his will.
>
> (Randy Alcorn, *The Treasure Principle*, Multnomah, 2017, p. 26)

Day 316

Read: Mark 12:28–34
Key verses: Mark 12:29–31

....

> [29] "The most important [commandment]," answered Jesus, "is this: "Hear, O Israel: the Lord our God, the Lord is one. [30] Love the Lord your God with all your heart and with all your soul and with all your mind and with all your strength." [31] The second is this: "Love your neighbour as yourself." There is no commandment greater than these."

What is the relationship between loving God and loving your neighbour?

In the Promised Land, Moses taught the people to observe God's laws carefully:

> For this will show your wisdom and understanding to the nations, who will hear about all these decrees and say, 'Surely this great nation is a wise and understanding people.' What other nation is so great as to have their gods near them the way the Lord our God is near us whenever we pray to him? And what other nation is so great as to have such righteous decrees and laws as this body of laws I am setting before you today?
> (Deuteronomy 4:6–8)

Moses is saying to the Israelites, 'If you obey this law, then the nations will see something about your lives, your ethics, your love for God, and it will captivate, compel and convict them.'

This idea in Deuteronomy 4 and Mark 12 is that our love for God is itself a witness. There is something proclamatory about our lives lived in front of neighbours, colleagues, unbelieving family and a watching community. And our witness is not just as individuals but also as a church when we feed the poor, provide debt counselling and get involved with groups for abused women or those struggling with addiction. As we love a community, they see something of a love for God and a love for neighbour, and it captivates them.

Lesslie Newbigin, a well-known writer on mission in the twentieth century, described the church as the plausibility structure for the gospel. If you say, 'God loves you,' and you don't live it out, you undermine the message. But church members who genuinely love God, one another and their community provide a plausibility structure for the message of a God who loves a broken world.

This is profoundly challenging. We say we want our churches to grow and people to become Christians but, at the same time, we want church to stay the same, be a size in which we all know one another. We profess to love the world but, truthfully, we like life to remain small, safe, secure and personal, and we'd rather our churches were like members' clubs. But that's not the raison d'être of the church; that's not why we're still here. We are here because there's a world in desperate need of the grace and love of God.

> The primary reality of which we have to take account in seeking for a Christian impact on public life is the Christian congregation. How is it possible that the gospel should be credible, that people should come to believe that the power which has the last word in human affairs is represented by a man hanging on a cross? . . . The only answer, the only hermeneutic of the gospel, is a congregation of men and women who believe it and live by it.
> (Lesslie Newbigin, quoted in Michael W. Goheen, *The Church and Its Vocation*, Baker Academic, 2018, p. 81)

Day 317

Read: Mark 12:28–34
Key verses: Mark 12:32–34

. . . .

> ³² *"Well said, teacher," the man replied. "You are right in saying that God is one and there is no other but him.* ³³ *To love him with all your heart, with all your understanding and with all your strength, and to love your neighbour as yourself is more important than all burnt offerings and sacrifices."*
>
> ³⁴ *When Jesus saw that he had answered wisely, he said to him, "You are not far from the kingdom of God." And from then on no one dared ask him any more questions.*

Can you feel the tension?

The religious leaders are looking for a way to arrest and kill Jesus (Mark 12:12), so they ask him questions in the temple to try to catch him out. Up to this point, Jesus' answers rebuke the rabbis but this one ends with a commendation. The man speaking understands that faith and grace lead to actions, and that a real relationship with God is more important than burnt offerings. So Jesus replies, 'You are not far from the kingdom of God.' There is a word of commendation for this religious leader, but it's also a bit of a slap.

This man would have studied for thirty years to be a rabbi. He knows his Bible far better than we do; he's probably got students of his own. And Jesus says, 'You're not far from the kingdom.' Can you imagine the crowd's response? If this guy can't get in, what hope is there for any of us? In some ways, that's the point. This greatest commandment should drive us to our knees as we realize how far we fall short of God's holy standards. God's standard of perfection – to love him with all our heart, soul, mind and strength and love our neighbours as ourselves – leaves us nothing to say but 'Lord, forgive me, I'm a great sinner in need of a great saviour'.

Where can we find forgiveness? Jesus. He is the only man who has ever kept the greatest commandment perfectly. He is the only one who has ever truly loved God his Father with all his heart, soul, mind and strength. He's the only one who has ever truly loved his neighbours as himself, laying down his life for them. Jesus lived the life that we should live but can't, and died the death that we deserve so that we can find forgiveness and reconciliation. He is the sacrificial substitute. He takes my sin and credits me with his perfect record of righteousness: the great divine exchange.

Does Jesus' death nullify the law? Jeremiah 31:33 says it's written on the heart. My obedience to the law now is not (and never was) to earn favour; it's a response to grace, to all that Jesus has done for me. God gives me his Holy Spirit and he writes his law on my heart, enabling me to live a life that, not perfectly but truly, shows love for God and neighbour.

Jesus is indeed a great and all-sufficient Saviour. He forgives our sin, gives us his righteousness and makes it possible to live a life of love. Thank God for Jesus, today.

Day 318

Read: John 13:1–38
Key verses: John 13:34–35

....

> ³⁴*A new command I give you: love one another. As I have loved you, so you must love one another.* ³⁵*By this everyone will know that you are my disciples, if you love one another.*

Final instructions are important.

Jesus' last command, recorded in John 13:34–35, leaves us in no doubt about the priority of love. He makes it clear that love is imperative, innovative and internal.

Imperative. 'Love one another' is not a word of advice or wishful thinking; it is a command. But can an emotion really be commanded? The Bible continually commands us to love (Deuteronomy 6:5; Matthew 22:37) because, in Scripture, an emotion is not an instinctive reaction that you can't control, shape or discipline. According to the Bible, emotions are an indication of what we truly believe and value. As Christians, we love things that are good rather than things that are worthless. So Scripture can command us to love because love isn't just an unbridled, instinctive emotion; it is an aspect of our being that is linked to knowledge and that leads to action which we can consecrate to Christ. It's when we surrender our emotions that we begin to feel true affection for God.

Innovative. Leviticus 19:18 tells us to love our neighbour. So why does Jesus say that this is a new command? It is simply because he sets a new standard. We are to love one another not, in the Old Covenant way, as ourselves but, rather, as Jesus says to his disciples, 'As I have loved you.' Jesus is about to go to the cross, and this new commandment exhorts us not to love partially but as Jesus has loved us. The cross and resurrection will bring in a new era in God's salvation plan. Soon, Jesus will ascend, the Holy Spirit will be given and the age of the church will be launched. The old command is being repeated and intensified for the New Covenant era.

Internal. Elsewhere in the Bible we are told to love the world but, on this occasion, Jesus tells us to love those in the church. Sometimes it's easier to love the world than it is to love a fellow church member. The church is a diverse mix of ages, ethnicities, educational backgrounds, emotional intelligence and physical abilities. Our love is not optional or reserved for those who are like us. We cannot choose whom we want to love. We are to love without qualification.

William Temple, who was the Archbishop of Canterbury from 1942 to 1944, pointed out that this simple command is actually impossible. We don't have it within us. But then he added: 'Except so far as we are in Christ. He himself will make it possible for us' (William Temple, *Readings in St John's Gospel*, Macmillan, 1961, p. 215). Christ is inviting us to be a channel of his supernatural grace, flowing through us, into the lives of other people.

Heavenly Father, thank you that obedience is possible. Thank you that, because we belong to Christ and draw on his power, we can love other believers as he does – without reservation and without qualification. Help us to surrender our emotions to you and become channels of your grace, blessing the lives of others today. Amen.

Day 319

Read: John 13:1–38
Key verses: John 13:34–35

....

> ³⁴*A new command I give you: love one another. As I have loved you, so you must love one another.* ³⁵*By this everyone will know that you are my disciples, if you love one another.*

Whom do you measure yourself against?

When it comes to love, the person we are to compare ourselves to is Jesus. We are to love as he has loved. Jesus loved practically, selflessly, patiently and sacrificially.

Practically. The same night Jesus gave this command to his disciples, he took off his outer garments, picked up a basin and a towel and washed their feet (John 13:3–5). His love was down to earth, with 'sleeves rolled up'; it was practical.

Selflessly. Jesus didn't love just when it suited him but when he was caught off guard and at inconvenient moments. Think of the occasions when he slipped away from the crowds to get some rest and they followed him. He ministered to them and did some of his greatest miracles even in those trying circumstances. Or think of the times when he appeared to be focused on one agenda. Remember the Canaanite woman who asked for help (Matthew 15:21–28)? Jesus said he wasn't there for her; he'd come for the Israelites, but her persistent faith led him to change his agenda and serve her. We can slip into the professional 'I'll care' mode: the 'I'll love when I'm on duty, when I'm the Christian leader or when I'm working' mode. But Jesus loved selflessly.

Patiently. John 13 begins:

> It was just before the Passover Festival. Jesus knew that the hour had come for him to leave this world and go to the

Father. Having loved his own who were in the world, he loved them *to the end*.
(verse 1, emphasis added)

Likewise, Paul says that Christians are to be patient, 'bearing with one another in love . . . [and to] be kind and compassionate to one another, forgiving each other, just as in Christ God forgave you' (Ephesians 4:2, 32). We often judge people by standards that we don't apply to ourselves. Instead, we need to put ourselves in the other person's position and not give up loving too deeply or too soon.

> *Sacrificially.* The command comes as Jesus talks about his being 'glorified'. That's a code word in John's Gospel for being lifted up on the cross as if it were his coronation throne. Stripped of his clothes, battered, bruised and denied his human rights, Jesus is to be crucified. This was his moment of glorification. Like Jesus, we are called upon to love sacrificially – to open up our homes when it's inconvenient, to be available when we're tired, to spend money, time and self, laying down our lives for others.

That's what it takes to love as Jesus loved us.

> See how he loved him!
> (John 11:36)

The Jewish leaders' comment on how much Jesus loved Lazarus could apply to each one of us. We are so loved! Reflect on the infinite scope of God's love in Christ: the practical evidence of his daily care, his patience in forgiving our sins, his relentless compassion when we are weak and, most of all, his sacrificial death to save us.

Today, thank God for his love for you and ask for help to love like Jesus.

Day 320

Read: John 13:1–38
Key verses: John 13:34–35

....

34 A new command I give you: love one another. As I have loved you, so you must love one another. 35 By this everyone will know that you are my disciples, if you love one another.

What about loving the world?

Surely, we should look to do mission, not just maintenance ministry; we should be outward-looking rather than staying in our 'holy huddle', shouldn't we?

Yes! But unless we love those inside the church, we undermine the gospel message by the way we behave and relate to one another. Francis Schaeffer said that love is the 'final apologetic', the ultimate argument for the gospel (*The Mark of the Christian*, IVP, 1971, p. 13). Jesus has commissioned us to share the gospel, but if we talk without loving in true, practical, down-to-earth ways, then we'll never engage in a convincing mission. The early Christians were known by their love. The ancient Father of the Church, Tertullian, was able to write to his critics and say, '"See," they [those outside the church] say, "how these Christians love one another" (for they themselves hate one another); "and how they are ready to die for each other" (for they themselves are readier to kill each other)' (*Apologeticus*, ch. 39, sect. 7).

Jesus calls us to love not only because it's the final apologetic but also because it demonstrates the family likeness. Jesus says, 'If you love like this, everyone will know that you are *my* disciples.' This is how you'd expect the disciples of Jesus to live and behave. They wear the family uniform. The tragedy is that, so often, we wear a different uniform. In the name of Christ, we have incited people to hatred and violence, and we have engaged in false nationalism.

What about you? Do you love those in your church or have you been the cause of dissension and unhappiness? Are there people you've been avoiding? If you feel loving towards everyone in your church, are you showing it? The love of Jesus takes a meal to the family who is struggling and washes the car of the person under pressure; it rolls up its sleeves and gets stuck in.

The disciples weren't a worthy bunch; they were sinful and their backgrounds were messy. And yet Jesus loved them so much that he went to the cross for them. Today, as we share life with those in our church, an equally sinful and messy group (ourselves included), Jesus says to us what he said to his first disciples: 'As I have loved you, so you must love one another.' We are to love those in our local church with a Calvary love. When we do that, we are proof that the gospel is true. Be patient with one another, be kind, be forgiving and bear one another's burdens because people who don't know how much they need God are watching. Cause them to question and to wonder: 'See how these Christians love one another!' Amaze them with God's love in action and stir their hearts for more.

Day 321

Read: Colossians 3:12–14
Key verse: Colossians 3:12

....

Therefore, as God's chosen people, holy and dearly loved, clothe yourselves with compassion, kindness, humility, gentleness and patience.

One of the great surprises and disappointments of the Christian life is the discovery that other Christians can actually be quite difficult to get along with. It is a tough reality check to discover that relationships within the Christian family can be immensely challenging.

Of course, the reason is that we still have our old sinful nature and inclinations. None of us has reached complete godliness – we have our blind spots, flaws and failures. And if you take a group of saved but still sinful people and bring them together in community, there is going to be messiness and even occasional misery.

Paul knows this and in Colossians 3 he calls us to nurture God-honouring, life-giving Christian communities. In the opening verses of the chapter his focus was on what we need to stop doing to achieve this. Now Paul turns to the positives, what we must embrace and seek to do through God's strength if we are to be churches that flourish and enable the flourishing of each believer.

The first thing we must do in and through the power of the Holy Spirit is to love the people of Christ (verse 14).

But notice, the basis of our love is not the loveliness of each other, but rather the fact that we ourselves are 'chosen, holy and dearly loved' by God (verse 12). This challenge to love others is grounded in gospel truth. We who know Christ are God's chosen ones, upon whom he has set his saving love, not for any merit of our own, but because of his own boundless grace and unfathomable wisdom. We are holy, not because we have done good things, but because the Lord Jesus Christ has made us holy by his blood. He set us apart from the world to be God's own possession. We are loved of God, not because of anything lovely within us, but because God has poured out his saving love in Jesus upon us. God saw all our sin and failure from eternity past and yet, in love, determined that he would give his own Son to save us.

This good news of the gospel changes everything.

Are you waiting to be appreciated for your service in church before you love God's people? Are you waiting for your hurts to heal? The way other people love us cannot determine our love for them or we will never become the communities God designed us to be. Loving God's people is not a matter of doing more and trying harder, it is not about gritting your teeth or ignoring the painful experiences of the past. Loving God's church is only possible when we realize how very much we are loved by God. Let this gospel truth settle in your heart and mind today: You are 'chosen, holy and dearly loved'.

Day 322

Read: Colossians 3:12–14
Key verses: Colossians 3:12–13

....

Therefore, as God's chosen people, holy and dearly loved, clothe yourselves with compassion, kindness, humility, gentleness and patience. [13] *Bear with each other and forgive one another if any of you has a grievance against someone. Forgive as the Lord forgave you.*

We learn to love by being loved.

Paul's aim is to get us loving one another in the family of God. That is why he reminds us that we have been deeply and radically loved by God at extraordinary cost. Paul is very strategic; he knows it's hard to escape the call to love one another when we have been loved like this.

You and I are God's chosen, holy and beloved people. In Christ, God has given us a new character and a new power by his Spirit, and we are to put on that which he has given us. God wants us to put on compassion. We naturally focus on our own needs and hurts and overlook the heartache and needs of those around us. But the God to whom we belong looked down from heaven upon a sinful people and sent his son to die for them; he had compassion upon them because they were as sheep without a shepherd (Matthew 9:36).

Put on God's compassion and with that put on kindness, not harshness or judgementalism. Also, Paul says, put on humility rather than pride or a sense of self-sufficiency or self-accomplishment. Put on gentleness. Do not demand the spotlight but be ready to be of little account, to serve, and to deal carefully with others. Put on patience because that reflects the heart of God, who delays his judgements so that none should perish, bears with us in all our folly and sin and does not disown us when we deserve to be disowned.

Loving the family of God also means we are to bear with one another and even forgive one another. If we struggle to do this, Paul tells us to remember how much we have been forgiven. We have been shown so much grace and treated incalculably better than our sins deserve; to refuse to extend the same forgiveness to others is a denial of the gospel.

Today, and every day, we need to put on the gospel truth that is ours in Christ and behave as a redeemed people.

What will you wear today? God wants his people, by faith, to clothe themselves with the character of Christ. God has given you garments of grace to wear – they are yours because they are Christ's, and you belong to him – but you need to actively put them on. Today, in God's strength, determine to put on compassion and put off indifference; put on kindness and put off criticism; put on gentleness and put off abrasiveness; put on patience and put off irritability; put on forgiveness and put off resentment. Pray that as you clothe yourself in Christ, the truth of the gospel would be seen in you and work through you, for the glory of God.

Day 323

Read: Colossians 3:12–14
Key verse: Colossians 3:14

. . . .

And over all these virtues put on love, which binds them all together in perfect unity.

How do we hold together all the relational pieces that Paul has set out for us in verses 12–13? How can we always be practicing compassion, kindness, humility, patience, and forgiveness?

Paul says what holds all these virtues together is love: 'And over all these virtues put on love, which binds everything together in perfect unity' (verse 14). We do not naturally overflow with love toward others, especially those with whom we have differences or disagreements; those who have been difficult, frustrating or rude; those who have let us down and worse. But God is love. We know this because he sent his Son to die for our sins. We have experienced his love and now in Christ we are united to this God of love and his Spirit works within us to enable us to love. There is now a new fundamental reality that unites us together with other believers; together we are his chosen ones, his dearly beloved. We are brothers and sisters in Christ and the family relationship binds us together in an unbreakable way.

So, how are you getting on loving those in your church and showing compassion to those in need? How easy are you finding it to show kindness to them and interact with humility? How well are you able to be meek in a situation where other believers are failing to do the same? To what extent are you able to be patient when a brother or sister is sorely testing your patience? How easy are you finding it to bear with believers who are being difficult and to forgive those who have hurt you?

If we are honest, these things are not at all easy. Our challenge is to put on the characteristics that belong to God and that are ours in Christ. We are a chosen for no merit of our own, and so we learn humility toward one another and seek to bear with one another. We are a holy people, and so we seek to be godly in our behaviour toward one another. We are a beloved people, and so we put on love. We are a forgiven people and so we learned to forgive.

Imagine for a moment a church family where verses 12–14 were truly being lived out with perfect consistency. Just imagine what that kind of a church would be like. Wouldn't you love to be part of such a marvellous community?

How are you and your church doing as a Colossians 3:12–14 community? Where are you excelling in compassion, kindness, humility, gentleness, patience and forgiveness? Thank God for every evidence of these virtues. Pray for your home group, the people on the ministry rota with whom you serve, those who look after your children and grandchildren in the Sunday school, your church leaders – that with God's help you would live together as his chosen, holy, and loved people and daily put on love.

Day 324

Read: Romans 8:31–39
Key verses: Romans 8:32–34

. . . .

32 He who did not spare his own Son, but gave him up for us all – how will he not also, along with him, graciously give us all things? 33 Who will bring any charge against those whom God has chosen? It is God who justifies. 34 Who then is the one who condemns? No one. Christ Jesus who died – more than that, who was raised to life – is at the right hand of God and is also interceding for us.

Does God stop loving me when I sin?

When we're feeling wretched about a particular sin we've committed in the past or disappointed with ourselves for giving in to habitual sin, it is easy to imagine God metaphorically throwing up his hands in despair. Surely there must come a point when God looks at our sin and says, 'Enough is enough'?

Paul frames the question differently. He asks, 'Do you think the living God who sent his Son to die for you – that's the hard part if you like – will not finish the job and take you to be with him for ever?' (See verse 32.) God loves you. He will not let you go. Yes, we will fail. We will commit terrible sins, and there will be all sorts of accusers – the devil, individuals we have wronged, even our own consciences – but, however grievous our sins, the prosecution cannot win because God has already delivered the verdict: we are justified (see verse 33).

The moment we sin, we can imagine Satan accusing us before God. Then Jesus stands and speaks to God on our behalf (see verse 34). He says, 'Father, I died for their sin. I've dealt with it already. I faced your wrath; I faced the judgement.' If you are trusting in Christ today and believe Jesus died for your sin, then you can be sure that Jesus has dealt with it and you are clean before a holy God.

The moment we believe, God imputes Christ's perfect performance to us as if it were our own and adopts us into His family. In
other words, God can say to us just as He once said to Christ, 'You
are my Son, whom I love; with you I am well pleased.'
(Timothy Keller, *The Freedom of Self-Forgetfulness*, 2012,
10Publishing, p. 40)

Fallen, anxious sinners are limitless in their capacity to perceive
reasons for Jesus to cast them out. We are factories of fresh
resistances to Christ's love . . . [But we] cannot present a reason for
Christ to finally close off his heart to his own sheep. No such reason
exists. Every human friend has a limit. If we offend enough, if a relationship gets damaged enough, if we betray enough, we are cast
out. The walls go up. With Christ, our sins and weaknesses are the
very resumé items that qualify us to approach him. Nothing but
coming to him is required – first at conversion and then a thousand
times thereafter until we are with him upon death.
(Dane Ortlund, *Gentle and Lowly*, Crossway, 2020, pp. 63–64)

Day 325

Read: Romans 8:31–39

Key verses: Romans 8:35, 37

....

[35] *Who shall separate us from the love of Christ?*
Shall trouble or hardship or persecution or famine or nakedness
or danger or sword? . . . [37] *No, in all these things we are more*
than conquerors through him who loved us.

'If God really loved me, he wouldn't let me suffer like this!'

When our bodies are wracked with pain and our minds are flooded
with anxiety, depression or bitter disappointment, we may find
ourselves doubting God's love. But Paul is clear: just as our sins
cannot separate us from God's love (Day 324), neither can our
circumstances.

He asks, 'Who shall separate us from the love of Christ?' Then he lists
all sorts of possible candidates: trouble, hardship, persecution,
famine, nakedness, danger or sword (martyrdom). Why does Paul
ask these questions if he doesn't imagine that they could happen to
Christians? We can't have a naive spirituality that leads us to think, 'If
I'm really faithful to God, terrible things will never happen to me.'
Paul's point is that these things may happen. You might face every
one of them. Christians loved by God can face terrible suffering.

He quotes from the Old Testament: 'For your sake we face death all
day long; we are considered as sheep to be slaughtered' (verse 36).
Believers are crying out, 'We have been faithful to you, Lord, and it's
because of our faithfulness to you that we are suffering, that we are
like sheep to be slaughtered.' Suffering can happen not just because
of the general circumstances of living in a fallen world; it can happen
even because of our faithfulness to Jesus. Perhaps you are a pastor
desperately trying to preach Bible truth but your congregation or
people in the community don't like what they are hearing and want

to get rid of you. Perhaps you are being faithful to Christ at work; you stand up for him and colleagues are giving you the cold shoulder. Maybe you are the only Christian in your family and you feel alienated. These things can happen.

But, when suffering comes, it cannot separate us from the love of God in Christ. Paul says, '*In all these things* we are more than conquerors through him who loved us' (verse 37, emphasis added). Literally, we are super-conquerors, not by escaping the suffering but by being in it and going through it. No doubt we will be battered and bruised, physically and emotionally, but we will come through because all things, including our suffering, are leading us to glory.

Whatever your suffering – betrayal by a close friend, ill health, loss of a loved one, loneliness, miscarriage, abuse at work because of your faith – be assured of God's love for you:

'Though the mountains be shaken
and the hills be removed,
yet my unfailing love for you will not be shaken
nor my covenant of peace be removed,'
says the LORD, who has compassion on you.
(Isaiah 54:10)

Day 326

Read: Romans 8:31–39
Key verses: Romans 8:38–39

. . . .

> ³⁸ For I am convinced that neither death nor life, neither angels nor demons, neither the present nor the future, nor any powers, ³⁹ neither height nor depth, nor anything else in all creation, will be able to separate us from the love of God that is in Christ Jesus our Lord.

If sin and suffering can't separate us from God's love, can anything else?

Paul gives a comprehensive list to answer this question with a resounding no!

'Neither death nor life': death may separate us from one another but not from God, and life won't either, with all its eventualities. 'Neither angels nor demons': in other words, no spiritual forces will have sway in our lives; they are powerless before Christ. 'Neither the present nor the future': you may be going through a bad patch now – you are lonely, depressed and discouraged; you may not feel God's love but he is with you. What is your greatest fear as you face the future? Perhaps the loss of friends, family, job, reputation or your mind? All those things could happen. You could lose them all but, in Christ, you cannot lose God. 'Nor any powers', whether spiritual or temporal, can come between us and God. Oppressive regimes can deprive Christians of property and freedom, even our lives, but they cannot separate us from God's love. 'Neither height nor depth': we can go up to the moon or down to the bottom of the sea, or into a difficult non-Christian family situation or a secular workplace – it doesn't matter where we go because God is there. Then, just in case Paul has missed anything, there is a catch-all phrase: 'nor anything else in all creation'. Nothing 'will be able to separate us from the love of God that is in Christ Jesus'.

Other human beings may let us down, even the best of them. It's only in Christ that we find the eternal security we long for. And when he says, 'I will always love you,' he means it.

> The soul that on Jesus has leaned for repose,
> I will not, I will not, desert to its foes;
> that soul, though all hell should endeavour to shake,
> I'll never, no never, no never forsake!
> (Anon., 'How Firm a Foundation', 1787)
>
> Is it a small thing in your eyes to be loved by God – to be the son, the spouse, the love, the delight of the King of glory? Christian, believe this, and think about it: you will be eternally embraced in the arms of the love which was from everlasting, and will extend to everlasting – of the love which brought the Son of God's love from heaven to earth, from earth to the cross, from the cross to the grave, from the grave to glory – that love which was weary, hungry, tempted, scorned, scourged, buffeted, spat upon, crucified, pierced – which fasted, prayed, taught, healed, wept, sweated, bled, died. That love will eternally embrace you.
> (Richard Baxter, *The Practical Works of the Late Reverend and Pious Mr Richard Baxter*, 1707, vol. 3, p. 21)

Day 327

Read: 1 John 3:10–18
Key verses: 1 John 3:10–11

• •

¹⁰*This is how we know who the children of God are and who the children of the devil are: anyone who does not do what is right is not God's child, nor is anyone who does not love their brother and sister.*

¹¹*For this is the message you heard from the beginning: we should love one another.*

What is the evidence of genuine Christianity?

The New Testament repeatedly tells us that the two marks of authenticity are our faith in Jesus Christ and our love for God and other believers (Colossians 1:3–4; Ephesians 1:15; 1 Thessalonians 1:3).

If we are children of God, we cannot disguise who our Father is because our habitual behaviour towards one another will demonstrate it. It is the nature of God to love, so the centrepiece of the law, which reflects his nature, is this: 'Love the Lord your God with all your heart . . . Love your neighbour as yourself' (Matthew 22:37–39). It was the new commandment Jesus gave his disciples, and no one can come into a real personal relationship with a God who is love without being transformed into a loving person.

By contrast, Cain was characterized by hatred, like his father the evil one, and he murdered his brother (Genesis 4:1–8). The root of the problem was not just that Cain disliked his brother; there was also a moral battle, which Cain lost. Cain offered God his crops instead of a blood sacrifice, the means God had determined for entering into his presence. In that sense, Cain's actions were evil (1 John 3:12); he would not accept God's authority, which is why his sacrifice was rejected. John's point is that when individuals determine to go their own way, when they follow the evil one as their father, the result is always disintegration in one's personal life and, eventually, in society.

Cain hated Abel's obedience, so we shouldn't be surprised if the world hates obedient Christians, however much we seek to express God's love (verse 13). At one time we, too, followed the example of our father, the devil. But Christians have passed out of that sphere (verse 14). How can we be sure we belong to God's family? Because we love our brothers and sisters in Christ. We have one Father and we belong to one another because we belong to him. The mark of our new lives as believers is this love for one another.

It would be easier if the evidence of our new lives in Christ were marked by the worldly things we avoid or the church ministry we do. But 'from the beginning', love for one another has been the mark of those who belong to Christ. Love is not something that can be regulated or ticked off our 'to do' list; rather, it is the overflow of a life transformed by faith in God. It is no wonder that the refrain of the New Testament and God's message for us today is still to 'love all of God's family . . . Yet we urge you, brothers and sisters, to do so more and more' (1 Thessalonians 4:10).

Day 328

Read: 1 John 3:10–18
Key verses: 1 John 3:16–17

....

¹⁶*This is how we know what love is: Jesus Christ laid down his life for us. And we ought to lay down our lives for our brothers and sisters.* ¹⁷*If anyone has material possessions and sees a brother or sister in need but has no pity on them, how can the love of God be in that person?*

What you believe affects how you behave.

Cain's hatred of Abel led to murder. In fact, anyone who hates is a murderer; they share the same moral character, which is incompatible with being a child of God. The devil's family reveals its hatred by taking life. By stark contrast, divine love revealed its character when Jesus laid down his life for us on the cross. Love doesn't take another's life in thought or deed; it gives its own life so that others may live. As Jesus said, 'I am the good shepherd. The good shepherd lays down his life for the sheep' (John 10:11).

This love, not in word but in deed, is the sort of action that God looks for in his children. John links belief and behaviour together: the truth that Christ died for me inevitably leads to the outworking of that truth in love for my brothers and sisters (1 John 3:16). God's love was unique. We cannot die for one another so that we may be forgiven. But if that unique love has brought us to the point of true repentance and faith in Jesus, then the love we have begun to recognize will be reproduced in our lives. In Jesus, we see that love in perfection and, if faith is real love, it will not be beyond us. There will be evidence of its beginning to grow in our love for one another.

It may come as a shock how practical this love is. The proof of genuine Christianity is not just that I sing songs of praise but also that I am prepared to give without any thought of return, just as

Jesus gave; it's that I am prepared to give without first weighing up the worthiness of the person who receives. A love like this will have an impact on my diary, finances, possessions and energy. It is an attitude of mind that will result in specific, sacrificial action. God is love so the more we receive the life of God, the more that life will flood into us and overflow to others.

> Love calls you beyond the borders of your own wants, needs, and feelings . . . Love calls you to lay down your life in ways that are concrete and specific. Love calls you to serve, to wait, to give, to suffer, to forgive, and to do all these things again and again. Love calls you to be silent when you want to speak, and to speak when you would like to be silent . . . Love calls you to stop when you really want to continue, and it calls you to continue when you feel like stopping . . . Love again and again calls you away from your instincts and your comfort. Love always requires personal sacrifice. Love calls you to give up your life.
> (Paul David Tripp, *What Did You Expect?*, IVP, 2010, p. 188)

Day 329

Read: 1 John 3:11–24
Key verses: 1 John 3:19–20

••

> [19] *This is how we know that we belong to the truth and how we set our hearts at rest in his presence:* [20] *if our hearts condemn us, we know that God is greater than our hearts, and he knows everything.*

Do you feel guilty that you don't love other Christians enough? Do you look at the high standard God has for loving others and feel so inadequate that you wonder whether you are truly saved at all?

John is aware that genuine Christians' hearts often condemn them. We know our own inner motives and how often our love for our brothers and sisters falls far short of what it ought to be. There are individual believers whom we struggle to love.

But the hearts that condemn us can be set at rest in the presence of God. John doesn't deny the condemnation of our hearts but he encourages us to see that God knows more (verse 20). This doesn't mean that God overlooks our failures; he knows them better than we do. God also knows that the measure of love we do have is irrefutable evidence that we are truly saved, that we have crossed from death to life (verse 14). Yes, we are imperfect. Our hearts cry out for more consistent love but that doesn't destroy our assurance; it confirms it. It shows that we are children of God and that we have begun to love our brothers and sisters. The eighteenth-century Methodist preacher and evangelist John Wesley was said to frequently pray: 'Lord, cure me of my intermittent piety and make me thoroughly Christian.'

When we face the crisis of a condemning heart, our rest is found in the certain knowledge that we do belong to the truth. We can commit ourselves to a God who knows us far better than we know ourselves, and whose work of grace and love in our lives is not determined by our feelings but by his unchanging eternal purpose of faithfulness and love.

We often feel disappointed and ashamed that our love for others is so feeble. But God is not surprised and his love towards us is not determined by it:

> There is tremendous relief in knowing that his love to me is utterly realistic, based at every point on prior knowledge of the worst about me, so that no discovery now can disillusion him about me, in the way I am so often disillusioned about myself, and quench his determination to bless me.
>
> (J. I. Packer, *Knowing God*, Hodder & Stoughton, 2005, p. 45)

Today, trust God's Word and his knowledge of you. As you ask God for a more consistent love for him and for others, do not listen to your condemning heart or subjective feelings but find 'rest in [God's] presence', delighting in the truth that you belong to him.

Day 330

Read: 1 John 3:11–24
Key verses: 1 John 3:21–23

....

> [21] *Dear friends, if our hearts do not condemn us, we have confi-dence before God* [22] *and receive from him anything we ask, because we keep his commands and do what pleases him.* [23] *And this is his command: to believe in the name of his Son, Jesus Christ, and to love one another as he commanded us.*

Are you a confident Christian?

John's point is not that there are two types of Christians: those who are confident and approach God boldly, and those whose hearts condemn them for their lack of love. Rather, our condemning hearts find rest when we know that God loves us, although our love for him is weak and faint. When we realize that God's love for us doesn't depend on our love for him, there is a confidence (and a humility, too) in speaking to him face to face. Grasping how very much God loves us can transform our prayer lives.

The fact that God treats us like dearly loved children by answering our prayers is further evidence of his love for us (verse 22). We keep on receiving because we keep on asking in his will, and we do that because we keep on obeying him. Imagine our relationship with God as a spiral staircase: the more we let God's Word fill our minds, direct our wills and transform our affections, the more we please God, and the more we are sure of his love and are confident to approach him.

To increase our assurance of salvation even more, John coalesces all these commands one final time into one great statement: 'This is his command: to believe in the name of his Son, Jesus Christ, and to love one another as he commanded us' (verse 23). What does God want from us? Believing and loving. Belief here implies a definite,

once-and-for-all action in the past, but love is in the present continuous tense. Believing 'in the name of . . . Jesus' is more than just
believing in orthodox theology. It means believing in the person and
believing that Jesus has the power signified by his name, which
enables us to trust in him. To believe in the name of Jesus is to
believe in his nature and that he is God, the Son of God, the Saviour
and Lord. The natural outcome of that sort of believing is obedience
in loving others. And that daily, detailed obedience is an increasing
assurance of this life of Christ within by the power of the Holy Spirit
(verse 24).

Believing in Jesus and loving others – our confidence as believers
is inextricably linked to these two commands, which cannot be
uncoupled.

> You cannot truly love others unless you are convinced that God's
> love for you is unconditional, based solely on the merit of Christ,
> not on your performance. John said, 'We love because he first
> loved us' (1 John 4:19). Our love, either to God or to others, can
> only be a response to His love for us.
> (Jerry Bridges, *Transforming Grace*, NavPress, 1991, p. 132)

Day 331

Read: 1 John 4:7–21
Key verses: 1 John 4:8–12

. . . .

[8]Whoever does not love does not know God, because God is love. [9]This is how God showed his love among us: he sent his one and only Son into the world that we might live through him. [10]This is love: not that we loved God, but that he loved us and sent his Son as an atoning sacrifice for our sins. [11]Dear friends, since God so loved us, we also ought to love one another. [12]No one has ever seen God; but if we love one another, God lives in us and his love is made complete in us.

God is love – what a claim!

John isn't pointing to a quality that God possesses; he is making a statement about the essence of his being. This is one reason why God is revealed in Scripture as Trinity. At the very heart of God, there is a dynamic relationship of love. The Father loves the Son, the Son the Father and the Spirit the Son. To imagine that God does not love us is to deny his very nature. His love doesn't depend on our worthiness or even the response of those being loved; he loves us because he is love (see Deuteronomy 7:7–8).

The cross of Christ demonstrates the extent of God's love (1 John 4:9–10). He had only one Son whom he sent into a rebellious world to redeem and reconcile us to God. He sent him to die as a sacrifice that atones, which meant taking upon himself all the guilt of sinful men and women. It also meant carrying the wrath of God, until he quenched it in himself, so that we would not have to face it. This is love: a love that sacrifices, forgives, that goes deeper than sorrow, sin and death itself; a love that restores and reconciles.

The mark of the reality of Christ's love is seen in the transformed lives of his people (see verse 12). Once we begin to see the greatness of the love of God that Jesus showed by giving his life for us, we are motivated towards that sort of love. The world should be able to look at the church and say, 'I can't see God. I don't understand about his love, but when I see these Christians loving one another, I begin to understand.' The Word was made flesh once perfectly in Christ, but the invisible God has a body on this earth; his love is to be seen in that body, and to be content with anything else is to deny the gospel.

Today, meditate on and praise God for his love.

> To know that from eternity my Maker, foreseeing my sin, foreloved me and resolved to save me, though it would be at the cost of Calvary; to know that the divine Son was appointed from eternity to be my Saviour, and that in love he became man for me and died for me and now lives to intercede for me and will one day come in person to take me home; to know that the Lord 'who loved me and gave himself for me' . . . has by his Spirit raised me from spiritual death to life-giving union and communion with himself, and has promised to hold me fast and never let me go – this is knowledge that brings overwhelming gratitude and joy.
> (J. I. Packer, *Celebrating the Saving Work of God: Volume 1*, Regent College Publishing, 2008, pp. 158–159).

Day 332

Read: Revelation 2:1–7
Key verses: Revelation 2:3–4

....

^{3}*You have persevered and have endured hardships for my name, and have not grown weary.*
^{4}*Yet I hold this against you: you have forsaken the love you had at first.*

Have you forsaken your first love?

In about AD 62, Paul wrote to the church in Ephesus.

He prayed for the believers to know what it meant for Christ to be at home and living in their hearts by faith. He prayed for them to know, in their personal experience, the love of Christ, which surpasses all intellectual understanding.

> I pray that you, being rooted and established in love, may have power, together with all the Lord's holy people, to grasp how wide and long and high and deep is the love of Christ, and to know this love that surpasses knowledge – that you may be filled to the measure of all the fullness of God.
> (Ephesians 3:17–19)

He pleaded with them to live a life of love and set before them the standard: 'live a life of love, just as Christ loved us and gave himself up for us as a fragrant offering and sacrifice to God' (5:2).

More than thirty years had passed since that exhortation to 'live a life of love', and what do we find? In John's vision, the risen Lord commended the Ephesian believers for their service, good deeds and doctrinal purity, but his complaint was that they had 'forsaken the love they had at first'. Perhaps it happened so slowly that they failed to notice their drift away from loving God wholeheartedly. But the other commendations counted for nothing if there was no love.

Have you left your first love? Do you remember, when you were first converted, how thrilled you were to read your Bible? Do you remember going to church and drinking in what the preacher was saying? Do you remember how hurt you were when you discovered that Christians were not quite the people they ought to be? Do you remember how keen you were to share the gospel and tell other people about how you became a Christian? Do you remember going to Communion and being so moved thinking about Jesus dying for you?

And now what? When did you last speak to somebody about Jesus? When did you last spend time alone with God in prayer and Bible study? When was the last time you went to church with a sense of expectation that God would speak to you through his Word? The novelty is bound to have worn off if you have been a Christian a while, but the love need not.

Passion for Christ is not reserved exclusively for new Christians. In fact, as we mature our love should deepen because we've passed through difficult circumstances; we've found God sufficient and we've experienced his faithfulness, despite our sinfulness. Pray that, in a fresh way, you would 'know this love [of Christ] that surpasses knowledge' and, with a sense of joyful gratitude overflowing from that, you would 'live a life of love, just as Christ loved us and gave himself up for us' (Ephesians 3:19; 5:2).

Day 333

Read: Revelation 2:1–7
Key verses: Revelation 2:3–4

....

³ *You have persevered and have endured hardships for my name,
and have not grown weary.*
⁴ *Yet I hold this against you: you have forsaken the love you
had at first.*

How do I know if I truly love the Lord Jesus?

Love is not a gushy feeling; it is not mere sentiment. Gratitude is at
the heart of love. We are grateful for what God has done, for what
he has given us and for who he is. When we love someone, we don't
just make empty declarations; we show our gratitude.

If we love people, we think about them. Do you think about Jesus
often? It is easy to be so consumed by thoughts of doctrine, ministry
and church duties that we don't actually think about Jesus. We are
pressed down and weighed under with all the responsibilities we
carry for the Christian cause, but we don't think about him.

When we love people, we are eager to hear their voices. Are you
listening for the voice of Jesus? Are you eager to study God's Word
to hear from him?

If we love people, we do not like to think of their going away and we
look forward to their return. Are you longing for the Lord Jesus to
come back soon? Does your heart echo the words at the end of
Revelation: 'Come, Lord Jesus' (22:20)?

When we love people, we are anxious to know what will please them
so that we can do it. Are you longing to know what brings God
pleasure? Do you read your Bible, not just to sign off on the task but
also because you are keen to find out what you can do to please
God?

When we love people, we are keen to introduce them to others. Are you passionate about telling others about Jesus or have too many knock-backs and awkward conversations meant you have given up sharing the gospel?

When we love people, we are concerned for their good name. We cannot bear people talking about them in a way that is detrimental. Are you concerned about Christ's reputation and the way he is spoken of by others?

When we love people, we do not find it hard to trust them. Sometimes our trust in Jesus wavers. We allow doubts about his good purposes and bitterness about disappointments to swamp our thinking. Grievances over the way the Lord has dealt with us creep into our hearts and minds. That sense of injustice and unfairness festers until, before we know it, we have forsaken our first love.

Which of these markers of love do you recognize in your own life? Don't let bitterness, busyness or familiarity choke your love for God. He is your Everlasting Father (Isaiah 9:6), Chief Shepherd (1 Peter 5:4) and Rock (1 Samuel 2:2). Keep him at the centre of your thoughts and attention for he is 'altogether lovely' (Song of Solomon 5:16).

Day 334

Read: Revelation 2:1–7
Key verse: Revelation 2:5

....

5Consider how far you have fallen! Repent and do the things you did at first. If you do not repent, I will come to you and remove your lampstand from its place.

Were you once known as a very keen Christian but, now, you are lukewarm?

When Paul wrote to the Ephesian church, he commended them: 'Ever since I heard about your faith in the Lord Jesus and your love for all God's people, I have not stopped giving thanks for you, remembering you in my prayers' (Ephesians 1:15–16).

Now the risen Christ calls the believers to 'consider how far [they] have fallen!' Like the Ephesians, the first step is for us to admit our current state and recognize how far we have fallen. Once, the Lord heard our love rising to him in grateful praise; now, he just hears our pattered prayers with no freshness left. The second step is to repent. This means turning away from our sin, and trusting the Lord to cleanse us from our lovelessness and give us the strength to go on living as we ought to live.

The third step, after considering how far we have fallen and repenting, is to 'do the things [we] did at first'. We must do again what love made us do in the first instance, so that we may learn to love again: read the Bible and spend unhurried time with God. We are to seek his wisdom about those to whom we ought to witness, ask for help when those 'first things' have become routine, and come back to him in sheer dependence like newborn Christians.

If we have substituted activity for adoration, busyness for communion and duty for devotion, we must tell the Lord. If our acts of worship have become habitual rather than heartfelt and we have 'forsaken the love [we] had at first', God is waiting to meet us and welcome us back. His mercy, love and compassion for us are overwhelming. He will pick us up despite the people we have put off with our hardness of heart, despite those to whom we have misrepresented him with our lukewarm Christianity.

God longs to give us something we can never whip up within our own hearts – the love which is a gift of God and the fruit of the Holy Spirit. He delights to impart that love in fullness and freshness as we bow before him and confess our need.

Is this message really for us? Yes! John says, 'Whoever has ears, let them hear what the Spirit says to the churches' (Revelation 2:7). God has made the way back to him clear; he has set out a three-step plan for how to do it. And now, like the father in the story of the prodigal son (Luke 15:11–32), he stands with his arms open wide, ready to welcome us home. What is holding you back?

Further study

If you would like to read more about God's love and ours, you might find the following selection of books helpful.

Books about God's love:

- Julian Hardyman, *Jesus, Lover of My Soul: Fresh pathways to spiritual passion* (IVP, 2020)

- Patrick Mitchel, *The Message of Love*, The Bible Speaks Today (IVP, 2019)

- Dane Ortlund, *Gentle and Lowly: The heart of Christ for sinners and sufferers* (Crossway, 2020)

- Phil Ryken, *Loving the Way Jesus Loves* (IVP, 2012)

- Martin Salter, *So Loved: 26 words that can change your life* (IVP, 2021)

Books about love and relationships:

- Paul E. Miller, *A Loving Life: In a world of broken relationships* (IVP, 2014)

- Jason Roach, *Swipe Up: A better way to do love, sex and relationships* (The Good Book Company, 2019)

A book about loving other Christians:

- Tony Merida, *Love Your Church: 8 great things about being a church member* (The Good Book Company, 2021)

Hope

Contributors

Day 335

Read: Matthew 24:36–25:46
Key verses: Matthew 24:37–39

. . . .

³⁷ As it was in the days of Noah, so it will be at the coming of the Son of Man. ³⁸ For in the days before the flood, people were eating and drinking, marrying and giving in marriage, up to the day Noah entered the ark; ³⁹ and they knew nothing about what would happen until the flood came and took them all away. That is how it will be at the coming of the Son of Man.

What does the Bible teach about the context of Jesus' second coming?

Jesus says it will be like 'the days of Noah' (verse 37). The parallel he draws is not with the wickedness but with the normality of the times. People in Noah's day were not transcendently more wicked than any other group in the history of the world. So, in the days before Jesus returns, people will go to the pub for a drink; they'll marry; they'll give their daughters in marriage. In other words, the Son of Man will come the way the flood came: unexpectedly, to all but those who are waiting for it.

The other vignettes are similar. In the ancient world you ground your flour, either with large millstones dragged around by oxen or small hand mills, usually controlled by two women. Typically, those women would be sisters or a mother and a daughter – family members. When Christ comes, one will be taken and the other left behind. Whether this means individuals are taken and transported to glory or taken in judgement doesn't make any difference. The point is about the absolute separation of people whom you would think, because of family ties, should be together. But one will be ready for the Master's return and the other will not (verse 41). In the same way, two will be working in the field – in the nature of first-century farming, probably a father and son or two brothers, or similar – and, again, one will be taken and the other left behind (verse 40).

Then (in verses 43–44) we're given the most startling image that keeps recurring in the New Testament: Jesus will come like a thief in the night. The point here is the unexpectedness, not the immorality, of the theft.

The message from these three scenes is that because we don't know when the Lord Jesus is coming back, we must make sure we're ready. If we don't want to be surprised at his return, we need to be waiting expectantly.

As we wait for Christ's return, it is easy to become complacent, living comfortably in our fallen world, enjoying its pleasures, consumed with routines and responsibilities. Our lives can look almost indistinguishable from those of the unbelievers around us. Ask yourself, 'If Jesus came back today, would I be surprised, ashamed or delighted?' Pray through your day – about your work and conversations, the money you'll spend and the people you'll serve. Think and act in such a way that you are always ready for the Lord's return. His return is not unexpected, so let's make sure we're not surprised when it happens.

Day 336

Read: Matthew 24:36–25:46
Key verses: Matthew 24:45–47

....

[45] *"Who then is the faithful and wise servant, whom the master has put in charge of the servants in his household to give them their food at the proper time?* [46] *It will be good for that servant whose master finds him doing so when he returns.* [47] *Truly I tell you, he will put him in charge of all his possessions.*

How should we wait?

A pattern that immediately emerges from this parable, and repeats itself throughout the rest of chapters 24 and 25, is that each fresh parable picks up on one or more themes from the previous material. Verses 36–44 emphasize the unexpectedness of Christ's coming; so here, too, in verses 45–51, the wicked servant discovers the master returning at a moment when he does not expect him.

It picks up the previous theme, but it adds something else – it enriches the notion of *how* we are to wait for the Master's return: we are to wait for the Lord Jesus as stewards who must give an account of their service, faithful or otherwise.

The judgement pictured here is not reserved for utter outsiders (pagans) but for people who seem to be the Master's faithful slaves: those who view themselves as his stewards but forget that *they must give an account*. These are nominal Christian leaders who, instead of feeding the sheep, are exploiting them; instead of nurturing and building up the flock of God, they are fleecing the animals and eating the mutton. And they must give an account.

Many clergy will fall under this judgement. And not just clergy – doesn't James warn us that not many of us should be teachers, knowing that we shall face stricter judgement (James 3:1–2)? We put

Christian leaders into places of authority, and sometimes they become so egocentric that this authority is more important to them than faithfulness to the Master. We got rid of the pope and then generated our own popes. It's not that these leaders are saved by good works; that's not the point at all. Rather, if they really are the Master's, they will live and serve in a certain kind of way. If they are really not the Master's, they will view whatever position of authority they have been assigned as a perk for themselves, and use their gifts, leadership and office to push down, hurt and exploit others.

This parable reminds us that we must wait for the Lord's return like stewards who must give account of their service. Like the good servant, we are to be prepared for the Lord to come at any time. If we are faithful throughout the long delay, we will be highly rewarded at the end (verses 45–47). In contrast, unfaithful servants will face judgement, where there is gnashing of teeth (verses 48–51).

Jesus' return will be a day of reckoning, when the worth of our service will be examined. Knowing we are to give an account, the only way to be prepared is to live faithfully now. Today, ask God to help you to be a good steward of the money, time, responsibilities, gifts, roles and relationships he has entrusted to you.

The world asks, 'What does a man own?'
Christ asks, 'How does he use it?'
(Andrew Murray, a nineteenth-century pastor)

Day 337

Read: Matthew 24:36–25:46
Key verses: Matthew 25:1–5

• •

> [1] *At that time the kingdom of heaven will be like ten virgins who took their lamps and went out to meet the bridegroom.* [2] *Five of them were foolish and five were wise.* [3] *The foolish ones took their lamps but did not take any oil with them.* [4] *The wise ones, however, took oil in jars along with their lamps.* [5] *The bridegroom was a long time in coming, and they all became drowsy and fell asleep.*

What happens when the bridegroom is delayed?

In the first century, weddings started with the groom meeting the bride and her family for some celebrations. Then, at some point, there would be a procession through the street and everybody else who was invited to the real celebration would join in. Knowing that time could slip by, these guests would be waiting on the route with their torches ready, signifying that they were part of the invited group. Together, they would process down to the groom's place where the celebrations would continue. The torches they held were passes to get into the party. Then the gates were shut and the wedding festivities proper began.

In this parable, five virgins who are waiting along the way have enough oil for their lamps to burn, but they don't have any additional oil if it runs out. The five others are wise, prepared for a long delay. When suddenly the cry goes up, 'Here's the bridegroom!', those with their lamps flickering out run into town to find more oil. When they return to the street, everybody has gone. Finally, they get to the party: 'We belong here, too!' they cry. But they just look like gatecrashers. If they really did belong, surely they would have been waiting? That's the way the culture works. They weren't waiting for the groom; they were off doing something else. So they are excluded.

The Master's coming may be long delayed. This is important for many reasons. At the lowest level, it should engender within us perseverance. At a slightly higher level, it should engender a sense of strategy. What do we do about training the next generation? What do we do about mentoring? How do we ensure that our children have learned biblical truths and are living them out? We begin to think about writing books and courses, building projects and other trajectories – all because we realize that the Lord could be long delayed.

It is part of our Christian responsibility to think not only 'Could it be today, Lord?' but also, assuming that it's not, 'How can I give, plan, pray and serve, so that I'm showing by the way I live that I, too, recognize that the Lord's return could be long delayed?'

If you knew that Jesus was not going to come back in your lifetime, what difference would it make to your priorities and prayers?

If the Lord Jehovah makes us wait, let us do so with our whole hearts; for blessed are all they that wait for Him. He is worth waiting for. The waiting itself is beneficial to us: it tries faith, exercises patience, trains submission, and endears the blessing when it comes. The Lord's people have always been a waiting people.
(C. H. Spurgeon, *The Treasury of David*, Psalm 130:5, <https://archive.spurgeon.org/treasury/ps130.php>)

Day 338

Read: Matthew 24:36—25:46
Key verses: Matthew 25:19–21

....

> [19] *After a long time the master of those servants returned and settled accounts with them.* [20] *The man who had received five bags of gold brought the other five. "Master," he said, "you entrusted me with five bags of gold. See, I have gained five more."*
>
> [21] *His master replied, "Well done, good and faithful servant! You have been faithful with a few things; I will put you in charge of many things. Come and share your master's happiness!"*

Who will hear the words, 'Well done, good and faithful servant'?

Jesus tells the parable of a master who assigned money to his slaves (the Greek word *doulos*, translated as 'servant', actually means 'slave'), according to their ability and character, and then went off on a long journey.

Now, slavery in the ancient world was very different from later practice. People became slaves for different reasons, such as personal bankruptcy, and exercised different levels of responsibility. Some were badly treated but others were accountants in family businesses, for example.

The slave who had received five bags put his money to work. Perhaps he bought a boat and started a fishing business, or a farm and started to work it? When the master returned and wanted the accounts settled, the slave sold everything off and brought in the bags of gold. Instead of five bags, there were now ten: he'd doubled it – a 100% return!

Similarly, for the slave with two bags of gold: he'd worked faithfully according to his ability and doubled his money as well. The master said to both, 'You have been faithful with a few things; I will put you in charge of many things. Come and share your master's happiness!'

Here's a glimpse of eternity. You are not going to sit around on a puffy cloud playing a harp. You're going to have fantastic responsibilities, and the Master will give you the gifts and graces to take care of them. Even more, you will enter into your Master's happiness. When the earthly master comes back, he is supposed to be served by slaves who ensure that *he* is happy. But this Master ensures that all the *slaves* are happy with the same happiness that he has. In the new heaven and the new earth, the happiness of Jesus himself will be given to those who are only slaves!

We might be sympathetic towards the third man. If he is successful, none of the result will be his; it's owned by his master. If he loses the capital, what would the master say? In the master's response, Jesus is not justifying slavery any more than he was justifying theft in Matthew 24:43. It's an analogy. His point is that the slave *owes* his master something, just as you and I are slaves of Christ. In the New Testament, this image is continually used to depict what our true discipleship to Jesus looks like. We have been bought for a price. We are no longer our own; we owe him everything and everything is his.

While we wait for Jesus' return, we are to improve the Master's assets by living lives of obedience, mentoring others, bearing witness to Jesus, and using the gifts, graces and money that God has given to us. Today, ask yourself, 'Given that I am Christ's, that all that I've got is Christ's, that whatever abilities or resources I have are all Christ's, what am I doing with what's entrusted to me in order to improve the Master's assets?'

Day 339

Read: Matthew 24:36—25:46
Key verses: Matthew 25:34–36

....

> ³⁴ *Then the King will say to those on his right, "Come, you who are blessed by my Father; take your inheritance, the kingdom prepared for you since the creation of the world.* ³⁵ *For I was hungry and you gave me something to eat, I was thirsty and you gave me something to drink, I was a stranger and you invited me in,* ³⁶ *I needed clothes and you clothed me, I was ill and you looked after me, I was in prison and you came to visit me."*

The stakes are high. When Christ returns, the ultimate division will take place: those who go into eternal life and those who go into eternal punishment.

But this parable is not teaching that if you're kind to a homeless person or you work for an organization that helps prisoners, you are doing it unto Jesus and he will look favourably on you on the last day. Jesus refers to those to be helped as 'the least of these brothers and sisters of mine' (25:40). We want to extend that to everybody who is poor, but that's simply not what the expression means. It certainly never means it in Matthew. Jesus' 'brothers' refers to his half-brothers through Mary or, if the word is used in any sort of metaphorical sense, invariably it refers to his disciples (Matthew 12:48–49 or 28:10).

Besides, if you serve others so that Jesus will welcome you into eternity, surely you'd be expecting him to notice your endeavours? But both the sheep and goats are surprised. When individuals helped the least in the kingdom, they didn't do so thinking, 'Oh, I'm doing this for Jesus' sake.' They did it because they were brothers and sisters in Christ, part of that community.

Do you see how closely this ties in with a massive theme in the New Testament: how Jesus identifies with his church? When Jesus appears to Saul on the road to Damascus, he doesn't say, 'Why are you persecuting my church?' No. He says, 'Why are you persecuting *me*? For inasmuch as you do it to the least of these of my brothers and sisters you are doing it unto me' (see Acts 9:4 and Matthew 25:40). Christians, because they have been transformed by grace, form a network; they constitute the church, the people of the living God. So they will care for one another. When Christians go into prison, they will look after them. When believers are starving elsewhere, they will send money, not to earn Brownie points but because they are part of the redeemed family of God. We are to wait for Christ's return as people whose lives are so transformed by the gospel that we unselfconsciously serve our brothers and sisters in Christ.

What importance Christ places on the church! He never intended the wait for his return to be a solitary experience. Let's love and pray for one another so that care becomes instinctive. Be so transformed by gospel truths that serving one another is the natural overflow. And may our devotion to one another point people to Christ, so that they, too, will be ready for his coming.

Day 340

Read: Romans 8:15–30
Key verses: Romans 8:17–18

....

¹⁷ Now if we are children, then we are heirs – heirs of God and co-heirs with Christ, if indeed we share in his sufferings in order that we may also share in his glory. ¹⁸ I consider that our present sufferings are not worth comparing with the glory that will be revealed in us.

Is following Jesus worth all the sacrifice and suffering?

The apostle Paul has 'considered' (verse 18) this question and concluded that, compared with the weight of glory to come, our sufferings now don't even register on the scales.

Paul is not minimizing our suffering. His point, in verse 17, is that we don't just suffer for Christ; we suffer with him. Following Jesus is hard; each day, we take up our crosses (Luke 9:23). But suffering with him means he goes with us as our faithful Friend. The pain you feel, he feels and he bears.

But, more than this, the Bible promises that our present sufferings are not robbing us of our happiness; they are achieving for us 'an eternal weight of glory' (2 Corinthians 4:17, ESV) – our own personal gravitas. We hate being trivialized; we long to stand tall with dignity. God created us for it. So don't be embarrassed by your longing; it is of God. But this existence we're stuck with right now *cannot* satisfy us. This life is good. But it is good the way air is good. I enjoy breathing. But when I'm hungry, air cannot satisfy, no matter how much I inhale. We are hungry for the weight of glory here in a world of breezy air. And God promises to satisfy our glory-hunger.

The author and philosopher Peter Kreeft explains what our future glory is worth now:

Suppose both death and hell were utterly defeated. Suppose the fight was fixed. Suppose God took you on a crystal ball trip into your future and you saw that despite everything – your sin, your smallness, your stupidity – you could have free for the asking your whole crazy heart's deepest desire: heaven, eternal joy. Would you not return fearless and singing? What can earth do to you, if you are guaranteed Heaven? To fear the worst earthly loss would be like a millionaire fearing the loss of a penny – less, a scratch on a penny.
(Peter Kreeft, *Heaven*, Ignatius Press, 1989, p. 183)

This is why we keep on walking with the Lord, no matter what the cost is here and now.

Our suffering, sadness and grief often feel raw and overwhelming but, in the light of the glory that will be ours one day, they are like a mere scratch on a penny. Today, keep that image in mind as you persevere in the faith, loving Christ and living for him. Hold on to the hope of future glory, remembering that Christ knows about your suffering. He loves you, is with you and is praying for you.

How did Paul handle his sufferings and encourage the church to face theirs? Not by trying to produce heaven on earth, but by recognizing that for the Christian the best is yet to be. He took the moment and put it in the larger context of God's unfolding purpose, not only for time but also in eternity.
(Alistair Begg, *Made for His Pleasure*, Moody Press, 1996, p. 116)

Day 341

Read: Romans 8:15–30

Key verses: Romans 8:19–21

....

19 For the creation waits in eager expectation for the children of God to be revealed. 20 For the creation was subjected to frustration, not by its own choice, but by the will of the one who subjected it, in hope 21 that the creation itself will be liberated from its bondage to decay and brought into the freedom and glory of the children of God.

What are you longing for?

Creation is longing for the 'children of God to be revealed'. J. B. Phillips puts it another way: 'The whole creation is on tiptoe to see the wonderful sight of the sons of God coming into their own.' We ruined everything in the Garden of Eden when we disobeyed God. But his remedy is not a blind natural process. God himself reversed the decline through the second Adam, Jesus, the perfect man. And, right now, the creation longs for the day when we all will be made royal again, trustworthy again, like the risen Jesus. That Greek word translated 'eager expectation' suggests someone craning his or her neck to see what's coming: 'the children of God to be revealed'. That's us – along with millions and millions of other ordinary stumblers who have found their future in stumbling towards Jesus. On that great and final day when the whole universe is renewed, God will gather us together, even from the grave, and crown us with *his* radiant immortality, and it will have nothing to do with our superiority but only with the glory of his grace.

God has structured into reality a forward tilt. He has built in our advantage and scheduled the happy inevitability of our debut as the children of God, fully clothed in the glory of the risen Jesus. Not that it *looks* or *feels* like that right now. The futility of this present world is formidable. You try to build something with your life but it's like a sandcastle on the beach: the waves of time wash over it and, soon, no one can tell anything was even there. But this futility isn't a flaw in God's design. That's why Paul says in verse 20, 'not by its own choice'. Reality was built against futility; futility is not intrinsic or permanent. Two thousand years ago, a second Adam entered in. We blamed him for our misery; he took it to his cross and it weighed him down into death. Then he rose up from it all with a new power of life that won't stop until the whole universe is renewed. Soon, God will uncork the cosmic champagne bottle and the whole universe will burst into explosive joy for ever. And we'll be there then, just as surely as we are here now.

Perhaps our longing for the future God has planned for us is weak because our expectations are low? Romans 8:19–23 expands our horizons exponentially. The return of Christ will not simply signal an end to suffering and futility; the whole universe will be renewed. God will dwell with redeemed humanity in the new heaven and the new earth, and we will reign with him in glorious immortality. Let's join creation, full of expectation – standing on tiptoe and craning our necks – as we pray and live in anticipation of that glorious day.

Day 342

Read: Romans 8:15–30
Key verses: Romans 8:22–23

. . . .

[22] We know that the whole creation has been groaning as in the pains of childbirth right up to the present time. [23] Not only so, but we ourselves, who have the firstfruits of the Spirit, groan inwardly as we wait eagerly for our adoption to sonship, the redemption of our bodies.

Can you feel creation groaning?

It isn't just a problem here or there; a million things are broken everywhere, with endless distress, continuous sighs and unrelieved yearnings. But in this massive ordeal, God is bringing new life – creation is in 'the pains of childbirth'. God is promising us that nature 'red in tooth and claw' is only a chapter and not the conclusion. The story ends in a new world, ruled by a new human race, with God in our midst: ' "He will wipe every tear from their eyes. There will be no more death" or mourning or crying or pain, for the old order of things has passed away' (Revelation 21:4).

We groan too, don't we? If you belong to Jesus, he has given you the firstfruits of the Spirit, with foretastes of your eternal glory. God has resurrected your heart from the dead so that you feel longings you never thought were real. Now you have new life within, a first instalment on your final inheritance. A person being prepared for the new universe feels not fewer but more groanings.

C. S. Lewis called it an 'inconsolable longing' (C. S. Lewis, *Surprised by Joy*, Collins, 2016, p. 82). This ache can pierce your heart at any moment. It's when you feel a yearning to be complete and finally with Christ. It can happen while in church, listening to music, holding your newborn baby or saying goodbye to a friend. The Spirit awakens this groaning with an 'Oh!' in our hearts. It's eternal life welling up within us.

And it's wonderful to think that our eternal life in the new heaven and new earth will not be ethereal, cloudy and vague. Our adoption as God's children will include 'the redemption of our bodies' (verse 23). Our whole being will finally become what God had in mind from the start. This is why Jesus died *and rose again*. The philosophers of Paul's time had a low view of the body; Paul put the resurrection of our bodies at the pinnacle of his gospel. He called it our hope (verses 24–25), the very thing we wait for with patience, because it is so worthy and glorious.

Soon our 'inconsolable longing' will be completely and utterly satisfied. Until then, our groanings serve as reminders that our hope is not in this world, although good things hint at it. Today, set your heart on God's gospel promises and wait patiently. In a little while, we will be saying with joy: 'I have come home at last! This is my real country! I belong here. This is the land I have been looking for all my life, though I never knew it till now' (C. S. Lewis, *The Last Battle*, HarperCollins, 2009, p. 210).

Day 343

Read: Romans 8:15–30
Key verses: Romans 8:24–25

....

24 For in this hope we were saved. But hope that is seen is no hope at all. Who hopes for what they already have? 25 But if we hope for what we do not yet have, we wait for it patiently.

How would you feel if God were to give you a huge salary, a big estate and vigorous health but not himself, and the instant you died, it would be over for ever? If you were happy to settle for that, your desires would be what Pascal, the French mathematician and Catholic theologian, called 'licking the earth' (Blaise Pascal, *Penseés*, no. 666). Alternatively, your heart might say, 'This world is a nice place. God made it and will redeem it. But I'd rather have Jesus and be his than all the money in the bank. I don't mind waiting for a happiness so big that this world can't contain it.' If that's how you feel, then there is only one way to account for it: the Holy Spirit lives in you, never to leave.

And with his presence in our hearts, we wait for this glorious day 'patiently' (verse 25). Now, we don't like patience, yet this is how the early church prevailed against all the persecution and suffering. Yes, there were miracles. But look at how Paul describes his friends in Romans 16: 'they risked their lives', 'worked hard', '[fellow Jews who have been] in prison with me'. They were powerless, but they prevailed. How? By patience. They just wouldn't quit. The early theologians called patience 'the greatest virtue', 'the highest of all virtues', the secret ingredient that was 'peculiarly Christian'. They believed God was in no hurry, so they were in no hurry. They believed God was in control, so they felt no need to be in control. They believed God was powerful, so they did not become pushy and forceful. They were resilient and resourceful in the quietness of patient endurance.

Bishop Cyprian, writing to his suffering people in the third century, told them, 'As servants and worshippers of God, let us show the patience that we learn from the heavenly teachings. For that virtue we have in common with God' (Cyprian, quoted in Alan Kreider, *The Patient Ferment of the Early Church*, Baker, 2016, p. 14).

Do we want to show our modern world what God is really like? Of course. The world is facing final judgement. But God exists. He sent Jesus, who died and rose again. All the promises of God are true. And now, in this generation, it's our turn to bear witness. How? Keep going! We will prevail by hopeful patience.

In the Old Testament, Job was a righteous man whom God allowed Satan to test. In his suffering, Job asked:

What strength do I have, that I should still hope?
What prospects, that I should be patient?
(Job 6:11)

This side of the cross, we reply confidently that we are waiting for God's glory to be fully and finally revealed, and to spend eternity with him. So, with patient endurance, resilience and resourcefulness, we witness to those who are 'licking the earth' that there is something far better to live for.

Day 344

Read: Romans 8:15–30
Key verse: Romans 8:29

....

> [29] *And we know that in all things God works for the good of those who love him, who have been called according to his purpose.*

This is one bold, industrial-strength promise!

Imagine a continuum. At one end is 'All things work together for good'; at the other end is 'Nothing is good'. Most of us probably find ourselves somewhere in the middle of that continuum, saying, 'I hope things work out OK.'

But, if we believe in God *at all*, we can't hold this middle position. What kind of God would promise us that some things work together for good and expect us to build a courageous life on that foundation? If there is any hope for us, it is an extreme hope that covers the worst that life throws at us. *Either* nothing is good, we suffer for nothing and have no future, *or* all things work together for good, everything about us matters and our sufferings are accelerating us into a glorious future.

How can we 'know' for sure that this gospel promise is true? Jesus. We crucified him, we chose evil, but God was working our malice for our good. He was bending our evil round to advance his good. And the resurrection of Jesus is now our wonderful destiny. When the apostle Peter preached about Jesus only months after his death, he said:

> But God knew what would happen, and his prearranged plan was carried out when Jesus was betrayed . . . You nailed him to a cross and killed him. But God released him from the horrors of death and raised him back to life.
> (Acts 2:23–24, NLT)

God does not have good days now and then so that some things work together for good; he has a good day every day so that all things work together for good. God proved that in Jesus. God has wrapped his arms widely around all things, including all evil, all your suffering, all your sins, all your tears, everything that's against you, and God is holding you. Maybe the most wonderful word in this verse is the little word 'for': '*for* those who love [God] . . . *for* [those] who [are] called according to his purpose'. You don't have to do this for yourself. You don't have to orchestrate the happy ending you long for. If you are in Christ, the resurrection of Jesus is your future, and nothing can take it away from you because God has determined to do this *for* you.

God is *for* you. It is often hard to believe but God's arms are wrapped around you; they are wrapped around your depression, cancer, strained family relationships, hurts endured in church, disappointments, sins – all of it – and he is working it together for your good. Today, trust God with 'all [your] things' and thank him that, even on the darkest of days, we can know for sure that he is on the throne and in control.

Day 345

Read: Romans 8:15–30
Key verses: Romans 8:29–30

....

²⁹For those God foreknew he also predestined to be conformed to the image of his Son, that he might be the firstborn among many brothers and sisters. ³⁰And those he predestined, he also called; those he called, he also justified; those he justified, he also glorified.

These verses are not a pep talk; they are announcing to us a hope so big that it will get us through anything in this life, because our hope lies *beyond* this life.

Romans 8:29–30 is in the Bible to help us all to become confident, cheerful, resilient, pain-tolerant men and women who display Jesus in the madness of our times. Verses 29–30 explain how we can know verse 28 is true – that all things work together for our good. What larger reality guarantees that assurance? Paul doesn't point to favourable sociological trends or the latest scientific research. Nothing observable can give us certainty from beyond this world. Verses 29–30 are about God. It is as if Paul were spreading out a huge blueprint, showing us the great purposes of God spanning from eternity past to eternity future, and all of human history as a brief parenthesis within that vast field of eternity. He helps us to see just how big God's plan for us is, so that all things work together for our good.

God 'foreknew' us, which means he chose us by setting his heart on us long before we set our hearts on him (Ephesians 1:4). God 'predestined' us – he decided how we would turn out in the end – to be with Christ, like Christ and for the glory of Christ. He 'called' us. God did not hold out until we called to him; he called to us through the gospel. And because we're sinners and God can't get involved with us without forgiving us, he 'justified' us. At the cross, Jesus took our damnation so we wouldn't have to. God brought us back into his good graces, not by submerging his holy law but by satisfying it in Jesus, our willing substitute. Jesus lived for us the worthy life we have not lived and died for us the atoning death we cannot die. All we can do now is receive him with empty hands of faith. This justification does not make us morally unserious people. It makes us love the Lord and fiercely fight temptation.

In eternity future, God will perfect our personalities with the likeness of Jesus; he will raise our bodies invincible like that of the risen Jesus. Paul is so confident, he even puts it in the past tense: 'glorified', not 'will glorify'. God's plan is so unbreakable that the future is as settled as the past. No wonder all things work together for our good.

What amazing hope we have! God's plan is unbreakable; our future glory is certain. We will be with Christ, like Christ, for ever, and all things are helping us to get there. Today, praise God for all that he has done in the past, is doing for us now and will do in the future. Rejoice and rest in the glorious truth that his purpose is the power driving the universe, now and for eternity.

Day 346

Read: 2 Corinthians 4:16—5:10
Key verses: 2 Corinthians 4:16–17

....

16 Therefore we do not lose heart. Though outwardly we are wasting away, yet inwardly we are being renewed day by day. 17 For our light and momentary troubles are achieving for us an eternal glory that far outweighs them all.

Why should we not lose heart?

Paul's testimony – and the testimony of countless other believers – is that the worse it gets, the better we become. Christians can grow under pressure and can have resilience in the midst of trials. Paul explains that while we're wasting away, our inner nature is being renewed day by day for a very special purpose. Our momentary affliction is preparing us for an eternal weight of glory, beyond comparison. Glory is the fullness of God's quality and character; his stunning, awesome reality. It is every aspect of his being. The Hebrew word for glory is 'weight' or 'heavy': the substance of God. Paul is saying that this trajectory of inner growth is getting us ready to receive the glory of God to ourselves. Inwardly, we are becoming increasingly like him all the time. One day 'we shall be like him, for we shall see him as he is' (1 John 3:2). In that moment of transform-ation, we will take on all the communicable characteristics and qualities of the almighty God, and we will be like Christ. This refreshing and renewing of our inner selves, day by day, to be ready for that moment when we become completely like Christ is the goal of every believer.

How do we get on this trajectory of inner growth? Through reading and being challenged by God's Word, the 'reproofs' of life, the counsel of friends and, especially, through affliction. James 1 tells us that God uses suffering as a friend because it works to perfect us, to form us and to give us character. I find that when trials and tribulations come, I suddenly become very God-focused. My values change. I become introspective – I look at my heart and ask, 'Lord, is there something in my life that brought this on? Is there a mistake I made in a relationship? How much of this is my fault?' I plead for God's grace; I long for his nearness. That's exactly why James 1:2 tells us to count it all joy when affliction comes our way, because God is using it to make us ready for that great day when we shall see him. It's why John writes that the one who has the hope of becoming like Christ, of receiving this eternal weight of glory, purifies himself to get ready (1 John 3:3).

Don't lose heart. Instead, be on an upward trajectory to receiving the wonderful weight of glory, the likeness of Christ that we will carry in ourselves for eternity.

> Let all true Christians remember that their best things are yet to come. Let us count it no strange thing if we have sufferings in this present time. It is a season of probation. We are yet at school. We are learning patience, gentleness, and meekness, which we could hardly learn if we had our good things now. But there is an eternal holiday yet to begin . . . It will make amends for all.
> (J. C. Ryle, *Expository Thoughts on the Gospel of Matthew*, Aneko Press, 2020, pp. 143–144)

Day 347

Read: 2 Corinthians 4:16—5:10
Key verses: 2 Corinthians 4:18—5:1

....

> ^{4:18} *So we fix our eyes not on what is seen, but on what is unseen, since what is seen is temporary, but what is unseen is eternal.* ^{5:1} *For we know that if the earthly tent we live in is destroyed, we have a building from God, an eternal house in heaven, not built by human hands.*

Are you focused on the future?

Paul urges us to take our eyes off what is 'seen', the transient – our suffering and material possessions – and focus on what is eternal, the 'unseen'. Jesus had the same challenge for his disciples: 'Stop being bound to your possessions and worrying about where you're going to get your next meal or next robe. Seek first the kingdom of God, and your Father will take care of you. Sell what you have. Give it to the poor. Put your treasure in heaven instead of where moths and rust corrupt. For where your treasure is, there will your heart be also' (adapted from Luke 12). The message is that instead of being bound to the things of this earth, invest your finances, time and effort in eternity.

We also need to get our eyes off this present body and on to the future body. Can you think of anything more fragile, more vulnerable to the elements than a tent? Like a tent, our bodies are pretty fragile, but we each look forward to an eternal, resurrected body, not made with human hands. At the moment we 'groan' because of our sinful nature (2 Corinthians 5:2, 4). We each still struggle with sin and groan under its burden, longing for that heavenly body, liberated from frailty and failings.

On that day, we will no longer be ashamed because we will not be 'unclothed' (verse 4). Paul is probably referring to Adam and Eve, who saw their nakedness and were ashamed. If Jesus were to return now, like Isaiah and John, we would fall on our faces in shame before him because we are sinners still under the groaning weight of our sin. But when we finally receive those eternal, resurrected bodies, we will be clothed. Our robes will be washed white in the blood of the Lamb (Revelation 7:14). We will not be found naked before him. We will live in unhindered fellowship with him. He will be the joy of our lives.

As you feel this groaning, remember the day is coming when 'what is mortal may be swallowed up by life' (2 Corinthians 5:4). I think of all the times when I've said to my wife, 'Ah, this is the life!' No, it's not. That day when I go home, that's when my mortality will be swallowed up in life.

Have you ever said, 'Ah, this is the life!' on these occasions?

• When you were enjoying a holiday in the sun.
• When you were relishing a good meal with friends.
• When you were appreciating your retirement.

If so, your hope is too small! Savour these and every other moment of pleasure God gives you today. But recognize that each one is a taster, whetting your appetite for the far greater eternal pleasure you will one day enjoy – being with God for ever.

Day 348

Read: 2 Corinthians 4:16—5:10
Key verses: 2 Corinthians 5:5–8

. . . .

[5] Now the one who has fashioned us for this very purpose is God, who has given us the Spirit as a deposit, guaranteeing what is to come.

[6] Therefore we are always confident and know that as long as we are at home in the body we are away from the Lord. [7] For we live by faith, not by sight. [8] We are confident, I say, and would prefer to be away from the body and at home with the Lord.

How can we be so sure that all God has promised will really happen?

This isn't just smoke-and-mirrors religious stuff. Look at Genesis 1: we were made in the image of God, to be image bearers, to share his glory. He prepared us for this; it's why he built us; we're wired for it. In Genesis 3, the fall left all of us, even the very best of us, severely damaged. We don't think, act, live or respond rightly. I learned a long time ago that my first instincts are almost always wrong. If you offend me, my first instinct is not to think, 'How can I forgive you and love you?' My instincts are always fallen, always broken. But Jesus came to suffer on the cross, to reclaim this damaged material of me. I wasn't for the rubbish heap; he still wanted me.

Romans 8:29 tells us, 'Those God foreknew he also predestined to be conformed to the image of his Son.' God has prepared you for this eternal weight of glory. Paul reminds us, 'He who began a good work in you will carry it on to completion until the day of Christ Jesus' (Philippians 1:6). And we can be sure about this because he's sealed us with the Holy Spirit (Ephesians 4:30).

How do you know you're going to heaven? You've been sealed. It's a done deal. The contract has been signed. The presence of the

Holy Spirit in you has sealed you for the day of redemption. There's no turning back. It's guaranteed.

This knowledge breeds confidence, so Paul declares, 'We are always confident' (verse 6). It's almost as if he were saying, 'Put me on a trajectory that makes me more like Christ as I move towards that eternal weight of glory. Suffering? Bring it on! Death, you want to destroy me? You want to kill me? Hey! I'm just going home. It will accelerate the process. I'd rather be at home with the Lord. Bring it on!' Like Paul, when we grab hold of these truths by faith, we grow in confident courage.

Every time you read your Bible, pray, serve others, sacrifice for God's kingdom, submit to God's agenda and share the gospel – however weakly – these other-worldly impulses are evidence that God is transforming you. God always finishes what he starts; so these flickers of Holy Spirit life are guarantees that one day you will be like Christ. Until then, be confident that God is at work in you and join him in it – more and more relying on his Word, surrendering to his will and living for his glory.

Day 349

Read: 2 Corinthians 4:16—5:10
Key verses: 2 Corinthians 5:9–10

• •

⁹So we make it our goal to please him, whether we are at home in the body or away from it. ¹⁰For we must all appear before the judgement seat of Christ, so that each of us may receive what is due to us for the things done while in the body, whether good or bad.

Why do we live to please God?

Because we're all going to stand before the *bema* seat of Christ. In Corinth, there was a seat on which the governor sat and pronounced judgement as he heard different court cases. Paul himself had come before the *bema* seat for judgement, and he pictures Christ there. We will all be judged for what we have done, whether it be good or evil. If this were the only verse, you might imagine an old set of scales, hoping that the good would outweigh the bad so that you'd make it into heaven. But we also have the rest of Paul's writings, and the rest of the Bible, which teach us we're not saved by our works, and that appearing before Christ's judgement seat is a moment of accountability.

In 1 Corinthians 3:12–13, we are told that, when we stand before Christ, the works that we have done in the flesh will be shown to be either gold, silver and precious stones or wood, hay and stubble. The fire will prove the point. I think the fire might be the glorious presence of Jesus himself. All the things that we've done in our bodies – all those poor choices – will be the wood, hay and stubble, which will be burned away. What lasts will be only those things we've done to please God – the gold, silver and precious stones. Francis Schaeffer, the American theologian and pastor, wrote a book called *Ash Heap Lives* (Norfolk Press, 1975). I'm afraid that there are going to be a lot of 'ash heap' Christians, standing knee-deep in the ashes of their wood, hay and stubble.

Revelation 4 says that the elders worship Christ by casting their crowns at his feet, and 1 Corinthians 3 says that we'll receive rewards for the good things we've done to please God. I wonder whether, when we see Jesus, with the crowns and the rewards in our hands, we will throw them at his feet in a supreme act of worship to the worthy Christ whom we love so much. If that were to be the case, I wouldn't want to be without crowns or rewards. I wouldn't want to bring a bucket of ashes. I would want to have something. So I live to please him.

None of us wants to be an 'ash heap' Christian. We don't want to be empty-handed as we stand before God. But to be rich in rewards *then* demands a change of lifestyle and attitude *now*. People say, 'You can't take it with you,' referring to the uselessness of earthly treasures in the next life. But that's not true. A Christian does take the treasures from this world into the next. How we spend our lives now determines whether we will take wood, hay and stubble or gold, silver and precious stones into eternity. Today, in your conversations, decisions, actions and thoughts, will you truly make it your goal to please God?

Day 350

Read: 1 Thessalonians 4:13–18

Key verses: 1 Thessalonians 4:13–14

. . . .

> ¹³ *Brothers and sisters, we do not want you to be uninformed about those who sleep in death, so that you do not grieve like the rest of mankind, who have no hope.* ¹⁴ *For we believe that Jesus died and rose again, and so we believe that God will bring with Jesus those who have fallen asleep in him.*

What will happen to Christians who have died before the second coming of Christ?

This is the question the Thessalonians were asking. Paul is keen to reassure these sorrowing believers that their loved ones would not miss out on Christ's coming. Indeed, they would return with him and, together with us (verses 14 and 16), receive resurrection bodies.

The return of Christ is a central part of Paul's gospel message: 'You turned to God from idols to serve the living and true God, and to wait for his Son from heaven . . . Jesus, who rescues us from the coming wrath' (1 Thessalonians 1:9–10). Clearly, these new believers must have been taught by Paul to cultivate a real spirit of immediacy in their expectation of Christ's return. Otherwise, why would they be anxious when they saw Christians in the church dying?

Paul himself certainly has this expectation. That's why he says in 1 Thessalonians 4:15, 'According to the Lord's word, we tell you that we who are still alive, who are left until the coming of the Lord, will certainly not precede those who have fallen asleep' (emphasis added). He doesn't say 'they', but 'we'. Is he dating the second coming? Not at all. He goes on to tell the Thessalonians, 'About times and dates we do not need to write to you, for you know very well that the day of the Lord will come like a thief in the night' (1 Thessalonians 5:1–2). Paul subscribes to the teaching of Jesus that nobody knows the day of his coming: 'But about that day or hour no one knows, not even the angels in heaven, nor the Son, but only the Father' (Matthew 24:36). Not even the Lord Jesus, as the Son of God, knows the day of his coming.

Paul, therefore, is not claiming to know the date of Jesus' second coming. It is not as if he taught that the Lord was coming soon, and events then proved him wrong. Rather, he wants these Thessalonian believers to live in a moment-by-moment expectation of an undatable event. This is how every Christian should view the coming again of Christ, and this is the spirit of expectation we should cultivate every day. We do not know when he is coming – but we are to long for it, to live in the good of it and expect it.

No believer – alive or dead – will miss out on the glories of the second coming. We will all share in the triumph of the Lord's return. Death is not the final event; rather, we live in the certain hope of Christ's imminent return. Today, in your grief or your ordinary everyday struggles, let your meditation on this great day bring encouragement and joy to your soul.

Day 351

Read: 1 Thessalonians 4:13–18
Key verses: 1 Thessalonians 4:13–14

....

> [13] *Brothers and sisters, we do not want you to be uninformed about those who sleep in death, so that you do not grieve like the rest of mankind, who have no hope.* [14] *For we believe that Jesus died and rose again, and so we believe that God will bring with Jesus those who have fallen asleep in him.*

Death is one of the few certainties of life.

Paul, full of pastoral concern, wanted the Thessalonians to be well informed. As we saw yesterday, they were anxious that fellow believers who had died would miss the second coming. So Paul allayed their fears and reminded them, and us, that we can face the sorrows of life and look forward to Jesus' return because we know that death, grief and hope have been transformed.

Death has been transformed. For us believers, death is the impenetrable and irreversible reality, but for Jesus, it is the sleep from which he will shake us awake. Just as he did with Jairus' daughter in Mark 5.

Grief has been transformed. How is our grief different from that of those who don't know Christ? Surprisingly perhaps, our grief is sharper. We feel grief more keenly because our emotions have been sharpened by the regenerating work of the Holy Spirit. Our grief is also different because it is in the context of eternal hope; while we grieve, we also have the glorious expectation of a joyful reunion.

Hope has been transformed. The Christian hope is sure and certain because it is based on Jesus' finished work. When he died and rose again, we were associated with that death and resurrection so that we both died and rose with him. Therefore, after our death, we have the sure hope that resurrection and transformation will follow.

As Christians, we are not immune to sorrow. We face the death of loved ones just as our non-Christian neighbours do. And like Jesus weeping at Lazarus' tomb, we feel that grief keenly. But Jesus' death and resurrection mean that, for believers, death and mourning are transformed. We grieve only for a short time, knowing that one day those who are asleep in Christ will return with him and, together with them, we shall receive our resurrection bodies. If you are mourning today or facing your own mortality, allow these truths to penetrate your grief. Lift your eyes and wait expectantly for the imminent return of Christ – our sure and certain hope.

> If death tells us we're not too important to die, the gospel tells us we're so important that Christ died for us. And not because death's message about us is wrong. It isn't. On our own, we are dispensable. But joined to Christ, through our union with him, we are righteous, we are children of God, and God will not let us die any more than he left Jesus in the grave.
>
> (Matthew McCullough, *Remember Death*, Crossway, 2018, p. 24)

Day 352

Read: 1 Thessalonians 4:13–18

Key verse: 1 Thessalonians 4:16

....

16 For the Lord himself will come down from heaven, with a loud command, with the voice of the archangel and with the trumpet call of God, and the dead in Christ will rise first.

Have you ever wondered what the return of Christ will be like?

We do not know many details, but one is guaranteed: his second coming will be very different from his first. Christ's return will be heralded with a loud command, presumably from God the Father, for who else knows when Christ is going to return and who else has the authority to give this command? God spoke when his Son was baptized (Matthew 3:17); he spoke when his Son stood on the Mount of Transfiguration (Matthew 17:5); he spoke in anticipation of Calvary: 'I have glorified [my name], and will glorify it again' (John 12:28); and, finally, he will speak the ponderous words of command: 'My beloved Son, go back again.'

The archangel Michael (see Jude 9; Daniel 10:13, 21; 12:1; Revelation 12:7), the leader of the angel armies, will announce Christ's victory. What will he say? I think he will cry out, 'The victory is won, the kingdoms of this world have become the kingdoms of our God and of his Christ and he will reign for ever and ever' (see Revelation 11:15).

And then the trumpet will sound. Why will there be a trumpet?

• It is the trumpet of Exodus 19:16 that indicates 'God is here'.

• It is the trumpet of Joel 2:1 that signals the great and awesome day of the Lord has at last come.

- It is the trumpet of Jubilee in Leviticus 25:9 that announces the release of slaves and the remission of debts.

- It is the trumpet of Isaiah 27:12–13 that sounds so the people of God scattered in Egypt and Assyria may be brought home to Zion.

- It is the trumpet of Matthew 24:31 that galvanizes the angels of God to gather God's people – past, present and future – from the four corners of the earth.

Are you looking forward to that day?

We can become so easily caught up in the good things – family, friendships, celebrations, work and holidays – that Jesus' return is not a top priority. We talk about it but don't yearn for it. We pray for it but don't tell people about it. We believe it but don't let it shape our behaviour. Today, intentionally dwell not just on the present realities of life but also on the future certainties.

Imagine the scene: Jesus returning to earth in a blaze of glory; the skies shuddering as God the Father gives the command and the archangel announces his victory. The trumpet blasts, gathering all the family of God. The glory and majesty of Christ is unmistakable. Fix this vision in your mind, let it ignite a passion in your heart for loving Christ and living for him more and more.

Day 353

Read: 1 Thessalonians 4:13–18
Key verses: 1 Thessalonians 4:16–18

••

> ¹⁶ For the Lord himself will come down from heaven, with a loud command, with the voice of the archangel and with the trumpet call of God, and the dead in Christ will rise first. ¹⁷ After that, we who are still alive and are left will be caught up together with them in the clouds to meet the Lord in the air. And so we will be with the Lord for ever. ¹⁸ Therefore encourage one another with these words.

What will happen to us at Jesus' second coming?

Paul explains that the bodies of Christians who have died will be raised to meet their souls, which once left them, and there will be a mighty reconstitution of those who are fully redeemed. But what about those who haven't yet died? Paul says, 'We who are still alive and are left will be caught up together with them in the clouds to meet the Lord in the air.'

There is obviously symbolism here. In the Bible, the clouds represent the presence of God. After the exodus, God lived among the people in a cloudy, fiery pillar. The cloud indicated that 'God is here'. When Jesus, Peter, James and John stood on the Mount of Transfiguration, a cloud overshadowed them, and out of the cloud came the voice that said, 'This is my Son.' The message which rang out loudly and clearly was: 'God is here.' And believers will be caught up in the clouds, into the very presence of God. The air is the dominion usurped by Satan, the prince of the power of the air (Ephesians 2:2). But we will enter into his usurped dominion because he will have gone for ever. Only Jesus reigns.

The symbolism is important: with Jesus, we will be caught into the presence of God; we will enter into his eternal triumph. But there is also objectivity and reality: we will be caught up. The phrase is literally 'we will be snatched'. We will be snatched from the earth. And if we are alive on that day, we will be lifted bodily to stand before Jesus, in the fullness of redemption, as he reconciles all creation to himself.

Paul wrote these verses not to satisfy our curiosity or to give us a timeline for future events but to encourage us. We can press on through suffering and grief because we know that, one day, we will meet the Lord and then be with him for ever.

Just as the Holy of Holies contained the dazzling presence of God in ancient Israel, so will the New Jerusalem contain his presence. The new earth's greatest miracle will be our continual, unimpeded access to the God of everlasting splendour and perpetual delight . . . God's greatest gift to us is now, and always will be, nothing less than himself.
(Randy Alcorn, 'Heaven Would Be Hell without God', 24 April 2018, <www.desiringgod.org/articles/heaven-would-be-hell-without -god>, accessed 20 September 2021)

Therefore encourage one another with these words.
(1 Thessalonians 4:18)

Day 354

Read: 1 Peter 1:1–12
Key verse: 1 Peter 1:3

....

³ *Praise be to the God and Father of our Lord Jesus Christ! In his
great mercy he has given us new birth into a living hope through
the resurrection of Jesus Christ from the dead.*

How has your hope in Jesus, and the future he has promised,
changed your life?

For Peter, this living hope, grounded securely in Jesus' resurrection,
proved life-transforming. From Caesarea Philippi on, Jesus had
spoken of his death and resurrection. But like the other disciples,
Peter didn't have a category for a crucified Messiah. Messiahs weren't
supposed to die; they were supposed to win and emerge triumphant.
So when Jesus spoke of his impending death, Peter rebuked him:
'Never, Lord . . . This shall never happen to you!' (Matthew 16:22).
Peter promised, 'Even if all fall away on account of you, I never will'
(Matthew 26:33), but later that same night, he denied ever knowing
Jesus. After Jesus' crucifixion, however, when the reports from the
women said that Jesus was alive, Peter ran with John to the tomb
(John 20). Then, according to Paul in 1 Corinthians 15, Jesus, in his
resurrected body, appeared privately to Peter before he met with
the eleven other disciples. Hope sparked into life, followed by a
restoration to service: 'Simon son of John [Peter], do you love me
more than these?' (John 21:15).

Yet there were more massive dimensions to this hope. By this point,
Peter had understood the implications. He knew that with the death
and resurrection of Jesus came God's final provision for the forgiveness of sins. The promised messianic kingdom was dawning. Eternal
life could be experienced now, even if not consummated until the
end. And with Jesus' resurrection, there was, one day, every hope of

our gaining resurrection bodies like Jesus' resurrection body. In fact, in due course, Jesus' return would come to be referred to as the 'blessed hope' of the church (Titus 2:13).

In some measure, we participate in all of this now by means of the new birth; so, with Peter, we joyfully declare, 'Praise be to the God and Father of our Lord Jesus Christ! In his great mercy he has given us new birth into a living hope through the resurrection of Jesus Christ from the dead.'

We have hope in this life and the next because of Jesus' resurrection. His death and resurrection are the irrefutable proof that our sins are forgiven, our relationship with God is restored and eternal life can be experienced now. We also have the promise that we will have resurrection bodies and spend for ever with God in the new heaven and new earth. Today, praise God for his 'great mercy' towards us: 'he does not treat us as our sins deserve' (Psalm 103:10). Thank God that, through Christ, we have new birth into a living hope, which transforms our lives now and for ever.

Day 355

Read: 1 Peter 1:1–12
Key verses: 1 Peter 1:3–5

....

> [3] *Praise be to the God and Father of our Lord Jesus Christ! In his great mercy he has given us new birth into a living hope through the resurrection of Jesus Christ from the dead,* [4] *and into an inheritance that can never perish, spoil or fade. This inheritance is kept in heaven for you,* [5] *who through faith are shielded by God's power until the coming of the salvation that is ready to be revealed in the last time.*

Are you looking forward to your inheritance? Not from your parents or a distant relative, but the inheritance God has for you.

There is a parallel in verse 3 and verses 4 and 5 between new birth into a living hope and new birth into an inheritance that can never perish. When Peter writes of this imperishable inheritance, doubtless he is recalling Jesus' teaching about treasure in the Sermon on the Mount:

> Do not store up for yourselves treasures on earth, where moths and vermin destroy, and where thieves break in and steal. But store up for yourselves treasures in heaven, where moths and vermin do not destroy, and where thieves do not break in and steal.
> (Matthew 6:19–20)

Here, the focus is not on treasure quite so much as on inheritance. Peter and his readers have an Old Testament background in mind, picturing the Israelites' inheritance first and foremost to be the land – not only given to the Israelites as a whole but also parcelled out to each clan, each extended family, with lasting rights of ownership, at least on paper. The Old Testament people of God were aliens and pilgrims until they entered the Promised Land and received their inheritance.

This does not mean they were utterly destitute, for there was a sense in which, although they were not yet in the land promised to them, the land was in principle theirs. It was therefore the Promised Land; they looked forward to it with hope. In due course, God brought about the accomplishment of that hope, and they entered into their inheritance.

Peter's description of our inheritance emerges from this God-ordained Old Testament model. We, too, are aliens and pilgrims. This does not mean we are paupers waiting for an inheritance that is in no sense ours. We are enriched in the certainty of the promise, and Peter insists that some part of it has already come to us. We have a clear title to the inheritance that God has reserved for us, and we also possess a down payment.

Because of Christ's work on the cross, you qualify to receive the inheritance God has planned – your name is on the title deeds (Colossians 1:12–13). The Holy Spirit living within you is the first instalment and the promise of the full measure to come (Ephesians 1:14). Today, if you are feeling hopeless or find yourself doubting God's promise, make Paul's prayer your own: 'I pray that the eyes of your heart may be enlightened in order that you may know the hope to which he has called you, the riches of his glorious inherit-ance in his holy people' (Ephesians 1:18).

Day 356

Read: 1 Peter 1:1–12
Key verses: 1 Peter 1:3–5

· ·

³Praise be to the God and Father of our Lord Jesus Christ! In his great mercy he has given us new birth into a living hope through the resurrection of Jesus Christ from the dead, ⁴and into an inheritance that can never perish, spoil or fade. This inheritance is kept in heaven for you, ⁵who through faith are shielded by God's power until the coming of the salvation that is ready to be revealed in the last time.

Can we be sure of receiving our inheritance? Can we bank our lives on it?

Peter says that our inheritance can 'never perish, spoil or fade'. These words are used in various Old Testament descriptions in Greek, concerning things that happened to the land. Sometimes the people are run out of the land or marauding troops come in, but the land is still there and does not perish. According to 2 Peter 3, the whole universe will finally burn up with such a fierce heat that even the elements will be devoured, but our inheritance won't burn up; it's reserved in heaven for us.

In Ancient Israel's concept of things, the land could also be polluted by the sins of the people, but the new heaven and the new earth have no sin in them. They are never defiled; they cannot be spoiled. Peter actually calls the new heaven and the new earth 'the home of righteousness' (2 Peter 3:13). There will be no shred of bitterness, hatred, arrogance, greed, lust, envy, jealousy, murder or resentment – nothing to spoil or corrode our inheritance.

The land could even be parched; its fruitfulness could fade, as in the days of drought imposed by God himself under the ministry of Elijah. But our inheritance is salvation consummated in the new heaven and the new earth, where there will never ever be any sort of drought again.

This inheritance is kept in heaven for us, and we are kept for it. God keeps your inheritance for *you* (verse 4). At the same time, he keeps *you* for the inheritance, shielded by God's power (verse 5). Otherwise, the inheritance could be nicely parked up while we wander off in rebellion and are damned. But no, God keeps his own people by his power, preserving us as he preserves the inheritance for us; as we hope for it and eagerly anticipate our inheritance, we are shielded by God's power, through faith. This is God's means of keeping us (verse 5), as it is God's means of saving us. This faith and hope are both grounded in God: 'Through him you believe in God, who raised him from the dead and glorified him, and so your faith and hope are in God' (1 Peter 1:21).

Our inheritance is utterly secure. It could not be more so because God himself is our guarantee. It will be everlasting and infinitely satisfying.

> We will be less sinful in the next life than we are now [indeed, for we won't be sinful at all], but we will not be any more secure in the next life than we are now. If you are united to Christ, you are as good as in heaven already.
> (Dane Ortlund, *Gentle and Lowly*, Crossway, 2020, p. 195)

Day 357

Read: Revelation 4:1–11
Key verses: Revelation 4:1–2

....

¹*After this I looked, and there before me was a door standing open in heaven. And the voice I had first heard speaking to me like a trumpet said, "Come up here, and I will show you what must take place after this." ²At once I was in the Spirit, and there before me was a throne in heaven with someone sitting on it.*

What is God doing now?

He is on his throne in heaven.

This vision of God's throne room in chapter 4 comes naturally after chapters 2 and 3, where God is giving the church a spiritual health check. There are lots of wonderful things to commend, but also some serious problems and challenges. The church is under attack: virtually all the seven churches are facing persecution. They are being invaded by false teachers. The most alarming thing of all is the spiritual decline within the churches, almost bordering on apostasy.

Christ looks at the church in Ephesus and says, 'Your love for me was so strong, how sad to see how weak and cold it has become.' To the church in Sardis, he says, 'You have such a fantastic reputation! Everyone's talking about how alive you are, but it's only a reputation. You are spiritually dead.' Worst of all, to the church in Laodicea, he says, 'You're so compromised, you make me sick.'

You can imagine the apostle John feeling discouraged and fearing for the future of the church. But God takes him to heaven and shows him this glorious vision. The point is that even when the church is feeble, even when the world seems to turn its back on God completely, the ultimate place of authority in the universe is his throne. The word 'throne' is a key word in Revelation. It is used about sixty times in the New Testament, forty-seven times in the book of Revelation and fourteen times in this chapter. The theme of this chapter of Revelation, and of the whole Bible, is the absolute authority of the throne of God.

God isn't looking at the universe, wringing his hands and getting frustrated. He is on his throne. God has plans for his cosmos, his church and you. Perhaps you have trials and troubles. You need to take this to heart: God is still on the throne – you are in God's hands; your children are in God's hands; and your church is in God's hands. There is a God in heaven who reigns, and he loves you. The sovereignty of God is the softest pillow on which Christians can lay their heads.

Are you fearful about the future for your children, for Christian believers or for the nation's spiritual health? God is on the throne. Meditate on this truth as you pray about world events, your family relationships, circumstances and sadness. Rest and rely on God's gracious sovereignty, trusting that he is working for your good and for his glory.

You, LORD, reign for ever;
  your throne endures from generation to generation.
(Lamentations 5:19)

Day 358

Read: Revelation 4:1–11
Key verses: Revelation 4:3, 5

....

> [3] *And the one who sat there had the appearance of jasper and ruby. A rainbow that shone like an emerald encircled the throne . . .* [5] *From the throne came flashes of lightning, rumblings and peals of thunder.*

Have you ever been awestruck? Have you been left speechless, gazing at a breathtaking sunset or holding a newborn baby?

John is awestruck in heaven's throne room. When he describes Christ's majesty in Revelation 1, he says that Jesus is like 'a son of man'. When Jesus went back to heaven, he didn't leave his humanity behind; he still has it. But when John describes God the Father sitting on the throne, he can't use those kinds of pictures. Finite human language struggles to put God's majesty into words. He has the '*appearance* of jasper' and is encircled by a rainbow that shines '*like* an emerald'.

Surrounding the throne are twenty-four other thrones, and sitting upon them are twenty-four elders. These elders represent the totality of the redeemed community. They are dressed in white, with crowns of gold on their heads: redeemed by Christ's blood, they reign with Christ, his victor's crown upon each of their heads. Isn't it encouraging that those closest to heaven's throne are the redeemed community? The church, the people of God, are closest to God's heart. When we become disillusioned with the church and are tempted to criticize it, we need to remember, it is God's church.

John describes the 'flashes of lightning, rumblings and peals of thunder' coming from the throne (verse 5). The Greek uses the present tense: this is continually happening. Just as, at Sinai, the ground shook and the air was filled with light, this is a picture of the holiness of God. Before the throne, the seven spirits of God are blazing. There aren't seven spirits. Rather, seven is a picture of the fullness of the Holy Spirit. Here, we see the grand mystery of the Trinity: the Father on the throne; in front of the throne, the Spirit of God; and, in chapter 5, the Lamb who was slain.

Then, around the throne are four living creatures. They have faces like the cherubim in Ezekiel 1 and six wings like the seraphim in Isaiah 6. They represent the animate creation God has made. The lion represents the wild beasts; the ox, domestic beasts; the eagle, flying beasts; and man, the pinnacle of creation. This is a picture of the whole of creation joining the redeemed community in heaven to worship God.

What's the overall impression of this vision? The flashes of lightning, the sounds of thunder, the movement of angels . . . It is a picture of awe, mystery, majesty and wonder. Are you looking forward to spending eternity with God? It is going to be glorious!

The reality of the throne room of heaven is so awesome because God is glorious, majestic, magnificent and mysterious. We too easily settle for a pygmy god who is made in our image: one who is a friend but not fierce, and familiar but not flawless. Today, gaze on John's vision; recapture your awe and reverent fear of God. Don't settle for a God who is too small.

Who among the gods
  is like you, LORD?
Who is like you –
  majestic in holiness,
awesome in glory,
  working wonders?
(Exodus 15:11)

Day 359

Read: Revelation 4:1–11
Key verses: Revelation 4:8, 10–11

• •

> [8] *Day and night [the living creatures] never stop saying:*
> *'"Holy, holy, holy*
> *is the Lord God Almighty,"*
> *who was, and is, and is to come.'*
>
> [10] *The twenty-four elders . . . lay their crowns before the throne*
> *and say:*
> [11] *"You are worthy, our Lord and God,*
> *to receive glory and honour and power,*
> *for you created all things,*
> *and by your will they were created*
> *and have their being."*

What style of music is appropriate? What instruments should we use?

In many churches, worship is a hotly contested subject. In heaven, it is not debated, only demonstrated.

Every picture of heaven given in Revelation always speaks about the worship and adoration of the One who's on the throne and the Lamb. The creatures' worship is continual: 'day and night they never stop saying: "Holy, holy, holy is the Lord God Almighty"' (verse 8). The elders join this God-centred adoration. They are not concerned about themselves or their feelings; their attention is on God and on his majesty and wonder. These twenty-four elders (representing the redeemed) and creation (represented by the four living creatures) lift up their hearts in praise and worship.

The focus of this worship begins with who God is (verse 8). The simple, profound, fundamental truth about God is his holiness. It is the sheer *Godness* of God that marks him out as God: his awesome majesty, his absolute purity, his holiness. He is the Holy One, the Almighty One, the Eternal and Unchanging God, who was, and who is, and who is to come. We are creatures of a moment; like John, dust and ashes standing before the eternal One.

As the elders lay their crowns before him, the focus of their worship shifts from who God is to what he has done (verse 11). God created everything out of nothing, by the power of his word and for the purpose of his glory. The whole of the cosmos begins with God, belongs to God and exists because God wills it, and it will one day glorify God.

We need to recapture the wonder of God that the living creatures and elders proclaim so that we, too, respond with such praise. We were created, redeemed and destined for adoration. The purpose of Revelation 4 is to cause us to lift our eyes to the heavenly throne, to see the power, majesty and might of God, and cry, 'Wow! What a God!'

Worship will never be redundant. Our worship today, along with that of believers already in heaven, will continue throughout eternity because the worth of who God is and what he has done is inexhaustible. Today, worship God with holy abandon because he is forever worthy of our adoration.

Praise to the Lord
O let all that is in me adore Him
All that hath life and breath
Come now with praises before Him
Let the Amen sound from His people again
Gladly forever adore Him
(Joachim Neander, 1680)

Day 360

Read: Revelation 7:9–12
Key verse: Revelation 7:9

. . . .

⁹After this I looked, and there before me was a great multitude that no one could count, from every nation, tribe, people and language, standing before the throne and before the Lamb. They were wearing white robes and were holding palm branches in their hands.

Would you like a glimpse of heaven?

The book of Revelation presents to us the completion of the great drama of salvation. It lifts the curtain – it is, literally, an 'unveiling' – and, in chapter 7, we are given a vision of heaven.

John gives his first-century believers a glorious vision of God's throne surrounded by representatives from every part of the globe. He piles up the expressions – 'nation', 'tribe', 'people', 'language' – to show that the redeemed, God's family, aren't from a restricted group but from all over the world. And this international community is innumerable: 'a great multitude that no one could count'.

Do you remember when God said to Abraham, 'I will surely bless you and make your descendants as numerous as the stars in the sky and as the sand on the seashore' (Genesis 22:17)? This is John's vision: all Abraham's true offspring, all the servants of God from down through the centuries and from every part of the world, as far as his eyes could see – a countless number streaming in from every direction – but each one standing before the throne and in front of the Lamb. If God is drawing people from every tribe, language, people and nation, then his mission is by definition worldwide. As Christians, we are part of a global family, and we need to be passionately committed to making John's international vision a reality.

Today, we find it increasingly difficult to assert that the Christian faith is for the whole world. In an age that prizes tolerance, it is not easy to proclaim the absolute truth of a universal Saviour. And further, our own horizons are shrinking. It is not uncommon for Christians to focus almost exclusively on personal, family or local church life. These are proper concerns, but the tribalism, nationalism and individualism of our culture should not be allowed to extinguish John's vision. We can't truly worship God and at the same time appear to be totally indifferent about whether or not anyone else is worshipping him.

Jesus declared, 'This gospel of the kingdom will be preached in the whole world as a testimony to all nations, and then the end will come' (Matthew 24:14). Thank God, in recent years we have seen a greater advance of the church's global mission than in any previous century. John's vision is becoming a reality, and now, more than ever, God's international purposes must be in our hearts and on our lips, touching our wallets, shaping our prayers and transforming our churches.

> God is pursuing with omnipotent passion a worldwide purpose of gathering joyful worshippers for himself from every tribe and tongue and people and nation. He has an inexhaustible enthusiasm for the supremacy of his name among the nations. Therefore, let us bring our affections into line with his, and, for the sake of his name, let us renounce the quest for worldly comforts and join his global purpose.
>
> (John Piper, *Let the Nations Be Glad*, IVP, 2010, p. 62)

Day 361

Read: Revelation 7:9–12
Key verses: Revelation 7:11–12

∙∙

> [11]*All the angels were standing round the throne and round the elders and the four living creatures. They fell down on their faces before the throne and worshipped God,* [12]*saying:*
> *'Amen!*
> *Praise and glory*
> *and wisdom and thanks and honour*
> *and power and strength*
> *be to our God for ever and ever.*
> *Amen!'*

'Of this good man let this be written, heaven was in him before he was in heaven.' These words describe the Puritan preacher Richard Sibbes. The seventeenth-century writer Izaak Walton is said to have penned them in his own copy of *The Returning Backslider*, a book by Sibbes.

Are they true of you?

In the Greek, each of the seven qualities listed in verse 12 is preceded by 'the'. In each case, it is not 'a' but 'the' praise, 'the' glory, and so on, above all others that should go to our God for ever and ever. On that day, when all God's people are finally gathered in, the focus will be the glory of God. And we have cause to anticipate that celebration. Psalm 96:3 exhorts us to 'declare his glory among the nations'. We are to proclaim the greatness of God above all other gods. Our task is to call our friends, neighbours and all people to worship him. Indeed, we can say that Jesus came as an evangelist for worshippers.

> Missions is not the ultimate goal of the church. Worship is. Missions exists because worship doesn't. Worship is ultimate, not missions,

because God is ultimate, not man. When this age is over, and the countless millions of the redeemed fall on their faces before the throne of God, missions will be no more. It is a temporary necessity. But worship abides forever. So worship is the fuel and goal of missions. (John Piper, *Let the Nations Be Glad*, IVP, 2010, p. 7).

Perhaps the reason for our lack of concern, our limited giving to missions and our half-hearted prayers is our little-felt emotion of burning desire for God's glory. Henry Martyn, a nineteenth-century missionary to India said, 'I could not endure existence if Jesus was not glorified. It would be hell for me if he were thus dishonoured' (quoted in John Stott with Tim Chester, *The World: A Mission to Be Accomplished*, IVP, 2019, p. 78).

Do we have a similar passion for God's glory? That will be the focus in the new heaven and new earth – and if heaven is in our hearts now, that will be our longing, too. And if we are gripped by God's glory, we will want to further God's mission. Our prayer, and our consequent effort, will echo that of the psalmist: 'Let the peoples praise you, O God; let all the peoples praise you!' (Psalm 67:3, ESV).

When Christ returns Habakkuk's prophesy will be realized: 'The earth will be filled with the knowledge of the glory of the LORD as the waters cover the sea' (Habakkuk 2:14). How do we prepare for that day? How do we increase our desire for God's glory? As in heaven, it begins with worship, focusing on God's character and greatness, not our own. It is a prayerful, conscious, moment-by-moment obedience and willing surrender of ourselves and our lesser loves.

> For from him and through him and for him are all things.
> To him be the glory for ever! Amen.
> (Romans 11:36)

Day 362

Read: Revelation 21:1–27
Key verses: Revelation 21:1–2

. . . .

> [1] *Then I saw "a new heaven and a new earth," for the first heaven and the first earth had passed away, and there was no longer any sea.* [2] *I saw the Holy City, the new Jerusalem, coming down out of heaven from God, prepared as a bride beautifully dressed for her husband.*

What will the new heaven and new earth be like?

John describes it as 'the Holy City', not built by human hands but coming down from God (verse 2). God's city, his work, will be characterized by security, community, immensity, purity, luminosity and intimacy.

Security. There are wonderfully thick walls (verses 17–18).

Community. God is dwelling among his people (verse 3). The names of the twelve tribes of Israel are written on the gates, and the names of the twelve apostles are written on the foundations (verses 12–14). At the end of time, there is one great, united family of God. The barrier, the dividing wall of hostility between Jew and non-Jew, broken down in Christ (Ephesians 2:14), has produced the one people of God, sharing eternity.

Immensity. It measures 12,000 stadia cubed (Revelation 21:16). That is 1,400 miles by 1,400 miles by 1,400 miles. The holy city is huge! There is room here for everyone who comes to Christ. Sharing the gospel is not a sideshow in history; it is the Master's plan. His plan of the ages is to bring countless sinners home as sons and daughters of God: 'a great multitude that no one could count' (Revelation 7:9).

Purity. 'Nothing impure will ever enter' (Revelation 21:27). With great sensitivity, and tears in our eyes, we have to warn people of the judgement to come (Revelation 20:11–15). The stakes are high, for there is heaven to gain and hell to shun. That is what makes human decisions so important and gospel witness essential and urgent.

Luminosity. There is no more darkness because God gives light to the heavenly city and Jesus, the Lamb of God, is its lamp (Revelation 21:23–25).

Intimacy. We are heading to a new depth of intimacy with God. In the new heaven and new earth, God will dwell with his people (verse 3). There is no need for a temple where people come to worship God because he is everywhere (verse 22). The city is also described as a perfect cube (verse 16). Why? Because that is what the ancient holy of holies in Solomon's temple was (1 Kings 6:20). Now this whole city, this whole new creation, is a holy of holies, where we will see the Lord: 'they will see his face, and his name will be on their foreheads' (Revelation 22:4). This is what we were made for!

I have heard of him, and though I have not
seen his face, unceasingly I have adored him.
But I shall SEE him!
Yes, we shall actually gaze upon the exalted Redeemer!
Realize the thought!
Is there not a young heaven within it?
You shall see the hand that was nailed for you;
you shall kiss the very lips that said, 'I thirst';
you shall see the thorn-crowned head,
and bow with all the blood-washed throng!
You, the chief of sinners, shall adore him who washed you
in his blood; when you shall have a vision of his glory.
Faith is precious, but what must sight be?
(C. H. Spurgeon, *Spurgeon's Sermons, Volume 05*, Anthony Uyl (ed.), Devoted Publishing, 2017, p. 338)

Day 363

Read: Revelation 22:1–21
Key verses: Revelation 22:1–2

¹*Then the angel showed me the river of the water of life, as clear as crystal, flowing from the throne of God and of the Lamb* ²*down the middle of the great street of the city. On each side of the river stood the tree of life, bearing twelve crops of fruit, yielding its fruit every month.*

Home is the place where you can raid the fruit bowl without asking.

In God's home, there is fruit to eat and refreshment after a long journey. There is a river of cool, fresh, unpolluted water, flowing out from the throne of God. God has been providing water for his people all the way through the Bible: water from the rock in Exodus 17, and Psalm 46:4 declares, 'There is a river whose streams make glad the city of God.' Jesus said, 'Let anyone who is thirsty come to me and drink' (John 7:37). All these images and events point to a truth about God's home – it has a source of never-failing refreshment, and you will never have tasted water like it.

'On each side of the river stood the tree of life' – is it one great tree, which the water flows through, or are there trees down either side of the river? It doesn't really matter. The point is that every month there is different, fresh fruit to eat, and there are no restrictions as there were in Eden.

Neither is there any curse – not on the ground, not on childbirth; no curse of the law, no death. All are completely overcome through Christ, his cross and his coming. We shall 'see his face' (Revelation 22:4): all the instincts to hide that started to arise within the human race in the Garden of Eden will be gone. He will write his name on our foreheads: his name of ownership, the expression of his character will be in us and on us. The Jewish high priest used to bear God's name on his forehead, and he alone could enter God's presence – only one man, from one tribe, on one day, once a year. But we are going to be able to have access to the Lord all the time.

And all this will never end: we 'will reign for ever and ever' (verse 5). We will never be thrown out like Adam and Eve were thrown out of Eden. This 'for ever' security is one of the deepest gifts that a bridegroom can give his bride. It doesn't always work out that way in life, sadly. The best any of us can offer a spouse is 'til death do us part', but God is never going to die. The safety and security he offers us is endless.

Our 'forever home' is waiting. It will be a place of many longed-for gifts, such as security, peace and refreshment. But it will be 'home' simply because God is there. We will delight in his presence endlessly.

We will constantly be more amazed with God, more in love with God, and thus ever more relishing his presence and our relationship with him. Our experience of God will never reach its consummation . . . It will deepen and develop, intensify and amplify, unfold and increase, broaden and balloon.
(Sam Storms, quoted in Randy Alcorn, *Eternal Perspectives*, Tyndale, 2012, p. 240)

Day 364

Read: Revelation 22:1–21
Key verses: Revelation 22:6–7

. . . .

> ⁶*The angel said to me, "These words are trustworthy and true. The Lord, the God who inspires the prophets, sent his angel to show his servants the things that must soon take place."*
> ⁷*"Look, I am coming soon! Blessed is the one who keeps the words of the prophecy written in this scroll."*

How can we know for certain that the new heaven and new earth will be established?

It comes down to whom we trust. Powerfully, we are reminded that the One who speaks to us is the Lord himself: 'He who was seated on the throne said, "I am making everything new!" Then he said, "Write this down, for these words are trustworthy and true"' (Revelation 21:5). The same emphasis continues in chapter 22: 'These words are trustworthy and true' (verse 6). We can trust these promises about Christ's return and the new heaven and the new earth because they are God's words and 'the word of our God stands forever' (Isaiah 40:8, NKJV).

Jesus himself reminds us three times, 'I am coming soon' (Revelation 22:7, 12 and 20). So, why such a delay? 'Soon' does not mean 'immediately'; it means 'imminently', or perhaps 'surprisingly' better captures the idea. The point is that every day we are to anticipate and look forward to his coming and so live each day to his glory.

Because the Lord is returning, what kind of churches do we need? Obedient and responsive ones: 'Look, I am coming soon! Blessed is the one who keeps the words of the prophecy written in this scroll' (verse 7). We also need to walk closely with Christ, worshipping God (verses 8–9) and staying spiritually clean: 'Blessed are those who wash their robes, that they may have the right to the tree of life and may go through the gates into the city' (verse 14). We need daily and hourly to respond to the invitation: 'The Spirit and the bride say, "Come!" And let the one who hears say, "Come!" Let the one who is thirsty come; and let the one who wishes take the free gift of the water of life' (verse 17).

In short, we need to share with others this invitation of a wonderful, ultimate, eternal home.

When friends or colleagues mock the certainty of our future hope, when doubts overwhelm us or our 'momentary affliction' (2 Corinthians 4:17, ESV) seems never-ending, lean on Christ's true and trustworthy words: 'I am coming soon.' As you hold fast to this promise, keep coming to Christ – in worship and obedience, and for forgiveness and cleansing. Pray today that the cry of our hearts truly would be: 'Come, Lord Jesus' (Revelation 22:20).

For further study

If you would like to read more on the theme of hope, you might find this selection of books helpful.

- Randy Alcorn, *Heaven* (Tyndale, 2009)

- Randy Alcorn, *We Shall See God: Charles Spurgeon's classic devotional thoughts on heaven* (Tyndale, 2011)

- D. A. Carson and Jeff Robinson Sr (eds.), *Coming Home: Essays on the new heaven and new earth* (Crossway, 2017)

- Sharon James, *The Dawn of Heaven Breaks: Anticipating eternity* (Evangelical Press, 2007)

- Scot McKnight, *The Heaven Promise: Engaging the Bible's truth about life to come* (Hodder & Stoughton, 2015)

- Bruce Milne, *The Message of Heaven and Hell*, The Bible Speaks Today (IVP, 2002)

- Marcus Nodder, *What Happens When I Die? And other questions about heaven, hell and the life to come* (The Good Book Company, 2013)

- James Paul, *What on Earth Is Heaven?* (IVP, 2021)

- N. T. Wright, *Surprised by Hope* (SPCK, 2011)

Day 365

Read: Jude 1–25
Key verse: Jude 24–25

....

To him who is able to keep you from stumbling and to present you before his glorious presence without fault and with great joy – ²⁵*to the only God our Saviour be glory, majesty, power and authority, through Jesus Christ our Lord, before all ages, now and forevermore! Amen.*

When we look at the problems in our world, the state of the church in our nation, even the troubles within our own family, we can feel overwhelmed by despair. Can we really keep going?

But, these difficulties are not new. Even in the first century the church was beset with problems. False teachers had been given positions of authority and were intent on 'perverting the grace of God' (verse 4). Jude graphically describes them as 'shepherds who only feed themselves. They are clouds without rain' (verse 12).

In the face of these threats, Jude calls for believers – then and now – to stand firm (verses 20–23). He urges us to build each other up in the faith, supporting each other as we fight against sin and encouraging each other with gospel truth. He tells us to 'pray in the Holy Spirit'. We each have the Holy Spirit, and we need to pray in his power and according to his promptings. We are to 'keep ourselves in God's love' by obeying his commands. While we 'wait for God's mercy' we are to show mercy and help restore those who are falling away from the faith.

As we are faithful to Christ we can be confident because overarching and underpinning all we do is the precious promise of God: We are 'called . . . loved in God the Father and kept for Jesus Christ' (verse 1). Jude's concluding words underline this truth by pointing to the steadfast assurance that Christ will not only hold us fast until the end, but he will also share his purity with us and present us before God blameless.

A doxology is a fitting way to close our devotional series because it centres our hearts and minds where they should be – on our infinitely glorious, majestic and powerful Saviour who keeps us, now and forever. It also ties together the themes we have been reflecting on. One day all our *perseverance, prayers* and *suffering* will be over; the truth about Jesus' death on *The Cross* and his resurrection plain for all to see; the *Holy Spirit's* work in our lives accomplished. On that great final day, the *love, grace* and *faithfulness* of God will be fully revealed, our *confidence* and *hope* seen to be well-founded, and our *holiness* and *joy* complete.

How do we respond to a God who does this? We worship him, now and for eternity.

> *Praise, my soul, the King of heaven;*
> *to his feet your tribute bring.*
> *Ransomed, healed, restored, forgiven,*
> *evermore his praises sing.*
> *Alleluia, alleluia!*
> *Praise the everlasting King!*
> (Henry Francis Lyte, 1834)

Bible acknowledgements

KESWICK MINISTRIES

Our purpose
Keswick Ministries exists to inspire and equip Christians to love and live for Christ in his world.

God's purpose is to bring his blessing to all the nations of the world (Genesis 12:3). That promise of blessing, which touches every aspect of human life, is ultimately fulfilled through the life, death, resurrection, ascension and future return of Christ. All of the people of God are called to participate in his missionary purposes, wherever he may place them. The central vision of Keswick Ministries is to see the people of God equipped, inspired and refreshed to fulfil that calling, directed and guided by God's Word in the power of his Spirit, for the glory of his Son.

Our priorities
There are three fundamental priorities which shape all that we do as we look to serve the local church.

Hearing God's Word: The Scriptures are the foundation for the church's life, growth and mission, and Keswick Ministries is committed to preaching and teaching God's Word in a way which is faithful to Scripture and relevant to Christians of all ages and backgrounds.

Becoming like God's Son: From its earliest days, the Keswick movement has encouraged Christians to live godly lives in the power of the Spirit, to grow in Christlikeness and to live under his Lordship in every area of life. This is God's will for his people in every culture and generation.

Serving God's mission: The authentic response to God's Word is obedience to his mission, and the inevitable result of Christlikeness is sacrificial service. Keswick Ministries seeks to encourage committed discipleship in family life, work and society, and energetic engagement in the cause of world mission.

Our ministry

Keswick Convention. The Convention attracts some 12,000 to 15,000 Christians from the UK and around the world to Keswick every summer. It provides Bible teaching for all ages, vibrant worship, a sense of unity across generations and denominations, and an inspirational call to serve Christ in the world. It caters for children of all ages and has a strong youth and young adult programme. And it all takes place in the beautiful Lake District – a perfect setting for rest, recreation and refreshment.

Keswick fellowship. For more than 140 years, the work of Keswick has affected churches worldwide, not just through individuals being changed, but also through Bible conventions that originate or draw their inspiration from the Keswick Convention. Today, there is a network of events that share Keswick Ministries' priorities across the UK and in many parts of Europe, Asia, North America, Australia, Africa and the Caribbean. Keswick Ministries is committed to strengthening the network in the UK and beyond, through prayer, news and co-operative activity.

Keswick teaching and training. Keswick Ministries is developing a range of inspiring, equipping, Bible-centred teaching and training that focuses on 'whole-of-life' discipleship. This builds on the same concern that started the Convention, that all Christians live godly lives in the power of the Spirit in all spheres of life in God's world. Some of the events focus on equipping. They are smaller and more intensive. Others focus on inspiring. Some are for pastors, others for those in different forms of church leadership, while many are for any Christian. All courses aim to see participants return home refreshed to serve.

Keswick resources. Keswick Ministries has produced numerous books, devotionals and study guides to inspire and equip Christians to live for Christ. Our range of digital resources helps you to make the most of Keswick Convention teaching throughout the year including podcasts, study notes, and sung worship. Convention talks and seminars are available via our website, YouTube and the KesTalks podcast.

Our unity

The Keswick movement worldwide has adopted a key Pauline statement to describe its gospel inclusivity: 'All one in Christ Jesus' (Galatians 3:28). Keswick Ministries works with evangelicals from a wide variety of church backgrounds, on the understanding that they share a commitment to the essential truths of the Christian faith as set out in our statement of belief.

Our contact details

T: 017687 80075
E: info@keswickministries.org
W: www.keswickministries.org
Mail: Keswick Ministries, Rawnsley Centre, Main Street, Keswick, Cumbria CA12 5NP, England

APPENDIX
Overview of Bible books

Genesis
'In the beginning God . . . ' The early chapters of Genesis set the scene for the whole Bible, introducing us to an eternal and powerful, yet loving God. As the book traces the story from Adam to Joseph, we discover that God spoke, created and designed us for fellowship with him and with one another. This opening section of the Bible introduces us to a number of firsts – the first individuals, the first sin and the first sacrifice for sin. Even though sin ruptured the relationship between a holy God and his people, he did not abandon them. Rather, he set in motion his eternal plan of redemption, and established covenants pledging his love and faithfulness. As God called his people to obedience, he proved himself to be a God who speaks truth, keeps his promise, and is faithful to his character, purposes and glory.

Leviticus
In the book of Exodus, the tabernacle had been completed. The book of Leviticus explains how people could worship God there and live as a holy nation. The chapters are filled with rules and regulations, most of them received by Moses on Mount Sinai. They cover moral purity, ceremonial cleanliness, holy days and all that the children of Israel needed to know to be God's holy people and worship him in a holy way. Leviticus also describes what was to happen when someone broke the law. The sacrifices prescribed point forward to Jesus' death on our behalf, which makes us holy and able to approach our holy God. Although many of the regulations find their true fulfilment in Christ, and so no longer have to be observed in the same way today, Leviticus reminds us that we worship a holy God who must be approached reverently, and that personal holiness still matters.

Ruth
The story is set in the time of the judges; it does not focus on heroic figures such as Samson or Gideon but on Naomi, an ordinary woman who found herself in Moab grieving the loss of her husband and two adult sons. The book traces her transformation from despair to hope because of the selfless love of her daughter-in-law Ruth and her relative Boaz. Ruth was from Moab but she left her home, family and religion to return to Bethlehem with Naomi. She also embraced Naomi's God, signalling that inclusion in God's

family is dependent not on place of birth or family heritage but on faith expressed by obedience (Romans 1:5). Ruth's loyalty and love for her mother-in-law reflect God's unfailing love for his people. The book ends with a genealogy naming Ruth as a great-grandmother of King David and an ancestor of Christ – a testimony to how God can use our love and obedience for his sovereign purposes.

1 Samuel
Israel had never had a king before. God had appointed judges to lead the people, but now a monarchy was to be established. 1 Samuel charts this transition to a new type of leadership under God. We don't know who wrote this book, but it is named after Samuel, the prophet and judge. He established the monarchy in Israel and anointed the first two kings: Saul and David. As well as providing historical detail, 1 Samuel highlights what personal faithfulness to God looks like, as well as the reasons for, and consequences of, unfaithfulness.

Nehemiah
King Cyrus of Persia had allowed the Jewish exiles to return to Jerusalem. But when Nehemiah, cupbearer to King Artaxerxes, heard that almost 100 years later the city walls of his homeland had not been rebuilt, he was heartbroken. The King sent him to oversee the building project. The book recounts the rebuilding of the wall, the opposition the Jewish people encountered, the new residents chosen to live in the city, the spiritual revival when Ezra read God's law and Nehemiah's reforms.

Psalms
Jesus, like many Israelites before and after him, used the Psalms in his public and private worship. The Book of Psalms is a collection of prayers and songs, gathered over a number of centuries and written by a variety of authors, including King David. They are full of personal testimony, but direct our focus to God as King, Creator, Judge, Redeemer, Helper and Deliverer. Each psalm is carefully crafted poetry, rich in imagery, and, although written for a specific context, contains timeless truths. On any and every occasion, we can go to the Psalms and find words to express our emotions, words of Scripture we can use to speak to God.

Isaiah
The catalyst for Isaiah's ministry was his vision of God on the throne (chapter 6). His unenviable task was to warn the people of Judah that

continued sin would result in judgement at the hands of the Babylonians. They would be carried off into exile, the city of Jerusalem would be destroyed, and restoration would only begin when God's servant, King Cyrus of Persia, allowed the Jews to return home. The prophet also spoke about a servant of God greater than Cyrus. He prophesied about a Messiah, descended from David, who would rule righteously, and through whose suffering complete salvation would be achieved. Written about 700 years in advance, chapter 53 points forward with breathtaking clarity to Jesus' death on the cross for our sins.

Daniel

Daniel was one of the young Jewish men carried off into exile in Babylon by King Nebuchadnezzar. He was given a job in the palace, and his work ethic and integrity meant he quickly rose through the ranks to become one of the king's most trusted servants. His book is made up of historical narrative (chapters 1–6) and highly symbolic prophetic visions (chapters 7–12); it reveals Daniel to be an interpreter of dreams and a man who cultivated the habit of prayer. God's sovereignty is a key theme: 'the Most High God is sovereign over all kingdoms on earth' (5:21).

Hosea

Hosea was a prophet living in the northern kingdom of Israel who called God's people to repentance for almost forty years. Like Isaiah, Jeremiah and Ezekiel, he lived out his message in a dramatically symbolic fashion. God told him to marry Gomer, a promiscuous woman, love her and take her back when she was unfaithful. Hosea's marriage was a picture of God's unfailing love for his people, who had been unfaithful, worshipping the Canaanite gods and attributing their prosperity to them. Despite their disobedience, God longed for the Israelites to return to him so that he could take them back. The love and intimacy of the covenant relationship God has with his people – then and now – is described graphically throughout the book, not only as a marriage relationship but also as that of a father and child.

Jonah

The book of Jonah is named after God's prophet who lived during the reign of King Jeroboam II. The king had restored the borders of the northern kingdom of Israel after almost a century of conflict. Although Assyria remained Israel's great enemy, the people became complacent, enjoying their favoured relationship with God. The story records Jonah's unwillingness to call the Assyrian city of Nineveh to repentance. He was reluctant to share God's grace and love with those he deemed to be unworthy of it. The challenge of the book is to recognize we are all unworthy of God's grace – that's what makes the gospel such good news and that's why we can't keep it to ourselves.

Habakkuk
We don't often get an insight into a prophet's private prayer life. But in the book of Habakkuk, we see the prophet crying out to God.

Habakkuk was a contemporary of Jeremiah and lived in Jerusalem. Under King Jehoiakim, wickedness, violence and anarchy were rife and the prophet couldn't understand why God did not intervene. When God answered his prayer and told him judgement would come through the hands of the evil Babylonians, Habakkuk was even more stunned. What changed the questions of 'Why?' and 'How long, Lord?' in chapter 1 to the worship of chapter 3? When God doesn't answer our prayers as we had hoped, when we don't understand what he is doing, how can we say with Habakkuk, 'Yet I will rejoice in the Lord, I will be joyful in God my Saviour'? (3:18). This book teaches us how to be confident in God's character and purposes, regardless of our circumstances.

Matthew
Matthew was one of the twelve disciples. He left his work as a tax collector to follow Jesus. His assumption of Jewish customs, extensive quotations from the Old Testament and emphasis on Jesus' descent from King David seems to indicate he wrote his Gospel account primarily for Jewish Christians. His aim was to confirm that Jesus is the Messiah and the fulfilment of Old Testament prophecies. His Gospel is arranged around five discourses, the most famous of which, the Sermon on the Mount (chapters 5–7), includes Jesus' radical call to be like God by loving our enemies.

Mark
This Gospel was written by the young man who abandoned Paul on his first mission trip. Barnabas wanted to give Mark a second chance and invite him to accompany them on the next journey, but Paul refused and, ultimately, Paul and Barnabas parted ways. Thankfully, over time, Mark proved his commitment to Christ and he and Paul were fully reconciled (2 Timothy 4:11). Mark based his Gospel on Peter's preaching and it is a fast-paced, easy-to-read account of Jesus' ministry. It was most probably written for the

Gentile believers in Rome who were facing the Emperor Nero's persecution. Mark encourages them to persevere by highlighting themes of suffering, discipleship and the cross. He records Jesus' teaching on the greatest commandment and the kind of love that God requires.

Luke

This gospel is a companion volume to the book of Acts and, although no author's name is mentioned, the most likely writer is Luke – a doctor and missionary companion of Paul. Luke wrote so that his patron Theophilus 'may know the certainty of the things you have been taught' (1:4). The distinctive emphases of Luke's gospel are the Gentiles' place in God's salvation plan and God's particular concern for women, the poor and the marginalised. We are challenged to extend God's grace to the unworthy and the outsiders, just as Jesus did.

Acts

Acts was the second volume written by Doctor Luke. His first, his Gospel, sets out what Jesus 'began to do and to teach' (Acts 1:1), and this book explains what Jesus continued to do through the apostles' preaching and the growth of the church. Acts is a selective account of the first thirty years of the church's life. It describes the relentless progress of the gospel from Jerusalem to Rome, the lives and ministry of Peter and Paul, and the role of the Holy Spirit.

The book of Acts shows believers being faithful to Jesus' commission to be his witnesses (Acts 1:8). Their obedience meant being faithful to the message and spread of the gospel, regardless of suffering, and faithful to God's vision for the church.

Romans

Paul had always longed to visit Rome. Probably during his third missionary journey, on the way back to Jerusalem, with the collection he'd received for the poverty-stricken believers there, Paul wrote to the church in Rome, anticipating his visit. Because this church had never been visited by an apostle, Paul was at pains to convey the basic truths of the gospel. Chapters 1–11 are almost like a theological essay, as Paul presents God's plan of salvation to this mixed congregation of Jews and Gentiles. In the rest of the letter, he urges these believers to put this theology into practice and live holy lives.

1 Corinthians

1 Corinthians is a response to a letter the church sent Paul (7:1) and a visit he had from concerned members of the congregation (1:11). As such, he sought to address a number of issues facing the church: challenges to his apostolic authority, division and rivalry among believers, immorality seeping in from the surrounding culture, false teaching about the resurrection, and abuse of communion. Paul wanted believers to understand that the gospel is not just for salvation, but for life – it must have an impact on our character and our conduct.

2 Corinthians

The apostle Paul had a close association with the church he founded in Corinth. He wrote to them four times (two of those letters are lost, with 1 and 2 Corinthians being preserved in Scripture), and he visited them at least three times. It wasn't always an easy relationship; Paul describes his second visit as 'painful' (2 Corinthians 2:1) because he had to deal with a disciplinary issue. He delayed his next visit, not wanting to cause the congregation further grief, and instead wrote to them about his continuing concerns (in one of the lost letters). Paul wrote 2 Corinthians to pave the way for his third visit, explaining his delay and expressing his delight that the matter had been resolved (chapter 7). He encourages the believers to resume the collection for the Jerusalem church so that it would be complete when he arrived (chapters 8–9). Finally, in the last three chapters, he addresses the issue of his authenticity as an apostle and the 'different gospel' (11:4) false apostles are peddling. This letter includes more autobiographical material than any of his others as Paul responds to the vicious opposition of those he led to faith. His response teaches those who trust in Christ how to think about suffering, death and eternity.

Galatians

No warm greetings open this letter. Paul is astonished that believers are turning to a 'different gospel' (1:6). Some Jewish Christians are proposing that Old Testament ceremonial laws still bind believers. Paul strenuously denies this, explaining that having and doing the law do not end in freedom but slavery (4:21—5:2). He reminds them of the true gospel: we are justified by grace through faith in Christ, which sets the pattern for our Christian lives. We can't earn God's favour by good works. Rather, we grow in Christlikeness by obedience as we live by faith in Christ and rely on the Holy Spirit's power.

Ephesians

God's high calling for the church is the resounding theme of Ephesians. Paul had stayed in Ephesus for three years, planting a church. This commercial centre was a strategic place for evangelism, from which the gospel spread to the surrounding communities. No doubt Paul's letter was intended to be circulated to all the churches in the area.

Unusually, Paul is not addressing a particular error or heresy; he is writing to remind believers that the church displays God's 'manifold wisdom' (3:10), and so they should serve one another, seeking unity and maturity. He explains that we are saved by grace alone so that no one can boast and that God promises to continue his work of grace changing us into Christ's likeness.

Philippians

Paul is writing to the church in the Roman colony of Philippi to thank them for their financial gift and update them on his work. He writes about a wide range of issues relating to Christian living. He exhorts them to 'rejoice in the Lord' (4:4), grow in love, and stand firm in the face of persecution. Chapter 2:6–11, perhaps an early Christian song, describes Jesus' humility going to the cross and his subsequent exaltation by his Father. Paul is not just providing theological information, but urging believers to share Christ's mindset and strive for unity in the church.

Colossians

The church at Colossae was founded when Epaphras, a convert of Paul's from Ephesus, took the gospel back to his home town (1:7–8). Heresy had invaded this young church and Paul wrote from his prison cell in Rome, or perhaps Ephesus, to help these new believers hold fast to the truth of the gospel. His letter emphasizes the complete adequacy of Christ, who is the image of God, the head of the church, the first to be resurrected from the dead, and the Reconciler of all things. He reminds the Colossians what they once were and the difference Jesus' death has made for their present and future.

1 Thessalonians

The first epistle to the Thessalonians is essentially a follow-up letter to new Christians. Persecution had forced Paul and his companions to flee the busy seaport city of Thessalonica sooner than he would have wished, leaving behind a group of very new Jewish and Gentile converts (Acts 17:1–10). Paul wrote to these believers from Corinth to encourage them to stand firm in the face of persecution. The letter also provides instruction about the second coming of Christ that Paul had hoped to give in person. He prays for these believers, who had started off so well, to be faithful and to continue making spiritual progress.

2 Timothy

This letter records Paul's last words. He was in prison, chained to a Roman soldier, dictating this letter to Luke for his young pastor friend, Timothy, Paul's 'true son in the faith' (1 Timothy 1:2). Timothy had been his travelling companion on missionary journeys, had visited churches on his behalf, was with him during his first stint in prison and was now the pastor of the church in Ephesus. Paul wrote to Timothy, encouraging him to visit but, more importantly, pleading with him to stay faithful, keeping Christ and the gospel central to his life and ministry.

Titus

After Paul's release from his first imprisonment in Rome, he and Titus briefly visited Crete. Paul asked Titus to stay on the island to establish the church and appoint elders (1:5). It was not easy to be a Christian on Crete, as the island was rife with immorality, gluttony and laziness (1:12). Paul is keen to remind these new converts that accepting the grace of the gospel results in a change of lifestyle. In a depraved society, believers are to be recognized by their holy living. Titus is to teach the people to know and do 'what is good' (1:8, 16; 2:3, 7, 14; 3:1, 8, 14).

Hebrews

We don't know who wrote the book of Hebrews, but we do know why it was written. In the face of persecution, some Jewish Christians were drifting away from the gospel. Unbelief had crept in, they were not making spiritual progress, and they had given up meeting together. Like the previous generation of Israelites in the desert, they were in danger of facing God's judgement. The writer made it clear that returning to the comfortable ways of Judaism was not an option, because Christ's coming had changed the spiritual landscape for ever. Christ was God's full and final revelation; he completes Israel's history, law, ceremonial rituals and priesthood. This book urges believers to remain faithful and persevere in the faith, by pointing them to Christ's absolute supremacy in divine revelation and his absolute sufficiency in Christian experience: 'fix your thoughts . . . [and fix] your eyes on Jesus' (Hebrews 3:1; 12:2).

James

Stephen's martyrdom in Jerusalem signalled a mass exodus, as believers fled throughout the Roman Empire. As leader of the Jerusalem church, what words of encouragement would James write to these persecuted believers? Perhaps a little surprisingly, his key message was: faith works. Genuine belief inevitably transforms our speech, suffering, priorities, and every other aspect of life. In just five chapters, James briefly touches upon a whole variety of issues that concern these new believers. He doesn't give an exhaustive treatise on any one topic, but simply urges them to live out their faith, knowing that there is a value and purpose to their suffering.

1 Peter

The believers scattered through Asia Minor (modern-day Turkey) were not prepared for the persecution they were facing. So Peter reminded them of God's eternal purposes. He urged them to rejoice in the hope of their inheritance, knowing that suffering was only temporary, and paled in comparison to the eternal glory they would enjoy. He also encouraged them with the example of Jesus' suffering and the privilege of belonging to God's people. The purpose of his letter was to give these pilgrims confidence in God's grace, whatever circumstances they faced: 'I have written to you briefly, encouraging you and testifying that this is the true grace of God. Stand fast in it' (1 Peter 5:12).

1 John

In his later years, John, Jesus' beloved disciple, was pastor of the church at Ephesus. It seems that this letter was probably a circular written to the other churches in the province of Asia. John was primarily writing to combat the early signs of Gnosticism. This heresy taught that the spirit was entirely good, and matter, the body, was entirely bad. The teaching had three main consequences – Jesus' humanity was denied; salvation was seen as an escape from the body, not by having faith in Christ but by possessing special knowledge; and lack of morality was rife because it didn't matter what you did with your body. John wrote to oppose this false teaching and assure believers that they were truly saved: 'I write these things to you who believe in the name of the Son of God so that you may know that you have eternal life' (5:13). He wanted the Christians to know that they could base their whole lives on the truths of the gospel. His first letter points us to Jesus' death on the cross as the grounds for our unshakeable confidence in God's love and our salvation.

Revelation

As early as the end of the first century, the future of the church hung in the balance. False teaching and internal division were rife. Domitian, the Roman emperor, had instigated persecution against those who would not worship him as lord. The apostle John, exiled on the island of Patmos, wrote to encourage believers to resist the demands of the emperor. He exhorted them to stand firm against the devil's schemes, secure in the knowledge that God was with them and that, one day soon, they would be vindicated.

Written in an apocalyptic style, the book of Revelation is full of highly symbolic visions that can seem strange to us. We won't understand every detail, but the certainty of Christ's triumphant return comes across loudly and clearly, so we can be confident in God's sovereignty and love, as well as our salvation and glorious future.

Food for the Journey THEMES

The **Food for the Journey: Themes** series offers daily devotions from much loved Bible teachers at the Keswick Convention, exploring how particular themes are woven through the Bible and what we can learn from them today. In a convenient, pocket-sized format, these little books are ideal to accompany you wherever you go.

Available in the series

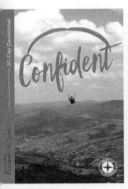 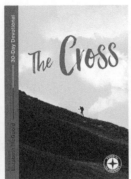 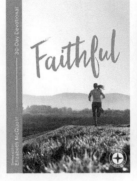 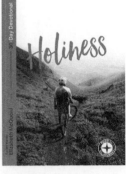

Confident
978 1 78974 190 2
'A beautiful collection.'
Elinor Magowan

The Cross
978 1 78974 191 9
'A must-read.'
Gavin Calver

Faithful
978 1 78974 341 8
'Gripping.'
Sharon Hastings

Holiness
978 1 78974 196 4
'Life-giving.'
Marcus Honeysett

Hope
978 1 78974 194 0
'Thought-provoking.'
Linda Allcock

Joy
978 1 78974 163 6
'A rich feast!'
Edrie Mallard

Persevere
978 1 78974 102 5
'Full of essential theology.'
Catherine Campbell

Pray
978 1 78974 169 8
'The ideal reboot.'
Julian Hardyman

Available from your local Christian bookshop or **www.ivpbooks.com**

Related titles from IVP

Food for the Journey

The Food for the Journey series offers daily devotionals from well-loved Bible teachers at the Keswick Convention in an ideal pocket-sized format – to accompany you wherever you go.

Available in the series

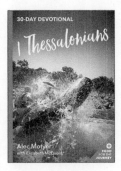

1 Thessalonians

Alec Motyer with

Elizabeth McQuoid

978 1 78359 439 9

2 Timothy

Michael Baughen with

Elizabeth McQuoid

978 1 78359 438 2

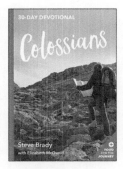

Colossians

Steve Brady with

Elizabeth McQuoid

978 1 78359 722 2

Ezekiel

Liam Goligher with

Elizabeth McQuoid

978 1 78359 603 4

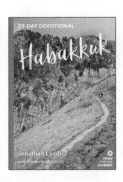

Habakkuk

Jonathan Lamb with

Elizabeth McQuoid

978 1 78359 652 2

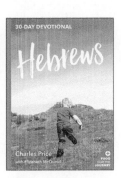

Hebrews

Charles Price with

Elizabeth McQuoid

978 1 78359 611 9

James

Stuart Briscoe with

Elizabeth McQuoid

978 1 78359 523 5

John 14 – 17

Simon Manchester with

Elizabeth McQuoid

978 1 78359 495 5

Available from your local Christian bookshop or **www.ivpbooks.com**

Food for the Journey

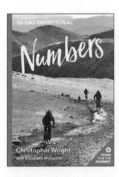  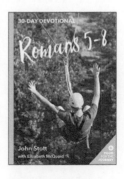 

Numbers
Christopher Wright with Elizabeth McQuoid
978 1 78359 720 8

Revelation 1 - 3
Paul Mallard with Elizabeth McQuoid
978 1 78359 712 3

Romans 5 - 8
John Stott with Elizabeth McQuoid
978 1 78359 718 5

Ruth
Alistair Begg with Elizabeth McQuoid
978 1 78359 525 9

Praise for the series

'This devotional series is biblically rich, theologically deep and full of wisdom . . . I recommend it highly.' **Becky Manley Pippert**, speaker, author of *Out of the Saltshaker and into the World* and creator of the Live/Grow/Know course and series of books

'These devotional guides are excellent tools.' **John Risbridger, Minister and Team Leader, Above Bar Church, Southampton**

'These bite-sized banquets . . . reveal our loving Father weaving the loose and messy ends of our everyday lives into his beautiful, eternal purposes in Christ.' **Derek Burnside, Principal, Capernwray Bible School**

'I would highly recommend this series of 30-day devotional books to anyone seeking a tool that will help [him or her] to gain a greater love of Scripture, or just simply . . . to do something out of devotion. Whatever your motivation, these little books are a must-read.' **Claud Jackson,** *Youthwork* **Magazine**

Available from your local Christian bookshop or **www.ivpbooks.com**